IDEOLOGY AND THE EVOLUTION OF VITAL ECONOMIC INSTITUTIONS:

Guilds, The Gold Standard, and Modern International Cooperation

IDEOLOGY AND THE EVOLUTION OF VITAL ECONOMIC INSTITUTIONS:

Guilds, The Gold Standard, and Modern International Cooperation

by

Earl A. Thompson
University of California, Los Angeles

and

Charles R. Hickson
Queens University of Belfast

KLUWER ACADEMIC PUBLISHERS
Boston / Dordrecht / London

Distributors for North, Central and South America:
Kluwer Academic Publishers
101 Philip Drive
Assinippi Park
Norwell, Massachusetts 02061 USA
Telephone (781) 871-6600
Fax (781) 871-6528
E-Mail <kluwer@wkap.com>

Distributors for all other countries:
Kluwer Academic Publishers Group
Distribution Centre
Post Office Box 322
3300 AH Dordrecht, THE NETHERLANDS
Telephone 31 78 6392 392
Fax 31 78 6546 474
E-Mail <services@wkap.nl>

 Electronic Services <http://www.wkap.nl>

Library of Congress Cataloging-in-Publication Data

Thompson, Earl A.
    Ideology and the evolution of vital economic institutions : guilds, the gold standard, and modern international cooperation / by Earl A. Thompson and Charles R. Hickson.
        p. cm.
    Includes bibliographical references and index.
    ISBN 0-7923-7878-4 (alk. paper)
        1. Wealth. 2. Income distribution. 3. International trade. I. Hickson, Charles Robert.   II. Title

    HC79.W4 T49 2000
    338.9--dc21   00-040549

Printed on acid-free paper.
Printed in the United States of America

TO OUR ECONOMICS TEACHERS,
WITHOUT WHOM THIS BOOK WOULD NOT HAVE BEEN POSSIBLE.

TABLE OF CONTENTS

LIST OF TABLES

LIST OF FIGURES

LIST OF GRAPHS

FOREWORD

Why does a book have a foreword? To tell what it's about? Apologize for it? Summarize it? One purpose is to prepare the reader for the "journey". Thus this foreword first warns that standard, strongly held beliefs about policies for development and survival of nations are severely challenged. And if your are not willing to run the high risk of having your present confident understanding turned upside down, you shouldn't read this book. I speak from prior personal experience with Thompson's publications. What appears upside down at first begin to look right-side-up -- from the newly acquired but very lonely Thompsonian perspective. The ideas in this book will surely haunt, alter and broaden your view of history and development of national political and economic actions.

More explicitly, Thompson and Hickson strongly challenge the standard interpretation of the basis of growth and viability of dominant wealthy nations. Briefly, efforts of the economically wealthy and the government leaders to increase their wealth and protect it from aggressors, internal and external, are cast in a new evolutionary light. The challenge is to the idea that societies leading intellectual formulators of political and social policy have been helpful. Their alternative, and persuasive, interpretation is that the rise and survival of wealthier nations has been achieved because of an "effective democracy". That's one in which: (a) investors participate in advising pragmatic legislators to protect their investments from private and public expropriation, and (b) a civilly reverent bureaucracy faithfully administers apparently unfair, inconsistent and ideologically unjustifiable legislation. Thompson-Hickson explain why an effective democratic state must avoid "narrow, short-sighted", rational appearing concessions to a sequence of aggressors. This successful avoidance requires that military leaders have emergency, and only emergency, taxation power to thwart aggressors. Examples of temporary emergency taxation are "conscription, rationing, price controls, money creation" and other actions regarded usually as "inefficient" actions under a narrower focus of analysis. Still other surprising examples explained by Thompson and Hickson are the gold standard, the guild system, international trade barriers, and exchange controls. These all fly in the face of modern popularly espoused "appropriate" domestic and international policies. In short, the Thompson-Hickson interpretation of the rise of wealthy dominant nations does not rely on advice of superior intellectual advisers, but instead rests on the pragmatic, almost ad hoc, actions of democratic legislators. This implies that "superior" actions (arrogantly popularly labeled as "programs") in the wealthy dominant nations evolved through adaptive adjustments and natural selection.

Thompson-Hickson thus provide a healthy antidote to intellectual arrogance. The reliance on a God -- or rationally designed -- path of events is replaced by a competitively evolving filter of pragmatic experimental events which is well in conformity to a modern evolutionary paradigm. And yet, quite unique to their process, ideas and intellectuals themselves evolve and, through their effects on vital institutions, play a critical role in the rise and fall of dominant states.

Armen A. Alchian

PREFACE

One of us started out his professional life as a libertarian, the other a Marxist. Soon thereafter, serious economic research taught each of us, as it did numerous other young economists, that practical solutions to real-world problems did not emerge from the engaging ideologies taught us by our activist economics teachers. Realistic transaction and protection costs, and a correspondingly complex array of unmistakable externalities, vitiated the libertarian conclusions of classical economists. And competition, whether economic or political, possessed none of the devastating inconsistencies charged to it by Marx and his intellectual descendants.

But these straightforward escapes from ideology furnished us with no analogously constructive policy framework. Rather, we, again along with many other young economists, were cast adrift in a sea of perplexing analytical questions.

Yet the ensuing swim-for-shore that preceded this writing, although lengthy in that it has been steadily proceeding for well over three decades now, has been remarkably easy. For the adventure has been accompanied by a growing realization of the ready solvability of many of the alleged imponderables raised by the initially right-minded critics of standard ideology. It now appears that these critical thinkers had been collectively exaggerating the difficulty of many of the theoretical problems that they had posed. These thinkers -- including several, more talented, would-be competitors in the supply of a new economic paradigm -- have been hierarchically organized into coordinated intellectual cliques so they could, and would, if they collectively found a particular class of logical and realistic solutions to be psychologically "unappealing", simply ignore it and continue on unperturbed. A likely reason for the collective ignoring of such solutions, as economic reasoning itself suggests, is that the material welfare of a group of specialized thinkers is founded upon their abilities to provide a long series of moderately useful, ideally demand-creating, future solutions. One-fell-swoop solutions, especially ideas whose content alone reduces the future demand for such thinkers, are simply unprofitable. The accepted leaders of a long-surviving group of critical-minded professionals therefore tend to psychologically regard such market-destroying theoretical solutions with detached amusement and to say that such solutions "cut the Gordian knot," even though the two ends of the rope are hanging free and there is no visible evidence of any such cut.

We shall correspondingly begin by dismissing our priestly intellectual heritage and thereafter weave a long series of empirical observations into a sacrilegious set of theoretical propositions to create what we believe to be a logically consistent and uniquely defensible world-view and policy approach. While economists typically regard themselves as entertained by sacrilege, we would be surprised if the highly socially integrated intellectuals in the group were able to tolerate our deicidal heresies, no matter how logically our arguments hang together or how accurately they fit reality. We would like to be popular. It's just that we have found the truth, or at least a continuously logical and empirically disciplined approach to finding it, too socially important to make the appropriate sacrifices.

Having just fired a round of buckshot into a roomful of well-protected kings, we had better produce a one hell of a good explanation.

ACKNOWLEDGEMENTS

We are grateful to Professor David Levine of UCLA for his extremely valuable organizational comments helping us to tame the relatively wild first draft of this book. Chapter 3, on guilds and tariffs, was substantially improved through numerous discussions, over many years, with colleagues Armen Alchian, Ron Batchelder, Jack Hirshleifer, and George Murphy, each of whose interest in our earlier work was a great source of inspiration and encouragement. Chapter 4, on the gold standard, was substantially improved through the numerous comments and substantial encouragement of David Glasner, one of the very few modern authors to display an understanding of our earlier work on monetary theory. Chapter 5, on international cooperation, was substantially improved by numerous comments and suggestions of Don Allison and Silke Reeves, whose backgrounds and open minds on these issues uniquely qualified them as pre-publication judges of the argument. David Levine also contributed several helpful insights regarding the dynamic argument in Chapter 6.

These extremely helpful individuals are in no way responsible for whatever errors may appear in the basic argument, whose conception and written execution are the sole responsibility of the senior author. The junior author, performing a service perhaps much more unique than the senior one, was chiefly responsible for digging up, organizing, and processing the hard facts that ended up eliminating a large number of provisional arguments. Very few creative theorists, whose hyperactive imaginations typically lead them to produce a large number of separate, empirically quite inconsistent, economic models, have been fortunate enough to find a polyhistor whose institutional and historical perspective, sophisticated economic understanding, tolerance, and extraordinary patience have allowed for the gradual elimination of all models except those that appear to fit together into a single, empirically consistent, world-view.

In this regard, it is interesting, at least to us, to compare the rough historical illusions of the previously unpublished, or "A", Appendices, which were essentially completed prior to our joint association, to the historically connected, hopefully cohesive, story comprising the central economic argument of the text. These critical Appendices nevertheless substantially benefitted from relatively theoretical discussions with several economists, especially Armen Alchian, David Friedman, Steve Goldman, Jack Hirshleifer, David Levine, Joe Ostroy, Jim Mirrlees, and Gordon Tullock.

Readers familiar with some of our already-published institutional histories may recognize that Chapter 4 (the shortest chapter) is a revision and extension of a previous publication while Chapter 3 (the longest chapter) is a revision and very substantial extension of a previous publication. Such readers are advised, to gain a maximal accretion to their knowledge in a limited amount of time, to concentrate on: The first two chapters, including the critically important underdevelopment-trap theory in the appendix to Chapter 1; the tariff analyses, war-and-ideology model, and democracy theory of Chapter 3; Chapter 5, including the Graphs; and, of course, the 6th and concluding Chapter.

Finally, it is doubtful that this work would have been completed without the 20-foot high stack of earlier drafts, which were promptly, cheerfully, and accurately typed by Lorraine Grams. We fear we have worn her out, as she was a youthful 1960s rebel when this project began and has recently entered semi-retirement.

PROLOGUE

"He who believes that by studying isolated histories he can
acquire a fairly just view of history is much the same as one who,
after having looked at the dissevered limbs of an animal
once alive and beautiful, fancies he has effectively been an
eyewitness of the creature itself in all its action and grace."

Polybius

CHAPTER 1

OVERVIEW

If the authority to which he is subject resides
in the body corporate, ... in which the greater part
of the other members are or ought to be teachers;
they are likely to make common cause.
Adam Smith, p. 718

One thing old about our new world view is that it is fundamentally economic. Our analysis will retain throughout the same basic methodological individualism that Schumpeter assured us is the common heritage of virtually all economists. We believe that the social and economic regularities dealt with in this work cannot be usefully understood other than as the consistent outcomes of the individually rational choices of each of the relevant individuals. Yet, for all of our iconoclasm, we could hardly be calling upon hallowed tradition or higher authority to justify our assumption of individual utility maximization. Nor are we presumptuously asserting a universal methodological principle.[1] Rather, as we shall soon see, our maximization assumption is derived from evolutionary processes. Others have traveled a similar route. And, as we shall come to stress, they have greatly improved the road that we shall travel.

---

[1]More generally, we shall adopt no moral stances and assume no affirmative normative principles of any sort. Rather, our policy evaluations will come from a general model of society in which economists, as endogenous economic agents, may or may not play a constructive role as policy advisors to actual or potential ruling classes. Before labelling this a brand of "might-makes-right welfare economics," the reader is urged to read on, especially through the distributional analysis of this overview.

Perhaps the only feature of our work reflecting an unsupported methodological principle is a negative one. It is our presumption that facts do not "speak for themselves". None of the factual assertions in the text is intentionally left alone, untied to an explicit theory. All of our qualitative empirical assertions are thus intended as "stylized facts", empirical generalizations serving as building blocks or direct tests of explicit alternative theories. We shall correspondingly omit an enormity of facts that may have indeed been important in shaping the particular events under discussion. All this is because our basic goal is not to explain particular events. Rather, as indicated by our Polybian prologue, our goal is to explain persistent patterns of events, regularities that are left unexplained by existing hypotheses, and to do so with a single, logically cohesive and policy-relevant, political-economic theory.

Similarly, because we do not wish to interfere with the clear development of our policy-driven theory, which contains no error terms, we describe our facts as certain, stylized, facts rather than realistically portraying them as somewhat uncertain. This absence of empirical caveats, together with the systematically anti-establishment tone and content of our argument, will surely turn-off many scholarly readers. We apologize but have no practical solution to the problem, other than to ask these cautious scholars to consider the work as a mere conceptual possibility.

For us, however, individual rationality comes in one of two possible forms, one which we call "narrow" and the other "broad". "Narrow rationality", what is conventionally called "economic rationality," describes the choices of those ordinary decisionmakers who exhibit no strategic domination over others. Such choices amount to the familiar, impersonal, utility-maximizing, quantity choices of all consumers and producers appearing in any standard economic model. Somewhat less conventionally, "broad rationality" describes the choices of individuals who <u>do</u> exhibit strategic domination over some other individuals. These latter choices amount to the strictly personal, utility-maximizing, <u>reaction-function</u> choices of professional bargaining agents, bosses, top administrators, and social leaders generally. Although substantial resource costs, ultimately education costs, are entailed in evolving a set of broadly rational decisionmakers, there are strong efficiency and distributional implications of an equilibrium arising out of a strategic interaction among perfectly and completely informed individuals capable of choosing to exhibit either broad or narrow rationality.[2] These implications are developed in the rational communication model of Appendix B.1. (The B-Appendices appearing at the end of the book represent reprints of past studies that are particularly relevant to this work.)[3]

I. AN EXAMPLE: SIGNIFICANT BILATERAL EXCHANGE

To see how broad and narrow rationality work together to produce an equilibrium, consider a bilateral exchange between perfectly and completely informed parties: The first strategy-selector adopts a broadly rational strategy of offering a Pareto optimal, all-or-nothing, take-it-or-leave-it, price just sufficient to induce a narrowly rational acceptance. At this price, the accepting party receives only a minimal surplus from the trade.

The standard academic response to the simplicity of this old, one-sided, Schelling-type, bargaining solution is a legitimate initial perplexity concerning the determinacy of prices in the bilateral monopoly. Absent an often prohibitively expensive third-party-enforcer, offering parties have no legal contrivance forcing them to stick to their initial price requests. Their future economic rationality may then

---

[2]Elsewhere (Thompson, et al.), optimal economic policies are identified for worlds containing proper subsets of ordinary non-dominant, economic actors who (because of their lack of maturity, objectivity, or consciousness) are narrowly irrational in that they are unable to make utility-maximizing choices.

[3]These preliminary discussions of "rationality" refer only to what Hirshleifer (1984) calls "rational results" in that individuals evolve, although generally with less than ideal information, utility-maximizing <u>behavior</u>. With respect to Hirshleifer's "rational methods", which refer to conscious <u>thought processes</u>, we will find that this latter kind of rationality arises from an evolutionary process only under specified conditions. Once we have identified these conditions, our meaning of the term, "rational," will be clear from the context. Before our evolutionary model is introduced, our discussion concerns only the "results" form of rationality.

dictate that the initially offering parties seriously consider less favorable counteroffers in subsequent negotiations. This objection indeed holds when there are several competing price-setters, which is another matter, or possibly when there is a small number of low-surplus bilateral trades, which possess little economic significance.

However, for high-surplus or frequent bilateral trades, if neither trader can sustain a price commitment, professionals will enter as middlemen or agents, either on one side of the market or the other. Such individuals, like dominant bilateral traders who would not induce such intermediation, generally have special training giving them "values", or "ethics", that pre-commit them to follow their announced strategies. If they initially say to another individual that they are going to stick with their initial price offer, they will. It's part of their broad rationality. Subsequent counteroffers are ignored, even if the offering party thereby incurs a substantial material loss. For example, part of their publicly recognizable training may have been that "good people do not break their promises"; their biologically justifiable (Thompson, et al., Vol. I, Ch. 1, Pt. II) utility for thinking of themselves as "good people", or for "self-respect", then forces such offering parties to continually refuse to accept a less favorable price in the future.

This rationally selected education, which exploits the individual's natural utility for a high self-evaluation, induces the person to adopt a broadly rational reaction-function. Although one might still object to this resolution of the significant-bilateral-monopoly problem by arguing that theory does not tell us whether the buyer or seller invests in the precommitment, what usually makes the bilateral monopoly significant is that either the buyer or the seller is faced with a relatively large number of such transactions. Thus, in the case of specifically invested labor, the relatively large number of bilateral monopoly transactions engaged in by the buyers has led us to conclude that buyers of labor will, consistent with a large set of related empirical observations, outbid sellers for the resources required to win those bilateral monopolies (Thompson, 1980); and in the case of collective goods such as industrial technology, the large number of buyers relative to sellers has led us to conclude that the sellers of collective goods will, also consistent with a large set of empirical observations, similarly win their bilateral monopolies (Thompson, 1968).

Despite the abundance of empirical support for this higher form of rationality and its economic implications, critical-minded economists and game-theorists typically persist in arguing that ethics are actually of little real consequence, that offering parties are sometimes observed to stubbornly maintain their initial price offers, but only because they stand to benefit in the future from a narrowly rational "reputation effect" (e.g., Rosenthal, Diamond-Maskin, or Klein-Leffler). However, this reputation argument obviously fails in the last conceivable transaction. The argument therefore fails in the next-to-last conceivable transaction, etc., until it fails in the current transaction. To escape this familiar "last-period-problem", proponents of "reputation effects" and universally narrow rationality typically adopt an infinite horizon. But then a "folk-theorem" tells us that any technologically feasible, individual utility-enhancing, program is a possible outcome, i.e., that although reputation effects are possible in an infinite-horizon model, so are countless other bargaining effects and grossly inefficient equilibria (Aumann-Shapley, Fudenberg-Maskin). Subsequent work by leading economists and game-theorists, work done in response to this infinite-horizon indeterminacy, has predictably created a plethora of models featuring either: (a)   incomplete information and a few conveniently irrational players (e.g., Kreps, et al.), which is indefensible in the presence of either contractual assurances or replicated play; or (b) some arbitrary set of trading rules (e.g., Rubinstein), which is indefensible in any case. These influential thinkers and their colleagues have thus found a growing maze of basically unrealistic theoretical models preferable to a simple, realistic, model admitting broad rationality.

The only inference we can draw from all this, as suggested in the Preface, is that the broad rationality assumption is too powerful to be profitable to an intellectual cartel of economists. Broad rationality may feel, psychologically, like it's cutting a knot; but perhaps all it's really cutting is the market for the incessant calculations of reality-avoiding academics.

II. GENERALIZING THE EXAMPLE:
A THEORY OF SOCIAL ORGANIZATION

Essentially the same phenomenon repeats itself as regards existing theories of oligopoly, trading of goods whose qualities are better-known by some traders than others, political interaction, international relations, and, most importantly, social organization itself. In this last respect, as elaborated in Appendix B.1, the same reasoning tells us that the broadly rational reaction functions that characterize an entire society analogously lead to complete-and-perfect-information outcomes that are both: (1) economically efficient, and (2) distributionally skewed to satisfy the preferences of the society's hierarchial leaders.

Because incentive problems do not appear, informational problems, which are basically non-objective educational choices generating broadly irrational strategies, become the sole source of avoidable inefficiency once the social hierarchy is formed. In our bilateral monopoly example and related business contexts, the Darwinian pressure of business survival forces objectivity on educational choice. Surviving education systems thus teach students to appropriately violate narrow rationality either through traditional business education, which teaches its students to exaggerate the value of "responsible" or "purely pragmatic" (i.e., purely empirical and backward-looking) business practices, or through inferable religious or family training, which teaches its students to exaggerate the value of truthfulness. However, in a broader societal context, the generally weaker evolutionary pressure permits systematic educational errors to emerge, and even thrive in some cases as part of a long-term 2nd-best equilibrium.   The problem is that alternative education systems need never be objectively evaluated because certain intellectual cartels, by teaching teachers and journalists far beyond their narrow specialty, have their ideas entrenched as an "ideology" in the general education systems and thereby generate biased and substantially Pareto non-optimal institutions (Thompson, et al., Vol. I). Nevertheless, other institutions (i.e., reaction functions) in the same economy also generally exist, social institutions that will come to define the subject of this work, in which certainly non-objective,   intellectual-cartel-influenced,   educational   systems   and   their correspondingly ideologically biased social policies systematically devastate a state and thereby fail to persist as a significant part of a long-term social equilibrium.

Regarding this long-term equilibrium, the internal hierarchial dominance of each society's leaders, most basically its founding military leaders, gives our abstract social theory a highly distinctive flavor. In particular, in the absence of systematic individual decision errors, civilization-wide changes in the military technology, which determine changes in the broadly rational reactions and therefore the rational values of successful leaders, become the sole cause of important civilization-wide changes in social organization.[4] It will therefore not be surprising when we subsequently find that basic changes in military technology explain universalistic social movements, including the medieval rise of democratic trading towns and feudal countrysides, the 14th and 15th century replacement of these towns and countrysides with centralized provinces and nation states, the 16th century emergence of European empires, the 17th century emergence of national democracies, the 18th century revolutions, the 19th century emergence of popular national democracies and steadily growing real wages, the early 20th century emergence of multinational economic cooperation, the late 20th century "growth miracles", and, most recently, the beginnings of a world empire. The simplicity and coherence of the theory will, it is hoped, offer a welcome contrast to related social theories.[5]

---

[4]For example, during the 7th century BC, just prior to the beginning of our broad institutional histories, the emergence of the light-iron age began to substantially increase the productivity and quantity of armed warriors. This induced the previously quite aristocratic city-states to compete much more vigorously for potential warriors. In the West, this meant offering warriors formal legal rights, and soon, in the subsequently most economically success-ful regions, effective democracy. The Greco-Roman roots of our current legal and political systems were laid down during this period. At the same time, the far less constitutionally bindable, more authoritarian, Far East, began to adopt new and similarly durable governmental philosophies (e.g., Confucianism and Taoism) that promised relief from the harsh bureaucratic oppressions of the past. Even among the relatively well-established near eastern civilizations, Persia quickly adopted a relatively tolerant, humanistic, outlook through Zoroastrianism while India established its similarly more humane religions in Jainism, Buddhism, and Post-Brahmanic Hinduism. In contrast, Egypt and Palestine, which failed to improve the incentives of their warriors by failing to substantially reform their ancient religions, fell easy prey to their less religiously conservative neighbors.

An evolutionary reason for the rapidity of the religious adjustments of the Indo-European states compared to others (the same intellectual adjustments in the Far East experienced gestation periods in excess of 400 years) will be noted in Chapter 2, footnote 32.

[5]Regarding generalist-authors, the social philosopher whose work is most closely related to our own is perhaps Frederick Nietzche, whose lifetime inquiry centered around the "value of values", or the search for a socially optimal system of social values. The earlier political philosophy of Tocqueville implicitly reveals an identical search. Nietzsche's, and implicitly Tocqueville's, "solution" (a rejection of the emergent humanism of their day in favor of a brand of cultural elitism) is not, however, determined (as it should be according to Appendix B.1), by the real preferences of the state's underlying rulers. Criticizing this "solution" in terms of our theory, the utilities of a society's evolved military founders generally depend much less upon their desired commitments to reward a small number of cultural high-achievers than on their desired commitments to reward the possibly large number of allies that must be

In any case, our discussion will not have any direct policy relevance until we admit systematic decision errors, in particular, errors in social policy. Regarding these legislative errors, a subsidiary advantage of a general theory of social organization (a society-wide sequence of announced reaction-functions followed by a related sequence of narrowly rational actions) is that it places us economists, and presumably social thinkers generally, within the social system. We can, of course, produce any information we want. But, viewing ourselves as part of a larger social system, we economists should recognize that the information upon which our livelihood is based consists of informed suggestions as to how a society's rulers are

---

compensated for their personal sacrifices for the state's future military survival.

The generalist-political-economist whose theory is most closely related to our own is perhaps Max Weber, who, like most political scientists (see, e.g., O'Kane), builds his analysis of the state on the possession of a "monopoly of violence" and proceeds by weaving his theory of underdevelopment and bureaucracy into a theory of an optimal political system. Our problem here is that Weber is an economic ideologue (a Classical Liberal to be more specific). This means that he takes the assumptions of the standard competitive model to be sufficiently realistic to derive unqualified policy recommendations from the model. The corresponding, distinctively Weberian, view of democracy is that it is only useful to assure relatively egalitarian philosopher kings. Legislative democracy is an encumbrance in such a world. Besides being repeatedly and obviously contradicted by historical reality, this approach ignores simple externalities (Appendices B.2 and B.3) and fails to provide a legitimate theory of underdevelopment (Appendix A.1 at the end of this chapter).

Regarding historically-oriented philosopher-generalists, our theory is quite unlike the quasi-rational theories of the German and British idealists (Kant, Hegel, and Spencer) and their numerous intellectual descendants in that we will find that civilizations do not naturally progress toward an optimum through some sort of endogenous enlightenment. Also, quite unlike Spengler and similarly inspired fatalists, we find no reason to conclude that western civilization is inexorably doomed to fail.

Further, contrary to Marx's call for raising the political consciousness of workers and completely eliminating private property, we find that the political decisions of workers are already subconsciously rational. And completely eliminating private property is a formula for generating gross long-run inefficiency in that it gives the ruling elites perverse incentives as regards educational policy (Thompson, et al., Vol. 1, Ch. 3, and Thompson, 1996).

More like a long string of western generalist-historians from Thucydides and Polybius to Gibbon and Toynbee (1988), we argue that decline can be averted if the consciousness of societal leaders is externally stimulated to intervene in the evolutionary process. What is missing from these often-wonderfully-descriptive historical arguments (and the similar arguments of more recent authors such as those summarized in Eisenstadt, et al.) is a welfare-economics-based model that is adequate to the task of generating large expected changes in economic efficiency and correspondingly powerful policy recommendations.

Moreover, as suggested by the title of this work, previous influential authors -- besides failing to supply us with either a logically cohesive theory of social organization (Appendix B.1) or a rational theory of economic underdevelopment (Appendix A.1) -- do not endogenize ideology, fail to systematically consider vital institutions, do not analyze history with a coherent evolutionary model, and do not apply their theories to explain the historical emergence and decay of previously universalistic institutions.

to choose their broadly rational reaction-functions, or utility-maximizing policies.

III. HOW OPTIMALITY CRITERIA DEPEND UPON THE POLITICAL ENVIRONMENT

In eras when the political system is stable, the market for policy information is limited to sales to the collectively secure political leaders. These leaders have much better ideas than any intellectual about which politically active individuals or groups they would like to currently benefit. So economists cannot earn an honest profit by communicating distributional advice in such an environment. In contrast, advice on how to achieve efficiency, a purely Paretian form of optimality, is potentially profitable. This is because politicians in states with an initially inefficient allocation themselves possess profit opportunities in that, as elaborated in Section I.A. of Chapter 3, the politicians could use the advice of competent economists to profitably promote reforms that increased everyone's utility. But efficiency is the only concern of society-serving economists when advising collectively secure political rulers. In such a world, we should eschew distributional advice and act as economists proper.

However, when the political system is unstable, the society's actual and potential rulers have qualitatively different demands for information. Such demands obviously include the distributional, as well as the efficiency, characteristics of alternative political systems. The material success of economists engaged in supplying this political information-market, who are then called "political economists," is then dependent upon their abilities to serve actual or potential rulers (including collectively insecure leaders within an existing political system) by determining a broadly rational polity for them. The predominant efficiency-orientation of the classical economics of Turgot and Adam Smith prior to the French Revolution was thus profitably generalized to emphasize the distributional recommendations of the Classical Liberalism of Bentham and J.S. Mill during the subsequent period of political transformation (1789-1870), an era during which the dominant western polities were increasingly converted, either by new military rulers or by collectively insecure political leaders, into popular national democracies.

Since, at least as regards international relations and world governmental institutions, political instability is currently the rule, the current work is aimed at the more general, political-economic, level. Our central policy recommendations will correspondingly concern the nature of world government and have a distributional as well as an efficiency component.

The above discussion of the social role of economists can be thought of as Copernican in that it attempts to move the center of the world of economists away from themselves and -- quite realistically we believe -- towards the society's future leaders. But the thought is not at all original. The predominant social views of the ancient (pre-Indo-European) Middle East, the pre-20th century Far East, and various 20th century totalitarian governments have all accurately placed military or political leaders on top of the social hierarchy and represented intellectuals as social servants. These thought systems have produced a long string of failed economies not because they represented an incorrect view of society, but, as we shall see, because they inevitably tempted their naturally hubristic military authorities, aided and abetted by their self-serving policy advisors, to excessively centralize legislative authority.

The contrasting claim of all dominant Indo-European policy thinkers, at least since Aristotle and including all dominant western political economists since Bentham's work on the maximization of what we now call "social welfare", is that our political-economic advice should be based upon the metaphysics of ethical philosophy rather than the actual preferences of military or political authorities. It matters not that metaphysical ethical notions, including the buried metaphysics of enforceable-contract-imagining legal philosophers from Hobbes and Locke to Rawls and Nozick, have little direct empirical relevance. We cannot go beyond the informed preferences of real social decisionmakers and maintain empirical relevance. Hume saw something like this long ago but, like Rousseau, never specified exactly which of the several conflicting preferences we should adopt. Critical-minded modern economists who have similarly understood the irrelevance of metaphysical goals have, largely under the influence of Robbins, Samuelson (1950), or Arrow, nevertheless come to regard the implied social welfare function as respectively indeterminable, arbitrary, or generally unethical, as if the preferences of a society's actual leaders were not concrete realities worthy of both theoretical and empirical determination.

In summary then, our policy teachers have persistently revealed a stubborn unwillingness to simply accept our role in society as sellers of information to actual and prospective rulers, information designed to characterize the broadly rational choices of these rulers. Accepting this realistic subservience, and thereby giving economic and political-economic research a clear direction, is, as above, psychologically regarded as some sort of illegitimate knot-cutting. The entire class of teachers, taken as a thought-coordinating social subgroup, or "profession", can alternatively create a substantial artificial demand for their policy advice by grossly exaggerating the extent to which the scope, durability, and value of their recommendations transcend the interests of actual or prospective societal rulers. Leading economic thinkers in this broader subgroup have thus seen little reason to voluntarily put themselves and their ideas in a subservient social role. Indeed, asserting the ultimacy of the preferences of the state's military leaders in determining social optimality has been explicitly rejected by the relatively independent thinkers of the West since the very beginnings of moral philosophy. Aristotle's teacher, Plato, set the pattern by having Socrates attack the assertion by attacking the straw-man, "might-is-right", hypothesis of the skeptical Thrasymachus in Book 1 of The Republic. Missing from the high-level sophistry is the possibility that the actual preferences of the military or political leaders -- although determining the actual standards of rightness -- can be far from the individually optimal preferences of these leaders, far from their truly utility-maximizing standards of rightness.[6]

---

[6]An analogous critique applies to moral philosophy, which examines the "rightness" of choice of all individuals, not just social leaders. While 20th century thinkers present us with a wide range of theories (e.g., Wittgenstein, Broad, and M. White), none acknowledge that an individual's search for private moral correctness is simply a search for a broadly rational reaction function. For example, while it may be narrowly rational for a seller in a given legal environment to deliver an inefficiently low-quality of merchandise, it is not broadly rational

IV. RATIONALIZING CITIZEN-EFFICIENCY AND DISTRIBUTIONAL ADVICE

As we have already indicated, since the maximization of the utilities of a state's basic military leaders implies a Paretian form of optimality, given a fundamentally military determination of the people deemed worthy of positive endowments, society-serving political economists, like economists proper, attempt to advise a Paretian form of optimality. However, as we have also noted and will elaborate in Section I of the next chapter, there are some evolution-supported exceptions to the achievability of broadly rational institutions in that well-entrenched, non-objectively evaluated, intellectual cartels may actually enhance social survival despite their inefficiency. Not accidently, we shall see, these deeply rooted intellectual cartels have yet to arise among cartels of economists. Rather, they are concentrated in various national legal and political ideologies (Thompson, et al., Vol. I). We shall use these exceptions to define the parametrically given "costs of citizenship". We thereby accept these legal and political constraints and limit the Paretian goals of the current study to the achievement of "citizen-efficiency". By thus isolating deeply rooted evolutionary traps and leaving these national political and legal inefficiencies for another, more idealistic, study (*ibid.*), we can apply the same, citizenship-constrained, concept of social efficiency throughout this work.

Regarding distribution, each military-technology shock examined in this study generates a predictable distributional shift, a shift in the class of individuals whom the societal rulers want to attract or motivate. We shall use these predictable changes in the contemporaneously optimal distribution of wealth to outline a new role for political economists. This role, which requires only the most basic of characterizations of actual and intertemporally optimal distributions of wealth, will lead us to a correspondingly new characterization of an optimal world political reform. Here, we should be more specific.

Suppose that the state and its present and future political representatives are facing a new military technology, one in which the existing political system will no longer generate the previously intended distribution of tax burdens. More specifically, say that the initial military technology and corresponding political system previously reflected an international environment in which states competed for people while the new military technology confers an international political monopoly, an unprecedented world-empire, on a single state. The mechanisms previously employed to attract people away from other states will then, in the absence of informed current intervention, be increasingly replaced by mechanisms that redistribute wealth to the ruling classes of the world's hegemonic leader, thereby commencing a subsequently self-rationalizing trend toward an increasingly inegalitarian tax distribution. Useful political economists, reflecting the relatively humanistic distributional values of the

---

("moral"). This is because informed buyers will pay the visibly uncommitted ("amoral") seller much less than the broadly rational one. While moral private education can thus be understood as selfishly profit maximizing, one's total reward for benefiting others generally comes from more than just prospective transaction partners (Appendix B.1).

current society (including its underlying military leaders), and using Buchanan's commitment-theory of constitutions, would then work to promptly identify and constitutionally correct the unintended, time-inconsistent, distributional defect in the world's political system.

Political economists may be able to supplement and enhance this purely distribution-oriented advice by also suggesting reforms that substantially extend the life of the existing, relatively humanistic, political regime through improving its citizen-efficiency. Adding this to the above-described distributional role, similarly suppose that, in the absence of the current input of political economists and a corresponding world-constitutional reform, there would be both an avoidably increasingly inegalitarian distributional trend and a substantial allocational inefficiency stemming from the same general fault in the geo-political institutions of the current regime. To sufficiently work to produce the appropriate constitutional reform, existing political economists must be able to recognize both the threat to their society's current distributional preferences and the violation of citizen-efficiency. These economists must recognize where the trends of their times would lead in the absence of a preemptive constitutional reform. Armed with this information, they can adequately advise current and potential future rulers similarly desiring to eliminate both the anti-humanistic distributional trend and the violation of citizen-efficiency.

The latter sections of both Chapters 2 and 6 will attempt to put some empirical meat on these theoretical bones. In any case, the new, distribution-oriented, policy role for political economists reinforces our early argument in that political economists cannot even begin to specify the requisite geo-political reforms if they either retreat into distributional metaphysics or accept any set of distributional goals to be as good as any other.

V. THE NEED FOR A RAPID ADJUSTMENT PROCESS

A methodologically individualistic and citizen-efficient social equilibrium; a corresponding endogenization of economists into a positive theory of welfare economics; and a new, preemptive, variety of constitutionalism: these are only part of what has emerged from our long search for a logical and realistic policy framework. Rapid institutional evolution is necessary if any of the equilibria that we are discussing is to be empirically relevant. For, as we have already noted, every few generations or so, the institutional equilibrium has been radically transformed by a sudden change in the military technology. Since the institutional equilibrium has thus presented a moving target, one that sporadically jumps to new social terrain in response to basic exogenous shocks, our model would be of little practical value unless there also happened to be a rapid adjustment process.

VI. ACHIEVING RAPID ADJUSTMENT: VITALNESS AND EFFECTIVE DEMOCRACY

The model's requisite dynamic adjustment speed is provided by the fact that many states cannot long survive without certain, "vital", institutions. An important class of such states is that characterized by "effective democracy". No effective democracy can survive to maturity without special economic institutions (Appendix B.3 (Section 2.1)). Non-democratic states can generally survive, although perhaps at a lower level of efficiency, without any of these institutions. In contrast, an effective democracy, in order to have survived to maturity, <u>must</u> have been able to both initially create such a special set of institutions and rapidly adjust these vital institutions in response to subsequent technological shocks.

A good part of Chapter 2, including Appendix A.2, is devoted to showing how the necessarily rapid evolutionary adjustments are possible, and indeed exist, both for societies and for biological organisms.

Now the same basic political process that is responsible for creating, and occasionally rapidly adjusting, the effective democracy's vital economic institutions can also be used to generate its other economic institutions. Whatever special characteristics have enabled a surviving democracy to rapidly generate its vital economic institutions should therefore have also enabled it to similarly generate citizen-efficient levels of a significant class of its non-vital economic institutions. This argument is elaborated in Section I.B of Chapter 2 and then complemented by the democratic efficiency theorems of Sections I.A and I.B of Chapter 3. Moreover, were it not for the <u>uniquely</u> high overall efficiency level, democracy itself would be a paradox in that it would be quite foolish for military founders to adopt a democracy in the first place. For democracy is both administratively expensive and exposes the leaders to a uniquely high risk of losing the entire state.[7]

---

[7]The manifold academic objections to democracy have little empirical relevance. The "special-interests" objection, wherein the mass of middle-class citizens find it relatively costly to form effective democratic interest-groups compared to small special-interest-groups comprised of relatively wealthy investors (i.e., the attack on narrow special-interest-groups popularized by a long line of political economists from Adam Smith to Mancur Olson), explains only distributional, not allocational, features of democratic legislation. Moreover, this common argument fails to recognize that direct democracy (e.g., voting on popular referenda with severe restrictions on political advertising), as in Classical Athens, severely biases legislation toward time-inconsistent redistributions <u>away from</u> wealthy investors.

A second objection is Tocqueville's popular "tyranny of the majority" objection, wherein voters with relatively rare characteristics are left unserved by a democracy. However, as we have just argued, such a tendency is held in check by the relative ease with which the economically significant victims of such potential "tyrannies" can form effective political associations to protect their interests.

A third, existence, objection -- wherein unconstrained voters cannot generally reach a legislative solution (i.e., the cyclical majority problem first posed by Condorcet and generalized in modern times by Arrow) -- disappears once we realistically allow logrolling or vote-trading among the legislators. Such dealing constrains the votes of future legislators (in a way that is <u>not</u> independent of otherwise irrelevant alternatives) so as to eliminate cyclical majorities and yield theoretically efficient solutions (Thompson-Faith, 1981, Sec. V).

Finally, there is the "uninformed masses" objection, wherein popular democracy places decision authority in the hands of relatively uninformed individuals. (This argument was popularized by Plato and Aristotle and has been kept alive in modern times by the free-riding-voter argument of Buchanan and Tullock (1962).) The argument ignores (or arbitrarily discounts) the ability of only partially informed individuals to select suitably motivated legislative agents,

VII. THE ECONOMIC BENEFITS OF EFFECTIVE DEMOCRACY: EFFICIENCY TESTS

An extraordinary feature of effective democracy is its unique ability to overcome laissez faire underdevelopment traps. Appendix A.1 at the end of this chapter establishes the existence of such traps and indicates a critical feature of democracy that enables it to escape such traps. The basic idea is that, under laissez faire, potential investors face the chilling prospect of having to defend the future returns on their investments against the perfectly legal predations -- both public and private -- of others with whom it is too costly to contract prior to the appropriate investment period. What democracy does is offer the potentially victimized investors an inexpensive process -- one that does not require anything like unanimity -- of initially cooperating with other concerned individuals, possibly including their would-be predators, in order to create a set of ad hoc laws or regulations that preclude the future attacks on their private capital. (Once again, broadly rational legislatures are never subject to voters' paradoxes or related Arrowian difficulties (Thompson-Faith, 1981)). Section I.A of Chapter 3, following the heuristic argument of Section III.I of Appendix B.3, provides us with an evolution-supported democratic efficiency theorem. Since effective democracy is domestically vital to its threatened investors, which implies that many threatened investors generating substantially ineffective democratic institutions will fail, there is a rapid co-evolution of investors and democratic states towards profitability and effective democracy. Our subsequent institutional histories in Chapters 3 through 5 will then regularly supply direct political-economic evidence for the implied theory of economic development.

Several other tests of the citizen-efficiency of effective democracy will be supplied in Chapters 3 through 5. (Still others are provided in Thompson, et al.) Here, several, generally non-vital, institutions unavoidably arise in our examination of vital institutions. We shall use our observations on these generally non-vital institutions to test a critical implication of simultaneously maintaining our model of defense and our model of democracy. In particular, effective democracies should internalize certain, ideologically unrecognized, domestic externalities that are implied by the basic defense model of Appendices B.2 and B.3.

An important member of this set of what we call "defense-externalities", one that is a source of vital economic institutions only under special circumstances (Section I of Chapter 5), arises because the domestic accumulation of capital that is coveted by enemies of the state will burden the other members of the survivable state with a greater collective expenditure on national defense. Although the introductory discussions of Appendix B.2 and B.3 respectively indicate the theoretical and empirical simplicity of this external diseconomy, it has been traditionally ignored in all influential political and economic ideologies. Indeed, the persistent ideological neglect of this simple defense-externality goes all the way back to the Book of Kings in the Old Testament: Solomon, of course, was King of the relatively small, unified and prosperous, 10th century BC nation-state of Israel. Now, in the highly respected

---

who in turn are in a position to gather the advice of suitably informed individuals.

Biblical account of Jeremiah, writing about four centuries later, Solomon was given the gift of wisdom and effusively praised for deciding to build a magnificent public temple in which almost everything was gold or covered in gold. Immediately after Solomon's death, the North of Israel seceded and attacked the government of Solomon's son; but, before victory could be achieved, previously peaceful Egypt attacked and confiscated all of the gold in the Temple. Although a large gold temple would seem to be a folly, it was approvingly restored by Solomon's pious grandson, who almost immediately thereafter suffered a very similar humiliation at the hands of the Syrians. After that, until Babylon's enslavement of the eventually quite artisanally skilled population over two centuries later, every descendant son or grandson was similarly occupied in either reaccumulating gold and substantially rebuilding the opulent Temple or trying in vain to defend its gold from stronger neighbors. Yet it apparently occurred to none of the numerous subsequent biblical redactors that something other than praise should have been heaped upon all of those royal builders of golden temples.

Thus, if effective democracy really is much more efficient than authoritarian government, we should see democratic governments pioneer economic policies that internalize these ideologically unrecognized defense-externalities. Moreover, since the externalities must be internalized through a suitable form of taxation in all efficient states, all long-surviving states must eventually adopt such taxation if the efficiency-predicting social theory of Appendix B.1 applies. More specifically, if such taxation were not typically pioneered by democracies and subsequently spread to other states, the defense model, the democracy model, or the abstract social theory would have to be abandoned, which would destroy the simplicity of the entire story.

Fortunately for the story, it will become quite apparent in Chapters 3 through 5 that the appropriate taxes were both popularized by democratic governments and subsequently adopted by almost all geographically related states despite a centuries-old barrage of economic-ideological attacks. Import tariffs and related non-tariff barriers, guild entry restrictions and apprenticeship rules, capital and income taxation; these notorious economic institutions will all be seen to possess structures and histories that strikingly reveal a developmental process in which democratic states pioneer, and long-surviving states of all varieties subsequently maintain, ideologically condemned tax-policies that efficiently internalize their society's not-consciously-well-recognized defense-externalities.

VIII. THE IMPERMANENCE OF DOMINANCE

In civilizationally dominant democracies, the same histories will also reveal a systematically perverse movement <u>away from</u> the efficient equilibrium. The quality of policy information has systematically deteriorated in civilizationally dominant democracies. This has occurred through the education-induced over-influence of the same class of professional teacher-ideologues that our Preface identified as the initial spark for this intellectual work. These well-meaning individuals, working as part of a cooperative endeavor, form the same class of intellectuals that have historically spearheaded the unjustified condemnation of the vital economic institutions of the world's wealthiest countries. The inevitable economic consequence has been, rather than a uniform Spencerian path of civilizational improvement, either a periodic replacement of each civilizationally dominant state, i.e., a circulation of the civilizational elite, or a total civilizational decay. After developing these observations in Chapter 3 through 5, Chapter 6 will suggest a political economic reform designed to cut short the ongoing world-civilizational decay by inducing the dominant countries to stop imposing their debilitatingly inappropriate economic and social ideologies on the world's less fortunate countries.

IX. A BRIEF READERS' GUIDE FOR SPECIALISTS

The above summarizes the practical aspects of our political-economic argument, the way in which the various components of this work fit together into a new world view. Nevertheless, each chapter and appendix tells its own story and can be read as an independent intellectual treatment of a separate subject, one suitable for specialists and described in the title of the chapter or appendix. The same conceptual independence holds for the theoretical arguments of Parts I and II of Chapter 1, Part I of Chapter 3, Part II of Chapter 4, and Parts I and III of Chapter 5. The critical histories that make up a good part of the remainder of the book can also be consumed as conceptually independent arguments. To us, of course, what is most attractive about these separate arguments is the way they fit together.

Although we have already indicated how the arguments fit into the above intellectual framework, the dynamical inevitability of our political-economic argument cannot be appreciated unless we tie the entire argument to an explicit evolutionary process. Therefore, since our basic dynamic framework is evolutionary, it may be helpful to restate the above overview in a way that concentrates on the exact evolutionary logic of the argument. This more specific framework will also enable us to provide a more specific readers' guide to the various parts of this book.

X. THE EVOLUTIONARY ARGUMENT: A MORE DETAILED READERS' GUIDE

Like the only-sometimes-vital defense-externalities discussed above, the economic institutions vital to the survival of an effective democracy, as emphasized in Chapters 3 through 5 as well as Appendix B.3, have never been appreciated by significant numbers of intellectuals. The development of these institutions must therefore have arisen through an evolutionary process. Policy experimentation, pragmatic imitation, and natural selection -- i.e., a complement of both Lamarckian and Darwinian forces -- must have been involved in the necessarily rapid adjustment from one effective democratic equilibrium to another. Indeed -- except for the critical fact that our special evolutionary process refers to a form of broad, rather than narrow, rationality -- we shall see that the implied evolutionary process is a theoretical equivalent of the evolutionary process described first by Alchian (and, thereafter, most influentially, by Friedman; most optimistically by Winter; most powerfully by Foster and Young; most usefully-to-us by Weibull; and most persuasively by a long series of experimental social scientists). In particular, in Section I.A of Chapter 2, we shall see that the rapid demise of the failures in this harshly Darwinian process, together with the complementary nature of these two evolutionary forces, imply just what the empirical applicability of our social theory requires, viz., a theoretically rapid adjustment process. It is apparently because of this implicitly rapid, vital-institution-containing, evolution that these authors have found it empirically plausible to argue for replacing the anticipatory rationality assumption of standard economics with an informationally-less-demanding assumption of experience-oriented choice, pragmatic imitation, and harsh natural selection.[8] We shall also come to adopt such a replacement, but only when the so-evolved decisions are utility-superior to those resulting from anticipatory rationality. In particular, we shall employ such evolution as a necessary part of the process generating <u>broadly</u> rational decisions.

Section I.B of Chapter 2 builds on the fact that any evolutionary mechanism generating a long-surviving effective democracy must also generate a vital polity, a set of basic political values (implying various rules and procedures) that exploits the subconscious (or "Pascalian") rationality of the political decisionmakers so as to rapidly respond to changes in the military environment by appropriately adjusting its vital economic institutions. A by-product of these vital political institutions -- complemented by additional political institutions analogously evolved because they are vital to co-evolving private investors for the protection of their investments from subtle <u>private</u> expropriation -- is a large set of highly efficient economic institutions.

Nevertheless, we must again emphasize that we are certainly not claiming -- despite the contrary assertions of the contemporary Panglossian school of "new-institutionalist" economists -- that "all institutions evolve toward efficiency." We can be certain that evolutionary processes uniformly converge to the social optimum of Appendix B.1 only under a critical "payoff-positivity" assumption briefly described in Section 7 of Appendix B.1 and elaborated upon in Section I.A of the next chapter.

Under payoff-positivity, relatively high-utility, partially adopted, pure strategies have positive growth rates. Now objectively pragmatic social learning is the same thing as payoff-positivity in the special case that the evolutionary model possesses a permanently fixed population. So objective learning would lead to a Pareto optimal evolutionary equilibrium in this case. Therefore, the only way to violate payoff-positivity and a steady approach to Pareto optimality in a long-surviving state is to introduce biased, non-pragmatic, social learning. Such a bias is generated here by introducing non-objectively evaluated, teacher-educating, intellectual cartels and thus what we shall call "ideology".

In any case, Section I.A of Chapter 2 explicitly derives payoff-positivity with respect to any survivable state's vital institutions. Employing this result in a general political-economic model, we predict the efficiency of a large set of historically evolved economic institutions. However, due to the general absence of payoff-positivity elsewhere, other broadly rational institutions may be secularly selected

---

[8]Although Blume and Easely have presented an interesting model in which economic evolution favors irrationally patient entrepreneurs, a more realistic evolutionary model would have these eventually "successful" investors pay a cost for their investments in the form of a smaller number of expected offspring. Otherwise, biological evolution would not have allowed impatient individuals to survive.

against. Certain, non-vital, broadly irrational, institutions may generate higher rates of both private and collective survival. If a society could somehow coax such strategies out of its given population, long-term social evolution would then favor Pareto-inefficient institutions. Thus, when a society's educational system leads to a systematic overvaluation of an intellectual cartel whose internally profitable ideas also happen to increase military survivability despite the social inefficiency, that society's long-term survival, and dominance over more objective societies, is nearly assured. Only a consciousness-raising, idealistic, brand of political economy will enable the society to eliminate these deeply rooted evolutionary traps (Thompson, et al., Vol. I).

Fortunately, these evolutionary traps have been concentrated in certain legal and political institutions (*ibid.*) The corresponding social losses take the form of what we shall call "citizenship costs". This handy compartmentalization will enable us to demonstrate, in Section I.A of Chapter 3, the existence and citizenship-constrained efficiency of an effectively democratic equilibrium.

It is, of course, conceivable that an economic or social ideology (e.g., social Darwinism) could have joined these inefficient but survival-enhancing legal and political ideologies in attaining the dubious status of a deeply-rooted evolutionary trap. Societies have re-evolved to out-compete their rivals by appropriately accommodating these inefficiency-creating legal and political ideologies. However, as noted above and elaborated in Chapters 3 through 5, economic and social ideologies are part of a broader class of quasi-rational ideologies in which the ideologues (perhaps because of their confidence-inducing abilities to understand the predictable order that markets or hierarchies create out of potential chaos) are hedgehogs who theoretically evaluate broad sets of institutions rather than foxes who pragmatically (from their own standpoint) evaluate particular processes within an accepted institutional setting. The former intellectual cartels have promptly stripped dominant states of vital institutions and inevitable military disasters have followed.

The ideology-induced impermanence of these dominant states is thus a critical part of our positive social theory. More specifically, our positive theory endogenously generates an emergence -- but only an isolated emergence -- of teacher-educating, demand-creating, cartels of economic or social thinkers in a world with several independent states. Perhaps the most direct confirmation of the theory is the relatively large number of once-historically-dominant social and economic policy theories, the fact that applied economic and social theories have, over the past 2000 years, been relatively temporary, fashion-oriented, phenomena compared to the more internally pragmatic subjects of law and political science.

As developed in Section I.C of Chapter 2, an internally secure world empire represents an extreme case, one in which no institutions are collectively vital. An inefficient economic or social ideology in such an environment will simply deteriorate world efficiency without generating any evolutionary response. Indeed, as elaborated in Chapter 5, this theoretical possibility has, for at least a decade now, come to represent a harsh reality.

Chapter 6 correspondingly proposes a world political-economic reform that responds to these inefficient economic and social ideologies. The reform, a re-evolutionary response to the normal evolution of such ideology, is robust in that its optimality is retained, becoming first-best-optimality, once all ideologies -- political and legal as well as economic -- have been ideally exorcised (Thompson, et al.)

Our discussion of the evolution of specific vital economic institutions, the chief subject of our specific theoretical and empirical explorations, will run from Chapters 3 through 5. The details of these middle chapters will reveal a series of economic institutions that, despite the persistent attacks of contemporary profession-serving intellectuals, have each been evolved, and with successively increasing rapidity, to meet the contemporaneous survival requirements of an effective democracy. First guilds, then the gold standard, and finally a whole complex of dependent-country responses to international institutions arising after World War I, will all be revealed to have evolved as vital economic institutions during their respective heydays. Although each institution is still typically condemned by modern intellectuals, both on the left and on the right, as a gross example of the inefficiencies that result when special-interest-groups attain "excessive" political power, a more realistic theoretical and historical appraisal will reveal that, with successively increasing rapidity, each of these institutions has been pragmatically evolved as a timely solution to a critical problem of state-survival.

Note that none of these three chapters will, by itself, produce a full-blown evolutionary treatment of the subject at hand. Each chapter makes substantial use of a basic theorem demonstrating the convergence of the evolutionary path to our general social equilibrium of Appendix B.1 (Foster and Young; Weibull). However, these chapters are highly complementary in that each emphasizes different key aspects of the evolutionary process:

Chapter 3 (A New Interpretation of Guilds, Tariffs, and Laissez Faire), besides providing an analysis of specific adjustment mechanisms in Section I.B, establishes a broad historical pattern of pragmatic institutional learning. It also establishes a pattern of subsequent institutional decay in dominant regions through the predictably negative effect of the spread of economic or social ideology. It will also uncover an example of how a highly profitable legal and political ideology (Church-supported feudalism) can induce extended yet entirely predictable war and misery in attempting to resist the emergence of a newly vital political institution.

Chapter 4 (On the Gold Standard) also displays a guild-type evolutionary pattern of the troubled-country rise and premature, dominant-country elimination of a vital economic institution. But it is concerned more with the specifics of how designers of a vital institution use practical experience as a guide and how economic ideologists subsequently use predictably excessive political influence and sheer economic error to prematurely dismantle the vital institution.

Chapter 5 (On Modern International Cooperation) enables us to witness both the pernicious character of securely ideologized institutions and the way in which both natural selection and pragmatic learning among numerous weaker states have worked to shape an institutional environment that enables the participants to rapidly and reliably achieve domestically efficient responses to externally imposed trade policies without having any idea of the nature of the economic problem they are solving. At the same time, it will show, as does the tariff discussion of Chapter 3, how broader policy "principles" (e.g., tight-budgets, income taxation, and popular elections) are evolved in order to induce only partially informed government decisionmakers to adopt efficient policy reactions to various exogenous disturbances.

XI. EXTENSION TO BIOLOGY: AN EVOLUTIONARY PRINCIPLE

A biological application of our basic evolutionary argument is described in Chapter 2 and specified further in our 6th and concluding chapter. In it, we find, in the life cycle of any high-rent-receiving species, that the successful evolution of a new species of this sort inevitably induces the subsequent evolution of ever-more-sophisticated mobile aggressors that increasingly feed off of its surpluses. Thus, what follows an era of exceptionally rapid growth -- at least within the class of carnivorous mammals (Simpson, Van Valen, Vermeij) -- is an era of subsequent decay through its victimization by new predators.

The long-run views of Darwin, like the "dismal" long-run views of Ricardo and the mature Reverend Malthus, are therefore too optimistic. For such views fail to adequately consider the induced evolution of ever-more-effective predators that survive by attacking the high surpluses of the classical system.

No high-rent-receiving species -- and, similarly, no species that exists in very large numbers -- can be expected to survive such escalating warfare for an extended length of time. Rather, to long survive, the species must adapt itself to live in a symbiosis with its mobile parasites, re-evolving into a higher form that converts the by-products of the winning parasites into sources of positive net benefits. Thus, for example, the only successful species of plants, the only species that have survived to coexist with their animal parasites for an extended length of time, are those early species that subsequently evolved an ability to live off of the waste of the animals. Without some such re-evolution, it would have been virtually impossible for any of the early plants, regardless of its ability to naturally evolve new defense mechanisms, to survive the ever-more sophisticated evolution of herbivorous animals.

XII. A SUMMARY OF THE POLICY FRAMEWORK

In the same way as biological organisms, the only high-surplus states that can rationally expect to coexist with their intellectuals for an extended length of time in a world with militarily competing states are those that eventually re-evolve constitutional conditions enabling them to live off of the opinions of these intellectuals. A re-evolution to a second-best, non-payoff-positive, equilibrium has already occurred with respect to our currently deeply rooted legal and political ideologies. But, since economic ideologies have not had a chance to become deeply rooted because they have historically impinged upon vital economic institutions, and since dominant states are a predictable source of new economic ideologies, civilizational dominance has consistently been a temporary phenomenon. Aggressive neighbors have persistently arisen to permanently dethrone dominant states.

But, as we have also pointed out, a world empire is not subject to such checks on its economic and social ideologies. Since a world empire, such as the one that is currently emerging, has no civilizational competitors, its prospective economic decline -- even more than the familiar economic declines of the Ancient Roman Empire, the Carolingian Empire, the Byzantine Empire, the Ottoman Empire, and Imperial China -- threatens to be a permanent plague on the entire world. A constitutional reform that would prevent this worldwide economic decay, a reform enabling us to re-evolve so as to successfully co-exist with our economic and social intellectuals, and eventually permit the achievement of a first-best equilibrium, is outlined in Chapters 2 and 6. This sketch of a world-constitutional reform will define the efficiency-part of our policy agenda.

The distribution part of our policy agenda builds upon the argument, emphasized in Chapters 2 and 6, that our military technology has recently changed so that a world empire characterizes the emerging political equilibrium. As our social theory shows, and as history has repeatedly shown, such an imperial distributional equilibrium is radically inegalitarian. If we wait until the radical redistribution is upon us -- and the trend is certainly there -- it will be too late. Nevertheless, the prospective future redistribution, the prospective world-wide decimation of the middle-class, is completely avoidable. We can work now to institute a political-economic reform that will impose our current distributional preferences on the otherwise increasingly inegalitarian equilibrium.

A P P E N D I X   A.1
POTENTIAL COOPERATION, UNDERINVESTMENT TRAPS AND THE ECONOMIC EFFICIENCY OF EFFECTIVE DEMOCRACY

ABSTRACT

This appendix will identify a new type of noncooperative equilibrium. Solution actions in this new type of equilibrium differ from familiar noncooperative actions in that certain equilibrium actions are undertaken in order to avoid the prospect of costly future cooperation. Since cooperation is not observed in these interactions, empirical analysts have generally overlooked it. The situation is analogous to that which arises under the beneficial constraint of "potential competition." But the efficiency implications of the new hidden constraint, which we call the constraint of "potential cooperation", are quite the reverse.

For example, a potential cooperation constraint will be seen to be necessary and sufficient, within complete information environments, to explain certain forms of gross economic underdevelopment. At the same time, the theory will enable us to correspondingly explain certain forms of observed democratic regulation, without which the country would be economically underdeveloped.

Recognizing the constraint of potential cooperation similarly enables us to see new problems stemming from old policy recommendations and thereby to rationalize the observed democratic response to small-numbers externalities problems, i.e., the widespread reliance on: (1) direct governmental production; (2) a fully compensatory tort liability system; (3) quantity-regulation rather than simple Pigouvian taxation.

With the new market-force of "potential cooperation" leading to a new form of market failure, and new principles of optimal policy, the appendix then identifies a set of qualitative empirical applications necessary to establish the theory's empirical scope. What eventually emerges is a new theoretical and empirical appreciation for the economic efficiencies of a special kind of democracy.

INTRODUCTION

A. Underinvestment Traps Under Cournot-Nash Interaction

It has long been well-known that Cournot-Nash solution sets may contain points that are worse for everyone than other points in these same solution sets (Nash, J. Friedman). The corresponding games are popularly called "coordination games." In the absence of technological externalities, economic examples of such games arise whenever the different potential producers of complementary, indivisible inputs, although able to internalize all of the incremental benefits flowing from their separate inputs, each find it unprofitable to produce their particular input only because none of the other potential suppliers produce theirs. Each of the potential producers would rationally provide his or her input if and only if all of the other potential producers were assumed to be providing their inputs (Makowski, Thompson, 1968).

More concretely, suppose that an initially undeveloped region contains: (1) a single natural site for a port, (2) an exploitable mineral deposit in a second location, and (3) space for a road connecting the port site with the mineral deposit. Each of these sites is independently owned and controlled by a separate potential investor. A port, a mine and a road must all be built before any one of the three resources can generate a positive net private or social benefit; and once any pair of these three indivisible capital inputs are supplied, independently supplying the third is highly profitable, both privately and socially. One possible Cournot solution to the corresponding investor interaction problem has a zero supply of each input: each potential supplier rationally provides no input because the others provide none. Another possible, highly Pareto superior, Cournot solution has each potential supplier providing his or her input and earning a significantly positive profit.

Since we are discussing a market economy, not just some abstract quantity game, the payoffs in the above Cournot production game must be consistent with those generated from prices formed in a separate game of exchange. For example, if there were many independent buyers of all outputs, the payoffs would have to be consistent with Bertrand-Marshall, market-run, price-taking behavior on the part of such buyers. This eliminates payoffs that would induce inefficient underinvestment traps for private-good complements (such as the "traps" described by Scitovsky, Hart, and Salop). We are in no danger of underinvestment traps in the likes of turkey and cranberry sauce. For even if neither private good were produced, the low prices necessary to induce both types of producers to choose zero outputs would also induce excess demands and price increases for both goods by the globally rational final users.[9] This comes in sharp contrast (as elaborated in Thompson 1968) to a world with collective-good complements, like an actual port, road and mine. Here, the low prices that induce zero supplies of these inputs do not induce excess market demands and price increases for the inputs. For the many buyers of the services a collective-good-input cannot analogously assume that they individually influence the quantities produced of collective-good-inputs and must therefore assume, starting at the zero investment point, that two such inputs are unavailable when they bid for the services of the third. (This rules out price offers contingent on the supplies of other producers; such cooperative behavior will be considered later in the argument.)

Multiple-equilibrium-type underinvestment traps are also encountered in models with externalities, where Pigouvian taxes are applied in attempting to correct external diseconomies. Since there may be several, Pareto-distinct, allocations satisfying the necessary marginal conditions for a Pareto optimum and qualifying as an equilibrium under a Cournot-Nash interaction with Pigouvian taxes, Pigouvian taxes are generally insufficient to achieve globally Pareto optimal allocations (Thompson-Batchelder). An empirical example is provided by a pollution externality occurring in Slippery

---

[9]These excess demands could not raise these prices if the markets for turkey or cranberry sauce were "closed" because of the existence of slightly positive transaction costs (Hart). Such a "market failure", however, is illusory because the demand prices for turkey and cranberry sauce at zero quantities both far exceed the supply prices and thereby generate a substantial entrepreneurial profit to jointly opening the unjustifiable closed markets.

Rock Creek, Pennsylvania, where both acid-creating coal mines and alkaline-creating limestone mines both dump their waste into a stream and thereby neutralize one another's effluent even though any one mine, operating alone, would pollute the water and kill millions of fish (Harder). One Cournot-Pigou equilibrium has no mining on the stream and understandably heavy Pigouvian taxes while another, Pareto superior, Cournot-Pigou equilibrium has both types of mines present and zero Pigouvian taxes.

B. A New, Purely Informational, Role of Exchange Markets

An additional, previously overlooked, consequence of including an exchange game, which extends to the case of externalities, is that it informs each of several possible investors -- who cannot observe one another's outputs under the Cournot-Nash assumption -- which one of the multiple equilibria the other investors are adopting. Without such prior price observations available to so inform the investors, a multiplicity of Cournot-Nash solutions would make all Cournot-Nash solutions inappropriate because the players would then have no basis whatever for assuming any of the alternative solution points. Under such confusion, each rational investor would base his output decisions on his prior probability distribution over the other players' adopting these, and many other, strategies.[10]

However, once we allow exchange markets to remain active over time, they take on an additional, informational, role. Investors, armed with the price-signals generated by the exchange markets, can then almost always infer the prior investments of others before making their own investments. The Cournot-Nash solution is then economically inappropriate to important investor interactions. As in any important interaction, such as in a real mine-road-port example, or in real Slippery Rock, the investors know -- either directly or indirectly through observed exchange markets -- the relevant prior investments of the others. So a sequential investment interaction -- not a simultaneous, Cournot-Nash, interaction -- applies.

---

[10]This "Bayesian" solution -- which is not a mixed-strategy Nash solution because the players are not subjecting their strategies to a predictable mixing device -- admits almost any behavior and is apparently too general to be of much use: To say that each person behaves rationally given his or her prior probability distribution over all possible behaviors -- while almost always admitting a solution -- has little empirical power. It's akin to describing a single position in a dynamic model. It is, however, all that we should ever expect in a single-period, simultaneous-choice model with multiple Cournot-Nash "solutions".

As we shall note in footnote #1 of Chapter 6, replicated play, using intergenerational learning and natural selection, may easily generate a single Cournot-Nash equilibrium. However, the untenably long time lags involved, as well as the unreality of the Cournot assumption, forces us to eschew such a framework. We could, following Fudenberg and Levine, respond to the long-lag problem by abandoning the small numbers assumption. Instead, regarding the strategies of states, we introduce the idea of "vital" strategies, where certain errors immediately eliminate whole classes of players, quickly replacing them with players adopting survivable strategies. Also, regarding individuals rather than states, as we are about to explain, we drop the Cournot assumption.

C. The Absence of Underinvestment Traps Under Sequential -- But Still Purely Noncooperative -- Investor Interaction

When potential investors know the prior investments of others -- and cooperative interaction is still entirely absent so that investors still cannot communicate committed reaction functions to others so as to influence their decisions (Appendix B.1) -- the appropriate complete-information solution concept becomes the von Stackelberg-Zermelo-von Neumann-Morgenstern "perfect information" solution concept. Here, the essentially lumpy investments are sequential in that each investment is made subject to observed, past investments and in view of accurately forecasted, uncommitted, future investment responses.

Section I of this appendix will show that adopting this perfect information form of noncooperative interaction completely eliminates the possibility of a multiple equilibrium-type of underinvestment trap: No point in such a perfect information solution set is strictly Pareto superior to any other point.

This is easy to understand. In our Pigouvian taxation example, if the investment decisions were sequential, any one of the investors would be willing to enter first, as the investor knows that his or her investment would inspire the other investor to enter, the latter's entry being induced by the absence of positive Pigouvian externalities and taxes once the former has entered. The possibility of an externalities-based, Pigouvian-taxation-induced, underinvestment trap would be gone. With it would go the theoretical possibility of a small-numbers multiple-equilibrium explanation for the widespread use of direct quantity controls (through governmental production or quantity-regulation) rather than Pigouvian taxes or subsidies for sizeable externality-creators (Thompson-Batchelder). These enigmatic governmental "interventions", which are apparently groundless in the absence of multiple equilibria, will play a substantial role in our subsequent empirical argument.

Similarly, in our underdevelopment example, any one of the collective-input suppliers, say the port-producer, is now willing to enter first because the producer knows that a second collective-input supplier, say the road-producer, will then enter because that producer knows that once a port and road are both supplied, the mine-producer will enter. Again, the investment coordination afforded by a perfect-information interaction serves to always exclude situations in which some outcomes in a noncooperative solution set are uniformly inferior to others.

The competitive pricing of collective-good-inputs still produces a substantial free-market undervaluation of durable inputs that are complements of subsequently purchased collective-good-inputs. This is because buying one such input raises the demand price -- and thus the actual price -- of the buyer's subsequently purchased collective-good-inputs (Thompson, 1968). A substantial laissez-faire underinvestment in the durable-input complements of a later-purchased collective good therein remains whether there is a Cournot or a perfect information interaction between the investors. However, this underinvestment problem, in the guise of a pseudo-logical "infant-industry" problem, has long been substantially ameliorated around the world through various investment subsidies.[11]   Accordingly, we assume the presence of a tax-subsidy policy eliminating these collective-good-based misevaluations so that a pure Pareto optimum would result if the interaction were purely noncooperative.

The upshot of the above argument, complemented by Section I below, is that we cannot assume a purely noncooperative interaction between completely informed investors if we are going to explain observed underdevelopment. Nor can we assume a purely noncooperative output interaction if we are to rationalize the widespread governmental eschewal of Pigouvian taxation in favor of a heretofore unexplained reliance on direct production, quantity-regulation, and fully compensatory liability payments in resolving small-numbers externality problems. Somewhat cooperative forms of private investment interaction -- where some investors can communicate committed reaction functions to others before certain investments are undertaken -- must be admitted if we are to rationalize such phenomena with models that allow individuals to have complete information about their environment.[12]

D. The Necessity and Sufficiency of Moderately Expensive Cooperation

It may appear a bit paradoxical to conclude that we must admit the possibility of private cooperation in order to explain underdevelopment; we've become accustomed to thinking that the ability to communicate and cooperate among all individuals under complete information can only enhance social efficiency. Indeed, if the costs of strategic communication were sufficiently low that there were initial strategic communication (i.e., if communication and commitment costs were sufficiently low that the informed economic decisionmakers initially presented reaction functions to the others, each function being rationally chosen from the set of all technically feasible reaction functions), then both underinvestment traps and externalities would be impossible (Appendix B.1).

It follows, again viewing the investors in the sequence as completely informed, that economic underdevelopment logically implies that the costs of private cooperation are "moderate" in that the costs are sufficiently high to preclude initial

---

[11]The U.S. Investment Tax Credit, permanently repealed in the 1986 Tax Reform, was the most recent general investment subsidy in the U.S. It created the costly U.S. investment slump of the late 1980s and early 1990s while the capital stock depreciated sufficiently to warrant a return to the previous investment rates during the mid-1990s. As noted in the text, this repeal is just part of a visibly ideology-based reduction in the quality of U.S. legislation over the past 45 years. Nevertheless, more pragmatic elements remain in subsidies to technology development, both through all immediate income tax write-offs and support from various agencies of the U.S. government (e.g., NASA and SBA).

[12]Implicit in the above discussion is the assumption of physical property (e.g., land) ownership. We assume this throughout. When a society lacks a territorial ethic sufficiently strong to maintain the property endowments of its initial leaders across generations, "tribal" underdevelopment arises (Thompson, et al., Vol. I, Ch. 3, or Thompson, 1996). None of the substantially-above-subsistence societies, or "states", that are the intended subject of the current work are tribally underdeveloped.

cooperation but not so high that private cooperation is <u>permanently</u> precluded.[13]

Section II of this appendix will show, in a multiple-investor model, that the converse of the above underdevelopment proposition is also true, thereby establishing an equivalence between underinvestment traps and moderate cooperation costs. That is, Section II will show that underinvestment equilibria are <u>inevitable</u> whenever the costs of strategic communication are neither so low that initial cooperation occurs nor so high that subsequent cooperation is precluded when prior investors adopt their parts of an efficient, noncooperative, investment sequence. Early investments in an efficient noncooperative sequence would necessarily induce costly cooperation, a net loss to at least one of the earlier investors, and therefore some degree of underinvestment.

Thus, with cooperation costs fixed at a "moderate" level, an early subsequence of investments in an efficient sequence of related potential investments would <u>always</u> generate -- rather than the continuation to an optimum that occurs in an entirely noncooperative, perfect-information-cum-subsidy, investment model -- a sufficiently high return to establishing later reaction commitments that these later commitments would be made. These later commitments would, in turn, make at least one of the early investments in the efficient sequence necessarily unprofitable. Therefore, a rationally adopted, jointly efficient sequence of related investments is always impossible under "moderate" cooperation costs.

Our port-road-mine economy provides a simple example. Say, as in the sequential investment interaction described in the preceding subsection, two of the three investors in our port-road-mine economy independently make their privately and socially optimal investments. The third would then, under "moderate" rather than prohibitive cooperation costs, be willing to devote the requisite resources to making a commitment <u>not</u> to supply his or her input unless appropriately paid by the other investors.[14] Since the costs of cooperation exceed the aggregate net return to the

---

[13]The efficiency of direct governmental production or regulatory controls, which implies both externalities and the inefficiency of Pigouvian tax-subsidy policies, has the same logical implication. In other words, if such direct governmental intervention is to be rationalized in a complete-information, sequential investment, framework, then the rationalization must be found in some special difficulties arising from <u>intermediate</u> levels of cooperation costs.

[14]While the "hold-up" problem in this particular example has long been recognized by men of affairs, the first discussion we are aware of by an academic economist appears in Rothenberg. A static equivalent is developed in the "coveted capital" analysis in Section I of Appendix B.2. More recent applications appear in Batchelder, Goldberg, Klein-Crawford-Alchian, V. Thompson, and Williamson. Our theoretical contributions here will be to: (1) generalize the problem to where moderate cooperation costs are the source of the problem, (2) show that moderate cooperation costs imply inevitable underinvestment traps, even when no actual "hold-up" is involved, and (3) describe optimal policy responses to the resulting underinvestment traps. We shall utilize these theoretical results to offer explanations of both previously unexplained underdevelopment traps and various widespread forms of direct governmental intervention, policies that have been heretofore widely considered to be economically inefficient relative to Pigouvian tax-subsidy policies.

three investments, and since the third investor is "earning" a profit from the induced cooperation, at least one of the first two investors must be making a loss. In other words, the induced commitment would gain the committer a transfer from at least one of the previous investors of an amount that necessarily exceeds the amount that the investor would have to earn to economically justify the original investment. Anticipating such transfers, at least one of the first two potential investors would rationally refuse to invest. The port-road-mine example thus illustrates a strong form of our general underinvestment result, a form that recurs whenever the investments in a potential-cooperation-constrained set of investments are all necessary complements in that none is profitable unless all are undertaken. As is obvious from the example, under this necessary complements condition, moderate cooperation costs make a zero-investment trap theoretically inevitable.

A second, alternative, source of extreme underinvestment arises whenever the potential cooperation between potential investors is asymmetric in that only one party would receive a significant surplus from a cooperative interaction with the others. In this case, regardless of the complementarity or substitutability relationships between the related potential investments, none of the potentially expropriated investors would initially invest. A zero-investment trap again necessarily occurs. This technologically quite general, robber-baron, type of zero-investment result is formally described and proved in Section III.

Note that, in either case, a basic economic feature of all interactions generating such traps is that the potential investors are able to affect and internalize prices that the other investors are able to receive in their transactions with still other individuals. (Such internalizations arise whenever there are privately marketed collective goods (Thompson, 1968) or, more generally, when there are two or more natural monopolists selling related goods (Thompson, 1969), whereas the standard, single-monopoly, welfare problem arises because of the ability of the monopolistic producer to affect and internalize only those prices that others are willing to pay directly to that monopolist.) Since, in particular, the present welfare problem arises because of the ability of at least one of the potential investors to affect and internalize the prices paid to other investors by making a costly commitment to supply, or not supply, a related investment good, the relevant indirect price-effects can only be practically internalized among sequences of sufficiently large-scale investors. Our analysis is therefore concentrated on indivisible, or "lumpy", investment decisions.[15]

---

[15]Lumpy investments directly imply the existence of collective-goods in that the scale economies implied by the need for large-scale investments imply the existence of overhead factors of production within the firm. When costs fall with the firm's quantities produced, at least until the firm reaches a sufficiently large scale, it is because certain inputs do not have to be duplicated along with the other inputs in order to double the firm's output. The initial operation and its duplicate are simultaneous consumers of those overhead factors. The factors are thus "collective goods" under the conventional definition of Samuelson. (However, input monopolies or positive transaction costs are also required to generate the scale economy because if these overhead inputs were competitively rented under zero transaction costs, the rents would vary with scale in such a way that the decreasing costs that induce the assumed

Let us now return to our Pigouvian taxation example, where the affected third-party price is the government's externality-internalizing tax. We have already noted how the observability of prior investments eliminates the underinvestment problem posed by the possibility of multiple Cournot-Pigou equilibria. However, just as in the port-road-mine example, the observability of prior investments also creates the possibility of a unique underinvestment equilibrium once we recognize that cooperative interaction, which again is initially prohibitively costly, may easily become profitable after a certain number of individuals have made their observable investments. Returning again to Slippery Rock, one miner, having seen the other enter, would, under moderate cooperation costs, rationally commit not to enter (even though it is profitable to do so) unless paid substantially for his "acid-neutralizing services". The first miner, realizing that such a payment would make net profits negative, would not enter. Thus, with cooperation costs down into the moderate range, the grossly inefficient Pigouvian equilibrium reappears despite the perfect observability of previous investments, and moreover becomes a unique, theoretically inevitable underinvestment trap rather than a mere theoretical possibility.

This inefficient Pigouvian equilibrium differs from the above-discussed potential cooperation traps only in that it contains technological externalities. Nevertheless, optimal policy considerations will often lead us to discuss the two problems separately. In particular, the optimal policy response in the trap-cum-externalities case is more likely to be market-replacing intervention because the externalities aspect of the problem generally induces a significant level of governmental monitoring even without the extra complication of a possible underdevelopment trap. This policy-difference will be elaborated upon in the next subsection.

Again, our new type of underdevelopment trap is fundamentally different than the Cournot-Nash type discussed at the beginning of this appendix. Besides being incapable of rationalization under realistic observability conditions, the Cournot-Nash trap represented a mere multiple-equilibrium possibility. In contrast, a potential cooperation trap, which infects any related sequence of large investments when cooperation costs are moderate, represents a unique underinvestment equilibrium.

While this uniqueness does help simplify the design of an optimal anti-trap policy, very little else is straightforward in designing policies to deal with a potential cooperation. In particular, governmental encouragement of the privately underdone quantities has a negative social value in the presence of our new -- more pernicious -- form of underinvestment trap. Simply encouraging private investments until they are undertaken would just induce cooperation, the costs of which are revealed to necessarily exceed the net internalizable economic surplus from the unrealized

---

large-scale investments would always completely disappear (Thompson, 1968).)

The reason we keep referring back to collective-goods is not that this environment is one in which Nash-Cournot underdevelopment traps can emerge. We have already criticized such theories by introducing exchange markets and a natural sequencing of investments. Rather, it is that non-laissez-faire policy principles apply in a collective-goods environment so that nondevelopment policies must generally be complemented with the appropriate tax-subsidies policies to arrive at a Pareto optimum.

investment sequence. Also, any general lowering of transaction costs among investors, by creating more traps than it eliminates, may as easily exacerbate the society's underinvestment problem as alleviate it.

E. Optimal Policy

1. *Governmental Production*. Direct provision by governmental bureaucrats would always achieve an efficient outcome if top governmental decisionmakers had sufficient prior knowledge of both the identities and the personal effort levels of the various decisionmakers in an efficient investment sequence. The authorities could then simply hire these knowledgeable individuals as specialized authoritarian bureaucrats, grant them salaries to compensate them for their known efforts, and rely on their common social benevolence and informed status to efficiently select and manage the relevant investments.

Since personal effort levels are, in fact, unobservable, the bureaucrats must be efficiently motivated by having them exaggerate the social values of their decisions. Although such exaggerations can sometimes be achieved by simply providing the bureaucrats with exaggerated estimates of the social values of their particular decisions (Thompson, 1972), more generally the bureaucrats must be guided by an exaggerated view of the value of governmental services generally. We shall further describe an optimal government-service ethic (viz., "civil reverence") later in the argument, after we have developed an alternative, complete-information, description of the interaction between these bureaucrats and other members of the society.

The assumption that central authorities know the identities of the optimal decisionmakers is also generally inappropriate. A harsh Alchianian selection of entrepreneurs makes the free-market a generally superior mechanism for selecting efficient decisionmakers. However, the presence of sizeable small-numbers-external-ities substantially weaken this conclusion, thereby admitting a plausible argument for direct governmental production.   This is because the extraordinarily complex governmental monitoring that efficiently arises in small-numbers externality cases (Thompson-Batchelder) makes private decisionmakers somewhat of a redundancy.

2. *Laissez Faire Legal Principles*. In sectors where we can ignore these bureaucracy-requiring externalities, the selection of an authoritarian bureaucracy is generally very costly, especially because policies involving absolutely no control by governmental bureaucrats may well be efficient (Faith-Thompson). Here, in a laissez-faire bureaucratic environment, a legal policy that would conceptually eliminate any potential cooperation trap would have suitably informed judges treat all post-investment cooperation between private investors as if the parties had previously made an initial, pre-investment contract (Macaulay and Part 5 of Appendix B.1 below). By distributing the returns from post-investment cooperation as if the parties had initially cooperated, such a judicial policy would eliminate all investment-induced future cooperation and thereby entirely eliminate the potential cooperation constraint from the laissez faire economy. The prospective confiscatory reaction functions that threaten the profits of early investors in an efficient non-cooperative sequence would be illegal because the early investors would obviously not have initially chosen to

join the confiscatory cooperative. Cooperation would remain prohibitively expensive throughout the investment sequence.

However, to implement this legal solution, judges would have to be mentally able to apply a rule enforcing payments between previous investors according to what an ideal pre-investment contract between all of the various investors would have dictated. This may be a reasonably feasible judicial task under certain, simple, technologies, wherein a judge, with some significant effort, can learn the relevant past investments of the litigants and the outcome of these investments. The judge need then only grant litigants the original opportunity costs of their individual investments, plus (or minus) fractions of the net value of the outcome, according to the normal sharing arrangements used in explicit contracts involving such investors, contracts designed to eliminate the threat of potential cooperation. In plausible special cases, this awards investors with their productive contributions plus (or minus) a conventionally distributed lump-sum payment sufficient to achieve product exhaustion.

We can use this trap-avoiding distributional ethic to further specify what we earlier defined as "territoriality". J.B. Clark was perhaps the first to explicitly argue that a marginal-productivity-based distribution of investment returns, because it satisfied popular, "reap-what-you-sow", distributional feelings, was the ethically best distribution of such returns. Most classical economists similarly took such a distributional rule as the "sensible" or "practical" way to distribute investment returns (Robbins), although none of the above authors appears to have appreciated the legal or underdevelopment problems that arise under non-competitive conditions.

Note that an "ethic", which we can take here to mean an objectively unjustifiable or exaggerated belief that is taught to the believer in order to improve the believer's social decisions, is necessary here. For any truly objective, normally humanitarian, judge will -- in the last legal decision of his or her career -- distribute investment returns in an egalitarian fashion regardless of the specific sacrifices made by the various investors. Everyone knows the character of this last decision. So there is no point in the judge's trying to invest in a reputation by making a more efficient next-to-last decision. The result is another purely egalitarian decision. The same argument then applies through backwards induction to each of the judge's earlier decisions so that an intertemporally consistent, objective, normally humanitarian judge will make purely egalitarian decisions.[16] In so doing, the judge is giving the relatively poor investors in an efficient investment sequence an obvious incentive to use the courts -- or convincingly threaten to do so -- after the relatively wealthy have made their investments, thereby engendering cooperation costs that were not initially incurred because they exceeded the aggregate net profits from the sequence. A "territorial" ethic, by allowing suitably indoctrinated magistrates to replace their trap-

---

[16]We might attempt to assign some sort of salary-and-pension-setting super-judge(s) the project of rewarding other judges according to their cumulative strictness. This, however, would create a "who judges the judge" problem, whose finite-horizon solution is equivalent to the single-judge case. In other words, considering the judicial system as a whole, since the world's last judgment is egalitarian, so is the next-to-the-last, etc. It follows that ethics must be employed by the judicial system if it is to have any social value.

creating, egalitarian preferences with a manufactured belief in the sanctity of a reap-what-you-sow distributional ethic, enables economies with sufficiently simple technologies to completely avoid these underinvestment traps.[17]

3. *Statutory Intervention and Regulation.* When a sufficiently complex technology vitiates the above legal solution, and it remains impractical for the government to identify and employ the natural investors (which is even more likely in a complex technology), various trap-threatened private investors will want to democratically cooperate -- that is cooperate through a less-demanding, non-unanimity-requiring, legislative process -- in order to initially establish statutory restrictions on their future cooperative interactions. With objective legislative representatives, bureaucrats are thereby given a theoretically efficient (Appendix B.3, Section IIIi; or Chapter 3, Section 1) and therefore trap-avoiding set of statutes with which to determine the distributional consequences of any private investment sequence.

Because this regulatory policy alternative substitutes seemingly arbitrary legislative controls for the seemingly efficient principle of freedom of contract, at least in the eyes of an intelligent or professionally educated bureaucrat, effective democratic legislation obviously requires honest and humble, "civilly reverent", regulatory bureaucrats, individuals who are willing to let the intentions of a democratically elected legislature of investor-influenced politicians dominate their private or profession-serving views on what is more efficient or more fair.

For an example of such counter-intuitive policy principles, there are many realistic technical environments in which the government can, via special regulatory principles, implicitly tax the returns to certain investments so as to reduce the returns to cooperation to where potential cooperation is no longer a binding constraint. This non-Pigouvian tax on the returns to these complementary investments, by removing the otherwise inevitable underinvestment trap, has the paradoxical effect of dramatic-

---

[17]Our definition of the term, "ethic", mirroring the term's practical usage, is thus much more general than the standard intellectual identification of an "ethical optimum" with a "true social optimum". The latter, as argued in Chapter 1, is, or should be, merely the utility-maximizing outcome of the particular employers of intellectuals. For example, the utility-maximizing choice of a political system by the underlying military leader(s) represents the ethical optimum for efficiently motivated political economists; and the utility-maximizing institutional choices of the subsequent political decisionmakers, all such choices having the property of Pareto optimality, represent the ethical optima for efficiently motivated economists proper. Generalizing, for example, the utility maximizing choices of an individual patient defines the ethical optimum of an efficiently motivated doctor. Members of competing professional disciplines (as "agents") are broadly rational in pre-committing themselves to adopt the target of their respective employers (or "principals"); and the term, "ethic", is appropriate because exaggerating the value of achieving the target is necessary in order to correctly motivate the otherwise excessively narrowly rational members of the profession.

Referring back to Chapter 1, note 6, we see that ethical behavior a special kind of moral behavior. The evolutionary psychology rationalizing such behavior is developed in Thompson, et al., Vol. I, Ch. 1.

ally <u>increasing</u> total investment.

F. Empirical Applications: Summary and Illustration

Our qualitative empirical applications, developed within a relatively familiar economic model, appear in Section IV. The applications will reveal a definite tendency for the real-world legislatures of developed countries to develop efficient forms of policy intervention, frequently despite the near-universal disapproval of economists and other social thinkers. Where we have not observed this sophisticated policy pattern, we have observed significant economic underdevelopment. In particular, economic underdevelopment will be seen to be nearly inevitable in modern economies lacking the policy structure of an effective democracy (i.e., a legislature of objective investor-representatives with a bureaucracy dedicated to carrying out its seemingly inefficient mandates.)

For a simple illustration, consider an <u>almost</u> fully developed residential neighborhood. A noisy, smelly, externality-generating plant might enter to complete the neighborhood's development. The owner's resulting Pigouvian tax bill would be so high that the profit from operating the plant in that neighborhood would be quite negative. Therefore, under a wholly noncooperative, perfect information, Pigouvian solution, the plant would certainly locate elsewhere and no inefficiency would occur. But, progressing from Section I to Section II or III assumptions by reducing the cost of cooperation to an only moderate level, the plant builder would commit to building the plant anyway, unless all of the neighboring homeowners forked over their huge potential Pigouvian damages for memberships in the potential builder's alternatively proposed neighborhood country-club. Looking ahead to such effectively extortionary, but perfectly legal, country-club bills, the landowners would never have invested there in the first place. Pigouvian policy, in failing whenever there is potential cooperation, <u>should be</u> replaced with quantity restrictions that harshly outlaw the obviously inefficient entry of creators of such external diseconomies.

In fact, local policymakers and large land developers all over the developed world have eschewed simple economic theory by pragmatically rejecting Pigouvian taxation in favor of zoning restrictions or restrictive covenants that effectively eliminate the possibility of a grossly inefficient, potentially cooperative, solution. With such regulations in place, inappropriate investments are excluded from the possible interaction, and potential cooperation is removed as a relevant economic constraint; our Section I model therefore becomes empirically relevant, and optimality is achieved. Zoning laws and restrictive covenants thus become practical trap-avoiders, as long as bureaucrats or judges are available who are intellectually prepared to carry out the laws. And those nations employing corrupt or ideologized bureaucrats, in failing to employ a civilly-reverent bureaucracy, have failed to effectively implement such seemingly arbitrary regulations and have therefore remained relatively underdeveloped (Thompson, et al., Vol. II, Ch. 5).

I. THE ABSENCE OF TRAPS UNDER WHOLLY NONCOOPERATIVE, PERFECT INFORMATION, INTERACTION

As in Appendix B.1, assume that each of n decisionmakers, $i = 1,2,...,n$, has a real-valued utility function, $U_i(x_1,...,x_n)$, over the actions of all the various decisionmakers, where the ith individual's set of actions, x_i, is chosen from a <u>finite</u> set, X_i, of feasible actions for that decisionmaker. (This is more realistic than assuming an infinity of feasible actions in that effective utility differences only exist between <u>measurably different</u>, and therefore discretely varying, actions.) The action sets are sequentially selected in the order of the indices. Each decisionmaker knows all the previously selected action sets and the preferences of later decisionmakers. (This is called "perfect and complete" information.) But here there is never any strategic communication so the interaction is purely noncooperative.

To describe the resulting, noncooperative, perfect-information solution, we first have the last decisionmaker, n, choose an $x_n \in X_n$, in particular x_n^*, that maximizes $U_n(x_1,...,x_{n-1},x_n)$. This sets up a dependence of x_n^* on $x_1,...,x_{n-1}$, expressed in the correspondence, $x_n^*(x_1,..., x_{n-1})$. Decisionmaker $n-1$, in attempting to choose an x_{n-1} that maximizes $U_{n-1}(x_1,...,x_{n-1},x_n^*(x_1,...,x_{n-1}))$, may find that his or her maximizing solution is ambiguous in that it depends on the particular value of x_n^* chosen from the $x_n^*(x_1,...,x_{n-1})$ correspondence for any given x_{n-1}. To remove this "assignment", or "selection", ambiguity, decisionmaker $n-1$ need only alter his or her action to one that is "near" x_{n-1}^* but generates a suitably unique solution to individual n's maximization problem. A formal approximation of this realistic procedure is achieved by simply allowing $n-1$ to choose, not only among the x_{n-1} in X_{n-1}, but also among the several possible values of x_n satisfying n's response correspondence, $x_n^*(x_1,...,x_{n-1})$.[18] Decisionmaker $n-1$'s choice solution is then described as the set, (x_{n-1}^*, x_n^{**}), that maximizes $U_{n-1}(x_1,...,x_{n-2},x_{n-1}, x_n^*(x_1,...,x_{n-1}))$, where x_n^{**} is a subset of $x_n^*(x_1,...,x_{n-1}^*)$. Note that $n-1$'s solution set, besides presenting some possible ambiguities in his or her own choices for earlier movers, may fail to resolve ambiguities in n's moves in that $n-1$ may also be indifferent

---

[18]A more standard approach, due to Selten, is to have $n-1$ choose an action that is optimal given the uncertainty regarding n's response. While the resulting, "trembling hand perfect", equilibrium is more realistic than ours for certain problems, it is not more realistic when $n-1$ has a lot at stake in n's subsequent decision. It is obvious that, with a lot at stake, $n-1$ is going to try to break n's indifference in $n-1$'s favor rather than simply living with the resulting uncertainty.

between several x_n^* belonging to $x_n^*(x_1,..., x_{n-1}^*)$. So, applying the same underlying argument, n-2 chooses the set $(x_{n-2}^*, x_{n-1}^{**}, x_n^{***})$ that maximizes $U_{n-2}(x_1,...,x_{n-3},x_{n-2},$ $x_{n-1}^*(x_1,...,x_{n-2}), x_n^{**}(x_1,...,x_{n-2},x_{n-1}^*))$, where x_{n-1}^{**} is a subset of $x_{n-1}^*(x_1,...,x_{n-2})$ and x_n^{***} is a subset of $x_n^{**}(x_1,...,x_{n-2},x_{n-1}^*)$, etc.

The non-emptiness of the solution set, $x^* \in \prod_{i=1}^{n} X_i = X$, to this series of problems follows immediately from the real-valuedness of $U_i(\bullet)$ and the finiteness of every X_i. Had we allowed infinite X_i's and continuous $U_i(\bullet)$'s, our method of resolving ambiguities would have precluded any general existence result (Peleg-Yaari), although Goldman has shown that a solution always exists for some, not-necessarily-rational, method of resolving ambiguities.

Our main interest is in Pareto dominance. In particular, we wish to show that the perfect information solution set (in contrast to the Cournot-Nash solution set) cannot contain solutions that are strictly Pareto inferior to other members of the solution set. That is, the solution set, x*, contains no points that are strictly Pareto inferior to other points in the solution set.

The proof is quite simple. Consider a solution point, $x' \in x^*$, and another, strictly Pareto inferior, point, x", i.e., a point with the property that $U_i(x") < U_i(x')$ for all i. Since the first decisionmaker's particular choice uniquely determines the outcome, and $U_1(x') > U_1(x")$, this decisionmaker would only choose $x_1^"$ over x_1' if $U_1(x_1^", x_2(x_1^"),...) \geq U_1(x')$, in which case the choice of $x_1^"$ would imply an outcome unequal to x". But since a choice of any $x_1 \neq x_1^"$ also implies an outcome unequal to x", <u>any</u> choice by 1 would then preclude an outcome equal to x". So, regardless of the first decisionmaker's rational choice between x_1' and $x_1^"$, x" cannot be in the solution set.

It may seem hopelessly artificial to have each decisionmaker take only one move. We may, however, without affecting the above anti-trap result, interpret some of the later decisionmakers as the same individuals, i.e., the same biological entities with the same $U_i(\bullet)$-functions as earlier decisionmakers. This procedure (i.e., the conversion from a "normal form" to an "extensive form" and a corresponding switch to "subgame perfect" equilibria) is explicitly adopted in Section III below. It will be clear then, and may even be clear now, that the essence of the above proof, and therefore the absence of Pareto-inferior points from perfect-information solution sets, is not altered by such an interpretation.

II. INEVITABLE UNDERINVESTMENT TRAPS UNDER POTENTIAL COOPERATION

We now introduce the possibility of strategic communication. We temporarily assume that the overhead costs of commitment and communication are fixed at an intertemporally constant level, C, delaying our more general discussion until Section III below. We assume throughout that these cooperation costs are high enough to preclude <u>initial</u> strategic communication, which is modelled in Appendix B.1. A purely noncooperative solution, such as appears above in Section I, is nevertheless not implied here because the corresponding actions by early movers may make it privately profitable for a subsequent mover to announce -- rather than a simple, noncooperative action -- a committed reaction function to then-subsequent actions.

The condition on the intertemporally fixed overhead cooperation cost defining the interaction as neither initially cooperative nor permanently noncooperative, i.e., as "constrained by potential cooperation", is

$$\sum_{i=1}^{n} B_i^o(x_i^c) < C < \sum_{i=r}^{n} B_i(x_r^c),$$

where the term on the far left is the aggregate capital value of the net investor profits from an initially cooperative, jointly optimal, investment sequence and the term on the far right is the aggregate capital value of the net profit to movers r through n from choosing their cooperative action set, x_r^c, <u>after</u> 1 through r-1 have made their simple noncooperative investments.

An explicit description of the underlying investment dynamics and corresponding utility structure is provided in Section III below. It suffices here to note that the full sequence of returns for individual i is denoted by $x_i = (x_{i1}, x_{i2}, ..., x_{iT})$ and that we are interpreting x_i^c as implying a current "investment", an avoidable sacrifice of current benefits for the purpose of obtaining future benefits, if x_{i1}^c is negative. We are also assuming that the investments are "lumpy", or $X_{i1} = (0, -1)$.

A. The Implications of "Moderate" Cooperative Costs

Our introductory theorem, the impossibility of efficient solution investment sequences whenever investor cooperation costs are only "moderate", makes more use of the notion of "coveted" (Appendix B.2), or "appropriable" (Klein, Crawford, and Alchian), capital. As developed in Appendix B.2, coveted capital is created whenever the corresponding, initially non-cooperative, investment activity increases the joint return to others from a subsequent expropriation of the previous investors' capital. Including these returns in the otherwise quite amorphous benefits appearing in the above right-hand inequality will enable us to produce an existence result. Let us be more specific.

Cooperation costs are, by definition, "moderate" whenever they exceed, as on the left above, the aggregate net investor benefit from a jointly optimal investment sequence, but, for some r < n, fall short of the <u>sum</u> of: (a) the transferable benefits produced by the first $r-1$ investors, $\sum_{j=1}^{r-1} B_j'$, and (b) the net benefit from initial

cooperation to the subsequent investors, $\sum_{j=r}^{n} B_j^o(x_i^c)$. I.e., under "moderate"

cooperation costs,

$$\sum = \sum_{i=1}^{n} B_i^o(x_1^c) < C < \sum_{j=1}^{r-1} B_j' + \sum_{j=r}^{n} B_j^o(x_1^c).$$

Now, from the assumption that the prior investments produce some coveted capital,

$$A + \sum_{j=1}^{r-1} B_j^o(x_1^c) = \sum_{j=1}^{r-1} B_j', \qquad \text{where} \quad A > 0.$$

Substituting the above equality into the immediately preceding inequalities,

$$1 < \frac{C}{\sum} < 1 + \frac{A}{\sum}.$$

Thus, whenever capital is coveted, for <u>any</u> jointly efficient investment sequence, there is a range of cooperation costs such that, whenever actual cooperation costs fall within this "moderate" range, the jointly efficient non-cooperative investment sequence never occurs. The right-hand inequality implies that subsequent cooperation would be induced by an efficient investment sequence without initial cooperation while the left-hand side assures us <u>both</u> that initial cooperation does not occur and that the induced cooperation must leave some investor with negative net benefits. With cooperation costs in this intermediate range, the jointly efficient investment sequence can never be a solution. The result is underinvestment. All jointly efficient investment sequences are precluded when there are "moderate" cooperation costs.

B. Quantitatively Strengthening the Result

There are at least two ways to strengthen the above, rather obvious, theoretical result. First, when the investments are necessary complements, like the port-road-mine example in our Introduction, then an extreme, zero-investment, solution is inevitable under moderate cooperation costs. The introductory example made this quite obvious. Section III below will offer another, somewhat less straightforward, strengthening of the result.

C. A Theoretically Optimal Policy

As also indicated in the Introduction, and shown in greater detail in the following section, there is a theoretically first-best policy eliminating all underinvestment traps. It is to make $B_j^o = B_j'$ by constraining all cooperative interactions so that the returns from <u>current</u> cooperation are shared as if the parties had <u>initially</u> cooperated. This, in effect, outlaws the coveting and appropriation of capital by granting early investors utility endowments ("territorial endowments") sufficient to prevent others from attempting to confiscate their capital investments, and, like the utility-endowing legal system assumed in Part 5 of Appendix B.1, leads to a social optimum. Implementing effective substitutes for this policy when it is not informationally feasible will be the main subject of Section IV.

III. ZERO-INVESTMENT SOLUTIONS AND AN OPTIMAL LEGAL POLICY

A zero-investment solution inevitably arises, even in the total absence of complementarities, under the robber-baron assumption that an investor can commit to undertake future reactions that would leave the others with no more than their initial, pre-investment endowments. This, our strongest result, is now obtained in a model designed to both explicate the dynamical structure of above investment arguments and relate the entire discussion to our basic model of social interaction.

A. Punishability in an Explicit Investment Model

1. *Preliminaries.* A special form of strategic interaction arises when actions are available to the first committer that can, directly or indirectly, make all subsequent actors worse off than if they had selected actions most preferred by the first committer, subject only to the achievement of minimum subsequent utility levels of these subsequent actors.[19] The punishment may, for example, be generated by sufficiently large increases in the production of substitutes for, or decreases in the production of complements of, the victim's investment goods. Under this "punishability" condition, the actions following the first commitment are simply those maximizing the utility of r, the first committer, given all actions prior to the establishment of the commitment and given the implicitly endowed subsequent utility levels, U_{r+i}^o, of the subsequent actors (Appendix B.1, Parts 4 and 5). In other words, if r is the first to adopt a cooperative strategy, then

$$(1) \qquad U_r = \max_{x_r,\ldots,x_n} U_r(x) - C_r$$

subject to $U_{r+i}(x) \geq U_{r+i}^o$, $i = 1,\ldots,n\text{-}r$, where C_r represents r's, positive, utility-equivalent of the resource cost of establishing a committed reaction function.

---

[19]These endowed levels replace private property endowments described in any standard competitive environment. The rationale for, and efficiency-under-zero-cooperation-costs of such utility endowments for more general environments is developed in Part 5 of Appendix B.1. For example, in the new formulation, individuals are compensated for all torts committed against them. More germane to the present discussion, these endowments are best thought of as the various individual standards of living allowable by a bankruptcy court.

We restrict our attention to interactions featuring a threat of potential cooperation. Thus, there is always at least one relevant action-sequence inducing cooperation and at least one that does not. Regarding the latter, within a given subset of X, call it X^p (p stands for "peacefully avoiding prospective cooperation"), none of the subsequences, $x_1^p,...,x_{r-1}^p$ are sufficient to induce r to choose the commitment strategy described in (1) above. In other words, an interaction solution when all x are in X^p is simply:

(2)
$$x_1^{p*} = \arg\max_{x \in X^{p}} U_1(x_1,x_2(x_1),x_{r-1}(x_1),...,x_n(x_1)),$$

$$\bullet$$
$$\bullet$$
$$\bullet$$

$$x_n^{p*} = \arg\max U_n(x_1^{p*},...,x_{n-1}^{p*},x_n).$$

Regarding the complement of X^p in X, or X^b ("b" stands for "bad"), each $x^b \in X^b$ has a subsequence $(x_1^b,...,x_{r-1}^b)$, such that a special form of (1) applies, or

(3)
$$U_r(x^b) = \max_{x_r,...,x_n} U_r(x_1^b,...,x_{r-1}^b,x_r,...,x_n) - C_r$$

$$\text{subject to } U_{r+i}(x^b) \geq U_{r+i}^o, \ i = 1,...,n-r,$$

where we assume the existence of unique maxima so as to avoid repeating much of the discussion of Section I. On the other hand, if, in the same general X-environment, the first r-1 choices are made so that it will never pay an individual to establish a reaction function, i.e., r's utility in a (2)-sequence is higher than in (3) above, then we are in X^p and have a special kind of noncooperative solution, x^p.

This special noncooperative solution is identical to the purely noncooperative x* described in Section I, except that the solution must be in X^p rather than X so that $x_1,...,x_{r-1}$, labelled $x_1^p,...,x_{r-1}^p$, must satisfy, for all r and subsequent $x \in X$,

(4)
$$B_r(x^p) = \max_{x_r,...,x_n} U_r(x) - U_r(x^p) \leq C_r.$$

The first actor will pick either such an X^p-constrained optimum, x_1^p, or x_1^b, given that one of these actions presents a higher utility than the other. This first choice sets the course: If the first potentially constrained actor picks x_1^{p*}, thereby satisfying the above constraint, the second such actor will find it utility-maximizing to pick x_2^{p*}, the third x_3^{p*}, etc. For, suppose that some of these later x_i-choices violated the above inequality constraint. Subsequent cooperation would therefore be induced, in which case individuals 1 through (r-1) would, as we are about to elaborate, <u>all</u> rationally choose an x in X^p. Such unanimity would contradict the supposed contrast in these investor preferences. If the solution is x^{p*}, then we say that the equilibrium is "constrained by potential cooperation."

Any theory of underinvestment traps requires a definition of an "investment". To simplify the notation for this, we first partition our n actors, or "movers", into T equal subsets. The first $\frac{n}{T}$ actors are in set n_1, the second in set n_2, etc.

We regard the jth, $(\frac{n}{T}+j)^{th}$, $(\frac{2n}{T}+j)^{th}$, and $(\frac{(T-1)n}{T}+j)^{th}$ actors as the same biological entity (or a sequence of bequest-receiving offspring). There are no commitment-inducing, Strotz-type, "inconsistencies" between these formally distinct actors because -- from a generalization of the theorem of Blackorby, Nissen, Primont, and Russell established in Appendix A.2 -- $U_j(x) = U_j(x_1,...,x_{n_1+j-1},U_{n_1+j}(x))$, where U_{n_1+j} may or may not be sensitive to values of x prior to n_1. Now an "investment" is an action undertaken only because it increases one's future benefits. Thus, letting the action-sequence $x(x_j)$ represent the solution resulting from j's choosing x_j, an "investment" by j relative to x_j^o is simply an x_j' such that $U_j(x(x_j')) \geq U_j(x(x_j^o))$ implies $U_{n_1+j}(x(x_j')) > U_{n_1+j}(x(x_j^o))$.

Investments are "coveted" (Appendix B.2) when they subsequently increase the gross return to other individuals from robber-baron-type cooperative interactions with the original investors. Thus, recalling that x^* represents an unconstrained noncooperative equilibrium, if j's investment of x_j' is "coveted", there is generally an $r > j$ such that $U_r(x^b(x_j')) - U_r(x^*(x_j')) > U_r(x^b(x_j^o)) - U_r(x^*(x_j^o))$. Hence, using (3) and the equation in (4) above, the covetedness of the investment in the context of our current model, wherein $X^P \in X$, simply states that $B_r(x(x_j')) > B_r(x(x_j^o))$.

Since, under punishability, a "cooperating" r will punish j, $j > r$, unless j surrenders an amount of the commonly consumed numeraire generating j's zero-investment utility endowment, U_j^o, punishability implies that every investment in a sequence of investments by $r-1$ individuals will be coveted.

2.   *The Theorem.*   We can now substantially strengthen the earlier underinvestment results by showing that: <u>Under punishability, in any noncooperative equilibrium in which potential investments are constrained by potential cooperation, no such investments occur.</u>

Given our lengthy set of preliminaries, the actual proof is quite simple. Say individual j is constrained by potential cooperation in the solution, x^{p*}. This means, from the above preliminaries, that none of the constrained potential investments would induce the requisite an increase in utility of $\frac{n}{T} + j$. For all such investments would be coveted and would therefore induce cooperation and generate a minimal utility level for this actor, $U^0_{j+\frac{n}{T}}$. The committer, r, would reap the returns from j's implicit sacrifice.

Some non-cooperative investment will generally occur before the potential cooperation constraint becomes operative. But, once operative, the right-hand side of the constraint will remain operative even though alterations in j's preferences (or the technology underlying them) place greater and greater values on $U_{\frac{n}{T}+j}$ relative to U_j. For any attempt to generate some non-cooperative investment by increasing the potential future return to individual j will just result in a greater expropriation. Of course, greater potential returns will increase the private returns to initial cooperation, thereby eventually lifting the left hand side of the constraint and limiting the extent to which the society is impervious to increasing investment values. However, realistically speaking, several forms of typically necessary early investment, such as exploratory informational investments or speculative real investments with an initially low probability of a high return, are extremely costly to contract over. So x^{p*} is typically impervious to technological improvements favoring j's investment. Increasing inefficiency is nearly certain.

And even where initial cooperation finally <u>does</u> become profitable, there are hopefully much less costly ways of responding to the problem than to wait for the potential returns to naturally rise sufficiently for the concerned investors to dissipate a large part of their prospective profits on initial cooperation expenditures.

B. An Optimal Policy Under Ideal Legal Information

Recall that an ideal legal policy treats subsequent cooperative interaction is if it were <u>initially</u> cooperative (e.g., Macaulay), granting all cooperating individuals the prospective utility levels that they would have received in an hypothetically costless, <u>initially cooperative</u> interaction between the economically related investors (Part 5 of Appendix B.1). To do this, judges would assume -- by statutory instruction (e.g., anti-predation laws) if necessary -- that the benefits of the subsequent cooperation would be distributed to others <u>as if</u> the interaction were initially cooperative. The corresponding, $t = 0$, prospective utility levels, $U^0_1,...,U^0_{r-1}$, therefore become new investment-contingent-utility endowments of individuals 1 through $r-1$ in all of the subsequent, $t > 0$, cooperative interactions between these individuals.

Since it would not, recalling the first inequality of Section II, pay r to set up a surplus maximizing, $t = 0$, reaction function if r had to refer back to the <u>pre-investment</u> endowments and grant $U_1^0,...,U_{r-1}^0$ to the corresponding actors, it would also not, under the optimal policy, pay r to set up such a reaction function after they have chosen their noncooperative actions. For such actions cannot work to increase the surplus obtainable by r. The prior investments are simply not coveted.

This optimal policy obviously applies whether or not r's reaction function satisfies a punishability condition. Potential cooperation can eliminate components of an investor-efficient sequence of noncooperative actions only when some early actors in the sequence can be subsequently made worse-off than they would be under their initial utility endowments. Punishability and robber-baronage, by broadening and magnifying these losses, and thereby broadening and magnifying the underdevelopment traps that would result from the constraint of potential cooperation, alter the ideal legal policy only by increasing the compensations that are due the first $r-1$ investors.

IV. APPLICATIONS

To simplify the economic environment, our applications will be restricted to an economy whose only trap-inducing effects work through indivisible inputs or externalities.[20]   Otherwise, we assume an economy with private resource endowments, productive opportunities, several price-taking buyers and sellers for each good, generally positive bilateral transaction costs, and prohibitive equilibrium transaction costs for all multilateral transactions.

The main advantage of adopting this specific economic environment, besides its relative familiarity, is the simplicity of its optimality properties. In particular, if both indivisibilities and technological externalities were absent, a general equilibrium would be Pareto optimal (Foley, Kurz, Thompson, 1977). The first set of applications of our potential cooperation theory will consider worlds with indivisible investments but no technological externalities. The second two sets of applications will bring in technological externalities.[21]

---

[20]An "indivisible" input here is any efficiently employed input in a firm that employs at least one sufficiently important overhead input that a large output must be produced before that firm reaches a minimum long-run average cost of production.

[21]"Technological externalities," or simply, "externalities", are restricted here to potentially beneficial multilateral trades at existing prices, trades that are implicitly excluded by the prohibitive equilibrium transaction costs of multilateral trades. If we did not restrict our definition of "externalities" to multilateral cases, a Pigouvian subsidy to simply transferring a good to another individual would then be a feasible "externality-internalizing" policy. This uninteresting policy would have to be eliminated in a realistic model by introducing governmental informational costs, costs that are assumed away in conventional externalities discussions.

So, under our definition, and in the conventional example, when A, who owns a potentially smoke-producing factory, produces a good and sells it to B while C simply stands by and suffers the smoke, there is, following Pigou, an "external diseconomy", the cause

Optimal government policy toward each problem will be discussed in each of the following two subsections. The theoretical goal in each subsection is to indicate how relatively familiar principles of efficient economic policy must be reformulated when a potential cooperation constraint underlies the observed noncooperative equilibrium. The empirical goal is to show how these efficient policy principles have actually been pragmatically implemented by the legislatures of most of the world's developed countries.

A. Potential Cooperation and Underdevelopment Traps in the Absence of Externalities

1. *The Simplest Case.* Large, initially risky, *ex-post* successful, business investments are often privately expropriated by self-interested workers subsequently claiming injury, customers claiming implicit contractual damage, or neighbors claiming tort damages to their properties. Many substantial investment opportunities are correspondingly rejected in anticipation of the subsequent domestic expropriation of the investors' coveted capital stocks. But the usual policy suggestions following this common observation are to either subsidize investment or to "secure private property rights". We have already pointed out the inefficiency of the former policy, noting that subsidizing private investment in such cases is tantamount to subsidizing private warfare. And the "securing" of private property rights by reducing the cost of each transaction will also facilitate the post-investment attacks on property. Thus, when reducing the total cost of cooperation means reducing previously prohibitive transaction costs to only "moderate" levels, the "securing of private property rights" actually creates underinvestment traps where none had previously existed. Regarding more extensive reductions in cooperation costs -- i.e., when reducing the cost of each transaction is so extensive that it induces initial cooperation -- it correspondingly creates expensive cooperation costs that investors that had previously been able to avoid. The standard policy recommendations simply do not work.

In general, the correct criterion for Pareto optimal policy in a competitive economy with transaction costs is the minimization of the costs of achieving a given allocation of resources to real, or non-transactional, activities (Thompson, *ibid.*). This involves achieving an optimal sequence of transactions, where the total quantity of transactions necessary to achieve the allocation becomes particularly relevant. Simple

---

of which is the prohibitive cost of a multilateral transaction between A, B, and C. But no one would say there was an "external diseconomy" if a smoke-free factory failed to operate because of a sufficiently high cost of bilateral transaction between A and B, despite the fact that the net social loss resulting from the failure to transact could still be theoretically eliminated by an appropriate tax-subsidy policy.

Nevertheless, an analogous situation arises when transaction costs completely preclude the provision of a collective-type of service to several individuals. Dealt with in Section B below, we will call these "qualitative externalities" to denote the fact that the efficient government here does not simply tax or subsidize an observable laissez faire quantity (e.g., smoke). It must unilaterally determine an optimal quality of the unprovided service.

economic rules for achieving such an optimum do not exist. This was already pointed out in the Introduction, at least for the case of a complex technology, and will be further elaborated in the next section's discussion of optimal policy in a world with externalities.

The only optimality theorems covering the general situation in this section concern collective decision processes, where the significant gainers and losers from each policy alternative all freely participate, either directly or through interest-group-sensitive representatives, in the legislative process. The process that mankind keeps re-evolving out of its various self-imposed dark ages, a process featuring voting on plausible legislative alternatives by all people favored by the military leaders, is popularly termed "democracy". Democratic processes are unable to induce exact preference revelation. But when we put aside this weakness by assuming complete information regarding one another's preferences, we find effectively democratic incentives to be internally correct in that they lead the process to theoretically select internally Pareto optimal economic rules (Appendix B.2, Sec. IIIi, and Section I.A of Chapter 3). We would therefore expect to find that democracies generate economic rules eschewing simple-minded economics in favor of a complex of pragmatic rules, rules responding to the potential cooperation problem by significantly reducing total transaction costs for a given set of real investments and corresponding real benefits.

A measure of the effectiveness of the pragmatic complex of rules, other than their effect on aggregate income, is their effect in eliminating large numbers of private transactions involving successive large-scale investments.

The familiar history of U.S. economic legislation during its relatively populist periods (1865-1905, 1932-1956) provides a steady stream of cases in point. The internal laissez faire policy-ideology fashionably emerging during the early 19th century led, in only a few decades, to a public outcry against the wastes of robber-baron economic warfare and the corresponding monopolization of the railroads, the result being a complex of state-regulatory laws, the so-called "Granger Laws" from the late 1860s to the late 1880s. The potentially expropriative slew of local court cases finally produced our first federal regulatory act, the Interstate Commerce Act of 1887. Clearly designed to relieve railroads of a growing avalanche of new local laws and corresponding local lawsuits, the Act, as steadily amended over the subsequent 20 years, relieved society of the drain of future such lawsuits by legislatively evolving a mutually acceptable set of regulatory guidelines (largely non-discriminatory pricing rules) to replace the almost-certain financial collapse of the industry through what had been a series of lawsuit-encouraging, potentially expropriative, judicial opinions.[22]

---

[22]While fully informed, risk-averse, plaintiffs and defendants would be jointly discouraged by such rent-absorbing judicial decisions, most people substantially exaggerate, even to themselves, the justice of both their own claims and the objectivity of the legal system they were raised to believe in. Legal uncertainty, therefore, invariably leads to some economically expensive trials, especially in an adversarial legal system such as our own, where the members of the legal profession benefit from, and therefore subtly encourage, lawsuits rather than

More generally, the reaction of the Federal government to a whole series of populist-inspired, state-law or common-law-based, anti-monopoly suits during the 1880s resulted in the Sherman Anti-Trust Act of 1890. Here, too, economists have trivialized the effects of the Act. Section 1 of the Act, which outlawed "conspiracies in restraint of trade," has been universally interpreted by economists as referring to the formation of output-restricting, uniform-price-increasing, cartels. While the social costs of such investor-cooperation may itself be significant (Tullock), probably much more significant are the additional social costs incurred in conspiracies to economically isolate high-surplus investors in order to monopolistically or monopsonistically <u>discriminate</u> against those investors. The rational anticipation of such discriminatory private rent-seeking had substantially deterred the investment of many potential industrial customers and input-suppliers. (A detailed specification of the economic effects of these laws, and a theoretically ideal antitrust, law is developed in Thompson, et al., Vol. III, Ch. 2.) Section II of the Act, which outlaws all attempts, including predatory ones, to monopolize, has an analogously substantial value as a trap-deterrent.

U.S. Workmen's Compensation Laws were similarly evolved during the 1890s as a populist response to a wave of rent-attacking, private lawsuits during the 1880s. This wave understandably followed the late 19th century judicial abandonment of the notoriously employer-protective, irresponsibility-inducing but investment-trap-preventing, legal doctrines of "contributionary negligence", "assumed risk", and the "fellow-servant rule". Workmen's Compensation Laws thus allowed large employers to substitute a relatively efficient process (a fixed-compensation, employee insurance plan) for the aggressively expropriative litigation system that immediately preceded it (L. Friedman, pp. 586-88).

Natural local monopolies, such as local electricity, water, natural gas, and related "public utilities", are particularly subject to expropriative discriminatory pricing, given the obviously prohibitive pre-entry cost of contracting between the typically numerous landowners and the prospective utility providers.   As in the zoning-regulation example presented in Section F of the above Introduction, the obvious laissez-faire underdevelopment traps in worlds potentially providing these expropriatively priced laissez faire utility services explain the near-universality of the interventionist policy responses observed throughout the developed world.

2. *Underdevelopment as an Ethics Problem.* Although it is easy to accumulate such evidence for our theory -- what we have outlined is just a small sample from what is available -- we must ask why severe underdevelopment persists among many modern countries that emulate the statutory institutions of the developed countries. The answer, as we have already emphasized, is that effective democracy requires an

---

settlements, if in no other way than to induce the state to bear a substantial burden of the costs of civil lawsuits.

An efficiency-justification of the specific economic guidelines that actually emerged with the Hepburn Act in 1906, although beyond the scope of this appendix, is developed elsewhere (Thompson, et al., Vol. III, Ch. 2).

ethically suitable, civilly reverent, bureaucracy.

It is plausible to assume that potentially benefiting parties often find it prohibitively costly to <u>initially</u> cooperate via private contracting to insure against subsequent legal expropriations of the coveted capital stocks of subsequently successful investors. Yet, once the success of a set of investments is established, economically related private individuals begin a costly process of cooperation with the successful investors. The same costly sequence occurs <u>within</u> the bureaucracies of non-civilly-reverent democracies. Certain governmental officials, although finding it impractical to initially cooperate by establishing commitments providing definite rewards for various investments, once certain investments are made, vigorously work to expropriate, even if only for the "social good", the efficient returns from the investments. The potential cure becomes part of the problem. It is difficult to deny that such expropriation has often characterized the bureaucracies of poor countries and has increasingly characterized our own over much of the past third-of-a-century. (All this is elaborated in Thompson, et al., Vol. II, Chs. 4 and 5.)

Underdeveloped countries have chronically suffered from an initial lack of cultural cohesion and linguistic homogeneity (Eisenstadt), and so pre-investment, democratic, cooperation has been much more difficult in these countries. An efficient policy for some of these underdeveloped countries would therefore be to replace their poorly communicating legislative representatives with authoritarian leaders. Because the resulting private systems then suffer from many unresolved threats of potential private cooperation, and because such states are usually brutocracies (Chapter 5, Section 1), it may also be efficient to have the government make the society's large-scale investments.[23]   However, once communication abilities and civil reverence, through cultural-educational investment, reach the levels of the more developed countries, it would pay these centralist systems to adopt democracy, especially in view of the obviously superior internal efficiency of mixed democracies such as the U.S. The post-WWII period has clearly followed this natural pattern.

But we do not wish to over-simplify the problem. Since there is no applicable formula to eliminate underinvestment traps under a complex technology, initial, non-unanimity-based, cooperation through ideologically unconstrained investor-participation is apparently the only solution. Cultural education to produce an effective democracy must therefore teach, rather than some economic ideology, social values of generalized respect for governmental institutions. The two great heroes in basic U.S. education, George Washington and Abraham Lincoln, serve as fruitful heroes because U.S. citizens are taught about their dedication to the U.S. government, not about their economic philosophies. Similarly, the mainline Protestant education

---

[23]We must be careful here not to make our government officials too smart. Our traps would not occur in private-property systems with sufficiently informed authoritarian leaders. Depending on observability conditions, such leaders could simply <u>impose</u> one of our three policy solutions to remove his system's underinvestment traps. In particular, we must assume that our authoritarian officials are no more capable of isolating the typically complex underinvestment chains in their countries than our laissez faire judges. Central planning is, by implication, quite imperfect.

from which this education sprang elevated governmental service above all other "callings" and made heroes of the founding fathers of their local governments. This, in turn, goes back to the extreme rejection of ideology ("reason") found in Luther. In sharp contrast, strict Calvinist training, which greatly elevated private property, and work and savings values as well, produced nothing but a string of still-visibly suffering local economies. (So much for Max Weber, as already pointed out by Viner.) As elaborated in Chapter 3, similar evidence is found in the economic failures of both the post-Thomist (ideologized) Catholic States and the analogously ideological, Enlightenment-inspired, 19th century reactions in the same states, which produced little economic progress until the emigration-induced abandonment of these ideologies in favor of pragmatic democracies during the last third of the 19th century.

Since that time, there have been two secular educational values responsible for our most impressive economic success stories. One is pragmatic professionalism, which is inherently anti-ideological and is emphasized in our graduate schools of business and public administration. This system exaggerates the value of experience, being backward-looking to the point that no questions arise with respect to last-period-rationality problems and time-inconsistency. The second is Hellenism, which has come to dominate modern undergraduate education, as discussed at several points of the text. Formally, Hellenistic values exaggerate the likelihood of unlikely hypotheses. The exceptionally broadminded thought system of the educated Hellenist creates ideal bureaucrats and middle-level managers, generally because of their trained ability to believe in and plausibly communicate the goals of the legitimate leaders, thereby facilitating the large scale organizations observed in the West. Unfortunately, the Hellenist is also an "ideal" ideologue when directed to a graduate program or a professional school of a world-class university. Such receptive students become effective carriers of the ideology into the succeeding generations and, as argued in the text, become a powerful source of the ideologization that has infected all historically dominant Western states and been responsible for the subsequent economic retardations of these states.

(3) *Other Theories of Underdevelopment.* A review of the failure of alternative, "critical variable," theories of underdevelopment can be found in Papenek. Our theory differs from existing "cultural" theories (e.g., Banfield) mainly in that our own is a more specific theory of the effects of costly cooperation and thus of how to remove the resulting underinvestment traps. For example, ours implies that: (1) Either reductions or increases in cooperation costs may help; (2) neither change does any predictive good until private cooperation costs are raised to a level at which post-investment cooperation becomes unprofitable, and, most importantly, (3) once an effective democracy is created, the economy "takes-off" a la Rostow. Alternative cultural theories do not have this critical-variable feature. Thus, even if we ignore the issues of logical correctness and empirical relevance, welfare-oriented theories of underdevelopment that emphasize both cultural failures and a single critical policy-variable are apparently quite rare (Papenek).

B. Optimal Policy in the Presence of Zero-Trade Solutions

Economists have long observed -- and left unexplained within simple rationality paradigms -- that certain varieties of theoretically-valuable trades almost never occur, regardless of the values of these trades. Perhaps the most common examples are the absence of: (a) full insurance against catastrophes such as floods or devastating personal accidents and (b) transactions providing on-the-spot, high-risk, aid to victims of emergencies such as fires, crimes, or critical health failures.

Once again, we have no reason to consider, at least for reasonably complex technologies, idealistic legal reforms that might induce such transactions. And we have already seen how a uniform lowering of cooperation costs generally creates more problems than it solves. Rather, we ask how transactions costs could possibly be so high that they would make such obviously useful transactions impractical, and how observed legislatures should and do respond to the problem.

Catastrophe insurance is typically impractical because, once the initial contract is written and something resembling a catastrophe subsequently occurs, it typically pays the victim to cooperate with others (such as witnesses, professional damage-estimators, or insurance company employees) in an attempt to receive the maximum possible compensation unless the insurance company takes its own, correspondingly expensive, transaction-prohibiting, precautions. And risky emergency aid transactions are impractical because, once the costly aid is provided, the returns typically would justify the almost-equal-costs of either: (1) charging the entire value of the saved asset as the appropriate payment and committing oneself to marshalling the resources necessary to prove the case unless a correspondingly high payment is received, or (2) working to avoid the above charges by devoting similarly valuable resources to protect one's legal interest. Given the high physical risk of providing emergency aid, the aiding party would almost never be able to earn a positive return on the investment.   So, in the absence of one of our potential-cooperation-inspired interventions, an efficient investment sequence would almost never occur.

In either example, the necessarily refined, prior-to-service, specifications of the conditions under which alternative compensations are to be paid are extraordinarily impractical. So there are no substantial pre-service commitments. In each example, then, given the conditionally likely prospect of future cooperation, significantly costly investments are simply not remunerative and our inevitable underinvestment solution emerges. In this case, as in Section III, there is a zero-trade solution.

Despite the absence of a supporting economic ideology, developed countries around the world have responded by providing: (1) governmental insurance against various catastrophes (especially floods and earthquakes), and (2) high-risk, emergency governmental aid to victims of fires, crimes and critical health failures. Although individual government employees have underincentives similar to individual private providers of highly incomplete, pre-emergency, service contracts, the government can, and does, compensate for this by supplying employees with both special training and ostensibly unprofitable additional inputs that are exceptionally complementary with the production of high-risk emergency services. Thus, in addition to providing a higher-risk brand of service, public fire departments in the U.S. supply much more physical capital and many more trained, full-time, firemen than do their occasionally observed, insurance-providing, private counterparts (Poole).

The rational refusal of uncommitted private individuals to provide these high-risk emergency services can be thought of as setting up an "external economy" in the provision of such services. The usual argument for governmental subsidy in response to this variety of externality is, however, insufficient because the laissez faire quantities are zero. In this case, optimal policy requires the government to determine the quality of the good so that it is more accurate to say that the government is engaged in "direct production" rather than "subsidy" and theoretically isolate the corresponding "externality" by calling it a "qualitative externality".

C. Optimal Policy in the Presence of Quantitative Externalities

1. *Compensatory Liability Systems*. Consider now the damages that individuals suffer because of the observable laissez faire actions of other individuals. We shall concentrate here on damages, although similar results emerge when benefits are included in the analysis. When the damage victims must be legally compensated by the imposers (such as occurs in the ideally informed property-rights system of Part 5 of Appendix B.1), the victims' prior investments cannot be jeopardized by damage-threatening reaction functions such as those illustrated in Section F of our Introduction. Indeed, the elimination of damage-threatening, extortionary, reaction functions is the only economic rationale for fully compensatory (non-multiple-damage) "tort" liability systems under ordinarily assumed and realistically imperfect information. This is because the prospect of full compensation is, realistically speaking, also socially costly in that it gives victims substantial underincentives to mitigate damages in a myriad of unobservable ways.

The phenomenon of quantitative externalities that we wish to discuss requires victims to be unable to practically collect damages through a compensatory liability system (in which case there would be no "externality"). For example, the high costs of the legal system in a complex technology may induce an efficient government to prohibit compensation, efficiently creating the externality that it then controls via less costly regulation. The inability to collect compensatory damages in significant small-numbers cases has indeed come mainly through a statutory abandonment of traditional compensatory liability rules whenever a sufficiently complex technology arises. The earliest and most notorious examples are the abandonment of railway accident liability (Coase, Atiyah). Here, and later in the area of pollution externalities, democratic legislatures, rather than straining the intellects of judges and juries by unrealistically relying on them to impose the conditions of theoretically ideal, pre-investment contracts in an increasingly complex technological environment, have replaced compensatory private-property coverage with pre-externality, quantity regulation by moderately informed, professional governmental bureaucrats.

Pigou's original externalities discussions also concern these railroad examples. Pigou thought so little of quantity-regulation (relative to non-compensatory taxation) that he basically ignored the fact that Britain's abandonment of the railways' legal liability was accompanied by governmental regulation. Had Pigou imagined that the railroad company might rationally adopt a strategy committing the company to essentially destroy a locality despite its Pigouvian tax liability unless that local government pays a huge, underdevelopment-inducing, side-payment to the company, he would have doubtless become an understanding supporter of such government regulation rather than taxation.

As a rule, non-compensatory, or "Pigouvian", tax systems have, quite efficiently, been traditionally maintained by democratic legislatures only when the external effects involve large numbers of <u>both</u> victims and imposers (e.g., Appendices B.2 and B.3), i.e., only when potential cooperation is not a relevant constraint. Similarly, compensatory liability systems have been traditionally employed only for idiosyncratic externalities in which there are small numbers <u>on both sides</u>, i.e., only when government investments in a regulatory level of understanding of the interactive technology are generally not worth the cost.[24]

2. *Quantity Regulation and Externalities in General.* Since, whether by design or nature, the costs of initial investor cooperation are prohibitive when externalities exist, externalities definitionally place us in an environment satisfying the left-side condition for "moderate" cooperation costs. But the right-side condition, expressing the subsequent profitability of cooperation, is likely when and only when there is a relatively small number of imposers. Thus, with only a small number of externality imposers, an efficient sequence of investments by potential pollution victims could easily subject them to the confiscatory reaction functions of destruction-threatening externality imposers. For example, an airport facing only Pigouvian taxes could fairly easily commit itself to concentrate its noise emissions in one particular region despite the noticeable increase in its Pigouvian tax bill unless the victims agreed to sell out below cost to the airport. In contrast, it would be very difficult for a large set of small airlines to join together for the sole purpose of collectively extorting payments from this little region. Applying the theorem of Section III, this would produce a zero-level of laissez faire investment by the potential victims of the extortionary airport. An efficient legislature would prevent the resulting lack of housing around the airport by quantity regulation, either by strictly outlawing excessive, obviously inefficient, noise pollution levels or by directly operating the airport as a governmental facility. This policy is, indeed, what has emerged from the legislatures of our developed democracies even though there has been no economic ideology available to motivate the obvious deviation from Pigouvian taxation principles.

We thus have an efficiency alternative to popular political explanations for the prevalence of regulation of small-numbers externality-imposers by quantity-imposition or direct governmental operation rather than taxation. These inefficiency explanations typically rely on the greater private profitability of quantity regulation to the imposers, who are, it is surmised, more politically influential than the victims. (The clearest available political argument, that of Buchanan and Tullock (1975), has the imposers a smaller, more readily cooperating, group than the victims. Polluting oil refiners would be an example.) Such political arguments do not explain the

---

[24]This ignores class-action suits and related recent disasters, which are discussed at length in W. Olson.

simultaneous popularity of legislation directly redistributing wealth away from large-scale imposers, such as large oil refiners. Nor can they explain the presence of the anti-large-investor zoning laws described in Section F of the Introduction.

V. SUMMARY

Economists have long been aware of the force of <u>potential competition</u>. Potential competitors in simple, all-private-goods economies, by flattening out industry demand or supply curves, provide an invisible force toward <u>efficiency</u> in private-property systems. But there is also a force of <u>potential cooperation</u>, an invisible force toward <u>inefficiency</u> in private property systems.

By eliminating the profit from what would otherwise be the early investments in an efficient sequence of investments and leaving a private-property economy looking as if its interactions were simply innocent, noncooperative interactions, the force of potential cooperation creates grossly Pareto-inefficient underinvestment traps. Left unattended, these traps generally create: (1) extreme underinvestment by a myriad of occasional recipients, as well as providers, of all sorts of emergency aid; (2) extreme underinvestment by a myriad of potential victims of large-scale polluters; and, most importantly, (3) extreme underinvestment by a myriad of potentially large and interacting investors. In short, these traps, left unattended, will produce extreme aggregative underdevelopment.

Pragmatic governments, appropriately sensitive to the benefits of its various consumer and producer interest groups, have evolved qualitatively efficient policy responses. In particular, regarding the three underinvestment cases mentioned above, they have: (1) adopted <u>local provision of police, fire and emergency medical care</u> to prevent extreme underinvestment by local investors in occasional need of high-risk emergency aid and <u>state-provided disaster relief</u> from collective natural disasters; (2) adopted <u>zoning laws and quality controls on pollution</u> to prevent extreme underinvestment by potential pollution victims; and (3) introduced <u>compensatory legal systems (torts)</u>, subsequently replacing them with <u>direct bureaucratic regulation</u> when the technologies became sufficiently complex, in order to eliminate underinvestment by the potential victims of damage-threatening reaction functions.

The fact that <u>traditional economic thinking argues against the efficiency of essentially all of these observed policies</u> is indicative of a complete absence of the constraint of potential cooperation from existing economic thought.

Finally, while the point to democratic government is to use legislation to <u>protect</u> the returns of private investors, the positive profit to engaging in confiscatory redistribution creates a positive return to insufficiently committed governmental representatives to <u>attack</u> the returns of private investors. Democracy is both ill-suited and seldom-used in such insufficiently committed, "civilly irreverent," countries (Chapters 3 and 5). With the resulting authoritarian governmental forms dependent on the inherited economic wisdom of social planners, rather than grounded in the real self-interest of interacting political interest groups, it is not surprising that non-democratic governmental forms have uniformly displayed only limited economic success in the real world.

CHAPTER 2

THE EFFICIENCY PROBLEM,
THE DISTRIBUTION PROBLEM, AND A POSSIBLE SOLUTION

"For want of a nail ... the kingdom was lost."
Poor Richard's 1752 version of George Herbert's
Outlandish Proverb No. 499 (1640).

I. THE EFFICIENCY PROBLEM[1]

A. The Evolution of Vital Organs in General

1. *The Efficiency of the Decentralized Development of a Nonconflictual Team.*
If an organism, biological or social, lacks one of its vital organs, the organism dies
before it reproduces. The organism survives to reproduction only if all of its vital
organs survive. Therefore, no conflict exists among the vital organs. They all live
or die together. In decision-theoretic terms, the vital components of an organism
form a nonconflictual team; they all share the same objective. This absence of
conflict substantially simplifies the development of the organism. As shown in
Appendix A.2 at the end of this chapter, even without the costly sequence of status-
determinations that characterizes ordinary cooperative interaction (Appendix B.1),

---

[1]Some readers of our introductory efficiency analyses may be put-off by our gross level
of social-scientific simplicity. Even though this apparent coarseness is actually the unavoidable
consequence of our continual imposition of a single, cohesive, model of social interaction on
the entire discussion, it may make reading our introductory efficiency-analyses intolerable. For
such individuals, who may nevertheless have a substantial interest in some of the relatively
applied portions of this work, the subsequent two parts of this chapter, like each of the
succeeding chapters and appendices, are written as self-contained units. We also offer the
following, much more brief, substitute perspective on the role of efficiency in our work: Our
investigations began well over three decades ago as separate price-theoretic inquiries into the
nature of the apparently quite inefficient, yet strangely durable and widespread, institutions
listed in the book's subtitle. The work has given us great intellectual satisfaction because it
has convinced us that we have finally come to understand the evolutionary inevitability of both
the emergence and the often premature decay of such institutions, as well as the role of both
efficiency and economic ideology in generating each institutional life cycle. We hope, in the
following chapters, to share some of this understanding with our patient readers.

For readers without much interest in evolution or game theory but with a healthy demand
for a social-theoretic framework, together with an understanding of the essence of our political-
economic argument, we recommend beginning with Section B below.

The distributional part of the work, which is introduced in Part II below, is much simpler
than the efficiency part. It's simplicity should not conceal its importance. Were it not for the
serendipity of this distributional discovery, which emerged about six years ago as we were
attempting to tie together a few empirical loose ends in the efficiency story, our
recommendations of world-constitutional constraints would possess none of their current
urgency.

each vital action is a narrowly rational choice; each actor unconditionally adopts an allocatively efficient action. An "invisible hand" thus inexorably guides the self-interested decentralized decisions of all vital decisionmakers to a social optimum.

The laissez faire efficiency result applies to any sequential social decision process in which the decisionmakers share the same objective function. Regarding social-organization decisions, whenever the reaction functions, or "roles", in the model of Appendix B.1 are necessary for the group's collective survival, they formally define the social organism's "vital institutions". Here, the reaction-function-selecting individuals all share the same objective, e.g., preventing an imminent total loss to a potential military aggressor. (As elaborated in Subsection 10 below, this unanimity arises when the shared gains from a decision dwarf the private costs or when the society's basic distributional conflicts are settled prior to the selection of the society's joint-survival-relevant institutions.) It thus follows from the central efficiency theorem of Appendix A.2 at the end of this chapter that the specific characteristics of each of a sequence of vital components are determined without the usual, costly, hierarchical struggle among the individual decisionmakers.[2]

It similarly follows that, during the later developmental stages of a survivable organism, after the relevant information has been widely disseminated so that the information among the various micro-decisionmakers has become quite accurate, the theorem predicts close approximations of an ideally efficient equilibrium. Nevertheless, we still have a choice of developmental paradigms. We can assume, as in all of the appendices, purposefully rational utility maximization by the increasingly well-informed individuals.

Or we can adopt an "evolutionary" approach by assuming that the institution-determining individuals are replicating, mutating, and imitating machines and then, as we shall see, apply the general convergence theorems of Foster-Young and Weibull to steadily approach the perfect equilibria described in the appendices.[3]

---

[2]Viewing all of our major anatomical organs as vital, macrobiological evidence for the sufficiency of unmonitored sequential optimization in the development of an organism can be found in the surprisingly close resemblance of the young embryos of later-emerging animals (e.g., mammals) with the almost-mature embryos of earlier-emerging species (e.g., fish). (See, e.g., Alberts, et al., p. 889.) If the development of the later-developing organs would have substantially conflicted with the development of its earlier-developing organs, surely the natural evolution of the organism would have led to a substantial alteration in the early developmental pattern.

[3]These theorems demonstrate the uniform convergence, under a payoff-positivity assumption, of various evolutionary processes to a strict, non-symmetric Nash equilibrium. The strict and asymmetric nature of the equilibrium in Appendix B.1 is obvious. That the Appendix B.1 equilibrium is a particular Nash equilibrium of some game (e.g., von Neumann's majorant game or Howard's "j-k metagame") is discussed in Thompson-Faith (1981) and illustrated in Figure 2 of Appendix B.1, where we: (1) reject most Nash equilibria, maintaining only those that arise under strategic communication, and (2) assume that leaders possess strict preferences over the social alternatives to obtain a unique equilibrium. The payoff-positivity assumption will be discussed in the text below.

Although our approach is basically evolutionary, evolution generates consciously rational decisionmaking over certain matters, as explained in footnote #7 below. As a result, our description of various evolutionary equilibria will contain some consciously rational, although not generally completely informed, choices.

Our reason for selecting a basically evolutionary approach is not simply the psychological unwillingness to adopt an affirmative methodological principle described in the first footnote of Chapter 1. As explained in Section I of that chapter, the beliefs that individuals adopt in order to execute an optimal reaction function are exaggerations necessary to motivate the individuals to carry out what would otherwise be irrational acts. It would be extremely unlikely for either successful students or effective teachers of these values to recognize the necessary inaccuracy of their beliefs. Effective priests and their dedicated parishioners are not agnostics, etc. Although possibly objectively pre-selected, this optimal set of exaggerated beliefs is subsequently taught and learned because it is, through some critical exaggerations, held to represent a sort of objective truth. Therefore, since we are arguing that certain kinds of false beliefs survive because they are objective-profit-maximizing beliefs, we are going to have to argue that these beliefs endure in the real world because they pass a Lamarck-Darwin market-test in which objective practical experience -- not objectively rational thought -- demonstrates their usefulness. Our optimal reaction functions are the result of objective social learning and natural market selection rather than thoroughly rational decisionmaking.

Within this evolutionary context, the only substantial condition for Weibull's uniform convergence (or "asymptotic stability") result, besides an essential asymmetry and strictness that all of our static models possess, is that the evolutionary adjustment process is "weakly payoff positive." This means that, among those partially adopted pure strategies that have higher-than-average payoff rates, some such strategies have positive growth rates. A given society cannot survive unless vital, initially only partially adopted but clearly very high-payoff, strategies gain supporters as the society develops. So vital strategies (i.e., "vital institutions") are necessarily payoff-positive strategies among the survivable states. Therefore, the presence here of vital institutions implies the satisfaction of Weibull's condition for uniform convergence. Furthermore, from the identity of payoff-positivity with objective learning pointed out in Section X of Chapter 1, vital institutions, being payoff-positive in long-surviving states, are objectively evaluated in these states. Such necessary objectivity inevitably carries over to the evolution of related non-vital institutions and thereby predicts a significant set of efficient non-vital institutions.

As regards other non-vital institutions, we have already noted that several cases arise in which an entire class of high-payoff strategies -- in sharp contrast to the high-payoff strategies that comprise a set of vital institutions -- systematically decreases the growth rate of their societies as well as their subsequent numbers of adopters despite the efficiency that would be generated by the adoption of these strategies. The resulting evolutionary inefficiencies, although occurring within societies in which the members nevertheless come to adopt their vital strategies, are the main subject of Thompson, et al., Vol. I. Nevertheless, as we have just noted, the presence of some payoff-negative, non-objectively evaluated, institutions does not disturb the uniform convergence to an equilibrium. Moreover, we are going to find a way to isolate these inefficiencies to prevent them from confounding our welfare argument.

Having, of necessity, chosen a substantially evolutionary approach to social organization,[4] we now show that vital-strategies-inducing evolutionary models produce <u>extremely rapid</u> adjustment processes. We must do this because, as explained in Chapter 1, a rapid adjustment process is also necessary if we are to justify using an equilibrium-model to explain the development of observed states.

2. *Rapid Evolution.* Lamarckian evolution -- which is clearly a significant part of <u>social</u> evolution -- is comprised of: (a) experiments consisting of new designs, not just piecemeal random variants on pre-existing designs; and (b) durable learning among survivable individuals (the actually pre-Lamarckian idea of "the inheritance of acquired characteristics"). Such a process contrasts sharply with Darwin's familiar random mutation, natural-selection process (which similarly had been expounded long before Darwin, by Empedocles, but negatively reviewed by Aristotle, who couldn't believe that life had no higher purpose). The Darwinian process contains neither the functionally correlated (design-oriented) mutations nor the durably learned adaptations among above-subsistence beings that occurs under Larmarckian evolution.[5]

The existence of vital organs unavoidably <u>adds</u> a harsh Darwinian component to any Lamarckian process. This Darwinian component is "harsh" in that the process is highly unforgiving in the case of a vital organ. The continual absence of a vital organ means the entire organism's certain and premature death.

Now Darwinian and Lamarckian evolution are not always substitute forces. Indeed, they may be quite complementary (Waddington). Moreover, this complementarity is magnified when it regards the evolution of vital organs, either biological or social. This is because, when the relevant organ is vital: (i) the prospect of harsh Darwinian extinction significantly increases the seriousness and intended accuracy of Lamarckian learning, and (ii) the accuracy of Lamarckian learning itself becomes a critical object of Darwinian natural selection. The evolutionary emergence of any vital organ, which we already know exhibits a uniform rather than a continually cyclical path, is an exceptionally rapid process.

---

[4]We are nevertheless going to allow, as rationalized in Footnote #7 below: (1) a rational-decision approach to certain non-institutional (i.e., non-reaction-functional) decisions; and (2) an intuitive filter to humanize social decisionmaking, our "Pascalian" approach to institutional decisionmaking described in Section C below. The latter is especially important because it enables us to treat certain decisions of appropriately evolved, "Pascalian," decisionmakers as if they were rationally calculated and then apply the optimality theorem of Appendix A.2 in a suitably evolved decision environment.

[5]The actual, historical, Darwin accepted Lamarck. In the larger picture, both were evolutionists as opposed to rigid creationists, people that were being increasingly embarrassed by the fossil evidence throughout the 19th century. It was Weismann, as we shall explain in Chapter 6, who worked, perhaps too successfully in the West but not successfully enough in the East, to discredit Lamarck and create the impression in the West that all biological evolution was limited to Darwin's relatively simple, replication-mutation-selection, process.

Nevertheless, the form taken by this rapid evolution is radically different for organisms that ordinarily live near subsistence than it is for organisms that ordinarily live far-above subsistence.[6]

3. *Rapid Evolution in The Near-subsistence Case.* For an economically familiar example of the near-subsistence case, consider a pre-existing competitive equilibrium consisting of: (1) a single industry comprised of many individual owner-operators, each of whom produces a physically homogeneous output and earns an insignificant long-run profit; and (2) a non-produced consumer durable, which serves as a numeraire. An institutionally adventurous seller now somehow decides to merge with another seller. Say, because of various complex incentive effects, average production costs under this partnership form of organization are uniformly lower. The partnership earns a substantially positive profit and correspondingly expands its output, while its competitors now earn a slightly negative profit in the new, temporary equilibrium. The subsequent path of institutional evolution in this industry will, for two reasons, be faster than would be a simple Darwinian path. First, the imitative mergers of others, which are Lamarckian rather than Darwinian responses, will obviously hasten the social response to the successful experiment. Second, as the remaining single proprietorships become increasingly unprofitable and fail at an increasing rate, a point in time will be reached at which single proprietorships have become so unprofitable that their owner-operators simply cannot survive for any substantial length of time. At that point, the partnership form of organization has become a "vital" business institution; a firm simply cannot survive for a substantial length of time unless it is a partnership. The remaining single proprietorships thereafter rapidly become extinct, reflecting a complement of both Darwinian and Lamarckian forces. Few economists would deny either the existence of vital business institutions or the super-Darwinian

---

[6]Near-subsistence living does not mean that every moment of an individual's life is spent near subsistence. It means that the worst pre-reproduction moments of a successful life are spent near subsistence. An important implication, at least for individuals whose survival probabilities uniformly decrease with increases in the number of their siblings, is that an increase in an organism's fertility will fail to increase the organism's population. Consequently, the organism is living near subsistence if and only if its fertility has been set so as to unconditionally maximize its sustainable population.

The corresponding equilibrium is Malthusian in that fertility rates are socially excessive because each individual among a group of competing organisms residing in a given niche imposes crowding costs and a likelihood of premature deaths on the others, which makes the marginal social costs of fertility exceed the private costs. While each organism's privately optimal fertility rate maximizes the organism's own expected representation in the future sustainable population, if all competing organisms simultaneously reduced their fertility rates, the exact same population could be sustained while the saved parental resources could be spent on projects that would raise the entire population above its original subsistence, projects that would generally raise the ability of each organism to survive future shocks despite the slower rate of natural selection.

speed of the evolutionary path.[7]

Since an organ is vital whenever its absence would force the organism to soon die, all of the substantial organs of a barely subsisting organism are vital. This steady survival pressure on near-subsistence organisms -- combined with the correspondingly high reward to innovation described in Subsection 7 below -- helps explain the remarkable rapidity of the early evolution of sophisticated and durable micro-organisms (early eukaryotes such as fungi and amoeba), the subsequently rapid evolution of various multicellular organisms, and the almost unbelievably rapid subsequent evolution of essentially all of what we now consider our vital macrobiological organs (e.g., brains, hearts, lungs, digestive systems, legs, sex organs, jaws, eyes, ears and noses) in the near-subsistence environment that existed from about 0.9 to 0.5 billion years ago (e.g., Alberts, et al., Ch. 1).

But the above partnership process, with all of its simplicity and speed, ceases to generally apply once organisms multiply to where they begin to effectively establish prior claims to certain family territories (somewhere around 0.5 billion years ago) and thereby come to regularly live above-subsistence lives (as, e.g., proto-sharks

---

[7]Indeed, Alchian argues, no doubt with such examples in mind, that economic competition is such a powerful force that rationality is a redundant part of laissez faire economics. Many modern game theorists -- building on the evolutionary models of Foster and Young, Young, and Kandori, Mailaith, and Rob -- are evidently willing to entertain a similar position.

Nevertheless, evolutionary thought actually provides substantial support in favor of the assumption of individual rationality. For imagine infiltrating one of these purely pragmatic, experience-oriented, societies with a being who organizes these past experiences into mental models of the prospective future environment and evaluates alternative courses of action on the basis of the effects of these alternative courses. As economists and social thinkers often argue, such "rational decisionmakers" (Hirshleifer's "method-rational" decisionmakers) have a selective advantage in making important, largely unique, one-shot, decisions. For direct experience is of little help in making one-shot decisions. Decisions with respect to education, marriage, residential location, etc., are thus normally regarded as systematically improved by "rational contemplation". We accordingly allow conscious individual rationality (or "method-rationality"), when it will improve private decisionmaking.

One of our main efficiency-findings will be that the dominant arguments of economists and social thinkers are so biased in the collective interest of the arguers that the citizens of a democratic government would be systematically worse-off if they accepted the attempt at consciously rational thought reflected in standard economic policy conclusions. It is thus to this institutional decision case that Alchian's evolutionary argument best applies.

This claim is supported by the results of Weibull, which show that a specialization of the Foster and Young convergence result extends over to a world with a complement of Lamarckian and Darwinian effects, thereby generating a fairly rapid evolutionary path to the efficient equilibrium of Appendix B.1 even in the absence of vital institutions.

Although our efficiency-generating model adopts this evolutionary mechanism by having citizen-optimal legislators employ experience-based pragmatism rather than economic ideology to predict the utilitarian consequences of various institutions, our evolved legislators will further hasten the adjustment by transforming this experimental information into new, perhaps vital, institutions only after consulting an interpersonally sensitive utility function. We shall call such legislators "Pascalian", as described and rationalized in Section C below.

(placoderms), most land animals, or trees).[8] In the same way -- as will also be shown in Subsection 7 below -- the high evolutionary-speed of the industry process no longer generally applies once we allow a large number of firms to earn substantial Ricardian rents. Before elaborating on the evolutionary analysis that <u>does</u> apply when the organisms live well-above subsistence, we should be more specific in characterizing the above-subsistence social organisms dealt with in this study.

4. *States*. The main body of this work concerns the evolution of <u>vital social institutions</u>, where the vital organs are society-wide institutions rather than business institutions or biological organs, and where the relevant organisms are well-above-subsistence, internally cooperating, self-governing, societies, called "states". What defines a "state", and elevates its economic potential far beyond that of other societies, such as "tribes", is the mental "ability" of its members to generate and believe any conceivable set of exaggerations (i.e., myths, values, ethics, etc.), thereby enabling it, albeit at some overhead education cost, to approach the ideally efficient social equilibrium described in Appendix B.1. ("Tribes", which are economically limited by an inability to generate or believe any of the myths sufficient to maintain radically inegalitarian territorial inheritances, are analyzed elsewhere (Thompson, 1996, and Thompson, et al., Vol. I, Ch. 3)). Hence, once we specify that the equilibrium consists of a group of "states", the general absence of subsistence pressure on the rent-earning organisms means that the rapid and efficiency-generating process contained in our partnership-examples no longer generally applies.[9]

The near-subsistence process does, however, continue to apply for sufficiently large innovations. Thus, consider an innovation necessitated by a collective shock so large that, even though the states all comfortably survived prior to the shock and will also comfortably survive in the new equilibrium, no state can long survive in the new equilibrium if it maintains the old social institutions. A "dark age" (the social analogue to widespread economic losses for previously substantially profitable business firms or widespread starvation for previously above-subsistence biological organisms) temporarily arises in response to such large changes.

---

[8]This early evolution is discussed in greater detail in Chapter 6. The kind of territoriality relevant to our argument is neither food-territoriality, wherein various strategies are devised to lay personal claim to food resources, nor "mating-territoriality", where the relevant claims are to mates. Rather, it is "nesting territoriality", where the relevant claims are to territories within which parents may freely raise their young offspring (Brown, pp. 124-29). It is a generally accepted hypothesis that such territoriality curtails reproduction rates and population density (e.g., Brown, Chapter 6, or Scott, pp. 220-23).

[9]The near-subsistence process will also continue to apply when governments must actively compete for all of their important citizen-investors, who must then be able to transfer their valuable capital across the relevant boundaries. The initial competition of early American colonies for important citizen-investors is a case in point. The apparently small number of historical examples of this obviously efficient sort induces us to relegate our evolutionary discussion of such near-subsistence governments to footnotes.

For example, following an unfortunately durable, Greek-philosophy-inspired, late 3rd century monetary "reform" that left the Western Roman Empire essentially indefensible (Thompson, et al., Vol. II, Ch. 4), there was a rapid series of subsequently profitable brutalizations (see Chapter 5, Section 1.B) of the Empire's increasingly aggressive neighboring confederations. The ensuing destruction of most of the Western Empire's capital assets and a subsequent, restorative, monetary reform occurring late in the 5th century (Thompson, *ibid.*), completed a sequence of innovations that were so large that the various new leaders of the West suddenly found themselves vigorously competing for the allegiance of competent bureaucrats and tax-paying local counts. Suffering through several failures, these previously brutalized leaders quickly learned (initially from Constantinople) that they could not survive the competition with neighboring states unless they decisively switched away from brutalism and toward new, humanistic and property-respecting, social institutions. In particular, unless the previously brutalized leaders of these 6th-7th century states quickly adopted commitments to a maximally humanistic and property-respecting domestic religion, one based on the maximal heroization of Jesus or Mohammed, they could not attract sufficient bureaucrats to maintain or expand their states.

Before continuing on to describe a second dark-age example, where the shock-induced specter of below-subsistence institutions creates a rapid evolutionary path, we back-up to consider how the broadly rational political system chosen by a state's military founder is constrained by historically-determined ethics of others in the social hierarchy. First, note that, although there is no reason for founding military leaders to grant immobile individuals substantial utility endowments when the individuals make no militarily valuable sacrifices for the state, broadly rational military leaders will (because of the prohibitive cost of widespread punishment) positively reward those who make substantial military sacrifices (Appendix B.3). Such rewards extend, as noted above, to the heirs of those who were rewarded in previous generations. A handy way to so-reward the initially sacrificing individuals, especially in Western Civilization,[10] is to grant them and their descendants a democracy or at least a right to elect future rulers, the former to protect their family's initially earned benefits against expropriation by imperfectly educated future state authorities and the latter to assure their compensation for future sacrifices (Section III.C. of Chapter 3). But democracy is not granted when, because of a multiplicity of earlier rivalries, many of the initially sacrificing families do not possess values sufficiently respectful of other such families in their state. Broadly rational military founders -- in response to substantial resources that such families would devote to subsequently acquiring political dominance (see Chapter 5, Section I.B) -- then rationally proceed by sharply restricting the political power of the initially sacrificing families (say to no more than a collective veto over peacetime tax increases and an occasionally requested election). Only one, especially popular or militarily potent, "autocratic", family is rationally

---

[10]A "civilization" is a group of states that has evolved a common, deeply rooted, legal or political ideology. Its biological analogy is an "order" (e.g., primates). The basic ideological feature distinguishing Western Civilization from others is elaborated upon in Footnote 32 below. Unlike states, civilizations do not strategically interact.

granted the right to rule.

Returning to the 9th century for our second "dark-age" example, soon after the Christianized, Carolingian Franks had succeeded in unifying most of western Europe, the increasingly ideologically dominant Church succeeded in replacing the newly monopsonistic market for its services with a more competitive buying environment by inducing a decentralization of the military holdings of the Carolingian Empire among Charlemagne's three grandsons (e.g., Wallace-Hadrill, pp. 141-42). The result of this ideologically induced shock was internecine warfare between the Christianized and the traditional Frankish leaders, which left western Europe open to invasions from the increasingly aggressive Norsemen and Magyars and escalated the decentralizing trend towards castle construction and armored knights. A second "dark age" thus descended upon western Europe from the mid-9th through the mid-10th centuries. As the increasing malevolence of the relations among the Carolingian kings spread to their increasingly self-defensible dukes and counts during the late 9th and early 10th centuries, the newly emerging leaders were necessarily less reliant on agreements among these fragmented nobles. Although it was infeasible to maintain anything like the scale of the old states, the rapidly forming new states featured much more aggressively authoritarian local leaders (e.g., the dukes of Normandy, Flanders and Saxony and the Capetian and Burgundian "kings"). These brutalized leaders, by the late 10th century, were commonly insisting that the similarly brutalized counts and barons work to reform themselves by both: (1) swearing oaths accepting a fixed code of unlimited local military obligation whereas the now-limited monarch could not command anything but nominal support (feudalism) and (2) adopting chivalric values, which correspondingly taught an exaggerated respect for individuals who operated within and excelled under an acceptable code of conduct. The gradually decreasing brutality, the corresponding growth of customary (or "feudal") rights and political participation, and the gradually restoring piety in the area of the old Carolingian Empire (and the ignominies of the Crusades tell us it was only gradual) over the late 10th and 11th centuries then allowed these timely authoritarian institutions to gradually recede (e.g., Strayer and Gatske, pp. 195 and 213).

Besides illustrating the relatively rapid evolution that occurs when new social institutions (first Christianity and then European feudalism and chivalry) become vital as a result of large collective shocks, the above two historical sequences will provide a backdrop for our first detailed empirical examinations of the evolution of vital institutions in Chapter 3. There, we will examine both the rise of medieval European guilds (in Sections I.B.4 and II.D.2-3) and the costly defeudalizations that occurred near the end of the middle ages (in Section II.D.4).

None of the subsequent collective shocks or innovations in our detailed empirical study were sufficient to produce a "dark-age". So none of the innovations covered by our further empirical examinations of the state are sufficient to enable us to apply the vitalness-logic of the partnership examples.[11] Rather, we must consider a

---

[11]Nevertheless, as in footnote #9 above, the vitalness-logic of the partnership examples does apply to competing pioneer governments, such as the early American colonies, which are essentially zero-profit operations because they must compete for essentially all of their large

separate vitalness-logic, one that applies to an above-subsistence world with relatively small innovations, a logic illustrated in the little prologue to this chapter.

  5. *Vitalness and Rapid Evolution when the External Shocks are Not Large and Organisms Live Well-Above Subsistence.* If an organism regularly lives well-above subsistence, vitalness can still arise in the absence of large external shocks if a certain deficiency (whether it is a policy error or a single genetic defect), would have irreversibly disastrous consequences.[12]   Irreversible disasters arise only from an internal weakness in the organism's defense system. Non-defense defects may also work against the future existence of an existing organism, whether a state, a firm, or a species. But the consequences of such a defect (e.g., "genetic drift"), being essentially continuous in nature, must, if the non-defense defect is somehow overlooked and left uncorrected, only gradually push the state, firm, or biological organism close to subsistence. If such a point is reached before arrested by a further evolutionary adaptation, then the analysis of Subsection 3 above begins to apply.[13]   This is not the case for defense systems, where the loss is sudden, complete and irreversible.[14]

---

investors. We will have more to say about such rent-eliminating competition when we consider the corresponding rapidity of investor-sensitive political institutions.

[12]We do not consider all conceivable deficiencies. We do not wish to spend time considering the dubious survivability of a society that would, say, criminalize all production. Just as standard biological analyses of survival ignore most conceivable technologies of life, our empirical discussions ignore most conceivable economic institutions. In particular, we restrict the empirical analysis of this study to varieties of institutions that have been observed or commonly suggested. This history-dependent simplification is totally dropped in a subsequent, more idealistic, study (Thompson, et al.) The latter study considers theoretically ideal (not historically observed) institutions, including both pre-historically vital and would-be vital institutions (Vol. I, Ch. 3, and Vol. II, Ch. 3, respectively).
  Nevertheless, the policies emerging from these two studies are quite complementary because the separate analyses both stem from a single, over-arching, evolutionary model and social theory. In particular, the policies of the current study accepts ideologization as part of the social process while the policies of subsequent study does not and therefore applies to a much less constrained set of allocative problems.

[13]Before that happens, the defect -- in an objective learning environment -- is almost certain to be corrected. For the same process that led to the convergence to the original equilibrium implies that the error will be perceived and corrected. However, non-objectively learning, ideologized, states can, and actually have, as we shall see, be easily brought to and beyond such a precarious subsistence.

[14]When "drift" affects a vital-organ, whether genetic or social, it is quite dangerous. As a result of this danger, while we may observe some *ex-ante* efficient organisms in a given population mutating themselves out of existence through *ex post* excessive experimentation with their vital organs, very-high-surplus organisms will efficiently mutate their vital organs at extremely low rates. Indeed, the strict convergence result in our cited evolutionary models formally requires some such anti-drift mechanism. Thus, for very-high-surplus, dominant

In terms of our above business analogy, a "vital organ" of a significantly profitable firm is a necessary and irreplaceable capital input, an input that will depreciate only if the firm's maintenance or defense of its property is inadequate, in which case the input and firm will collapse as does a "one hoss shay". Note that the protection of Ricardian rent has each firm defending itself against attacks from either nature, extortionary bureaucrats, or private rent-seekers. Whatever the source of the threat, unless a firm has an appropriate defense strategy, it will soon die. Since these threats can be assumed to be continuously present, firms that let their guards down are soon eliminated. The only surviving firms are those able to constantly protect their Ricardian rents. The adjustment in defense tactics in response to new threats must be correspondingly fast. The only firms that can survive in this environment are those that are able to rapidly and appropriately respond to a variety of attacks on their Ricardian rents. These survivable, profit-defending, firms were analyzed above in Appendix A.1 and correspondingly appear as co-evolving agents in our discussions of political systems that evolve to avoid underdevelopment traps.

Regarding the survivability of states, the continued presence of a significant error in defense policy means that a sudden loss of state sovereignty is imminent. Collective defense institutions preventing such uniquely costly policy errors are obviously necessary for the near-term survival of the state. Those states unable to quickly produce a full set of vital organs providing for the collective defense of the social organism cannot long survive. The evolution of the defense-providing institutions in response to a new defense technology must be correspondingly fast among any surviving group of states.

The analogous micro-biological situation also possesses such evolutionary speed. Consider the historical emergence of a small but deadly, completely mobile parasite (e.g., a pandemic virus) in a pre-existing above-subsistence population. In the absence of Lamarckian effects, the effect of the historical emergence of the predator was to quickly eliminate an entire subspecies. Other subspecies in a collectively surviving species survived only if they initially possessed defense systems that were prepared to ward off the attack. Surviving populations were soon free of such destruction because those whose systems could not defend against such attacks were all eliminated. The species was thus systematically altered, perhaps eliminated, by the attack. Yet, as with the case of vital social economic institutions, without detailed historical knowledge of the attack and its necessary consequence, it is very difficult for subsequent intellectuals to appreciate the set of surviving "idiosyncrasies" and the anomalous observational gaps that rapidly evolved from the attack. [15]

---

states, it is virtually always optimal to free-ride on the vital-institution experiments of low-surplus states, who have much less to lose from such experimentation.

[15]Since viruses, which were among the first replicators on Earth, still abound, viral infections have probably wiped out a long series of prototypical territorial species that were not around long enough to leave a convenient fossil imprint. The resulting extinction of intermediate phenotypes before they could appear in the fossil record is probably sufficient to complement our earlier, subsistence-and-rapid-evolution, analysis to explain the major

We shall further specify the evolutionary process -- and show how we can further exploit the rationality-based efficiency theorem of this chapter's appendix despite the generally evolutionary character of the model -- in Section C.3 below.

6. *Inferring Vitalness.* The necessary speed with which vital institutions evolve enables us to empirically identify the visible vital organs of a state with a conceptual simplicity analogous to the simplicity implicit in the identification of the vital organs of existing biological organisms. Although the number of persuasive post-mortems on observable states has been far fewer than the number of persuasive post-mortems on observable biological units, the identification of the vital organs of a state is facilitated by the imitability of the organs of a state.

In particular, suppose we hypothesize, on the basis of some plausible theoretical argument, that an observed institution of a successful state has been vital. To test this, we need only look back to the point in time that the institution first emerged. The institutional imitations of subsequently successful neighboring states, together with the non-imitations of subsequently failing neighbors, will clearly verify the vitalness of the institution. When a new institution is vital, neighboring institutional imitation and continuing state success, along with non-imitation and state failure, will empirically follow on the heels of the innovating state's introduction of the new institution.[16] This double-test will be employed throughout this study whenever we empirically identify the vitalness of a particular institution.

7. *Innovation When Organisms Live Well-Above Subsistence.* There are biological analogues to "states" (again, states are well-above-subsistence, internally cooperating, independent societies). These are found in territorial biological organisms. As indicated above, the arrival of territorial animals around 0.5 billion years ago converted a zero-surplus, Malthusian, world into a positive-surplus, Ricardian, world.[17] All of the intricate systems (nervous, circulatory, respiratory, digestive, skeletal and ambulatory, reproductive, masticatory, auditory, ocular, and olfactory) that we casually use to characterize the vital organs of today's commonly

---

macrobiological anomalies that modern evolutionary biologists have found in the standard Darwinian story (e.g., Gould and Eldredge). The same sort of gaps appear, of course, in comparing civilizations.

[16]Non-imitation by an exceptional survivor will lead us to suspect, and often verify, the survivor's lack of military independence.

[17]The Malthus we are referring to is the 1798 Malthus. This, the first edition of his First Essay on Population, had population expanding within the land-owning family to where even the landlords lived at subsistence. Later, he was to argue, in line with what we are calling a "Ricardian world", that property-owning families could afford the education necessary for them to restrain their rate of population growth and earn a substantial surplus on the land. (Darwin's positive-surplus view of the world would thus have come from his reading of something beyond Malthus' first edition (which was intentionally bleak because it represented a debater's attempt to counter the "perfectibility" views of Godwin, Owen and Condorcet).

visible animals had <u>already</u> been evolved, again with the help of the super-Darwinian, efficiency-demanding, partnership-effects discussed above and biologically elaborated upon in Subsections 10 and 11 below.

Thereafter, various sophisticated organisms acquired portions of the newly scarce living-space for their families by staking-out and defending certain territories (e.g., Demsetz). These successful organisms were then free to appropriately adjust their domestic family sizes to where the territorial family maximized its eventual survival probability on the claimed territory, which entailed a substantial reduction in the territory's population because the family then internalized the crowding costs that had previously been imposed on external competitors within the territory. Positive surpluses could thus accrue to organisms that had evolved the appropriate territorial claims (through gigantism, ferocity, or cunning intelligence).

Some non-territorial niches, of course, have remained. Thus, for example, cottontail rabbits, field mice, and grasshoppers all rapidly expand their populations in a Malthusian fashion to where they must live their typically predator-abbreviated lives in a phrenetic search for food, shelter, and safety compared to the relatively comfortable Ricardian lives of birds, large mammals, and social insects, whose territoriality has resulted in relatively small representative family sizes, low rates of morbidity, and stable population densities (e.g., Scott).

The evolved rate of non-militaristic (or "civilian") innovation in a territorial, or Ricardian, ecology is much lower than the corresponding rate of innovation in the pre-territorial, Malthusian ecology. The reason for the exceptionally high rate of civilian cost-reduction in the near-subsistence ecology is that each such innovation clears the environment of the initial competitors, thereby rewarding the Malthusian innovators and their immediate offspring with an enormous, albeit temporary, redistributional benefit.[18] This internalized redistributional benefit is entirely absent from the Ricardian world because the environmental competitors in the Ricardian world remain in existence despite the reduction in their surpluses occasioned by the appearance of a more efficient rival. Thus, while the hyper-competitive Malthusian organisms are socially overzealous innovators in that they maximize their family's own likelihood of future existence in a collectively shared environment by innovating whenever it increases their family's expected representation in the shared environment (which maximizes the cumulative rate of civilian cost-reduction), the Ricardian organisms are naturally rewarded for a civilian innovation only if it increases their family's ability to survive on their exclusive territories. In contrast to the Malthusian world, the marginal private benefits of peacetime innovation in the Ricardian world does not contain a substantial redistributive component. An "ecological economist", one hired to oversee the joint welfare of all of the existing organisms, would approve only of the Ricardian rate of civilian innovation.

---

[18]While economists typically approve of the "creative destruction" entailed in such competition-eliminating innovations, Barzel has pointed out that this laissez-faire innovation is analogously excessive because of the correspondingly excessive reward to discovering a new technology <u>prior to</u> one's competitors when property rights to develop ideas are not somehow pre-determined.

But these Ricardian surpluses create a persistent attraction to new species evolving to attack the relatively durable surpluses and gradually consume the previously prosperous species. Relatively low-surplus species can handle these parasite problems by co-evolving, with territoriality, defense mechanisms that will divert the efforts of aggressor-species to relatively high-surplus species.[19]

8. *Vital Re-Evolution and Long-Term Survival: The Bottom Line.* But high-surplus species, like high-population species, are targets for a growing variety of parasitic attacks. A high-surplus or high-population target's only chance at long-term survival is, as argued in Chapters 1 and 6, to re-evolve so as to benefit from the attacks of the surviving parasites. Many examples of such symbioses are found among durably surviving high-total-surplus hosts observed in nature.

An example of a vital re-evolution from social history is the emergence, during secularizing times, of Hellenistic, or "liberal arts" education in the West, wherein various, by-themselves-dangerous-but-together-inconsistent, social philosophies (e.g., those of Pythagoras, Plato, Aristotle, Lucretius, and numerous, more modern, social thinkers) are all taught as if they were simultaneously quite reasonable. Students survive this ideological barrage by learning to tolerate all of these views, thereby effectively learning an ethic in which they subconsciously exaggerate the likelihood of unlikely hypotheses.[20] This learning prepares students for managerial or bureaucratic roles in large organizations by inducing them to take as very reasonable each of the unstable or inconsistent pronouncements of various organizational leaders,

---

[19]The "wastefulness" of such arms races has a different significance in biology than in economics, where policies are often available to discourage anti-social behavior. On a positive level, switching to a Ricardian world means that most of evolution has changed from a mechanism for generating more efficient civilian organisms to a mechanism for generating more efficient military organisms. But, on a normative level, where again we put ourselves in the position of advising a government containing a constituency that has a positive utility for the utilities of other organisms (say the animals in a "preserve" dedicated to the general welfare of the easily visible animals), the "wasteful" territorial system is generally superior to the non-territorial one. This is because the militaristic territorial system offers some fairly durable surpluses while the non-militaristic system has the survivable animal populations expand to where all are living at subsistence.

[20]Just as for other ethics, as we have already pointed out, most adherents deny that they possess exaggerated beliefs. In this context, the adherents will admit that their university education has made them much more mentally flexible in their approach to the world. But when challenged that this flexibility might be excessive, that actually there is only one, ideally discoverable, objective truth, they will typically come to argue that they are simply much more "open-minded" and "intellectually tolerant" than they were before college. At this point, to test their self-understanding, the interviewer need only ask college graduates of their opinions of a thinker who passionately endorses the adoption of a single theory to the permanent exclusion of all existing alternatives. The induced <u>absence</u> of intellectual tolerance in their responses will then simultaneously contradict the graduates' claim to self-understanding and reveal the nature of their shared exaggeration.

even in a conceptual last period. Secular societies have thus successfully evolved a way of actually benefiting from the half-baked, often quite dangerous, ideas of its stock of famous reformers. Less expensively taught, much simpler, obedience ethics have existed (e.g., the Stocism of Zeno); but they have never been complemented by a social policy that would make these states impervious to the facile ideological attacks of competing social ethics (e.g., the "Stoicism" of Seneca).

As regards high-surplus, civilizationally dominant states, this Hellenistic re-evolution has been far from efficient. For advanced professional education exploits the Hellenistic ethic of intellectual accommodation to readily mold allegiances to "advanced", profession-serving, ideas. This is especially dangerous in a dominant state, where the "advanced" ideas of the state's civilizationally dominant professional elites are taken much more seriously by its relatively highly educated ruling classes.

A new social policy is required if we are to substantially mitigate the social losses from the resulting, ideology-based, inefficiencies. Our specific policy reforms, as well as a policy-oriented biological analysis of parasitic challenges and re-evolution, are discussed further in Chapter 6. But we cannot hope to be taken seriously unless we elaborate upon the specific nature of the problem, past and present. Chapters 3 through 5 will provide such an elaboration. Without the threat of ideologization, our efficiency-theory generates nothing but citizen-efficient equilibria. With it, our efficiency-theory generates a self-conscious reconstruction of social institutions so as to substantially mitigate the social losses from purely profession-serving, historically debilitating, ideological "innovations". Such a reconstruction represents our central efficiency problem.

9. *Existence Paradoxes.* Because of the unrelenting evolution of new predatory organisms against high-surplus organisms that do not re-evolve to live in symbiosis with their predators, it is virtually impossible for their defense systems to evolve to keep pace with the subsequent evolution of an increasing variety of predators. Indeed, as the variety of visible predators (including humans) has grown over time, the rate of extinction of the various genera of territorial animals has become increasingly rapid (Simpson). These organisms have no real chance of long-term survival. Such survival requires that they find a way to benefit from their predators.

A different sort of existence paradox would arise within a strictly Darwinian world if we ever observed a territorial organism adopting a surplus-increasing, non-vital, characteristic that sufficiently increased the vulnerability of the organism that a new vital organ would have to accompany the new characteristic. The time requir-ed to independently evolve the new vital organ in a Darwinian world would clearly preclude the emergence of the new characteristic, the likelihood of a random mutation creating both of these complementary features being extremely remote.

A mixture of Lamarckian and Darwinian forces such as occurred through our various partnership-effects could conceivably provide the requisite speed. However,in a biological context, the likelihood of hitting upon the correct defense innovation before the death of the biological organism is extremely remote. Indeed, we know of no biologically vital organs, and no corresponding Lamarck-Darwin biological innovations, to have evolved among pre-existing, established, territorial organisms. Our concluding chapter considers an example of a mixed Lamarck-Darwin process in the biological world in which a newly vital organ gradually <u>co-evolved</u> with territoriality. Such co-evolution, which presumably gave the emerging vital organ time to evolve because surpluses are low when territoriality is only partial, takes us as close as we can come to the evolution of new vital biological organs in a territorial world.

However, several of the established territorial <u>societies</u> we have studied <u>have</u> generated newly vital economic institutions. The apparent existence paradox can be only partially resolved by noting that states are not restricted to simple Darwinian evolution. The paradox cannot be fully resolved until we understand the special way in which Lamarckian forces work within states to complement harshly Darwinian social forces to produce the otherwise quite anomalous evolutionary patterns. Section C.3 below begins our explanation. Chapters 3 through 5 will then become quite specific in characterizing of the evolution of vital institutions. But before progressing to this more specific societal analysis, we should elaborate upon the possible biological relevance of our evolutionary theory.

10. *Economic Reasoning and Biology.* Economic reasoning, at least when applied to the subject of biology, has been extremely fruitful. Darwin's revolutionary 19th century theory of natural selection was built upon a harshly selective process of Malthus. Similarly, the 20th century revolution in the sociobiological understanding of our animal nature through a neo-Darwinian analysis of within-species externalities (so admirably elaborated by Fisher, Lack, Williams, Hamilton, Alexander, Dawkins and Ghiselin) was presaged by a prior wave of Pigouvian externalities and free-riding arguments within the field of economics. Most recently, Van Valen's "Red Queen" hypothesis, wherein mammalian evolution is portrayed as an arms race in which we are merely running faster to stay in the same place, has dramatically altered the conventional Darwinian view of progress through natural selection. But this hypothesis is a simple extension of Tullock's earlier economic study of the social waste of rent-seeking behavior.[21]

Therefore, since economic reasoning has not been heretofore extended to vital institutions, it is no surprise that modern biology lacks an extensive treatment of the evolution of vital biological organs. Thus, however valuable has been the Darwinian revolution in separating religion from science; however valuable the neo-Darwinian revolution has been in enhancing our self-understanding (e.g., our deep feelings of kinship, our frustratingly stubborn senescence, and our ingrained psycho-sexual differences); and however valuable has been Van Valen's "Red Queen" hypothesis in dispelling the myth of evolutionary progress; there has been no correspondingly

---

[21]Many economists, although possibly not so many evolutionary biologists, would include more recent biological work extending: (1) Cournot-Nash, conditionally-cooperative, and cooperative equilibrium concepts over to the modern notion of a biological equilibrium (Maynard-Smith and Price, Hirshleifer (1987), and Appendix B.1, respectively), or (2) the synthesizing power of the Marshallian concept of short and long-run equilibrium to consistently combine the essentially anti-Darwinian subject of population genetics (e.g., Karlin) with the phenotype-dominated analysis of the Darwinians (e.g., Hammerstein, Eshel).

valuable discussion of the evolution of vital biological organs.

Yet, perhaps surprisingly, the development of the vital organs of any organism, social or biological, is conceptually much simpler than the development of non-vital organs. For the former admits no problem in determining the "unit of selection", no ambiguity between individual and group selection. There is no conflict between the survival goal of the individual micro-unit and the goal of the entire organism when the micro-unit's activity is vital to the organism's survival. Externalities among the various organs occurring within an above-subsistence organism ordinarily prevent non-cooperative strategies from coordinating to achieve a joint optimum.[22] But such externalities are entirely absent as regards vital organs.

In more familiar biological terms, whether the unit of selection is regarded as a "gene" (i.e., a portion of DNA whose physical structure determines the structure of the rest of the cell) or the entire organism in the abstract (i.e., an initially amorphous macro-unit filling a defined ecological niche), there is no conflict within an organism that is shaping its vital organs. So, employing the central theorem of the appendix to this chapter, the individualistic micro-decisions made within the organisms are the same as if the organism possessed an ideally informed centrally planner. Maynard-Smith and Price's "evolutionarily stable strategies" for vital organs are equivalent to the maximizing behavior of the corresponding "selfish genes" of Hamilton, Williams, and Dawkins.

Since, in general, several substitutable inputs can be used to produce a given vital organ, a conflict does arise in the production of vital organs for above-subsistence organisms if the inputs have private opportunity costs. The individual components of an efficient organism might then be pre-screened for an absence of private opportunity costs. In a social context, military personnel and governmental officials are regularly screened for their absence of foreign political connections and their sacrificial nature. In the absence of such central direction, the conflict is resolved through the pre-establishment of rent-acquiring (e.g., Ricardian) claims to the various components of the surplus-generating organism. Thus, on the genetic level, most of the space on our chromosomes is occupied by free-riding DNA: This so-called "selfish DNA" merely works to colonize the chromosome while apparently contributing nothing to the development of the cell or the organism (e.g., Maynard-Smith (1993, pp. 8-9)). Once all of these rent-acquiring (Ricardian) territorial claims are established, the remaining spaces on the chromosome will be (through natural selection) surrendered to genes, or "expressive DNA", which guide the RNA and Amino Acids that efficiently contribute to the ultimate survival of the biological organism.[23] Given such prior claims, there is no conflict, either within or among

---

[22]Economically and biologically interesting examples of such "coordination failures", at least for sexual reproduction, are found in both Waldman and Bergstrom. An example for simple, or asexual, reproduction is provided in the first footnote of Chapter 6.

[23]Foreign invasions of free-riding DNA into the chromosomes of the vital organs of an above-subsistence organism, viz., retroviral infiltrations, are considered in Chapter 6, after we have studied such infiltrations at the societal level.

the active components of the various vital organs of a survivable organism.

On a societal level, it is more realistic (and on any level more survival-enhancing) for the above-subsistence components of an organism to sacrifice significant peacetime rents in case of a defensive emergency. Indeed, we shall find that the pre-arranged ability to proportionally draw upon the society's entire asset base during defensive emergencies represents a critical part of an efficient social organism's vital economic institutions. Here, too, given the prior, efficiently conditional, wealth claims of the surplus recipients, there is no conflict either within or among the vital components of the survivable organism.[24]

Now the origination of vital organs has always presented a vexing problem for Darwin's random mutation theory. If an organ were truly vital, how could the prior organism from which it sprang as an independent mutation have survived? The only viable conjecture open to Darwinian thought (e.g., Maynard-Smith, 1993, pp. 303-34) has been that, to the earlier species, the organ was not vital. It is nevertheless no mean feat to explain the evolution of any particular vital organ, say, the heart, given the multiple fixed-proportions between the appropriate valve-shapes, blood vessel-shapes, and the coordinated neurological reflexes. There is no obvious reason why, for example, valves would evolve to open and close in the absence of a pumping mechanism, and vice versa. Whether or not the heart itself was originally vital, the formative rates of independent random mutation necessary to simultaneously evolve the many separately vital components of this multiple-component organ through Darwinian selection would have had to be so high that the organism would have had virtually no chance of survival relative to its more conservative competitors.

This nearly impossible Darwinian mechanism comes in stark contrast to the design-oriented mechanism used by Lamarck. The latter author, whose main concern was the evolution of genera rather than species, explicitly dealt with gross phylogenetic discontinuities. Although Lamarckian authors have still left us guessing as to the nature of their evolutionary process, we have filled in this gap with a primordial partnership-process working under the extreme innovative pressure of a Malthusian world. Our hypothetical heart-story would thus feature two primordial mergers, the first between an organism specialized in pumping and an organism specialized in controlling internal fluids through a system of valves and the second between a master decisionmaker organism and the earlier partnership. We now illustrate our biological theory with some actual microbiological studies that lend substantial empirical support to the theory.

---

[24]The actual selectors of vital institutions in a democratic state are political representatives, who form a distributional as well as an allocational equilibrium. These individuals can be thought of as selecting vital institutions with a given utility distribution in the background and so will appropriately compensate groups who make extraordinary emergency sacrifices. Given this basic distributional equilibrium, political decisions concerning important defense-relevant institutions are so important to the shared livelihoods of the politicians that they typically forego their usual partisan wrangling and make such decisions as a non-conflictical team.

11. *Microbiological Application.* Concerning near-subsistence organisms, modern evolutionary biologists, many of whom are dissatisfied with the ability of classical Darwinians to explain the rapid, sophisticated, and sometimes discontinuous nature of early evolutionary adjustments (e.g., Gould and Eldredge), should be willing to accept the following biological analogy to our partnership process: Begin with a biological niche containing several competing organisms, each of which has previously expanded to where the organism is barely able to survive. A new organism is then formed out of a Lamarckian merger, say a mutation-induced phagocytosis ("cellular eating") by a host "prokaryote" (a primitive, nucleus-free, cell such as a bacteria) of another, differentially specialized, prokaryote to create a "eukaryote" (a nucleated cell). The increased efficiency of the host, its ability to survive more hardships than its initial competitors, allows it and its replicated offspring to compete better for the available resources. (Say the absorbed prokoyote, or "endosymbiont", was evolved to excel at breathing while the phagocyte was evolved to excel at eating; the host, after protecting its newly formed chromosomes with a nucleus, then efficiently feeds and shelters the symbiont, converting it into a eukaryotic mitochondria, which then efficiently and completely specializes in breathing for the new, much more environmentally versatile, cell (Margulis, or, more recently, Dyer and Obar)). This then forces the other organisms either to similarly merge (which is extremely unlikely because it requires a similar mutation) or to die prior to reproduction, thereby opening up the entire niche for the easily multiplying offspring of the newly formed organisms. Once the new equilibrium is established, i.e., once the new organisms' population and niche have quickly expanded to where each new organism is barely able to survive, it becomes similarly open to the destructive creation of new, still more efficient, endosymbiotic partnerships. A new mutation might, for example, allow the newly established eukaryote to absorb another kind of prokaryote, say one that had gradually evolved in an environment that put a unique premium on a cell's ability to appropriately circulate internal fluids, thereby putting survival-pressure on the other, less versatile, eukaryotes to where the new zero-profit equilibrium similarly eliminates all of the previous eukaryotes in the niche.

More generally, the early eukaryotes were quick to evolve meiosis, which regularized symmetric chromosomal mergers between different cells and a consequent hybridization of the eukaryotic offspring. Soon thereafter, species-specific partnership formations ("sexual reproduction") evolved as mutation-generated endosymbiotic partnerships merging "hostess" cells that were specialized in the production and domestic maintenance of multiple offspring with distant relatives that had become much more mobile and specialized in environmental adaptation. Some of the resulting hostess offspring would generally have an enhanced ability to compete with their originally specialized, asexual, form by maturing into a more mobile and environmentally adaptable form, thereby efficiently exploiting the competitive advantages offered by the hybrid vigor of any such offspring capable of surviving to the age of reproduction.[25]   If the sexually reproducing organisms later come to live far above subsistence, the advantage of such competition-eliminating organizational effort may well fall short of the cost.   Indeed, the hostess would biologically gain (i.e., dramatically increase her type's frequency in the subsequent population) from a return to asexual reproduction, ignoring the now-modest return to hybrid vigor. Thus, once a secure niche becomes long-established, it is not unusual for the male-female dimorphism to disappear, usually signalling the species' return to asexual reproduction (e.g., in tuberous plants, snails, and fruit flies).[26]

B. Effective Democracy and Vital Economic Institutions

1. *Two Critical Features of Democracy.*   Democracy, which is formally defined in Section I.A of Chapter 3, can be heuristically defined as the ability of all of a state's private investors to freely participate in the state's rule-making process.[27]

---

[25]The symmetric nature of meiosis should not obscure the fact that only the hostess's "preferences" determine the success of endosymbiotic partnership.   If a hostess's survival probability falls after such a merger, a temporarily successful endosymbiont will soon run out of properly nurtured reproductive material.   On the other hand, if an endosymbiont's initial survival probability were reduced by the merger, surviving hostesses will nevertheless breed a suitable form of endosymbiont in order to provide fresh supplies for future mergers.

More generally, an endosymbiotic merger succeeds according to its effect on the host's survival probability.   Even if the offspring of the endosymbiont (which would be a "parasite" if its mobility were retained after the merger) would have had a higher survival probability in the endosymbiont's pre-merger niche, they are essentially trapped in the host and will thereafter survive according to whether the family of the host survives.   Because a surviving endosymbiont thus becomes a vital part of a successful host, the endosymbiont's surviving offspring will generally evolve to further accommodate the host.

A similar conclusion applies to mobile parasites, but only in a long-run setting.   Although a sufficiently mobile parasite can temporarily enhance its survival despite the failure of the hosts, this is not a viable long-term strategy.   And there is no short-term return that will rationalize a mobile parasite's evolving to benefit its hosts.   So the long-term survival of both mobile parasite and host is vitally dependent on the ability of the high-surplus host to re-evolve to benefit from their parasites.   Although this process eventually favors mobile parasites that benefit their hosts, it is the surviving hosts that must be counted on to find a way to benefit from the visitors rather than vice versa.   This is again because mobile parasites receive no short-term evolutionary advantage from independently evolving to benefit their hosts.

[26]Such returns to asexual reproduction are nevertheless extremely rare among mammals and social insects.   A straightforward resolution of the resulting "paradox of sex" (Ghiselin) is outlined in Appendix B.1, Section 7.

[27]The term "investor" here includes investors in coveted human capital (Appendix B.2). However, in view of the fact that inegalitarian societies usually contain large numbers of people who are neither investors nor in possession of any rights to political participation, we shall have occasion to refer to our democracies as "investor-democracies".   This is done to emphasize the fact that some governments are democratic in our sense even though the propor-

Democracy possesses two critical features. First, as developed in Appendix A.1, complemented by Section III.I of Appendix B.3 and Section I.A of Chapter 3, democracy has a <u>unique</u> potential to provide legislation that eliminates the severely inefficient underdevelopment traps that arise under laissez faire.[28] Democracy thus possesses a unique potential for economic efficiency. However, as is consistently illustrated in the empirical examinations of Chapters 3 through 5 below, the potential cannot be realized -- i.e., the democracy is not "effective" -- unless the legislation is the result of pragmatic negotiation between representatives of the affected interest groups and a legislation-respecting "civilly-reverent" bureaucracy is available to enforce such non-ideological laws. The fact that efficient legislation is often ideologically unsupportable makes it especially important for bureaucrats to support the actual legislation rather than a popular ideology whenever a conflict arises.

The second critical feature of democracy, at least when it is effective, is that the efficiency of <u>future</u> legislatures forces rational <u>current</u> legislatures to somehow tie the hands of the future legislatures in order to commit the state to reaction policies that would otherwise <u>not</u> be adopted because they are not in the narrow interests of the state's future legislatures. This is especially true of the willingness of future legislatures to go to war over small territorial infringements. The sequentially efficient state that ignores this commitment problem will soon be lost in "efficiently" avoiding war with a series of concession-seeking foreign aggressors. We shall see that overcoming this time-consistency problem requires some very special economic institutions. That is -- as pointed out in Appendix B.2 (footnote 4), elaborated in Appendix B.3 (especially Sect. II.B), and summarized at several points below in order to allow each chapter to stand alone as an independent exercise -- independent states adopting an effective democracy become <u>uniquely</u> fragile in that they cannot long survive unless they quickly adopt a special, vital, set of economic institutions.

The many previous writers on democratic institutions have possessed no theory rationalizing either: (1) the uniquely superior levels of economic prosperity consistently observed in mature democracies, or (2) the existence of vital economic institutions. We know of no other authors who have argued either: (1) that "effective democracy" has been theoretically required in the process of eliminating the grossly inefficient underdevelopment traps that arise under laissez faire, or (2) that certain economic institutions -- such as guilds, the gold standard, and international economic alliances -- have arisen in effective democracies to provide defense commitments necessary for the survival of these democracies. Moreover,

---

tion of the population that privately invests, even if only in coveted human capital, is quite small. Our definition, of course, contrasts with various, legal-morality-based, forms, including Tocqueville's classic definition of democracy as an "equality of condition".

[28]Briefly, democracy gives certain potential investors, those who would, under laissez faire, have their potential profits unavoidably dissipated in future economic wars with others in their society, a practical method of cooperating, one that does not require unanimity, with their cohorts, and perhaps their prospective rivals, in order to create ad hoc laws or regulations that serve to preclude the prospective economic strife.

judging from the literature, theories akin to our underdevelopment-trap theory (Appendix A.1 again) and our defense-of-democracy theory (Appendices B.2 and B.3 again) are apparently required before the evolutionary pattern can be detected despite the regularity of the observed pattern. As we shall see, previous authors, lacking both theories, have been respectively able to coherently explain neither the great ascendancies nor the persistent declines of economically dominant states.

2. *The Efficiency of Long-surviving Democracies.* <u>Some</u> degree of commitment is a necessary component in the administration of any institution. But extremes must be avoided in this regard. Unalterable commitment, or "hard-wiring", is not a naturally selected characteristic of human institutions.[29] Let us be more specific. A surviving democracy must regularly provide a sufficient level of peacetime preparedness for defensive warfare. Only two kinds of democracies can achieve this sufficiency. The first, hard-wired, kind is dominated by military fanaticism. Classical Sparta provides a familiar example. The Classical Spartan state was formally democratic in that its constitution encouraged the political participation of all mature male citizens. But early Spartan state education was so centered on military heroes (especially the Atreids, along with Heracles and his favored Tyndarids) that the Classical (7th-5th Century BC) Spartan state could not be conquered. (She was, for example, the only Classical Greek democracy that survived without relying on government money to finance her wars (Martin).) She could die only by withering away (through shrinkage due to excessively restrictive citizenship requirements). The hard-wiring of Classical Sparta meant that she was no more than a formal democracy. Long-term efficiency cannot be expected from such a democracy because efficient economic institutions change with the environment.

The second, Classical Athenian, kind of democracy is what arises when the citizens of a formal democracy are given a practical option of substantially escaping the influence of centralized state education.[30] This latter, intellectually much freer,

---

[29]Note here the contrast of human societies to insect societies. The only source of the reaction commitment produced by social insects is biological. Myth is not available to insects as a source of broadly rational reactions. The hard-wiring of reactions is, therefore, a naturally selected characteristic of the social insects. As a result, the sophisticated variations in economic and political institutions that represent the subject of this work play no role in insect societies. With social learning correspondingly absent from insect societies, the Lamarckian element we have been praising is absent from the social evolution of insect societies. The observed inflexibility of insect societies compared to human societies therefore provides striking evidence for the evolutionary value of adding Lamarckian to Darwinian selection.

[30]Although historical evidence concerning schools that are relatively free of state-serving values is sketchy, the presence of such schools can typically be inferred from their effect on adult values. Since the interests of young children are ordinarily concentrated on athletic competition and the arts, societies in which schools cater to the interests of the children rather than the political interests of a state, past or present, will generate adult populations with exceptional interests in organized sports and beautiful things. Thus we find, in those adult western societies most noted for their interests in athletics and beauty -- in ancient Etruria,

"soft-wired," democracy -- which we hereafter simply describe as a "democracy" in order to economize on adjectives -- does not have its peacetime defense institutions dictatorially determined by its education system. Rather it achieves an efficient quality of defense (rather than the excessive quality produced by a "hard-wired" democracy) only if it also evolves political and economic institutions that are efficiently sensitive to the state's actual survival requirements.[31] A surviving democracy must therefore be continuously prepared to deftly alter its political and economic institutions in response to subtle environmental changes.

Long-surviving democracies could therefore hardly have been dominated by the charlatans, simpletons or crooks that economists typically portray in characterizing democratic representatives. Indeed, we shall find, in an independent theoretical model of democracy and a series of historical studies (Section I.A. of Chapter 3 and the subsequent inquiries), an evolution of citizen-efficiency in both the political and the economic institutions of the surviving democratic competitors. Efficiency findings of this sort are entirely predictable because -- in order to have survived evolutionary competition -- these democracies must have been regularly capable of legislatively detecting and internalizing a wide variety of varying and sophisticated defense-externalities that arise among investors (Appendices B.2 and B.3).

An important by-product of this latter, generally necessary, legislative sensitivity to sophisticated defense-externalities is a corresponding legislative sensitivity to investor externalities generally, including those transaction-costs-externalities responsible for the significant underdevelopment traps to which all laissez faire economies are subject. For any mature democracy, having survived by generating a long series of investor-sensitive defense-institutions, should also have been able to employ the same investor-sensitivity to efficiently internalize a wide range of externalities and thereby eliminate its significant underdevelopment traps. Although non-partisan political incentives, which Section C.3 and Appendix A.2 below show to facilitate the development of vital institutions, are not generally present in the case of non-vital institutions, underdevelopment traps, as characterized in Appendix A.1,

---

Archaic Athens and Ionia, Medieval Florence, pre-Napoleonic France, early modern Holland, and modern England and America -- vivid reflections of the educational pre-requisite of the democratic states under discussion.

[31]Actually, Classical (5th century BC) Athens became too expansionist after a mid-century Periclean "reform" granting substantial salaries to military officials. With such officials -- who were popularly elected on an annual basis and already receiving substantial perquisites from the state -- so highly rewarded, young Athenian citizens-to-be naturally began to develop the physical and mental attributes that would enable them to compete for such exalted positions. In this way, the following generations of classical Athenian citizens came to greatly exaggerate the value of military achievement (much as our youth has come to exaggerate the value of athletic achievement). What followed was a succession of popular, but excessively ambitious, aggressive wars and predictable military collapse (Thucydides).

Despite all of the sophistication and "rationality" of Aristotle to teach him, Alexander the Great, the next century's resource-rich heir to Athenian values, repeated the same tragic mistake on a larger scale.

threaten the potential investors with an elimination of their profit potential if they do not succeed in inducing the investor-sensitive political process to appropriately respond to their joint interest. Therefore, viewing the private economic warfare that can be prevented by the appropriate investor-sensitive legislation in the same way as we have been viewing collective warfare, it is clear that the prevention of private economic warfare is vital to the relevant investors. So a similar analysis can be employed to induce the co-evolving democracy to supply the appropriate institutions. In particular, the evolving property owners and their potential customers will all face a non-conflictual team payoff in inducing a solution to their trap, a solution that would convert their expensive-but-dormant projects into profitable ventures. Their non-partisan support for these investor-vital institutions (e.g., the zoning laws discussed in Appendix A.1) therefore creates the same sort of rapid evolutionary adjustment that occurs for collective defense-institutions.

Again, although we have no reason to expect effective democracies to generate such speed in solving other, non-vital, allocation problems, those involving neither collective defense nor underinvestment traps, the investor-sensitivity that is evolved in solving defense and underdevelopment problems will undoubtedly carry over into these non-vital areas. This is reflected in the democratic efficiency theorems of Chapter 3, Section I. It should therefore come as no surprise when we find that long-surviving democracies have historically produced uniquely impressive rates of economic growth and eventually uniquely high levels of economic prosperity.

From the standpoint of our social theory, it could not have been any other way. Democracy poses a unique burden on any society. Even when it is effective, democracy is expensive and generates an extra set of vital economic institutions, institutions required for the state to survive its military emergencies despite the special handicap of a wartime legislature. So any democracy must be expected to substantially compensate its evolved-to-succeed military founders by producing uniquely superior civilian legislation and consequently superior economic performance.[32]

---

[32]Western democracies have long been much more formal, participatory, educationally free, and legislatively flexible than Middle Eastern and Far Eastern democracies. The following dynamical explanation will simultaneously offer the interested reader an alternative view of the problems addressed in this study.

Slightly more than seven thousand years ago, a relatively insignificant village of partially sedentary people in what is now in the steppe north of the Caucasus Mountains began to slowly expand, spreading its influence to neighboring villages, gradually forming new alliances and expanding in all feasible directions (Gimbutas) until, during the current century, its people and culture have come to dominate the entire world.

Since intermarriage with indigenous peoples has seldom slowed this advance, which simultaneously progressed at roughly the same rate in numerous geographical directions, any racial supremacy argument can be, and certainly has been, dismissed out of hand. And, since the separate advances have been fitful, more than once falling into "dark ages" or utter domination by foreign peoples, we cannot attribute the success of the Indo-Europeans to some sort of first-mover-advantage. Nor does the historical record support the recent hypothesis of Diamond in which the Indo-European and related civilizational success stories are attributed to a superior geographical heritage relative to their initially geographically segregated

A large part of this study is devoted to theoretically and empirically confirming the above conceptual argument. Perhaps the most important implication of the argument is that, whenever social evolution results in an intellectually free, pragmatically evaluated, competition to produce political and economic institutions that ultimately appeal to the expressed interests of the various investors within their states, an impressive degree of efficiency emerges, both in the military and the civilian arenas.[33]

---

neighbors. For example, an internationally systematic pattern (most noticeably in Africa and Indochina) has emerged regarding previously dispossessed neighbors of the Indo-Europeans in which the restored natives have proceeded to quickly return their regions from a relatively developed to a relatively underdeveloped status. More generally, the surrender of Indo-European lands to non-Indo-Europeans (most noticeably in Asia Minor, the Balkans, and Russia after the fall of Byzantium) has produced systematic economic degeneration. Thus, it is widely agreed, we must look to culture, especially the victorious western European culture, if we are to understand our civilizational success story.

Fortunately, identifying a strikingly unique aspect of Indo-European culture, or mythology, is a fairly simple matter. While competing social thought systems had granted mystical powers to existing military rulers in order to extend and facilitate social control, the Indo-European mythologies systematically subordinated existing military authorities to intellectual authorities as a social class (Dumezil, Lincoln), authorities such as priests, lawyers, and social philosophers, as we have already seen in Section III of Chapter 1.

This primary subordination myth of any Indo-European society (most likely some prehistoric state's vital re-evolution built upon an elsewhere-socially-debilitating effort to exaggerate the social value of a particular variety of priests or spiritual communicators), freed their actually dominant military sector (Appendix B.1) from the burdensome activity of producing and administering a system of civil law. At the same time, it enabled intellectual specialists within the society to separately evolve an appropriate civilian incentive system (e.g., formal democracy). Functional specialization has thus allowed both the military and the civilian systems of successful Indo-European civilizations to each become more highly evolved -- more sophisticated and complex -- than their more centralized civilizational competitors.

At the same time, such specialization has exacerbated a couple of delicate institutional coordination problems. In particular, the specialization has forced: (1) surviving Indo-European legislatures to internalize the problems that private citizens create for the future militaries (Appendix B.2); and (2) surviving Indo-European militaries to effectively over-ride civilian power in defensive emergencies (Appendix B.3). The ability of a state to solve the former coordination problem is as an indicator of its legislative efficiency. The ability of a state to solve the latter problem is necessary for the survival of the state and therefore defines a critical set of structurally vital economic institutions.

[33]Note that even non-democratic, what we call "authoritarian", societies cannot militarily survive unless their leaders are willing and able to defend their state against foreign aggression. But the ability to mount a successful defense is wholly expected because it is very highly correlated with the leader's definitional ability to maintain internal order. Although the evolved authoritarian state lacks the efficiency potential of a democracy, its capacity for generating positive surpluses is not insignificant. And so the ability of a long-surviving authoritarian state to rapidly furnish appropriate institutional responses to important exogenous shocks is also not insignificant. Our empirical studies will correspondingly reveal an ordinarily

C. The Consequences of Economic Ideology

1. *Democracy vs. Received Economic Theories.* Economists and social thinkers -- like Edmund Burke's "sophisters, economists, and calculators" -- have almost universally regarded optimal economic institutions as the province of consciously rational policy analysis, i.e., of abstract professional theories determining how an economy does and should operate. Nevertheless, decisions regarding the choice of economic institutions may or may not be aided by the rational policy analysis that our teachers have led us to make. Indeed, as emphasized in Chapter 1, one of our central conclusions will be that the teacher-serving biases that came to so annoy the mature Mr. Burke (1790) have been so strong that highly successful states (including both pre- and post-revolutionary France) have been systematically ruined by economic policies based upon such ideological calculations.[34] In contrast, a pragmatic and intuitive approach to democratic legislation will be seen to have uniformly yielded citizen-efficient outcomes.[35] This central result will appear both as the theoretical

---

impressive responsiveness of legislatively pragmatic authoritarian governments to important exogenous shocks.

[34]This is not to say that <u>all</u> social decisions have been best made without abstract theories. An over-riding constitutional theory has helped prevent current legislators from passing laws that would perpetuate the power of current legislators. An over-riding military and legal theory of territoriality has helped social leaders commit themselves to respond to various private aggressions within the state. Regarding economics, as shown in Thompson (1981), the inability of current democracies to escape their own future efficiency has also been responsible for their establishment of independent bureaucracies of politically isolated professionals to carry out economic policies that future legislatures would find too painful. Although the corresponding professions, to be efficiently non-objective, must generally be cartelized, there must also be an objective evaluation, perhaps through genuine competition among these alternative professional cartels, and a corresponding ability to prevent the winning cartels from exploiting their positions by becoming teachers of the future ruling class. <u>Legislative</u> decisions, including decisions to establish independent bureaucracies, should not be affected by abstract theories taught to them by intellectual cartels of policy advisors. Our complaint here is thus not against theory per se; it is against those specific, ideology-based, economic and social theories that have carried with them a specific legislative program.

[35]In many respects, Burke, who used his skepticism to <u>criticize</u> the revolutionary creation of new democracies, is of little help. If Burke really believed in the value of experience, why wouldn't he support Revolutionary France's attempt to replace their "enlightened" national aristocrats with more practically oriented individuals such as observed democracies had been producing? In fact, the entire Enlightenment debate over democracy is of little help. Regarding the anti-Burkian side of the debate, if the Enlightenment intellectuals that came to support democratic revolutions really knew, following the economics of the physiocrats and Adam Smith, how an economy should be run, what was the point to the risk and expense of democracy? Under Enlightenment assumptions, a benevolent authoritarian leader (popularly elected in order to avoid the widely-feared corruptibility of absolute power), once armed with an enlightened bureaucracy, would be surely superior to democracy (as Adam Smith and the

prediction of a specific political-economic model (Appendix B.3 (Section III.I), Appendix A.1, and Section I of Chapter 3) and as a recurrent empirical conclusion in every one of our institutional studies.[36]

2. *The Difficulty of Maintaining Democratic Effectiveness.* The study will uncover a systematic institutional deterioration in any politically dominant state, wherein a singular weakening of intellectual competition from other states lays the unusually high surpluses available to the citizens of such states wide open to ideology-based, parasitic attacks on the initial legislative pragmatism of the dominant state. The resulting civilizational dynamic is straightforward:

a. Endogenous Dominance Cycles During Civilizational Advances

In the historically common presence of several military challengers to a dominant state within a given civilization, a dominance cycle is an inevitable consequence. The predictable economic decay and military losses of a previously dominant effective democracy induce a new competition-for-dominance until a new effective democracy becomes politically dominant. The newly dominant state then increasingly loses its own internal efficiency due to the growing influence of its own legislative ideologues until it too is overtaken by a competing state.

This would continue on indefinitely in a simple cyclical equilibrium if there were an unlimited supply of competing states in the given civilization and the military technology were fixed. But there is only a finite number of legitimately competing states, and, ordinarily, an ideology will remain within a society at least as long as the

---

aristocratic Austrians recognized, but Western Europe's Classical Liberals did not). The unfortunate legacy of the convoluted arguments of both Burke and Western Europe's Enlightenment intellectuals is a widespread confusion over the rationale for democratic legislatures. (As we have already noted, a famous exception representative of a small group of unconfused 20th century liberals, is Max Weber, who advocated an elected authoritarian leader, what Jefferson derisively called a "Polish King", over democratic legislatures in order to effectively implement the economic ideology of the Enlightenment.)

As elaborated in Appendix A.1, and Section I of Chapter 3, the basic problem is that political economists have lacked a theory of how severely inefficient underdevelopment traps can arise under laissez faire and how democracy can theoretically eliminate such traps.

[36]A revealing aside here is that Alchian, with whom we have seldom agreed as regards social policy, has nevertheless consistently been one of the most interested readers of our earlier, non-evolutionary, works. These works (e.g., the B-Appendices) consistently illustrated, to Alchian's only temporary consternation, the extraordinary efficiency of traditional democratic legislation. We now believe that Alchian soon came to see, in each of these works, an implicit extension, to the societal level, of his basic idea that evolutionary forces eventually convert experimental and pragmatic decisions into optimal decisions. We (the senior author) had long failed to recognize this because, like others (e.g., Leijonhufvud), we had ungenerously attributed Alchian's Burkian view of so-called "economic experts" to mere skepticism rather than an implicit belief in the efficiency of competitively evolved social institutions.

civilization remains.

(b) The Inevitability of Civilizational Empires

So, once all states but one become ideologized, it is no trouble for the late bloomer, the last of the non-ideological states in the given civilization, to create an empire in which all of the other, still ideologized, states become her clients.[37] Alternatively, before that, the military technology might become so sophisticated that what would be merely a dominant state in a civilization of independent states becomes a hegemonic rent-collector from her imperial dependencies.   In either case,[38] the result is the same: mature civilizations develop empires.

So, the only historical end to this depressingly regular cycle, this circulation of the civilizational elites, has systematically appeared when an empire has arisen, wherein an initially pragmatic state has come to militarily dominate and substantially legislate for all of its would-be competitors within the civilization.

(c) The Persistent Decay of Civilizational Empires

In such cases, even more depressingly, ideologization has caused the entire empire to suffer a steady and lengthy legislative and thus economic deterioration, down to where even its initially unlikely, extra-civilizational, aggressors could defeat it. The bigger they have been, the harder they have fallen. A long and momentous civilization-cycle has thus been the predictable historical outcome, wherein the long upturns have been accompanied by smaller cycles representing a circulation of the

---

[37]An important example of a civilization whose states do **not** retain their economic or social ideologies after they have been subjugated is Asian Civilization, the premier example of which is China. Here, as noted in the introduction to Chapter 4, a newly dominant state endogenously drives out the failed economic and social ideologies of the previous dominant state. Although the traditional Chinese state is often called an "empire", the dominant state (or "dynasty") is traditionally only slightly militarily superior to its client states.   The traditional Chinese state is a feudal state. So when the economic or social ideology of an ancient Chinese dynasty began to inadequately serve the Chinese gentry, a new dominant state would, after some bloodshed, take over the bureaucratically endorsed "mandate of heaven". There is no endogenous end to this theoretically and historically quite impressive "dynastic cycle". What can, and actually did (e.g., Wakeman), end the cycle was the 19th century arrival of European powers (especially England), which created the need for a regular national Chinese army and thus a true Chinese "empire". Since the failed late-18th century economic ideology of the Manchu leaders (Thompson, et al., Vol. I, Ch. 7) lacked the traditional check, the imperial state kept declining until its loss of independence and political collapse in the 20th century (see Chapter 5).

[38]These two effects are actually quite complementary: As a civilization matures and the number of subjugated, ex-dominant, states grows, the resources that are at the disposal of the later independent state correspondingly grow. Innovation, including military innovation, is an increasingly socially profitable use of the growing resources of these successively larger states.

civilizational elites while the typically long downturns have soon become characterized by the relatively relentless and intra-civilizationally uniform economic deteriorations characteristic of all famous imperial states.[39]

(d) The Economic Free-Fall of a World Empire

The economic prospect facing a world empire is even more bleak in that there is no military check of any kind on the prospective decline in economic efficiency. Our suggestion of a new world constitution will be correspondingly designed to prevent a permanent economic decline, the otherwise inexorable economic decay of a true world empire.

3. *The Pascalian Mind-Set of the Social Leaders.* As suggested above, our emphasis on the social value of special interests and legislative pragmatism rather than consciously rational welfare maximization does not mean that economic development and state survival were not sometimes explicit goals of the intuitively driven, non-ideologized, social leaders adopting the appropriate institutions. "The heart has reasons that reason does not know" (Pascal). Indeed, the predominant psychological approach to legislative decisionmaking taken throughout this study can be interpreted to be effectively Pascalian (Thompson, 1995). Socially successful legislators, we shall see, have been able to approximate broad rationality by remaining within their evolved, seemingly arbitrarily constrained, policy roles and following intuitions based upon the civilizationally traditional values and pro-social intentions that earned them, like their predecessors, the rights to fill these roles, at the same time following the flexible democratic pressures of existing special-interest groups and their lifetime accumulations of empirical policy knowledge.

Thus, when two objective Pascalian leaders with conflicting interests meet in an attempt to resolve their conflict to avoid a mutually costly war, they will, like any pair of private traders, be able to see their way to a joint optimum. If they know one another's entire preference map, this is just an application of the theoretical model of Appendix B.1 to the simple case of significant bilateral monopoly, as discussed in Section I of Chapter 1. Even if they do not know one another's preferences, the

---

[39]Note that our use of the word "imperial" or "imperialistic" throughout this study is a simple derivative of the word "empire" which applies when a single state militarily dominates an entire civilization. We certainly do not have in mind the pejorative Marxist-Leninist definition in which "imperialism" is where a few monopolistic-capitalistic countries selfishly tax their colonies (Lenin). Thus, what we shall label an "empire" is not just a state and its colonies but a single, civilizationally controlling, legislating state like the Roman, Byzantine, Carolingian, Habsburg, Ottoman, or 2nd British Empires.

Although imperialism (in our sense) may be a good or a bad thing, there is nothing that any political economist can do about it. So we don't treat it as a good or a bad thing. The same is true of colonialism, wherein a dominant state taxes and defends its subordinate states. We therefore also have no *a priori* prejudice against "imperialism" in the Marxist-Leninist sense. We will, however, extensively criticize contemporary "neo-colonialism" because it will be seen to be a quite inefficient, broadly irrational, imperial policy (see Chapter 5).

disputants need merely share the same probability of the outcome of a war (which could be inferred from the behavior of the country's relative bond prices) for our theory to predict an absence of war among objective international negotiators. As long as both sides correctly see the disaster that awaits them, one side or the other will capitulate in the bargaining before incurring these costs. Systematic war will arise in our model only when ideology has worked to make at least one of the negotiators non-objectively estimate the probability of success in war (Section II.D.4 of Chapter 3 and Section I.D. of Chapter 5). In particular, systematic, socially inefficient, war will arise when ideologized negotiators persist in the incorrect belief that their adversaries do not understand the true benefits of capitulation but will, soon, after not-too-much fighting, come to understand them.

Another critically important example occurs when several objective legislators meet to adjust the vital institutions of their society in response to recent experience. Although institutional natural selection has worked to determine the identities and income constraints of these Pascalian decisionmakers, their objectively shared interest in survival and intuitively correct sense of the pending disaster leads them, using Appendix A.2 below, to quickly and efficiently adjust these institutions. The process is illustrated in Chapter 4's introductory discussion.

Although the correspondingly practical intuitions of the legislators thus often greatly facilitate the adjustment process, unconstrained Pascalian decisionmakers do not generally understand, even subconsciously, the nature of the social problem they are solving and would make serious mistakes in the absence of these institutional constraints. Correspondingly, we will, in the course of the empirical argument, offer several examples of the way in which evolved institutional constraints have transformed these otherwise highly inefficient intuitive decisions, these otherwise misguided attempts to maximize social welfare, into remarkably efficient social decisions. Since top social leaders theoretically face no institutional (or higher reaction-functional) constraints (Appendix B.1), the current, similarly Pascalian, top leaders of evolved democracies institutionally earn their positions through a procedure that selects especially tradition-respecting or constitution-respecting individuals.

Thus, as in our model of the private sector, consciously rational governmental decisionmaking works well in important special cases but breaks down and gives way to institutional evolution in the general case of multilateral bargaining.

Simple evidence for the power of such institutional evolution to determine an efficient institutional form, i.e., to efficiently constrain Pascalian leaders, is the great similarity of the organizational forms selected by large modern business organizations. The efficiency of a shareholder-elected board of directors, who in turn select and constrain the analogously Pascalian chief executives of these companies, is extremely difficult to doubt because of the now-over-400 years (Adam Smith, p. 713) of vital-institutional evolution of such joint-stock companies.

It is true that the rapid rise of national democratic institutions over the past two centuries stems largely from the imitation of the observable successes of the particular institutions of a single pair of countries, Great Britain and the U.S. However, the former's democratic institutions had earlier been sporadically evolved, often under harsh Darwinian pressure, since even before the Magna Carta. And, as noted above, the latter's democratic institutions (as reflected in the U.S. Constitution) were the culmination of 150 years of close-to-Malthusian, competition among American colonies for significant investor-immigrants.

It is easy, then, to see how the education-induced adoption of fashionable economic or social ideologies would pervert a successfully evolved, citizen-efficient, political mechanism. Indeed, we shall frequently see how the pro-social intentions of important government officials betray them and lead to the adoption of citizen-inefficient economic or social ideologies whenever these ideologies become sufficiently fashionable. We shall correspondingly see how various economic and social ideologies have systematically come to transform Pascalian decisionmakers and thereby deleteriously influence the legislatures and bureaucracies of politically dominant, educationally "advanced," states.

4. *Pascalian Intellectuals.* Viewing the same problem from the standpoint of the simultaneously evolving sellers of information, Pascalian thought also extends over to intellectual hierarchies, wherein most thinkers psychologically evaluate alternative assumptions on the basis of whether or not the assumptions, and the corresponding conclusions, feel intuitively "right", or "useful", or "interesting". These evaluative feelings, shaped as they are by a desire for the approval of one's professional colleagues, are best represented as profession-serving evaluations. In the case of an intellectual hierarchy, where entry is not artificially limited, the only way to benefit from its internally joint-maximization, hierarchical, organizational form (Appendix B.1), is to create an artificial demand for its professional service. Profession-serving evaluations thus bias the cooperating intellectuals toward the promotion of demand-creating ideas at the cost of objective truth. Because the market for these ideas rewards the appearance of truth, rather than truth itself, the evolutionary successful cartel will, *ceteris paribus*, maximize its externally perceived social value. Nevertheless, rational and objective buyers suitably discount the cartel's informational representations so that, as we have argued, the profession's self-flattering bias is only substantially costly to others when the informational product of a professional cartel is not objectively evaluated. This occurs when the cartel educates the buyers and thereby creates what we have called an "ideology." So non-objective evaluations will only emerge in civilizationally dominant countries, where the intellectuals -- largely because of their singularly impressive sophistication and effect on education -- have a noticeable impact on the thoughts of educated government officials. The subconscious nature of this gradually evolved, demand-creating, ideological bias among hierarchically organized thinkers means that the individuals involved are unaware of the problem.

Yet the bias is surely there, as elaborated in Thompson et al., Vol. 1, Ch. 1, in a study that also proposes a relatively idealistic decartelization of science in order to quickly eliminate an entire class of professional cartels and thereby eliminate the evolution of an entire class of profession-serving biases and the resulting social problems. The less idealistic analysis of the current study complements the ideal solution by suggesting: (1) a world constitution that promises to immediately reduce the civilization-wide costs of this failure in the market for legislative ideas; and (2) an isolation of intellectual cartels from the broader educational system so as to gradually eliminate their ideology.

5. *The Efficiency Problem: Summary.* The world-constitutional reform suggested in our concluding chapter is explicitly designed to induce a replacement of ideologically inspired policy with policy based upon experience-inspired design, trial-and-error learning, and pragmatic imitation. Although no policy generated from this volume's research is sufficiently refined to achieve this idealistic goal for the hegemon of a world empire in a timely fashion, our suggested policy <u>would</u> work to both reduce the return to ideologization and eliminate an ongoing spread of the hegemon's policies and thus an unimpeded decline in worldwide economic efficiency. In view of the imminence, if not existence, of a secure world empire, and the corresponding prospect of a continuing, historically unprecedented, deterioration in worldwide economic efficiency, the concluding chapter will outline a constitutional reform that would quickly immunize the world against such an otherwise inevitable free-fall in economic efficiency.

II. THE DISTRIBUTIONAL PROBLEM

A. The Free International Competition for People

A classic study of the history of real wages by Thorold Rogers reveals that real wages in England, and probably all of western Europe, varied within a narrow band, remaining essentially constant, from at least the height of the Middle Ages to 1820, slightly after the end of the Napoleonic Wars. A price-theoretic interpretation of Roger's running political commentary is that a conveniently-timed series of <u>aristocratically-imposed tax-increases</u> on workers -- not the supply-side speculations of either Malthus or Ricardo and not the stagnant-technology speculations of neoclassical and modern authors -- was the cause of the wage-constancy. Reinforcing our tax interpretation -- besides the social theory of Appendix B.1 -- is the aristocratic wisdom, especially widespread prior to the mid-19th century, that workers must be kept poor in order to assure a healthy abundance of labor inputs. The subsequently well-documented positivity of the effect of income on leisure thus implied a dual redistributive benefit to an aristocracy from a tax increase on the laboring population. There is correspondingly no reason why a world with a unified aristocracy would not -- unless constitutionally constrained -- come to rely on a similar "wisdom" and thereby generate a similarly near-subsistence wage rate.

Also, regarding the common neoclassical-modern explanation of a heightened rate of innovation in modern times, 1760 is increasingly used to mark the dramatically heightened rate of innovation represented by the industrial revolution. In view of the 1820 date as the start of the climb in wages, this neoclassical-modern explanation can only be objectively maintained by arguing for a highly implausible, 60-year, lag in the determination of real wages.

The huge reduction in labor supply during the war-and-plague-ravaged 14th century provides us with perhaps the simplest simple test of the theory. While before-tax real-wages jumped during this calamitous century, a reflection of the accuracy of the neoclassical theory as regards inessentials such as before-tax distribution, taxes on labor also jumped so that after-tax labor income (largely the income of free peasants) generally failed to increase at all (e.g., Rosener, pp. 271-73).

This, of course, was also the age of futile peasant revolts.

While Rogers' study ends in the early 1860s, the subsequent 110 years of wage history impressively confirmed Rogers' hypothesis that a sea change had occurred at the end of the Napoleonic Wars. Never explained, however, is just what happened in the 1820s that would allow for a complete break in the historic pattern, a 15-fold explosion in real wages over the ensuing 150 years.

Now an obvious military lesson of the peace-producing Napoleonic Wars to the nations of the West was that any attempt to acquire the surplus of a neighboring nation by military aggression would induce such a widespread defensive involvement by ordinary civilians that much of the basic labor force of the victimized country would be destroyed in the essentially Pyrrhic victory. Thereafter, the typical response of neighboring nations to the significant increase in the basic labor productivity of a nearby nation -- which had been military attack against the more productive nation -- was peaceful emigration to that nation. Correspondingly, what had been the traditional military response to the significant emigration of a western nation's labor to a more labor-productive neighbor -- i.e., punitive warfare against the labor-acquiring neighbor -- came to an abrupt end.[40] And, quite symmetrically, what had been a successful state's traditional military response to its own high domestic productivity growth, i.e., military aggression against less economically successful neighbors in order to acquire additional inexpensive labor, was transformed into a purely civilian response, i.e., allowing after-tax wages to rise in order to legitimately attract immigration from the neighboring countries.

As labor was economically attracted to the more productive country, the shrinking neighbors could only respond by competitively lightening the tax burdens on their own urban laborers and peasants, correspondingly extending voting rights to the masses. The source of the previous five centuries of wage constancy -- secularly increasing labor-taxation by politically exploitative aristocratic investors in land and capital rather than some imaginary (Ricardian or Malthusian) "iron law" of wages or some similarly imaginary (neoclassical or modern) assertion of a relative lack of prior technical inventions -- was finally being reversed by the simple international competition of free and independent countries for the labor of other countries. Emigration into the high-wage countries thus proceeded along-side the mass-army-induced popularization of democracy, both continuing to grow at an unprecedented rates after the Napoleonic Wars. The taxation of labor could no longer expand with the productivity of labor. "Nations" were converted from the enserfing racial or cultural entities of the past into the peacefully competing legal entities of the subsequent 170 years. Cosmopolitan cities, immigrant rights, and popular democracy reawakened

---

[40]Most familiar to the United States is the War of 1812, which Britain fought to regain its emigrating seamen. The ensuing war, which ended in 1819, was the last war Britain fought in response to the emigration of its labor force.

This basic military change brought a correspondingly abrupt end to what had been the long-standing, quite rational, labor-import policy in Europe prior to the 1820s, a guild-enforced refusal to hire the labor of a foreign nation.

after an at least 500-year slumber.[41]

One can only imagine all the grief and suffering that the world would have been spared if only Marx or his followers would have understood the international distributional benefits that had already begun to flow from this early 19th century change in military technology.

B. Earlier Civilizational Blossomings

The same introduction of widespread civilian participation in warfare -- followed by a competitively induced popularization of democracy, cosmopolitan cities, and widespread per-capita income growth -- had arisen earlier among the city-states of Classical Greece; among the Italian city-states of both the Hellenistic Era and the Middle Ages; and among the trading towns of High Medieval England, France, Spain, Portugal, and Germany up until the emergence of professional armies during the last two centuries of the Middle Ages.   Moving eastward, the same sequence had occurred among the competing city-states of ancient Sumer, the early Egyptians, and much later, among the 7th and 8th century Saracens, and still later, within the feudal states of both the Fatimid and Safivid dynasties. Moving further eastward, we see a duplication of this pattern among the Feudal states of Aryan-India up through the 5th century, and the similarly among the peacefully competing feudal states of China during the later Tang, Sung, and early Ming dynasties.

In each case, the remarkable explosion in technological innovation that suddenly emerged probably represented the simple exploitation of what had been an expanding latent technology, inventions that had been accumulating for centuries as reflected in artistic achievements and increasingly sophisticated weaponry but nevertheless largely unexploited by the masses because of the absence of a mass market and corresponding presence of historically cheap skilled labor (Thompson, 1961). The underlying competition in these repeated civilizational blossomings was more than an efficiency-generating competition among policy ideas pragmatically designed to efficiently serve the increasingly valuable civilian populations.   It was also a competition among states for immigrants. The latter competition is what generated the skilled-wage and middle-class income growth necessary for the predictable

---

[41]Popular democracy represents a kind of democracy in which citizens who invest only in human capital are granted the same political participation rights as owners of non-human capital. As we shall see in Section I.A of Chapter 3, citizen-efficiency generally requires this complete form of investor-democracy. Moreover, as shown in Section III.C of Chapter 3, popular elections by militarily-sacrificing individuals represent a vital institution in the presence of inter-regional labor mobility. The explosive growth of real wages in the modern Anglo-Saxon countries following the Napoleonic Wars, for example, was immediately preceded by voting-rights legislation that suddenly converted upper-middle-class (e.g., Jeffersonian) democracies into popular (e.g., Jacksonian) democracies.

Note once more, however, that a popularly elected government is not a popular democracy unless the citizens may also freely participate in the legislative process. The 19th century boom was in both popular government and popular democracy.

realization of the innovational golden ages.[42]

C. The Costly Reversion to Empire

The elimination of the international competition among states for people -- an elimination that has recently commenced in modern times by what establishment intellectuals are widely portraying as a "progression" to centralized world institutions, an effective world empire -- would thus represent a devastating distributional regression. Indeed, a major ruling-class "economy" of governmental scale stems from the ability of the ruling class to monopsonize the masses.

The imperial centralizations of the Merovingian and Carolingian Franks, whose main idea was to exploit, through taxation, the Gaulish countryside, is thus easy to understand despite their high cost of internal organization. Although, during the subsequent political decentralization represented by the age of feudalism, wages should have correspondingly increased, an alternative form of exploitation was found in serfdom, at least outside of the solidly Germanic communities (Rosener, pp. 19-20; Strayer and Gatske, p. 193). Since imperial taxation was no longer possible, the only way to continue the monopsonization of labor was to physically and legally tie workers and their offspring to the soil in effective slavery despite the substantial efficiency costs of such an institution (Appendix B.1, Section 6). Where, of course, a feudal province came to be extraordinarily wealthy, serfdom was phased out even before the wave of re-centralizations of the 13th-15th centuries (Section II.B.4 of Chapter 3), for there was relatively little provincial exit to fear from even highly taxed freemen because of the attraction of its urban life and the province's relatively large scale (Pirenne, Ch. 3). And where, as northeastern Europe, a post-15th century province or nation was relatively poor, it retained serfdom because, for them, centralization into a nation-state was not sufficient to prevent mass emigration.

So, with the basically exploitative preferences of these various ruling classes, most of whom were quite Christian, revealed by their evolved institutional choices, labor's numerous centuries of secular stagnation up to the period of international labor competition beginning in 1820 should come as no surprise. The lesson is quite clear: Ruling classes simply do not pay higher wages than they have to. If, as economists commonly surmise, the persistently growing inequality of income in our increasingly imperial world merely reflected a change in civilian technology, it would find little historical precedent.

In a similar vein, referring to the above-mentioned civilizational history, we find a corresponding sequence of distributionally devastating imperial centralizations.

---

[42]Investments in innovation are typically just part of the complex of complementary investments that characterize the escape from any underdevelopment trap. It is efficiency (perhaps achieved in part by an effective patent system), not innovation per se, that constitutes the escape. Indeed, the theoretical and empirically estimated marginal social rate of return to innovation in the United States is not substantially higher than the return to other investments (Thompson, et al., Vol. III, Chapters 5 and 6). Nevertheless, these innovational waves serve as quite visible measures of economic progress.

Corresponding to the above sequence of Western civilizational blossomings, we find: the increasingly oppressive Athenian imperialization arising in the temporarily successful states of the Classical Greek city states and the even more oppressive imperializations of the Hellenistic Age; the notoriously inegalitarian formation of the Roman Empire, and the middle-class-eliminating centralizations of an imperializing late 15th and 16th century Europe. In the Middle-East, we find the similarly distributionally devastating centralization of the previously democratic city-states of ancient Sumer by various Emperors from Urukagina and Sargon to Hammurabi, the similarly inspired centralization of the initially democratic feudal kingdom of ancient Egypt by the later pharaohs of each of the various Kingdoms, the centralizing Abbasid Caliphs of the 9th and 10th centuries, and the even more centralizing Ottoman Emperors during the 15th and 16th centuries. Moving further eastward, we find the later Guptan and later Manchu centralizations. Every one of these historic imperial centralizations, once secure, produced both a rapid economic decline as well as a dehumanizing impoverishment of a previously vibrant middle class.[43]

Such episodes, taken as a whole, should vividly alert us to the distributional as well as the allocational dangers posed by our rapidly centralizing institutions of world government. How these dangers are reflected in current geo-political trends is elaborated below in Chapters 5 and 6.

D.   The Prospective Rational Surrender of Popular Democracy

The intellectuals and the masses living in the dominant states of the modern era have been taught that we have "natural" rights and that we exercise these rights in a social contract in which we hire a leader who protects us from foreign and domestic enemies. However, the logic of social organization complements history by telling us that quite the opposite is true (Appendix B.1). Natural social organization begins with a prior commitment from the social leaders. Ultimately, these primary social leaders are the military founders of the state. George Washington decided against a monarchy; so we don't have a monarchy. But note that the original U.S. and British democracies were not popular democracies. They were property-owner, or "aristocratic", democracies. As we have argued, it was only during the late 1820s and 1830s, reflecting the new, market-based, international competition for people through peaceful immigration movements, that ushered in popular democracy and secularly growing real wages. Moreover, this popular democracy is not irreversible, even within the confines of a popularly democratic legal system.[44]

---

[43]The evidentiary basis for the less well-known of these stylized facts is summarized in Thompson, et al., Vol. II, Ch. 6.

[44]A U.S. trend away from egalitarian tax and expenditure systems began with the U.S. defeat in Vietnam and the corresponding replacement of conscripted citizen armies with professional armies. The subsequent decrease in the feeling of indebtedness of the wealthier voters for the military sacrifices of the country's youth has obviously accompanied the sharp decrease in the extent of these sacrifices. The result has, of course, been a sharp decrease in the tax

The new, post-cold-war, worldwide dominance of the U.S. and its European allies, and the corresponding ability of our ruling classes to use this control over third-world polities and worldwide lending agencies (e.g., the World Bank and International Monetary Fund (IMF)) to determine the tax and expenditure policies of essentially all of the other nations of the world (see Chapter 5), has given our ruling classes an ability to end the worldwide competition among nations for people that has been responsible for our moderate middle-class tax rates· and growing real wages since the 1820s. IMF "globalization", which essentially buys cheap-labor and free-trade policies from the voters of third-world countries in exchange for emergency government finance (Chapter 5), has recently put such a policy in place. The correspondingly new profit opportunity for the wealthy property owners in the dominant countries, which has certainly not failed to impress buyers of common stock, is also being domestically exploited.

To the extent that this emerging decimation of the domestic middle class requires something beyond the deceptions achieved by progress-suggesting shibboleths such as "globalization," the wealthy ruling class can achieve their emerging distributional goal by essentially buying regressive changes in their domestic political systems from their relatively poor contemporaries. For these poor voters have relatively high time preferences and little ability or willingness to efficiently sacrifice for their children, as indicated by the relative infrequency with which we observe relatively poor parents granting lump-sum transfers to their recently grown-up children (Thompson, et al., Vol. I, Ch. 3). We have thus observed a continued weakening in our legislatively determined rules limiting campaign spending, thereby generating a continuing trend toward legislatures that favor wealthy property owners. (Meanwhile, the masses are assuaged with leaders who ostensibly represent them but actually adopt policies supported by the wealthy property owners and their representatives.) Eventually, the equivalent of a poll tax could be passed, giving current tax relief to the poor but inducing a dramatic fall in their future political participation and distant future income. It would, in effect, represent the rationally voted end of popular democracy.[45]

---

contributions of the wealthy to programs that benefit our country's youth and, more ominously, a purchase of political power from the poorer voters and their descendants through a political purchase of campaign-finance laws favoring large contributors. Nevertheless, such a trend cannot be taken too far because a mere professionalization of the local armed forces does not eliminate the international competition for people. It is only when there is a single, militarily dominant, country -- an imperial leader -- that there is genuine, world-wide, threat to popular government. This threat is the subject of the remainder of this chapter.

[45]Other, less direct, and much less efficient, means of redistribution -- methods generating higher incomes to cartels of lawyers and related professionals at the expense of all others in the world, including the wealthy investors -- are increasingly likely as we approach a long-run equilibrium. But discussing them here would take us too far afield.

III. A CONSTITUTIONAL SOLUTION

The only apparent way to prevent the wholly predictable reoccurrence of yet another civilizational-wide disaster, another relentless distributional as well as allocational retrogression, is for the world's dominant nations to quickly move to establish a decentralization-based world constitution.

Such a constitution would maintain what would otherwise soon become an obsoletely egalitarian fiscal structure. This currently valuable distributional goal would be constitutionally achieved by permanently allowing each nation-state to legislate its own tax, expenditure, and welfare system, independent of the desires of any other nation, or even of multinational corporations having significant political influence in the dominate nations. An uncompromising "states-rights" value system, as well as a world anti-monopoly policy, would be required to maintain such a world-constitution and the resulting free competition of states for people. This political ideal -- which is diametrically opposed to the hot new "globalization" trend that has predictably come to dominate our international economic agencies since the collapse of the Soviet Union -- and the corresponding world-constitution would have to be supported and defended by the world's militarily dominant nation. So, to gain the support of the dominant nation, its elected national leader should appoint, with the approval of a constitutionally constrained world legislature, a conditional world leader.

First-best efficiency, again according to Appendix B.1, requires the complete absence of ideology. Under current conditions, this would entail an elimination of the educational and political influence of professional elites. As elaborated in the concluding chapter, the above constitutional recommendation works significantly towards this elimination. And future work will recommend further tailoring to fully achieve this efficiency goal. Nevertheless, we must establish the nature and magnitude of this efficiency problem before we can hope to be taken seriously.

The investigations that immediately follow will center upon democratically-evolved institutions that have been widely criticized by existing economic ideologies. Taken sequentially, these long-maligned institutions are guilds and tariffs, the gold standard, and various post-WWI international financial innovations such as fixed exchange rates and foreign exchange controls.

APPENDIX A.2

THE SOCIAL OPTIMALITY OF NARROWLY RATIONAL BEHAVIOR IN NONCONFLICTUAL INTERACTIONS

ABSTRACT

The "1st and 2nd Welfare Theorems of Economics" establish a basis for praising the free and narrowly rational decisions of individuals living under an idealized form of private property. This Appendix proves an analogous pair of theorems for collectivist worlds, i.e., a "Collectivist's Optimality Theorem." An analogous application is to unconditionally praise the free and narrowly rational decisions of the members of a non-conflictual team.

The theorem is then generalized to admit a limited form of conflict, one in which subsequent decisionmakers do not appreciate the consumption decisions of their predecessors. This generalized form is most appropriately applied to intertemporal individual decisionmaking and an explanation of the observed lack of personal consumption commitments in stable informational environments.

The theorem and its generalization apply to a states' current choices of vital institutions. In particular, the theoretical results predict that a state's equilibrium choices of vital institutions, as well as being theoretically efficient, are made in an honest and nonpartisan fashion.

INTRODUCTION

It is commonly observed that in non-conflictual interactions -- i.e., when all of the individuals in a group share the same basic preference orderings over all of their alternative social states -- individuals openly communicate. The team members behave neither deceptively nor aggressively toward others in the group. Even when the physical environment prevents some members of the group from making decisions with the same effectiveness as others in that group, the former individuals willingly submit to the directions of a more informed central coordinator, or "team captain."

These empirical regularities suggest that the theoretical outcome of narrowly rational individual decisions in non-conflict interactions are always best for the group. In other words, if non-conflicting individuals sequentially maximize, then they will always reach their commonly-desired optimum. The purpose of Part I of this appendix is to prove a special case of this result, which we call a "collectivist optimality theorem". More specifically, the purpose of Part I is to prove that, in non-conflictual interactions, narrowly rational individual actions under perfect information (a la von Stackelberg and Zermelo-von Neumann-Morgenstern): (1) always generate a solution and (2) that solution is always a joint optimum.

It would be peculiar if (2), our optimality result, which is the simple converse of Bellman's optimality principle, had not been proved elsewhere. We just haven't been able to find the theorem explicitly stated or proved elsewhere. Regarding (1), the existence result, we do find a way to avoid the indifference conundrums posed by Peleg and Yaari for perfect information games when later decisionmakers are indifferent between various solution points. (While Goldman has proved a fairly general existence result for these environments, we are still left without an algorithm for resolving the Peleg-Yaari indifference conundrums under generally conflicting preferences.)

The combined existence and efficiency results, the "collectivist optimality theorem", can be used to test for the existence of conflict. In particular, if individuals are observed to act deceptively or aggressively toward one another, activities that definitionally subtract from the social total, the payoffs are not "team" payoffs. The theorem can be used, for example, to determine whether or not a single consumer -- viewed as a sequence of distinct decisionmakers -- represents a set of conflicting decisionmakers.

A long chain of economic theorists (Strotz, Pollack, Peleg-Yaari, Hammond, Thaler-Shefrin and several other, no-less-sophisticated, thinkers) have argued that our unconstrained future selves are likely to choose future consumption streams that differ from (or are "inconsistent with") the streams that our current selves would most prefer, and that the resulting conflict, an external diseconomy from future to present selves, leads current selves to make commitments constraining the behavior of future selves. However, the standard empirical examples of consumption-commitments -- viz., joining Christmas clubs, avoiding vice-inducing situations (like Odysseus ordering himself tied to the mast), and hiring budget-enforcing agents -- are not unambiguous examples of such constraints. Rather, a bit of introspection suggests that these are merely examples of constraints narrowly rationally imposed on narrowly rational future selves that are less informed, impulse-buying, selves than the current, more thoughtful, self. The literature's inability to isolate clean examples of such consumptive "time inconsistencies" speaks for a genuine empirical rarity of intrapersonal consumption externalities from informed future selves to informed present selves.

We can thus take the absence of consumption commitments in situations where the individuals are continually well-informed to imply an absence of consumption externalities from future selves to current selves. A person's informed future consumption choices do not displease the person's informed current self. But an absence of commitments does not imply a complete absence of conflict. Current selves may still impose externalities on, or do things that displease, their future selves. Part II of this appendix correspondingly shows that, under perfect information, a no-commitment solution under this limited form of conflict remains optimal for the externality-imposing current decisionmaker. Viewing the current individual as the appropriate social target, the theorem -- which generalizes a consistency theorem of Blackorby, Nissen, Primont, and Russell -- is a generalization of our "collectivist optimality theorem" to worlds with exclusively forward-looking, or "ungrateful", future decisionmakers.

Part III of the appendix indicates how the optimality of a radically decentralized equilibrium extends over to imperfect and incomplete information cases, including those covered in the pioneering work on nonconflictual teams by Marschak and Radner.

The generalizations of these theorems to the territorial interactions that form the central subject of this work are discussed in Part IV of this appendix.

I. A COLLECTIVIST'S OPTIMALITY THEOREM

A convenient description of the first non-conflict situation has the utilities of each of the individuals in a group represented by monotone increasing functions of a common, continuous, real-valued function of individual actions, $f(x_1,...,x_n)$, where the action, x_i, of the ith individual, $i = 1,...,n$, is chosen from a compact set of feasible actions, X_i.

If the individuals in this situation independently (or simultaneously) chose their actions, each selecting an x_i that maximized f for given $(x_1,...,x_{i-1},x_{i+1},...,x_n)$, the resulting, Cournot-type, solution set might obviously contain many local maxima that are not global maxima. There would be nothing to guarantee the achievement of a globally maximal value of f. The source of the problem is that the decisionmakers have no information about one another's actions, and therefore there is no genuine "coordination" of their activities (as in Footnote #1 of Chapter 6).

To represent genuinely "coordinated," noncooperative decisionmaking, we assume "perfect information" in the von Stackelberg-von Neumann-Morgenstern sense, meaning that the individuals choose their actions in sequence, where individual 1 chooses first and then, in full knowledge of this move, individual 2 chooses an action. This continues on until the nth individual chooses an action x_n in X_n that maximizes $f(x_1,...,x_{n-1},x_n)$ for the known, previously chosen, values of $x_1,...,x_{n-1}$. We first show that an unambiguous (pure-strategy) solution to the above game always exists.

The existence of an optimal x_n for the last mover is assured by the compactness of X_n and the continuity of f (for a proof, see Apostol, p. 73). There may be several such maximizing values of x_n. We shall let $x_n^*(x_1,...,x_{n-1})$ represent n's solution correspondence. Since x_n^* is going to be so picked, individual n-1 will attempt to pick an x_{n-1} that maximizes, for given $x_1,...,x_{n-2}$, the common function $f(x_1,...,x_{n-2},x_{n-1},x_n^*(x_1,...,x_{n-2},x_{n-1}))$. Since the value of f for a given x_{n-1} is the same regardless of the value of x_n subsequently chosen from the non-empty image set of $x_n^*(x_1,...,x_{n-1})$, the actual choice by n from this set is a matter of indifference to n-1 as well as to n and therefore does not affect the choice by n-1. Momentarily assuming the existence of a maximizing solution for individual n-1, an assumption validated in the next paragraph, the maximization yields another non-empty correspondence, $x_{n-1}^*(x_1,...,x_{n-2})$. Similarly, individual n-2 attempts to pick, prior to the choice of both n-1 and n, an x_{n-2} that will maximize, for given $x_1,...,x_{n-3}$, $f(x_1,...,x_{n-3},x_{n-2},x_{n-1}^*(x_1,...,x_{n-3},x_{n-2}),x_n^*(x_1,...,x_{n-3},x_{n-2},x_{n-1}^*(x_1,...,x_{n-3},x_{n-2})))$. A solution set to this sequence of n maximizations, (x^*), may, of course, contain several elements.

To prove that the set is non-empty, it is sufficient to prove that the above-described response correspondences, $x_{n-1}^*(\ ),...,x_1^*(\ )$, are all non-empty. Again, $x_{n-1}^*(\ )$ is non-empty if the domain of the objective function variables controlled by n-1 (i.e., $(x_{n-1},x_n^*(x_{n-1})))$ is compact (Apostol, *ibid.*). Since the domain of x_{n-1}, X_{n-1}, is compact by assumption, we need only show that the range of $x_n^*(x_{n-1})$,

or $\displaystyle\bigcup_{x_{n-1}\in X_{n-1}} x_n^*(x_{n-1})$, is compact. This is done in the following three steps:

First, because $(x_{n-1},x_n^*(x_{n-1}))$ maximizes a continuous, real-valued objective function for a given x_{n-1}, we know that $x_n^*(x_{n-1})$ is upper-semicontinuous (Berge). Second, $x_n^*(x_{n-1})$ is closed for any given value of x_{n-1}. For suppose otherwise; then the set $x_n^*(x_{n-1})$ would not contain all of its limit points. Call one of these excluded limit points z. Since X_n is closed, $z \in X_n$. And since z is not in $x_n^*(x_{n-1})$, $f(x_1,...,x_{n-1},z) < f(x_1,...,x_{n-1}, x_n^*(x_{n-1}))$. From these two facts, it would follow that

$$\lim_{x_n^v \to z} f(x_1,...,x_{n-1},x_n^v(x_{n-1})) > f(x_1,...,x_{n-1},z),$$ which contradicts the continuity of f.

So $x_n^*(x_{n-1})$ is an upper-semicontinuous function with a closed image for any given x_{n-1}. We can now complete the proof by applying the result of Nikaido (Lemma 4.5) stating that such a function defined over a compact set produces a total image set,

$\displaystyle\bigcup_{x_{n-1}\in X_n} x_n^*(x_{n-1})$, which is compact. So $x_{n-1}^*(x_1,...,x_{n-2})$ is non-empty. The same

procedure can be repeated to show that $x_{n-2}^*(x_1,...,x_{n-3})$ is non-empty, etc.

This completes our existence proof. We are now prepared to discuss optimality.

In general, that is, when conflict may be present, perfect information solutions are not generally jointly efficient. Standard Prisoner's Dilemma games illustrate this simple fact. But we are dealing here with a non-conflict situation, where the possible payoffs do not permit the redistributional opportunities presented in a standard Prisoner's Dilemma game.[46]

We now prove that a perfect information solution will always achieve a joint optimum in the above, non-conflict situation:

Suppose that a member of the solution set, say x^*, were not a global

---

[46]An additional, well-known difficulty with perfect information solutions is that, when a later mover is indifferent between several possible actions, prior movers -- not knowing which among the later mover's indifferent actions will actually be selected -- do not really know what to do. This difficulty also disappears in non-conflict situations because, as we have already indicated, when prior movers always share the indifference of later ones, the particular actions of later movers within their solution correspondences have no effect on the utilities or decisions of prior movers.

maximum point. Then, there would exist be an alternative, $x^\circ \in X = \prod_{i=1}^{n} X_i$, such that $f(x^\circ) > f(x^*)$. Had individual n been presented with $x_1^\circ, \dots, x_{n-1}^\circ$, the individual would have picked x_n° (i.e., $x_n^*(x_1^\circ, \dots, x_{n-1}^\circ) = x_n^\circ$); and x° would have resulted instead of x^*. It follows that n was not presented with $(x_1^\circ, \dots, x_{n-1}^\circ)$. It similarly follows that if individual n-1 had been presented with $x_1^\circ, \dots, x_{n-2}^\circ$, the individual would have picked x_{n-1}°; for $x_n^*(x_1^\circ, \dots, x_{n-1}^\circ) = x_n^\circ$ and $f(x^\circ) > f(x^*)$. So n-1 was not presented with $x_1^\circ, \dots, x_{n-2}^\circ$. For the same reason, n-2 was not presented with $x_1^\circ, \dots, x_{n-3}^\circ$, etc., up to individual 1. But individual 1 has no excuse. Individual 1 must have not maximized utility. For, according to the above sequence, wherein $x^* \neq x^0$ implies $x_1^* \neq x_1^\circ$, if individual 1 had picked $x_1^* = x_1^\circ$, then the outcome would have equalled x° and individual 1's utility would have been higher. So the supposition that x^* is not a global maximum contradicts the assumption of individually rational choice. The solution point x^* must be a global maximum.

Jim Mirrlees has privately suggested an alternative, more direct, optimality proof. It can be paraphrased as follows: Pick any x. Then change x_n so that it maximizes f for the given $x_1, \dots, x_{n-1}$. The resulting f defines a particular value of a function, $f_{n-1}[x_1, \dots, x_{n-1}]$. Then pick an x_{n-1} that maximizes the latter function, thus yielding an f that defines $f_{n-2}[x_1, \dots, x_{n-2}]$, etc. By definition, $f_1 \geq f_2[x_1] \geq \dots \geq f_{n-1}[x_1, \dots, x_{n-1}] \geq f[x_1, \dots, x_n]$. Since f_1 depends on no variables, it is, according to Mirrlees, unique and therefore the same regardless of what value of x we initially chose. In particular, if $x = x^0$, $f_1 = f_2 = \dots = f_{n-1} = f(x^0) = \max_{x} f(x_1, \dots, x_n)$. So f_1 is our maximum and the theorem is proved.

Maxim Engers has pointed out that the optimality theorem leads to a simple alternative, albeit less direct, existence proof: Since the converse of this optimality theorem, Bellman's Optimality Principle, also holds, a sequential maximization solution is equivalent to a maximum. Therefore, since a maximum in our model exists, so does a sequential maximization solution. Unfortunately, this existence proof does not extend to the generalized problem of Section II while our more cumbersome, direct, proof does.

II. A GENERALIZATION ALLOWING FOR
UNGRATEFUL FUTURE DECISIONMAKERS

As noted in the Introduction, the absence of incentives to devote resources gaining transfers from others implied in the above non-conflict situation continues to hold under a weakening of the conditions on preferences. In particular, it continues to hold as long as each future decisionmaker has the same preferences <u>over future actions</u> as the immediately preceding decisionmaker. In this case, the successive objective functions are:

$$f_1(x) = U_1(x_1, f_2(x))$$
$$f_2(x) = U_2(x_1, x_2, f_3(x))$$

$$\cdot$$
$$\cdot$$

$$f_{n-1}(x) = U_{n-1}(x_1, ..., x_{n-2}, x_{n-1}, f_n(x))$$
$$f_n(x) = U_n(x_1, ..., x_{n-1}, x_n),$$

where $f'_{i+1} > f''_{i+1} \rightarrow U_i(x_1, ..., x_i, f'_{i+1}) > U_i(x_1, ..., x_i, f''_{i+1})$. Thus, for any given $x_1, ..., x_i$, the ith individual's objective function is a monotone increasing function of the $i + 1^{st}$ individual's function.

A particular perfect information solution, x', is, as above, an x such that: x'_n is picked so as to maximize $f_n(x)$; x'_{n-1} is picked so as to maximize $f_{n-1}(x)$ given $x_1, ..., x_{n-2}$ and the dependence of x'_n or x_{n-1}; etc. The existence of a solution holds under the same conditions on preferences, and through the same argument, as in the direct proof of Section I; the exercise will not be repeated.

What we wish to show is that no decisionmaker has an incentive to influence later decisionmakers, i.e., that all subsequent decisionmakers will choose a sequence of actions that maximizes the utility of a current decisionmaker. From this it follows that a current decisionmaker has no incentive to threaten to punish, or withhold information from, future decisionmakers.

The result holds trivially for $i = n$. To show it for $i = n-1$, first note that our above specification on the forms of the successive objective functions implies that any x_n that maximizes f_n given $x_1, ..., x_{n-1}$ will also maximize f_{n-1} given $x_1, ..., x_{n-1}$. Therefore, n will choose the x_n that maximizes the utility of $n-1$, say n's mother, as long as any pair of actions resulting from $n-1$'s first rationally picking an x_{n-1} in anticipation of a subsequent choice of x_n that maximizes her initial utility function given the previously chosen x_{n-1} -- call the pair x'_{n-1}, x'_n -- unconditionally maximizes her utility, $f_{n-1}(x^*_1, ..., x^*_{n-2}, x_{n-1}, x_n)$ over all x_{n-1}, x_n in $X_{n-1} \times X_n$. Now, because no decision would be affected in that $n-1$'s decision would be the same as n's, we can transform $f_n( )$ into $f_{n-1}( )$ without altering the solution. Theorem 1 -- that rational, perfectly informed, sequential choice under a common utility function achieves an unconditional maximum of that function -- then tells us that x'_{n-1}, x'_n does indeed unconditionally maximize $f_{n-1}(x^*_1, ..., x^*_{n-2}, x_{n-1}, x_n)$. Building on this, in the same way, that x'_{n-2}, x'_{n-1}, x'_n unconditionally maximizes $f_{n-2}(x^*_1, ..., x^*_{n-3}, x_{n-2}, x_{n-1}, x_n)$, and so on until we arrive at individual 1, at which point our theorem is proved.

III. IMPERFECT AND INCOMPLETE INFORMATION

While the above results are restricted to perfect information environments, where each decision maker knows the prior actions of the others and correctly estimates the information that will be available to future decision makers, our optimality conclusions extend over to substantially imperfect information environments. For example, regarding the correctable coordination failures described in Marschak and Radner's pioneering study of "teams" (our "non-conflictual teams") of imperfectly informed individuals, such teams actually have no reason to benefit from the central command structures introduced by these authors (*cf, ibid.,* pp. 312-3). When, for example, the social payoff is increased by revising an initial order of moves, the individuals (ex-commanders) who see the problem will find no rational resistance to their (necessarily prior) actions suggesting a revised order of moves. The same is true for actions in which more informed individuals share their information with others or advise others of their correct moves. In other words, any practical proposal that would better coordinate the decentralized decisions of the imperfectly or incompletely informed individuals would itself describe a rational action in a more general, yet-still-radically-decentralized, team equilibrium.

IV. SUPPLYING VITAL INSTITUTIONS TO A TERRITORIAL SOCIETY

In independent territorial societies, called "states" when referring to human societies, the basic object of rational choice, as emphasized in Chapter 1 and Appendix B.1, is the reaction function. What we have been calling "rational", or "narrowly rational", choice in this appendix would then apply to a choice among alternative reaction functions.[47]

In particular, once the rent-determining reaction functions that define the territorial state are established, the joint-survival-determining reaction-functional choices necessary for the defense of these above-subsistence societies are not the subject of internal conflictual interaction. Thus, once the initial distributional issues are settled, there should be no disagreement among equally informed individuals on the existence, for example, of a continued armed response to an attack, its method of finance, an intermediate military hierarchy, etc. The political and military decisions that set up such non-controversial institutions should therefore possess the same lack of deception and inter-personal aggressiveness -- the same lack of rent-

---

[47]The term "broad rationality" used in the text is generally preferable in order to distinguish it from a sequential choice problem that does not entail committed reactions. However, to apply the formal argument of the current exercise, we maintain the term "narrow rationality" for this discussion. The only caveat is that we are implicitly following the logic of Appendix B.1 in initially setting up the sequential choice problem. The remaining difference between the discussions, of course, is that here we are presenting the various decisionmakers with a common utility function. In particular, the commonality of this survival-relevant utility function will enable us to analyze the status-determination interaction informally discussed in Appendix B.1 with the same model that appears in Sections I through III above.

seeking when interpreting these activities in a social context -- that exists in the above model.

In other words, equilibrium social decisions as regards various vital institutions, besides being efficient, are made in an honest and non-partisan fashion. Moreover, applying our generalized theorem (Section II above), the vital military obligations that current political decisionmakers impose on their future selves must be similarly regarded as efficient obligations despite the possible disagreement of the future decisionmakers.

Unlike the other applications mentioned in this appendix, some commitments are essential. If the announced responses to foreign aggression are not substantially carried out, if the announcements are hollow threats, the state will be lost. Nevertheless, an individual may easily feel better off as a probably-live coward than a probably-dead hero; and even the whole society may easily feel "better red than dead", or that war debts are negotiable. Aggression against cowards and conflict at the onset of a war or over the payment of war debts are thus inevitable. The non-conflictual interaction, and hence the theory of this appendix, must therefore be care-fully restricted to the strictly pre-war setting in which defense institutions are being established.

Although ideal defense institutions may provide commitments so persuasive that they never have to be executed, actual defense institutions, even the best of them we are assuming, provide commitments that are occasionally tested. And, since, when they are so tested, internal conflictual relations are inevitable, the test of a state's continual ability to supply itself with vital institutions is not its absence of observed wartime conflict. Rather, the test should come during peacetime, especially during emergency preparation. The "methods test" suggested here is the absence of ordinary rent-seeking, or "partisan", politics in choosing to adopt a set of clearly vital institutions.

The subsequent "results-test", for the ability of a state to supply its vital institutions, as we shall emphasize in the next three chapters, is found in the nature of the institutions adopted, and, of course, in the continued existence of the state. [48]

---

[48]The same bottom-line test applies to the extended families of territorial biological organisms discussed in the text.

It may, at first blush, appear that these biological applications, the most important of which have dealt with subsistence organisms, have little in common with our societal applications, which are to above-subsistence "states". However, as discussed in our concluding chapter, a suitably long view of the biological evolution of above-subsistence organisms, and a suitably evolutionary view of a state's vital economic institutions, reveals a strikingly common pattern. The few territorial organisms that have long-survived the necessarily increas-ing sophistication of their mobile attackers have so-survived because they re-evolved to where they could symbiotically benefit from the presence of the attackers. We have similarly uncovered some 2nd-best solutions revealing the same re-evolutionary process in human societies. Nevertheless, no dominant state has, as yet, displayed an analogously durable survival pattern with respect to its economic and social ideologies. No dominant state has, as yet, learned how to symbiotically benefit from the presence of its increasingly sophisticated attackers.

CHAPTER 3

A NEW INTERPRETATION OF GUILDS, TARIFFS, AND LAISSEZ FAIRE

ABSTRACT

This Chapter theoretically derives and tests a new explanation of historically observed variations in guilds, tariffs and laissez faire policies. The traditional view, based upon classical economics, is that guild and tariff policies have been unambiguously inefficient, and that the political associations formed to effect such redistributional policies represent a net drain on society's resources. In contrast, our view, based on a new theory of political association formation in investor-democracies and a more realistic model of collective defense than that implicit in the traditional analysis, is that such institutions have been rapidly evolved and efficiently retained by naturally selected, legislatively pragmatic, states whenever the institutions have been vital to the state. Conversely, such a salutary evolutionary pattern has failed to occur in legislatively ideologized states, wherein producer interest groups have been systematically damaged in the name of laissez faire efficiency or social justice and the entire citizenry has substantially suffered as a consequence.

An analogous pattern will be found in the rise and unnecessarily painful decline of ideologically defended medieval political institutions.

INTRODUCTION

A. An Evaluation of the Traditional View of Political Economy

The inefficiency of rent-seeking "special interest groups" has been the dominant political hypothesis of the world's most influential economists since Turgot and Adam Smith, working their way into modern thought through the influence of such diverse 19th century adherents as Marshall and Marx.[1] The two primary historical examples of allegedly inefficient, rent-seeking, political associations have been entry-

---

[1]See Turgot, pp. 269-70; Smith, pp. 99-118; Marshall's Principles of Economics, pp. 610-11, 619-20, 640, and Marx's Capital, vol. 3, pp. 800-01. In fact, as has been artfully developed by Tom Sowell, classical political economy largely represented a systematic attack on special interest groups.

In contrast, J.B. Clark's Philosophy of Wealth, probably the most penetrating and insightful discussion of rent-seeking inefficiencies in the entire economics literature, makes no mention of inefficient political rent-seeking or special interest lobbies. This omission reflects the mainline Protestant belief in the efficiency of government that implicitly dominated American policy thought through the institutionalist school until a classically inspired literature on political rent-seeking began to develop in America in the late 1960s and early 1970s (Tullock, Krueger (1974), Posner, and M. Olson). While the current paper suggests that Clark's implicit belief is much more empirically accurate than the now widely accepted classical view, our argument in support of observed political interest groups is based upon an explicit political and economic model and direct empirical testing rather than an act of faith.

restricting guilds and tariff-seeking political lobbies.

1. An Evaluation of the Monopoly Interpretation of Guilds

The work of Gross, Pirenne, Mickwitz, Hibbert, and Postan has gradually elevated the classical monopoly view of entry-restrictive guilds to where it is now dominant among historians as well as economists (see, e.g., the recent survey of Black). Earlier scholars (e.g., Toulmin Smith, Commons, Thrupp (1948), Ashley and Unwin), writing in an anti-classical tone and alleging that early medieval guilds were probably socially beneficial in that they served to facilitate direct mutual aid and enforce product quality, could not explain why these trade associations would have systematically reduced the entry of quality-enhancing capital inputs (e.g., Renard, Chs. V-VII). As a result, virtually all of these institutionalist authors eventually acceded to the classical monopoly view, at least as regards the mature, substantially entry-restrictive, guilds of late medieval and early modern Europe.

But any monopoly interpretation of entry-restrictive western European guilds has serious problems. There is little evidence that these guilds implemented anything like a rational monopoly policy. Although frequently cited as evidence for a short-run monopoly policy is that these guilds, in conjunction with town administrators, often set domestic price levels, these price controls always specified maximum, never merely minimum, nominal prices (Thrupp (1963), pp. 246-65; Renard p. 42, Ashley pp. 31-34, Coornaert pp. 92-93, and Unwin, pp. 38-46). And guilds were seldom allowed to set maximum quality levels, some such restrictions being required by price-setting monopolistic cartels to prevent quality competition from converting above-competitive nominal prices into competitive real prices. Rather, guilds typically set only minimum observable quality standards (Renard pp. 34-35, Ashley pp. 17-34, Coornaert pp. 104-05, Unwin pp. 86-92, and Johnson, pp. 116-117).[2] The

---

[2]One social function of the essentially universal guild policy of imposing minimum observable quality levels, as well as of the sometimes-observed city prohibitions of sales below the maximum price, was to reduce the market participation of beggars, petty thieves, and the more disease-carrying elements of society. This social function, however, can be easily supplied in the absence of guilds. Observable quality minima were set long before guilds appeared and are commonly observed today in the cities of poverty-plagued third-world countries.

Consequently, this social function, like several other guild functions we shall mention below, can be considered only ancillary in that provision of the function by producer organizations does not lead to substantial net changes in social welfare. This is because the ancillary function is either socially unimportant or can be easily provided by alternative social institutions. Our concern in this paper will not be with ancillary, but with primary guild activities, activities that are both socially significant (either positively or negatively) and that would not be readily provided in the absence of these producer organizations. To keep this in mind, we restrict our definition of guilds to include only those producer organizations whose policies and economic activities are primary to their respective societies.

For this reason, our definition probably excludes modern "guilds", groups of freely entering service-providers who, because of the peculiarities of their trade, contract in such a complex manner that it pays them to join together to provide their customers with self-only conceivable rationale for a peacetime policy fixing both maximum nominal prices and minimum observable qualities, thereby establishing maximum <u>real</u> prices, is that such a policy serves as a short-run <u>anti-monopoly</u> device. Such a policy could obviously serve to prevent the already-organized masters from working to set monopolistic real prices.[3]   Most economic historians attempting a general interpretation of western European price regulations have indeed concluded that the actual regulations created essentially competitive short-run behavior (e.g., Thrupp (1963), p. 246; de Roover (1958), p. 434; Unwin, p. 92; Pirenne, pp. 181-188).

Therefore, the only economically consistent way to interpret western European guilds as monopoly institutions is to argue that these guilds worked mainly through <u>long run</u> effects, i.e., through restricting the entry of human or non-human capital. This was Adam Smith's view. (Smith, Book I, Ch. X, Part II, argued that guild policies monopolistically restricted the entry of <u>both</u> human and nonhuman capital.) It has also become the view of essentially all serious students of medieval and early modern western European guilds. We concur in the belief that western European guilds, including early medieval guilds, significantly restricted factor entry.[4]   But if the purpose of these entry restrictions had been monopolistic, the systematic work of the same guilds and town governments to establish <u>anti-monopolistic</u> prices and short-run outputs would have been perversely self-defeating. In particular, a <u>strictly</u> Pareto-improving policy would have been to lighten-up on the capital restrictions and simultaneously allow firms greater freedom to raise prices and discourage one another's outputs so as to leave prices and outputs, and thereby consumer interests,

---

regulation as a substitute for the ordinary legal system. Although the magnitude of this presumably positive net social benefit in modern times is clearly increasing, the aggregate effect of such guilds upon social welfare probably remains quite small.

[3]As the regulators did not buy and sell to absorb surpluses and fill deficits at the controlled prices, it would be ridiculous to assume that these regulatory policies established <u>actual</u> real prices. Rather, the <u>maximum</u> real prices set by the observed policies had to be above-equilibrium prices set sufficiently low to prevent guild members from attempting to either: (a) collude on short-term quantity and therefore real price or (2) aggressively discriminate against certain classes of customers. In this way, the policies induced free competition, at least in the quality dimension, and therefore essentially competitive real prices.

Moreover, during wartime and analogous emergencies, when the government <u>did</u> become substantial purchasers at the preestablished prices and quantities, current real prices were typically subcompetitive (e.g., de Roover (1958)). This policy is rationalized, and its additional policy implications are identified, in Appendix B.3.

[4]Nevertheless, guilds could not generally limit factor entry at will. For instance, a prospective entrant, either master or journeyman, upon being refused membership in a London guild, could appeal to the city council. The city council then could, if the refused individual proved his competence, either force the guild to accept the disputed membership, or grant the refused individual the "freedom" to practice his craft in the city. Guild entry-restrictions were thus jointly negotiated consumer-producer entry restriction rather than purely monopolistic. (See, e.g., Gross, pp. 61-103, Ashley, pp. 78-88, and Cunningham, pp. 98-99.)

totally unaffected. Besides saving administrative costs, the policy would generate improvements in input proportions for firms that would, following the logic of the neoclassical model, have amounted to an increase in welfare for everyone.

The absence of a logically disciplined theory of political economy has allowed the proponents of the classical view to escape the above-described inconsistency of their monopoly view with rational public choice. Later, in Section I, we explicitly set forth a simple model of political economy in order to logically discipline our own theory sufficiently to avoid such political-economic absurdities.

More obvious inconsistencies infect the traditional view. If the classical monopoly view of guilds were correct, the consuming landlords in Royal Towns, such as Paris, London, and Winchester, where guilds had no independent policy influence, would never have rationally selected the standard sets of guild entry restrictions that they regularly did select (Biddle, pp. 422-447; Johnson, pp. 20-27; and Van Werveke, p. 29, respectively).

Similarly, if the standard monopoly interpretation were correct, those producing medieval towns politically dominated by middlemen and traders (i.e., "merchants") would never have granted their unenfranchised local artisanal suppliers (i.e., "craftsmen") the standard capital and entry restrictions that they regularly did grant (DuPlessis and Howell).

Broadening our scope beyond these persistent structural inconsistencies, we must recognize that the classical monopoly view leads to the belief that, whatever the various ancillary welfare effects of guilds may have been, they could never have accumulated to where the social benefit of politically influential guilds was large enough to significantly exceed the alleged social cost of guild monopolization and to the corresponding belief that increased economic growth was brought about by laissez faire policies (e.g., Pirenne, Nef, and Postan on the right and Hobsbawn, Tawney, and the Webbs on the left). However, these beliefs are strangely inconsistent with the simple evidence on both the rise and the fall of medieval and early modern European guilds.

Regarding the rise of medieval European guilds, as described in I.B.4 below, politically influential guilds sequentially evolved among the more legislatively pragmatic, non-church-dominated, investor-democratic town-states of Europe largely on the basis of the impressive economic successes of neighboring regions experimenting with these new institutions.[5] Moreover, the rapid growth to maturity throughout most of western and west-central Europe of merchant guilds beginning late in the 10th century, followed by craft guilds beginning late in the 11th century, was accompanied by unusually high rates of economic growth all the way up to the devastating wars, famines, and plagues, starting around the beginning of the 14th century (e.g., Thrupp (1972); Russell, pp. 40-41). Similarly, many subsequent, quite extended, increases in economic growth immediately followed sudden increases in

---

[5]We shall say that such learning-based, Lamarckian, changes are the result of "legislative pragmatism" and contrast this intuitive trial-and-error process with processes based on "legislative ideology", which have presumably well-intentioned political leaders selecting economic institutions by relying upon existing social or economic theories.

guild strength. Examples include 15th and 16th century Iberia (R. Smith, Ch. 1; Kellenbenz, pp. 465-67), 17th and 18th century Scandinavia (Kellenbenz, *ibid.*), and 18th and 19th century Russia (Lyashchenko, p. 297; Clarkson, Chs. 16-19).

Regarding the demise of these politically influential guilds, as briefly described in I.B.4 and detailed in II.D.5 below, the sudden widespread guild eliminations throughout southern and west-central Europe accompanying the emergence of laissez faire ideology in the second half of the 18th century were systematically followed by historically unexplained <u>decreases</u> in both output and sovereignty until the last third of the 19th century. Earlier cases of ideologically inspired guild weakening, followed by sudden, similarly unexplained, <u>decreases</u> in both relative income and sovereignty occurred in Renaissance-inspired late 15th century northern Italy, in domestic-free-trade-inspired late 17th century Holland, and in complete-laissez-faire-inspired late 18th century France, as elaborated at several points in the ensuing discussion. Russia's sudden, similarly ideologically inspired, elimination of guilds in 1900 will provide us with a later example (Section II.D.5.a below).

The sovereignty losses are particularly important in that they reveal the vital nature of guilds and the consequent existence of a harsh form of natural selection against states that substantially weakened their guilds for no reason other than the emergence of an "enlightened" economic ideology.

2. An Alternative Interpretation of the Rise and Fall of Guilds

a. *Interpreting the Strengthening of Guild Entry Restrictions.* The above-noted empirical inconsistency regarding the early relative success of guild-dominated medieval towns is traditionally dismissed by arguing that guilds became seriously monopolistic only an <u>extremely long time</u> after guilds had become established institutions. The argument has been based largely upon a monopolization interpretation of the commonly observed jumps in guild entry-restrictions and concurrent decreases in economic growth following the wars and related famines and plagues of the "calamitous" 14th century (e.g., Gross, Pirenne (1948), and Unwin). We do not want wish to deny that there was a sharp increase in labor taxes during this period. We have already pointed this out that this tax increase (e.g., Rösener) is indeed a logical implication of our subsistence-wage story in Section II of Chapter 2.

However, since a sharp drop in the <u>socially efficient</u> rate of investment would obviously follow a series of negative population shocks, the late medieval retardation in the rates of guild investment and economic growth and the corresponding 14th century consumption boom (the Early Renaissance), can be easily interpreted as qualitatively <u>efficient</u> responses to an unfortunate series of population shocks.[6]

---

[6]Consistent with our broader theory, there is, as detailed below in Section II.D.4, an endogenous explanation of the devastating wars, and associated famines and plagues, during the closing two centuries of the middle ages. The section will show that these calamities can be consistently interpreted to be the logical result of a profession-serving ideology of the powerful late-13th century church, one that spent the following two centuries repeatedly resisting the obviously successful introduction of a newly vital political institution.

While guild entry-restrictions would have no reason to jump under the guild literature's old, quality-enhancement alternative to the classical monopoly argument -- which is why most historians have been reluctantly converted to the classical monopoly view -- the guild literature has completely overlooked the possibility that a social optimum may require the equivalent of an externality-internalizing tax on coveted capital, capital whose presence increases the state's defense burden (Appendix B.2, B.3, and Section II.A below).   The higher degree of European military insecurity throughout the 14th and 15th centuries would then have generated a substantial increase in the optimal degree of entry restriction.

Moreover, regarding the population shocks, increased guild entry-restrictions would have been required to optimally reduce business investment even if the defense-externality and efficient capital tax rate had not increased.   In other words, socially optimal entry-restrictions necessarily jump in response to a negative population shock, the jump being required to reflect the new, suddenly much lower, optimal rate of business investment.   The subsequent maintenance of relatively high entry-restrictions during and after the European population recovery that began late in the 15th century could, under the same capital tax theory, be explained by the steadily increasing defense expenditures, and correspondingly increasing rates of optimal capital taxation, characterizing the development of modern nation states, the entire movement being the result of a sharp increase in the overhead cost of defense following the development of mobile, gunpowder-based weaponry.[7]

Contrast this simple efficiency interpretation of the data with the standard one in which guilds suddenly became severely monopolistic -- irreversibly for some peculiar reason -- throughout Europe during the plagues, famines and wars of the 14th century.   This standard monopolization interpretation of the 14th century jump in entry restrictions is immediately faced with a familiar insurmountable difficulty: How could the plague-induced increases in entry-restrictions, if they indeed reflected increases in the degree of monopoly, have been normally accompanied by the simultaneously observed introductions of substantially tighter, frequently sub-competitive, price-regulations (Cunningham, pp. 330-32; Coornaert, pp. 99-100)?

In short, classical economists, and now historians as well as economists, have been too quick to infer increases in the degree of monopoly from observed increases in entry restrictions.   Increases in entry restrictions could alternatively, and in contrast quite consistently, reflect increases imposed by efficient governments using investment restrictions to implement the policy-equivalents of efficient capital taxes.

The failure to see this simple, efficiency-based, alternative interpretation of early, guild-strengthening, policies has no doubt been responsible for a pro-laissez-faire bias in subsequent economic thought.   In any case, classical economics -- and the costly

---

[7]Section I.B of Chapter 5 will complement this argument by providing a reason for increasing capital taxes even more than the costs of external defense during this imperializing early-modern period, a reason based upon the higher internal defense costs resulting from a rational attempt to establish new, imperial, federations.   (See Appendices B.1 and B.2 for theoretical models in which a shift in military technology that increases the effectiveness of military aggression or the overhead cost of defense will increase the optimal size of the state.)

laissez faire policy experiments that immediately followed -- emerged largely through errors in the interpretation of later, guild-weakening, policies, errors misattributing the source of the impressive growth rates of early-mid 17th century Holland and mid-late 18th century England to their respective anti-guild policies. We obviously should be more specific here.

b. *Interpreting the Weakening of Guild Entry Restrictions.* The first modern attack on European guilds occurred in the third quarter of the 17th century, when Holland and neighboring Protestant provinces substantially reduced the entry-restricting power of guild artisans supplying her large merchants and trading companies.[8] The immediately prior, quite dramatic, economic success of relatively laissez faire Amsterdam throughout the 1st half of the 17th century had supplied the empirical inspiration for Pieter De La Court, a pioneer of the modern theory of domestically free markets, and his apparently politically astute co-author, Jon de Witt, the ideologically and politically influential leader of the uniquely successful, investor-democratic, United Provinces during the 1660s (Blok, Ch. 10, Rowen, Ch. 19). These policy pioneers, like subsequent free-market authors, failed to recognize that uniquely low defense costs -- such as those lying at the foundation of Amsterdam's early 17th century economic boom -- justify uniquely low effective local capital taxes (Appendix B.2) and therefore uniquely low levels of local guild capital restrictions. So it was a serious mistake for de Witt to extend Amsterdam's weak-guild policies to the rest of the United Provinces. De Witt's subsequent inability to obtain

---

[8]Rather than a commonly asserted fact, the timing of this attack on craft guilds is our inference from available 17th century Dutch histories. Van der Wee tells us that Dutch guilds declined throughout the 17th century (p. 360) while noted Dutch historians (J. De Vries), p. 56; Smit, pp. 61-66) tell us that Dutch guilds had become insignificant by the end of the 17th century. Since, from Unger (Ch. IV,) we know that guilds persisted in the important Dutch shipbuilding industry throughout the 17th century (and even developed into an all-input-restrictive form early in the 18th century) we can conclude that entry-restricting Dutch guilds, other than shipbuilding guilds, significantly declined during the 17th century. (Later we shall point out a special advantage of having all-input-restricting guilds in export industries such as the Dutch shipbuilding industries.) More detailed 17th century Dutch histories further isolate the period of decline of entry-restricting guilds to the second half of the 17th century. For example, Van Dillen (Ch. 1) mentions no case of guild decline (other than in a relocating industry) during the first half of the 17th century, but (in Ch. 2) notes many such cases occurring during the third quarter of the 17th century. Also, from other sources we find, for example, that Middleburg guilds were abolished in 1658 (Unger, p. 86), that Groningen guilds repeatedly rioted over new anti-guild laws in the early 1660s (Blok, p. 314), and, even in rela-tive conservative Leiden (where entry restricting guilds did not fully decline until the end of the 17th century) that guilds were subjected to substantially relaxed entry-restrictions during the early 1660s (DuPlessis and Howell, p. 63). The reason, we believe, that this concentrated decline in the effectiveness of entry-restricting guilds in the Protestant United Provinces has not been commonly acknowledged is that Jon de Witt, the unusually autocratic Dutch leader of the era (e.g., Blok, p. 354), though decidedly against the entry restrictions that guilds used to raise the costs of the goods traded by the large merchant class that he represented, was a master of political appeasement and clearly saw the advantage of having relatively contented groups of suppliers (Blok, Ch. 9; Rowen, Chs. 3-12, esp. pp. 58-59, 188-89).

provincial guild support for his Great War of 1672 (Blok, Ch. 14; Rowen, Ch. 29) spelled the end to the great Dutch ascendancy despite Holland's subsequently benefiting from both a huge immigration of Huguenots and a favorable junior partnership with increasingly powerful England in the succeeding 100 years. The even-less-democratic Dutch leaders that followed de Witt (Blok, Ch. 17; Wilson, Ch. 1) -- failing to detect the institutional weakness causing the obvious jump in Dutch defense costs (Blok, p. 480, Smit, p. 62) -- did little to restore guild influence or do anything else to change basic Dutch institutions (Blok, p. 474, Wilson, p. 18). Classical economists similarly failed to recognize that democratic states, whose tax rates are continually constrained by investor-democratic legislatures, cannot survive unless their military leaders are somehow able to command large involuntary wartime sacrifices from their citizens (Appendices B.2, note 4, and B.3; and Section II.A below). These economists therefore similarly failed to see that Holland's attack on her guilds without a prompt replacement of the wartime contributions of the guilds, i.e., her ideologically inspired elimination of a vital economic institution, was the source of Holland's sudden subordination to foreign powers.

It was over 70 years before another nation was to strip guilds of their power to restrict entry. A similarly recently democratized, pragmatic England -- her monetary practitioners mindful of the Dutch experiment in national democracy and eventual failure in the area of emergency finance (Chapter 4) -- cautiously delayed granting her politically powerful merchants this favor until the 1730s, <u>after</u> pioneering the development of a flexible gold standard around the turn of the 18th century. The new monetary standard provided a superior, national rather than local, source of emergency war finance by allowing for temporary suspensions of gold payments and, correspondingly, a capacity for emergency purchasing power limited only by the national government's entire future power to tax.[9] England's subsequent elimination

---

[9]The reason, as elaborated in Chapters 4 and 5 below, is that the expectation of resumed gold payments creates an expectation of capital gains on cash balances that increases money demand as the emergency money supply increases, thereby providing the government with emergency purchasing power limited only by government's expected ability to retire the money after the emergency is over by resuming gold payments at a suitably depressionary rate. Although money has a distinct advantage over bonds in that money is more liquid and thereby poses no interest cost to the government, long-term bonds are often employed by gold-standard governments in order to reduce the anticipated fiscal strain of post emergency gold payments and spread the burden of the war over several generations. Emergency bond finance also reduces the magnitude of the expected post-emergency depression.

Other authors (e.g., Dickson; Wilson; and Neal) have noted the correlation between long-term bond financing and economic success that resulted from England's rational wartime adoption of long-term bonds during the wars following her introduction of a gold standard in the late 1690s. However, this correlation cannot be taken to support a hypothesis that marketable long term debt causes economic success. The easiest counter-examples are all of the failed pre-gold-standard economics that widely employed such debt (most notably, 16th and 17th century Holland (Tracy) and 15th century Florence (Becker, v.2, Ch. IV).

The reader may well wonder why emergency debt-flotations were not a sufficient means of emergency finance, even in the absence of a gold standard. Politically speaking, the pre-of guild entry-restrictions, therefore had nothing like the disastrous military consequence that it had for Holland.

Also, again contrary to the predictions of classical theory, a peacetime business boom did not result from the English demise of guilds. The reason is that one peacetime tax was merely being replaced by another. The English, and eventually the rest of Europe, as detailed in II.D.5.b below, were merely replacing their entry-restrictive, previously defense-providing, guilds with an alternative, more broadly-based, national source of peacetime taxation, a national capital tax, to support their enlarged national armies and navies. This policy replacement has somehow escaped serious notice. Rather, the mainline literature has treated the pioneering Dutch and English guild eliminations in isolation, regarding them as fortunate eliminations of monopolistic incentives, peculiarly ignoring both the subsequent collapse of the Dutch defense system and England's steady military success through a prior introduction of a gold standard. It has also ignored England's simultaneous imposition of national capital taxes and the corresponding absence of any noticeable acceleration in England's growth rate in response to her guild elimination.

As a result of the above-described oversights by classical economists, the remarkably superior economic performances of both early 17th century Holland and late 18th century England came to be thought of as due to their weak-guild, internal laissez faire, policies. Simple guild elimination (i.e., guild elimination without replacement by a substitute source of emergency finance) thus became an ideologically fashionable, vital-institution-eliminating, policy of the late 18th and early 19th centuries. Such an easy, basically physiocratic, doctrine served the newly-forming "schools" of economics because it also served the Enlightenment aristocracies, who could hardly have retained their elevated social positions without an easy policy explanation for the embarrassingly high 18th century growth rates being experienced by democratic England. What followed was an entirely predictable series of military disasters throughout the legislatively ideological southern and west-central sections of Europe from about 1760 through 1870 (described in II.D.5.c below). Also, quite predictably, the continuing relative successes of the relatively pragmatic and democratic Anglo-Saxon countries finally led the surviving military leaders of their embattled western and central European neighbors to adopt the non-laissez-faire-constrained, politically pragmatic, highly successful, democratic revolutions of the last thirty years of the 19th century.

The correspondingly vital gold standard adoptions beginning in the final third of the 19th century were thus the predictable evolutionary result of finally following England and the U.S. in letting at least some degree of pragmatic empiricism rather than economic ideology be the guide for fledgling democracies. Southern and eastern

---

gold-standard legislatures did not vote to surrender the power to borrow to the administration. It was only after a country had adopted a gold standard that its legislature came to grant the independent power to float war-bonds to the central administrators. This is because the ability to print temporarily inconvertible money during an emergency was soon understood as a full administrative tax-power, in which case the emergency legislatures had little to gain by withholding the right to float bonds from their central administrators.

European leaders are only now in the process of learning the same lesson and beginning to develop legislatively pragmatic democracies

The remarkable economic success of the most legislatively pragmatic democracies has been due to more than their evolved ability to protect their externally coveted capital from foreign aggression. The source of the remarkable economic success of these more legislatively pragmatic regions of Europe can be gleaned from a brief consideration of the rise and fall of guilds -- not in their role as entry-restrictive defenders of coveted capital from <u>collective military</u> aggression -- but in their role as administratively active defenders of coveted capital from the various sources of <u>private civilian</u> aggression (Appendix A.1).

    c. *Interpreting the Fall of the Bureaucratic Function of Guilds.* The capital -- especially inventories -- of medieval towns must have been highly coveted by <u>domestic</u> authorities. It is therefore no surprise, as detailed in I.C.4 below, that the towns employing bureaucratically active guilds to administer their own legal systems (e.g., the "guild merchant" that soon came to characterize medieval towns (Gross)), and thereby control the redistributive tendencies of local nobles and church officials, noticeably succeeded relative to their more ideologically affected neighbors. A position of this sort regarding the early <u>rise</u> of guilds has often been stated and is rarely disputed, at least in the secular literature.

    However, this conventional position is rationalized by applying a standard competitive model to the guild towns. The position is therefore accompanied by the seriously mistaken classical belief that <u>purely private rent-seeking</u> is no problem. There is therefore no appreciation of the basic development problem that was being solved by early democratic legislation in even the most critical-minded of literature on medieval contract law (W.H. Hamilton; and Greif, Milgrom, and Weingast).)[10] As a result of this error, the conventional approval of guilds is unfortunately

---

[10]Both of these studies accommodate us by providing several examples of severe investment-induced cooperation that is efficiently eliminated by guild-induced contracting procedures. Yet neither study correctly represents this as eliminating an underinvestment trap! In the former study, underinvestment is alleged to appear because of a laissez faire lemons-problem, in which case the combination of an <u>ad valorem</u> subsidy and revenue-equivalent per-unit tax would induce an optimum without the costly change in the liability system endorsed by the author. In the latter study, underinvestment is alleged to appear because of a standard discriminating monopsony against certain merchants, in which case up-front cash bonuses to the subsequently victimized merchants would solve the problem under laissez faire without the resource-costly legalization of guild boycotts endorsed by the authors.

The theoretically ambiguous welfare effects of the approved policy changes in each study, in the first study because of the extra resource costs of the seller-liability (frankpledge) process and in the second because of the discriminating <u>monopolistic</u> implications of boycotting guilds, should have made the respective authors wonder whether they had indeed theoretically captured the initial market failure. In particular, given the substantial boost in prosperity following both of the observed legal changes, the authors should have realized that there had to be some very severe, rent-seeking, type of underdevelopment traps (as in Appendix A.1) that were being eliminated by the socially costly legal changes.

withdrawn in conventional discussions of later, "enlightened", societies, where complete guild elimination is almost universally thought to unleash the presumably beneficent forces of unfettered domestic competition. Summarizing results detailed in II.D.5.a below, the first effective attacks on the administrative function of European guilds occurred during the High Renaissance. The Hellenistic-elite-inspired towns of Florence and Milan replaced their guild bureaucrats with the intellectually liberated and immediately suffered severe local depressions and subsequent foreign dominations from which they are still attempting to recover. A similar attack on guild participation in local bureaucracy was repeated in a partially restored, but still highly ideological, late 18th century Florence under a combination of Romantic (anti-investor) and laissez faire (anti-regulatory) ideologies. Although the literature treats this as a political-administrative change with few short-term economic consequences, an immediately ensuing economic depression and subsequently retarded growth rate again occurred. Late 18th century France -- under the growing influence of an "enlightened", complete laissez faire, ideology -- similarly weakened their guilds prior to their costly and, we shall see, quite premature Revolution. Spain in the 1830s and Russia in 1900 similarly replaced their guild bureaucrats with strongly ideological local magistrates and immediately suffered similarly unexplained and costly economic depressions. The literature, by consistently failing to appreciate the economic value of guild bureaucrats relative to educated ideologues, has failed to detect the source of the highly disappointing economic performances of the most heavily ideologized parts of Europe following their premature guild eliminations.

In other words, while the secular literature has regularly acknowledged the efficiency of investor participation in a church-influenced bureaucracy, it has regularly failed to acknowledge the efficiency of investor participation in a secularly ideologized bureaucracy. It appears that secular social thinkers, besides perpetuating the incorrect political and economic theories of various Late Renaissance and Enlightenment ruling classes, have been unable to acknowledge the systematically negative effects of the application of Late Renaissance and Enlightenment economic theories on observed economic prosperity. In view of more accurate theories of internal investor protection and democratic legislation (Appendix A.1 and Section I below), it is actually predictable that internal efficiency would suffer whenever guild participation in local administration was surrendered over to a legislatively ideological bureaucracy, one largely insensitive to democratically evolved laws that are vital to investors in order to protect them from internal expropriation.[11]

---

[11]We shall see that effectively democratic rule-making provides an exceptional method of internally protecting investor rents despite the traditional economic argument that democracy induces rent-seeking behavior. In particular, we shall see that a democracy requires, in order to be "effective", (a) a degree of political and intellectual competition sufficient to eliminate non-pragmatic legislation such as that due to an economic or religious ideology and (b) a principled commitment to its strange laws by a loyal, or "civilly reverent," bureaucracy. What made the early Dutch and English bureaucrats civilly reverent was the Protestant value (the Pauline in contrast to the Johannine Ethic (Saunders)) treating the laws of one's government (rather than the opinions of a single mind) as divinely inspired (Romans XIII, 1-7). In any

It is also no surprise that wherever guild bureaucrats were replaced with law-respecting, or "civilly reverent", bureaucrats, no such depressions occurred. Rather, as reported in II.D.5.a below, the subsequent economic prosperity in investor-democratic states is readily apparent. It is such observations, and the theory of Appendix A.1 and Section I below, that led us to define a democratic government as "effective" when its bureaucrats are "civilly reverent" and its legislators are pragmatic rather than ideological.

3. The Traditional Theory of Tariffs: A Critique and Alternative View

A political distortion, or inefficient-special-interest, view of observed tariff systems similarly fails to satisfactorily explain the structure, economic effects, and incidence of commonly observed tariff systems.

a. *Tariff Structure.* There are historically countless instances of persistent tariffs on imports having no clearly identifiable domestic substitute, tariffs that substantially benefit no particular group of producers whatsoever (e.g., S. Litman, Ch. 6). Going back to early U.S. history, when tariffs were a continual political issue and our basic tariff policies were being formed, examples of such tariffs were: (i) the high tariffs regularly placed on molasses, flax, and hemp initiated in the notorious "Tariff of Abominations" in 1828; and (ii) the similarly high and controversial 19th century tariffs on tea, coffee, and sugar (Taussig, Ch. 2).

According to the conventional approach, whenever no organized group of protected producers can be identified, the tariff is inferred to exist for "revenue purposes" rather than monopolistic protection (e.g., S. Litman, Taussig, *ibid.*). This inference, however, is empirically contradicted by the frequent insignificance of total government revenue, net of collection costs, from non-special-interest-based tariffs (Towle, p. 220; Taussig, *ibid.*). Moreover, under the conventional model, a theoretically superior revenue source exists. Under the standard model, a broadly-based domestic tax, such as a general excise or consumption tax, will always generate more revenue to the government for a given social cost than will a tariff. Since the revenue argument for tariffs is free of references to special-interest politics, this standard economic argument also implies that the broadly based domestic tax is theoretically more politically acceptable than a revenue-equivalent tariff.[12] Without

---

case, the importance of effective democracy for economic success was certainly not appreciated by intellectuals at the time. Nor does it appear to be appreciated by modern economists despite the enormous economic success of effective democracy. In contrast, the more-than-once-bitten leaders of Europe have gradually come to abandon economic ideology for a more pragmatic, effectively democratic, approach to domestic legislation.

[12]In the case of large-country effects, wherein the tariff-imposing country receives a monopsony benefit from the tariff (Bickerdike), the country would benefit even more by threatening to impose the tariff and correspondingly receiving an appropriate lump-sum subsidy from the exporting countries for not doing so. Although transaction costs may preclude such

the fallback of a theoretically respectable revenue-defense for tariffs, traditional tariff rationalizations become hopelessly inconsistent with real-world tariff observations.[13]

A similar inconsistency of standard tariff theory with the structure of observed tariffs is found in the fact, elaborated in III.A below, that peacetime imports of almost all forms of industrial machinery have almost always received very lenient tariff treatment. Also, peacetime tariffs on perishable foods and raw material inputs have uniformly been way below the tariff rates on finished consumer goods (e.g., Yeates, p. 47).[14] Such enduring patterns find no rationale under existing tariff theory. No revenue-benefits are apparent, and some of our most politically powerful interest groups -- allied producers of a wide variety of industrial machinery, consumer perishables, and raw materials -- regularly lose from these traditionally low tariffs.

As elaborated in III.A below, once the simple defense-externality (Appendix B.2) is again acknowledged, the above-discussed historical tariff pattern can be quite easily rationalized as economically efficient. Certain capital goods -- most notably imported consumer durables -- can be practically taxed to efficiently reflect their significant defense-externalities only when the goods are initially brought into the country; and these are the only goods that have historically borne very high tariffs!

b. *The Effects of Relatively High Tariffs in the Developed World.* Regarding the allegedly negative effect of higher national tariffs on economic growth, this efficient-tariff theory will be used later to explain the success stories that are popularly acknowledged to contradict the classical view: Modern Japan and China, the fastest growing and probably the most import-protected of the developed countries of the late 20th century; the U.S., Russia, France and Germany, which experienced the highest growth rates of the late 19th and early 20th centuries while maintaining probably the highest tariff levels in the developed world (Haight, p. 52); late 18th and early 19th century England, which experienced the world's highest growth rate of that period under similarly high tariff rates; late 17th and early 18th century France, which

---

deals, if the monopsony or revenue arguments explained observed tariff systems, imports with relatively elastic demands would be relatively tariff-free. But any perusal of any modern tariff book reveals a large number of high tariffs on categories of imports that clearly have good substitutes coming from a wide variety of mutually competing domestic sources.

[13]At this point in the argument, many economists and public-policy-types, are wont to argue that the superior tax system is not "politically feasible". This identifies the level of rationality of the economic argument as Pascalian in that the policy advisors, like the political decisionmakers, are allowing themselves to be constrained by politically evolved economic rules. What distinguishes Pascalian policy "rationalizations" from genuine economic rationalization is that the latter are devoid of artificial policy constraints. In any case, it is quite obvious that, once we introduce a political constraint, it must itself be explained if we are to understand the policy. Several examples will arise in the course of the argument.

[14]Several 20th century exceptions exist. These recent exceptions -- producers of domestic capital goods, consumer perishables and raw materials that have benefitted from substantial tariff protection -- are discussed at length in Appendix B.3.

experienced Europe's highest growth rate in that period while under the notoriously protectionist policies of Colbert; and 16th century Spain, whose great mercantilist expansion provided the initial inspiration for the subsequent national success stories (Cole, p. 214).

The same pattern arose among the strong city-states of the Middle Ages. As elaborated in III.B below, the most successful European towns of the Later Middle Ages also effected highly foreign-trade-restrictive policies. Earlier, the Byzantine Empire, easily the most successful city-state of the Early Middle Ages, had adopted the same general set of trade-restrictions. While Byzantium subsequently experienced a free-trade movement throughout the 12th century (e.g., Jenkins, p. 84), the free-trade trend began with her retrenchment following her late 11th century loss of highly profitable eastern colonies and ended with her total collapse. Continuing further back in time, extremely high tariff restrictions were applied by the Ancient Roman Empire against imports from the East throughout her highly prosperous Pax Romana (e.g., Frank, p. 49; Walbank), and the root of this entire pragmatic sequence was probably the great 3rd Century BC economic success of Hellenistic Egypt under the unabashedly protective tariffs of the aggressively mercantilistic investor-democratic government of Ptolemy II (Botsford; Bengston; and Finley, p. 148).

We are not suggesting that an efficient tariff policy produces exceptionally high long-term growth-rates. Rather, we are suggesting that, among a set of relatively developed, property-respecting, countries, when a country's political system is sufficiently pragmatic and investor-sensitive that it will ignore anti-mercantile ideology and eliminate the country's most significant potential underdevelopment traps and rapidly grow, it is also sufficiently pragmatic and investor-sensitive that it will ignore such ideology and adopt efficiently high tariff rates.

However, since anti-mercantile or free-trade ideologies are not always present, this is, at best, a partial explanation of the positive correlation between growth and tariff rates among developed countries. Later, in III.D, we shall find that the above tariff-growth pattern, which so persistently contradicts the standard theory, is also an implication of our defense-externality, efficient-government theory in that exceptionally high expected growth rates imply relatively high efficient tariff rates. We shall also elaborate on the evolved institutional constraint that induces Pascalian governmental authorities to adopt this efficient pattern.[15]

---

[15]Chapter 5 will discuss the military technologies and tariffs in many relatively underdeveloped "third-world", regions. For special reasons elaborated in Section I.B of that chapter, defense-externalities, and their optimal tariffs on consumer durable imports, are also extraordinarily high in these regions. In fact, the external imposition of free trade on such a high-optimal-tariff region amounts to the elimination of a vital institution and forms the central economic problem of that chapter.

It is also pointed out there, and will be elaborated in Part III below, that the imperial governments of the 16th and 17th centuries belong in this high-optimal-tariff category. Since, as we have noted, some of these governments grew quite significantly during this "mercantilist" era, we can only guess how much they would have grown under a more advantageous military technology.

c. *Eras With Extremely High or Low Defense Costs.* Traditional tariff theory cannot explain why domestic producers typically continued to benefit from substantial trade protection throughout the first three quarters of the 20th century, during which time consumer interests dramatically grew in political influence (evinced by the corresponding growth of anti-producer regulations regarding monopoly and product quality). In contrast, the defense-externality, efficient-government, theory correctly predicts relatively high tariffs during this high-defense-cost era.

Tariffs in the developed West, of course, have fallen over the past quarter century. As this most recent period has been increasingly pro-producer relative to consumer, the classical explanation of tariffs predicts increasing tariffs in the developed West. In contrast, because the increasingly revealed decrease in the probability of warfare is producing a decreasing defense-externality, the efficient-government theory, which has correctly predicted a widespread decrease in the entire set of income taxes and special defense subsidies (Appendix B.3, Section III.H), similarly predicts the recent widespread trend toward decreasing tariffs, especially since the collapse of the Soviet Union at the beginning of this decade.

d. *Pre-20th Century Experiments in Free-Trade Policy.* Despite ideologically dominant France's notoriously ill-timed tariff reductions of 1786-87 (Haight, p. 12; Bosher), a series of similarly ideologically inspired switches to external free trade arose throughout Europe during the 1850s in response to the spread of and classical economics. As detailed in Part III below, these liberal experiments in external laissez faire policy had little positive effect on economic development.

But it was not until the embarrassing military victories of high-tariff Prussia at the expenses of Francis Joseph's free-trading Austria and Napoleon III's free-trading France from 1866 to 1870 that the ideologically inspired experiments were pragmatically abandoned on a broad scale (e.g., Bastable, Ch. 10).[16] The two main exceptions had been the two most dominant mid-19th century states. Low industrial tariffs were retained until WWI by belatedly ideologizing, decreasingly dominant, increasingly militarily vulnerable, England and Austria.

4. Summary and Generalization: Introducing Our Political Model

To summarize the above critique, the classical view qualitatively fails in its central predictions of: (a) the internal structures of both guild and tariff regulations; (b) the effects on economic prosperity of the rises and declines of both guilds and high tariff levels; and (c) the historical incidence of both guilds and high tariffs under different political conditions. How could such a totally inaccurate view of the world come to gain such widespread academic acceptance?

Before attempting to answer this broad question, we should consider the most sweeping argument presented as support for the classical view. Promoters of the view typically take as conclusive support for the classical theory the fact that areas

---

[16]Although France, in 1881, was the last country on the Continent to restore high tariffs, she established the highest tariff barriers (except for Russia) in Europe (Haight, pp. 52-6).

with <u>both</u> relatively low tariffs and light domestic investment restrictions, areas with a comprehensive (both external and internal) laissez faire policy, systematically generate better concurrent economic performance than neighboring areas. We have already discussed the early 17th century success of relatively free-trading Amsterdam. Similarly famous historical examples run all the way from the increasing distress of the increasingly regulated 3rd and 4th century Roman Empire to the modern success of relatively free-trading Hong Kong. Still more impressively, hundreds of related episodes can be recounted in which successful investments in confederation resulted in lower capital taxes, substantially lower internal trade barriers, and substantially increased economic welfare.

However, as we have already noted, under our defense-externality theory, relatively high tariffs and heavy domestic capital restrictions are both efficient responses to an area's relatively high defense cost, a cost that <u>directly</u> reduces the area's economic welfare. The dismal economic performance and the increasingly restrictive economic policies of 3rd and 4th century Rome were thus both, simultaneously, attributable to the Empire's rising defense costs. The extraordinary economic success of 20th century Hong Kong and its status as a center of free trade were both, simultaneously, due to its uniquely low defense cost through a unique contract between Britain and China. And the hundreds of economically successful investments in confederation and correspondingly huge observed reductions in internal trade barriers can similarly be simultaneously attributed to huge reductions in internal defense costs. The universality of such observations goes to further confirm our theory rather than classical theory by showing that relatively high defense costs have normally induced governments to select relatively high levels of capital restrictions, which are efficient policy responses to their underlying defense problems.

This predictably efficient response underscores our earlier question of how such a totally unsupportable economic argument could have come to so predominate the intellectual environment. We believe that the classical view has predominated despite its gross empirical failure largely because it reinforces a profession-serving bias against the ability of common people to have their real economic interests represented in a legislatively pragmatic democracy. In particular, the traditional view that common consumers and their elected representatives systematically undervalue the real price-increasing effects of the output-reducing policies, policies promoted by various political associations of producers, amounts to a profession-serving undervaluation of the political-economic rationality of the common consumer and a corresponding undervaluation of the economic efficiency of popular democracy.[17]

---

[17]The Classical Liberal argument of Bentham and Mill attributed tariffs and guild entry-restrictions to the aristocratic nature of the democracies of their day, to the absence of voting rights by laborers and common consumers, not to any lack of political-economic acumen on the part of ordinary people. However, even though popular democracy came to replace these aristocratic democracies throughout the 19th century, high tariff policies were no less popular at the end of the 19th century than at the beginning of the 19th century. Indeed, as we shall see in Section I below, there is little logical support for any such political inefficiency argument of the Classical Liberals. (Continued, next page.)

The static political-economic reason for our seemingly harsh inference is simple: If, as may often be the case, consumers could not politically protect their interests from the subsequently redistributive policies systematically promoted by certain producer interest groups, these potential victims -- assuming they were at least aware of their political bargaining weakness -- would rationally prevent the potentially pernicious political associations from forming by buying-off their benefiting members. This simple political efficiency argument, which generally runs quite counter to existing political-economic thought, is the economic basis of the statical political efficiency theorem that supports the central empirical argument of the entire work.[18]

The dynamical, or evolutionary, source of efficiency of surviving democracies is the fact that democratic polities cannot grow to maturity unless they first pass the unique speed-and-efficiency test discussed in Chapter 1. The current chapter will show that, indeed, observed democratic states that have survived to maturity have also been able to rapidly generate certain, critically efficient, sets of economic institutions. This evolutionary argument for the efficiency of long-surviving democracies has been completely ignored in the conventional literature on political economy, as has the laissez-faire underdevelopment problem that effective democracies are uniquely qualified to solve (Appendix A.1).

B. A New Approach to Political Economy

In Section I below, the heuristic political rationality arguments that we have just used to counter the traditional inefficiency presumption are developed into the theoretical proposition that an effective democracy will generate a citizen-efficient set of political associations.[19]

A glaring exception to the above-noted tariff pattern, as we pointed out earlier, is England, the wealthiest and most dominant nation in the world throughout the final three quarters of that century. As predicted by our broader theory, the previously pragmatic English were becoming ideologized during their period of world supremacy. They correspondingly erred in maintaining a uniquely free-trade policy all the way up to WWI. We shall be more specific about the unfortunate consequences of this ideologization later in the argument.

Another Pre-WWI exception is Austria, the leading imperial power in eastern Europe in the middle of the 19th century. Although Austria had, as we shall see, actively imposed free imperial trade on its dependencies in the latter half of the 18th century, it was not until the middle of the 19th century that she fatefully adopted the policy towards her own industries.

[18]This efficiency argument does not suggest a distributional contrast between popular and aristocratic democracy in that the cost of a political payoff should be independent of the political power of the paying parties. The way that popular democracy does translate into a more egalitarian distribution of wealth is through its generation of more humanistic representatives (e.g., III.C.3 below).

[19]"Citizen-efficiency" here need not be ideal Pareto optimality because the costs of establishing the existing system of "citizenship" or legal endowments rights, although possibly unnecessarily high, is taken as a given overhead cost of the inherited system. Moreover, the

What makes a set of costly political associations efficient in any sense of the term is the efficiency of the economic policies induced by its existence. In particular, if guilds and protectionist lobbies have historically represented a citizen-efficient set of political associations, then the economic policies created by their existence would have had to be citizen-efficient. A test of our political-efficiency result is therefore provided by seeing whether there is a specific economic model -- necessarily a non-classical one -- that rationalizes the actual economic policies historically generated by guilds and protectionist lobbies. Supplying and applying such an economic model is the main subject of Sections II and III of this chapter.

Before that, Section I theoretically characterizes both a static democratic equilibrium and an evolutionary adjustment path arriving at the equilibrium. It also describes the historical observations that led us to develop a theory about such paths. Section II provides an efficiency-based rationale for entry-restricting guilds and combines it with our political model to explain the once-universal existence of guilds, the structure of guild policies, the effects of guilds, and the historical rise and fall of guilds. Section III will then use the same general model to provide a new, efficiency-based, rationale for protectionist lobbies serving to explain the existence of tariffs, the traditional structure of observed tariffs, the economic effects of these tariffs, and the rises and declines of various forms of mercantilism.

The institutional rationalizations of Section II imply a time-consistency problem whose solution calls for vital economic institutions (Appendices B.2 (note 4) and B.3). This vitalness characteristic means that harshly Darwinian pressures arise to complement ordinary, Lamarckian, social learning processes. The same sort of hyper-evolutionary pressure will also arise in the discussions of Chapters 4 and 5, where we consider the same time-consistency problem in successively more militarily and financially advanced worlds. Since vital economic institutions must sensitively respond to changes in the military and financial environment, a long-surviving government evolved under this harsh Darwinian pressure must be correspondingly sensitive. This sensitivity will be tested by examining correlated variations in the nature of guilds, and later of guild-substitutes. As emphasized in Chapters 1 and 2, a necessary joint product of the evolved sensitivity is that a democracy also employs its unique ability for much more than the resolution of vital time-inconsistencies. Most importantly, a democracy that is *ex ante* rational for its founding leaders is one that employs its evolved investor-sensitivity to sense and eliminate the significant underinvestment traps that would otherwise characterize the laissez faire economy (Appendix A.1). Substantial economic success must therefore be expected to accompany the appropriately structured vital economic institutions. This correlation will regularly supply us with a stringent test our entire theory.

The theory can also be tested by examining the ability of surviving investor-

---

range of political and economic institutions (i.e., reaction functions) is limited by the political-economic imaginations and experience of the citizens of that state. An ideal political response to these possible inefficiencies, based upon a model generating evolutionary inefficiencies, is developed elsewhere (Thompson, et al.) The concept of "effective democracy," which we have already heuristically characterized, will be defined in Section I.

democracies to generate the often non-vital institutions that efficiently internalize a logically implied defense-externality (Appendix B.2). To supply these critical tests, Sections II and III of this chapter will respectively employ pre-WWI observations on guild and tariff policies. For the post-WWI period, Chapter 5 will test the theory by examining various innovative policies that have responded to external attempts to lower a country's effective tariff rates.

I. AN EFFICIENCY-BASED THEORY OF DEMOCRATIC POLITICAL ASSOCIATIONS

A. The Citizen-Efficiency of Effective Democracy

The political theory of this work is based upon the citizen-efficiency-generating proposition that any group of individual citizens -- say the information-sharing victims of some common externality -- will, in an effective democracy, incur the positive overhead costs of joining together into a political association that allows the individuals to subsequently costlessly cooperate with one another when and only when it is efficient for the state's entire citizenry that they do so.[20] The proposition can be derived from three conditions.

The first two conditions define a "democracy". The first condition is that the democratic state always contains <u>at</u> <u>least</u> <u>one</u> political association, one group of internally cooperating, legislation-promoting, citizens, and that <u>other</u> such associations can be freely formed. When we say here that political associations can be "freely" formed, we do not mean that there are no resource costs of such entry; we mean only that the admissible political ideologies neither impose nor countenance any institutional barriers to the entry. The allocational advantage of a political association (e.g., a political lobby or party), as emphasized in Appendix A.1, is that its members are able to help create, evaluate, and promote legislative solutions tailored to their particular allocation problems.

The second condition -- which is realistic only in an intellectually open political environment allowing <u>all</u> possible political ethics consistent with both (a) the endowed legal and political ideologies defining citizenship and statehood and (b) the above-specified free-political-entry constraint -- is that some individuals in each political association can freely adopt and communicate <u>any</u> technologically and informationally feasible reaction to the political behavior of all other citizens of that state.[21] Regarding citizens who have not worked to join a political association,

---

[20]"Citizens" are individuals who have received commitments (implicitly from the military rulers) assuring them of minimal utilitarian benefits (see Appendix B.1, Section 5).

[21]"Ethics" here, following the discussion of Chapter 1 or Appendix B.1, are taken in their most general sense. They are simply exaggerations enabling people to carry out their broadly rational reaction functions and thereby induce cooperation. For a familiar example, the exaggerations implied by a belief in high medieval epic poetry lead to the chivalrous ethical reaction functions that made feudalism a social success. The way in which the deeply rooted

although the society can objectively estimate their overall expected returns from joining an association, no one in the society can rationally produce a tailored estimate of their individual returns from specific legislative acts.

The third condition, which is not part of the definition of democracy, is realistic only in a political setting conducive to objective economic learning. It is that all citizens act, perhaps through appointed or elected agents, as if they <u>correctly estimate</u> the net welfare effects of the alternative political outcomes. To eliminate an ambiguity in the determination of these welfare effects when different sets of political associations generate different distributions of income (e.g., Samuelson, 1950), we proceed by considering each set of associations as a possible equilibrium, in which case the income distribution resulting from each hypothetical equilibrium is the one from which values are computed.

Under the above three conditions, which together define an "effective democracy", a political association will be part of a social equilibrium when and only when it is jointly efficient among all of the existing citizens of that state.[22]

To see this proposition, call it "Lemma 1", suppose that a group of individuals is considering forming a new political association (such as a political lobby), and that, although benefiting its members, the association would generate a commonly and objectively perceived net loss in the citizens' <u>aggregate</u> economic welfare. Then, since the commonly perceived aggregate benefit to the gainers is less than the aggregate loss to the losers, the leaders of the initial association would profit by making: (a) a fixed offer, e.g., an adjustment in a legislative platform, to pay each of these gainers a flow of benefits that slightly exceeds their expected individual benefits from the would-be association as long as they refrain from creating the new association; and (b) a correspondingly fixed demand that each of the potential losers also make their corresponding contributions to the bribe fund. All of these potential losers would rationally pay, and the would-be new association members would rationally accept, the payment and thereby prevent the formation of the inefficient association. By the same reasoning, the leaders of an existing association will always

---

political and legal ideologies of western Europe helped determine this social ethic is discussed in Thompson, et al., Vol. I, Ch. 7.

[22]Following the analysis of Appendices A.1 and B.1, a social equilibrium here is a perfect equilibrium with generally costly strategic communication. A politically non-authoritarian, or "democratic" form of such an equilibrium arises when the natural military leaders (the earliest strategy-selectors), who are generally "dictatorial" in the Arrowian sense, surrender legislative authority to the above-described process, wherein all of the state's citizens are invited to freely participate.

An obvious alternative, of course, is an authoritarian system based solely on prevailing legislative theory. A democracy may, in an extreme case, adopt an equivalent to an authoritarian solution by simply adopting, without reservation, a complete legislative theory. However, the resource cost of operating a democracy that chooses the equivalent of an authoritarian solution is, because of entry costs, uniformly higher than the resource cost of operating a directly authoritarian system.

be induced to accede to the entry of a socially efficient association.[23]   Similarly, the exit of inefficient associations occurs under our three conditions because the leaders of an existing association will rationally commit themselves to slightly compensate the losers for disbanding their inefficient associations, an offer that none of these individuals will rationally refuse.   Finally, the same reasoning assures us that the efficiency-enhancing members of an existing set of political associations will remain in the set.   It follows that the entry or exit of political associations will occur if and only if the existing set of associations is inefficient.

This suggests, for example, that the common allegation that special interest groups and political lobbies significantly deteriorate the quality of a democracy are too narrowly conceived.   If such political associations really did so detract from the efficiency of the democracy, their victims would rationally pay-off their potential members as long as the potentially injurious association remains dormant.

Under an additional, rather technical, assumption, this proposition leads to the citizen-efficiency of a democratic equilibrium.   The additional assumption is that each set of political associations generates a distinct set of legislative acts, or allocation-determining laws.   The society's set of feasible legislative acts is thus the product of the legislative acts of all possible sets of political associations.[24]

To construct an equilibrium, we consider, in turn, each feasible set of political associations.   If there is entry or exit from the initial choice, which makes it inefficient according to Lemma 1, we eliminate it from further consideration.   Once we have so eliminated all inefficient sets of political associations, all that remains are efficient sets.   Alternatively, once our elimination process arrives at a set of political associations for which there are positive returns to neither exit nor entry, it follows from Lemma 1 that there is no feasible change that can make everyone better off.

The sequential elimination process in the above optimality proof, together with the obvious existence of Pareto-optimal points among any finite set of utility

---

[23]Although we avoid the standard assumption of cooperative game theory in which the coalition containing all players generates an efficient outcome, our entry-prevention process is analogous to a society's using side payments to prevent the formation of blocking coalitions. What eliminates the corresponding spate of existence or indeterminacy problems that haunt cooperative game theory is our second assumption, wherein the association members follow the model of Appendix B.1 so that the association leaders commit themselves to maximally favorable bargaining solutions and interact in a sequential fashion.

[24]Although it may appear that the feasible laws described in this assumption include all possible laws, the pre-existence of citizenship and statehood and corresponding inheritance of deeply rooted legal and political values, as emphasized in Chapters 1 and 2, generally seriously restricts the set of feasible laws and correspondingly precludes the achievement of an unconstrained, 1st-best optimum.   So the optimum we are about to generate is not generally 1st best.   Rather, it is a citizenship-constrained, or "citizen-efficient", outcome.

The behavioral meanings of citizenship and statehood are implied by the respective models of Appendices B.1-B.3.   The particular feasibility constraints that this imposes on the reaction functions, although partially described in the appendices, are more fully described in Thompson, et al., Vol. 1.

possibilities, simultaneously generates a simple existence proof for our finite model.[25,26]

The existence result is an important complement to the optimality result. For, regarding mere optimality, following the argument of Section III.I of Appendix B.3, it is easy to see, and many subsequent authors have argued, that any political equilibrium, at least among completely informed individuals, is Pareto optimal. What is a bit more difficult is to simultaneously escape cyclical majority problems and show that a political equilibrium actually exists. We have also allowed for an important element of realism, one that gives a central role to lobbies and special interest groups, an element of substantially incomplete information.

---

[25]Alternative existence and optimality proofs can be generated by suitably applying the theorems in Appendix B.1. First, when the initial political association suffices to achieve a constrained-efficient outcome, we need only repeat the existence and optimality proofs in the Appendix (altered only by the transformation of feasible political actions into feasible legislation and then into feasible economic actions). This is constrained-efficient in that those who may be excluded from the association, and therefore do not register their specific legislative preferences, do not lose so much from the resulting legislation that it is worth the joint cost of entering into a political association. When the initial political association does not suffice (i.e., when Pareto-superior policies can be generated by using the legislative input of some initially excluded citizens), this optimality proof can still be applied by taking the following, intermediate, logical step: The members of any subsequent political association supply tailored information about specific legislation to the appropriate members of the original political association, and then the latter proceed as if they initially had complete information concerning the preferences of the additional individuals even in the absence of the secondary association. The original optimality proof then again applies. This proof helps us see that: (1) effective democracy works because special interest groups, when they justify their overhead costs, work by inducing individuals to reveal their specific legislative preferences, and (2), as we know is necessary from Appendix A.1, the efficiency-generating process is generally far from unanimous. The existence and constrained efficiency of the equilibrium resulting from specifically evolved legislative and voting mechanisms, a subject beyond the scope of this work, is established in Thompson, et al., Vol. I, Ch. 8.

[26]The presence of utility-endowments in our model, together with the fact that our multiple-association case assigns payoffs to "coalitions", appear to move us into the payoff ("characteristic") functions and the corresponding strategy sets of cooperative game theory. However, our new associations are collectively negotiated and sequentially considered. We correspondingly adopt a non-cooperative, perfect equilibrium, solution concept, which is implied in the model of Appendix B.1 and violates a basic symmetry condition found in the conventional theory of cooperative games.

Our terminology may nevertheless be criticized as non-conventional in that we are calling "effective democracy" something that many game-theorists would call a form of "cooperation". However, the terminology of game theorists is highly imperfect in this regard because it fails to capture both: (a) the necessarily confining, narrowly irrational, component of genuinely cooperative behavior, and (b) the fact that free participation in social rule-making has, at least since the time of Aristotle, conventionally meant that the systems are to be called "democratic". In contrast, "cooperative", at least to economists and game theorists, merely means always-joint-utility-maximizing, or Pareto optimal, among the members of a group.

B. The Effect of Faulty Political Values and Erroneous Economic Information

1. Three Dimensions of Evolutionary Adjustment

The assumptions of costless political strategy formation and correct economic information, and the resulting citizen-efficiency conclusion, are justifiable in a suitably "long run" setting (keeping in mind our Chapter 2 result that citizen-efficiency means that we have already allowed for cases in which evolution favors non-objective evaluations of certain, non-vital, legal and political institutions). But serious citizen-inefficiencies are likely in the short run. Individuals will, in the short run, generally be seriously constrained by both obsolete political values and erroneous economic beliefs. The empirical success of our efficiency-predicting social theory therefore depends largely on how individuals adjust their initially faulty political values and respond to initially incorrect economic expectations. We distinguish three separate dimensions of evolutionary adjustment.

First, besides the harsh Darwinian selection that supports a rapid and objective selection of vital institutions, there is the evolution of political theory based on the observable performance of different political theories. Founders of political associations promoting new political processes and theories consider the recent performances of similarly situated states with different political theories before choosing one for their own. The objectivity of the decisionmakers employed in the theorem above inevitably leads the chosen political theories (e.g., support for decentralized political decision processes) to systematically approach citizen-efficiency.

Although there is, in the background, an evolution toward the above-mentioned, non-objectively evaluated, inefficient, legal and political ideologies, we have isolated these inefficiencies here by accepting them as given in the definition of "citizen-efficiency". What supports our objectivity assumption here is the fact that the evolved objectivity that does hold for vital institutions (Section I.A.1 of Chapter 2) carries over to all of those institution-selecting decisions that do not overvalue the teachings of cartels of professional thinkers. Empirical support for this citizen-efficiency conclusion in cross-sectional evidence running across different civilizations is thus found in Thompson, et al., Vol. I, Chs. 3 and 6; and Vol. II, Chs. 4 and 5. The current study will complement these with time-series evidence that indicates a frequently rapid dynamical adjustment to constrained-efficient political theories.

A second dimension of evolutionary adjustment concerns the extent to which economic thought is used in the estimation of the welfare effects of legislative alternatives. Consider what happens when there is an initial, uniform, belief in a complete economic theory. This has the advantage of saving the state the costs of political bargaining over all laws. Although one political association would then suffice as there is no social efficiency gained by adding a second group, the resource costs of running a democracy that wound up with only one political association would still exceed the costs of an authoritarian system (e.g., fascism or communism). If, however, the available legislative theories were substantially incomplete or incorrect, an effective democracy would evolve. This evolution would occur in initially single-association states through a complement of gradual Lamarckian learning (of a more conflict-tolerant political theory and a less doctrinaire, more experimental, approach to economic policy) and occasionally harsh Darwinian selection. We need only assume, as we shall throughout, that intellectually competing states always have <u>some</u> pragmatism, i.e., some "soft-wiring," and therefore some ability to learn from experience and experiment with participatory rule-making. Moving to the other extreme, to complete "legislative pragmatism", no explicit welfare-economic theory whatever is used to make legislative decisions. Only actual policy experience and special interest calculations are referred to in devising legislation.

All of our evidence favors the competitive evolution and efficiency of this extreme form of legislative pragmatism.[27]   Appendices B.1 through B.3 present cross-sectional evidence, while the present chapter will present time-series evidence, for the competitive evolution of extreme legislative pragmatism.

Only in maturing dominant states, where the competitive pressure to pragmatically simulate the successes of other states is no longer present, do we find an evolution away from extreme legislative pragmatism and toward ideologically inspired legislation. Moreover, to the extent that this ideology comes to dominate an entire civilization, it is a threat to the entire civilization rather than merely the temporarily dominant state. Fortunately, as indicated in our final Chapter, this civilizational inefficiency is constitutionally removable. But we are getting way ahead of our story.

Given both an existing political theory and an existing degree of legislative pragmatism, we still cannot determine either the actual set of political associations or the actual set of economic institutions resulting from their existence. <u>Specific legislative beliefs</u>, as determined by the nature of both existing economic theory and existing policy experience, must also be evolved. Our third, and final, level of evolutionary adjustment thus concerns these specific legislative beliefs, which may or may not rapidly adjust to observable legislative errors. However, when certain economic institutions are vital, either the state is sufficiently perceptive and flexible that those specific economic institutions will quickly evolve, or the state will fail. The same is true of the degree of legislative pragmatism.

In other words, once a state has arrived at a political theory that makes certain economic institutions vital to the state's survival, a harsh, super-Darwinian, process of natural selection is activated. If this potentially fatal political theory nevertheless survives, it is because the harshly selective process has rapidly weeded out both many inefficient ways of adjusting policies to experience and many specific economic beliefs.

Before proceeding to examine where these three, simultaneously adjusting variables lead, we should further consider the effect of both economic ideology and economic theory generally on the evolutionary path. For, as noted in the foregoing discussion, our historical studies have provided us with a fairly extreme specification on the nature of the equilibrium in this regard.

---

[27]As economists, we hope that future economic theories are practically useful to our states. But we cannot follow the cartel convention of allowing such hopes to disturb the objectivity of our evaluations of the past empirical effects of actual economic theories.

2. Economic Ideology and Institutional Evolution

The possession of a correct economic theory -- which follows Appendix A.1 in admitting the superiority of pragmatic learning with respect to a wide range of important economic policies -- would make a state appropriately responsive to policy experiments and the recent policy experiences of neighboring states. However, states whose political leaders are initially taught an overly assertive economic theory -- a kind of economic ideology -- are slower to develop an efficient set of both political associations and economic institutions than states whose political leaders are legislatively pragmatic and therefore objectively evaluate observable legislative successes and failures. Although the state cannot be expected to know whether or not an initial economic theory is correct, the presence of a profession-serving, significantly teacher-influencing, ideological bias creates an excessive likelihood of an initial error and an overly slow dynamic adjustment toward an efficient state.[28] In states whose legislatures are sufficiently burdened with such an ideological bias (states often empirically identifiable by their past dominance over other states), effective democracy is either excessively slow to emerge or excessively quick to die.

We have already mentioned that any complete legislative theory, such as is generated by classical economic theory or Marxism, is inconsistent with the efficiency of a democratic system. For if the legislative theory were substantially correct, the democratic policy would be an expensive superfluity; and if the theory were not substantially correct, then the society would suffer from its effects on legislation. However, correct, incomplete legislative theories, such as those consistent with Appendix A.1, do not pose this problem; incomplete legislative theories are consistent with efficient democracies. Effective democracies, presumably out of pragmatic learning, would then surrender permanent legislative control over to independent bureaucracies in those spheres of an economy where a permanently correct legislative theory would hasten the achievement of an optimum. Our historical studies, however, have yet to reveal such a case.[29]

---

[28]The bias typically works by having a cartel of teacher-advisors mix self-serving messages in with productive lessons so that students cannot separate one kind of message from another. The rational student therefore ends up both undervaluing the productive messages and overvaluing teacher-serving messages. The productive messages emanating from contemporary real-world observations are further undervalued if the teachers responsible for the initial error supply an ongoing flow of ideological "information" to the state. In any case, accompanying any "successful" ideology is a set of what Popper calls "immunizing stratagems," methodological positions that protect an established ideology from obviously contradictory data. We discuss these, and the nature of various biases in economic thought, elsewhere (Thompson, et al., Vol. I, Ch. 1).

[29]There are, of course, important policy spheres in which observed democracies voluntarily, and sometimes even objectively, surrender temporary rule-making control over to economic authorities. These are spheres in which legislative time-inconsistencies would make continually rational decision-making severely inefficient (Appendices B.2, note 4; B.3; and Thompson (1981)). The only important cases in which surviving democracies surrender rule-

This strong empirical result is what allows us to assert the sufficiency of the intellectually humble bureaucratic ethic of "civil reverence" in order to achieve an effective, citizen-efficient, democracy. The ethic, which empirically arises in various forms but is always the result of a powerful mythology whose heroes sacrifice their private wishes for the expressed wish of the state, is necessary because distributional preferences would lead an objective high-level bureaucrat to forsake the administration of socially optimal laws for distributionally more attractive outcomes.[30]

3. An Evolutionary Theory of Dynamic Adjustment for Objective States

If, because of some sort of miscalculation, a noticeably citizen-inefficient political association should arise in an objective state, other such states, commonly observing the resulting decrease in the miscalculating state's relative prosperity, would certainly not adopt the new institution. So the citizen-inefficient institution would not spread to these objective states. Rather, if the error does not eliminate a vital economic institution, the miscalculating state would eventually correct the miscalculation and the corresponding institutional inefficiency. And, if the error does eliminate a vital institution, the state is eliminated and soon replaced with one that does not repeat the error. Similarly, if one of several, common, pre-existing, political associations (or political or economic theories) suddenly becomes citizen-inefficient, those states without the association (or theory) would become relatively prosperous. Seeing this, other objective states, assuming that they are not yet swallowed up because they may temporarily lack a vital institution, would quickly disband the association and thereby adjust away from the correspondingly inefficient institutions. In the case that they remain without a vital institution, they soon become a replicate of the newly successful state. Hence, whatever the case, a citizen-efficient institutional equilibrium, which exists within the group of objective states, is asymptotically stable in that it is constantly being approached.[31]

Thus, once we admit the possibility of inadequate vital economic institutions and harsh Darwinian selection into a relatively peaceful Lamarckian process, we add a

---

making power over to economic authorities are thus second-best cases in which democracy would be "too rational" for its own good (i.e., narrowly, but not broadly, rational). If popular economic theory were really a source of broadly rational policies, there would be no reason for these evolved bureaucracies to be either politically chosen or temporary.

[30]The time-consistency aspect of this distribution problem is discussed at length in Thompson (1981), at least for a case in which the bureaucrats require substantial economic training. The first-best -- quite idealistic -- solution is for the government to permanently employ technically proficient economists who are trained to completely ignore distributional issues. However, when such broadly rational people are not available, it may be optimal to temporarily employ economic ideologues for the job.

[31]The uniqueness of the equilibrium, at least under strict preferences (Appendix B.1), allows us to infer global stability from the above, local stability, argument. The argument, of course, is a special case of the Foster-Young-Weibull convergence result employed in Ch. 1.

fast and unforgiving element to the developmental discussion. Either the state fails to quickly create the newly vital set of institutions, in which case the state is soon eliminated, or it does not so fail, in which case the state survives until the next challenge of this sort. Before long, then, the entire population of states possessing vital economic institutions is comprised solely of such rapidly responding states. The asymptotic stability of the Lamarckian adjustment process is not only retained when we add a Darwinian element (Weibull); the institutional adjustment process is substantially hastened, especially when the Darwinian element is harsh.

In particular, because effective democracies must create special, vital, economic institutions, fledgling democracies would have soon failed if their detailed political processes (i.e., myriad rules concerning elections, legislative procedures, vetoes, the education of bureaucrats, etc.), all of which emerged from a series of empirical observations and political ideologies, had failed to legislate timely and citizen-efficient institutional responses to changes in the military environment. Moreover, as stressed in Chapters 1 and 2, democratic institutions, because of their relatively high overhead costs as well as military risks, could not have long survived their evolutionary competition with authoritarian institutions were it not for a substantial legislative efficiency-advantage of effective democracy.[32]

This substantial efficiency-advantage -- although no such advantage is apparent from pre-existing economic theory -- is that effective democracy is uniquely qualified to eliminate the underdevelopment traps inevitable under laissez faire (Appendix A.1). Our empirical observations will repeatedly confirm this implication.[33]

We will also have abundant occasion to verify a degenerative tendency toward the elimination of the intellectual conditions for an effective democracy in certain kinds of states. This elimination, or "ideologization", which again has invariably occurred in dominant states, has had two predictable consequences. First, by violating our objective-evaluation condition, a dominant state's efficiency, and typically its observed growth rate, declines. Second, unless the dominant state possesses the external control and corresponding military security of a world empire, the ideologized dominant state sooner or later falls victim to the military aggression of neighboring states that have not so degenerated.

---

[32]We have been repeatedly using the term citizen-efficiency to emphasize the non-idealistic concept of social efficiency adopted throughout this work. It has, by now, hopefully served this didactic purpose and we will frequently hereafter shorten the term to "efficiency" in the interest of brevity and because the discussion is about to demand that we concentrate on a series of important cases containing vital institutions.

[33]From a rational choice perspective, discussed in Chapter 1, if such an advantage did not exist, there would be no reason for an objective founding military leader to risk the entire state by adopting a democracy in the first place. Using Appendix A.1, the specific form of this compensatory efficiency can be directly derived by noting that investors in a democratic system regard trap-eliminating legislation as vital to their interests and will therefore call upon the same non-partisanship that provides the economic institutions that protect their state. The same, non-partisan, Pascalian sensitivity should thereby analogously generate economic institutions that are vital for the protection of their jointly threatened investments.

We have been arguing that an effective democracy's unique military survival requirement, one entailing rapid and efficient legislative responses to occasional changes in the military environment, implies that steadily surviving democracies have the capacity to rapidly eliminate some large economic inefficiencies. The practical success of democracy thus implies that democratic legislatures have the time to produce superior sets of civilian laws in between their separate bouts of super-Darwinian selection. Without some such "surplus-capacity" of legislation time, there would be no point to democracy. In particular, the legislatures of rationally chosen democracies must have sufficient time to employ their exceptional legislative capabilities to eliminate serious allocative problems such as their laissez faire underdevelopment traps. Therefore, granted that the surviving democratic legislature has sufficient time in between its military concerns, the argument of Appendix A.1, which not only establishes the existence of such traps but shows that the institutions that eliminate them are vital to several classes of investors, implies a rapid improvement in civilian institutions.

The surviving classes of such threatened investors are those that participate in the political process sufficiently to protect their profits from the rent-seeking activities of other citizens of their fortunately democratic state. Note that, in the elimination of underdevelopment traps, this surviving class of new investors may also somewhat enhance the democracy's ability to prepare for defense emergencies.

Finally, regarding non-vital issues, given still further surplus legislative capacity, the purely Lamarckian features of the evolutionary process imply that steadily surviving, non-dominant, democracies will also use their necessarily refined problem-solving capabilities to eventually establish the theoretically predicted, citizen-efficient, non-vital economic institutions.

Testing the above political-economic theory is now this study's central goal.

4. Brief Examples of Dynamic Adjustment: The Rise and Decline of Both Guilds and Complete Laissez Faire in Western Europe

An example of the dynamic evolution of an equilibrium political association and corresponding economic institution is the development of the European guild. Let us first describe the historical sequence.

The compulsory, tax-paying, sometimes voting, trade associations, or *collegia*, of the Classical Roman Empire were either absorbed by the church or disbanded by the Germanic invaders during the closing years of the Western Empire. However, through the colonizing efforts of Byzantium late in the 6th century, the combination of authoritarian Germanic rulers and Roman Catholic bureaucrats which was developing a dark age for western Europe lost its suzerainty over large parts of Italy. Among the numerous new Byzantine protectorates was the oligarchic republic of Naples,[34] whose traditional independence from the church in Rome had left it an enclave of Greco-Roman culture. Naples quickly took advantage of her emancipation

---

[34]Our theoretical model classifies these oligarchies as "democracies" because citizens were typically free to join any of the state's freely formable political associations.

by reintroducing a strengthened form of *collegia* in which independent groups of tradesmen were granted, in addition to their Classical political and tax-paying role, a direct role in civil administration (Mickwitz; Headlam. Ch. 9).

The Byzantium-supported democracies of refugee merchants forming at about the same time at nearby Amalfi and at Venice were similarly administered by merchants rather than counts or clerics and similarly financed by the lump-sum contributions of the merchants (Hyde, pp. 20-22; Lopez). The subsequent economic successes of each of these three little merchant-democracies amid the general decline elsewhere (Sedgwick, Ch. 8; Hyde, Ch. 1) were not lost, either on their northern neighbors of Pisa, Genoa, and Pavia (Mickwitz), or, more significantly, on the Frankish Emperor Lothar I, who was kept regularly informed of Venician activities (Scholz, p. 116). Lothar reacted quickly to an 824 Papal forgiveness of the torturers and murderers of his two chief representatives in Rome by imposing his "Constitutiones Olonenses" on the succeeding Popes, thereby permitting seven inland centers for the formation of independent associations of both merchants and craftsmen (Staley, p. 36). The subsequent relative successes of these guild towns (Sedgwick, p. 70), especially Florence (Staley, p. 6), the continued relative successes of Naples, Venice, and Amalfi, as well as the successes of the subsequently formed coastal merchant democracies of Pisa and Genoa (Hyde, p. 29; Sedgwick, *ibid.*), created the conditions for a guild boom beginning late in the 10th century once the feudal hierarchy was stable enough to secure inland towns and trade routes.[35]

In particular, European guilds evolved through the rapid spread of new investor-oligarchies to the Flemish and French towns with which the Italians traded at the Champagne fairs (Mundy and Riesenberg, Chs. IV and V). The increased prosperity observed in such towns as Liege, Paris, Arros and Rouen resulted in a spread of merchant-run guild towns into neighboring western Germania and England beginning the 1st quarter of the 12th century, then to the trading towns of southern France such

---

[35]The accelerated guild expansion from the 11th through the 13th centuries followed on the heels of an area-wide military strengthening concentrated in western Europe, where there had been a similarly evolutionary maturation of feudal orders and a corresponding chivalric ideology. The resulting increase in security of both internal and external trade routes (often attributed to incidentals such as the military victories over the Moors (esp., Pirenne)) fostered the substantial increases in trade and wealth in western Europe and was, we shall argue, both a cause and an effect of the blossoming of western European guilds.

While no scholar concentrating on guilds has failed to note the highly military function of these early guilds, our contribution in this regard will be to explain the rapidity of the rise of these guilds by arguing that their military input made them a vital institution to the medieval city. Moreover, by viewing guilds as political associations vital for protection of the rents of the investors in these typically investor-democratic cities, we are able to explain the corresponding economic booms.

Also, applying our defense-externalities model, we are able to explain the details of various guild institutions as a necessary consequence of the evolution of survivable investor-democracies. These institutional details have previously been misunderstood by failing to recognize the economic problems posed by both the general need for military protection and the investor-need for protection against civilian aggression.

as Marseille and Toulouse (Mundy and Riesenberg, *op. cit.*), then to various north-eastern Spanish coastal trading centers around the middle of the 13th century (R. Smith, Ch. 1), and finally to eastern Germania with the Hanses in the late 13th century (Mundy and Riesenberg, Ch. 1). With the coming of merchant guilds and guild-administered towns in the middle ages, western and central Europe grew all the way up to the height of the middle ages in the late 13th century, by which time it had achieved a quasi-long-run equilibrium.[36]

This description of the spread of a form of political association based on its observed economic success in neighboring areas does not reveal the underlying source of its success. Nor is it likely that contemporaries understood the source. Indeed, most scholastic writers, the predominant ideological force during the later middle ages, consistently criticized the guilds for monopolistic practices (de Roover (1958), p. 431). Nevertheless, the remarkable economic success of the guild-run investor-democracies was normally sufficient to overcome the frequently overt church opposition to their independent existence. It was practical economic success, not ideological approval, that accounted for the spread of guilds.

Guild decline was similarly emulative in legislatively pragmatic regions, regions not dominated by contemporary legislative ideology (Renaissance elitism or laissez faire economics). This will be elaborated upon in Section II.D.5. We have already given late 15th century Florence and Milan and mid-17th century Holland as unfortunate early examples of ideologically based, premature, guild-declines. Several later examples will emerge in the surveys of guild-decline provided in Section II. These surveys will once again reveal a great contrast in economic performance between legislatively pragmatic investor-democracies and all other states.

Complete laissez faire requires, in addition to the absence of entry-restrictive trade associations, the absence of government interference in foreign trade through protectionist trade lobbies. As we shall see, such a thoroughgoing free-trade policy first began to emerge in intellectually dominant late-18th century France, and, although stalled in the early years of the Revolution, came back with the Jacobin capture of the Revolution and the Napoleonic era as an ostensibly final "victory" for the physiocrats. Although Protectionism returned in 1814 with the legislatively constrained Bourbons and was retained by the Second Republic, the liberal regime reemerged soon after Napoleon III declared himself Emperor in 1852. Complete laissez faire policy gradually spread to increasingly dominant, gradually ideologizing, Britain during the late-second and early-third quarters of the 19th century, on the heels of the rapid rise of the Second British Empire.[37] As we have already

---

[36]Regarding craft guilds, the subsequent, rapid spread of these entry-restricting political associations from Italy in the 12th century follows a similar pattern (e.g., Black, p.6; Pirenne, p. 180), the trend similarly beginning only after the capital stock of a typical investor had grown to an economically significant level.

[37]As we shall elaborate in Section III.B.1 below, the great bulk of this "free trade" policy was, in effect, an internal free-trade policy, efficient because the great bulk of Britain's dealings were with her many colonies. Nevertheless, there was an initially small, genuinely

mentioned, several European countries soon began to follow the British example by moving toward a complete laissez faire policy early in the third quarter of the 19th century; but they, along with France, quickly abandoned the policy in the late 1860s and 1870s as the embarrassing Austrian and French military failures at the hands of high-tariff Prussia, and the lack of observable economic benefits, freed the more pragmatic countries from their infatuation with laissez faire ideology. Genuinely democratic reforms rapidly ensued. But the Austria-Hungarian Empire, which had been dominant in eastern Europe and greatly influenced by laissez faire ideologues, continued to maintain a basically free trade policy, at least for manufactured goods, and essentially perished in WWI. And, in western Europe, even more dominant, similarly legislatively ideologized, Britain also maintained free trade but, with U.S. intervention, survived the War and eventually, by the end of World War I, discarded laissez faire policy, but only after having been economically overtaken by the U.S. and German democracies. The latter democracies, to their good fortune, had long been politically captured by economic interest groups rather than economic ideology.

And post-WWI Britain, in line with a long series of other once-dominant nations, was merely trading one economic ideology for another. As detailed in the next chapter, her new ideology soon led her, and her European neighbors, out of the frying pan and into the fire.[38]

---

external, component to her free trade policies. And, although the external trade component had grown to significance by the 1880s, an ideologically inspired Britain maintained her free-trade policy and faltered all the way up to WWI while a previously struggling France finally abandoned her free trade ideologues in the 1870s and correspondingly took-off.

Coinciding with the growth in British imports from non-Commonwealth sources, Britain's industrial laws were changed during the 1870s. The new changes made it easier for unions to form closed shops and thereby monopolize whole industries. This served as a substitute -- albeit an inferior, increasingly costly, substitute -- for nationally optimal, export-monopolizing, export taxes, a substitution necessitated by the ideological constraint imposed by free-trade teaching. Thus, union monopolies were appropriately achieved in, and only in, those sectors where England exported outside of her Empire and had a substantial initial effect on world prices (viz., iron, ship-building, coal, and machine tools). But this monopoly-union policy became an allocative burden once England permanently lost her world monopoly power during the last quarter of the 19th century. Also, as discussed in Section III.B.1, British free-trade policy was inefficiently subsidizing her imports of foreign manufactures.

[38]This historical regularity of ideology-switching rather than returning to legislative pragmatism will eventually lead us to treat ideologization as a nearly incurable disease. The reason, of course, is that intellectuals conveniently interpret the previous failure as simply an inappropriate ideology, a situation in which an opposing ideology should have been employed. This has obviously been the case, for example, in several, struggling, late 20th century, Eastern European states that have replaced communist ideology with laissez-faire ideology. An efficiently pragmatic reaction is dynamically likely only when more than one ideology fails within the experience of a single generation. We are, indeed, currently witnessing such an effect emerge in Eastern Europe. However, unless there then is a total reform of the education system, such as occurred in France during the Bourbon Restoration, the subsequent teacher-intellectuals will still have it in their power to distort the interpretation of this pragmatic

II. EFFICIENT GUILD POLICIES

A. The Two Primary Social Functions of Guilds

The primary social functions of guilds concern the security of capital.

1. *Guild-Provided Protection Against Civilian Aggression.* The first primary function of guilds deals with the civilian security of capital. It applies when highly law-respecting (i.e., "civilly reverent") bureaucrats are unavailable. Investors in internally coveted capital are, in the short run, subject to both private and bureaucratic expropriation (Appendix A.1). To prevent such internal expropriation, intentional or not, when bureaucrats are not civilly reverent requires the steady administrative as well as legislative input of the potential victims.[39] Political associations of the potential victims, such as guilds, may perform this investor-vital bureaucratic function. It was thus through their own, self-enforced legal system, the "guild merchant", that the merchants in the early guild towns were able to produce

---

reaction, thus returning the state to some economic ideology.

Consider, for example, the U.S. experience during the 20th century. The century opened toward the end of the legislatively pragmatic, "Populist", era, a quarter-century of great economic expansion. The liberal ideologization represented by the "Progressive" movement, an intellectual import from Europe by Teddy Roosevelt, lasted up through WWI, which punctured the balloon of the idealistic Progressives. The conservative reaction during the 1920s yielded the "Great Depression" of the early 1930s and thus a wholesale rejection of both liberal and conservative ideologies in favor of the pragmatic populism of Franklin Roosevelt, which was predominantly a pragmatic policy-import from Europe. However, rather than correctly representing these highly successful structural policies as a victory for political pragmatism, post-WWII educators (essentially all of our teachers) represented the policies as the result of liberal theory, which they most certainly were not. The result was an unfortunate degeneration of the U.S. polity of the post-WWII period into a liberal/conservative contest, a maturation of the ideological debate of the pre-depression decades.

[39]Mature (esp. St. Thomas' Aristotelian form of) Roman Catholicism -- being founded upon the infallibility of an independent, morally inspired, legal authority -- is far from a civilly reverent religion. Mainline Protestantism -- being founded upon a replacement of this moral authority with a civil leader, or a domestic political process, as the legitimate rule-making source -- is a civilly reverent religion. As a result, we shall assume that investors in regions with mature Catholic or noble bureaucracies should, for efficiency, actively participate in the rule-enforcing process while investors in regions with mainline Protestant bureaucracies, should not. Early, Pre-Thomian, Platonic Catholicism, although similarly respectful of civil authorities, was too other-worldly to provide a commercial bureaucracy. So efficiency was also served by the participation of early guilds in their own regulation.

Our interpretations of these religions should not be taken to represent any assertion as to the net social values of the religions. Such thought systems may obviously serve society in ways beyond the scope of this study (e.g., Thompson, et al., Vol. I, Ch. 3). Similarly, our criticism of laissez faire policy should not be taken as a criticism of the standard competitive model, which has a tremendously valuable role to play in the coordination of various, sector-specific, optimal policies (Faith-Thompson). Ideology is our only target.

their unique economic success (e.g., Gross, Ch. 1). Civilly reverent bureaucrats -- when available -- obviate these costly administrative inputs.[40]

2. *Guild-Provided Protection Against Military Aggression.* The second primary social function of guilds concerns military appropriation. The function has two general subfunctions, each corresponding to one of the two kinds of "defense-externalities" that we have already discussed at several points in the argument. The first recognizes that, because the leaders of large towns or nations defend the collectively coveted capital stocks of their regions from military aggression, investors must pay the equivalent of a peacetime capital tax if they are to internalize the defense cost they impose on their area's leader (Appendix B.2). This tax is only sometimes vital, only sometimes necessary for the survival of the state (Chapter 5).

The second -- always vital -- subfunction requires that certain citizens make substantial net contributions to emergency war efforts (Appendices B.2 (Note 4) and B.3 (Section I.H)). In particular, whenever an effective democracy has its capital stock coveted by military aggressors, it must be defended during wars with centrally forced emergency contributions from the citizenry, state-survival requiring such authoritarian over-rides. Also, for efficiency, and possibly state-survival, the democracy must somehow provide heavily war-supporting investors with peacetime tax favors to compensate for their net wartime contributions (Appendix B.3, Section 2.1). Authoritarian and democratic governments alike require commitments to both heavy wartime sacrifices and substantial postwar debt repayments to domestic contributors, the future policy representing a substantial violation of the narrow economic interests of both the authoritarian leaders and the contemporaneous legislatures. But authoritarian leaders are psychologically trained to impose large sacrifices on their societies. Whatever economic institutions may be required to override this narrow, self-defeating, legislative "rationality" in democratic governments, such institutions are seldom required for survival in authoritarian states. The military values psychologically required to effectively assert <u>domestic</u> authoritarian leadership are themselves typically sufficient for authoritarian leaders to directly induce the sacrifices appropriate to both fighting and financing a defensive war against foreigners. So the particular economic institutions that are vital to a democracy are generally not vital to an authoritarian government. Nevertheless, the institutions vital to a democracy may well serve as administrative conveniences in authoritarian polities.

Vital economic institutions thus exist for the essentially unprincipled citizens of a democracy because the citizens require special laws to establish substantive collective commitments to both state-preserving wartime defense and the postwar

---

[40]Optimal governmental policy in the face of a redistributive bureaucracy, as illustrated by the policy set described in Appendix A.1, is, in general, only second-best policy. Nevertheless, such not-directly-controllable imperfections do not call for violations of familiar, first-best, optimality conditions in the directly controllable areas of the economy (Faith-Thompson). This theoretical result rationalizes the conventional, piecemeal, policy approach adopted throughout this study.

fulfillment of wartime obligations. The evolutionary pattern is therefore quite different as between authoritarian and democratic states. In particular, a ruthless Darwinian force rapidly eliminates those democratic states lacking the legislative capacity to flexibly adopt complete sets of vital economic institutions. In contrast to authoritarian states, whose leaders operate directly from initially evolved principles of social order and collective defense, any continued absence of a sophisticated legislative capacity in a democratic state will soon lead to the state's military downfall. In the ancient Greco-Roman West, for example, both the emergence of democratic government and the fall of the entire civilization were immediately preceded by the respective emergence and elimination of the vital economic institution of seignorage-bearing government money (Thompson, et al., Vol. II, Ch. 2). The political-economic difference between the rise and the fall -- and we shall repeatedly see the same phenomena recur in the current study -- is that while harsh evolutionary competition continually forced pragmatic policies on the rising states, subsequently, the intellectual leaders of the eventually dominant states were soon able to gain sufficient influence to burden their unsuspecting citizens with a devastating legislative ideology.

Empirical observations correspondingly reveal that the prospering early medieval trading towns, finding guild-organized investors contributing substantially to emergency local defense, competed for such investors by pragmatically offering them legislative and regulatory powers. The evolved towns thus universally granted guild investors essentially democratic political influence. This influence was efficiently spent obtaining the right to (1) administer local regulations, and (2) restrict one another's peacetime investments in coveted capital. These favors thus came, in effect, in exchange for their substantial wartime contributions (e.g., Unwin, Chs. III and IV, and R. Smith, Chs. I-V; Coornaert, Chs. II and III; Thrupp (1963), p. 263; Staley, Ch. II, esp. pp. 44 and 59). As a theoretically implied by-product, the corresponding investor-sensitivity of these democratic and legislatively pragmatic medieval towns led to extremely impressive economic growth in and around these towns.

B. Ancillary Defense Functions of Guilds

1. *Medieval Military Manpower: The Efficiency of Apprenticeship Laws.*
Ordinary human capital was too mobile to be a burden to medieval towns in the form of human capital that is substantially coveted by the potential foreign aggressors of these towns. Rather, militarily capable young men were significantly socially valuable as potential future draftees. This combination of mobility and fighting potential is probably what led towns to require trained apprentices to serve as dependent residents of a master, making the youth readily available for defense emergencies. It is similarly what led medieval and early-modern towns to almost universally establish laws lengthening an apprentice's years of service with his master substantially beyond that which free contracting would produce. Particularly revealing is the fact that although minimum local apprenticeship periods differed significantly across different industries, essentially all apprenticeship rules kept a young man bound to his master until he was at least 25 years of age (Thrupp (1963), p. 193), an age limit encountered in numerous modern systems of military

conscription. And women were essentially excluded from these guilds.

Also, since towns could easily refuse to deliver future favors to workers fleeing military emergencies, towns substantially withheld favors from their workers until a fairly distant future. Fleeing apprentices, and journeymen as well, would thereby surrender their initial entry fees, leaving behind their correspondingly accumulated investment in the rights to become a master (open a shop) at a substantially reduced tax rate. Once the attachment of shop ownership served to keep the person around during emergencies, no such bonding system was required. An analogous attachment, working through family ties, also helps rationalize the much-maligned laws of many mature guild towns allowing a master to pass on his privileged position only to his own sons (people who, because of familial attachments, are especially likely to meet the challenge of future emergencies.)

Note that this military-manpower-type of defense-externality, like the resulting apprenticeship law, is largely independent of the existence of guilds. Guilds had only a supportive role, an "ancillary function" (recalling Footnote #2) in administering these apprenticeship laws. Guilds existed primarily because of their social value as: (1) participants in the formation and administration of the commercial laws of the towns and (2) collectors and payers of defense-relevant taxes on non-human capital. Even in the complete absence of guilds, governments could -- and frequently did -- administer stringent laws providing for minimum apprenticeship periods. England, for example, imposed minimum 7 year apprenticeships on all towns in 1563, whether or not the towns had guilds. And these national apprenticeship laws were maintained all the way up to 1813, long after guilds had substantially disappeared in England. And Russia, for example, had apprenticeship laws long before she had guilds (Kellenbenz, p. 468).

What has been overlooked in the traditional literature on apprenticeship is that apprentices, being natural soldiers and therefore efficient draftees when providing emergency defense, have a natural incentive to avoid providing these under-compensated services. Accordingly, the apprentice's master was induced to carefully watch over what the labor law, through its extended periods of servitude, had induced to become his long-term personal investment.[41] Indicating the extent to which masters

---

[41]Adam Smith (Book I, Ch. X, Part II) naively considered the "artificially" long apprenticeship terms to be substantially monopsonistic. Subsequent authors have similarly regarded these lengthy apprenticeships as redistributive institutions facilitating the exploitation of politically unenfranchised labor, akin to the serfdom and debt-peonage that was indeed common among the peasants of the feudal countrysides. However, apprentices from the countryside were free sons of the nobility or free peasants rather than bound serfs. Therefore, given that competitively bargained up-front lump-sums were involved in the hiring of new apprentices, the statutory length of an apprenticeship could not have significantly affected the total opportunity cost of labor. Artificially long apprenticeships merely produced a higher average quality of such laborers, and therefore a higher negotiated average wage, with no substantial effect on the real cost of labor and therefore no significant internal allocational effect, other than through the important defense considerations discussed in the text.

The refined level of efficiency of these long-maligned apprenticeship institutions is another example of our theory in action, where the only democratic governments able to

received a substantial net return on their early investments in training apprentices, guild records abound with examples of masters going to great lengths to retrieve runaway apprentices (Thomas). Moreover, both the master and towns alike were careful to look into the "quality" of the prospective apprentice's family (its feudal nobility, chivalric character, etc.), sometimes rejecting the applicant for his unsuitability for future military combat, but never rejecting the applicant for his unsuitability for learning the trade (*ibid.*).

In any case, by first substantially delaying an apprentice's "freedom of the city", his freedom to enter the town's free labor force, and then inducing him to stay on as a journeyman through the near-term prospect of opening his own shop at a substantially sub-market entry fee, the medieval and early-modern town was greatly enhancing its region's supply of emergency draftees and thereby greatly facilitating its survival-determining defense commitment.

It was only during the Napoleonic era -- when western Continental countries began to rely on nationally educated, registered, and drafted armies -- that western European national apprenticeship laws, almost as quickly, came to an end. Nevertheless, at least up until very recently (the 1970s), modern nation states continued to withhold substantial future national benefits (the vote, subsidized advanced education, subsidized housing, etc.) from potential conscripts. The causes and consequences of the post-Vietnam-War reduction in the military participation of civilians will be discussed in the concluding sections of both Chapter 4 and Chapter 6.

2. *Maintaining an Egalitarian Distribution of Medieval Shop Ownership: The Efficiency of "Pre-Capitalistic" Fraternalism.* Regarding mastership, a medieval town's defense effort was similarly improved by strongly encouraging masters to own shops rather than working for other masters. The potential loss of one's shop then served the master's town by giving him an extra incentive to prepare for and participate in the defense of the town. Guild rules strictly limiting the size of each shop-owner's operation, along with correspondingly "fraternal" guild rules tending to keep masters in business despite the relative inefficiency of their shops, provided such an encouragement (e.g., Unwin Ch. 1; Black, Ch. 10). While mutual insurance is usually offered as an efficiency justification for this producer-egalitarianism, just like the generalized fraternalism found in the master-apprenticeship relation, efficient insurance payoffs come in the form of lump-sums, not entrepreneurial rights. This "pre-capitalistic" fraternalism was, however, important only when guilds provided direct military services, not merely financial assistance to the town.

Thus, almost immediately after confederational and national border defenses began to substantially replace the more local defense system (elaborated below in Section D.4), and thereby substantially obviate the direct military role of guilds in western Europe -- which occurred first in various 14th and 15th century confederational and national wars, then in the militarily most advanced 16th century nations such as Spain and Portugal, and finally throughout Europe over the next two

---

survive were those that were able to generate a level of institutional efficiency not even imagined by existing intellectuals.

centuries (e.g., Black, p. 144) -- the traditional fraternal structure of these guilds was correspondingly replaced through a sociologically jarring switch to a system of state acceptance, and subsequent mercantile encouragement, of large-scale enterprise (e.g., Black, Chs. 12 and 13, and Thrupp (1948), pp. 438-457).

This switch to a non-fraternal policy is popularly regarded as a birth of "capitalism" (e.g., Unwin, Ch. 1; Commons). However, the change actually represents little more than an efficient response to a switch from one defense system to another, a switch away from a largely local emergency defense system, one relying on the military participation of local civilians, to a confederational or national defense system that increasingly employed field armies and successively more expensive equipment. The change, albeit unnecessarily painful for labor as reflected in various strikes and riots (Unwin, *ibid.*), was thus a locally rapid institutional reversion to specialization in society's trading and defense functions, a return to the specialization that was characteristic of the decidedly non-fraternal Ancient Roman Empire.

Thus, early modern France, Iberia, and Holland, followed by large German Provinces such as Brandenberg-Prussia and Saxony -- which were relatively quick to sequentially follow England, Austria and northern Italy in developing specialized national or provincial militaries -- were also quick to allow high degrees of inequality between their masters. In sharp contrast, various developed regions of southern and western Germany, which were exceptionally slow to develop specialized national militaries because of the protection services offered by the Holy Roman Emperor during the 16th and most of the 17th centuries, were correspondingly stubborn in their "non-capitalistic" maintenance of exceptionally high levels of guild fraternity throughout the early-modern period (Walker, Black, Ch.10).[42]

It is therefore a mistake to follow modern economists and other social thinkers in regarding the early modern "capitalist" states as somehow more self-interested, forward-looking, "rational", adventurous, or in any fundamental sense economically superior to their predecessors or their more socially conservative neighbors. These larger states simply faced a different -- as it turned out, more modern -- defense technology. More generally, by failing to see "capitalism" as merely an incidental part of a larger set of efficient institutional responses to a special class of sometimes-historically relevant defense technologies, economists and related social thinkers have failed to see economic history as part of a repetitive evolutionary political-economic process, one in which they themselves play a pivotal role.

---

[42]Following the above argument, it is tempting to hypothesize that European guilds rose and fell with the social efficiency of local militia. However, local militia need not be organized along industrial lines; wholly integrated local militia could easily supply this military function, as they have throughout U.S. history, in the complete absence of guilds. More importantly, as already noted, European guilds were typically strengthened for extended periods following the emergence of professional armies in the early nation-state period. Hence, the direct military role of guilds must be regarded as purely ancillary to their primary functions. As we have already stressed, the primary functions of guilds include emergency military support of some kind, financial if not direct. This financial function, and wealthy guilds too, greatly expanded with the switch away from local defense systems.

C. The Interaction Between The Two Primary Functions of Guilds

We have already noted that modern systems of national taxation and finance, which served the defense-tax function for most late-19th and 20th century nations, have aggregate resource costs that appear to be substantially lower than the resource costs of nationally organizing and controlling a large number of local guilds. However, before concluding that guilds should have been abandoned with the early-modern emergence of modern systems of national taxation and finance, recall that guilds in the early-modern period were already historically organized to provide the first primary function, the prevention of highly inefficient civil administrations. It was therefore relatively inexpensive, especially in those early-modern nation-states lacking a civilly reverent bureaucracy, to have the guilds continue to provide a system of capital taxation and emergency military aid. All that was involved was to allow these administratively active investor-organizations to continue to restrict the entry of capital inputs into their industries in exchange for the guilds' developing expanded tax bases and expanded amounts of borrowing power that governments would tap during a subsequent emergency. This, of course, is what actually happened.

However, once guilds lost their essential administrative function in some of these newly emergent nation-states, which appropriately occurred with the development of civilly reverent bureaucracies, we shall see one pioneering government soon came to successfully replace their entire guild system with: (a) national capital taxation and (b) a new system of emergency military aid. Once its two parts were in place, the new solution obviated the substantial expenses of both local anti-monopoly regulation and interregional political bargaining during national emergencies. The substitution, we shall see, correspondingly had two separate components. The first had guild entry-restrictions partially replaced in the emerging nation states with incentive-equivalent capital taxes, and the second had guilds completely eliminated upon the complementary adoption of a substitute system of emergency finance.

A state suffers no net loss in its vital economic institutions when it introduces a modern system of emergency finance <u>before</u> it utilizes capital taxation to replace the previous system of guild military contributions as a payment for peacetime entry restrictions. Thus, as we shall see, when modern systems of emergency finance were introduced <u>before</u> the substitution of peacetime capital taxation for the previous system of guild military contributions and civilian investment-restrictions, the policy replacement occurred without serious incident. This will contrast greatly with the impact of the unconditional elimination of all guild investment restrictions and corresponding military contributions, which uniformly ended in sudden military disaster in investor-democratic states that had not, as a pre-condition, previously adopted an alternative system of emergency finance. Thus, we shall find a costly series of late-medieval and early-modern policy errors, ideologically based attacks on guilds or guild-entry restrictions that regularly reduced guild liquidity and incentives sufficiently to eliminate guild support during the subsequent military emergencies. These policy errors eventually produced a total switch in political and economic domination away from the initially faster growing, initially politically dominant, subsequently ideologized states of southern and central Europe and toward the northwestern, then more legislatively pragmatic, Anglo-Norman states.[43]

D. Actual Guild Policies and Related Institutions

We proceed now to examine the broad historical pattern of rise and decline of European guilds and related institutions in light of the above theories of both efficiency and institutional evolution.

1. The Ancient Societies of the Hellenic World and Rome

Since Ancient Hellenic and early Roman tradesmen, producers and merchants alike, were typically transient and had relatively small amounts of fixed capital, the cost of defending these capital stocks from both foreign aggressors and local bureaucrats must have been of minor importance.[44] Our efficiency theory therefore predicts an early absence of guilds. And indeed, there were no "guilds" in our sense of the word in early antiquity. Although there were organizations of craftsmen, they were granted neither administrative powers nor rights to restrict the entry of physical capital inputs; these organizations were involved only in the "mysteries" of their craft (Burford, pp. 155-56; Moore, p. 164; Finley, p. 158), apparently established to locally

---

[43]The trend actually began around 1300, the economic peak of the Middle Ages. The legislative pragmatism that had earlier led the sons of the chivalrous knights to develop the guild-run towns into prosperous city-states by the height of the middle ages was declining throughout the subsequent period, eroded in the especially church-influenced European countrysides by ideologization through Thomist Aristotelianism. Section D.4 will elaborate on the disastrous 14th and 15th century consequences of this sort of religious ideology among the powerful lords. Soon thereafter, we shall see in Section D.5, a new set of ideology-based policy disasters emerged. The late 15th and early 16th century Italian disasters occurred through a different ideology, the intellectual elitism of the High Renaissance. Spanish and German catastrophes then occurred in the early-modern period out of the harshly ideological Reformation-Counter Reformation dialogues. Holland, France and the provinces of Austria began to suffer the effects of laissez faire ideology even before the 19th century. Throughout this string of early-modern disasters, the relatively practical and anti-intellectual English -- whose civilly reverent constitutional mind-set was maintained by the power of the Beowolf, King Arthur, Robin Hood, and anti-Papal Christian legends among both their largely Anglican ruling classes and their Protestant Dissenters -- were the military beneficiaries of a long series of neighboring policy blunders.

[44]While tradesmen often had several slaves, the low capital value of these slaves (Finley, Ch. IV), implying a near-equality of wages to subsistence meant that a craftsman's tax-relevant, or "coveted", capital stock in the form of slave capital was typically insignificant.
    Regarding the merchant inventories that were to later impose substantial defense-externalities on medieval towns, the length of the wars required to acquire one of these large ancient states was sufficient to enable the state to export or consume these inventories before they could be substantially acquired by a foreign aggressor.
    While large scale projects, e.g., mining projects, obviously utilized large amounts of fixed capital, the government was typically a partner, if not a full owner, in these ventures.

disseminate and protect technological information.[45]

As the Roman Empire matured, the typical tradesman's fixed capital investment grew to significance. Correspondingly, primitive guilds developed from the 2nd century onward. Craftsmen organizations, known as *collegia sodilitia*, became actively involved in selecting Roman towns officials, in particular the *Aediles*, to help protect these fixed investments from bureaucratic expropriation. Regarding military defense, guild members, as others, paid the general property tax (Seligman, pp. 36-37).[46] Therefore, as our efficiency theory predicts, the *collegia* restricted neither entry nor the use of capital by their members (Burford, pp. 155-56; Finley, p. 158).

2. The Dark Ages

The exceptionally high military defense costs stemming from Rome's collapse caused merchants to suffer large reductions in their fixed capital stocks and, in line with our theory, to transform their relatively expensive, domestic-expropriation-protecting, primitive guilds into simple, church-dependent, "fraternities" (e.g., Black, pp. 4-5). These ancillary Church fraternities, as well as the fraternities stemming from Germanic tradition, engaged mostly in ceremonial communal feasting and mutual oaths (Coornaert, p. 34), thus existing mainly to mutually insure one another against unexpected hardships and carry out their ancient, pre-guild, function of internally disseminating trade information among their members.[47]

---

[45]Since such information services are fairly easily provided by alternative existing institutions (e.g., local schools and governments), the Greek mystery cults appear to have maintained little in the way of primary social activities and therefore do not appear to qualify as "guilds" according to our definition in footnote 2.

[46]The Roman tax on trade capital was collected through the *collegia*. *Collegia* craftsmen were required to use their skills and tools to undertake certain public works. As might be expected, membership in the *collegia* became compulsory in the later Empire.

[47]The relatively high defense costs characterizing the western European dark age meant that relatively high capital tax rates were in order. The uncomfortably church-dependent Germanic invaders (the Ostrogoths and Visigoths, the Burgundians and Lombards, and the Saxons), all setup property tax systems, known in England through the Saxon Chronicles as the "Fumage" (hearth tax), and known through the Church to be essentially continuations of the old Roman property tax systems throughout southern Europe. The less Church-dependent invaders, those remaining closer to their ancient homelands (viz., the Angles, Franks, Danes, Normans and Suebians), were less committed to Church institutions and thereby able to substitute property-based military obligations or their monetary equivalent (e.g., England's "Scutage") for property taxes while enhancing investment dis-incentives by granting the local lords relatively temporary property rights. (The fact that temporary rights help to create an efficient capital tax has been pointed out, and applied to the case of the Spanish economienda, by Batchelder and Sanchez.) The French property tax, or *taille* was introduced only after the area was stabilized under the decreasingly Frankish Capetian dynasty. While these Germanic tax institutions are usually taken to be a part of "feudalism", we shall soon see that what basically defined the feudal system was its radically decentralized defense technology.

As outlined above in Section I.B.4, the 7th through the 10th centuries saw a gradual evolution of a new form of commercial organization centered upon the guild. The Byzantium-supported coastal Italian towns adopting this new form were uniformly towns experiencing large increases in foreign trade. These trading towns grew up not as centers of production but rather as storage and trading centers for travelling merchants. Because of the positive correlation between transportation distances and the optimal qualities of the traded goods (Adam Smith, Book IV, Ch. I, pp. 412-3, and Alchian and Allen), most of the goods traded by the merchants of these towns were of relatively high quality. This, and the increased volume of trade, must have made it relatively difficult for the contemporary, non-trade-oriented, Church bureaucracies to monitor the qualities of merchant deliveries, as well as to resist the temptation of redistributing resources to more worthwhile causes than the continuing enrichment of merchants. To effect laws reducing the high potential bureaucratic error and expropriation, investors in these freely competing towns were given new political rights. In particular, the emerging merchant-democracies, which organized into separate merchant guilds to represent the interests of (and accept responsibility for) each trade, appointed knowledgeable guild members rather than counts or clerics to their town legislatures and bureaucracies. Thus, with internally coveted capital stocks of the towns during this period predominantly in the form of merchant inventory holdings, town regulations and contract laws were established and administered by merchants as well as defense-providing local lords (e.g., Martines, p. 47 and Gross, Ch. 1).

In return for their new political, legal, and administrative rights, the town's investors were obliged to pay the local lords and king occasional lump-sum-taxes, or specific services, usually collected during local defense emergencies (e.g., Black, Ch. IV). Guilds were vital local institutions because the overlord was often militarily unreliable and guilds were the only local institutions available to commit substantial resources to the emergency defense of the new trade centers. Viewed from the perspective of Appendices B.2 and B.3, what the guilds obtained for their wartime contributions of money and manpower was the right to a self-administered form of capital regulation, and a corresponding freedom from peacetime local capital taxation, in order to efficiently restrict their peacetime capital stocks.

Because the *raison d'etre* of these towns was trade, all that was needed for this new organizational form to spread throughout Europe was a new economic reason for large commercial towns. This was provided by the dark-age evolution of chivalry and feudal orders, and a corresponding increase in the security of property and key European trade routes starting late in the 10th century (e.g., van Werveke, pp. 8-14).

3. The Growth Boom of the Later Middle Ages: 1000-1300

a. *The Blossoming of Medieval Guilds.* As described above, this rapid decrease in defense costs in western Europe in the 11th and 12th centuries produced the rapid growth of guild-supporting trading towns observed throughout the period (van Werveke, pp. 12-13). Urban production, or "crafts", which started to become significant in western Europe late in the 11th century, grew steadily until early in the 14th century, generating a correspondingly steady growth in both technology and fixed urban capital (e.g., L. White, pp. 157-171.) Therefore, applying our statical efficiency theory, because of the unavailability of competent civilly reverent, bureaucracies throughout the middle ages, it became increasingly efficient for the already established oligarchy of merchants and landlords to extend both political rights and an administrative role to craftsmen. In fact, the first politically and administratively influential craft guilds appeared early in the 12th century. Like the earlier merchant guilds, the impressive economic successes of the Italian towns that first admitted craft guilds led these new guilds to spread rapidly northward throughout western and central Europe during the 12th and 13th centuries (e.g., Black, p. 6).

Our analysis of the form of efficient local taxation during the height of the middle ages differs according to the number of competing landlords residing in a given town, and according to the political autonomy of the town.[48]

b. *Later Medieval Towns With Many Landlords.* The large 12th and 13th century increases in guild-owned fixed capital stocks (Thrupp (1971)) substantially increased the defense cost to the other guild investors and local landlords collectively protecting the town (van Werveke, pp. 9-15, p. 37). As we have argued, without some form of capital taxation, private investors in fixed capital in medieval towns with many landlords would not internalize the town's correspondingly increased defense cost as part of their private cost and thereby over-invest in fixed capital. Thus, in accord with our democratic efficiency theory, restrictions as to the maximum amount of fixed capital each investor could own became a standard guild policy.[49] And craft guilds, soon upon obtaining political representation during the 12th century, became much more entry-restrictive than had the earlier, less fixed-capital-intensive, merchant guilds (Thrupp (1948), pp. 92-102; Hibbert pp. 193-94; Coornaert, Ch. 2;

---

[48]Royal taxes on fixed capital, reflecting the king's cost of defense from area-wide (or multiple-town) attacks were appropriately maintained throughout each mature medieval kingdom. Now essentially all of a medieval king's tax collectors became some sort of tax-farmer, a reflection of the general lack of civil reverence among medieval bureaucrats. (For a detailed example, see Templeman.) Because tax-farmers, even when officially entitled only to lump-sums, collected more readily from wealthy taxpayers, a wealth tax was implicit. This worked together with the traditional royal capital taxes, such as England's originally feudal (Poston, p. 173) tallage and France's *taille*, to produce a general royal capital tax.

[49]In the countryside, where a single local lord both owned and protected capital from specifically local attacks, lower-level capital accumulation could efficiently be, and was, contractually discouraged through normal share-tenancy agreements. This is still true today. Like most of the other economic institutions discussed in this book, these share-tenancy agreements have long troubled economists, whose standard model regards such fixed-sharing agreements as generating insufficient investment incentives. This again ignores the existence of defense-externalities that tenants impose upon their lords.

The "countryside" differs from "cities with few landlords" in our analysis in that the lords of the latter use essentially all of the independently produced local output and neither import nor export these goods. A unique type of monopsony problem then arises. This problem is discussed in our next subsection.

Postan pp. 214-218).   Although some merchant guilds in the same period also introduced significant fixed capital restrictions, those were guilds whose fixed capital stocks had grown to significance (Thrupp (1948), p. 207).

Town governments typically held guilds responsible for the monopolizing attempts of their members.   For example, English and French guilds were required to elect wardens responsible to the town government.   These wardens monitored the compliance of guild members with the town-approved guild regulations, particularly those on minimum product quality.   In this way guild members could neither surreptitiously nor collusively lower their product quality, given the controlled nominal price.   Typical of the deception-preventing quality regulation were the restrictions on the London clothing guilds of the 14th century prohibiting the sale of "patched up work" passed off as new by their members. Regarding more commonly observable quality restrictions, these guild members were required to purchase raw materials in higher quality markets rather than from streethawkers (Renard, pp. 34-35; Johnson, pp. 116-17).   Such restrictions were clearly intended to prevent extreme, implicitly collusive, forms of visible quality deterioration. The rules still left plenty of room for visible quality competition to clear the market. Typical of the regulations in which the two forms of quality regulation occurred together were the restrictions on the London poulters requiring members to purchase their inputs at times of the week when the quality of the produce was abnormally high (Jones, Ch. 7).[50]

Guilds had many regulations serving to reduce the town's capital stock.   In addition to substantial entry fees, the long minimum apprenticeship periods rationalized above indirectly reduced the stock of capital because one could not set up a shop without first becoming a master. Similarly, the medieval master-egalitarianism rationalized above -- through rules against the ownership of multiple shops, rules against producing outside of a master's shop, and rules against producing in the physical absence of a master[51] -- also worked to reduce the town's coveted capital stock.

Finally, for production requiring relatively large amounts of machinery, like weaving, there were strict rules directly restricting the maximum number of machines a single master could employ (DuPlessis-Howell).

---

[50]Such observed minimum-quality regulations are what led the school of social historians mentioned in the Introduction to believe that guilds existed _primarily_ to induce potentially deceptive, but otherwise freely competitive, sellers to supply an efficient product quality. We have already noted that asserting this quality-assurance rationale as sufficient to explain the existence of guilds has been appropriately discarded not because it couldn't explain the visibility of some of the quality minima but because it couldn't explain the government-sponsored restrictions on the entry of high-quality capital inputs.   These social thinkers, although understandably somewhat unhappy with the traditional monopoly story, were simply unable to provide an alternative explanation of the observed entry restrictions.

[51]There were also rules limiting the use of labor of various qualities in a given shop. These regulations served the added function of enforcing the minimum quality restrictions necessary to effect anti-monopolistic real prices while simultaneously protecting several militarily-valued producers from being driven out-of-business by a few, slightly-lower-cost, producers.

The knee-jerk response of post-mercantilist economists to any efficiency-explanation of existing interventionist policies has been the claim that observed policies are better explained by a political-inefficiency model. However, the latter claim is theoretically unsupported in that it does not emerge from a political-economic model featuring individually rational decisionmakers suffering from informational deficiencies that systematically lead to the specifically observed policy regularities. Moreover, as stressed in the Introduction above, the familiar political-inefficiency, or "special-interest-capture", model, is inconsistent with the observed ceilings on real prices and cannot conceivably extend over to Royal Towns such as Winchester to explain the presence there of the same set of guild institutions.

The same critique, we shall now see, applies more generally to towns with small numbers of landlords.

c. *Later Medieval Towns With Few Landlords.* A few local lord-protectors were often, along with the church, the only landlords in small medieval towns.[52] These local landlords were also the principle customers of their local merchants and craftsmen. Nevertheless, such highly lord-dependent sellers were eventually organized into ordinary guilds during our period. As already noted, the classical monopoly explanation for the existence of guilds is extremely implausible in such consumer-dominated environments. Moreover, the defense-externality also becomes smaller and smaller as the individual lord becomes a larger and larger part of the market. This is because a freely contracting landlord who internalizes more and more of the additional defense cost created by new investments as the lord's ownership of the area approaches 100%, will contractually pass on such costs to his tenants. Although the defense-externality from new investments thus shrinks to zero, another problem in free-market efficiency simultaneously expands, a problem correctable by the same guild-type entry-restrictions that corrected the defense-externality problem in the many-landlord case. In particular, as an individual landlord consumes an increasing portion of the total output of the guilds, the landlord has an increasing incentive to encourage over-investment in guild capital by charging lower -- even subcompetitive -- rents to marginal entrants into local trades.

Consider a hypothetical guild town with a single landlord, who is also the principal guild customer. There is no defense-externality in this case because the single lord's rental agreement, perhaps a capital-tax agreement, will reflect the

---

[52]In Coventry, for example, the great majority of craftsmen, and some merchants, paid rent to either the local earl or to the prior, although, a few of the more wealthy merchants were landlords themselves (Harris; Adams). A 1553 survey of Birmingham shows that even at that late date nearly all the city merchants paid rent to Lord Birmingham (Holt). Palliser and Creswell tell us a similar story about York and Exeter, respectively.

In contrast, London had many great merchant landlords, as well as numerous aristocratic landowners (Thrupp (1948)). Also, in the relatively large royal city of Winchester, the rent of the seven great fiefs, which were the king and six church officers, accounted for only 30% of the total rents in the city (Biddle). There were numerous other landlords who were primarily members of the merchant and cloth guilds.

locality's entire cost of defending whatever durable improvements the tenants make to the property. But the landlord is unable to make future rent-commitments other than through long-term rental agreements with existing tenants. Existing tenants therefore have fixed long-term rental agreements in order to protect their specific investments from discriminatory rent increases. In such a case, the landlord would always offer sub-competitive rents to future, extra-marginal, craftsmen because attracting extra tenant-investors will drive down the product prices charged by the previous investors.[53] To remove the resulting threat of jointly inefficient over-investment, landlords and guilds could cooperatively agree to reduce investment in that town by introducing guild entry-restrictions.

Capital-restrictive guilds thus served the smaller medieval towns by counteracting the above tendency toward substantial over-investment. The result, of course, was that entry-restrictive guilds were an essentially universal efficiency-feature of later medieval town governments, both large and small.[54]

Guilds, however, came to these lord-consumer-dominated towns at a slow, relatively leisurely, pace. What explains the casual evolutionary pace is that guilds were not <u>vital</u> to these naturally authoritarian towns. Such towns could, and did, survive well for a long time without guilds. As expected, guild evolution was fast <u>only</u> in merchant-dominated towns, where guilds provided a vital defense function for the locality.

      d. *Trade Fairs*. A medieval analogue to low-defense-cost, free-trading, Amsterdam in the early-modern period and Hong Kong in the modern one is found in the famous medieval trade fairs.

Every year, during certain seasons, some medieval lords would open temporary markets, offering both internal and external protection to the traders visiting their markets. Like the few-landlords case discussed above, the contracts offered to the various participants reflected the lords' defense costs; so substantial taxes were not required to internalize these defense costs. However, unlike the town-case discussed above, since the sponsoring lords were <u>not</u> major buyers in these markets, there is no offsetting monopsony to rationalize the existence of guilds. This is important because it allows us to use our theory to predict a medieval trading environment in which

---

[53]The more familiar consumer monopsony effect, which <u>lowers</u> factor entry below the efficient level when there are increasing costs to the industry, does not apply here because the essentially dynamic nature of the sequence of rental agreements creates a dynamic equivalent of an output-subsidized decreasing-cost industry. As output gradually expands over time with a succession of profitable entrants (who implicitly receive the equivalent of an entry-subsidy), subsequent entry is explicitly subsidized in order to reduce the implicit subsidy of the early entrants. Actual industry costs of course, can be assumed here to be constant.

[54]Note that our monopsony-induced over-investment argument for guild entry restrictions works in a different way than our defense-externality argument because, as indicated in the following paragraph of the text, the monopsony-effect induces an entirely different evolutionary time-path than the defense-externality.

guilds would be <u>absent</u>. Indeed, guild regulations and contracting procedures were uniformly <u>unwelcomed</u> at the fairs. These were genuine free-trade centers.

Moreover, our theory can be used to predict, as for Amsterdam and Hong Kong, that these exceptionally low-defense-cost trading centers would simultaneously feature low prices <u>and</u> have minor economic influence (Poston, pp. 208-09). In contrast, standard economics discussions, which both ignore defense costs and enthusiastically endorse all such free-trade centers, leave as a paradox (or inconsistency) the fact that these relatively low-price, free-trade, institutions did not simply spread to where they drove the higher-price, more regulatory, institutions to near extinction.

e. *Autonomous Towns.* Certain guilds may have been <u>efficiently</u> monopolistic in that monopoly guilds in export industries in autonomous, or politically independent, towns may have provided the best method of extracting monopoly rents from foreign customers, including customers residing in the surrounding countryside. However, wherever there was a well-informed central authority over both the town and the potential victims, such a possibility would not be consistent with our general political theory because the central authority would internalize the welfare loss resulting from the monopoly. Indeed, both English and French monarchs frequently stepped-in to lower the local export prices, these monarchs having assumed the right to revoke the charters of both towns and guilds, and occasionally exercising this right, in response to unauthorized price increases (see, e.g., Jones pp. 109-111; Renard, p. 49, for English guilds; and Coornaert, p. 93, for French guilds.) The French king's monitoring of guilds was particularly comprehensive. He placed his own representatives in the guild towns. Before long, the approval of these royal represent-atives was needed by French guilds for any price increase.

Nevertheless, for politically independent towns, the potential wealth transfers to the town from foreign buyers would induce the internally efficient town to either: (1) adopt an export tax to restrict production in an optimally monopolistic fashion, or (2), for sufficiently export-specialized industries, allow guilds to impose labor as well as capital restrictions in order to approximate a simple monopoly solution and save the town the cost of computing and collecting the welfare-equivalent production or export taxes. Since the monopoly-inspired general input restrictions in either case should be complemented by special capital restrictions in order to internalize the defense-externality to the town as a whole, politically independent towns should have <u>both</u> monopolistic guilds <u>and</u> some form of separate local capital-tax.

Therefore, in medieval Germania (i.e., Germany, Austria, Switzerland and northern Italy), it was internally efficient for the many uniquely independent city-states or provinces to adopt <u>both</u> local capital taxes <u>and</u> monopoly guilds in their heavily export-oriented industries. Indeed, during the late middle ages, most large northern Italian and German towns, such as Florence, Augsberg and Hamburg, were distinguished by their support of <u>both</u> monopolizing, all-input-restricting, guilds in export industries <u>and</u> substantial municipal capital taxes. Cologne and Nuremberg, which had no property taxes, achieved the same result by complementing their qualitatively ordinary guild policy with a policy allowing guilds to set simple cartel outputs in their chief export industries (Irsigler, von Stromer, respectively).

4. The Calamitous Conclusion of the Middle Ages: 1300-1485

The remarkable European economic growth from the 11th through the 13th centuries did not fail to effect the education-providing intellectual cartel centered in economically dominant Italy. It was during this period that the Roman Catholic Church escaped from its traditional dependence on the state, a dependence which had made it a growingly valuable supplier of basic education and social services for the towns and of bureaucracies for the countrysides. Predictably exploiting its position as a monopoly supplier of basic education, the late 11th and 12th century Church successfully worked to establish itself (through a misrepresentation of feudal tradition that has been call the "Papal Revolution") as an arbiter of European political legitimacy and provider of legal services (e.g., Berman). This entry of the growingly influential medieval Church into the fields of secular politics and law might have had little effect if the military technology had not also been changing.

The prominently growing European capital stock over the 12th and 13th centuries invited the development of new siege technologies. Originally coming from similarly growing, but more this-worldly, 11th century China, first the trebuchet and then the cannon were fine-tuned (e.g., Oman, pp. 48-51; de Vries), largely through French metallurgy, into weapons that increasingly destroyed the viability of the previous defense system. In this previous system, as we have already noted, guilds protected the city walls while knights and castles protected the feudal countryside. With the trebuchet making possible the hurling of heavy and often biologically devastating objects (especially diseased animals) over the walled defenses and the early cannon beginning to threaten the walls themselves, the defense systems of the 13th and 14th centuries increasingly demanded territorial armies that would quickly engage the enemy in the field and occasionally combine with the armies of similarly threatened neighbors to intercept foreign armies that invaded their collective territory.[55] A reflection of the growing defense problems during the 13th century,

---

[55]Under the earlier, feudalism-generating, defense technology, such horizontal defense alliances were often of negative value -- both private and social -- to the neighboring armies. This was because the high cost of internal organization meant that the typical aggressor was content to take a small number of enclaves, usually a single territory, or "duchy". Since the territorial neighbors were thus typically substitutes to a potential aggressor, it was typically better for a local duke to provide a vigorous defense of only his own duchy, thereby inducing the aggressor to search for a weaker territory. Feudal military obligations were thus traditionally restricted to a single duchy. The negative externality that each duchy's defense system imposed on its neighbors therefore generated a much greater total defense effort than would have a cooperative, and relatively costly, "united we stand", defense effort.

Late 9th and early 10th century France, which began united by the Treaty of Verdun, thus could not defend itself against the attacks of its neighbors until it <u>decentralized</u> into relatively small, defensible, "feudal", duchies. Chivalry, and correspondingly serious oaths of fealty to the duke by the castle managers, or "counts", and related oaths by knights to their overlords, were necessarily evolved to prevent the system from over-decentralizing during military emergencies. (A single castle was not a viable political unit because it offered little in the way of trade-route or crop protection.) Monarchs were only formal lords over the

besides an enlargement of the typical political unit, was the steady advance in the height and design-sophistication of castle and city walls (Oman, Ch. 2).

But the huge expansion of warfare and misery during the subsequent "age of upheaval" was certainly not inevitable. The feudal institutions that supported the previous defense technology were appropriately breaking down throughout the 13th century, being steadily replaced by tradition-breaking interventions such as the lengthy emergency tax increases of temporarily authoritarian kings (Reynolds) possessing substantial mercenary armies (Wise, Ch. 1). Indeed, there can be little doubt that such a centralizing, emergency-finance-enhancing, field-army-expanding, set of political-economic institutions had become vital to many of the dukes and kings of the 14th and 15th centuries. The fact that appropriately de-feudalizing, defense-enhancing, 13th century centralizations had occurred with little or no conflict suggests that the final switch to centralized, modern type, nation states could have been similarly accomplished with no substantial increase in warfare.

Indeed, as elaborated in Chapter 5 (Section I.G), substantial and persistent information differences are required before rationally negotiating states will engage in a series of socially costly wars. But an education-providing monopoly church was supplying a feudalism-supporting ideology; and ideology is what we are using to generate systematic information differences. So it should come as no surprise that the monopoly church of the 13th century increasingly disapproved of the vital centralizations of the western European dukes and kings. Yet, throughout this prosperous century, the increasingly attended Church was growing more self-confident and influential. There were the successes of several Crusades, the continued "successes" of various Popes in radically decentralizing the German Empire, and finally the secularization of the interests of the Church Dominicans, culminating in the Thomist Aristotelianism of the last quarter of the 13th century. Thus, in contrast to the centralizing 13th century kings, the Church had been increasingly viewing itself as the appropriate central authority over a feudally organized, otherwise decentralized, Europe.

In other words, while the pragmatically evolving ideal of the late 13th century kings was one of a Europe composed of centralized, modern-type, nation-states, the intellectually evolving European ideal of the Church was one of an Aristotle-inspired "Papal Monarchy" (Flick, Vol. 1, Ch. 1). Perhaps nothing more vividly illustrates the

---

dukes; they were so legislatively constrained that their defense-commitment-ability was severely limited, and, even in the 11th and 12th centuries, their military role was largely restricted to leading Church-announced Crusades against threats to the entire civilization.

In any case, the substantially increased capital value of each duchy over the period, 1000-1300, combined with the significantly higher overhead cost and effectiveness of siege equipment, meant that neighboring duchies in the year 1300 were much more likely to be treated as complements by an attacking army than they were in the year 1000. So, cooperative, "united-we-stand" defense systems had, once again, become appropriate, if not vital, to the various duchies of a given nation. While technologically easy to supply institutionally, the almost unlimited emergency powers that monarchs possessed before the age of feudalism would have to somehow be restored, despite the resistance of the compensable barons and dukes and the not-so-compensatable Church.

conflict than the forced physical relocation of the Papacy to Avignon by the French King in response to a 1302 Papal refusal to accommodate a non-discriminating levy of war-emergency taxes on the Church in France (*ibid.*, pp. 24-25). Even before this "Babylonian Captivity", and the corresponding French slant to Papal policies over the following 75 years, the strengthening 13th century kings had been posing an increasing challenge to the secularizing religious authorities.

The threat to Church revenues was obvious. Empirically, the Popes needed to look no further than precociously centralizing England's attack on the independence and legal function of the Church, not to mention her increasing failure to pay the Pope his annual taxes and "provisions" (Keen). Theoretically, as we have already noted, a monopoly church is much better off selling its services to a large number of decentralized, competing, buyers than to a few, relatively monopsonistic, buyers. One might counter here that any surviving seller with as many buyers and, as much practical experience as the Church would, following Section I of Chapter 1, be able to win its various local bilateral monopolies and therefore have nothing to fear from a few centralizations among its several buyers. But, even if a monopoly church <u>were</u> able to win its local bilateral monopolies, larger-scale local buyers would be more able to afford the overhead cost of setting up their own, domestically protected, legal and bureaucratic systems, as had uniquely occurred in uniquely centralized England. Centralization among the buyers would therefore generate lower demand prices for the Church's services. Moreover, the increasingly national armies of Europe meant an expanding demand for an ethic of civil obedience and national patriotism, an ethic that we have already identified as being in conflict with the Christian universalism of the increasingly this-worldly Catholic church.

So, when relatively effectively democratic, centralizing and field-army-efficient, 14th century England began to assert property claims against her more traditional, more feudally defended, neighbors, suitable lump-sum transfers, accompanied by efficient and peaceful political centralization, rarely settled the issue. Rather, Church ideology worked to resist the proposed centralizations and a series of wars became a near-inevitability.[56]

---

[56]There are several ways to generate a jointly rational, yet jointly costly, war once we introduce suitable information differences. Regarding jointly costly revolutionary wars, Chapter 5, Section I.G presents one way. Another, relatively unsystematic, kind of warfare is generated in the introduction to Appendix B.3. Yet another, which includes a benevolent but ideologized third party as a potential peacemaker, is as follows: Say an objective potential aggressor stands to receive $100 of real benefits from acquiring control of and reorganizing a neighboring, decentralized, church-ideologized state. Church ideology ignores this benefit, but does see, say, $40 in Church rents and psychic benefits if it maintains a decentralized polity. Although the threatened state would actually benefit from the change, following the Church, this ideologized state attaches, say, a negative $201 value to centralization and does not believe it is really worth the cost of the pending, 50-50 war, to the potential aggressor. For simplicity, we assume that the threatened state would incur no resource costs in the war. Since the potential centralizer cannot economically compensate the ideologized state in order to avoid warfare, unless the church tells it otherwise, the uncompensatable state will fight to maintain its status quo. In pre-war bargaining, the Church allows that it is willing to pay $40

Thus, relatively centralized and field-army-efficient England could find no lump sum that would, in 1337, compensate the property-losing leaders of Church-ideologized, feudalism-supporting, France. The "Hundred Years War" lasted 116 years; and even that did not resolve the basic dispute. Even the centralizing inspiration of Joan of Arc and the most advanced and expensive artillery in mid-15th century Europe would not centralize France. It took, along with a sharp decrease in the Church's support for feudalism, a fanatic centralizer in the person of Louis XI (the "spider", d. 1483) to finally, by the end of his life, through guile and money, maneuver the duchies of France into a unified nation-state with a centralized administration and put an end to the suffering of late medieval France (Calmette).

Essentially the same series of long and devastating civil wars occurred in Spain, with England and her Spanish allies again consistently supporting centralization and the Church again supporting feudalism, until a similar series of late 15th century centralizations (featuring the marriage of Ferdinand of Aragon and Isabelle of Castille) created a nation-state (e.g., Altamira, MacKay). Tellingly, the truces that occurred in these wars roughly coincide with the truces elsewhere in Europe during the 1300-1485 period. We shall soon return to this revealing coincidence.

The best that the relatively Church-influenced cities of Italy and southwestern Germany could do during the 14th and 15th centuries was expand to where they had strong provincial defense systems for their inevitably independent city-states or duchies. Although frequent military confederations between these areas were attempted, they systematically failed as a result of Church-fostered intrigues (e.g., Waugh, Flick, Vol. I, pp. 210-224). Perhaps the simplest manifestation of the basic conflict responsible for the steady Italian warfare during this period was the predominant dispute between the Church-supported Guelphs of relatively democratic and decentralized Florence (and, to a lesser degree, Venice) and the Emperor-supported Ghibbelines of the extraordinarily centralized duchy of Milan (e.g., Ady, p. 206). Unlike the rest of Europe, the extremely strong influence of the Church in northwestern and southern Italy left it relatively decentralized, and so it became a prime target for its centralizing neighbors in the late 15th and early 16th centuries.

---

to the centralizer if it will cease its aggression. If the potential aggressor refuses the offer, it will still have to win a war, with a success probability of one-half, before it can implement its centralized policy. Say the cost of war to the potential aggressor is $9. Then, even though it passes up the $40 peace-subsidy and incurs an extra $9 in resource costs, the risk-neutral state (i.e., its Pascalian leader) is willing to incur these certain losses for the 50-50 chance of the $100 gain. Before concluding that war here is inevitable, consider the possibility that the aggressor state offers the Church $99 to advise its client state to accept centralization and thereby incur the $40 loss in rent and psychic benefits. If the Church were not benevolent, the payment would be accepted and there would be no war. But a benevolent church, which not only believes that there are net social costs of the centralization, suffers, say to the extent of two-third of the loss, when one of its clients suffers. So, the Church-perceived $99 loss to the potential aggressor represents a cost of $66 to the Church. This means that the net value of the potential aggressor's offer is less than $33. Since the aggressor state's $9 cost of the war only costs the Church $6, the Church cannot be compensated for its $40 loss and rationally supports the war.

Although the flatlands of southwestern Germany were similarly induced to abandon their various leagues and decentralize, the eventual acceptance of the idea of centralization by the German Electors in the 1480s (Tout) finally came to constitutionally offer these previously warring German "free cities" sufficiently centralized protection that the cities were able to survive through the early modern period with essentially 13th century domestic institutions (Walker).

In any case, Germany, like Italy, was in an almost constant state of civil war from 1300 to 1485, the typical battle being between Church-supported feudal Electors and a centralization-seeking league of cities supported by the Holy Roman Emperor and his centralized imperial duchies (Flick, Vol. I, Ch. 2 and 7).

The Church's systematic support for feudalism and weak monarchs during the middle ages is well-known. However, as for similar ideology-based actions in history, the Church is not recognized as a demand-creating intellectual cartel that has acquired an undue influence over its society by acquiring a basic teaching role in that society. Perhaps it strikes too close to home. In any case, what tells us that an intellectual monopoly is what was behind these wars is the precipitous fall-off in the frequency of such wars during eras in which the monopoly was peculiarly weak.

The "Great Schism", which ran from 1378 to 1409, represented a period in which there were two competing Papacies in the West, one in Avignon and the other in Rome. The religions competed in that each state could choose its own Papacy. And it was the same basic thought system. So the price received by each Papacy substantially fell (e.g., Flick, Vol. I, p. 280; Keen, p. 213). There was simply less profit to running a religion. Sensibly, then, the two sets of Cardinals met in 1408 and formally decided to end the self-defeating Schism in 1409. Although it took a few years for a single Pope to securely emerge from these religious councils, the Schism in the Church was over. Now, since investments in demand-creation are of lower profit in a lower-profit activity, and since the returns to such investments must be shared with a competitor in a duopoly relative to a monopoly market, economic theory tells us that there will be much less investment in industry-demand-creation under duopoly than under monopoly. This implies that the extent to which the Church was willing to share the costs of warfare with a client state in order to create a higher aggregate demand for their legal and political services was much lower during the Great Schism. In fact, the frequency of warfare dramatically fell everywhere in Europe during the years of peace and truce, 1378-1409!

The few wars that did occur during those years, e.g., a war expanding the Swiss Federation, were brief and mainly between non-feudal states, e.g., the Swiss and the Austrians. And, tellingly, although a locally monopolistic Church was the target of the initial uprising by a neighbor of the original Swiss confederation, the desperate Abbot appealed to secular powers such as Austria -- not a Pope -- in his attempt to quell the revolt (McCracken).

The absence of warfare does not mean that the gradual trend towards centralization was abated. In fact, it met less resistance during the Great Schism. It was during this period, and only during this period, for example, that the traditionally Church-supported defenders of Scandinavian feudalism ceased their fighting and peacefully merged themselves into a pan-Scandinavian union, the ill-fated Union of Kalmar (e.g., Koht).

Thus a whole spate of old-style European Wars broke out after the agreement to resume the Papal monopoly. Regarding the Prague, where, consistently, during the Schism, the University had been allowed to become an important center of religious toleration and a Wycliffe-style movement toward bible-based national churches for centralized governments outside of England, the Council of Constance that was finally charged with selecting a new Pope decided to burn the movement's intellectual leaders at the stake. This touched of over 20 years of bloody civil wars in Bohemia (the "Hussite Wars"). Such once-again-profitable, monopolizing predation did not enhance the Church's popularity at other continental universities.[57]

These less directly confrontational universities had been weakening the Church's intellectual cartel throughout the 14th and early 15th centuries. Renaissance scientism, the anti-Aristotelian nominalism of William of Ockham and the philosoph-

---

[57]A second outbreak of peace occurred in the decade from 1453 to 1462. If our hypothesis is correct -- that internally rational Church obstructionism was the root cause of the long rash of civil wars that bedeviled the closing two centuries of the middle ages -- then what would explain this period of domestic European peace would similarly be something that temporarily distracted the Church from her ongoing battle against political centralization. A source of such a distraction is easily found. 1453 was, of course, the year of the landmark shock to the West in which the neighboring Byzantine Empire was taken by the Ottoman Turks in their surprising sack of Constantinople. The Church then suddenly faced an even greater challenge than domestic political centralization. Domestically warring states would certainly not be an advantage to the obviously concerned Church. Although the regions that did not neighbor the eastern boundary showed little concern -- as evinced by their total lack of response to new Church appeals and subsidies to engage in a crusade against the Turks -- the Church obviously did (Flick, Chs. 26 and 27). So it would have to be Church concerns that would explain why: In 1453, six months after the sack of Constantinople, the French king declared victory over the steadily retreating English without bothering to remove them from their final beachhead at Calais; the nobles of Castile, having finally assassinated the successful absolutist usurper, Alvaro de Luna, in July of 1452, waited a full decade before proceeding to move against his autocratic government (e.g., Altamira, pp. 480-86; MacKay, pp. 135-38); in early 1454, to finally end the civil war engulfing Italy, church officials were employed in order to successfully plea for a confederation of Milan, Venice, Florence, Naples, and the Papal States in the Treaty of Lodi (Ady, pp. 214-16); in southern and western Germany, an ongoing series of "town wars" between the Emperor-supported, centralizing, confederational towns and the Church-supported feudal Electors finally resolved themselves through an abrupt, and highly unusual, simple monetary settlement in the famous Treaty of Lauf during the same month that the sack of Constantinople had been completed (Laffan, pp. 142-49).

None of these peaces lasted. By 1462 it had become clear that the fledgling nation-state of Hungary, with the financial help of the Church, was able to hold the Turks at bay while similarly defeudalizing Poland was similarly able to hold back the threatening Moscovites. It must thus have become increasingly clear that the centralizing nations were helping the Church's cause and that Europe generally had become too independent and too suspicious of Church motives to ever respond to its tired call for a crusade against the re-emergent Turks. With its own survival clearly at stake, at some point, the Church finally abandoned its losing, decentralizing, ideology. This is quite apparent from the Church's durable about-face and sudden support for highly centralized governments that began during the 1480s.

ical skepticism of Franciscans such as Dun Scotus were steadily eroding the intellectual credibility of the secular Church. This, complemented by the fact that the 14th and 15th century Church had repeatedly taken the losing side in its feudalism-supporting military positions outside of Italy and was coming to be popularly regarded as an immoral partner of the feudal lords in the unfair local taxation of the masses (Flick, Vol. II, pp. 34-35), was an important source of the demoralization of the Church leaders, which further contributed to the Church's nearly universal reputational low in the 1480s (*ibid.,* Chs. 26-27). It was at this point that the high overhead expense of artillery and the resuming threat of the Turks and Slavs in the East (e.g., Bury), led county after county to finally abandon the vestiges of feudalism and adopt centralized political institutions. For, by this point, the Church, having spent the previous 30 years in an utter failure to rouse a crusade against the still threatening Turks (Flick, Vol. II, p. 402), was rapidly reversing directions.

What was emerging was the "Renaissance Papacy," where, instead of concentrating on sales of its decreasingly popular bureaucratic and legal services, the still immensely wealthy Church (Flick, Vol. II, Ch. 26) was, outside of Italy, expanding its role in arranging for centralizing marriages and huge international loans in order to further strengthen the centralized states that were coming to represent the best of its clientele (Garnett).[58]

5. The Modern Period: The Decline of Guilds

a. *Explaining the Loss of the Guilds' Administrative Role.* Our statical efficiency theory predicts that the administrative role of guilds would decline within town governments as the result of the development of civilly reverent, professional bureaucracies. As reflected in Table 3.1, northern European states developed civilly reverent bureaucracies from the latter half of the 16th to the second quarter of the 17th century through mainline Protestantism.[59] Only much later, through the popularization of Hellenistic education, was this secular-state-respecting bureaucratic ethic spread to France, Flanders and Switzerland. This occurred there with the

---

[58]The analogue of the Renaissance Papacy to the current IMF, elaborated upon in Chapter 5 below, is, we shall see, no accident. Both institutions are natural suppliers of local emergency finance when the military technology favors the existence of a single imperial government. And both, we shall see, have harbored some socially very costly ideologies.

[59]Several early Protestants, most especially Lutherans, High-Anglican, and Arminian sects, believed that men served God by being dedicated to their profession or "calling". This belief made Protestant bureaucrats less inclined to follow their church's or their own preferences and more inclined to follow the intent of the civil legislators. These Protestants could thus, for example, be less redistributional than Catholics, which made the new, Protestant, breed of bureaucrats much more professional and less likely to subjectively redistribute away from successful investors. Nevertheless, it was only after the "Great Awakening" of the early-18th century that Protestant sects (e.g., Methodists) beyond Lutheran, High Anglican and Arminian sects could escape the theocratic dictates of the early Calvinist churches (e.g., Puritans) set up during the Reformation and join the other, secular-state-supporting, mainline sects.

TABLE 3.1

THE REPLACEMENT OF THE ADMINISTRATIVE ROLE OF
GUILDS WITH CIVILLY REVERENT BUREAUCRATS

State	Development of A Civilly Reverent Local Bureaucracy	Loss of Guild Administrative Roll
Holland and Zeeland[1]	Early 17th Century	Early 17th Century
England[2]	Late 16th Century	Late 16th Century
Denmark and Norway[3]	Late 16th Century	Late 16th Century
France & Flanders[4]	1870s	1760-1793
Southern Italy[5] and Spain	Present	Mid-19th Century
Sweden and Finland[6]	Late 16th Century	Late 16th Century
Northern Germania[7a]	Late 16th Century	Late 17th and Early 18th Centuries
Switzerland[7b]	1860s	1790s
Northern Italy and Bavaria[7c]	1860s	Two Steps: Late 15th/Late 18th Centuries
German Rhineland[7d]	1860s	1810s
Austria[7e]	1950s	1850s
Russia[8]	Present	1900

NOTES: [1]Dutch guilds lost their administrative role early in the second quarter of the 17th century, soon after they gained their independence from Spain. Following independence, guild regulations in Holland and Zeeland were administered by provincial authorities at the frequent expense of guild interests (Unger, p. 83, Kellenbenz, pp. 464-467). The militant Calvinism of the 16th Century was not replaced by more tolerant, Arminian sects until the late 1620s.

Table 3.1 (cont.)

[2]English guilds lost their administrative role under the Elizabethan Statutes, which were passed near the end of the 16th century. The statutes were enforced by local, largely Protestant, magistrates (Nef, pp. 35-57).

[3]Danish and Norwegian guilds were abolished by a decree of King Christian IV. When they were later restored, these guilds in these Lutheran states did not regain their administrative role (Kellenbenz, *ibid.*)

[4]France's guilds steadily lost influence with the growth of physiocracy from the 1760s onward (Root). France outlawed their still fairly administratively active guilds in 1793. Napoleon outlawed guilds soon thereafter in Flanders (Godechot, et al., Ch. 1). Although governmentally educated, professional bureaucracy was one of the chief reforms of Napoleon (Godechot, *ibid.*), Enlightenment ideology stubbornly hung on, even after the Bourbon Restoration as discussed later in the text, until France's final humiliating defeat in the Franco-Prussian War in 1870.

[5]Spain, although eliminating guild entry restrictions in the 1780s, retained guilds for their judiciary and bureaucratic services all the way up to the liberalization of 1829-33 (R. Smith, pp. 16, 116; Marshall, p. 53). Southern Italian guilds remained strong until the 1860's (Unwin, p. 1).

[6]The advent of central government regulation of Craft Guilds in Lutheran Sweden during the late 16th century is described by Heckscher (1954, p. 73).

[7a]7aThe elimination of the guild's administrative role in late 17th and early 19th century in the Lutheran states of northern Germania is described by Burford, Part III Chs. II and III.

[7b]Under heavy French influences, the Swiss eliminated the bureaucratic function of their guilds in the late 18th century, the same time that they eliminated the monopolistic privileges of their various cantonal churches (Oechsli, Ch. 23, and pp. 326-27). As in France and Germany, however, the education remained a variety of classical economics until the late 1860s, when political pragmatism in the form of either Hellenism or *Realpolitik* quickly came to replace laissez faire ideology.

[7c]As discussed in the text, Renaissance thought led to an essentially complete replacement of guild bureaucrats with ideologically inspired, elite Hellenistic bureaucrats in late 15th century Lombardy and a similar, but subsequently partially reversed, bureaucratic replacement in late 15th century Tuscany. Austrian hegemony imposed a final, laissez-theory-inspired, guild elimination on Tuscany in the mid-1780s (Woolf, Ch. 7).

The same two ideologies caused a similar, only slightly delayed, two-step decline in Bavaria, whose Counter-Reformed towns (e.g., Augsberg) replaced guild with magisterial control throughout the 16th century (Janssen, Vol. 15, Ch. III) while it was again only three centuries later that Bavaria completely eliminated the administrative role of guilds through new, laissez-faire-ideology-inspired, central governmental regulation in 1825 (Holborn, v. 3, pp. 4-5).

Table 3.1 (cont.)

[7d]The German Rhine states, under Prussian influence, maintained the guild-elimination laws of Napoleon even though Napoleon was long gone (Godechot, *ibid.*; Holborn, v. 3, p. 5). As discussed in the text, the pragmatic professionalism reflected in the philosophy of *Realpolitik* took over from both laissez faire ideology and Catholicism throughout southern Germania in the 1860s (e.g., Strayer and Gatzke, pp. 604-606; May, Ch. 3).

[7e]Although the "enlightened despotism" of Joseph II introduced professional bureaucracies to Austria (Woolf, *ibid.*), these elitist bureaucracies were too often imbued with a laissez faire spirit or Catholic morality (Schenk) to be regarded as civilly reverent. More generally, Austria, which was the dominant power in eastern Europe (from the Middle Ages to the mid-1860s), could not begin to develop a civilly reverent bureaucracy until their crushing, 20th century defeats and direct foreign intervention giving them a western-style, Hellenistic, education system. We will have more to say about the Austrian defeats after we introduce tariff policy because their guild elimination might not have been so hard on them without a simultaneous movement toward complete laissez faire. Austrian guilds remained strong through the 1st half of the 19th century (Holborn, v. 2, p. 451), and were not eliminated until the 1850s (Holborn, V. 2, p. 451), when their ministers under Francis Joseph came to adopt a fairly complete laissez faire policy.

[8]While Russia suddenly eliminated her guilds in 1900 (Lyashchenko, p. 553), she is only now beginning to replace her extreme legislative ideology with a more legislatively pragmatic approach under the same political philosophy of *Realpolitik* that came to dominate her central European neighbors over a century ago (Strayer and Gatzke, pp. 604-06).

practical success of modern-type, wholly secular, universities during the 19th century. The southern Germanic states of northern Italy, Bavaria, and the Rhineland, similarly failed to develop such professional bureaucracies until late in the 3rd quarter of the 19th century, when the Bismarckian revolutions, under a banner of the professionalist philosophy of *Realpolitik*, rapidly converted them (from either Church-based morality, Romantic humanism, or economic libertarianism) to a pragmatic professionalism in the execution of the rules of the state (e.g., May, Ch. 3). Several southern and eastern European states are only now in the process of developing similarly non-ideological, Hellenistic or pragmatically professional, bureaucracies.

With central governments in mainline Protestant countries much more able to effectively execute a state-determined legislative policy, these northern European governments commenced to completely remove the administrative role of guilds just after the Reformation. This is also reflected in Table 3.1. The policy was first implemented by placing guilds under the supervision of either local magistrates (England) or state bureaucrats (Holland, Denmark and Norway). In contrast, the administrative power of guilds remained strong in the more southern or central, Catholic states.[60] While some Catholic states codified existing local guild rules into national systems similar to their Protestant neighbors, these Catholic states maintained, or even strengthened, the administrative role of guilds. For example, the French Edicts of 1581 and 1582 elevated guilds to a prominent place in a national bureaucracy, which controlled all guild rules and prices, while the Elizabethan statutes of the same period placed English guilds under the local jurisdiction of common law magistrates. French guilds correspondingly maintained, and even

---

[60]This raises the alternative hypothesis that early modern guilds were an extension of traditional Catholic religious institutions. However, as we are about to see, the Hellenized Catholics of the northern Italian counter-Reformation, were quite successful in replacing guild bureaucrats with their own Jesuit magistrates. Also, guilds eventually disappeared even where Catholicism remained. Moreover, most non-Catholic, but also non-civilly reverent, urban societies have also been dominated by administratively active guilds. Ready examples occur in India, Egypt, and Turkey (e.g. Sjoberg).

An empirically more justifiable hypothesis is that guilds, which generally disappeared soon after the introduction of modern, national democracy, served as authoritarian, non-democratic, national institutions. The theoretical rationale underlying such a hypothesis is that guilds may serve to transmit the local economic interests of various trades to national legislators, such a role being relatively important in authoritarian nations, where many of the guild members had no other way to express their national policy preferences. However, such an argument would have to account for the fact that this political function could have been easily provided by simple trade lobbies. The fact that national lobbies did <u>not</u> systematically appear in after the demise of the guilds is strong evidence against this political-function hypothesis. In any case, the national political function of historic guilds was at best ancillary. Moreover, a political-function, authoritarian-role hypothesis would fail to explain a couple of elementary facts. First, on the local level, guilds were originally introduced in relatively democratic European city-states. Second, guild <u>political</u> decline was initiated by the quite authoritarian regime of Elizabeth and soon thereafter extended to the Scandinavian monarchies (Table 3.1).

increased, their influence and number while the English guilds substantially decreased in bureaucratic influence during the Protestant Reformation.[61] It was thus common for Catholic states to prohibit policies strengthening local governmental control over guilds. One such policy is that of the Spanish-dominated Dutch regime. Under the 1531 Buitennering Order, this regime granted Dutch guilds continued administrative control and prohibited industry from locating outside towns. Guilds also gained administrative influence in 17th century Catholic Portugal and Spain through the similar encouragement of their respective governments (Merino).

At the time that France was eliminating her guilds near the end of the 18th century, she, as indicated in the Notes to the Table, had not yet even begun to produce the semblance of a civilly reverent bureaucracy because of her temporary (albeit-century-long) ideologization by the Enlightenment and correspondingly extended loss in internal efficiency. Considering earlier France in this gradualist light, the early 18th century movement of the French capital to Versailles by Louis XIV, which provided the government with a steadily increasing stock of highly educated bureaucrats, increasingly under-represented guilds at the palace. Increasingly "enlightened" and physiocratic France therefore produced an increasing tax burden on the guilds throughout the latter half of the 18th century that was tantamount to a gradual guild elimination. Adam Smith thus generally approved of the pre-revolutionary French government, especially where the physiocrats were able to influence policy (Book IV, Chapter IV); he disapproved only of particular policies. such as the effort-discouraging tax burdens it had imposed on the peasantry.

It is therefore quite natural -- yet quite unacceptable to ideologized intellectuals both then and now -- to view the Revolution (1789-91) as an uprising of local nobles and investors to reestablish their pre-Bourbon political input, an uprising that <u>failed to achieve its essentially conservative goal of ousting the "enlightened" aristocracy until 80 years later</u>. It failed because the "Second Revolution," 1792-1795, was actually a counter-revolution in that transformed the original movement into one that represented an effective return to an "enlightened" government.

The apparently late elimination of the administrative role of guilds in the provinces of northern Germania, late in that civilly reverent (Lutheran trained) bureaucrats had been available since the late 16th century, was probably due to the fact that the naturally monopolistic export position of the typical 16th and 17th century Germanic city-state made it better for such states to allow their relatively informed guildsmen to control competition than to extend such decision power over to relatively uninformed town officials. A further implication of the relative appropriateness of export monopolization by the typical 17th century Germanic city-state is discussed in the following subsections.

Civilly reverent bureaucracies developed more slowly in the other, more southern and eastern, parts of Europe. Many of these initially quite successful, subsequently highly Renaissance-influenced, areas, as the Table indicates, prematurely

---

[61]See Nef, Chs. 1 and 2, who also points out that the decline in the administrative role of guilds, through a sudden growth in the commercial influence of the king's courts, took place in England despite attempts by the crown to protect the guilds from its legal bureaucracy.

abandoned their guilds long before developing civilly reverent bureaucracies. Besides France, which we have already discussed, this inefficiency occurred in Italy, Bavaria, Spain, and Russia. What sharply distinguished these countries from their more fortunate neighbors was their relatively permanent adoption of <u>elite Hellenism</u> in the early modern period. Let us elaborate.

Hellenism, whose evolutionary success was rationalized in Section I.8 of Chapter 2, is the Occidental ruling-class ethic born in Post-Classical Athens and spread by the subsequent conquest of Alexander and the Ceasars throughout the Ancient West. Hellenism -- formally, the exaggeration of the likelihood of unlikely hypotheses -- generally enables secularly educated managers or bureaucrats to rationalize the entire range of social actions that is requested of them. This is a highly effective bureaucratic ethic when the state is in performance competition with other states. However, when the state is far ahead of their competition, Hellenism makes advanced social thinkers susceptible to the adoption an unrealistically self-aggrandizing, quite elitist, self-image. As explicitly reflected in the conclusions of its pioneers (especially Aristotle), this intellectual elitism brings along a correspondingly <u>negative</u> image of the efficiency of popular-democratic ("mobocratic") and significant-investor-democratic ("plutocratic") legislation. Its effect on bureaucratic decisionmaking in dominant secular states, once injected into the state's popular education system, has thus been to give popular bureaucrats in those states a license to interpret facts so as to benefit the classes of people that they consider the most deserving. In particular, an elitist bias against successful investors is observed among Hellenists in dominant countries, a bias reflected in the negative attitudes of the school's pioneers towards the social value and social judgments of wealthy tradesmen. The upshot is that Hellenism, while facilitating civil reverence and therefore effective democracy among <u>competing</u> states, is a double-edge sword in that it works <u>against</u> effective democracy and facilitates major ideologization in <u>dominant</u> states.[62] This perversion occurs because advanced professional training, which is especially appreciated and popular in dominant states, greatly exaggerates the practical value of advanced ideas. Hellenistic education thus prepares subsequently professionally trained bureaucrats to whole-heartedly adopt intellectually elitist policy positions.

While it is beyond the scope of this study to inquire into the psychological roots, the impressive <u>intellectual</u> productivity, or the historical rise of Hellenistic thought (on all this, see Thompson, et al., Vols. I and II), it is not beyond our scope to describe the economic effects of the 13th century rebirth of Hellenism in the West.

---

[62]Since Hellenism, from Section I.8 of Chapter 2, has itself become a deeply rooted, evolutionarily successful, ideology, we should not expect first-best efficiency. Indeed, like Confucianism in the East, Hellenism generates relatively severe dominance cycles (Thompson, et al., Vol. II, Ch. 6). We should expect such a result because long-term ideological evolution generally selects those institutions whose <u>best performances</u> exceed their rivals' <u>best performances</u>. The fact that a slightly best-performing ideology generates far worse subsequent losses (e.g., the grievous losses from elite Hellenism) than alternative ideologies does not matter as long as the period of ascendancy is long enough to use the educational system to permanently intellectually subordinate its potential rivals within the given civilization.

In particular, the rapid maturation of Renaissance thought in the dominant 15th century states of northern Italy (Florence and Milan) had a decidedly negative effect on the bureaucratic function of guilds. The increasing abundance and influence of Hellenistically educated urbanites led both Florentine and Milanese guilds to finally surrender essentially all of their autonomy over to Hellenized elites in the 1480s (e.g., Ady, pp. 136-138, for Milan; and Trevelyan, p. 265, for Florence). The consequence for Florence -- besides an immediate collapse of investment and output (Luzzatto, pp. 181-82) that conforms to the predictions of our underdevelopment theory -- was a substantial reduction in government revenue, as reflected in the corresponding collapse in the market for government bonds (Becker, vol. 2, pp. 239-40). The subsequent threat of popular insurrection led the increasingly desperate Hellenistic despots to withhold both training and arms from their potentially rebellious artisans during the various French and Spanish sieges of the late 15th and early 16th centuries (Trevelyan, p. 344). By preferring instead expensive and frequently disloyal *condottieri*, these Hellenized elites quickly led the brilliant parents of the Renaissance into foreign enslavement (Symonds, p. 51; Trevelyan, Chs. 19-24; Bayley).

Relatively democratic Florence was able to restore a partial administrative and political input for her guilds despite foreign political domination and, correspondingly, noticeably outperformed unfortunate Milan (e.g., Carpanetto and Ricuperati, Ch. 1). Further in the direction of Florence was Venice, who remained almost completely immune to the intellectual Renaissance (as opposed to the artistic Renaissance). Venice thereby completely retained her guilds (albeit in their original, narrowly oligarchic, form), correspondingly retained her sovereignty, and significantly outperformed both Florence and Milan throughout the early-modern period (e.g., Carpanetto and Ricuperati, *ibid.*)

As indicated in the Table, as Renaissance thought spread north into Bavaria, largely through the Counter Reformation, the administrative role of guilds was largely surrendered to Jesuit-trained, bureaucratic elites (e.g., Janssen, Ch. III). Predictably, this movement left in its wake a string of failed local economies, including Augsberg and Cologne (e.g., Janssen, *ibid.*)

Finally, it was only during the decade of the 1780s, under the fashionably liberal, laissez-faire-inspired, Austrian despot, Leopold, that Florence completely eliminated her guilds, which up to then had stubbornly retained a substantial administrative influence. What immediately ensued was a devastating Florentine depression as many of the old craft guildsmen abandoned their fixed investments (Cochrane, Ch. 4; Woolf, Ch. 7). Our explanation, of course, is that many old Florentine masters knew they could no longer protect their investments from the nobles, clerics, and Romantic ideologues in the remaining bureaucracy. After all, a very similar experiment had occurred there 300 years earlier -- with very similar results. And the masters could not have failed to witness the steady economic decline in Milan, where guilds had long been administratively powerless.

Civilly irreverent Russia suffered a similarly unexplained, essentially permanent, loss of efficiency immediately after her sudden, ideologically inspired, guild elimination in 1900 by the modernizing Sergei Witte. We have found no plausible alternative explanation for the sudden, widely acknowledged (e.g., Lyashchenko, Part II, esp. p. 674; and Nutter), decrease in Russian economic growth. Russia's humiliating losses in the Russo-Japanese War and the short-lived democratic revolution of 1905 followed. The ideological reaction and Stolypin reforms of 1906 (1) substituted monopolistic cartels for many of the old guilds (Lyashchenko, Ch. 33, Harcave) while only mildly increasing her small, but similarly capriciously discriminatory, income tax (Bowman, pp. 274-81) and (2) artificially induced a boom in private agrarian investment (e.g., Korelin, esp. pp. 148-59) while continuing to exempt agriculture from the profits tax (Bowman). The only-apparently-healthy, further-modernizing, recovery lasted until, as we shall argue in Chapter 5, the accumulated excesses of various forms of capital produced the 1917 Revolution.

b. *Explaining the Loss of the Guild's Capital-Restricting Role.* Guilds in Protestant areas typically hung on long after guilds lost their administrative as well as their direct military roles. This, according to our efficiency-based theory, implies that guilds continued to supply a valuable tax-function to their governments. Guilds did indeed continue to serve as entry-restricting, tax-paying, trade associations.

Our peacetime tax theory and efficient-government theory further suggest that whenever guilds were finally eliminated, either by formal decree or by a removal of their ability to restrict entry, ordinary peacetime capital taxes would be introduced during the same general era. Table 3.2 illustrates the empirical accuracy of this prediction. Given the timing of the various demises of guilds, Europe appears to have been behaving in extremely close accord with our efficiency theory. Modern capital tax systems arose roughly simultaneously with, or fairly soon after, the death of guilds. (Only one exception exists, and we shall rationalize it momentarily.)

The impressive uniformity of this observation on the introduction of capital taxes should itself be explained. Although ordinary peacetime capital taxation is not a vital economic institution in the relatively civilly reverent, democratic nations, the citizen-efficiency of such governments implies that the substantial loss in revenue from guild wartime contributions would sooner or later be met by revenues from not only vital war-finance institutions but also from an efficient, capital-restricting, peacetime capital tax. In such nations, a failure to impose peacetime capital taxes and acceptance of more neutral taxes such as pure land taxes or consumption taxes, although costly, is not fatal. The evolution of an efficient capital tax in the relatively democratic regions thus appears to have proceeded in a simple Lamarckian fashion. This would explain England, Denmark and Norway on the Table. With respect to the less civilly reverent, less democratic, theoretically less efficient, nations, it is much more likely, following an argument developed in Section 1 of Chapter 5, that the defense-externality was especially high and therefore that capital taxes were vital to these more authoritarian nations. So a fairly harsh Darwinian mechanism probably threatened these regimes, meaning that the surviving authoritarian governments would have to possess substantial capital taxes. Nevertheless, since the democratic nations had already pioneered capital taxation, since physiocracy was about all the ideologists could muster to oppose capital taxation, and since the Pascalian response to the loss in revenues from the guilds was a search for an expansion of the tax base in the form of a related wealth tax, our observations display no examples of governments that

TABLE 3.2

THE REPLACEMENT OF GUILD ENTRY RESTRICTIONS
WITH NATIONAL CAPITAL TAXES

State	Development of The Modern Tax On Fixed Capital	Elimination of Guild Entry Restrictions
Holland and Zeeland[1]	17th Century	Late 17th Century
England[2]	18th Century	2nd Quarter of the 18th Century
Denmark and Norway[3]	1813	1800
France and Flanders[4]	1790s	1760-1793
Southern Italy Spain[5]	1790-1870	1780-1865
Sweden and Finland[6]	1840-1870	1840-1865
Germania[7]	13th Century	Late 18th and 19th Centuries
Russia[8]	1885-1917	1900

NOTES: [1]On the various 17th century Dutch property taxes, see Tracy, Ch. VI. Seligman similarly reports various irregular general property taxes throughout 17th century Netherlands. While entry-restricting shipbuilding guilds remained late into the 18th century (Unger), other such guilds in Holland and Zeeland had severely declined to insignificance by the end of the 17th century (Kellenbenz, p. 466).

[2]In 1692 England introduced a general property tax known as the "land tax". The tax assessed not only land rents but also urban property rents and capital stock interest (World Tax Series, Taxation in the United Kingdom; Houseman). While the tax initially failed to account for increased property values, a series of 18th century acts updated property values for tax purposes and finally produced the automatic updating characteristics of an ordinary general property tax system (Houseman; Seligman pp. 53-75; and Dowell pp. 81-98). English guilds declined slightly in the 17th century, but then declined much more rapidly until they were essentially extinct by the middle of the 18th century (e.g., Kramer, pp. 139-161).

Table 3.2 (cont.)

[3]Denmark and Norway abolished guilds through free trade legislation in 1800 and introduced a national tax on movable property in 1813 (Barton, p. 213 and p. 329, respectively).

[4]France introduced her first property tax and a substantial inheritance tax in 1789. She then introduced an income tax in the 1790s (World Tax Series, Taxation in France, pp. 79-86). The inheritance tax, known as the Registration Tax Law, taxed all capital as a proportion of its value when it changed ownership. Although France formally abolished her guilds after the Revolution in 1793 (Godechot, et al., Ch. 1), she steadily weakened her Guild entry restrictions from the 1760s onwards under the increasing influence of physiocratic doctrine. (See the text and the notes to Tables 3.1 and 3.3).

[5]The French tax system was also implemented, albeit slowly, shortly after in Italy and Spain (DeRosa and Godechot, et al. p. 265, respectively) The new property taxes were maintained after Napoleon left. As elaborated later in this section, Spain eliminated the entry-restricting role of guilds in the 1780s (Olivera, Ch 5; Godechot, p. 228) while the states of southern Italy restored their guilds after Napoleon left and kept them until 1864.

[6]Sweden and Finland, while experimenting with property taxes in 1840, did not introduce a regular income and property tax until the 1860s (World Tax Series, Taxation in Sweden, pp. 71-73). Their entry-restrictive guilds while weakened around 1840 were not abolished until their "Freedom of Trade Act" in 1864 (Schmidt).

[7]Prussia, as well as numerous Germanic city-states all the way down to and including the northern Italian city-states in the Po Valley, had an extensive property and income tax system by the mid-14th century (World Tax Series, Taxation in Germany, pp. 6-11; Staley, pp. 192-193; and Burckhardt, pp. 3-4), but nevertheless maintained strong entry-restrictive guilds until the late 18th and 19th centuries (Berner, p. 19; Godechot, Ch. 1; Holborn, v. 2, p. 414, vol. 3, p. 210). The apparent contradiction is discussed at length in the text. On the development of a general property tax in medieval Germania, see, e.g., Seligman, esp. p. 39.

[8]Russian guilds, after struggling through the modernization period of the 1880s and 1890s, were suddenly abolished in 1900 (Lyashchenko, p. 553; Clarkson, pp. 303, 355-56). Although Russia introduced a small profits tax in 1885 and, as discussed in the text, increased it to less than 10% by 1907 (Bowman), Russia's unfortunately belated imposition of a substantial national tax on fixed capital in 1917 may have been somewhat overdone.

actually failed because they neglected to replace their guilds with a capital tax.

The sole exception to the pattern in Table 3.2 is Germany, whose various provinces and city-states from the early middle ages onward maintained both selective property taxes and entry-restricting guilds up to the end of the 18th century. The case is nevertheless quite consistent with, and even implied by, our general theory. We need only reiterate that, up until the late 18th century, this region was unique in being composed mainly of largely autonomous city-states or provinces. Correspondingly, their foreign-trade-oriented guilds, like the export-oriented provincial Dutch shipbuilding guilds of the 18th century (Unger), had extensive work rules, making them labor-restrictive as well as capital-restrictive.[63]   Again, autonomous local governments should, in the absence of foreign trade agreements, grant simple monopoly rights to their foreign-trade-oriented industries in order to exploit terms-of trade effects. The observed local capital taxes are also called-for because export-monopolistic capital stocks are still excessive in the presence of a local defense-externality. The entire welfare argument stays relevant until the various German centralizations of the late 18th and late 19th centuries, when these cartelizing guilds were respectively eliminated.

This is not to say that export monopolies were irrelevant to the more centralized states of the West. However, the optimal form of monopolization against foreigners in a nation state, owing to the ordinary impracticality of national cartelization, is ordinarily selective export taxation. Export taxation was indeed the established policy of late Medieval England, Denmark, France, and Spain (e.g., Miller, Coornaert, Ch. I, and R. Smith, Chs. IV and V). Export taxation was also frequently observed in high medieval Florence, which often negotiated with the surrounding countryside and therefore found it useful to adopt a monopolizing technique that would facilitate flexible contracting over the degree of monopoly (Staley, Chs. IV and VII).

   c. *War Finance and the Timing of the Demise of the Guilds.* While guilds were predictably eliminated in nations with the introduction of a modern capital tax, the historical timing of the efficient policy substitution is another matter. The elimination of guild entry restrictions -- and corresponding elimination of the significant wartime contributions of the guilds -- generally represents the elimination of a vital economic institution. Guild elimination may therefore be quite untimely. This subsection will indeed show that, in many European nations, the "modernizing" replacement of guilds with ordinary peacetime property taxes was -- under the influence of laissez faire ideology -- grossly premature in view of wartime taxation problems.

We can begin the discussion by asking, from Table 3.2, why guilds were retained by the early modern Protestant states in Scandinavia all the way up to their 19th century introductions of modern property or income tax systems. Why didn't these Protestant states behave like early 18th century England by quickly substituting

---

[63]See Staley, Chs. IV and V for a description of Florentine input restrictions, including taxes on variable inputs. Our best information on the thoroughly labor-restrictive character of the export oriented German guilds comes from conversations with Professor Claus P. Clasen.

capital taxes for guilds?

These long, 65-130 year, lags in emulating the successful English policy replacement are especially puzzling because capital taxation had been no stranger to Europe. As we have already noted, Medieval European kings systematically employed capital taxes, efficiently internalizing the defense-externalities that certain investors imposed on them as protectors of the entire kingdom. (The English tallage and later their "10th's and 15th's", the traditional French *taille*, and similar taxes throughout western Europe all were levied against both real and personal property before the tax on movables was phased out in the early-modern period (e.g., Dowell, p. 70, Seligman, pp. 43-56)).

Let us review the entire argument to help clarify the question. It was only within the medieval trading towns, citadels often defended with the substantial military aid of local investors in fixed capital (e.g., Black, Ch. 1, Thrupp (1948), p. 43), that guilds were first evolved. Medieval towns did not simply impose their own capital tax similar in form to the kings', even though such a policy would have induced each investor to internalize the marginal local defense cost of his capital, because medieval guilds were also justified as producer collectives protecting coveted capital from bureaucratic expropriation. Such collectives obviously have a built-in monopolizing incentive. To convert this potential problem into a social benefit, the medieval town had only to limit guild "monopolization" to acceptable restrictions on fixed capital-inputs and call upon the favored capital owners for heavy support during military emergencies. This produced a qualitative equivalent to a system of both peacetime and wartime local capital taxation, a first-best-efficient policy in the presence of local defense-externalities (Appendix B.3). The growing military power of the successful European kings from the 13th through the 15th centuries -- occasioned as we have noted by the technical improvements in the trebuchet and cannon -- steadily reduced the relative military strength of local lords and correspondingly produced an increasing tax burden on these lords. With realty the chief asset of these local lords and thus increasingly taxed to finance the monarch's increasingly expensive national governments (Dowell pp. 81-98, Seligman pp. 53-73, Smith pp. 801-809), guilds were increasingly welcomed as additional tax sources by the financially strapped 16th and early 17th century monarchs, who were increasingly confronted with militarily obsolete and correspondingly tax-impoverished local nobilities. Thus, with the previously local defense-externality from guild capital now part of a larger, national, defense-externality, guilds were coming to make their effective capital-tax contributions to monarchs rather than local governments (Jones, pp. 144-152 and Renard, pp. 101-106).

The question that arises is, why didn't these early-modern Protestant monarchs immediately expand their pre-existing capital-tax systems and scrap their guilds? After all, guilds were, quite appropriately, being quickly stripped of their administrative role. Even England waited for over a century, essentially the entire 17th century, between the time she stripped guilds of their administrative role and the time she started to replace guilds with explicit capital taxes. Why so? And why did Scandinavia wait for over two centuries?

A straightforward answer is provided by our defense-finance theory. We have already emphasized that authoritarian assessments provide a source of <u>emergency</u> taxation that is far superior to the legislative tax assessments of a democratic government.[64]   Therefore, through a Lamarck-Darwin process elaborated in the following chapter, it was only <u>after</u> legislatively constrained states developed an adequate system of emergency finance -- viz., a gold standard -- that their financial dependence on the liquidity and borrowing power of guilds was eliminated. Only <u>after</u> the introduction of such an emergency financial system was it appropriate to replace guilds with a modern system of capital taxation. It would therefore have been highly inappropriate, if not fatal, for the countries of Protestant Europe to imitate England's successful 1730s abandonment of guilds without first introducing a convertible monetary system. Indeed, as indicated in Table 3.3 (including the Notes in the case of Northern Germania), Scandinavia, and similarly legislatively pragmatic and Protestant Prussia, were sufficiently resistant to ideological fashion to retain their guilds until they had firmly established a convertible monetary system.

A more complete answer would explain why these Protestant regions, and the rest of Europe for that matter, were so slow to imitate England's <u>financial</u> innovation. In fact, Protestant Sweden <u>did</u>, from 1719 to 1772, <u>promptly</u> attempt to follow England with both a democracy and a flexible convertible money of her own. However, the convertible money system was a less expensive, <u>copper</u> standard. The high storage and transportation costs of a copper standard made the standard incapable of financing a really substantial emergency war effort (against Russia). Yet

---

[64]One might well ask here why a sufficiently high peacetime tax rate would not create a war chest sufficient to finance any reasonable defensive emergency. The answer is that war chests are too liquid; they are liquid in peacetime as well as wartime. The mere threat of war will transfer a war-chest to a potential aggressor. Historically, war chests have thus frequently been used to buy peace from attracted aggressors, to ransom royalty, and to finance royal escapes to safer soil. In short, war chests are a sort of super-coveted capital because the state's all-or-nothing defense commitment does not extend over to such liquid wealth. Even more than ordinary forms of coveted capital (Appendix B.3), war chests provide more of an attraction than a repellent to aggression against the state. (The financial mercantilism of the 16th-18th centuries, which has traditionally been incorrectly represented as an argument for war chests, is rationalized in Thompson, et al., Vol. II, Ch. 2.)

Ideally, the services that are tapped for emergencies are specific to the victimized state. In any case, they are, unlike war chests, relatively immobile across state boundaries. This is, no doubt, why viable states are contained within borders and why most wars have been fought for control of the territory within the borders of a viable state.

What all this means for war finance is that the money used to finance wars must be created during the war, either through borrowing or money creation. For significant amounts of wartime purchasing power, as elaborated in Chapter 4, this paper must also, somehow. be significantly retired after the war, obviously by the surviving citizens of the successfully defended state. In the case of an authoritarian leader, debt or money-retirement can be simply commanded. In the case of a democracy, debt or money retirement is simply not in the interest of the rational voters. Therefore, special legal and monetary institutions must constrain the democracy for the system to be viable.

TABLE 3.3

THE INTRODUCTION OF CONVERTIBLE CURRENCIES
AND THE ACCELERATED DECLINE OF GUILDS

Country	Introduction of Convertible Currency	Accelerated Elimination Of Guilds
Holland and Zeeland[1]	1810s	1650s
England[2]	1690s	1730s
Denmark and Norway[3]	1803	1790s
France and Belgium[4]	1870	1760s
Southern Italy[5a]	1860s	1860s
Spain[5b]	1830s	1790s
Sweden[6]	1820s	1840s
Northern Germania[7a]	1850s	Two Steps: 1800s/1860s
Switzerland[7b]	1870s	1790s
Northern Italy[7c]	1850s	1770s
Bavaria and the Rhineland[7d]	1850s	1810s
Austro-Hungary[7e]	1810s	1850s
Russia[8]	1890s	1900

NOTES: [1]The United Provinces first issued a convertible paper currency in 1813 through the newly established, state-regulated Bank of the Netherlands (Conant, p. 289). However, guilds in Holland and Zeeland began to decline rapidly in 1652, as discussed in the Introduction.

[2]National convertible paper currency was first issued in England, though the government dominated Bank of England in 1696 (Vilar, p. 207). However, the accelerated decline of guilds occurred later, during the 1730s, when guilds lost their legal and political power to maintain their entry-restrictions (Kramer, pp. 139-61).

[3]Denmark and Norway first issued convertible paper currency in 1803 (Del Mar (1895), p. 304), and had officially abolished guilds in 1800 (Barton, p. 213).

Table 3.3 (cont.)

[4]National convertible paper currency, through the newly established government-owned Bank of France, was first issued in 1803 (Del Mar (1969), p. 204). However, France's convertibility system lacked the wartime flexibility possessed by the other systems. As explained in the text, subsequent events showed that France would not suspend payments during her military emergencies until the 1870s, when she adopted a conventional gold standard. Before that time, France merely switched from gold to silver payments during emergencies. This limited her emergency authoritarian financial capability to her silver supply, thereby putting her at a substantial disadvantage.

The accelerated attack on French guilds began in the 1760s with a steady series of physiocrat-inspired laws permitting the entry of non-guild suppliers (Root). These dates also apply to Belgium since during this period Belgium was under French jurisdiction (Godechot, et al., p. 228).

[5a]Convertible paper currency was first issued in southern Italy during the period 1850-1870 through the various state banks. Examples of the first issuance of such convertible paper are: in the Papal states in 1850 through the Bank of Naples; and in the Kingdom of Sicily in 1870 through the Bank of Sicily, (Canovai, pp. 21-26).

Guilds in southern Italy, although temporarily disappearing during the Napoleonic era, remained relatively strong until they were abolished in 1864 (Godechot, et al., Ch. 1; Unwin, p. 1).

[5b]Spain first issued convertible paper currency, through the newly established government owned Bank of Spain, in 1829 (Del Mar (1969), p. 117). However, the entry-restricting role of guilds in Spain was first attacked over 20 years before under a French dominated liberal regime (Godechot, et al. p. 228; Olivara, p. 375). Some guild entry restrictions returned to Spain soon after the fall of Napoleon, fitfully coming and going until the final demise of Spanish guilds in 1835 (Olivara, Ch. 5).

[6]Sweden first issued a workable convertible paper currency in 1829 through the state owned Bank of Sweden (Del Mar (1895) p. 297). However, guilds did not rapidly decline until 1846 when, by statute, they lost most of their entry-restriction rights (Heckscher (1954), p. 236).

[7a]While Prussia first issued a convertible paper currency in 1765 through the state owned Royal Deposit and Loan Bank, it was not until the Royal Bank was reorganized as the Bank of Prussia in 1848 that the amount of convertible paper became highly significant (Flink, pp. 1-2). At this time, Prussian hegemony provided the financial base for the entire North German Federation. Although the various states of northwestern Germany failed to restore their guilds after the defeat of Napoleon, and became the client states of Prussia, Prussian guilds were restored, and remained until the industrial freedom decree of 1868, which only then removed the legal ability of guilds to restrict entry (Holborn, v. 3, p. 201).

Nevertheless, Prussian guilds were weakened substantially from 1798-1806 (Holborn, v. 2, p. 378), just prior to their sudden military defeats at the hands of the French. This ignominious collapse of the proudly militaristic Prussians was achieved,

Table 3.3 (cont.)

consistent with our theory, because of a simple lack of Prussian emergency funds (Holborn, v. 2, p. 417). Prussian guilds were substantially restored after the death of the reforming Hardenberg in 1822 (Holborn, p. 458). Correspondingly, Prussia reverted to her previous role of a successful aggressor-state.

[7b]Switzerland first issued a national convertible paper currency in 1875 when she placed the various privately owned banks under federal legislation (Conant, p. 303). However, Swiss guilds were abolished in 1798 under the French dominated liberal Helvetic regime (Oechsli, p. 326).

[7c]The northern Italian Piedmont state first issued a convertible paper currency in 1848, through the newly established state owned National Bank (Conant, p. 19). However, guilds in northern Italian towns were being dismantled as early as 1778 under a liberal regime (Berner, p. 20; Woolf, Ch. 7).

[7d]An imperial convertible paper currency was first issued in southwestern Germany in the late 1840's through various state owned banks. An example of such banks was the Mortgage and Acceptance Bank of Bavaria (Flink, p. 2). Guilds were permanently eliminated in the western German states soon after the area was invaded by Napoleon (Holborn, v. 2, p. 390).

[7e]Although the Austro-Hungarian Empire first issued a small quantity of convertible paper in 1762 (Del Mar (1969), p. 329), the quantity of such paper only became significant early in the Napoleonic era (Del Mar (1969), pp. 329-30). Austrian guilds remained strong and were protected by the government until the Austrian adoption of complete laissez faire ideology in the 1850's (Holborn, v. 2, p. 451). Guilds were finally abolished there during the period 1859-60 (Unwin, p. 1).

[8]Russia first issued a convertible paper currency through the state-owned Bank of Russia in 1890 (Lyashchenko, p. 557; von Laue, p. 113) and a conventional gold standard in 1897 (Riasanovsky, p. 441). Guilds were suddenly abolished soon after in 1900 (Lyashchenko, p. 553; Clarkson, pp. 303, 355-56).

the standard was still capable of producing a gold-standard-type, postwar depression in the 1760s and 1770s (Chapter 4) and an eventual end to both her convertible money and her democratic experiment (Heckscher, 1954). The Swedish failure suggested that a successful democracy required an English-type, precious-metal standard, with which they immediately began to experiment. With their observant neighbors similarly learning that an effective convertibility system required a precious metal backing for money, legislatively pragmatic Denmark was relatively quick to introduce an effectively convertible money to replace the guilds that were being eliminated during the 1790s. By the end of the 1st quarter of the 19th century, all of the Scandinavian countries had introduced some sort of convertible, precious-metal-based, monetary system. Soon thereafter, they would all be guild-free. Indeed Sweden, along with other pragmatic and highly successful 19th century states, e.g., Prussia and Metternich's Austria, were sufficiently non-ideological to keep their guilds around as a source of emergency finance until many years after an alternative means of finance had been introduced.

But the emerging classical theory led the more legislatively ideological countries of Europe to the wholly incorrect inference that it was simply internal laissez faire policy -- i.e., guild elimination -- that was responsible for the remarkable success of England. These countries were led, with the encouragement of ideologically dominant France, along the garden path of laissez faire ideology and became easy prey for aggressor-states in the first half of the 19th century. Thus, while the immediate neighbors of France predictably failed to abandon the path even after Napoleon left (Godechot, et al., Ch. 8; Holborn, v.2, Ch. 15; Walker, Ch. 9) and either paid dearly or introduced a gold standard, the more distant states did not really buy the new economic ideology and fortunately returned to their guild-supportive paths soon after Napoleon lost his hold over them (Holborn, Godechot, *ibid.*). The entire pattern is detailed in Table 3.3 (Notes 3-7e).

More generally, Table 3.3 illustrates a close overall relationship -- among all non-ideological, militarily successful, countries -- between the birth of a flexibly convertible currency and the beginning of the accelerated demise of guilds in militarily successful countries. The relationship indicates that guilds and convertible monies were indeed substitute sources of emergency finance.

Table 3.3 also supports the complementary conclusion that the more economically ideological nations first outlawed guilds and then -- after suffering Holland-type military disasters and losses of sovereignty due to their losses of emergency financial capability -- introduced English-type convertible currencies. Consider, in the view of Table 3.3, the four regions (other than Holland and France, which we have already discussed) that abandoned guilds for significant periods of time before adopting convertible currencies: Spain, Switzerland, northern Italy, and southwestern Germany. Following our theory, each of these guild-abandoning areas suffered dramatic losses in territory during this period. Spain lost her extensive empire in the Americas. Switzerland lost her traditional military and economic independence. And northern Italian and western German states all similarly lost what autonomy they had to the least internally liberal, guild-retaining, Germanic states of Austria and Prussia, although the former durably succumbed to a rather complete form of laissez faire ideology during the 1850s and paid dearly, as we shall see.[65]

With the most ideologically inspired countries failing and the contemporary effective democracies continuing to exhibit exceptionally high growth rates, 1870s Europe predictably saw a wave of pragmatic and successful democratic revolutions supported by belatedly established convertible currencies.

The long delays in the southern and west-central European implementation of England's viable policy combination were thus caused largely by a mistaken adoption of the very theory we are criticizing in this paper!

This traditional economic theory misattributed the early success of Holland and the continuing success of England to their anti-guild policies rather than recognizing that it was the effective, legislatively pragmatic, investor-democracies of early 17th century Holland and 18th century England that accounted for their great economic successes. England's early 18th century guild elimination had uniquely succeeded because she, unlike 17th century Holland, remained unencumbered by a strong economic ideology and could therefore pragmatically establish a reliable emergency financial system before replacing guilds with a modern system of capital taxation.

France, economically as well as geographically, is an intermediate case. She was thus, as shown in Table 3.3, slow to adopt a gold standard and predictably suffered as a result. The failure of John Law's Bank in 1720 and the Assignat debacle of the 1790s were merely two of a long series of examples of financial errors due to a fateful unwillingness of a long dominant, or ex-dominant, country to pragmatically imitate the successes of an emerging neighbor.[66] Thus, as discussed in the notes to Table 3.3, the 1803 "gold standard" that France adopted was unique in that it failed, until after the defeat of Napoleon III and the subsequent introduction of a genuinely democratic Republic, to allow for suspended payments. We have already argued, and will further elaborate in Chapter 4, that suspended payments are a *sine qua non* of an effective gold standard. France had managed to form a bimetallic standard, which allowed her to beneficially switch to silver rather than gold payments during emergencies, when real gold prices increased; but this benefit is an insignificant source of emergency finance when compared to the financial freedom offered by a suspendable gold standard. The Empires of Napoleon I and III, the independence of the 19th century French legislature, and the French people all suffered dearly as a result of this poor substitute for a true gold standard.

---

[65]Similar losses were not seen again in western Europe until a century later, when these countries systematically abandoned their convertible currencies and were saved by the U.S., the one country that maintained a convertible currency (Chapter 4).

[66]In this way, our dynamical theory, which predicts the ideologization of civilizationally dominant societies, allows us to replace our perhaps overly subjective comparisons of various economic thought systems with a more objective criterion. In particular, as discussed above, since a society that was once civilizationally dominant will find it extremely difficult to return to anything like its original pragmatism, ex-dominance may, perhaps for future studies, be used as a rough proxy for economic ideologization.

E. Geographical Extensions

1. European Colonies

Freshly settled European colonies -- those in the Americas, Australia, New Zealand, and Africa -- have never been granted broadly entry-restrictive guilds. This is usually considered paradoxical, both because the settlers have typically been citizens of a mother country in which guilds were concurrently quite popular (see, e.g., Commons), and because it would appear to have been especially appropriate to reward these information-providing pioneers with monopoly rights.   Indeed, monopoly rights were regularly granted to colonizing firms (e.g., the East India Companies) that were economically bound to the mother country. But guilds in freshly settled colonies were a rarity.

Our theory easily explains this anomaly. A mother country has a negative interest in the ability of politically inferior territories to fully defend themselves. Once a colony can fully defend itself, it becomes rational for the colony to actually choose independence by establishing a local defense commitment. As elaborated in Chapter 5, Section I.G, since the parent is unwilling to risk making an all-or-nothing defense commitment, as revealed by its refusal to grant the colony political equality, once the parent loses her cost advantage in defending the colony, an unconstrained colony will rationally make its own all-or-nothing defense commitment. Of course, once the colony becomes independent, it is no longer available for rent extraction. Therefore, under our defense-oriented theory of guilds, colonial guild systems would, by hastening colonial independence, be undesirable to the mother country. Guild systems, like high levels of colonial wealth, would make it very difficult for the mother to hold onto her profitable offspring and would correspondingly reduce the present value of the rent she could extract from them.

For the same basic reason, colonial governments have traditionally been forced to depend on the currencies of their mother countries despite their frustrated pleas for some financial autonomy and colonial complaints of chronic "shortages of money" (e.g., Bolino, ch. 2). We know of no case in which a colonial government has been allowed to issue its own, flexibly convertible, paper money.

Moreover, once freed from their mother countries,[67] surviving ex-colonies all immediately introduced convertible currencies of their own. Experience, again in spite of the prevailing classical ideology, has again been the teacher, at least in the case of the United States (e.g., Bolino, p. 71). For example, the U.S. abandoned their central bank in 1811, immediately began steadily losing a war to an already-busy Great Britain in 1812, and could not militarily recover until restoring a central bank in 1816 (Sheiber, et. al., pp. 105-106).

---

[67]Prior to the 20th century military technology treated in Chapter 5, these revolutions predictably occurred immediately after unexpected surges in colonial wealth, when it suddenly became profitable for some individuals -- least expensively, permanent residents of the colony -- to provide the region with an all-or-nothing defense commitment. A simple theory of efficient colonial revolution is provided in Section I.G.1 of Chapter 5.

Still more dramatically, following WWII, after the U.S.-led victors offered effective convertibility to all third-world currencies through the International Monetary Fund, an unprecedented wave of formal decolonializations immediately arose. (Chapter 5 will discuss the underlying causes and unique economic effects of these 20th century movements towards national independence.)

2. Historical Eastern Centers

Although it is beyond the scope of this study, and the ken of the authors, to examine the Lamarckian interactions generating the rise and fall of guilds outside of European civilization, it is not beyond its scope to examine the structure and broad Darwinian pattern elsewhere in order to further test the general theory.

a. *The Byzantine Empire*. Byzantium, in contrast to the impoverished West, predictably continued, and even strengthened, the *Collegia and Corpora* of the ancient Roman Empire (e.g., Mickwitz, Ch. 1; pp. 77-78) and, of course, dramatically succeeded until faltering during the middle of the 11th century and then falling to the revitalized West during the Fourth Crusade just after the turn of the 13th century (e.g., Jenkins, p. 79; Lindsay, Chs. 16 and 17). Like the *Collegia*, early Byzantine guilds made a substantial political contribution to Byzantium's unique form of democracy (Guerdan, Ch. I). Also like the *Collegia*, Byzantine guilds were never administratively active. The highly detailed guild rules in Constantinople, although fairly democratic, were administered by the prefect's bureaucracy with no discernable input from the guilds (e.g., Lindsay, pp. 158-159). According to our theory, this combination would be efficient only if the bureaucracy was civilly reverent, which it clearly was under their traditionally Caesaropapistic, orthodox form of state Christianity (e.g., Vasiliev, pp. 334, 469-75). Throughout the halcyon years of the Empire, Byzantine guilds had been highly successful, all-input-restrictive, guilds of the export-monopolistic Germanic type, efficiently imposing selectively restrictive, cartelizing controls on their large foreign trade sector (Mickwitz) while collecting uniformly high entry fees, periodic license fees, and substantial emergency contributions (Rice, pp. 101, 124; A. Cameron, p. 119; Lindsay, p. 157).[68]

The impressive success of the Byzantine Empire also predictably brought with it a gradual rebirth of Hellenism (e.g., Jenkins, p. 823). This intellectual trend was held in check through competition with Orthodox conservatism up to the death of Basil II in 1025, whereafter it greatly accelerated and became a dominant, elitist, ideology under the influence of Michael Psellus and the later Macedonian Emperors

---

[68]Byzantium did not have the long periods of apprenticeship characteristics of the West (Mickwitz). This is due, applying our theory, to the absence of large feudal countryside from which to recruit new members and to which apprentices could retreat during military confrontations. With recruitment into the guilds of Constantinople therefore largely from the families of existing guild members (Lindsay, p. 160; Rice, p. 122), there was little call for the state, even one as hyperactive as the Byzantine state, to impose institutions serving to tie potential soldiers to the city.

(e.g., Rice, pp. 91, 102; Jenkins).

Although the recurring financial disasters and territorial losses of these later Macedonian Emperors produced a temporary return of the Byzantine bureaucracy to Orthodox Ceasaropapism, there was also a continued underlying growth of Hellenistic (Aristotelian) humanism (e.g., Vasiliev, pp. 469-472, 478-479). It was not long before the urban-democratic rule-making process was surrendered to authoritarian Hellenistic elites (e.g., Finlay, pp. 270-71). Since popular insurrection was then the only means of political expression left to the decreasingly influential guilds by the late 11th century (Vryonis), and since the post-Macedonian emperors adopted personally highly protective bureaucracies so as to make themselves impervious to insurrection (Finlay, Ch. 1), there was a rapid emergence of the same Hellenistic despotism that, three centuries later and with eerily similar consequences, developed during the Italian Renaissance. Peacetime urban taxation under the Comneni and Angeli thus continued the rise begun under the similarly Grecophilic Macedonians. In the end, the hopelessly overtaxed common guildsmen, rather than filling their traditional role of defending the walls of Constantinople (Rice, p. 124), cheered on the enemy during the infamous Norman siege of 1204 (e.g., Lindsay, pp. 165-67)!

b. *The Middle East.* The Middle-East was not far behind Europe in the successful development of guilds as bureaucratically active, defense-providing, urban economic organizations of investors. Such investor-bands (or futuwwah clubs) were the backbone of the democratically driven Ismaili Shiite movement of the 10th-12th centuries that enabled the Fatimid Caliphate to elevate the Moslem centers at Cairo, Baghdad, Aleppo and Damascus to an Islamic golden age (Massignon, Hodgson, pp. 126-30). However, just as in neighboring Byzantium, the remarkable Moslem success was aborted by a late 11th and early 12th century growth of relatively secular humanism (von Grunebaum, Hodgson, Ch. 3). Sufism, the traditional Middle-eastern version of elite Hellenism, steadily infiltrated the political system through the relatively wealthy, educated Sunnies until the futuwwahs were irreversibly transformed into government agencies for the increasingly authoritarian, increasingly Turkish, governments (Hodgson, pp. 129-31, 192-221 and Ch. V; Massignon).

The more fundamentally democratic West, at least those states that were able to resist the economically stultifying effects of legislative ideology, increasingly succeeded relative to the various Turkish and Mongolian despotisms of the 13th-early 20th centuries. Nevertheless, an exception arose when bureaucratically active and entry-restrictive guilds -- together with a fundamentalist, *mujtahidic*, form of Shiism -- were restored to Persia in the late Safavid Empire of the later 17th and early 18th centuries (see, e.g., Hodgson, v. 3, pp. 53-5; Floor, pp. 105-08; Roemer, pp. 304-14). These guilds, however, provided little in the way of direct military services, and correspondingly had relatively weak systems of apprenticeship and fraternalism (Kuznetsova). The remarkable economic prosperity of early 18th century Ishfahan therefore did not prevent a coalition of banished Sunnies and disgruntled Turks from soon destroying the embarrassingly successful Empire and restoring the old, Sufi-dominated, authoritarianism (Roemer, Floor, p. 108).

c. *India.* Indian guilds had earlier followed a similar pattern. The worldwide, light-armor-based, urban centralizations of the 6th century B.C., which brought more humanistic religions to the entire world (e.g., Macdonnall), brought bureaucratically active, entry-restrictive guilds and correspondingly restored anti-Brahmanic, democratic forces to India during this critical century (Anstey). Supported by the development of Indian Buddhism and Jainism, these guilds led India to its golden age, only to be eventually absorbed into a resurrected, Brahman-dominated, bureaucracy under the Guptas during the 3rd-5th centuries. The predictably rapid submission of the region to foreign domination lasted well into the 20th century, just as the emasculation of the initially independent Byzantine and Islamic guilds by legislatively ideologized bureaucrats was to subsequently seal virtually identical fates for India's neighbors to the west, and just as a subsequent series of ideologically inspired guild eliminations was to wreak political and economic havoc in the West.

d. *China.* Chinese guilds traditionally worked outside of normal governmental channels (H.B. Morse) and therefore provided little in the way of emergency aid of any sort. Chinese guilds thus present us with a unique opportunity to examine a kind of guild whose only possible primary social function (besides collecting peacetime taxes) was protection from the bureaucracy. Indeed, probably because of the relative simplicity of such guilds, studies of Chinese guilds have consistently argued that these guilds were historically organized explicitly to provide a check on the corrupt, or ideologically inflexible, Chinese bureaucracy (Burgess, Morse).

Nevertheless, the same studies, largely under the inspiration of classical economics, also strenuously insist that the entry restrictions of the Chinese guilds soon became seriously monopolistic. Just as we found in evaluating studies of western guilds, these monopoly-claiming authors simultaneously note: (1) the common existence of real price maxima; (2) the fact that these politically weak guilds were typically well-represented in towns politically dominated by their so-called "victims"; and (3) the relatively high rates of economic growth in the traditionally guild-dominated Imperial regions, Peking and Canton. Ideologization is our only explanation for such non-objective economic arguments.

The traditional studies of Chinese guilds also fail to explain the central peculiarity of recorded Chinese guilds, their lack of emergency defense role. In contrast, our efficiency-oriented theory easily explains this unique feature of Chinese guilds in that China pioneered a widely accepted convertible paper money system in the 9th century, long before the beginning of the recorded history of Chinese guilds (Edkins, pp. 10-11; Burgess, Ch. II, and Ch. 3 below).

Finally, again following our efficiency theory, the traditional lack of a special emergency defense role for guilds and, more generally, urbanites in Chinese military history, explains China's corresponding absence of both the producer egalitarianism and artificially long apprenticeships found in the West.

e. *Japan.* Unlike those of China, the guilds of Japan served seriously military, anti-Ronin and anti-Hatamoto (Murdoch, vol. 3, pp. 40-49), functions as well as standard bureaucratic functions. Correspondingly, as we should by now expect, Japanese guilds rapidly developed both highly intensive apprenticeship programs and extremely high degrees of guild fraternalism (Takekoshi, Ch. 77). It should similarly be no surprise, at least as regards Japanese history recorded after the rapid centralizations under Nobunaga and Hideyoshi following the arrival of European firearms in the mid-16th century, that Japan's only two periods of sudden, anti-monopoly-inspired, guild-weakening -- prior to her adoption of the precious metal standard late in the 19th century (Murdoch, v. 2, p. 36) -- were also her only two periods of internal military collapse.   In particular, Japan's first ideologically inspired elimination of guild entry restrictions occurred just prior to the 250-year take-over in 1603 by the guild-strengthening Tokugawas (Allen, p. 221); and the second occurred in the mid-19th century, just prior to the Tokugawa loss to the relatively democratic, guild-strengthening, Meijis (Allen, p. 222.)

f. *Brief Summary.*   Although we have obviously failed to acquire sufficient information on interstate information flows to evaluate the Lamarckian evolutionary dynamics of guild development for these historic eastern centers, the above observations work both to confirm our static theory and indicate that powerful Darwinian forces were contributing to the creation of the theoretically predicted institutional pattern.

F. The Central Lesson of Guild-History

Examining the details of the rise and fall of European guilds has consistently illustrated the high social cost of economic ideology whenever the ideas of subtly self-aggrandizing intellectuals, on the left or the right, win-out over the special-interest compromises that characterize an effective democracy. By far, the most devastating have been the losses of state sovereignty that almost immediately arise in previously effective democracies. These repeated pre-WWI disasters will, as shown in the next chapter, find a 20th century descendent in an analogously premature, analogously ideologically inspired, fall of the very same gold standard that had earlier arisen to replace the guilds as a vital economic institution.

III. THE ECONOMIC POLICIES GENERATED BY PROTECTIONIST LOBBIES

We now apply the above political theory to observed tariff systems. Under this political theory, if such domestic-price-increasing trade intervention were not citizen-efficient, it could not have evolved to where virtually all states have come to adopt significant restrictions on a broad range of their imports. Under this theory, there can be no lasting ignorant-consumer bias, wherein consumers or their chosen representatives, according to the implicit logic of neoclassical and modern political economists, persistently underestimate the price-increasing effects of government policies such as tariffs or of the political lobbies that promote such policies. Under our political theory, universally adopted, domestic-price-increasing, import-restrictions must somehow confer corresponding external benefits on the citizens of the domestic economy.

We have already dealt with a foreign-trade-externality in which an exporting country receives substantial pecuniary benefits via export taxes that internalize interregional monopoly effects. Admitting the exploitation of such interregional monopolization opportunities, thereby assuming prohibitively high costs of interregional cooperation, we were able to economically rationalize the peculiar features of certain guild policies (the double taxation of certain Dutch, German, and Byzantine Export Guilds as well as the export taxation of the early nation-states.) So as not to disturb this monopolistic trade analyses, we shall restrict our subsequent analyses to states or markets that experience sufficient interregional <u>competition</u> that regionally monopolistic price-effects can be ignored. The same will be assumed true of the buying side so that monopsony-inspired import tariffs will be similarly ignored.

A negative import-externality will nevertheless arise. In particular, the <u>same</u> defense-externality that we have been discussing (Appendix B.2) will economically rationalize a negative import-externality. And recognizing the existence of this import-externality will enable us to rationalize the salient structural features of traditionally observed tariff policies. It will correspondingly allow us to explain the short historical lives of laissez faire policies and the long historical lives of various forms of mercantilism.

A. Optimal and Actual Trade Restrictions Under Interregional Import Competition

1. The Structure of Import Duties

Consider first the case in which a country is importing a consumer durable. Again, since we are assuming that goods are bought under conditions of interregional competition so that a single country cannot affect the real price that it pays for the import, no import duty is justifiable on the familiar "scientific tariff" grounds that it produces monopsony benefits for the importing country (Bickerdike). Nevertheless, since taxes on the ownership of existing stocks of consumer goods (excepting commonly visible goods such as houses and transportation vehicles) have rarely been significant in history (because of the ease of large-scale bureaucratic or taxpayer abuse under in-house property taxation), and since imported consumer goods cannot be taxed through an ordinary income tax simply because the goods are produced abroad, imported consumer durables create a defense-externality that can be practically internalized <u>only</u> through an import tariff.[69]

---

[69]Defense-externalities also arise when a consumer good is domestically produced. So, as emphasized in the Conclusion of Appendix B.2, if domestic producers were always perfectly competitive, the efficient governmental response would be to extend the tariffs as a tax on the local production of consumer durables. However, two problems arise. First, many domestic producers of domestically consumed durables goods are relatively monopolistic because they produce relatively unique, heterogeneous goods. The reason is simple: Certain consumers are willing to pay a substantial premium for tailored, necessarily heterogeneous, goods over homogeneous goods; and nearby, domestic, producers have a comparative advantage -- based

The magnitude of the optimal tariff is the present value of the future defense liability created by the imported consumer durable. Assuming the annual real estate tax rate reflects the annual defense liability of a unit of coveted capital, the optimal tariff would be the present value of the real estate taxes that could be hypothetically levied on these imports. For example, if we assume a real interest rate of 4%, and an annual real estate tax rate of 2%, the importation of an infinite-lifespan consumer durable should be taxed at 50%.

Regarding somewhat less durable consumer goods, since low-priced consumer goods are normally much less economically durable, and also less coveted, than high-priced consumer goods of the same general type, an efficient tariff system is progressive, concentrating its highest tariff rates (like the 50% in the above example) on the luxury end of the market for a given type of good.

Regarding imports of fixed capital goods, such as industrial equipment, since such goods are generally taxed by the importing country through an ordinary income or property tax, they should generally remain duty-free in an interregionally competitive market place. (Some 20th century exceptions, due to the 20th century emergence of wartime rationing schemes, are described in Appendix B.3.)

Finally, regarding imports of intermediate inputs, or circulating capital, a simple extension of the domestic property tax to inventories will not suffice to internalize the defense-externality from such capital: Considering first that part of the circulating capital stock that avoids inventory taxation because it is imported, processed, and re-exported all within successive dates of inventory tax assessment, the covetedness of the capital and hence the optimal import tax is quite small and can be ignored (see Appendix B.2). More significantly, consider intermediate inputs of the type that may be held across tax-collection dates. Here, an optimal domestic inventory tax rate is significantly below the optimal capital tax rate. This is because of the deadweight avoidance costs induced by socially costly inventory relocations around tax-collection

---

on both transportational and informational factors -- in supplying and informing these monopolizable consumers. (The overhead costs of informing users of the unique aspects of the locally tailored goods create a collective-good allocation problem that generates very high equilibrium mark-ups in the sales of the private good (Thompson, et al., Vol. III, Ch. 6)). Local producers therefore tend to be the suppliers of high-mark-up goods tailored to suit local tastes, leaving foreign producers to specialize in relatively homogeneous goods. The result is that taxes on the sales of such domestically produced consumer durables should be, and typically have been, insignificant compared to the taxes due on imported consumer durables.

Second, although high transportation costs, especially during defensive emergencies, also account for the efficient presence of several domestic industries producing homogeneous consumer goods that directly compete with low mark-up imports, such domestic industries are ordinarily due the wartime-price-control-based protection described in Appendix B.3. Hence, whether or not a domestically produced consumer good is a high mark-up, custom product or a basic, homogeneous, commodity, efficiency ordinarily dictates an effective forgiveness of national taxes on the domestic output as well as the benefits of tariff protection described in Appendix B.3.

dates. So an import tax on circulating capital is in order.[70] In other words, given the general insufficiency of the optimal domestic inventory tax, a small, non-internalized, defense-externality would exist in the absence of a tariff.[71] In any case, an optimal tariff on circulating capital is typically much less than an optimal tariff on the final goods represented by consumer durables. Assuming a holding period of three years, and the effective absence of an inventory tax, under the above numerical assumptions, the optimal tariff on circulating capital imports would be less than 7%.

Just as our efficiency theory predicts: Consumer goods have historically received much higher tariffs than raw material inputs; raw materials have faced higher tariffs than fixed capital goods; and fixed capital goods have typically been duty-free (e.g., Taussig, S. Litman, Yeates). Moreover, again as our efficiency theory predicts, observed tariffs have typically varied positively with durability and been progressive in that high-priced, or "luxury", imports of a given type of consumer good have typically been taxed at significantly higher rates, even in non-egalitarian societies such as mercantile Europe (e.g., Gray, Taussig, pp. 92, 247-48, 268).

Additional evidence, most obvious since the advent of large steamers during the early 1800s and the subsequent enhancement of international trade in agricultural products, results from the fact that the lives of agricultural inputs (e.g., grains and

---

[70]Note that an income tax will fail to tax circulating capital altogether. For, regardless of when a domestic producer sells the output from an imported raw material, the expected present cost of the producer's future income tax liability equals the producer's current tax writeoff from purchasing this material. Thus, consider a manufacturer who, in a competitive equilibrium, imports a raw material for a dollar. The income tax rate is again 25% and the interest rate 10%. The manufacturer immediately writes off the raw material expense and receives an income tax credit of $0.25. If the manufacturer waits a year to use up his material, the net product of the input will be sold for $1.10 and the additional income tax bill will be $0.275. If the manufacturer waits two years, the tax bill will be $0.3025, etc. However long the manufacturer waits, the present value of the additional income tax equals the initial $0.25 writeoff on the good. Thus, the income tax completely fails to discourage accumulations of circulating capital (for a generalization of the argument, see Appendix B.2.)

[71]This negative externality also exists for <u>domestically produced</u> circulating capital. However, under the positive-defense-externality developed in Appendix B.3, the traditional, efficient, wartime price controls on domestically produced intermediate-good inputs imply the efficiency of a roughly offsetting subsidy to the domestic production of these imports. Because high wartime transportation costs shut-off the foreign supplies of most such inputs, this offsetting subsidy is justified for only a small number of imported intermediate inputs. As developed in Appendix B.3, we have come to establish excess-capacity-inducing foreign cartels or domestic tax-shelters to accompany the severe underevaluautions generated by 20th century wartime rationing systems. As regards intermediate inputs that do <u>not</u> suffer from these 20th century wartime rationing systems, the optimal peacetime tax-favor is relatively small, depending merely upon the extent to which wartime governments directly purchase the intermediate inputs at the controlled prices. This relatively small Appendix B.3-subsidy is the same order of magnitude as the optimal tax (the 7% tax that we are about to calculate from the numerical example in the text above) on circulating capital according to the negative defense-externality appearing in Appendix B.2.

livestock) greatly exceed the lives of the corresponding final outputs, (e.g., bread and meat and dairy products). Again corresponding to our theory, and similarly unexplained within existing theories, imports of basic agricultural inputs have traditionally been burdened with much higher tariffs than imports of the perishable products of these relatively durable inputs (e.g., Yeates, pp. 44-46).

Tariff rates can be assessed either on an *ad valorem* or on a per-unit basis. (The latter tariffs are usually called "specific" tariffs.) Consider the present tariff cost to an importer of an out-of-season durable import, one that appreciates with the interest rate. This cost does not change with the date of import if the tariff is *ad valorem*. So *ad valorem* tariffs on these appreciating assets are inefficient in that the tariffs create no incentive to delay the importation of the assets. However, if the tariff on the appreciating import is assessed on a per-unit basis, the present cost of the tariff to the importer appropriately decreases the longer the good is kept abroad. Note that the value of a durable import can be expected to appreciate almost all of the time if the production or use of the good is seasonal, and that it is irrational to plan to hold inventories of such goods across either utilization or production seasons, during which prices are expected to drop. Therefore, according to our theory, seasonal commodities should receive a per-unit rather than an *ad valorem* tariff.

In fact, imports possessing a highly seasonal utilization or production pattern, largely raw material inputs of domestically processed goods such as clothing and food, have long received per-unit rather than *ad valorem* tariffs. In contrast, observed tariffs on imports of finished goods, whose production and use is not significantly seasonal, are, as predicted by our quality-sensitive theory, historically much more likely to receive *ad valorem* rather than per-unit tariffs (see, e.g., Taussig, p. 161, Bastable, p. 74). The theory similarly explains why basic raw materials should have systematically received per-unit tariffs while imports of the <u>same goods in finished form</u> received *ad valorem* tariffs. Typical is the 19th century British per-unit tariff on raw silk and *ad valorem* tariff on finished silk (Bastable, p. 92) and the French per-unit tariff on unfinished cotton but *ad valorem* tariff on finished cotton (M. Smith, p. 258). Also, regarding modern consumer goods, the decreasing importance of the seasonal factors responsible for periodic price appreciation have substantially reduced the incentive advantages of per-unit tariffs. Correspondingly, per-unit tariffs have been increasingly replaced with *ad valorem* tariffs.[72]

Our efficiency theory also helps explain other historically unexplained trade policies. For example, the typical medieval and early modern trading towns had effective laws against "engrossing", which imposed maximum restrictions on the storage time of circulating-capital imports (see Tuma, p. 91 and Hibbert, pp. 172-179). Such laws -- and similar laws against inventory speculation, or "regrating" -- substitute for local property or inventory taxes in taxing circulating-capital imports that are held in ports for exceptionally long time periods.

---

[72]The only known alternative explanation for per-unit, or "specific", tariffs over *ad valorem* tariffs is that addition is easier than multiplication for the customs officials. However, this theory has no way to explain the contrasting pattern of tariffs on raw materials and finished goods.

As indicated in the Introduction, the theory also helps explain why specialized trading centers, which locate in areas that are especially secure but not especially favorable to manufacturing, have regularly imposed extremely low tariffs. The low tariffs observed in these commercial centers reflect their comparatively low defense costs. We have already mentioned the famous medieval examples of the periodic Champagne fairs of the 12th century, the later medieval free German and Scandinavian ports serving as entrepots for cross-Baltic trade, 17th century Amsterdam, and 20th century Hong Kong. The modern international "freeport" provides an even more extreme example. The historical inability of such free-trade centers to induce competing buyers in neighboring regions to insist upon similarly low-tariffs is strong evidence for the presence of a negative import-externality such as the defense-externality employed throughout this work.

Similarly, any collectively defended federation of states, say the modern U.S., has no efficient reason to possess tariffs on intra-federational, or "interstate", trade because the federation's defense-externality is no different whether a good is located in one state or another within the federation. Hence, tariff-imposing federal governments are regularly observed to strictly outlaw tariffs between member states. For the same reason, federal income taxes should be, and typically are, on federation-wide income; this again reflects the fact that the defense-externality is the same regardless of the location of the income-earning asset within the federation.

Finally, the efficiency theory also rationalizes the external financial policies of colonizing European governments. In the early colonial period of the 16th and 17th centuries, European explorer-investors received state-granted protection if they formed investment companies giving the sponsoring state the fixed-percentage profit-share of an ordinary investment partner even though the state did not directly contribute, other than to overhead defense costs. In this way, colonizing nation-states were, in effect, able to tax for the defense-externalities imposed on them as protectors by their resource-rich colonies.[73] These imperial governments introduced colonial property taxes and tariffs only after it became sufficiently difficult to monitor the increasingly complex foreign operations of the investor-managers.[74]

---

[73]As we have already noted (footnote 47 above), Batchelder and Sanchez have pointed out that the much-maligned capital-consuming system of temporary property rights employed by early Spain in exploiting her lucrative American colonies can be rationalized by noting that the system internalized a defense-externality. Combining this with our rationalization of ancient Germanic (i.e., non-monetary) taxation in the same footnote, whenever an overlord can neither evaluate a local lord's holdings nor observe the activities under the local lord's control, an overlord wishing to efficiently discourage the locality's peacetime accumulation of coveted capital has no choice other than to artificially limit the lord's tenure.

[74]It is overly simple to argue that the American Revolution, like other colonial liberations, was basically caused by high imperial tariffs. Much higher tariffs were adopted by the early U.S. governments. Rather, as noted above in Section II.E.1, such liberations efficiently result from large unexpected increases in colonial wealth, together with the prudent unwillingness of the mother country to make an all-or-nothing defense commitment over an isolated geographic area (reflected in her prudent unwillingness to grant equal political status -- e.g.,

2. The Structure of Export Duties

Accumulations of exportables within a country are efficiently discouraged through a correct level of domestic income or property taxes. Traders, to avoid the efficient income or property tax on domestic exportables, would appropriately export their goods when and only when the assets are more productive, net of foreign defense costs as reflected in foreign taxes, in other countries. Thus, given efficient capital-tax levels, and an absence of export monopolies, optimal export taxes are zero.

Indeed, export taxes typically are very low, approximating user-charges on ports for competitively marketed exports. This is a useful first approximation. However, suppose domestic taxes on some goods were set at an overly high level. These goods would then be over-exported to avoid the overly high domestic capital tax. Such over-taxation would not arise in a citizen-efficient state unless some of the domestic tax -- due to expropriation by civilly-irreverent bureaucrats or private rent-seekers -- were hidden. Otherwise, if the government knew which of its capital goods were over-taxed -- i.e., which exports were leaving the country for the purpose of avoiding the tax -- it could simply eliminate the excessive domestic tax rate on those goods. But, since the expropriation is hidden from the government, the best the government can do is both lower the official tax rate on all such internally coveted capital and impose a tax on exports of the same class of goods. Although such an export duty, by discouraging exports, encourages expropriation, some of the returns to the rent-extractors are pure economic rent (to an endowed ability to expropriate resources) and hence not part of the social cost of expropriation. Some export tariff -- especially on raw materials, the processing of which is often subject to various governmental controls and therefore potential domestic rent extraction -- would therefore be efficient in an internally expropriative state.

Our efficiency theory thus helps explain why late medieval and early modern states imposed selective export duties on the outputs of industries where guilds were weak (Heckscher (1955), v. 2, pp. 80-90). A famous example is the English export duty on raw wools and hides, goods whose international prices England could have only slightly affected. Our efficiency theory also helps explain why export duties in the civilly reverent nations of Protestant Europe were eliminated soon after the middle of the 17th century but were not abandoned in the rest of Europe until the anti-ideological reforms of the late-19th century.

Since investment subsidies are justified by the same argument, and since the argument in modern times is restricted to lesser-developed countries, we should, and do, observe export taxes and domestic investment subsidies working together as unique policy complements in selective sectors of almost all lesser-developed

---

parliamentary representation -- to the colonial territories). Under such circumstances, it is rational for a colony to refuse to pay whatever charges the parent is levying to pay their relatively high costs of colonial defense. Colonial status is appropriate for an area only when it is sufficiently rich to be worth exploiting but also sufficiently poor that it cannot afford the overhead cost of establishing an all-or-nothing defense commitment. We shall return to this matter in the more explicit theory in Section I.G of Chapter 5.

countries (Meier, pp. 540-547).

Finally, with consumer goods seldom subject to hidden bureaucratic rent extraction, export duties have efficiently concentrated on producer goods (Towle, p. 233). (Export taxes for self-sufficiency are discussed in Section B.2 below.)

3. Transit Duties

Our efficiency theory predicts that moderate tariffs should be imposed on goods originating in one country and passing through a second country for a significant amount of time in order to get to a third. Such tariffs, known as transit duties, were common in the transportation-providing countries of Europe until the advent of the railroad in the mid-19th century. By shortening the time spent in transit within the intermediate country, rail travel made the optimal level of such duties insignificant. Correspondingly, the duties generally disappeared in countries soon after they introduced national rail systems (Bastable, p. 219).

B. The Historical Lives of Various Tariff Policies

1. The Rise and Fall of British Laissez Faire

The above efficiency theory also explains the relatively unique free-trade policy that arose in Great Britain after the first quarter of the 19th century, as the uniquely successful British Empire was becoming so widespread that Great Britain scarcely imported from countries other than her own colonies. There was little point to high tariffs under such conditions because the Empire's expected defense cost was not much higher than if Great Britain did not import the good.

At the same time, colonial capital owned by the British should have been taxed as if it were domestic capital. Britain achieved this by introducing a "wealth tax" to substitute for her previous national property tax and broadly based British tariff (World Tax Series, p. 32). A wealth tax differs from a property or modern income tax in that it also taxes the value of citizens' domestically protected overseas properties (Appendix B.2). Thus, after Britain's Second Empire quickly grew to maturity following the defeat of Napoleon, she soon introduced her unique wealth tax (part of the 1842 Income Tax Act (World Tax Series, 1947, pp. 32-35)) and steadily reduced her extraordinarily high tariffs of the early 1820s to unusually low levels by the 1860s. As discussed in the Introduction, although the subsequently rapid growth of extra-imperial imports made Great Britain's free-trade policy increasingly obsolete, ideologizing Great Britain unfortunately retained the program all the way up to World War I. Elsewhere, except in similarly ideologized Austria, the previously misguided continental attempts at their own laissez faire policies did not survive the 1870s. Great Britain's, and to a lesser extent Austria's, uniquely persistent laissez faire policies thus appear to be yet another instance of the self-destructive evolution of a teacher-favoring legislative ideology. Let us briefly re-examine the British sequence.

The early stages in the sequence were easily consistent with the systematic efficiency of the legislatively pragmatic English policy that followed the Glorious Revolution. As we have already explained, previously dominant France foundered in the latter third of the 18th century and first two-thirds of the 19th century, when her bureaucratic elite conveniently misattributed the success of Britain's 18th century democracy to her internally laissez faire policies and refused to adopt a true gold standard, one that would have suspended conversion payments during military emergencies. Nineteenth century Great Britain quickly capitalized upon France's growing weakness by cementing in the foundation of her Second Empire, aggressively expanding her colonial interests in Australia, New Zealand, the Cape Colony, India and Canada (e.g., Burt, Part II, and p. 207, J. Williamson, Part I). What soon followed was a mutual colonial tariff reduction, a system of "Imperial preferences" appropriately facilitating trade between the colonies while maintaining high tariffs to outsiders (e.g., O. Williamson, p. 53, Bastable, pp. 47-49). The rapid growth of imperial investment in these areas in the 1830s (e.g., Burt, *ibid.*) led to the above-discussed wealth tax of 1842 and another round of internal tariff reductions.

The 1842-1853 period marked a second stage in the development of British free trade policies (e.g., Bastable, p. 53, J. Williamson, pp. 56-7). The 1842 income-wealth tax and the rapidly increasing degree of Imperial self-sufficiency during the second quarter of the 19th century led to a sharply decreasing need to tax raw-material imports generally. The sharp drop in British raw-materials tariffs during the period was therefore no surprise under an efficient-government theory. There was also a gradual, empire-wide, lowering of tariffs on non-imperial imports throughout the period, which can be justified by the generally decreased military threat facing the increasingly dominant Empire.

But then there was a third, decidedly ideological, stage, the late Gladstone-Cobden stage, culminating in the extreme free-trade policy of 1860 (e.g., Bastable, pp. 55-60, Bowden et al, pp. 357-361). A temporary union with France during the Crimean war may well have justified this universalistic British policy for a few years, and free-trade policy spread throughout Europe, Prussia being a notable exception. But Prussia's successful aggression against Austria's "Liberal Empire" in 1866, and France's in 1871, without a bit of help from Great Britain, spelled a pragmatic continental return to narrow nationalism and tariff barriers.

Yet sufficient time had elapsed for Great Britain, like Austria, to catch the French disease.[75] Britain and Austria's free-trade policies remained. They became an article of faith to their well-educated elites all the way up to the Great War.

With no way to discourage post-1860 British manufacturing exports of monopolizable goods short of domestic monopolization, a decidedly second-best wave of trade union monopolies was quickly formed in Great Britain's export-

---

[75]The disease, of course, was free-trade ideology. Although France's free-trade ideology and policy came a century earlier than England's, the cost of free-trade ideology to France was interrupted by the Bourbon Restoration and the Second Republic (1814-1852) but was probably dwarfed by the hard-money ideology that we have seen prevented her from establishing a survivable democracy prior to the 1870s. Although French laissez faire ideology may be thought to be more extreme than England's in that France and Austria typically imposed imperial free-trade on their colonies while England did not, France and Austria also granted much less military and legislative independence to their colonies.

monopolizable markets (Bowden et al., pp. 548-51). Although well-justifiable in the 1870s given the free-trade constraint, all this labor policy did for the subsequent 100 years was burden Britain with another, pro-labor-monopoly, ideology to complement her earlier, pro-free-trade, ideology. For the original, export-monopoly, justification for these domestic labor monopolies was soon lost due to international competition from Germany, the U.S., and France during the 1880s and 1890s.

Moreover, with no ideologically acceptable way to discourage imports of manufactured consumer goods, Britain, along with Austria, its similarly dominant and ideologized counterpart in eastern Europe, essentially subsidized the post-1860 industrial development of Germany, France, Russia, and the U.S., while making themselves prime targets for early 20th century military aggression.[76] The British and Austrian examples thus complement our earlier examples in indicating both (a) the high costs of teacher-favoring legislative ideologies in dominant states and (b) the great difficulty in restoring legislative pragmatism to a once-dominant state.

As we have already seen, the typical response to a failed ideology, like Great Britain's after WWI, is the adoption of an alternative ideology rather than a return to legislative pragmatism. Chapters 4 and 5 will elaborate on Great Britain's post-WWI ideology. Indeed, the only cases we have found in which ex-dominant nations have been able to durably restore a semblance of its original legislative pragmatism and bureaucratic civil reverence are apparently due to the adoption of a centralized system of state education.[77] Probably the most effective such educational transform-

---

[76]Deriving the existence of a jointly rational war for our Pascalian representatives when there is an ideology-based excess in the country's capital stock is not quite the same as applying our "war and ideology" model at the end of Section II.D.4 above. When there is an ideology-based excessive accumulation, the country's ruling class feels that there is no real problem with such large accumulations (like Solomon's descendants). If the ideologized country were appropriately increasing its defense expenditures, the country's ruling class would very likely feel that the growingly expensive accumulation was inappropriate. So defense expenditures are not likely to appropriately increase and the ideologized ruling class does not feel that the country is becoming an easy target. What this amounts to is a growing underestimate of the probability of a foreign attack, an observable unwillingness of the ideologized leaders to take seriously the growing threats of foreign aggressors and corresponding overestimate of its probability of winning a war. Checking the more complex war and revolution examples at the end of Section II.D.4 above and Section I.G.1 of Chapter 5 below, it is easy to see that such incorrect estimates are the basis of the breakdown of prewar negotiations. For an extreme example, if a country that is objectively profitable for others to attack in the absence of bribes believed itself to be invincible, it would offer a zero bribe to objective aggressors and be rationally attacked.

[77]Although a centralized education system is contrary to what we have defined as a "democracy", once a country is ideologized, its optimal policy might well be a short-term acceptance of surface-democratic institutions (i.e., elections, representative legislatures, etc.) along with a centralized educational policy designed to de-ideologize the ruling classes. We shall, in our concluding recommendations of Chapter 6, complement this education policy with a more immediately effective and genuinely democratic de-ideologization policy.

ation followed the decade of the French Revolution. What emerged during the post-Napoleonic era was a new national system of intentionally practical education (Cobban), one that completely separated the education of future governmental officials from the education of professional scientists and technicians and explicitly downplayed the political and moral sciences (e.g., R. Cameron). Although subsequently enhanced by Louis Philippe and supported by Napoleon III, it took over half of a century to accomplish the task, the French ruling classes finally emerged in the 1870s with a new, finally nationally democratic, economically pragmatic, albeit radically nationalistic, political value system to replace their prior economic ideologies.[78] It is doubtful that the incomparable French aptitude for philosophy and political economy could have been controlled with anything other than a persistent dedication to a consciously fixed national education policy.[79]

2. The Rise of Mercantilism and the Rise and Fall of Classical Mercantilism

Local defense throughout the Middle Ages was essentially siege defense. Sufficient initial inventories of various basic consumer goods had to be available to the town to withstand a siege and its related trade embargo. As we have noted, emergency price controls were readily effected under normal guild practices. As a result, medieval towns had a problem in inducing sufficient peacetime accumulations of siege-relevant inventories, the appropriate response to which was the establishment of special policies encouraging the peacetime accumulation of these assets (Appendix B.3). This worked through "staple" and "provisionist" policies (Heckscher, 1955, Vol. II, Pt. III). The former policy, partially through the notorious "forestalling" laws, which outlawed selling certain outputs in a medieval state outside of its walled towns, appropriately encouraged the movement of inventories of "staple" commodities into the potentially embargoed towns (Heckscher (*ibid.*), Ch. II). Related, "provisionist" policies encouraged these and related goods to remain in the towns by taxing their export from the town (Heckscher (*ibid.*), Ch. III).

These provisionist policies gradually disappeared in early modern western Europe as sieges were, as we have already emphasized, increasingly overshadowed by longer term, more financially expensive, national warfare. Nevertheless, since early nation-states retained their guilds and therefore their effective emergency price

---

[78]Before the 1870s, a bureaucracy-serving, St. Simonian, form of scientific socialism had grown up to compete with the aristocracy-serving doctrine of laissez faire. However both faltered from the 1870s to the 1920s. For example, although one of the chief reforms of the democratizing Third Republic was to set up a new school for the study of political science and political economy that was free from governmental control (1872), the financial dependence of the school on governmental sources soon converted the school into just another *Grande École* for educating governmental administrators (Osborne).

[79]Thus, in economics, for example, we witness the spectacle of arguably the world's three greatest 19th century economic theorists -- Cournot, Du Puit, and Walras -- educated to be non-ideological French engineers and essentially ignored by governmental policymakers.

controls, and since national wars were much more lengthy than town sieges, providing efficient peacetime accumulation incentives required much more than encouraging the peacetime inventory accumulation of staple consumption goods. Thus, a new form of mercantilism arose, one reflecting new pressures to build up peacetime productive capacity and thus productive self-sufficiency (Appendix B.3). These mercantilistic policies were appropriate in and only in strong nation-states and, in fact, emerged in and only in such states. Moreover, although to an appropriately decreasing degree, these policies have remained to this very day (*ibid.*).[80]

But classical mercantilism, which is something else, began with the practical success of precious-metal-accumulating 16th century Spain. The enlarged scope of 16th century defense systems created a large jump in emergency financial demands, which Spain was uniquely qualified to supply. As convertibility systems were not yet available in the West, multiple coinage systems remained dominant. This meant that the demand for emergency national stores of precious metals dramatically rose in the West during the 16th and 17th centuries. (The theoretical basis of classical mercantilism, the proposition that the available amount of emergency military purchasing power in a multiple-coinage system increases in proportion to the country's stock of precious metal, <u>independently</u> of whether the precious metal is held by the government or its untaxed public, is demonstrated in Thompson, et al., Vol. II, Ch. 2, Section I.A.5). It was the practical success of accidently gold-accumulating Spain that inspired the other successes of the mercantilist period.

Thus, as the United States and Germany introduced gold-standards at about the same time they became nation-states, these countries never did adopt the classical, precious-metals mercantilism that characterized 17th century western Europe. Nor did they adopt the extreme self-sufficiency, harshly import-prohibiting, policies of the earlier period (Heckscher (1955), V. 2, pp. 326-89).[81]

Moreover, classical, gold-conserving, western European mercantilism declined with the spread of British-type convertible banking systems (Heckscher, *ibid.*, pp. 231-52). Thus, although, as explained above (in Section II.D.5), the emulative spread of the gold standard was overly slow, the eventually obvious successes of states with these new financial systems finally robbed the mercantilists of their previously politically successful role models (especially Spain and France). Gone with them was

---

[80]Tariffs levels in 16th and 17th century Europe exceeded those that followed despite the fact that military expenditures were a larger fraction of national income during the later period. A likely reason, as explained in Section I.B of Chapter 5, is that the domestic defense-externality, reflecting the cost of protecting against internal military takeovers, was exceptionally high during this and the preceding, federation-forming, "brutocratic," period. The following Section explains the subsequent humanization of European civilization.

[81]Following the argument of the preceding footnote, the generally lower degree of tariff protection that arose during the 18th and 19th centuries reflect, not simply a lower premium on gold imports, but the greater level of <u>internal</u> military security during these humanizing centuries. Those unfortunate 20th century nations that have yet to fall heir to this humanizing ruling-class trend are discussed at length in Chapter 5.

the practical force of their arguments for emergency war-chests (Bowden, et al. pp. 79-81), whose logic we have already severely criticized. Gone too were their policies imposing high tariffs on perishable-good imports and net subsidies to the export of finished consumer goods, policies that had survived because of their 2nd-best ability to simultaneously: (1) enhance the state's often-vital inflow of precious metals and (2) generate a regressive tax structure in an era when the masses were objects of exploitation. All that remained of mercantilism, at least for competing states with the new method of emergency finance, was the simple, defense-externalities-internalizing, form of "mercantilism" that spread from the democratic Egypt of Ptolemy I to the Roman Empire and has since been maintained in some form or another by successful Western states all the way up to the present day.

Briefly summarizing the above tariff discussion, except for a couple of unfortunately durable laissez faire experiments, significant tariffs have been almost continually adopted in the West, and in a qualitatively efficient form, for well over 2000 years. Moreover, since the emergence of nuclear defense systems after World War II, the dominant democracies, which have been offering decreasingly attractive targets to military aggressors, have been efficiently producing a steady trend towards lower tariffs, as well as steady reductions in self-sufficiency-oriented subsidies (Appendix B.3, Part III.H). The unique emergency finance and taxation institutions of non-dominant modern economies are taken up in Chapters 4 and 5.

C. An Evolutionary Reason for Humanization and Elected Government

While we have had little difficulty inferring the mechanism generating the evolution of entry-restrictions for self-interested tradesmen and capital taxes for needy Pascalian defense-providers, a special evolutionary mechanism is required to generate some of the capital subsidies, the peacetime-accumulation-inducing policies, discussed above and in Appendix B.3. Unlike the purely self-interested micro-process involved in the evolution of guilds and tariffs, the underlying evolutionary process here appears to require Pascalian decisionmakers who possess a significant capacity for humanistic gratitude. Without a political process containing a capacity to exhibit such gratitude, once the requisite sacrifices of the masses have been provided, the government, although fulfilling some formal promise, would simply add another burden so as to effectively neutralize the agreed-upon compensation. As a result, competing political institutions have necessarily evolved so that the determination of postwar subsidies for life-and-limb-risking citizens has come to be made out of ruling-class gratitude for previous wartime sacrifices. The citizen election of ruling-class leaders is historically the best way to assure the citizen-sacrifices of the presence of this humanistic gratitude-response. The ancient institution of elected leaders among mobile citizen-soldiers thus has an evolutionary foundation based upon these defense-externalities. Selfish tyranny has normally failed to persist in these societies not because people have "natural rights" but because selfish tyrants are unable to sufficiently reward people for their wartime sacrifices. The basic reason that elected government returned in the 17th century -- and even became vital during the late 19th century emigration waves -- is not that we suddenly became enlightened but that the military technology changed and the previously-professional-army-using ruling classes increasingly had to reward citizen-soldiers for their wartime sacrifices.

The radically egalitarian fiscal systems that swept across western Europe and the U.S. after WWII should therefore come as no great surprise. Also, as the frequency of such citizen-sacrificing warfare steadily has decreased over decades of extended peace, this gratitude-effect and the corresponding tax benefits have become smaller and smaller. The trend is efficient because the revealed probability of such warfare is correspondingly decreasing. Such disappearing tax benefits have been particularly visible in the U.S. since the professionalization of its military in the mid-1970s. Historically alternative political institutions -- those not employing elected leaders -- could not reliably achieve the appropriate gratitude-effect and the corresponding economic efficiency. So when states must actively compete for their many, substantially wartime-sacrificing, citizens, elected leadership is a vital institution.[82]

Furthermore, when governments compete for people generally, potential wartime sacrificers or not, the popular (e.g., post-1820s) governments that emerge (Section II.A of Chapter 2) offer political privileges that extend far beyond lifetime voting rights for potentially wartime-sacrificing individuals. Nevertheless, as emphasized in Section II.D of Chapter 2, both popular and elected governments are endogenously reversible. Indeed, non-competing governments, or "civilizational empires," have leaders that are materially better-off by adopting values that exclude humanistic gratitude. So do professional-army-defended states with an immobile population. The rapidity that we have seen "divine right" monarchies evolve in Ancient Egypt, Imperial Rome, Byzantium, various Moslem empires, and even the oppressive empires of 16th and 17th century Europe, not only lends credence to our general model but also flashes a bright warning light that we shall revisit in our concluding chapter.

D. Why Countries Experiencing Exceptionally High Growth Rates Have Concurrently Imposed Relatively High Tariff Rates

We noted in the Introduction that states with exceptionally high growth rates have concurrently imposed exceptionally high tariffs compared to other, similarly developed, countries. While dramatically contradicting traditional tariff theory, this observation can be easily understood once we admit defense-externalities into the picture. High tariff rates may then be a simple reflection of high defense-externalities. All of the continually high-growth regions we have described had initially experienced a sudden institutional change (viz., the introduction of effective democracy), resulting in visible upward shifts in resource productivity (i.e., the Fisherian marginal rate of productive return over cost.) Since future consumption is certainly not an inferior good, this is reflected in a jump in the regions' growth rates

---

[82]While this may appear to make democracy a vital institution, recall that democracy in our sense requires investors to participate in the rule-making process. What is a vital institution -- when a large number of politically mobile individuals are occasionally asked to make substantial wartime sacrifices -- is elected government, where voters may or may not participate in the rule-making process. It is only necessary that these voters elect their political leaders, thereby supporting the state's required humanistic response mechanism.

in the foreseeable future. Such a shift also immediately raises the aggregate wealth of the favored region without improving its short-term defensibility. (To our knowledge, early land booms characterize all of these high growth episodes.) We can also assume that there is a constant or decreasing marginal efficiency of defense expenditure. This is both: (a) a stability condition in a simple model of rational state-formation (the Introduction to Appendix B.2) and (b) statistically supported (the Introduction to Appendix B.3)). Sudden productivity increases in a country therefore generate suddenly high defense-externalities, and high optimal tariffs to accompany the country's exceptionally high growth rates.[83,84]

The specific evolutionary mechanism generating this efficient pattern is simply an evolved reliance on national income taxes and tariffs to finance peacetime national expenditures. A permanent increase in a nation's productivity and commonly perceived prospective growth rates will substantially increase the nation's efficient, presumably perceived, defense expenditures even though its current income has barely increased. Given the state's long-evolved reliance on capital (or income) taxes and tariffs, and it's similarly evolved unwillingness to incur extended peacetime deficits, the result of this efficient increase in defense expenditures is then, quite efficiently but non-rationally, an automatic increase in capital tax and tariff rates. We will have more to say about the evolutionary value of the implied, peacetime, "tight-budget principle" in Chapter 5.

E. A Contrast Between Pre-20th Century Tariff History and Guild History

The pre-19th century sequences discussed above reveal comparatively few regional disasters resulting from ideologically based errors in tariff policy. (The French Revolution was probably the worst case; and even there we also saw a similarly laissez faire-inspired, premature attack on guilds.) Compared to guild history, pre-19th century tariff history appears to be a success story. The reason, we suggest, is that the security of property, either from internal or external threats, is rarely substantially threatened by an incorrect tariff because the region has time to appropriately adjust its peacetime defense expenditures to moderate errors in tariff policy. Tariffs in non-ideologized states, like the peacetime property taxes summarized in Table 3.2 in the previous section, are thus amenable to simple

---

[83]It follows that efficient internal capital tax rates are also exceptionally high in these high-growth regions, a reflection of the same, high, defense-externality. While our preliminary test of the corresponding tax-rate prediction is encouraging, we shall leave a systematic treatment of this implication for another study.

[84]An alternative explanation for this pattern, also consistent with our general theory, is that some sort of free-trade ideology has been ubiquitous. It would follow that high tariffs measure a country's ability to avoid ideology, which would correspondingly account for the high growth rate of that country. Although we have yet to devise a test that would separate our alternative explanations as regards the past two centuries, the absence of an external free-trade ideology before the late 18th century is substantial evidence against this alternative.

Lamarckian evolution. We should therefore not be surprised when we see sufficiently accurate tariff responses to various external shocks, at least when the state is able to view legislation in a relatively objective light.

Only in the case of pronounced free-trade ideologization -- only where there is a substantially excessive accumulation of consumer durables over an extended period of time -- can tariffs become like guilds and gold standards, i.e., vital economic institutions. Complete free-trade ideology did not become a widespread phenomenon until the latter half of the 19th century. Only in the 1850s and early 1860s do we see free-trade-policy-induced over-importations of consumer durables and correspondingly increasing threats to the military security of the ideologized states, states whose pronounced liberalism also led them to deny the rationality of warfare and correspondingly display narrowly rational pacifism in the face of the growing military insecurity created by their free-trade policies. Nevertheless, it took only about a decade of extreme free trade in Napoleon III's "Liberal Empire" before France's humiliating and costly loss of property to uniquely protectionist Prussia in 1871. Similarly, in Austria, Francis Joseph's "Liberal Empire" had begun in the very early 1850s and it was during the period, 1859-66, that Austria suffered her own string of militarily humiliating property losses to conservative Prussia.

A major subsequent difference between these ill-fated Empires was that France -- due to her previous, counter-ideological, educational reforms -- was able to learn her lesson and adopt a pragmatic national democracy and protectionism during the 1870s and early 1880s. In contrast, Austria, like Great Britain, maintained relatively free trade policies all the way up to World War I. Predictably, then, Austria, under the political influence of intellectuals such as Karl Menger, made herself an increasingly juicy target for Serbian aggression. At the same time, Great Britain, under the free-trade-and-pacifism educational influence of Alfred Marshall and the mature English neoclassicists, similarly became increasingly consumerist and vulnerable and yet displayed an unfortunately narrowly rational decreased willingness to risk-it-all, as reflected in the Liberal isolationism of Britain's late 19th century foreign policy and the subsequently half-hearted attempts of her reascendant Liberals to help France resist German aggression in their joint effort to prevent the western European involvement in what eventually escalated into the Great War. Thus, although excessively low tariffs are largely a post WWI, or "modern", problem, the roots of this modern problem go back before WWI, back to the middle of the 19th century, when the classical economics of the day became durably entrenched in the ruling class mentalities of Europe's two then-dominant imperial states -- Austria and Great Britain.

When free-trade ideology is a basis for externally imposed tariff reductions by imperially dominant states, the costs that are externally imposed upon the dependent states may also be quite high. At the same time, the dominated countries, to survive as quasi-independent states, must quickly evolve special decision processes. These survival-oriented decision processes, and the resulting policy responses, can then be used to confirm hypotheses regarding the presence of an ideology-based attack on their vital institutions. We will take up these largely modern issues in Chapter 5.

IV. POLICY CONCLUSION: ON THE BEATING OF LIVE HORSES

We economists would serve both the social interest and our own long-run private interest if we adopted a more generous view of democratic legislation. The long-run economic institutions of a non-ideologized democracy are citizen-efficient. The harsh Darwinian pressures that effective democracy imposes on a state means that long-surviving non-dominant democracies can be expected to generate efficient economic policies. The traditional economic arguments against observed price-increasing policies such as tariffs and internal capital restrictions, arguments stemming from a teacher-serving view of the political judgment of the common citizens or their legislators, would be correspondingly eliminated.[85]

The traditional view of political economy would then, for the long-run good of the profession, be replaced with a logically disciplined theory in which a non-ideologized democratic political system would be presumed to generate citizen-efficient economic policies.

An economic policy proposal would then be recognized as possibly worthwhile within a long-surviving democracy only if the policy were qualitatively innovative, i.e., only if that kind of policy had not already been repeatedly tried. We would then cease our merciless flogging of live horses.

---

[85]This biased political-economic view is revealed by the standard conjunction of an assumption of costless rationality in the making of private economic decisions with the assumption of widespread error in the making of political decisions. The widely accepted, Buchanan-Tullock-Olson, rationalization for this asymmetry is that beneficial political decisions have such a large number of free-riders that we cannot expect ordinary individuals to devote a suitable amount of information to making rational political decisions. Although the general political model we have worked with in this Chapter does not explicitly consider the nature of specific political processes, democratic political systems have typically evolved to where ordinary voter decisions are typically restricted to the election of political representatives. Since judgments concerning the relative quality of alternative legislative representatives are probably best made on the same intuitive level as private economic decisions, our Pascalian assumption is probably quite reasonable as regards the evolved political system. The competitively evolved form of large-scale private organizations similarly limits the direct participation of individual investors to the election of representatives (boards of directors, etc.) An explicit theoretical model generating this efficiency conclusion with respect to specifically observed political institutions is developed in Thompson, et al., Vol. I, Ch. 8.)

CHAPTER 4

ON THE GOLD STANDARD:
WHY DEPRESSIONS HAVE BEEN A NECESSARY EVIL, OR
HOW THE ECONOMICS OF KEYNES DETHRONED EUROPE

ABSTRACT

Before the nuclear age, the emergency military defense of a wealthy nation was a prolonged and expensive affair. The main advantage of adopting the gold standard was that it provided the country with a unique ability to finance such large-scale military emergencies. Although necessitating post-war depressions, this financial advantage of a gold standard appears to have been necessary for the military survival of pre-nuclear modern democracies. Again, this financial <u>sine qua non</u> arises because there is a time-inconsistent, overly appeasing, response of any narrowly rational legislature to each in a series of broadly rational threats of all-out-war by external aggressors demanding individually small favors. A democratic nation whose underlying military leaders are unable to overcome this legislative time-inconsistency by independently financing the nation's expensive military emergencies is soon rationally subjugated by such aggressors. Britain's premature, Keynes-inspired, abandonment of the gold standard in 1931 generated a case in point.

INTRODUCTION: EMERGENCY FINANCE AND THE GOLD STANDARD

The gold standard first appeared in China during a 9th and 10th-century renaissance in ancient Chinese religion and investor democracy (e.g., Wagel; Edkins; Shyrock). Thereafter, the standard was steadily maintained throughout China's lengthy golden age of technological and economic expansion until the increasing philosopher-authoritarianism of the classically Confucian Ming dynasty gradually phased out the gold standard by 1620 (Huang). Not long thereafter, due largely to what had been a steadily increasing shortage of emergency finance (e.g., Huang, Eberhard, pp. 281-85), the world's largest and wealthiest empire was ignominiously over-run by a relatively small number of Manchurian tribesmen, who were <u>not</u> too Confucian to use a gold standard for emergency finance.

Although the idea of the gold standard was introduced to the West at the end of the 13th century by Marco Polo, who was greatly impressed by the convertible certificates of the initially silver-rich Mongol Emperors, not until four centuries later did the gold standard begin an independent life-cycle of its own in the West. As we have already seen, this occurred alongside England's establishment of the modern West's first successful democratic nation in the 1690s.

Economic folklore attributes the evolution of the gold standard in the West to 17th century English goldsmiths, whose deposit receipts began to circulate as negotiable debt, i.e., paper money. However, similar private banking institutions (theoretically characterized in Appendix B.4) had already developed much earlier without special comment in medieval Florence and Venice (e.g., Sherwood, Ch. IV, esp. p. 122). The true innovators of the gold standard were the <u>governmental</u> leaders of England's new democracy following her "Glorious Revolution" of 1688.[1] This pathbreaking democratic revolution, while providing a legal and political ("rights-of-man") commitment to compensate the citizen-soldiers of the large new armies of rifle-equipped Englishmen for their wartime personal sacrifices, had done nothing to prevent the new democracy from subsequently repealing its debts to those who had made large wartime financial sacrifices. Yet such financial sacrifices had been necessary for the survival of the fledgling national democracy, and, as emphasized above and developed in Appendix B.2 (note 4) and B.3 (Section I.B)), military leaders cannot defend such a democracy unless they can override the self-defeating -- but narrowly rational -- appeasement responses to potential aggressors that characterize any democratic legislature. The timely governmental invention of the gold standard, although creating a uniform sequence of postwar depressions, solved this critical problem in defense-finance for the newly forming democratic nations of the West and thereby cleared the path to modernity.

More specifically, during the early 1690s, the founders of the Bank of England were acutely aware both of the historical reluctance of independent parliaments to supply funds necessary for emergency military defense and of the recent military failure of neighboring Holland's pioneering, but short-lived, national democracy (e.g., Sherwood, esp. pp. 135-42). These perceptive English bankers, along with their new Dutch King, William III, saw that Holland's failure was due to the disastrous legal inability of the Bank of Amsterdam to expand her innovative paper money supply during a defensive emergency (the War of 1672). This unfortunate inflexibility was due to a rule in the bank's constitution limiting its issue of paper money to its effective gold reserve. (See, e.g., Adam Smith (Book IV, Ch. I, Part I, and Book V, Ch. III), who approved of such war-starving financial institutions.)

In any case, the war-troubled William III, his pragmatic English bankers, and a Scottish banking promoter, William Paterson, worked to create a national paper currency that would flexibly expand during military emergencies (Clapham), and do so without creating proportionate increases in the price level. Under a gold standard, extra paper money could be created and spent during the defensive emergencies, although convertibility would have to be temporarily suspended to prevent a "reflux" of the paper money back to the Bank. (The first formal suspension of gold payments thus occurred in 1695, barely one year after the new kind of money was first issued;

---

[1]Thus, among those practical-minded institutionalists represented by general and coinage historians, the term "gold standard" traditionally signifies a paper money economy in which the government is contractually bound to convert a unit of its circulating paper money into an intertemporally constant amount of a real commodity, usually a precious metal because of the relative transactional convenience of such conversion payments.

For the same reason, the wartime-suspension, postwar-resumption process discussed in Chapter 3 and elaborated below is also a necessary feature of a true gold standard. A case in point is the French monetary system during the 19th century. Although ostensibly adopting a "gold standard" from 1803 onward, both Napoleon I and Napoleon III failed to suspend precious-metal payments during their eventually ill-fated military ventures. Hence, under our definition, France's "enlightened" emperors failed to implement a true gold standard.

and the suspension lasted only the two additional years that William required to impressively defeat the formidable France of Louis IVX.) The suspension-induced expansion of the paper money supply would in turn cause some wartime inflation. But the new paper money represented a durable contract between the otherwise helpless individual money-holder and the powerful government. So English judges would likely attempt to enforce an eventual resumption of gold payments at the original conversion rate, and an implicit deflation to something like the pre-war price-level,[2] as a matter of common law.[3] Parliament, foreseeing a protracted legal battle (Acres), predictably ordered the resumption of gold payments at the old conversion rate -- and continued to do so until 1931 -- despite the need for both a postwar tax to finance the payments and a depressionary return to the prewar price trend.

It was the expectation of this post-war depression by the financial community, as we shall see in Section I below, that allowed the wartime expansion in governmental purchasing power that was in turn required for the survival of the democracy.

Early in the 18th century, after a couple of such wars, parliamentary support arose for large wartime issues of long-term national debt. For such borrowing served as a convenient <u>substitute</u> for wartime monetary expansion. Although moderate interest would be due on such borrowing (see Section III below), (a) repayment through postwar taxation could be delayed to dates that would distribute the intergenerational burden of the war in a more politically acceptable fashion, and (b) the debt issues would reduce the wartime inflation and thus moderate the social costs of the anticipated post-war deflation. War finance in gold-standard countries therefore became quickly marked by substantial issues of legislatively approved, long-term, governmental debt as well as by authoritarian, suspension-induced, monetary expansions. The effect on subsequent observers of economic history has been the dangerous <u>appearance of a simple willingness</u> on the part of the democratic legislatures to extensively borrow to support defensive warfare. Nowhere in the

---

[2]As elaborated in Section III below, under perfect competition, the pre-war price level is above the post-resumption price level by the accumulated real interest return on an investment in real capital. To mitigate the corresponding post-resumption unemployment costs, post-war governments typically worked to reform the gold-payments system in order to economize on gold and thereby reduce the magnitude of the resumption-induced increase in the relative price of gold. These policies succeeded to the point that the long-term inflation rate under the gold standard was approximately zero rather than the negative of the real interest rate.

[3]The underlying legal reason for this intertemporal commitment ability is that a wartime suspension of a straightforward governmental conversion promise is widely regarded as a temporary <u>force majeure</u>, an excusable but temporary supply interruption in an otherwise inviolable contract between a powerful government and an innocent individual citizen, the latter being chivalrously conceived of as requiring the substantial protection of the law. Post-emergency law courts -- especially Anglo-Saxon common law courts -- therefore typically induced depression-producing legislative resumptions of pre-war gold conversion payments on their paper monies, although usually only after several years of extended legislative debate during which time suitable revenue-increasing measures could be devised in order to finance the retirement of the large issues of wartime paper.

standard literature do we find a recognition of the simple fact that this unique "willingness" was based upon the existence of a gold standard. Nowhere do we find a recognition of the basic problem that the gold standard was solving.[4]

In any case, without the gold standard, emergency national finance would have doubtless remained in the hands of Renaissance elites -- clubs of wealthy noblemen, bankers, and guild aristocrats, groups whose peacetime compensation for their extensive wartime sacrifices depended on maintaining highly elitist religions and philosophies -- people whose anti-modern (although currently re-emergent) value system significantly disserved their countries by exaggerating the personal wisdom and benevolence of appropriately educated aristocrats.

Indeed, before the nuclear age, no independent nation evolved from aristocracy to a surviving national democracy without the aid of a gold standard. The gold standard pioneered in the West by the newly established Bank of England thus represented the financial foundation of what was to become our first successful national democracy. Then, almost a century later, after the failed Swedish experiment to establish a national democracy supported by a cumbersome copper-standard (1719-1772) described in the previous chapter, a second viable precious-metal standard was adopted in 1791 by the newly formed Bank of the United States in what was to become our second successful national democracy. Then, due largely to the remarkable successes of these two nations, the standard -- uniformly

---

[4]This includes the recent paper of Bordo and Kydland, which purports to treat the gold standard as a commitment device to assure creditors of a non-inflationary monetary policy. Actually, a suitably independent monetary authority is sufficient to optimally solve their commitment problem without resorting to a gold standard (Thompson, 1981). Moreover, although they follow our argument (Thompson, 1987; Hickson-Thompson, 1991) in introducing emergency suspensions of gold payments, there is actually no reason for such suspensions in their environment, wherein the emergency governmental authority is free to issue long-term bonds to finance their activities. In our environment, the legislature, not the emergency author-ity, controls the magnitude of such borrowing, in which case the emergency authority must suspend gold payments to over-ride the narrow rationality of the emergency legislature in order to finance the emergency. In the contrasting environment of Bordo and Kydland, the historic conflict between the rational, over-appeasing, legislature and the principled military leaders is entirely ignored. The only time-inconsistency relates to overall governmental repayment of debt and therefore can be handled with either foreign-currency-denominated bonds or the appropriately independent central financial authority mentioned above. Neither the gold standard nor suspended gold standards are called for.

More basically, the economic superiority of emergency monetary expansions over emergency debt expansions, and the corresponding efficiency of real -- not just nominal -- emergency monetary expansions, is not dealt with by the above authors. As a result, their theoretical argument contains no essential monetary or macroeconomic element. There is no mention, for example of the rational expectation of post-war deflation that we are about to see is necessary for the achievement of a suspension-induced increase in emergency purchasing power, and no mention, for another example, of the fact that standard Keynesian macroeconomics leads to the dangerously mistaken belief that fiat money-supply expansion during national emergencies will lead interest rates to fall so that convertible money is not a necessary part of an effective system of emergency finance.

accompanied by substantial democratization -- spread to Continental Europe, Latin America and Japan during the 19th century through the eventually pragmatic evolution described in Section II.D.5.c of the above chapter.

The restructured countries similarly enjoyed eras of remarkably successful national defense and exceptionally high, albeit fitful as elaborated in Section II below, overall economic growth. Eventually, as elaborated in Section I below, in the early-mid-1930s, based largely upon the cumulative impact of the "Cambridge School" of economics led by the increasingly influential John Maynard Keynes, each European nation separately abandoned its gold standard in order to give its central bank greater flexibility in fighting the unemployment predictably characterizing the post-resumption era identifiable as the downturn-years of the Great Depression.

Only the U.S. remained on a gold standard, albeit one with harsh curbs imposed on the export and private possession of gold. And only the U.S. could finance the military defense of the democracies during WWII.

After the end of WWII, an international "gold exchange standard" was set up. This was achieved by executing a 1944 agreement developed in an international monetary conference at Bretton Woods, in which financial representatives of the democratic nations of Europe all agreed to work to make their countries' paper currencies convertible into the U.S. dollar as long as the U.S. maintained a fixed conversion rate of the dollar into gold in exchanges with foreign central banks. This internationally cooperative kind of gold standard effectively served the emergency military requirements of the recovering European democracies. It thus worked, and in the same recession-producing way that the internationally individualistic gold standard had served prior to the early 1930s, to finance the Suez Crisis and the French war in Algeria during the 1950s. Then, upon the completion of a U.S.-centered nuclear defense system for the democratic nations of the West during the late 1960s, this last remnant of the gold standard was quickly phased out and finally eliminated when the U.S. permanently closed the gold window in 1971.

The emergence of substitute emergency-defense systems for non-nuclearly defended countries -- i.e., various forms of fixed-exchange rates enforced by international cooperation -- is briefly described in Section IV below. Then, in Chapter 5, we shall elaborate upon the economic consequences of these fixed-exchange-rate systems and the uniquely ideological form of international cooperation that has recently come to reject them.

I. MAINSTREAM MACROECONOMICS AND THE GOLD STANDARD

The emergency-defense function of the gold standard, although never a recognized part of mainstream economics, has been particularly obscured to modern economists by an error in basic Keynesian economics unfortunately leading to the theoretical conclusion that a permanent increase in an inconvertible money supply lowers interest rates (Appendix B.4, Section III). This theoretical error is the source of a major unresolved empirical paradox in Keynesian theory called "the Gibson paradox", wherein observed peacetime interest rates are always abnormally <u>high</u> during demand-side booms, which is inconsistent with Keynesian theory because some of these booms were obviously caused by essentially permanent increases in the money supply. In any case, the error led Keynes, and subsequent generations of economists, to a dangerously false belief.

This has been the belief that emergency expansions in an <u>inconvertible</u> money supply -- which have been correctly understood to be <u>permanent</u> increases in the money supply -- would be partially hoarded. Such induced hoarding would occur because of the theoretically induced decreases in the interest-cost of holding money. The increases in commodity prices during emergencies would then be proportionately less than the corresponding money-supply increases. If this <u>were</u> true, then the essentially <u>permanent</u> money-supply increases occurring during a wartime emergency in an inconvertible money economy <u>would</u> produce unambiguous increases in emergency governmental purchasing power, just as had the <u>temporary</u> monetary expansions induced by national emergencies under the classical gold standard.

But the above-mentioned correction of this theoretical error leads to the opposite theoretical prediction. A permanent increase in an inconvertible money supply in a capital-theoretically correct macro-model, by unambiguously increasing the marginal productivity of capital without decreasing the rationally expected inflation rate, implies an <u>increase</u> in interest rates and therefore an <u>increase</u> in the opportunity cost of holding money (Appendix B.4, Section III again). Dishoarding, not hoarding, is induced. Inconvertible monetary expansions therefore result in percentage increases in prices that <u>exceed</u> the corresponding percentage increases in money supplies. Emergency increases in an inconvertible money supply fail to act like gold-standard-increases because the real purchasing power from governmental money, which is a very small fraction of any economy's pre-emergency real wealth, fails to increase during state-threatening emergencies.

Thus, besides freeing us from the Gibson paradox, this theoretical correction of the basic Keynesian model enables us to understand why democratic Europe was so uncharacteristically weak in its response to Fascist aggression in the mid-to-late-1930s, and correspondingly why such populist-totalitarian governmental forms were so extraordinarily popular during this uniquely militaristic period. It also enables us to understand why the U.S., the only country that did not abandon the gold standard (at least in international transactions), was able to generate uniquely large increases in emergency governmental purchasing power and, as part of the same process, maintain exceptionally low interest rates throughout WWII. Democratic Europe's intellectually fashionable, Keynes-inspired (Harrod), abandonment of the gold standard in the early 1930s in order to forestall further depression therefore appears to have been a serious policy error. The fashionable abandonment left democratic Europe wide open to the threat of all-out attack by rationally selected military fanatics, who then naturally flourished during the mid-late 1930s. The only democratic nation sufficiently resistant to intellectual fashion to remain on the gold standard, the U.S., was therefore the only nation able to finance a wartime defense effort adequate to the task of defending the world's democracies.

Although it may appear peculiar, the mainstream literature on the gold standard (e.g., Eichengreen) has traditionally avoided the critically important political-economic issues discussed above in favor of much narrower, actually more speculative, discussions dealing with the dynamics of international price adjustment.[5]

II. BUSINESS CYCLES AND THE GOLD STANDARD

During periods of free convertibility of paper money into a real asset, where the public is free to exchange idle real commodity stocks for paper money, or vice versa, the total demand for this convertible paper completely determines its supply (Appendix B.4). Governmental monetary authorities then have no direct control over the money supply. The correspondingly passive money supply has been generally understood by political economists to be a property of a classical gold standard since the writings of Adam Smith (Book II, Ch. II). This property has been reflected in the policy-oriented writings of Thomas Tooke and the English "Banking School" in the 1840s (Appendix B.4, Section I), and of J. Laurence Laughlin and the U.S. "sound money school" of the 1890s, together with the early supporters of the Federal Reserve Act of 1913 (Girton and Roper). These classical and neoclassical authors correctly saw great benefits in the gold-standard's ability to automatically expand and contract its peacetime paper money supply in response to "the needs of trade" (i.e., changes in money demand) without affecting prices to any significant degree.[6]

---

[5]The latter include: (1) David Hume's seminal discussion of the laissez faire gold-flows, and corresponding price-level changes, occurring between nations in a suddenly disequilibrated, grossly hypothetical, world whose only money consists of full-bodied gold coins; (2) the famous "currency school" versus "banking school" debate leading to Peel's Bank Charter Act of 1844, which enshrined Hume's view of the natural adjustment process, except that the Central Bank could respond to a terms-of-trade shock inducing continual gold drains by Bank borrowing (i.e., by raising the Bank's discount rate) serving to raise the domestic relative price of gold and thereby hasten the final laissez faire price adjustment while at the same time preventing a costly overshooting of gold flows during the adjustment period; and (3) the increasingly acrimonious post-WWI discussions of the negative short-term employment effects on other nations of the above, "beggar-my-neighbor", borrowing policies (or restrictive short-term trade policies) and the corresponding international disapproval of gold-hoarding (perennially by France) to the point that such borrowing policies were condemned as "not playing according to the rules" of an imaginary international game (Bloomfield).

[6]Modern authors, failing to notice the switch away from a convertible currency, have generally ignored these counter-cyclical benefits of the earlier monetary system (Appendix B.4, Section I). They have preferred instead to inaccurately portray the above-described "real bills doctrine" as a ridiculously misguided attempt to vary an exogenous money supply so as to produce either a target interest rate or an equality of money supply changes to changes in the stock of commercial debt.

There are, however, also substantial <u>costs</u> of this monetary flexibility once we introduce exogenous peacetime shocks that substantially alter the real price of gold (Appendix B.4, Sections II and III). If, for example, the U.S. had continuously maintained, rather than abandoned, the gold exchange standards of the late 1960s, the 10-fold increase in the real price of gold since that time would have generated a current U.S. price level that is 1/10 of its level of the 1960s, or about 1/25th of its current level!

These counter-cyclical benefits of a passive money supply are absent during periods of suspended or non-existence convertibility.   During such periods, independent governments, such as the contemporary U.S. government, are free to fix their paper money supplies "exogenously", i.e., without regard to legal commitments. Thus, with observed governmental monetary authorities unwilling to surrender their discretionary control to an automatic mechanism, such as a gold standard, sudden expansions or contractions in the demand for inconvertible paper money have respectively depressed or raised commodity prices and correspondingly generated avoidable business cycles.   This has been well-recognized since the early days of classical economics, as reflected in Henry Thornton's famous analysis of the effects of an initial monetary shock on prices and interest rates during periods of suspended gold payments. This inconvertible-currency analysis was placed in a somewhat more explicit, mini-general-equilibrium-type, setting in the late 1930s by Keynes and John R. Hicks. It survives today -- capital-theoretic errors and all -- enshrined in textbooks as what is commonly called "neo-Keynesian macroeconomics".

In any case, examples of such avoidable business cycles, and correspondingly of the social value of a passive money supply, are easily supplied.   Indeed, the last two U.S. recessions provide almost identical examples of how sudden fluctuations in the demand for a fiat money create modern business cycles that would have been automatically avoided if we had adopted a suitable gold standard.   The suddenly higher mid-1982 and mid-1990 demands for U.S. paper money, necessarily the medium for the payment of U.S. taxes (Section II.B.1 of Chapter 5), following the Presidential announcements of near-future tax-rate increases immediately precipitated almost identical economic declines rather than immediate increases in the stock of paper money. In contrast, these recessions would have been automatically avoided if our paper money supply had been freely convertible (into a real asset whose relative price were unaffected by the tax-rate) and therefore automatically expanded with the tax-needs of trade.

However, a gold-standard produces its own unique brand of business cycle. In particular, gold-standard depressions occur when there are shocks that increase the equilibrium value of the conversion commodity relative to other commodities, thereby decreasing the general price level by the same percentage (Appendix B.4, Section III).   A correspondingly severe gold-standard depression induces a percentage reduction in the endogenous money supply approximately equal to the percentage reduction in the price of ordinary goods relative to the fixed-price conversion commodity. In sharp contrast, the same relative-demand shock would occasion no systematic change in the overall price level or aggregate output if there were an exogenously fixed currency stock.   Thus, given the gold-standard government's inability to so fix the paper money supply, its historic inability to avoid the employment recessions caused by shocks that decrease the price level by increasing the relative demand for the conversion commodity, it is clear that the ensuing business cycles are by far the main disadvantage of a gold standard.

Such business cycles, including the Great Depression, occurred regularly under the gold standard.   We should not fail to note the relative ease with which depressions could be -- and actually were -- predicted by financial experts, who implicitly understood that the European resumption of gold payments would substantially decrease the world's demand for commodities relative to gold. Nevertheless, the cycles in real output and employment under the gold standard were of much greater amplitude and duration than those observed under our recent, inconvertible, governmentally managed, monetary systems. Viewed solely from the standpoint of the economic costs of the business cycle, the gold standard was, therefore, almost certainly, socially disadvantageous.

III. THE BROAD PRICE TRENDS OBSERVED UNDER THE GOLD STANDARD

To describe the basic workings of the gold standard with added precision, it is helpful to assume a zero-transaction-costs, perfectly competitive, equilibrium in all markets. Then, multiplying the government's fixed, intertemporally constant, money price of gold by the perfectly competitive equilibrium price of any other commodity relative to gold, we can immediately determine the money price of that commodity. Since this can be done for all commodities, and without reference to the passively determined money supply, equilibrium relative prices in a perfectly competitive money economy can be determined independently of the monetary sector (Appendix B.4, Section II). The resulting "classical dichotomy" between the real and monetary sectors of an economy, which was implicit in most of classical and early neoclassical economics (Patinkin), greatly facilitates the quantitative analysis of the economy.

In a perfectly competitive economy with a gold standard, idle stocks of gold, like any other currently non-productive asset, must be expected to appreciate at a rate equal to the real rate of return to holding currently productive assets. It follows that perfectly competitive issuers of gold-convertible paper money do not pay direct interest on their monies. Indeed, convertible banknotes typically bore no direct interest while money prices in gold-standard economies generally fell slightly during peacetime, reflecting the slightly positive real interest rate on alternative investment goods.

During wartime, when gold-standard economies generated large increases in the money supplies and suspensions of gold payments, there were typically substantial increases in the nominal prices of most goods. Nevertheless, the rational expectation of postwar resumptions of the original gold conversion payments, and corresponding postwar reductions in commodity prices (which quickly became a predictable empirical pattern (Glasner)), implied higher-than-normal rates of return to holding paper money relative to goods during the wartime emergencies. Increases in the government's real wartime purchasing power therefore accompanied wartime increases in the government's nominal issue of paper money. This powerful financial weapon provided a gold-standard government with a potential wartime increase in zero-interest purchasing power limited only by the government's ability to repay the zero-interest loan after the war by suitably raising postwar taxes to finance future conversion payments. The rationally expected postwar deflation also generated, after the brief learning period of 1695-1725, nominal governmental borrowing rates that typically remained low (below 5%) during major wars throughout the gold-standard era despite the obvious wartime increases in both real interest rates and default risks (Evans).

But this main advantage of the gold standard also implied postwar depressions as the economies headed back to their pre-war price levels. Repetitive innovations economizing on gold conversion during these resumption periods -- first by including silver as an alternative conversion metal, then by limiting conversion to bullion, then by allowing conversion into another country's convertible currency, then by outlawing the private hoarding of gold, and finally by restricting gold payments to conversion payments made by a single country to foreign central banks -- beneficially served to mitigate these consistently depressionary resumption costs and create a long-term trend of money prices in the West that was not deflationary. In fact, the secular price trend was roughly constant throughout the entire quarter-millennial era of the classical gold standard, 1694-1944.

The demise of the international gold exchange standard in the quarter-century following WWII followed closely behind the development of an international system of nuclear defense. This is because, as already noted, a well-equipped nuclear power does not require large increases in cumulative expenditures during a defense emergency. Thus, as the underlying advantage of the gold-standard was being eliminated for the nuclearly defended democracies after WWII, the experience of emergency financial benefits provided by the gold standard was correspondingly eliminated in these countries. But the main disadvantage of the gold standard obviously remained. So when the U.S. faced the prospect of a huge potential depression in the early 1970s through a resumption of gold payments that had been suspended since 1968, it was an easy choice to permanently abandon the last vestiges of her gold standard. Also, viewed from the European perspective, since the U.S. nuclear umbrella had substantially spread across western Europe by the late 1960s, the European political pressure to resist the U.S. decision among the practical advisors of these allied democracies had substantially eroded by 1971 (e.g., Gilbert).

IV. EMERGENCY FINANCE AFTER THE GOLD STANDARD

Nevertheless, as elaborated in the following chapter, numerous nations still have been facing substantial emergency financial demands, especially to cover <u>domestic</u> political uprisings. Such countries, even after the abandonment of the Bretton Woods agreement in 1971, have typically attempted, quite rationally, to unilaterally keep their currencies convertible into the fiat currency of a large foreign country in order to maintain the financial advantages of a gold standard. However, the hyperinflations of the 1970s proved that the legal systems of these nations did not treat a domestic governmental promise to convert a unit of domestic currency into a fixed amount of an inconvertible foreign currency anything like a common law system would treat a governmental promise to convert money into gold.

The mid-late-1970s and the 1980s was thus a period in which these vulnerable countries increasingly enlisted the aid of the International Monetary Fund to commit themselves to a more durably fixed exchange rate. These 1975-1990 systems (e.g., Dell), which are analytically equivalent to the suspended-gold-payment systems of 1919 to 1925, are examined in the next chapter, as are the systems of the 1990s.

Finally, looking beyond the 1990s and into a political-economic future in which there may well be several alternative world-dominant governments, the problem of emergency finance in nuclearly armed democratic nations has not disappeared. Rather, there will likely be an increasing need for the leader among these mature democracies to provide a mechanism that will finance large emergency defense expenditures, if only because the leader should want to deter rivals and thereby forestall a 21st century arms-race to determine an alternative imperial leader. To exacerbate the problem, stemming from the reduction in gratitude for the military sacrifices of the young following the Vietnam debacle and corresponding replacement of conscripted armies with professional-army-dependent defense systems, there has been an upper-middle-class tax-revolt and correspondingly massive accumulation of governmental indebtedness over the past 25 years. So developed democracies will probably have little ability to finance extended future emergencies with ordinary borrowing. There will correspondingly be an increasing demand for mechanisms that finance future emergencies beyond ordinary borrowing. However, if no, new, depression-resistant, mechanism of emergency finance (Thompson, et al., Vol. II, Ch. 3) is adopted, and if no secure world empire and no emergency-precluding world-governmental reform (such as is outlined in Chapter 6) arise, the increasing tax usefulness of wealthy individuals relative to ordinary civilians during the ensuing high-tech arms race would inevitably lead (as it led the 16th-17th century rivals for European domination) to a tortuous degeneration of our elected governments back into elitist aristocracies such as those that had infected the world's governments under the similarly imperializing military technology that existed prior to the rise of drafted national armies and the gold standard.[7]

---

[7]As the evolution of democracy, a non-vital institution, goes somewhat beyond the scope of this work, the above analysis of our political-economic future is not a strict application of the central theory of this work. In particular, it uses several of the theoretical and historical analyses of Thompson, et al., Vol. I, chs. 3, 4, and 6, to establish the general dependence of effective democracy on the military contributions of significant numbers of civilian conscripts. Critical to the story, for example, are the evolution of deeply rooted cartels of legal and political thinkers and intra-familial externalities that have been largely suppressed in this study (through the devise of citizenship-constrained-optimality) in order to isolate ideologies whose roots have been unable to sink deep because of the inevitable effect of such ideologies on the vital institutions of historically observed nations.

CHAPTER 5

ON MODERN INTERNATIONAL COOPERATION: EXCHANGE CONTROLS, HYPERINFLATION, AND COSTLY SOCIAL REVOLUTION AS EFFICIENT NATIONAL RESPONSES TO EXTERNALLY IMPOSED TRADE LIBERALIZATION

ABSTRACT

The fitful decays of both classical colonialism and the gold standard after WWI created a world in which a large number of otherwise independent nations became vitally dependent upon the emergency loan support of dominant countries. In the West, this vital loan support, and even the right to trade on non-discriminatory terms, has regularly come on the ideologically rationalized condition that the dependent countries substantially lower their trade barriers. This chapter shows how the surviving governments have quickly and efficiently, but certainly not costlessly, responded to such ideological constraints with new peacetime institutions of their own. The inability of the concerned economists to see these as rational national responses, responses that take us a long way towards characterizing all that is unique in post-WWI economic institutions, furnishes us with striking evidence both for the social costs of free-trade ideology and for the subconscious efficiency of political systems that survive the harsh evolutionary process.

INTRODUCTION

The disasters represented by World Wars I and II reinforced one another in teaching the world's militarily dominant countries that classical colonialism was no longer profitable. In a world of colonial empires able to use modern technology to inflict massive destruction on one-another, it was no longer worth the costs of defense to assert military dominion over militarily much weaker nations. The "gunboat diplomacy" that dominated the world before WWI, and persisted in isolated regions during the interwar period, was essentially abolished soon after the end of WWII. Old colonial dependencies that had not been legally constituted protectorates became relatively independent nations, with new responsibilities for their own collective defense and new rights of domestic self-determination. And, of course, the form and language of international cooperation and control radically changed.

In particular, the post-WWI and post-WWII periods witnessed the steady spread (in both the East and the West) of international economic paternalism, where militarily dominant nations rapidly came to collectively impose what they professed to be economically efficient policies on militarily weaker nations.[1] These newly

---

[1]The leader of a dominant country rationally pre-commits to a tailored, all-or-nothing, offer. Thus, as in Section I of Chapter 1, the dominant country always wins the implicit bargain with the countries with which it deals. Although there may be more than one actively

imposed, still existing, policies rapidly came to be confidently regarded by the ideologized leaders of the dominant countries, and a supporting mainstream economic literature, as beneficial to the weaker nations, the latter often being relatively poor and presumed to be so because of their less informed political leaders.

Many social critics, however, have regarded the newly imposed economic policies as some sort of neo-colonialism, basing their conclusion largely on the empirical observation that many of the most dependent of the weaker nations (especially the neighboring dependencies in eastern Europe and in the northern and central portions of both Africa and Latin America) have typically under-performed the more independent of the weaker nations.[2]

---

competing leader (e.g., East vs. West, Cold-War, competition), each leader implicitly makes a single set of offers, the nature of which determines the particular allies obtained by that leader. Thus, when we say that the leader of a dominant nation "imposes" a policy on a weaker nation allying itself with that leader, we mean that the policy is the leader's all-or-nothing offer.

Note also that both the pre- and the post-WWI forms of international cooperation are client-by-client ("1st degree") discriminating monopolies despite what may be a theoretical expectation of price-equalizing competition between the alternative dominant countries. This is because the dominant leaders rationally exhibit economically predatory reactions to an adversary's attempt to attract away a small country in the formers' "sphere of influence". The basic differences between the two forms of cooperation are that post-WWI reactions: (a) are only economically, not militarily, predatory; and (b) artificially limit the collection of lump-sum rents from the smaller countries. We know from Appendix B.1 that the social equilibrium would be Pareto optimal if we only had to contend with condition (a), at least under costless strategic communication and complete information.

However, condition (b), the self-imposed restraint on post-colonial rent collection, reveals that the rivals are attempting to attract adherents by treating them as objects of affection. If this were true affection, optimality would be retained. However, finding little history or biological theory to support such benevolence, we can only suspect that the dominant country is masking an inefficient, unconscious, ideologically rationalized, form of exploitation. The question addressed in this chapter is whether or not the post-colonial reluctance to accept conscious transfers has, in fact, produced an inefficient form of rent collection, one that could be eliminated by accepting a world constitution that precluded such exploitation.

---

[2]That economic ideology, not simply military dependency, is the likely source of these economic retardations, at least in the West, is indicated by the relative economic success of the old-style military dependencies (e.g., the remaining U.S. territories and protectorates, the members of the British Commonwealth, and, most recently, the members of France's West African Monetary Union).

The generally progressive increase in the post-WWI growth rates as we proceed further and further away from the United States into increasingly ideologically independent Latin America similarly supports the neo-colonial exploitation charge. And here, too, the exceptions help isolate the negative effect of ideology: First, the increasing growth rates end abruptly at the Argentine border, which helps the argument in that this nation, being the farthest from the U.S. in the western hemisphere, has become an outpost for an anti-U.S., quite interventionist, authoritarian, ideology. Second, the high growth rate of exceptionally anti-ideological, but still nearby and physically dependent, Costa Rica similarly supports the hypothesis that it is

Western economists, of course, have found little difficulty in serving as such critics when examining the policy impositions of Soviet Russia, readily sensing that the economic retardations of Post-WWII Eastern Europe, Maoist China, and similarly inspired third-world regions were due to defects in communist ideology and that the self-professed paternalism actually amounted to a thinly veiled, highly inefficient, form of colonialism. But established western economists have refused to view the self-professed paternalism of the West in this exploitationist light. This is largely because the critics of the dominant countries in the West have never provided a rational economic argument to buttress their neo-colonialist inference.[3]

The central purpose of this chapter, beyond attempting to supply a simple framework within which we may understand the entire set of novel international economic institutions introduced during the 20th century, is to provide a theoretical and empirical model predicting the economic effects on dependent nations of imposing policies based upon the predominant economic ideology of the West. Besides reinforcing our earlier results on the ability of surviving governments, especially legislatively pragmatic investor-democracies, to quickly respond to external shocks with the appropriate economic policies, our model will clearly support the charge of neo-colonialism, the claim that the self-professed post-WWI Western paternalists have been unconsciously "exploiting" (i.e., inefficiently redistributing from) their poorer national dependents. Costly foreign exchange controls, hyper-repressive government, hyper-savings, hyperinflation, and even costly social revolution, besides emerging as rational amelioratives of the various dependent nations, will serve here to clearly reveal the underlying exploitation problem.

Nevertheless, in sharp contrast to the Marxian beliefs and revolutionary political goals of other critics, our optimistic belief is that the Western powers, once informed of the genuinely exploitative effects of their imposed trade-liberalizations, will

---

ideological, not physical, domination that retards economic development.

[3]The traditional economic "exploitation" arguments, which stem from the terms-of-trade pessimism of Prebisch and Singer, employ no clear means of exploitation and fail to explain why investors in industries with unfavorable price trends are not compensated with higher current returns. More recent arguments (e.g., Kemp and Ohyama) have introduced discriminatory export taxes to raise at least a theoretical possibility of genuine exploitation. However, such taxes are neither widespread nor consistent with the existing level of paternalism.

Probably the most persistent political-economic argument is that large multinational corporations dominate the politics of the smaller countries. Since substantial political power is essential to protect large investments from effective expropriation, the argument is not persuasive. Moreover, since alternative multinational companies ordinarily compete, prior to making their investments, for the rights to enter a small country, there is no grounds for believing that the winning multinationals either initially underpay for their future favors or contractually under-constrain their future exploitative activities.

In the same vein, although our eventual policy recommendation would greatly restrict the third-world political activities of multinational companies, an exemption would always apply allowing such companies to participate in the formation and execution of laws directly concerning their particular investments in those countries.

voluntarily adopt simple policy reforms completely eliminating the unconscious redistribution, or at least alter the policies of our international agencies so as to substantially increase the welfare of all of the concerned nations.[4]

I. THE PRIMARY WESTERN POLICY IMPOSITION AND THE RESPONSES OF THE DEPENDENT NATIONS

A. General Specification and Preliminary Critique

The central economic ideology of the West is the presumption that the standard competitive model is sufficiently realistic that it can be immediately applied to the construction of socially optimal economic policies. Internationally, this means that dependent nations, at least when operating in markets where they have no individually significant effect on world prices, should, in their own national interests, as well as the collective interest of the rest of the world, adopt free-trade policies. Because of the strength of this ideology,[5] the near-universality of effectively high tariffs by

---

[4]A more basic difference is that our arguments are all tied to a fundamentally rational, logically disciplined, social theory (Appendix B.1), one which recognizes the problem of order (i.e., "who guards the guards?") and solves it by showing that the basic institutions of all states are determined by the preferences of a militarily supported ruling class. These basic institutions cannot be expected to provide substantial surpluses to the masses unless the preferences of a survivable state's military founders permit such surpluses. A Marxian raising of the social consciousness of the masses in such a model does nothing to help them: when the masses are objectively informed and subconsciously rational, the only effect of social consciousness is to depress them.

And when the masses are not so well-informed, revolutionary ideologies bias the masses towards self-futile revolts. We already pointed this out in Section II.A of Chapter 2 in explaining the futility of the feudal-rights-driven peasant revolts arising out of the tax increases that followed the shock-induced wage jumps of the 14th century. Regarding more successful revolutions -- including the Cromwell-Sidney-Jefferson-Henry-Paine type of "rights-of-man"-revolutions in the West -- ideology has worked to artificially lower the operating costs of revolutionary leaders by biasing the masses toward participation. Supporting this bias-interpretation is the common observation that revolutionary foot-soldiers have typically been highly disappointed by the ensuing governments. Care must be taken here to distinguish such states-rights-type revolutionary ideologies from the much-more-centralized, post-revolutionary, Locke-Madison-Hamilton-Mason, "rights of man" ideology appearing in most of the world's constitutions. This latter ideology obviously helps central military founders to commit subsequent leaders to uphold the legal privileges that the founders wish to grant to their important compatriots and their descendants.

[5]Many activist economists deny an adherence to free-trade ideology. These, more liberal, economists profess an unrelenting interest in egalitarian, employment, or "infant industry" goals as critical components of their recommended trade policies. Our problem with these professed policies is that, as theoretical arguments, they are generally unsound because more direct policies (viz., respectively, lump-sum redistribution, monetary or fiscal policy, or temporary domestic investment subsidization) exist to efficiently address their specified market failures.

dependent nations has been traditionally taken by our economists and social thinkers to be a reflection of: (a) the inefficient political influence of special interest groups, (b) the unavailability of more efficient, first best, modes of taxation, or (c) widespread economic ignorance.

However, as argued in Chapter 3, none of these tariff-rationalizations is defensible. Regarding the political influence rationalization, high tariffs have often been regularly imposed upon imports for which there is no obvious protective effect (i.e., no clear import-substitute) and no identifiable political support from an economic interest group. Moreover, there is no reason for domestic interest groups to take their political transfers in a systematically inefficient form, a form that unfailingly repeats itself around the observed world. Regarding the 2nd-best taxation argument (or "revenue-argument") for tariffs, numerous non-special-interest tariffs have also been regularly prohibitive, generating no tariff revenue whatsoever for the tariff-imposing country. The only inference remaining in the standard set is that the tariff-imposing countries are systematically ignorant. However much comfort such an inference may give to the sellers of economic ideology, it is nonsensical to argue that a universally observed policy has evolved in widespread ignorance of the benefits of a policy alternative when, in fact, that alternative has been repeatedly tried. In short, none of the standard tariff rationalizations is defensible.

A non-standard, counter-ideological, Pareto-optimality-based, social-evolution-justified, explanation of tariffs (developed and tested in Chapter 3, Section III) is that such tariffs are necessary if a nation is going to internalize the defense-externalities resulting from the importation of consumer durables. Such imports: (i) add to the country's coveted capital stock and thus its overhead defense costs (Appendix B.2), and (ii) cannot be practically taxed with anything but an import tariff.[6]

There is no apparent reason for international economic efficiency to be sacrificed to achieve an indirect solution to any one of their allocation problems, especially since their societies, *arguendo*, refuse to adopt direct policy interventions to solve the alleged allocation problems. Besides, empirically speaking, these economists, reflecting the ad hoc character of their policy rationalizations, will almost always oppose foreign-country protectionism, as can be easily verified by a quick survey of textbook discussions of international economics.

Eclectic, constitutionally uncommitted, or uninvolved economists are obviously not relevant to our critique, which is implicitly restricted to activist economists, whose adherents regularly express unambiguous policy recommendations.

[6]Taxes on the sales of all consumer durables -- domestic as well as foreign -- would be theoretically optimal in a standard competitive model with Appendix B.2 defense-externalities. This is indeed called-for in the Conclusion of Appendix B.2, which was written in 1974. It was not until the late '70s, and the wartime-price-controls-based tax-exemptions of basic consumer goods explained in Appendix B.3, and the mid-1980s, when a consistent theory of retailing ("monopolistic competition") was produced (Thompson, et al., Vol. III, Ch. 6), that we came to see the complete lack of realism of the standard competitive model as regards domestically produced consumer goods. (As pointed out in Footnote 69 of Chapter 3, in the retailing case, locally produced consumer goods that are tailored to local tastes require more quality refinements and retailer-explanation than rationally more generic, imported, products.

Without such tariffs or their equivalent, states with very high defense-externalities will so over-accumulate consumer durables that they cannot long survive the acquisitive attacks on the existing governments. Significant trade restrictions are vital economic institutions to states with very high defense-externalities. Hence, at least for empirical reasons, it is important that we find some way of identifying countries that suffer from very high defense-externalities.

B. On Brutocracy

Consider a nation in which the ruling social hierarchy unavoidably contains a large number of productive individuals with such little respect for political constitutions and the welfare of people outside of their narrow socio-political clique that each of several such extended families poses a separate revolutionary threat to their own government. A survivable leader of such a government is necessarily concerned with the possibility of a domestic uprising. But the leader never knows which, if any, of several possible alternative cliques will actually stage a coup. Representing, *en masse*, a large part of the productive ruling hierarchy, the alternative ruling cliques (like the dominant families in a loose confederation of 15th century Italian city-states) cannot be practically eliminated from the state. Unlike states whose civil reverence precludes such domestic military rivalry, alternative leaders of a militarily rivalrous state rationally compete by showing how brutal they can be to their domestic political enemies (Thompson, et al., Vol. III, the Appendix to Ch. 3). A normally humanistic (St. Francis-Erasmus-Bentham-Mill-Bergson), or even an ethically neutral (Machiavelli-Kennan), punisher could not afford to run the government because such a leader similarly could not afford to buy-off all of the would-be rebels. The brutal Duchies of Renaissance Italy (e.g., Sedgwick), which inspired the unusually non-humanistic, ethically neutral, political advice of Machiavelli (advice that was still far too humanistic given his political environment), provide us with graphic Western examples of this anti-humanistic form of government. We call such governments "brutocracies". A successful leader of a brutocratic state, an Atilla-Clovis-Gheghis Kahn-Borgia-Stalin-Hitler-Samosa-Hussein type, necessarily places a significantly positive value on being cruel to his or her active rivals.

A coup is nevertheless avoided only if each one of the many rival families receive a real income sufficiently close to the real income that they estimate they could earn as part of a coup and an alternative ruling clique. A visible increase in

---

The result is a much higher retail markup, or excess of price over marginal cost, for such locally produced goods than for imports.) With wartime price controls justifying substantial tax relief for domestic producers of homogeneous consumer goods and the retail markup serving as a substitute for a tax on heterogeneous consumer goods, the only justifiable consumption tax is on imports. Once some more detailed institutional studies then revealed a historic tariff pattern that mirrored the modern pattern (Section III of Chapter 3), we abandoned the overly simplistic approach to consumer-good taxation of Appendix B.2, an approach we now consider to be of only indirect policy relevance.

luxury consumption by the existing ruling clique creates a problem in such states. Members of alternative ruling-cliques take any such increase in luxury consumption as a measure of (a) how much better they could live if they were in power or (b) an unwarranted increase in the resource drain going to the existing ruling clique. In either case, to avoid an increased probability of a coup at a given level of defense expenditure, each one of the alternative ruling cliques must all receive a compensatory income increase. To the existing ruler, who gains no humanistic benefit from these extra-familial income increases, the initiating increase in luxury consumption by the ruling elite thereby creates an enormous defense-externality.

Increased tariffs on imports of luxury consumer goods were thus a large part of the mercantilism of the 16th and 17th centuries, an era during which brutocracy came to rationally dominate the loosely-federated, putative empires of early modern Europe. The relatively extreme brutality of this period has not failed to impress students of political violence (e.g., Davies). As the increasingly massive, rifle-equipped, citizen national armies of the late-17th, 18th, 19th and early-20th centuries sporadically spread and eventually replaced the overhead-intensive, empire-supporting, cannon and professional armies of early-modern Europe, nationally elected and thus humanistic governments correspondingly arose to efficiently compensate the once-again-important commoner. Brutocracy, revealed by the practice of torturing and murdering one's political rivals, became increasingly restricted to regions of the world in which old rivalries between extended aristocratic families could not be practically eliminated. The leaders of these coup-threatened, professional-army-dominated, states distinguished themselves both by maintaining notoriously high tariffs and luxury consumption taxes and by moving their capitals to ruling palaces (such as Sforza Castle, the Uffizi Palace, El Escorial, Versailles, and the Delhi and Peking Palaces) surrounded by large and opulent cathedrals, opera houses and museums, or building beautiful, walled, capital cities (St. Petersburg, Vienna, etc.) In modern times, the beautiful capital centers at Buenos Aires and Brazilia exemplify the force, wherein leaders employ such sites both to improve their abilities to monitor potential coups and to help equalize the living standards of the members of the entire ruling class.[7]

Democracy is fairly rare in, and would be largely wasted on, brutocratic states. For brutocracies lack the civil reverence required of any effective democracy.

These economically handicapped states require extremely high rates of coveted-capital taxation in order to internalize their exceptionally high defense-externalities. The external imposition of free trade on a brutocracy, by inducing an extremely excessive accumulation of coveted consumer durables in the hands of the relatively highly paid ruling clique and their extended families, therefore generates a correspondingly increasing threat to the survival of the existing government. Because of the corresponding need for increasingly costly state repression and the near-inevitability of revolution in relatively independent brutocracies, the external imposition of free trade on a politically independent brutocracy is tantamount to the

---

[7]These are only amelioratives. Heavily subsidized and nearly universal state education, as we saw in Chapter 3 in the case of 19th century France, is the only practical cure, although it is an expensive and lengthy one, that we know for such severe civil irreverence.

external elimination of one of the state's vital institutions.

The exceptionally high durable-goods tax-rates characteristic of an efficient brutocracy imply that the criminal elements of brutocratic states are attracted into durable-good industries, which in turn means that predatory monopolies will be frequently encountered in these states (Thompson, 1995). Correspondingly extensive regulation will therefore appropriately accompany the high tax-rates. Applying the underdevelopment model of Appendix A.1, wherein civil reverence is shown to be necessary for effective democracy and the elimination of underdevelopment traps, the result is the widely acknowledged, but seldom rationalized, four-way correlation between corrupt business practices, the absence of democracy, the presence of extensive government regulation, and economic underdevelopment.[8]

Despite the extensive regulation and high rates of taxation, there is an important difference between this significantly private economy and socialism (governmental ownership of all durable capital) in that the absence of inheritance under socialism seriously distorts the broadly rational education decisions of the state's current leaders (Thompson, et al., Vol. I, Ch. 3, or Thompson, 1996). The reversion of the Soviet Empire to this essentially tribal ownership system at the end of WWI can, as we shall see, only be understood as an unfortunate effect of Marxian ideology. The costly spread of socialist revolution to several other, initially more objective, countries can, we shall also see, be understood as a consequence of a combination of: (1) free-trade policy impositions by the West, (2) brutocratic social structures, and (3) direct Soviet support. The second and third factors jointly imply an extraordinarily high cost of accepting the first, the pro-trade policies of the West. Thus, studies of post-WWII socialist revolutions consistently emphasize that pre-revolutionary states uniformly contained: (1) substantial economic intervention by the West, (2) severe militaristic splits among numerous groups of ruling elites along with high levels of corruption and an initial lack of both democracy and economic development, and (3) a reaction against the West that was politically and militarily supported by the East (e.g., Gurr and Goldstone, pp. 325-31). The end of substantial Soviet support for small-country revolutions against the West has correspondingly substantially reduced the pressure for revolution (Gurr and Goldstone, p. 340).

More specific empirical implications of this lengthy digression will become apparent only once we develop some relatively objective methods of determining how different kinds of countries react differently to the same initial external attempt to

---

[8]Although no economic policy implications follow from this commonly observed empirical relationship, the members of a brutocracy obviously would again collectively benefit from an effectively state-wide educational system that subtly induced a replacement of narrow family loyalties with an appreciation for the state and the wide variety of its people. This fact can hardly be lost on the leaders of a struggling brutocratic state. It is no surprise then that, once various underdeveloped regions that had been colonies of immigration-resistant England obtained national sovereignty in the 1950s and began having their students attracted to English and U.S. universities in the 1960s, the successful universities there came to teach, besides a previously taught respect for legitimate states, an extraordinarily high degree of respect for different kinds of people and their opinions, i.e., for a "diverse" community.

eliminate their import restrictions.

C. The Initiating Policy Imposition

Prior to WWI, the defense-externality-ignoring ideology of free trade -- although frequently the cause of excessively free trade during the ascendancy of classical economics (especially the third quarter of the 19th century) -- was seldom utilized to impose internationally free-trade policies on dependent countries. Pre-WWI colonial powers bore a large part of the costs of defending their dependents and so had little incentive to use their control over the central governments of these dependencies to impose low tariffs on durable imports from other nations. (Recall, for example, that the American Revolution represented a colonial refusal to financially provide for their defense by paying what the colonists claimed were excessively high, not low, tariff-impositions of the mother country.) The World Wars changed all this.[9] In particular, the "Versailles system" set up at the end of WWI both granted local autonomy to the defeated nations and imposed artificially low import tariffs upon each defeated nation. The imposed tariff reductions, being ideologically based and self-presumed to be for the benefit of everyone, were impervious to the defense costs that were now being borne by the ostensibly independent nations. (On all of this early background, see the 1921 study of the U.S. Tariff Commission.) Except for a temporary hiatus -- the uniquely successful Dawes' Plan era from 1924 through 1927 during which reparations were paid out of tariff revenues so that the dominant countries had a unique incentive to relax their ideological impositions and permit significantly higher tariff rates -- this new policy of externally imposing artificially low tariff rates on sovereign nations rapidly spread to other ostensibly independent nations. The policy worked by inducing cooperating nations to adopt artificially low tariff schedules in return for the right to trade with the dominant countries as "most favored nations", i.e., without facing discriminatorily high tariff rates (League of Nations). The well-known General Agreement on Tariffs and Trade (GATT) and its recent successor, the World Trade Organization (WTO), arose after WWII to further institutionalize the system.

D. The Primary Small-Country Response

A second novelty of modern international economics is the immediate post-WWI

---

[9]Thus, for example, in 1904 Teddy Roosevelt, in proclaiming his famous "corollary" to the Monroe Doctrine, unilaterally established the U.S. as the exclusive police department of the western hemisphere but stated no objection to the high Latin American tariffs on foreign imports. In contrast, following the official abandonment of this "corollary" in the Clark Memorandum of 1930, Franklin Roosevelt further reassured the nations of Latin America of U.S. respect for their military independence (through his still-effective "good neighbor policy" eschewing U.S. military intervention other than to protect U.S. lives and property) but could offer no such assurances with respect to trade policy.

emergence of peacetime foreign exchange controls, or simply "exchange controls".[10] Not accidently, as we shall see, these costly controls were introduced by the self-same Central European dependents upon whom the WWI victors had imposed low tariffs. Subsequently, peacetime exchange controls have also accompanied externally imposed tariff reductions in other dependent nations, persisting in tandem into the 1990s except in countries that have exhibited abnormally high or abnormally low degrees of dependency on the dominant nations, as we shall elaborate below.

Thus, with exceptions, when a small, post-WWI (i.e., "modern"), state begins to suffer a continuing deficit in its balance-of-trade at its initial exchange rate, a deficit that would not exist in the absence of the external imposition of low-tariffs, the state does not voluntarily allow the price of its domestic currency to fall (or lower its domestic money supply), which would be sufficient to eliminate the trade deficit. Rather, despite the almost universal disapproval of economists, the dependent state attempts to maintain its original currency value and exports and correspondingly employs a system of exchange controls to ration, among its existing importers, whatever foreign reserves are earned by its existing exporters.[11]

Like the small-country tariffs they replaced, albeit at a significant cost, these persistently condemned exchange controls have remained largely unexplained.[12]

Yet the strangely ignored post-WWI relationship between observed peacetime exchange-controls and the external imposition of freer trade -- exchange controls having consistently followed the external imposition of low tariffs -- has a quite straightforward theoretical interpretation: A small country's policy-neutralizing response to an externally imposed tariff reduction is simply to artificially maintain its original exchange rate rather than passively allowing its currency to depreciate. Since imports are then cash-constrained by exports because exports do not change

---

[10]Rationalizing <u>wartime</u> foreign exchange controls is a straightforward application of a pre-existing wartime efficiency-argument, which we will have occasion to summarize in Section II.B.1 below. As wartime controls immediately preceded the emergence of peacetime controls, the latter, although sometimes vital, cannot be regarded as an inspired policy innovation requiring a substantial gestation period or an evolutionary process.

[11]Post-WWII Germany and Japan, and subsequently Taiwan, South Korea, and Singapore, together form a theory-confirming exception. The unique postwar constraints imposed on these countries by the U.S. precluded the adoption of exchange controls and therefore overvalued currencies. As argued in the next subsection, the unique -- and wholly predictable -- response to externally imposed tariff reductions has been for all of these countries to rationally <u>undervalue</u> their currencies.

[12]The usual rationale for exchange controls, that differential import license fees are a convenient way to interpersonally price discriminate between different foreign buyers (e.g., Else or Bhagwati), does not apply to small countries. Besides, differential tariffs to different importers are at least as convenient as sales of import licenses. In fact, such discriminatory tariff reductions -- in preference to discriminatory import license fees -- are regularly granted to members of defense alliances, for whom the relocation of a consumer good within the alliance is of little military, and therefore of little tax, consequence in an efficient alliance.

while imports are in greater demand because of the imposed tariff reduction, imports must be rationed back to their initial level, assuming no change in loans from abroad. So the country immediately and efficiently achieves -- with an overvalued currency and import rationing -- what it can no longer achieve with tariffs.[13]

The neglect of this obvious historical regularity by leading academic economists is certainly not due to their inability to see the straightforward, Marshall-like, equivalence between tariffs and exchange-controls. (See, e.g., Bhagwati.) Rather, the neglect is likely due to an ideological blind-spot, a profession-serving unwillingness to view small-country trade restrictions as the result of an important political-economic efficiency. It is much more pleasant, and profitable, for economists to attribute these trade restrictions to some strangely universal political-economic illiteracy. More narrowly focused economists, examining the empirical effects of externally imposed tariff reductions, have apparently been thrown-off by the fact that the tariff-imposing countries -- seeing effective tariff-restoration via exchange controls emerge from the imposition of lower tariffs -- have sometimes delayed the dependent country's adoption of exchange controls by financially supporting their increase in import demand through temporary foreign exchange loan-subsidies to the recalcitrant dependents. In such cases, months, even years, may pass before the loan-subsidies, which theoretically decrease the welfare of the subsidizers, cease and exchange controls emerge.

Thus, from the very beginning of these post-Versailles programs, exchange controls were immediately adopted by the victimized nations who were not given the benefit of foreign-exchange loan-subsidies. Such a policy response is, of course, a theoretically optimal response to an externally imposed tariff reduction. Mere coincidence does not explain the policy response because the return to high tariffs generated by the 1924 Dawes' Plan induced the dependent nations to immediately dismantle their costly exchange control systems. Although the Dawes' system was uniquely successful in collecting reparations debt and inducing Central European growth, the ideological unpopularity of this colonial-style scheme forced it to be replaced after 1927, under both U.S. and League of Nations pressure, by a more "enlightened" system, one that both respected national autonomy and reimposed lower tariffs. To support the post-1927 system (the so-called "Young Plan"), i.e., to prevent a reintroduction of exchange controls, temporary foreign exchange loans from the promoters of the "enlightened" system were extended to Central Europe. The escalating accumulation of these loans had to come to an end, which it did in the middle of 1931. After France's highly publicized refusal of another loan increase and the immediate failure of the Austrian Credit-Anstalt, exchange controls were -- within

---

[13]Since the initial tariff rates were part of a long-term evolutionary equilibrium, where practical experience rather than ideology determined the policy outcome, we need not be concerned with the exact Pascalian rationale the victim uses to restore its original effective tariff rates. We shall, however, find it both necessary and enlightening to introduce a process that specifically evolves to induce the surviving countries to make the economically correct decisions when we come to environments in which small countries are suddenly given special incentives to lower their trade barriers and accept some degree of trade expansion.

days (Ellis) -- reintroduced throughout central Europe!

Economists examining the welfare effects of trade liberalization have been similarly thrown-off by the related fact that the empirically measured social benefits of a loan-subsidized free-trade policy are generally quite positive in the short run. The small-country costs of a continually excessive importation of coveted consumer goods only show-up, as we have seen, in the form of future military problems and political instability. Indeed, the main ostensible beneficiaries of continuing foreign-exchange loan subsidies (Central Europe from 1927 to 1931 (Ellis) and the Middle East, Africa, and Latin America after the early 1960s (M. de Vries)) have all subsequently suffered from both serious military problems and political instability.

Besides the above financial evidence (where exchange controls or temporary foreign currency loans immediately follow externally imposed tariff reductions), combined with the 19th and 20th century military and political evidence in Section 3.B of Chapter 3, there is additional, structural, evidence that peacetime exchange-control systems are policy-substitution-based responses to externally imposed reductions in efficient tariff levels. It is that import license fees, like tariffs, are concentrated on consumer durables (Bhagwati).[14]

As we have mentioned, certain kinds of nations do not exhibit the above, normal exchange-control response. The first such exception concerns extremely dependent nations.

E. Extremely Dependent Nations and Hyper-Repressive Government

Very highly dependent, what we shall call "1st-order" dependent, nations simply accept the externally imposed tariff reduction without countering them with severe exchange controls. These extremely dependent nations adopt trade liberalization because their political leaders are inevitably puppets of the dominant country. Thus, even when the highly dependent nations are brutocracies (e.g., most of Central America), direct political intervention will lead these nations to "voluntarily" adopt internally inefficient policies. Foreign exchange loans are then, at least during peacetime, unnecessary and only occasionally granted (Adams). Because of the eventually much higher level of defense costs in these highly dependent states, the ideologically receptive ruling elites will, especially in brutocracies, have to adopt abnormally high degrees of political repression and receive the timely military assistance of a dominant country in order to maintain political power. (A high degree of long-term political and economic success may be occasionally observed in such states (e.g., Chile), but only if the region is also fortunate in being simultaneously favored by exogenous decreases in the threat of internal military aggression.)

Since effective trade liberalization following an externally imposed tariff reduction implies currency depreciation in the dependent country, foreign owners of real capital in the dependent country are powerful beneficiaries, and therefore

---

[14]Recall that although the defense-externality that rationalizes such license fees also applies to the importation of producer durables, the producer-durable defense-externality is ordinarily internalized through domestic income and profit taxation (Appendix B.2).

powerful political supporters, of effective trade liberalization. It is therefore easy to see why the elimination of direct foreign investment soon became a major post-WWI rallying cry among the populists in the surviving dependent governments. The similarly understandable response of the dominant countries, at least in the 1st-order dependencies, has been direct political intervention at the behest of such foreign capital owners. This has frequently come in the name of anti-communism despite the almost purely nationalist nature of the movements in these countries (e.g., Miller, esp. Ch. XVIII). Since social evolution follows military strength, which in this case is in effectively ideologized, relatively popular governments have been systematically replaced by popularly despised, necessarily hyper-repressive, foreign-investor-supported, pro-trade regimes in these militarily coerced, highly dependent, states.

All of these effects, of course, are magnified when the 1st-order dependencies are brutocracies.

The remaining full sections of this chapter will concern less-than-1st-order-dependent nations. Although political puppetry and hyper-repression are interesting subjects, the difficulty of creating persuasive numerical measures of these political variables, and the subtle foreign military influence on them, makes satisfactory quantitative testing in this area extremely difficult. Nevertheless, before elaborating upon that which we can easily quantify -- the dominant-country financial reactions to small-country exchange controls and the secondary small-country responses, etc., etc. -- we consider two additional exceptional cases.

In the second exceptional case, some critically located, not quite so politically dependent, countries, which we call "2nd-order" dependencies, have simply been denied the right to adopt exchange controls.

F. 2nd-Order Dependencies and Hyper-Savings

1. *Post WWII Germany, Japan and the "Baby Tigers" -- Economic Miracles (unless you happen to have been living there).* The fear of a remilitarization of West Germany and Japan after WWII led the U.S. to eliminate the abilities of these re-democratized countries to independently defend themselves. Soon after this effective demilitarization, these countries, although allowed to freely elect their political leaders, were correspondingly refused the right to adopt foreign exchange controls. So these "2nd-order dependencies" could not respond as other, more independent, countries to the externally imposed post-WWII tariff reductions (e.g., Mayer). The response of West Germany and Japan was to undervalue their currencies (e.g., Reuss, pp. 54-65, and Minami, pp. 242-44; respectively). Such a policy, supported by the governmental creation of an artificial scarcity of foreign exchange, is efficient in that it represents an alternative route to the restriction of imports under fixed exchange rates. Nevertheless, currency undervaluation is, to the dependent country, quite welfare-inferior to the normal overvaluation policy we have been describing. For an undervalued currency implies -- and is implied by -- a continual domestic subsidy to capital imports, a subsidy-induced surplus in the dependent country's balance of trade. This has correspondingly been the explicit policy of west Germany and Japan throughout the Cold War (1948-1988). This subsidy-induced increase in exports amounts -- using now the converse of the Bickerdike theorem -- to a distinct welfare

loss to the capital-import-subsidizing country.[15]

Perhaps the most interesting feature of this predictable sequence is the tremendously high regard that economists and the popular press have expressed for the economic performance of these unusually high-savings, high-growth, economies. Although the popular press may be forgiven for failing to adequately discount future consumption, it is not immediately clear why economists -- many of whom are very well aware of the abnormal West German and Japanese post-WWII investment and savings subsidies and the force of consumption interest -- would abandon welfare economics for naive comparisons of growth rates.

A quantitative welfare analysis of these investment subsidies may thus be enlightening: First, up to the late 1980s, the various, U.S.-induced, post-WWII German and Japanese investment subsidies, including the above-described balance of trade surpluses and corresponding governmental subsidies to foreign investment, led these countries to save at rates more than twice their normal rates. (This is revealed by comparing each country's comparative savings rates in the early 1900s with their comparative post-WWII savings rates (see, e.g., King and Fullerton, and Minami, respectively)).   Second, again up to the late 1980s, since the financing of these various savings and investment subsidies came from income taxes (rather than fiscal deficits and national borrowing), consumer liquidity was directly sacrificed to generate the increase in savings.   This means that the typical consumer discount rate, which is at least twice the investor discount-rate, is the relevant rate of discount to apply to the induced investment.[16]   The welfare loss from the excess investment, the appropriately discounted present cost of the induced investment, is therefore at least as large as the present value of their normal quantity of aggregate investment.   Thus, in welfare terms, the adult post-WWII citizens of these countries were made worse-off than if they had saved and invested at their normal rates but the total returns from these investments were completely confiscated!

The underlying advantage to the U.S. from vigorously promoting these artificial investment stimuli, promotions that arose immediately after the USSR displayed their highly aggressive, nuclearly supported, intentions in 1947-48, was to furnish the victorious Allies with a rich and highly locationally convenient pair of ransom payments in case the balance of power shifted to the USSR, which it never did. Nevertheless, given the insecurity of Post WWII Germany and Japan, the unusual prohibition of exchange controls imposed a substantial burden on their citizens, whose

---

[15]Although corresponding benefits accrue to the rest of the world in the form of artificially low prices of imports from West Germany and Japan and artificially high supplies of savings from those two countries, lump-sum transfer mechanisms (like the post-WWI Dawes Plan) would alternatively generate higher utilities for all concerned under normal circumstances. The unusual circumstances that led the U.S. to rationally prefer the undervalued currency solution is identified later in the discussion.

[16]We could arrive at the same conclusion that we are about to reach by alternatively assuming perfect capital markets and reasonable variations in the marginal costs and benefits from the consumer sacrifice.

military insecurity and correspondingly high defense-externality would have led them to save at <u>lower-than-normal</u> rates if they had not been forced to do the opposite. The blameless descendent populations of these two ex-aggressor nations now happen to stand to benefit handsomely from the realizations of these forced savings policies and the 1991 dissolution of the once-threatening Soviet Union. The predictable, eventually welfare-enhancing, reductions in the domestic Japanese and German foreign investment subsidies and their corresponding reduced growth rates during the suddenly secure 1990s has been similarly mis-portrayed by economists as economically unfortunate, "miracle-ending", events.[17]

Somewhat later than the Soviet Union, Communist China became a Cold-War threat, both to the West and to their neighbors. Thus, almost immediately after Mao began developing a nuclear arsenal to complement his militarily aggressive stance during the late 1950s, the Western powers converted several of China's smaller neighbors (Taiwan, South Korea, and Singapore) into Japanese and German-type centers of savings-induced wealth-creation, again through a policy forcing these high-defense-externality nations to avoid exchange controls and thereby to rationally undervalue their currencies (Haggard-Pang and Cumings).[18] Since China has remained a military threat despite the break-up of the Soviet Union, the savings and

---

[17]The reason for the qualification with respect to the welfare benefits (viz., that they are "eventual") is that the recessionary macroeconomic effects of the reduction in exports should have been -- but were not -- accompanied by expansionary monetary policies. As a result, a large part of the observed reductions in Japanese and German growth rates represent real economic losses. (Also, as we shall soon see, the imposition of exchange-control limitations on most of southeast Asia in the early 1990s created a glut in many of their previously specialized export markets.)

Rational economic policy thought offers no explanation for the inability of these countries to switch to expansionary monetary policies to combat their now-quite-lengthy recessions. What <u>does</u> explain this policy anomaly are the special constraints on banking institutions (hyper-creditor-domination) that both countries had evolved to support their undervalued exchange rates. (Short-term inflation increases import demand and reduces export supply and thereby reduces the initially optimal degree of domestic currency undervaluation at the fixed exchange rate.) The Pascalian leaders of these essentially pragmatic countries simply see no reason to scrap the monetary institutions that so-well served them for so long a time. Institutional evolution can be very slow when vital institutions are not at stake.

[18]Taiwan and South Korea, the most responsive to U.S. policy pressure, have set the pattern for the rest of the "tigers". Thus, after the U.S. finally forced an end to both Taiwan and South Korea's currency overvaluation policies in 1960, a new pragmatic industrial policy immediately arose, one which, quite appropriately, directly subsidized the types of industries that had been evolved in Japan and Germany, e.g., foreign-capital-intensive export industries (Haggard and Pang, and Cumings, respectively). The initiating jumps in the domestic prices of dollars amounted to the same sort of currency undervaluations that appeared in Japan and Germany, the implicit purpose of which was to restore the imports of consumer durables to acceptable levels. The savings and growth booms, although excessive, have been repeatedly used by economists to praise such policies.

growth rates of these "baby tigers" has remained relatively high.[19]

It might be thought that the direct foreign investment that these export booms often attract would work to perversely increase the nation's coveted capital stock. However, since foreign investors involve their home nations in protecting their investments abroad, there should be no presumption of increased domestic defense costs stemming from such investment. And, although <u>domestic</u> investment may also expand during these booms, domestic investors compensate their nations for the investment-induced military insecurity with domestic capital and income taxes.

2. *Widespread Currency Undervaluation.* Based on the growing relative military strength of the U.S., the late 1980s saw the emergence of a new IMF policy. Many discretionary IMF loans have, during the 1990s, come to be conditioned upon entire fiscal and monetary packages that explicitly limit the dependent countries' use of exchange controls. Although not so-restricting the subsequently hyperinflating Eastern Bloc countries, the new policy still amounted to a widespread elimination of the previous freedom of IMF borrowers to employ exchange controls to neutralize unwanted tariff reductions and is partially responsible for the generally sharp reduction in exchange controls in the early 1990s (International Monetary Fund).

So a large number of borrowing, high-defense-externality, states were suddenly put in the same boat as West Germany, Japan, and the "baby tigers". While maintaining the import license fees offered by exchange controls as much as they could without losing their loan eligibility, the borrowing, high-defense-externality, states of southeast Asia and South America began to use some of their export revenues to purchase investments abroad, thereby creating the beginnings of artificial savings and export booms.[20]

---

[19]Note that West Germany, Japan, and the "baby tigers" all satisfy our Appendix A.1 efficiency condition in that they have all become investor-democracies and have long enjoyed highly civilly reverent bureaucracies. (The mythological foundations for the latter assertion are developed in Thompson, et al., Vol. II, Ch. 6.) Prior to the externally-imposed exchange-control eliminations that initiated their off-the-charts growth rates, these countries had pragmatically established themselves as capable of generating high levels of economic efficiency (Japan and Germany prior to the mid-1930s and the baby tigers following their achievement of domestic independence during the mid-1950s.) Employing the argument of Appendix A.1, the induced domestic investment subsidies would have been largely offset by domestic rent-seeking if these countries were not effective democracies. It is therefore somewhat likely that the affected nations would not have accepted the elimination of their exchange controls unless they were effective democracies. Overinvesting is far more tolerable when it generates abnormal growth than when it generates abnormal domestic rent-seeking.

[20]The standard textbook treatment of the southeast Asian Boom of the 1990s is that these countries, in accepting lower tariffs and weaker exchange controls, have simply chosen to accept the path of trade liberalization (e.g., Caves, Frankel, and Jones). But an official source reports that these booms were accompanied by such large export surpluses that total consumer imports substantially fell in the 1990-1996 period (United Nations). Nevertheless, we suspect that such perversions will not become common observations until some time in the future.

What distinguishes the experiences of these countries from the earlier experiences of Japan, Germany and the "baby tigers" is a predictable learning-response to the earlier, profit-inducing, currency devaluations. In particular, there has been an IMF-endorsed foreign financial participation in the newly induced expenditure on capital imports. The result has been a temporarily high foreign demand for certain southeast Asian and Latin American currencies and a substantial delay in the real depreciation of the currencies. A concurrently predictable consequence of the multi-country export boom is an induced deterioration in their common terms of trade, an end to the foreign participation boom, and an inevitable devaluation. The correspondingly predictable jump in real indebtedness in the 1990s "debt crisis" has been incorrectly but unanimously attributed by modern authorities to an irrational "herd effect" based upon Keynes' "animal spirits".

In this regard, it is interesting to note, as we shall emphasize in Chapter 6, that, along with the recent "globalization" of labor and commodity markets, the U.S. and IMF policy response has been to financially "bail-out" these currency-depreciating countries (including those in Latin America), and thereby induce massive debt-dependency and encourage further such glut-inducing export booms.

Our third and final exceptional case arises in <u>much less</u> politically dependent, almost independent, what we call "4th-order" dependent, brutocracies. Here, the dominant countries are not up to the task of preventing a wholesale revolution against the ideology-based imposition of pro-trade policies.

G. 4th-Order Dependencies and the Economics of Revolution

1. *Colonial Revolutions.* We can now continue the argument introduced in Section II.E.1 and Footnote 74 of Chapter 3, where we briefly analyzed historical revolutions against a colonial power (e.g., the American Revolution) as the outcome of unexpected increases in colonial wealth (e.g., the colonial windfall at the end of the French and Indian Wars). The cost of defending the territory to the essentially uncommitted mother country suddenly exceeded the self-defense costs of the inhabitants of the colony, who could suddenly afford the overhead costs of defending the suddenly more valuable territory and <u>were</u> willing to make a commitment to all-or-nothing war to defend their borders. With the cost of collective defense suddenly lower to the colonial inhabitants than to the mother country, the colonial inhabitants were suddenly willing to pay more for the territory than it was worth to the mother country. Efficiency dictated a transfer. But since neither the mother nor the colony was convinced of the military capability of the colonial inhabitants, the colony generally had to demonstrate its ability to defend itself before the transfer occurred. The same sort of parent-child contest is frequently observed in nature before parents send their predatory-offspring off to fend for themselves. This type of revolution was a necessary part of an efficient transfer given the uncertainty concerning the self-defensibility of the colony.

Similarly, in this chapter's introductory discussion of the wave of post-WWII anti-colonial movements, we noted that large and sudden increases in the cost of defending colonies would, again after a military demonstration period (e.g., Halliday, pp. 24-27), efficiently result in at least formal independence for the colonies.[21]

2. *Costly Social Revolution.* A wholly different sort of revolution, one that is efficient only from the standpoint of the revolutionary government, occurs when an ideology, say free trade ideology, is inappropriately imposed upon a state, say an almost independent brutocracy. The point to such a revolution is to free the state

---

[21]Perhaps the reader would benefit from the following outline of an economic theory of revolution: What maintains a state is a commitment to violence by its broadly rational military leaders (Appendix B.1). A revolution is a military challenge to this commitment from within the pre-existing state. The leaders of the pre-existing state match violence for violence in an exercise of their commitment. From an informationally idealistic standpoint (perfect and complete information), revolutions make no sense because a broadly rational pre-revolutionary offer would avoid the obviously heavy resource costs of violence. So the relevant parties to a revolution must be substantially uninformed. There are two major cases. In the first case, which is illustrated in the above discussion of colonial revolutions, both the pre-established leaders and the challengers are equally uninformed. Such a revolution, like the wars of Appendix B.3, establishes the military capabilities of the parties and thereby provides a positive expected social value.

The second case, which we are about to discuss, arises when there are substantial differences in information. In our discussion, one part of the population is objective and the other is not. Say, through the effect of an economic ideology, the existing authorities are over-optimistic about the value of their social leadership. An especially damaged collective of objective victims of this ideologized leadership would incur a resource cost of revolution of, say $100, which can be assumed to be lower than its objectively expected value of revolution, say $110 ($220, its value of control against any alternative leader, times the probability of a successful revolution). The existing authority is inefficient so that an objective estimate of its personal leadership rents relative to what it would obtain by submitting to the rebels is less than $220, say $180. So the rebels should be able to buy control for a jointly beneficial offer of anywhere between $180 and $200. But the ruling group is also ideologized so that it exaggerates its cost of living under the alternative rules and places the value of its control at, say, $300 and believes that it would likely win the war and so incur a cost of war of much less than $150 (half of $300), say of $30. The latter is plausible because, as in our war theory of Section II.D.4 of Chapter 3, ideologized leaders typically expect that their adversaries will soon come to appreciate their policies. So the leadership rejects the maximum $200 offer and, if no other options exist, fight the rational aggressor.

However, if there were very few dissatisfied groups, the existing leaders would rationally buy off the potential rebels, sequentially offering each of them assured benefits, say $11, thereby preventing each attempted revolution and retaining its inefficient control with certainty. But peace would reign. In contrast, when, as in a brutocracy, a large number of possible rebel groups exist, say 10, it becomes more profitable to either accept the first $200 offer or, in case the cost of employing a collective punishment strategy is less than $100, simultaneously exercise its commitment to lethal violence against the entire group of aggressive dissidents. This is of general importance because it tells us to expect non-colonial revolutions to engage all of a country's dissidents and to be concentrated among ideologized brutocracies. And, indeed, it does appear that non-colonial revolutions are broad-based and occur only in brutocratic states. However, as we are about to see, there are other reasons for 20th century non-colonial revolutions to be concentrated among brutocratic states.

from the influence of the ideology, say to free a brutocracy from a free-trade ideology, in order to somehow reduce the cost of domestic defense to manageable proportions and create a more viable or less repressive state. Since the initiating ideology prevents the leaders of the pre-revolutionary state from objectively estimating the extent of the social demand for such a change, thereby preventing them from sufficiently appreciating the increasing insecurity of coveted capital, some sort of military aggression against the state soon becomes objectively profitable. (The above footnote explains why monetary payments are infeasible.)

Such aggression, in particular excessive-capital-induced revolutions resulting from a free-trade ideology, are highly costly and could be entirely avoided by simply eliminating the initiating ideology. As in the case of colonial revolution, noticeable increases in aggregate wealth usually precede this externally induced form of revolution (Brinton, Goldstone). The revolutions empirically differ, however, in that excessive-accumulation-induced revolutions include an internally redistributional, "social revolutionary", component. This is because the attack necessarily comes from those who do not benefit from the excessive accumulation of real capital, i.e., from a coalition of disaffected segments of the ruling class and an army of perennially oppressed masses. Thus, in studies of the post-WWI revolutions of the Bolsheviks, the Chinese Communists, the Yugoslavian Communists, the Bolivian Communists, Castro's Cubans, the Viet Cong, the Nicaraguan Sandinistas, and Cambodia's Khmer Rouge, it is systematically observed that there is a lengthy build-up of severe resentment by several lower-levels of the ruling class against the increasingly obvious prosperity of the ruling elite (Gurr, Goldstone). The disaffected elites soon enlisted the support of much larger, more physically adept, groups of regularly oppressed masses, the revolutions predictably becoming "social revolutions" against the overly prosperous and [not incidently] cruel ruling elite (Skocpol).

The 1917 Russian Revolution thus followed a long sequence of west-inspired modernization programs (first under Reutern, then Bunge, then Witte, and finally Stolypin)[22] featuring: (1) a long period of insignificant taxes on industrial capital, as noted in Section II.D.5.a of Chapter 3; (2) a growing ruling-class division between those favored by tax-forgiving bureaucrats and those encumbered by the belatedly significant (but still only 10%) tax rate on profits (Bowman, pp. 274-81); (3) decreasing tariffs on luxury imports from France and Great Britain (Haight, esp.

---

[22]It is tempting to believe that the goal of modernization, being based upon simple imitation, is not an economic ideology. However, informed imitation in Russia would have accounted for the brutocratic social structure and would therefore have been correspondingly circumspect about lowering the extremely high Russian tariffs and guild restrictions that prevailed prior to the 1860s. More specifically, the pragmatic imitation that our theory requires would have led to a reversal of the modernization policy, probably before 1900 but certainly after the depression of 1900-04 or the French-style Russian Revolution of 1905.

More generally, even if we knew nothing about a state's eschewal of trial and error experimentation or its possession of teacher-favoring intellectual cartels, any overall economic policy based upon a singular conception of a socially optimal set of economic activities rather than pragmatic thought would imply its implementation of an economic ideology.

pp. 69-70); and (4) a substantially excessive, eventually militarily indefensible, investment in agricultural capital spurred on by Stolypin's pre-revolutionary agrarian banking and de-collectivization reforms and maintenance of a complete absence of taxation on agricultural capital (Bowman, esp. pp. 281-2).[23]

Regarding the post-1917 social revolutions, most authors (e.g., Skocpal; Halliday, Ch. 2; and Goldstone) emphasize our earlier-noted presence of both: (1) the initial involvement of western superpowers and (2) the subsequent involvement of the Soviet Union. We interpret these influences to be respectively: (1) a trade-liberalizing foreign influence on the original ruling elites; and (2) a subsequent, overall-dependency-reducing, counter-ideology to support the ultimately successful ruling elites.[24] Nevertheless, as emphasized by numerous authors, none of these revolutions did much to end the basic brutality of these societies (e.g., Sibley).

Another distinguishing feature of these 20th century social revolutions is their non-democratic character. This is implied by our efficiency-theory because the relevant countries, being brutocracies, lack the civil reverence to make a democracy effective. Still another unique feature is their tendency to eventually commit to an unfortunately extreme, anti-trade, ideology. Although this informational excess would be a plausible occurrence even without Soviet support in that the revolution is actually a revolution against a pro-trade ideology, we have yet to see what we really need: a post-19th century revolution against ideology itself.

The complementary dynamical reason for 20th century social revolution, one

---

[23]Because the eventual leaders of post-revolutionary Russia failed to see that the problem with the pre-revolutionary governments was excessive capital accumulation, socialism became their only viable option given their appropriately egalitarian post-WWI distributional goals and their revealed unwillingness to tax capital sufficiently to prevent domestic attacks on subsequently accumulated private wealth. Absent their modernizing ideology, the optimum, as in any brutocracy, would have been achieved by adopting (1) relatively high rates of capital taxation, rates somewhere in between the moderate rates the Russian revolutionaries inherited and the 100% rates that they eventually chose, and (2) a centralized, civil-reverence-producing, educational system. Although the socialism that they alternatively came to embrace can be rationalized under certain preference-assumptions (Appendix A.2), these assumptions are generally quite unrealistic. Assuming more human preferences, an absence of inheritable capital leads to devastatingly inefficient educational policies (Thompson, 1996 and Thompson, et al., Vol. I, Ch. 3). In any case, this anti-market ideology unfortunately became, largely through Soviet foreign policy, the model for subsequent 20th century social revolutions.

[24]The French, First Russian (1905), and Mexican Revolutions are close relatives. But what is missing in each of these three cases is the presence of an anti-trade counter-argument. (The argument against France's ideological imposition of relatively free trade was transformed into an attack on France's Austrian Queen.) The result, for France, as elaborated in Chapter 3, was excessively free trade and increasing political instability until their pragmatic democratic revolution of 1871. The immediate result for Russia was the same and therefore the second, more extreme, revolution occurred. The result for free-trade-ideologized Mexico has been increasing political instability and correspondingly increasing political oppression (Tutino). One would hope, as occurred in France, that the spread of civilly reverent (e.g., Hellenistic) education would eventually generate effective democracies in Russia and Mexico.

directly tied to an evolutionary process, is based on the fact that externally imposed trade liberalization simultaneously lowers the states' customs revenues and continually increases its efficient domestic defense expenditures as the stock of consumer durables grows towards its new level. Efficient domestic tax rates thus continually increase in a state that already features relatively high rates of capital taxation due to its brutocratic structure. Because the efficient taxes ascend to heights that are increasingly beyond their past experience and far beyond the contemporary experience of more successful (non-brutocratic) neighbors, defense expenditures will increasingly fall short of their efficient levels despite growing domestic tensions and thus partial increases in defense expenditures. This produces a growing fiscal squeeze and increasing political repression. These (according to Brinton's and Goldstone's studies) are important members of the set of precursors to social revolution, which will be protracted and bloody only if it is substantially resisted by the promoters or the free-trade ideology. In this way, Lamarckian learning propels the trade-liberalizing brutocracy into a financial and political crisis and hastens its externally supported, constrained-efficient, social revolution.[25]

3. *Revolution, War, and Ideology.* The careful reader (especially of long footnotes) will have noticed a great similarity between the above rationality-based model of non-colonial revolution and the rationality-based model of war developed in Section II.D.4 of Chapter 3. (The main theoretical difference is that "revolution" features several separate adversaries on one side of the fight.) In both cases, an information difference was present to generate substantial over-optimism regarding victory on one side of an extended dispute. And in both cases we introduced ideology to generate predictable, persistent, and very costly military conflicts.

Having developed these models of military conflict, we should explicitly relate them to the theory of ideology and vital institutions developed in Chapters 1 and 2. We have seen that military conflicts have persistently arisen from ideology-based eliminations of vital institutions. In none of these instances did the ideologized leaders believe that they had done something to eliminate the country's defensibility. Ideology thus made the state over-optimistic about its ability to win a war. The predictable result of this information difference was thus not merely an end to the original state. There was also a theoretical likelihood of a costly military conflict, whose persistent occurrence helps to confirm our basic ideologization hypothesis.

A different sort of ideology problem arose out of the simple learning effects of World Wars I and II discussed at the beginning of this chapter. Prior to that discussion, we had outlined ideology-and-rationality-based <u>causes</u> of WWI (in Sections III.B and E of Chapter 3) and WWII (in Chapter 4). Regarding the <u>effects</u>

---

[25]A different class of brutocratic revolution (e.g., Libya, Iran, Iraq, and Haiti) exists where Brinton's classic financial weakness precondition is violated. (We infer this because the ruling military exits even though it has the financial resources to continue the fight.) This class of state is discussed later, after we have taken the above evolutionary analysis a bit further by admitting the temporary existence and Darwinian failure of states that do not possess political values that efficiently constrain their Pascalian decisionmakers.

of these wars, substantial common learning occurred concerning the extreme devastation that war could produce under advanced technology. The increased cost of decision-error, whether due to ideology or not, dramatically increased imperial defense costs. So, following the defense model in Appendix B.2, the jump in imperial defense costs rationally resulted in much smaller territorial claims. An internationally acceptable form of border-respecting small-country nationalism thus arose through the rational attempt of developed countries to reduce their exposure to military confrontations. In the resulting international outcome, as outlined in Footnote #1 above, lump-sum rents were eschewed in favor of less transparent, quasi-paternalistic, demands that dependent clients adopt economic policies that, according to the dominant countries' ideologies, are actually beneficial to the clients.

H. Filling the Gap

Sections II-IV will show that certain, high-defense-externality, states have been led to rationally respond to externally imposed trade liberalization by adopting hyperinflationary price paths. A perusal of the involved countries indicates that these states are part of a broad class of states that have been able to choose simple monetary adjustments in response to externally imposed trade-liberalizing policies. What distinguishes this class is that they have been more politically independent than those high-defense-externality states adopting either political repression or currency undervaluation but less independent than those experiencing costly social revolution. In short, they have been "3rd-order dependencies".

Now any dependent state that is less than a 4th-order dependency is still vitally dependent upon the emergency financial support of the West. So an attempt at anything beyond a simple coup in a 1st, 2nd, or 3rd-order dependency would be doomed to failure because the new government would retain the same, relatively high, degree of dependency. This is especially obvious in the numerous revolutionary attempts in the 1st-order dependencies such as occurred in most post-WWI Central American "revolutions" (e.g., Kelly and Klein) and the more recent Filipino "revolution". Moreover, the financially conciliatory 2nd and 3rd-order dependencies should be anxious to avoid being forced into becoming 1st-order dependencies. For 1st-order dependencies, at least those that are brutocratic and find that a dominant country directly intervenes in their domestic politics, have inevitably been marked by retarded economic and social progress as well as by relatively extreme degrees of trade dependency and governmental repression.

Social revolution is practically available only to 4th-order military dependencies, a status achieved either because of: (a) such an unmanageably large size that there is little hope of practically asserting external central control over the region (the pre-WWII social revolutions); (b) profound religious differences (the Middle-Eastern revolutions); or (c) substantial and continual financial or military support from a rival superpower (the post-WWII social revolutions). Thus, regarding category (c), with the collapse of the Soviet superpower, many pre-1990 4th-order dependencies became 3rd-order dependencies. Likewise, with a correspondingly strengthened IMF, many 3rd-order became 2nd-order dependencies. Most recently, as we shall explain, an increasing number of these countries have jumped two orders of dependency.

Table 5.1 summarizes the above taxonomy for nations with very high defense-externalities. Many of the pre-1990s examples shown in the Table also apply to the post-1990 period, except at a stepped-up level of dependency. Needless to say, however, the Table is only a suggested theoretical interpretation of the complex observations before us; it serves mainly as a way for us to categorize the large variety of unfortunate domestic consequences of an external imposition of trade-liberalizing policies on countries with very high defense-externalities.

We are, in particular, most anxious to isolate those high-defense-externality states (usually, but not always, brutocracies) that are neither so independent that they respond with a social revolution nor so dependent that they either become puppet governments or lose control over their exchange controls and savings rates. For it is among states with this intermediate, 3rd-order, of military dependence, and only among such states, that we can expect to find that commonly acknowledged, easily quantified, policy perversity, regular peacetime hyperinflation.

II. PEACETIME HYPERINFLATION AS A RATIONAL RESPONSE TO DOMINANT-COUNTRY REACTIONS TO PERMISSIBLE EXCHANGE CONTROLS

As will be explained in Subsection B.1 below, exchange controls of some form have generally played a vital role during national emergencies. International agreements formally preventing nations from adopting exchange controls are therefore generally violations of national sovereignty. (Sovereignty here means that the country is domestically free to choose both its political leaders and its own vital institutions.) When post-WWII Germany and Japan, later the "baby tigers", and most recently an increasing number of post-Cold-War IMF dependencies, were denied the freedom to set these controls, they had lost one of the freedoms of a sovereign power and therefore became what we have called 2nd-order-dependencies.

Regarding less extreme forms of dependency and barring social revolution (which implies 4th-order dependency), dominant nations have been able to induce others to loosen their exchange controls only by inducing them to voluntarily select trade-expanding policies. But we can restrict to footnotes those cases in which a genuine free-trade ideology is successfully sold to a sovereign nation. Non-ideologized smaller nations will select such liberalization policies only if adopting the policies can be objectively expected to advance their national interests.

But directly subsidizing trade with these sovereign nations is obviously not in the interest of the dominant countries.[26] Therefore, the only cost-effective way for

---

[26]This again follows from the Bickerdike Theorem, which holds regardless of existence of external diseconomies from international trade. The same domestic welfare loss results from trade-conditioned loan subsidies. Since a dependent country's benefits from accepting any such form of trade subsidy must exceed the foregone benefits of the original system, the Paretian inefficiency of the entire operation implies that the dominant countries will come to experience net losses from such subsidy programs.

TABLE 5.1

DOMESTICALLY EFFICIENT RESPONSES TO EXTERNALLY
IMPOSED TRADE LIBERALIZATION IN DEPENDENT NATIONS
WITH VERY HIGH DEFENSE-EXTERNALITIES

Extent of Dependency	Rational Policy Response	Domestically Efficient Outcome	Pre 1990s Examples
1st-Order	fully accommodative increase in trade	hyper-repressive government	El Salvador, Guatemala, Honduras, Philippines
2nd-Order	eschewal of substantial exchange controls but corresponding currency undervaluation	hyper-saving	Germany, Japan, Korea, Singapore Taiwan
3rd-Order	severe exchange controls and currency over-valuation but partially accommodative increase in trade	peacetime hyperinflation during costly commitment eras	Argentina, Brazil, Bolivia, Peru, southeast Asia
4th-Order	only temporarily accommodative increase in trade	costly social revolution	China Cuba Soviet Union, Vietnam

a dominant nation to loosen the exchange controls, the effective tariffs, of smaller sovereignties is to provide these nations with a jointly beneficial non-pecuniary favor in exchange for trade liberalization. The observed favor is to provide these weaker countries with opportunities to lower their defense costs. Dominant-country commitments, financial as well as military, have thus arisen after both World Wars to lower the emergency defense costs of cooperating smaller nations, thereby lowering the exchange-control levels acceptable to the smaller countries.

Two cases naturally arise. In the first case, which we discuss in the following subsection, it is relatively inexpensive for the dominant countries to provide sovereign states with defense-support commitments.

A. Inexpensive Commitment Eras: Accommodative Trade Liberalization

Dominant countries, in this case, are in a position to cost-effectively commit themselves to providing weaker sovereignties with emergency-finance benefits sufficient to induce a substantial reduction in the optimal levels of exchange controls, a substantial increase in the effective acceptance of the externally imposed tariff reductions. This effect is especially quantitatively significant. For a dependent sovereignty's willingness to accept moderate exchange controls in exchange for the inexpensively provided defense benefits is magnified by the finance-induced reduction in their defense costs and correspondingly separate reduction in their defense-externalities and efficient demands for exchange controls. Indeed, where the U.S. has come to provide nuclear defense for certain countries -- viz., the NATO and ANZUS countries -- exchange-controls have, *pari passu*, voluntarily disappeared with the emergence of the commitment to provide such benefits.

As we shall elaborate in the following subsection, various gold exchange standards were relatively easily provided through the financial commitments of the dominant countries during several eras within the 1924-71 period. We shall find that such gold standards, through their salutary effects on defense costs and the magnitude of the defense-externality, substantially reduced both the incidence and severity of peacetime exchange controls.

After 1971, when the IMF could no longer offer its members the opportunity to fix the gold values of their currencies, emergency finance costs, and thus defense-externalities, substantially increased. Moderate exchange controls could no longer be either expected or demanded of these sovereign states. So exchange controls substantially increased and remained relatively high for the next two decades (Hansen) of this expensive-commitment era. Similarly, as we shall soon elaborate, almost immediately after western Europe began its wholesale abandonment of the gold standard in 1931, and before the Bretton Woods substitute began to take effect in the late 1940s and early 1950s, central and eastern Europe and the most Europe-dependent of the Latin American countries (Argentina, Bolivia, Brazil, Chile, Colombia, Uruguay and Paraguay) all adopted substantial exchange controls during this expensive commitment era (U.S. Tariff Commission).

The collapse of the Soviet Union in 1991 re-created a low-defense-externality environment for many western countries. This is partly because emergency loan support for an IMF member country facing a domestic uprising was less costly to provide because it no longer meant increased Soviet support for the uprising. The subsequent reductions in exchange controls through the 1990s were probably, however, due at least as much to: (1) the induced reduction in domestic defense-externalities because of the weaker revolutionary threats; and (2) the ability of a monopolist, a single world imperial leader, to raise the price of its emergency financial support and, therefore, as mentioned above, to switch 3rd-order to 2nd-order dependencies, especially in southeast Asia and Latin America.

In other countries, the Soviet breakup has similarly restored several 4th-order dependencies to the status of a high-defense-externality, high-exchange-control, 3rd-order dependency. And since some of the new 3rd-order dependencies (especially Russia) are much more costly to support than the prior 3rd-order dependencies, the post-Cold-War period has probably witnessed a net increase in the importance of high-commitment-cost, 3rd-order dependencies.

In any case, severe exchange controls appear to be widespread when and only when the dominant nations find it relatively expensive to supply the relevant 3rd-order dependencies with defense-cost-lowering institutions.[27]

B. Costly Commitments Eras:
Dominant-Country Reactions to Exchange Controls

Regarding costly-commitment periods (roughly: 1919-1924, 1931-1951, 1971-the present), we now return to our central economic argument by considering the ideologically rationalized reactions of the dominant nations to the efficient exchange controls adopted by the 3rd-order dependencies. These ideologically rationalized dominant-country reactions will be seen to account for our theoretically derived, and empirically observed, hyperinflations. We shall find this to be the case only in states with very high defense-externalities. For dependencies with less extreme defense-externalities, our theory, and our data, will have countries eschew hyperinflation and rationally adopt either excessively loose or non-existent exchange-controls. Such conciliatory policy responses, although quite commonly observed, represent socially inefficient capitulations, submissions to the unconsciously exploitative, joint GATT

---

[27]Exchange controls have been high during costly commitment eras despite the fact that artificially low exchange controls are discouraged as part of the IMF's official price for a commitment to provide countries with emergency financial support. For example, various membership privileges -- through the same ideological inspiration responsible for the externally imposed tariffs -- have been denied IMF members who seriously ration their foreign exchange. Nevertheless, to repeat, there have been several eras during which the quality of the available systems of emergency support was not sufficient for the IMF to charge a price that would prevent 3rd-order dependencies with high-defense-externalities from adopting severe exchange controls in response to the low-tariff policies imposed by the GATT or WTO.

(or WTO) -IMF, plan of trade liberalization.[28]

1. *Basic Monetary Background.* Understanding hyperinflation requires us to consider yet another economic novelty of the post-WWI era, viz., the introduction of permanently inconvertible paper money. Although such "fiat money" economies were already discussed in Chapters 3 and 4, before outlining our imposed-trade-liberalization explanation for a small country's efficient adoption of peacetime hyperinflation at the end of this section, and then elaborating upon our explanation in Sections III-V, we first review and elaborate in order to resolve certain persistent issues concerning the theory of inconvertible paper money.

First of all, a potential "last-period problem" exists for all inconvertible paper money economies. The world's last sale of a real asset in exchange for an inconvertible paper currency is apparently conferring a worthless object on the seller, who should then be unwilling to surrender a positive amount of any valuable real asset in exchange for the paper. The value of such currency in the next-to-last transaction should therefore also be zero. So then should the value in the 2nd-to-the-last transaction be zero. Continuing to apply this argument in each earlier period up to the present period, inconvertible paper currency should currently be value-less, which would certainly eliminate its potential usefulness as a medium of exchange. Nevertheless, once we recognize that the sovereign governments issuing such money also have an independent power to tax, we can see that the government can give positive value to its currency, even in the last private transaction with that currency, by requiring its future ad valorem taxes to be paid with the currency. Fiat money exists

---

[28]The static model assumes that the dependent countries are internally efficient, or "rational". Certain dependent nations do not fit the model because their leaders have been made into pro-trade ideologues in order to facilitate their acceptance of the international financial system. A dominant country may, for example, have subsidized small-country loans that are contingent on the country's political leadership, thereby saddling the small country with an ideologically inspired leadership. Relative underdevelopment is the predictable outcome (Appendix A.1). For example, in post WWII Mexico, where both the political and the monetary bureaucracy has become ideologized, the system has been suffering a market-clearing exchange rate, no hyperinflation, increasing repression, and increasing internal instability.

In the contrasting, Argentine system, U.S. ideology has been aggressively rejected and the old oligarchic families have remained in control of the bureaucracy. So the basic model still applies in that an internally efficient incentive still exists to employ a domestic monetary and fiscal policy that retains an overvalued currency and effectively high import charges. Hyperinflation during high-defense-externality, costly commitment, eras, we shall see, is the natural consequence of their ensuing rational interaction with the ideologized IMF, at least as long as Argentina remains a 3rd-degree dependency. While the numerous studies of Argentine-type currency problems, continuing without let-up into the current decade (Cavallo and Cottani, Edwards, Leijonhufvud and Heyman), predictably lay the blame at the feet of these old oligarchies or the related bureaucracies -- more or less explicitly condemning them for corruption, irresponsibility, or simple economic ignorance -- our view is that the old oligarchies or bureaucracies are actually responding in nationally optimal fashions to an unfortunate IMF attempt to impose an unconsciously exploitative ideology on these nations.

because it is a tax-anticipation note. Acknowledging this tax-payment demand for currency also simplifies our discussion of fiscal policy. For tax-increases are then recessionary, not merely because of the probable intergenerational redistribution-effect of the tax-increase (Thompson, 1967), but also because of the quite certain, money-demand-increasing, effect of the tax-increase. Aggregative tax policy can then be macroeconomically viewed as a form of monetary policy.

Our second point explains why successful, constitution-respecting sovereigns have -- ever since the 6th century BC emergence of constitutional democracies -- insisted upon creating their own monies. Following the argument of the Appendices B.2 (fn. 4) and B.3 (Part II.B), emergency money-creation -- like conscription, rationing-supported price-controls, and wartime exchange controls -- is vital to any continually democratic sovereignty. Without access to a flexible set of authoritarian over-rides to narrowly rational legislative decisions, the legislature would continually surrender property in order to rationally appease various potential aggressors, to the point that the state's property would all soon be in the hands of the future broadly rational aggressors. In other words, a broadly rational pre-commitment to defend the entire property of a state requires the state's military leader to impose emergency sacrifices on the members of the state, sacrifices that the members are collectively unwilling to make because the then-necessary sacrifices exceed the benefits of retaining the disputed property. Such efficient authoritarian over-rides have necessarily evolved because they are required to deter rational aggressors from acquiring more and more of the property initially controlled by the democratic state.

Thirdly, as was also stressed in Chapters 3 and 4, the financial advantage of a fully convertible paper currency, such as was common under the pre-1931 gold standard, is the ability of the government to suspend conversion payments during a defensive emergency and then subsequently resume the original conversion payments after the end of the emergency. Since the price level substantially increases during the emergency suspension and monetary expansion, the post-emergency resumption produces a corresponding deflation. It is the expectation of this post-emergency deflation that provides a survivable sovereign with the requisite cumulative increase in the emergency purchasing power. For only then does <u>each</u> emergency increase in the state's nominal money supply, by inducing an increase in the rationally expected future deflation rate, exceed the correspondingly induced increase in the emergency price level. Only then does each emergency increase in the state's money supply generate an increase in money's real purchasing power.

Contrast this conceptually unlimited governmental borrowing power to the potential cumulative increase in emergency purchasing power of a simple inconvertible paper currency, where there is no rational expectation of a post-emergency deflation. In this inconvertible-currency case, the emergency price-level rises more than in proportion to the emergency money-supply because of the corresponding rise in interest rates during the emergency (Appendix B.4, Part III). In symbols:

$$\frac{M_s^{t+1}-M_s^t}{M_s^{t+1}} < \frac{P^{t+1}-P^t}{P^{t+1}},$$

where M_s^t and M_s^{t+1} are the respective inconvertible money supplies at the beginning and end of the emergency and P^t and P^{t+1} are the corresponding price levels. It follows that

$$\frac{M_s^{t+1}-M_s^t}{P^{t+1}} < \frac{P^{t+1}-P^t}{P^{t+1}} \cdot \frac{M_s^{t+1}}{P^{t+1}}.$$

The inflation measure on the right is always less than unity. So, regardless of the size of the emergency inflation, the state's expected increase in emergency purchasing power (the left side of the inequality) is always less than the state's normal real currency supply, M_s^{t+1}/P^{t+1}, a number which is itself a universally tiny fraction of the state's real wealth.[29] In our modern world, the only democracies that can afford such a fair-weather monetary system are those defended by nuclear arsenals.

A small modern nation must rely on relatively expensive methods (conventional weapons, armies, and extortion payments) to deter potential aggressors. And, since no small nation is able to independently sustain a commitment to a convertible paper money, small democratic nations must obtain the emergency financial support of dominant states. Up until 1971, the IMF inexpensively provided this support by helping the smaller countries to fix the values of their currencies relative to the gold-backed currency of a dominant state. Temporary small-nation emergencies, usually politically inspired rebellions or negative shocks in export revenues, could then be adequately met by domestic authoritarian monetary or credit expansions. With a commitment to an intertemporally stable exchange rate, there could be a rational expectation of post-emergency monetary contractions and corresponding deflations. There could then be a significant restoration of the original value of the country's currency, thereby simulating gold convertibility by generating emergency price-level increases that fall short of emergency money-supply increases.

After the breakdown of the gold exchange standard in 1971, fixed-exchange-rate systems became much more discretionary and correspondingly less reliable. Although a post-emergency country is seldom able to fully restore the original exchange rate in the absence of gold convertibility, the expectation of a sufficient post-emergency deflation is all that is required to lower the interest rate and supply the "fixed exchange rate" country with its requisite increase in emergency purchasing power. With sufficient post-emergency deflation, each emergency expansion in the money supply -- although accompanied by a rational expectation of only a future deflation back <u>toward</u> the pre-expansion price-level -- will still exceed the emergency-induced

---

[29]The popular Cagan-Friedman measure of the potential revenue from an expected inflation, which exceeds our measure, is significantly biased upward by a simple economic error, a critical failure to date the relevant price levels, interest rates, and real money supplies at the end of the period. It is not reasonable to assume that people do not rationally expect wartime inflation; yet such an assumption would be required to rationalize the conventional calculation.

expansion in the domestic price level.[30]   Thus, the economic advantage of the literally fixed exchange rates during the inexpensive-commitment years of the gold standard (1925-1931) and the Bretton Woods agreement (1951-1971), was not completely eliminated in the subsequent, "costly-commitment" period (1971-present). Rather, it has remained, albeit shakily, in the minds of monetary authorities through the "advantage" they feel exists in the maintenance of "stable exchange rates".

More specifically, under the rules of the Bretton Woods System, which hit its prime from the mid-1950s to the mid-1960s, the IMF was forced to substantially tax small countries that devalued their currencies.   This gave the post-emergency rulers of a small country substantial incentives to deflate their economies back toward the original price levels and exchange rates.   Predictably, small country inflation rates became relatively low under this gold-based system.   But the entire system was based on the ease with which the U.S. could provide foreign central banks with an effective gold standard.   The Vietnam War inflation of the late 1960s, and the concurrently reduced value of a gold standard to the U.S.'s recently nuclearly defended European allies, abruptly ended this "inexpensive-commitment" era.   Under the subsequent, post-1971, "costly-commitment", system, IMF loan-support has become much more discretionary.   Nevertheless, such support soon became contingent upon deflationary macroeconomic policies (Dell, Edwards).   The post-emergency deflations, and corresponding achievement of "dirty floats" and "crawling pegs", were thus achieved by the re-emergence of a pre-WWII, creditor-inspired, form of macroeconomic "thought" perhaps best described as "inflationophobia".

As discussed in Chapter 4, such recession-producing policies quite irritate Keynesian macroeconomists (e.g., Turgeon), whose illogical capital theory prevents them from appreciating the critical advantage of monetary regimes that generate post-emergency deflations.   Although the evolved, creditor-inspired, inflationophobia that still, albeit decreasingly, resides at the IMF is often a good thing in view of the Keynesian alternative, a potentially superior policy would have a well-endowed IMF simply grant small member countries emergency lines of credit.   Although the IMF has indeed been moving toward large lines of credit, and reasonable collateral could no doubt be arranged, the IMF has been concurrently imposing tailored "packages" of economic and social policy conditions that are, at best, tangentially related to the probability of repayment.   Because of the ideological nature of these tailored loan conditions, as we shall emphasize in Chapter 6, what could be a very efficient change is actually a very inefficient one.   Thus, in view of the more discretionary and less reliable post-Bretton Woods system, we must regard the entire post-1971 period as entailing relatively costly methods of emergency finance.[31]

---

[30]For an extensive elaboration of this argument, see Thompson, et al., Vol. II, Ch. 2.

[31]Regarding the future, we conjecture that the decreasing IMF profit to supplying fixed-exchange-rate systems and the continuing influx of Neo-Keynesians at the IMF will soon eliminate the IMF's ability to produce sufficiently large post-emergency recessions.   At that point, or perhaps before, discretionary emergency IMF loans will have wholly replaced a dependent country's independent money and debt flotations and correspondingly quasi-fixed

During each one of these costly commitment eras -- 1919-24, 1931-51, and 1971 to the present -- dominant states in the West have persistently intervened in the determination of the exchange rates of their dependent states. In particular, dominant states have used their influence over the levels of their sovereign dependencies' exchange rates and related policy variables to liberalize trade and thereby immediately benefit from the resulting terms-of-trade effects while increasingly benefitting from "Ugly-American"-style (Lederer) increases in demand for U.S. military exports that have yet to receive significant academic recognition.

   2. *Background on Secular Inflation.* Switching to a permanently inconvertible paper money, would certainly not, by itself, induce hyperinflation. Although there would be a somewhat excessive rate of secular inflation in the presence of a narrowly rational monetary policy, the government can set up an independent peacetime monetary authority with a creditor-bias in order to provide the country with an optimal, typically modest, peacetime inflation rate (Thompson, 1981). This long-evolved policy, complemented by an empirical study (Lohani and Thompson), establishes for us the expectation of a non-ideologized government's ability to achieve statically optimal inflation rates.

   The standard theory of hyperinflation does little to enlighten us about its cause. Certain capital-theoretic errors, predominant in the hyperinflation literature since the paper of Cagan, are responsible for the idea that significant real governmental tax revenue, or seignorage, is available from hyperinflation. The errors are corrected in the simple revenue calculation of the above subsection. The actually insignificant seignorage resulting from a correct seignorage calculation means that the myriad of economists assuring us that hyperinflation results from "fiscal exhaustion" -- i.e., the need to complement the ordinary tax system in order to acquire additional governmental purchasing power -- must be quite wrong. For, even ignoring hyperinflation's substantial resource cost, given the tiny potential real governmental revenue actually available from hyperinflation, any such "fiscally exhausted" government would immediately collapse upon reaching its first military challenge.

---

exchange rates as sources of emergency finance. With sovereignty thus determined by the IMF rather than the nation and all dependency being either of the 1st or 2nd-order, the U.S. will emerge as a more explicit imperial leader of the world's democracies. The trend is certainly there, and has accelerated since the demise of the Soviet Union, which has clearly increased the IMF's monopoly power and converted previously 3rd-order dependencies into 1st or 2nd-order dependencies. The IMF has correspondingly been shrinking its currency-stabilization programs in favor of being a wholly discretionary grantor of short-term lines of credit, and member country exchange rates have correspondingly been moving toward a free float against the dollar. In response to this trend, various customs unions have grown in an attempt to tie their exchange rates to one anothers' currencies. But, so far, due largely to IMF influence, the typical built-in penalties for a country's depreciating its currency have been quite minor compared to the old Bretton Woods penalties.

   Chapter 6 will take up the important issue of labor and product market "globalization", the new and prospective future "price" that the increasingly dependent countries are being asked to pay for their discretionary lines of credit.

In fact, these states have not collapsed. The concerned governments must therefore have been able to increase their tax rates after all. Hyperinflation could not have represented these governments' <u>last resort</u> in funding fiscal emergencies. If it were, since little if any governmental purchasing power emanates from hyperinflationary money creation, hyperinflating governments would simply have been unable to survive their prior emergencies. We thus search the literature in vain for a rational explanation of persistent peacetime hyperinflation.

Nevertheless, we can find a clue as to the cause of these costly hyperinflations in the external conditions preceding the hyperinflations.[32] As observed in post-WWI Central Europe (1919-1924), post-Bretton-Woods South America (esp. 1971-1991), and post-Cold-War Eastern Europe (1991-1996), all regular hyperinflations have followed the conjunction of: (1) externally imposed (WTO-type) tariff reductions, and (2) liberalization-contingent (IMF-type) lines of credit from the dominant countries. Although traditional economic thought does not indicate how our consciously paternalistic international institutions could ever inflict such misery on their ostensible beneficiaries, the observed conjunction suggests that hyperinflation is somehow a theoretically predictable small-country response to these unique aspects of post-WWI international economic institutions. Indeed, given this familiar pair of policy impositions, a bit of reflection on the above economic arguments reveals that a high-defense-externality state's hyperinflation actually represents an internally efficient response to persistent external attempts to liberalize trade.

3. *Rationalizing Hyperinflation: Evolution and the Curse of Liquidity.* Consider a 3rd-order dependency with a very high defense-externality and a correspondingly high initial tariff rate.[33] As above, the external imposition of a low tariff rate (e.g., a tariff in line with the world's less-threatened countries) induces the imposed-upon country to avoid the potential real effects of the policy imposition by simply maintaining her pre-imposition exchange rate and adopting a relatively extreme degree of import rationing, correspondingly replacing her lost tariff revenue with license-sale revenue. Such rationing quickly alerts the ideologized international leaders (e.g., the IMF) to demand a more "realistic" exchange rate of the country, on

---

[32]Since hyperinflation obviously destroys almost all of the emergency-finance function of money, a function vital for the survival of independent democratic states, hyperinflating governments have invariably been quickly brought under the control of constitutionally unconstrained military authorities. Nevertheless, some of these military governments -- like the essentially money-less military governments of ancient Mesopotamia and modern Brazil -- may economically succeed as long as the Cincinnatian values of, or external pressures on, their military leaders make them willing to transfer their legally unconstrained legislative authority back to civilians during normal times.

[33]Anticipating our empirical results, all regularly hyperinflationary countries are "brutocracies," as characterized above in subsection IB. Nevertheless, some brutocracies have, at a significant cost, effectively escaped at least one of our sufficiency conditions and thereby completely escaped hyperinflation. Other, once Soviet supported, brutocracies have simply abandoned capitalism altogether.

the threat of eliminating the country's existing line of credit.[34]   A quantitatively significant, externally imposed, currency devaluation thus becomes a necessary part of effective trade liberalization. The liberalization, of course, is necessary to placate the concerned economists (and their allied, politically powerful, foreign investors and domestic exporters).

However, since the small country's post-devaluation flow of imports is significantly excessive in view of the defense-externality, it would be efficient for the country to generate a one-shot monetary expansion at the first available excuse, an expansion reducing exports and thus the cash-constrained flow of imports to where the country has restored its original stock of imported goods. Because excessive importation occurred prior to the monetary expansion, the restoration of the original stock requires a larger-than-original overvaluation of the country's currency.

Note that the direction of this domestic monetary expansion is perverse in terms of standard macroeconomic models because the devaluation that induced it was itself an expansionary shock. Moreover, although the small-country monetary expansion can be rationalized in terms of its ability to restore, and even expand, the original overvaluation of the country's currency, few monetary authorities would admit to such a trade-contracting target. We are talking here, as elsewhere, about evolved policy reactions, reactions that, because of the harsh evolutionary forces that generate the institutional constraints on Pascalian government officials, turn out to be broadly rational whenever state survival is at stake. Nevertheless, the small-country's monetary authorities, being Pascalian, must somehow view themselves as acting in the interests of their country, or at least of important special interests in that country. What the small country typically pre-evolves to satisfy this Pascalian constraint and still generate the monetary expansion is an elimination of all budgetary surpluses, liquid assets, and sources of discretionary peacetime governmental borrowing. Although an alternative evolutionary mechanism will be mentioned below, typically, governmental liquidity is evolved out of the system.[35] Since the immediate financial effect of a sudden devaluation on the fisc is to reduce its customs revenues, and since the financially strapped country has no remaining source of peacetime borrowing, it's authorities must increase the money supply to make up for the lost customs revenue. Otherwise, some bills will go unpaid, and a political or military uprising will be

---

[34]We are assuming, as we shall hereafter, that the dominant countries do not extend foreign exchange loans to the countries in order to overcome the induced shortage of foreign exchange at the initial exchange rate. One reason for this, as mentioned above, is that it is unambiguously welfare reducing to subsidize foreign trade. We have occasionally observed such development loans, but only for relatively short periods of time. Once foreign debt has risen sufficiently, the quality of the debt starts falling to where it is no longer tolerable to creditor countries. We can, if the reader wishes, allow such lending, and delay the beginning of our analysis to where the foreign-exchange debt has reached its limit.

[35]It also helps the argument if the country is continually coup-threatened so that any interruption in the government's cash flow would immediately represent a major threat to the regime. This military characteristic, as pointed out in Section I.B above, is indeed an important source of the high-optimal-tariff regimes under discussion in this subsection.

imminent. This is how the typical small-country banker -- and thus economists -- have come to the "fiscal exhaustion" hypothesis. It is, in fact, the way that a typical Pascalian bureaucrat sees the situation. But the money-supply-increasing country could actually, at a very moderate resource cost, have alternatively slightly increased its prior tax rate and created a mild fiscal surplus. As noted above, if the government could not regularly do such things -- i.e., if it could not provide for long-term expansions in its expenditures to finance truly adverse conditions -- it could certainly not have survived its previous extended emergencies and therefore could not have survived to where it is. What the pioneering countries have done -- without any conscious plan -- is evolve an easily comprehended financial excuse for its underlying efficient response to a devaluation. Without such an excuse, i.e., without artificially financially strapped governments, Pascalian decisionmakers simply accept such imposed currency devaluations, in which case the corresponding high-defense-externality governments suffer large accumulations of consumer-durable imports and fall in a coup, revolution, or foreign military takeover.

The highly liquid regimes of Cuba's Batista, Nicaragua's Samosa, the Philippines' Marcos, and the Shah of Iran thus all found themselves adopting insignificant currency overvaluations and correspondingly heavy imports of consumer durables into their brutocratic states before being predictably toppled by much more trade-restrictive and independence-asserting, revolutionary regimes. The practical lesson regarding the curse of central-governmental liquidity could hardly have been lost on the pragmatic fiscal authorities of high-defense-externality regimes elsewhere. In any case, a surviving 3rd-order dependency with a high defense-externality will have necessarily adopted an artificially illiquid fisc, or some other automatically trade-restricting political devise, in order to rapidly generate a suitable monetary expansion in response to an externally imposed currency devaluation.

The above, one-shot, monetary expansion then disturbs the ideologized international monetary authorities and induces them to insist upon another, correspondingly larger, devaluation in order to, at least temporarily, recreate a ration-less equilibrium in the foreign exchange market.[36] A "crawling peg" thus begins (providing relatively alert exporters and domestic importers the opportunity to transact on unusually favorable terms during the time intervals between the induced devaluations and the subsequent monetary expansions). The small country, of course, efficiently responds to the larger percentage devaluation by correspondingly increasing its subsequent money supply by an even larger percentage at the first available opportunity. Again, the step-up is required in order to reduce the country's trade flow down to where it will soon restore its original stock of accumulated imports.

And, again, the evolved domestic policymaker is consciously thinking of neither

---

[36]Although the small-country's monetary injection following the previously imposed devaluation cannot help but be seen by these international ideologues as macroeconomically perverse (again in that it responds to one expansionary policy shock with another), little is heard of the perversion. This is presumably because free trade ideology, which in this case serves the narrowly conceived interest of the dominant countries, has been much stronger than macroeconomic ideology, which in this case disserves the international investors.

the defense-externality nor the country's stock of consumer durables. What the decisionmaker is thinking about is the devaluation-induced loss of customs revenues and thus the need for a monetary expansion that is sufficient to immediately restore the liquidity of the government.

In an alternative, perhaps complementary, scenario, institutional evolution would constrain Pascalian bureaucrats by having them captured by special interests protecting their local consumer-goods industries. The domestic policymaker would then be thinking about the cumulative rate of domestic protection and thus restoring the original stock of imports. We do not, however, see this as prevalent.

Since, under either evolved constraint, the IMF's temporarily successful devaluation lowers the stock as well as the flow of governmental purchasing power and raises the stock as well as the flow of consumer durables, the induced percentage increase in the money supply must exceed the imposed devaluation (i.e., the percentage increase in the price of foreign currency) sufficient to induce a stock-restoring increase in the small country's flow of real customs revenues and a corresponding decrease in the flow of imports.

The international agency increases the devaluation crawl to a trot in order to keep up with the compensatory monetary expansions, although cumulative imports do not yet significantly increase from the original level. The process continues until the trot becomes a gallop and progresses to a point that each subsequent increase in the money supply becomes sufficiently allocatively painful that the small country would prefer an increase in its cumulative flow of imports and corresponding increase in general tax rates and imports to a further increase in its actual inflation rate, finally acceding to an inflation rate that does not exceed the agency's preceding devaluation rate, i.e., an equilibrium rate of hyperinflation.

Painful inflation is thus the only way for the international economic ideologues and foreign exporters to achieve, at least partially, their goal of trade liberalization.

This is elaborated in the rationality model of Section III below. Section IV then provides a series of empirical tests of the theory, including (a) an explanation of an anomaly uncovered by Krueger (1978) regarding the dynamic interaction between devaluation and hyperinflation; and (b) a regression analysis in which the regressor representing our theory repeatedly out-performs all competing regressors.

Finally, Section V presents a series of simple graphs displaying both the power of the theory and how a single, non-monetary, variate can be used to reliably forecast a country's peacetime rate of hyperinflation.

III. A MODEL OF RATIONAL HYPERINFLATION

We begin by restating the above sketch in order to further specify the general argument and greatly simplify that theory by assuming, again relying on our Lamarck-Darwin evolutionary process and the Foster-Young-Weibull convergence theorem, that the small countries are informed, rational, maximizers. The stringent system of small-country exchange controls that now rationally follows an externally imposed tariff reduction is again met by an IMF-imposed currency devaluation, which is in turn rationally responded to by a one-shot small-country money-supply increase that efficiently eliminates the unwelcomed increase in imports.[37]   The determined international agency responds by promptly imposing a second, inflation-neutralizing, currency devaluation.   Since the small country's initial monetary increase exceeded the initially imposed devaluation in order to correct for the devaluation-induced increase in the stock of imports, this second imposed devaluation must correspondingly exceed the first devaluation.   (The initial monetary increase is assumed to rationally anticipate the subsequent devaluation request of the international agency and therefore to be all the larger in order to squeeze the intended trade-contraction into the available time-period.)   The small country's second monetary increase, which must again await the satisfaction of various loan contingencies, will therefore exceed the first monetary increase.   Acceleration in the rate of inflation is thus implied.   As the resource costs of inflation become more and more significant, however, the small country's net returns to using monetary expansions to reverse the devaluation-induced trade-increases become smaller and smaller.   Sooner or later, the small country's rate of monetary expansion will cease to exceed the previous, inflation-neutralizing, devaluation.   At that point, when the successive devaluations are equal to the successive monetary increases, trade will obviously exceed its original level because each of the temporary, post-devaluation, trade-increases will have ceased to have the resulting increase in the stock of imports eliminated by the subsequent, post-monetary-expansion, trade-decreases.   The international agency will therefore achieve part of its initially desired expansion in cumulative exports to the small country.   The small country, although suffering substantially from the hyperinflation, will have limited the trade expansions to the post-devaluation, pre-monetary-expansion, time intervals.   So neither the IMF nor the dependent country totally surrenders to the wishes of the other, and the hyperinflation is quite socially stable.

The above argument can be illustrated with a simple pair of graphs.   First, Figure 5.1 contains a familiar set of international currency demand and supply curves for a dependent country, say Argentina.   M   is Argentina's flow demand-price for dollars to finance its steady level of imports from the United States.   X   is Argentina's flow supply-price of dollars from its exports to the United States.   The free-trade equilibrium peso price of a dollar is $P^F = X(F) = M(F)$,   while the corresponding dollar value of trade is $F.[38]   The expected defense-externality, E,

---

[37]In contrast, a gold standard taxes a country for any such monetary increase and thereby induces a relatively "successful" trade liberalization. The effective international gold standard achieved by the IMF from the mid-1950s to the late 1960s thus put an end of the "dollar shortage", as measured by the prevalence of severe exchange controls outside of the U.S. Where the defense-externality remained high and exchange controls were externally curbed, a rational "dollar surplus", or induced capital import, emerged (see Subsection I.E above).

[38]Capital movements based upon rational inflationary expectations are, in our final equilibrium, neutralized by interest rate differentials on short term financial instruments. For simplicity, our theoretical analysis will ignore policy-induced, temporary-equilibrium, increases in Argentine real interest rates. Accounting for these increases, and the correspondingly

FIGURE 5.1

THE EXCHANGE CONTROL EQUILIBRIUM

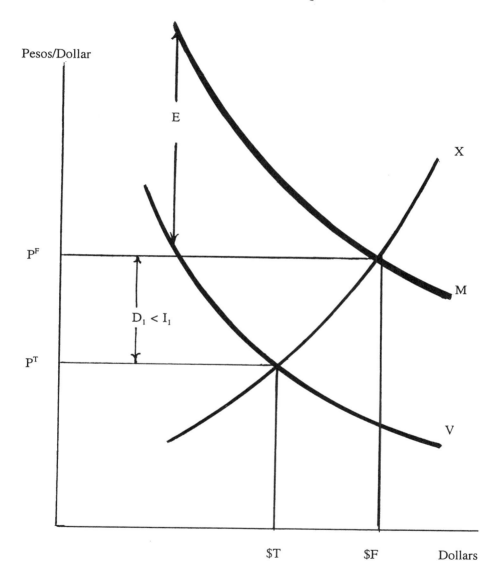

induced temporary influxes of foreign currency, would temporarily decrease the magnitudes of the market-clearing devaluations and increase the devaluation-neutralizing inflation rates.

created by a dollar of U.S. imports, lowers the social value of dollars for Argentine imports to $M - E = V$. E is also the average initial tariff on Argentine imports. These imports, along with exports, are reduced in dollar value to T by Argentina's initially optimal tariff system. Since Argentina has no influence over the dollar price of traded commodities, $F - T is also a measure of the reduction in the volume of trade induced by the optimal tariff. Meanwhile, the tariff-induced reduction in Argentina's demand for dollars lowers the tariff-induced equilibrium value of a dollar in terms of pesos to $P^T = X(F-T) = M(F-T) - E$.

Although the tariff reduces the peso price received by Argentine exporters, there is no change in the dollar terms of trade. Again, Argentina is too small to effect the world's relative prices between traded commodities. Domestically, of course, the prices of the taxed Argentine imports of consumer durables efficiently increase, while the domestic prices of exports all necessarily fall by the exact same percentage as the fall in the price of dollars. The lower equilibrium value of dollars relative to pesos in moving to the tariff-induced optimum is simply a reflection of an appropriately lower value of transforming certain U.S. goods into Argentine goods. Although Argentine imports generating no defense-externality and entering free of any tariff are correspondingly less expensive in Argentina, U.S. sellers of such goods to Argentina have the same incentive as before because the lower peso-price of such goods in Argentina is exactly offset by the higher dollar-price of Argentine pesos.

Enter the GATT (or WTO), which, on threat of a discriminatorily high tariff eliminating a very large part of the gains from trade going to Argentina, forces an elimination of the Argentine tariff in hopes of increasing the equilibrium value of trade to F. Argentina efficiently responds by accepting the tariff elimination but maintaining her exchange rate at its original, fixed, level of P^T. This enables her to ration the induced excess demand for dollars among the competing importers of consumer durables, while charging license fees to importers of consumer durables, thereby creating an average import license fee of E and restoring the original allocation.

But the IMF, the international agency in charge of facilitating the desired fixing of the exchange rate, is affected by the same political influences and the same economic ideology as the GATT. It regards the peso as "overvalued" because of the existence of the above exchange controls, i.e., the necessary rationing of foreign currency among competing domestic importers. To "correct" the situation, or "reform" Argentine exchange-rate policy, the IMF insists on an Argentine devaluation of the peso equal to D_1 in order to achieve a "realistic", free-market-clearing, trade-liberalizing, exchange rate of P_F. Otherwise, various pre-existing IMF loans, designed to encourage smaller countries to maintain a fixed exchange rate by offering foreign- currency lines of credit at sub-market fees, will be withheld from Argentina.

Once the "reformed," market-clearing, exchange rate is fixed, and Argentina has its line of credit, she responds by increasing her domestic money supply, which shifts both the M and X curves up by the same percentage amount as the increase in the money supply. The excess demand is then rationed back as above, which, for a suitable increase in the money supply, will restore the original allocation, only at a correspondingly higher price level.

Since the IMF-imposed austerity policy following the devaluation temporarily prevented Argentina from expanding her money supply, Argentina's money supply will have to increase by a percentage <u>greater than</u> the $(P_F-P_T)/P_T$ peso devaluation rate in order to restore her original stock of consumer durables.

The best the IMF can again respond with is a demand that Argentina return to a market-clearing exchange rate, the sooner the better, especially because of the even-lower-than-original post-inflation trade flow.[39]

Figure 5.2 provides a graphical description of the entire devaluation-inflation sequence, where I_t represents the tth inflation rate while D_{t+1} represents the subsequently imposed, equal, devaluation rate in the above-described sequence. The reason, of course, that the successively larger jumps in the price level do not continue to exceed the successively larger devaluations is that the price-level jumps eventually become quite costly.[40] The Figure shows how the accelerating early stages of the hyperinflation finally lead to an equilibrium at I^e, an exceptionally high, necessarily quite costly, inflation rate.

Note that the argument is critically dependent upon the durability of the unwanted imports. For the catch-up effect, where $I_t > D_t$ for all $I_t < I^e$, appears only because the current inflation offers the opportunity, albeit temporary, to compensate for the excessive imports during the immediately preceding, post-devaluation period. (If this catch-up opportunity were not present, even a tiny cost of inflation would make $I_1 < D_1$, in which case the successive inflation rates would be smaller and smaller, as illustrated on the lower broken-line path of Figure 5.2, finally inducing a solution inflation rate of zero!)

Since each early step is larger than the previous, which is in turn larger than a fraction (1/2 if the supply and demand curves have the same elasticity) of the initially observed average tariff rate (typically around 40% in the high-tariff countries), the eventually optimal inflation rate over a single devaluation-inflation cycle, as illustrated in Figure 5.2, is obviously a substantial number. Thus, even if the observed devaluations occurred only quarterly, and the costs of inflation rose very rapidly so that D^e were only twice D_1, the annual inflation rate would be $4 \times \frac{1}{2} \times 2 \times 40\% = 160\%$. We're not talking about low inflation rates. Although triple-digit inflation is conventionally regarded as "hyperinflation", our theoretical definition of "hyperinflation" does not signify an inflation number; it signifies instead an initial series of accelerating inflation rates, followed by a regular, abnormally high, average

---

[39]Insisting upon a larger currency devaluation would be perverse in that it would create a demand-constrained, rather than a supply-constrained, trade reduction, as discussed in Section I.E. above.

[40]Realistic uncertainty about the timing of the jump in the price-level would create, besides speculation costs, abnormally high short-term interest rates and thus the familiar transaction costs entailed in avoiding the interest cost of holding the non-interest bearing money. Even without this uncertainty, the cost of any jump in the price level increases with the magnitude of the jump in that the extent of the induced contractual adjustments and currency reforms obviously increase with the size of the jump.

FIGURE 5.2

THE HYPERINFLATIONARY EQUILIBRIUM

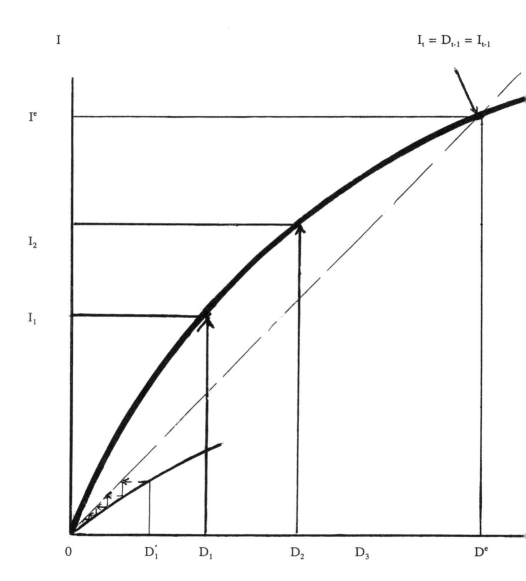

rate of inflation.[41]

Note that the steps in the above inflationary process are not part of a learning dynamic. The entire sequence is a perfect equilibrium. Even when the actors know the entire process and where it will end up, they will still go through the same gradual process to arrive at the equilibrium.[42]

Further Quantification

Our subsequent econometric specification will be aided by the following dynamical quantification of the above theory: Using Figure 5.1, letting the flows there represent daily flows, following an initially imposed devaluation rate of D_1, the country's desired exports (and therefore real values of imports) have been exceeded (assuming a linear export-supply curve and a unitary initial exchange rate), by

$$(1) \qquad \Delta Q = D_1 \; \frac{dQ}{dP} \cdot m,$$

where m is the number of days following the devaluation before the country can practically respond with a monetary expansion (because of final loan contingencies, meeting-lags, etc., during which time nominal interest rates, not prices, theoretically rise to reflect the expected response). After these m days, the country has, say, n days before a second imposed devaluation triggers another cycle, n days to reduce the flow of trade by initially increasing the money supply and price level. (Think m for "malignant"; n for ""neutralizing".) If the country is to compensate for the previously excessive imports, its trade flow must be reduced to where there is no change in cumulative exports, or to where the above increases in exports equals nC, or

---

[41]Cagan's 50% per month definition was designed to capture Germany's somewhat contagious 1923 experience, which, as discussed in Thompson, et al., Vol. II, Ch. 3, was a learning-affected episode for an economy that was apparently headed toward a zero demand for, and zero price of, domestic money. Because an unexpected shock occurred that headed-off this growing expectation, the price of the Mark did not fall to zero. This entirely different experience, this remarkable 1/2-year of German history, however, will not be analyzed in the current study.

[42]The idea of modeling the interaction between a firm and a trade-liberalizing government as a perfect equilibrium is not a novel one. See e.g., Matsuyama, who, under the influence of the standard economic literature, considers only the possibility of infant industry protection. Interestingly, Matsuyama ends up arguing against such protection despite its theoretically optimality within his model because, under the same influence, he believes the government is so incompetent that it is unable to withhold protection after the industry has grown up. In any case, neither inflation nor two-way optimization are part of Matsuyama's study.

(2) $$\Delta Q = nC,$$

where   C   is the compensatory, or "catch-up", reduction in the daily flow rate of imports. So the inflation has not merely to restore the original flow incentives by increasing the supply price of exports by D_1; it has also to reduce the flow rate of exports by C, which requires an additional increase in the domestic price-level of $C / \left(\dfrac{dQ}{dP} \right)$.

The optimal price level therefore increases by

$$I_1 = \Delta P_1 / P = D_1 + C / \left(\frac{dQ}{dP} \right).$$

$$= D_1 + \frac{\Delta Q}{n} \frac{1}{\left[\dfrac{dQ}{dP} \right]}, \quad \text{using (2).}$$

$$= D_1 + D_1 \frac{m}{n}, \quad \text{using (1), or}$$

(3) $$I_1 = D_1 \left(1 + \frac{m}{n} \right).$$

This occurs over a period of m+n days. The initial annual inflation rate therefore equals $\dfrac{365}{m+n}$ times the above number. With a desired tariff rate of 40%, and so initial devaluations of approximately 20%, equal lags, and quarterly devaluations (which is actually quite moderate by recent standards), this annual rate again calculates to 160%.

An immediate empirical implication of the above explanation for hyperinflation is that the inflation rate, rather than being steady, proceeds in predictable spurts. In particular, the inflation rate is relatively moderate immediately following a devaluation; then greatly accelerates; then slows up again before the next devaluation. In other words, inflation proceeds at its most moderate rate both before and after a currency devaluation.   This very special dynamic pattern among hyperinflating countries, which runs quite counter to standard economic stories purporting to explain why devaluations occur, was uncovered years ago by Anne Krueger (1978) but, to our knowledge, has heretofore gone completely unexplained.

Positive marginal welfare gains from inflation exist when the country's exchange rate is periodically devalued to accommodate international bankers and the corresponding average flow of imports is above the country's internally optimal level.[43] Figure 5.3 illustrates these marginal gains, as can be calculated from the triangular losses in Figure 5.1, where $MG(I_t,D^e)$ represents the marginal gains from an inflation rate of I_t, given the equilibrium rate of periodic devaluation, D^e. Of course, in a hyperinflationary equilibrium: (a) there are substantially positive marginal costs of inflation, where $MC(I_t)$ represent these costs; and (b) D^e has risen to where $MG(I_t,D^e)$ has been forced up to where the optimal inflation rate is equal to D^e.

As determinable from Figure 5.1, if D were set below D^e, say at $D^e - 1$, then since $MG(I_t-1,D^e-1) = MG(I_t,D^e)$, the resulting optimal inflation rate, $I(D^e-1)$, would, as shown in Figures 5.2 and 5.3, exceed the previous devaluation rate D^e-1, and so the inflation-devaluation cycle would continue until D^e were again reached.

Finally, once the equilibrium is reached, i.e., where $D^e = D_t = I_t = I^e$, the <u>annual</u> inflation rate, I^a, is given by

$$(4) \qquad\qquad I^a = \frac{365}{n+m} \bullet I^e$$

Notice, however, from Figures 5.1 and 5.3, that if a country's defense-externality, E, and therefore its marginal gain from inflation, $MG(I_t,D_1)$, were sufficiently low, say because it is on a gold standard or is protected by a dominant country's defense commitment, it would have an $I_t = I^o = 0$ corner solution, simply accept the nevertheless unwanted initial devaluation, and exhibit a zero abnormal inflation rate. Such countries would be identified by their freedom from exchange controls as well as their relatively low inflation rates. Less obviously, as also illustrated in Figure 5.3, suppose a country's E were sufficiently low that it's initial level of $I(D_1)$, or I', were positive but below D_1. As shown in Figure 5.2, both it's <u>eventual</u> inflation rate and induced devaluation rate would again be zero. (A perfect-equilibrium path is illustrated as the eventual no-inflation solution in Figure 5.2.) Such countries would be distinguished by only occasional bouts of inflation, ordinarily innocuous exchange controls, and relatively free trade.

Thus, in either one of these low-E cases, the trade-liberalizers "win" the game in that they eventually force their desired, socially excessive, amount of trade on the countries and make it stick by imposing currency devaluations that are simply too costly to avoid because of the need to hyperinflate to obtain any lasting relief. Viewed in this light, the hyperinflators represent only the most visible casualties of the system. All the rest are relatively invisible, the costs of the policy impositions arising from either excessive defense expenditures or subsequent political instability as a result of excessive accumulations of consumer-durable imports. In 4th-order-dependent brutocracies facing substantial western trade intervention (e.g., China,

---

[43]This induced increase in trade has the small country importing more durable goods, which lowers the overall demand for imports in immediately succeeding periods. However, since the same effect occurs under a simple devaluation, and since our general model does not assume stationarity, we retain here the same interdependent sequence of demand and supply curves as was implicit in our original discussion of devaluation.

FIGURE 5.3

THE MARGINAL RETURNS AND COSTS OF INFLATION

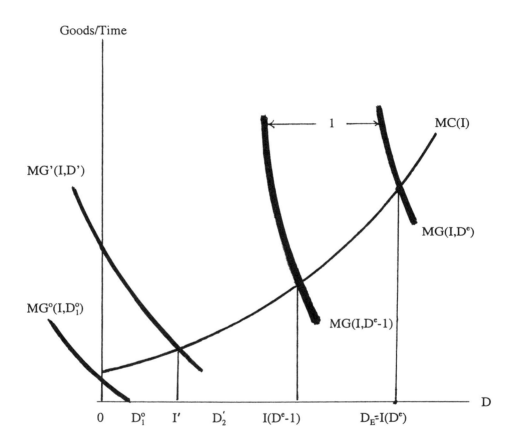

Cuba, Vietnam, and Nicaragua), the best the put-upon government has been able to do, based largely on their previously persistently excessive importations of consumer durables and consequently serious internal defense problem, has been to turn its back on the GATT and IMF and join communism-inspired alliances such as the old Soviet Blok in order to simultaneously: (1) reduce their internal defense costs, (2) receive vital military support, and (3) avoid the unconsciously oppressive Western policies. Nevertheless, the alternative economic ideology has, as we have stressed, created its own set of gross economic inefficiencies.

Regarding 3rd-order-dependencies, if the IMF had sufficient emergency-finance benefits to offer the countries, such as the indirect gold-convertibility offered under the Bretton Woods system, the IMF could induce price stability by simply applying its traditional policy of prohibitively taxing inflating member countries. However, in the post-Bretton-Woods, Cold-War world, taxing an inflating brutocracy, or even shortening the inflation-devaluation lag, would risk the defection of these hyper-inflating countries. These countries could quit the system and either collectively set up their own system of internationally tied exchange rates, which has proved very difficult because of the absence of IMF support, or join the Eastern Bloc in order to escape the IMF's onerous taxes or short inflation-devaluation lag. With the USSR beginning its exit during the late 1980s, we did indeed see a substantial reduction in this inflation-devaluation lag (Edwards). Correspondingly, the number of annual devaluations rapidly increased during this period. Using equation (3) above, and examining the empirical results below, the result was a sharp <u>increase</u> in the equilibrium rates of hyperinflation. The subsequent and sudden elimination of the worst of these hyperinflations, which were largely a Latin American phenomenon, in the early 1990s may thus be a reflection of a continuing aggressiveness by the IMF and resulting reduction of the returns to a single round of inflation to where it is, as illustrated in Figures 5.2 and 5.3, no longer nationally efficient for countries, other than the new 3rd-order dependencies from eastern Europe, to support a hyperinflationary solution. Of course, an arbitrarily short inflation-devaluation lag is essentially an internationally authoritarian elimination of exchange controls and hyperinflation as a means of avoiding trade liberalizing policies. Several of these countries have thus recently switched to undervalued currencies and new, "export-led-growth", development plans.

More ominously, the late 1990s is witnessing a rapidly decreasing frequency of hyperinflation on a worldwide basis. Although there has been a widespread reduction in Western defense-externalities since the end of the Cold-War, there is no reason to believe that countries have suddenly lost their brutocratic polities. The only plausible explanation, one entirely consistent with recent institutional observations, is that the increasingly powerful IMF has come to assert an authoritarian control offering uniquely large emergency lines of credit in exchange for entire packages of domestic policies, packages which typically include the elimination of exchange controls. In effect, the entire third world is losing its sovereignty and becoming a 2nd- or 1st-order dependency.

IV. STATISTICAL ANALYSIS

The above theory suggests that a country's observed annual inflation rate, I^a, can be predicted by: (1) its effective level of military conflict, MC, a country at war optimally increasing its money supply to help finance the wartime emergency; and (2) the excess, E, of its peacetime defense-externality over its allowable tariff rate, interacted with its dependency on international agencies.

As we have just seen, the effect of E on I^a is extremely nonlinear. To accommodate this, we constructed the following nonlinear index: Letting the extent of a country's exchange controls measure the excess of its desired tariff rate over its allowable tariff rate, we ranked all 100 some-odd countries in each of our samples from 0 to 6 (see the Statistical Appendix at the end of this Chapter), giving each country an E-ranking based on the existence, comprehensiveness, and severity of its exchange-control system. The anti-log of the raw measure, $T = e^E$, then served as our net externality measure.

Similarly critical was our measure of a country's dependency on international agencies, I. A country received a dummy level of unity if it were a member of the GATT, and a "zero" otherwise. But if its exports were a small fraction of its income, its dependency on GATT policies could not be assumed to be large (in particular, its willingness to incur inflation to avoid GATT policies could not be assumed to be large). So our GATT-influence measure was a 0-1 dummy times one plus the log of one plus the share of exports in the country's GDP (the logarithmic weighting being due to an otherwise exaggerated effect of the trade weight because the variance of the raw weight typically exceeded the variance of the primary dummy variable). A country that was not an IMF member (Eastern Europe before the 1990s and several small African countries with financial and military ties to France to the point of granting the latter internal monetary control) received a "zero", while IMF members received a "one". The extent of the dependency of an IMF member, measured by the extent of the government's short-term debt to foreign lenders relative to its GDP (or, more specifically, one plus the log of one plus this variable), was then multiplied by the zero-one dummy variable to obtain a final measure of IMF-dependency. The mathematical product of these two weighted dummy variables, I, which is described in greater detail in the Statistical Appendix, was our measure of a country's trade-relevant dependency on international institutions.

The interaction between the above two, inflation-predicting, variables, i.e., the product of I, the international-agency-dependency measure, and T, the transformed defense-externality measure, was thus our critical peacetime inflation-predictor.[44]

A "military conflict" variable was constructed by first examining whether the country had become engaged in a war within two years of the period in question, and continued the war throughout the period. If so, MC = 3. If not, but the country was

---

[44]One might wonder why peaceful countries with zero levels of GATT-dependency would adopt high levels of exchange controls (rather than unilaterally high tariffs). The answer is that, as we have already noted, other forms of international cooperation exist, non-GATT forms that, from a similar ideological inspiration, impose low tariffs on member countries.

politically unstable, as measured by whether it had a war during part of the decade in question, we gave the country a "2". If neither, but the country was not covered by a dominant country's nuclear umbrella (i.e., was a member of NATO or ANZUS), we gave the country a "1". The remaining countries received a "zero". Finally, to obtain our "war" variable, W, we doubled MC to approximately equalize its variance to that of our exchange-control dummy and weighted the variable by the severity of the country's current financial drain, one plus the log of one plus the increase in the country's fiscal deficit relative-to-income over the period in question.

We can force our IT- and W-centered theory to statistically compete with existing alternatives, mainly financial corruption and fiscal exhaustion, alternatives which have proxies that can be variously expressed by the financial indicators appearing in the weights on each of our variables.[45] We do this by simply generating a maximum likelihood approximation of our general inflation function, approximating the function with the quadratic form of F(W,T,I). In other words, we let the data tell us their own story by running the following least squares regression on an international cross-section of 100 some-odd countries for which data was available:

$$I^a = k + aI^2 + bI + cT^2 + dT + fIT + gW^2 + hW + iTW + jIW,$$

where the small letters signify estimated parameters.

A. Numerical Estimates: 1989-90

For the latest years of our study, 1989-90, the regression results appear on Table 5.2. As predicted by our theory, the W and IT variables explain most of the variation. Moreover, IT was, by far, the single most powerful predictor of inflation.

---

[45]We have already indicated our inability to make sense out of pre-existing hyperinflation stories. Conventional stories based on the financial corruption of the bureaucracy imply variable, not inflating, price levels and just make us ask why the victimized countries do not solve the problem by simultaneously paying higher salaries to their monetary officials and imposing much larger penalties for insider trading by the bureaucrats and their associates. And those stories based on the existence of genuine fiscal exhaustion and the use of money-creation as a last resort source of peacetime finance completely fail once we recognize (as we have) that the real government revenue from hyperinflation is necessarily a tiny fraction of a country's GDP and therefore that any small fiscal setback would leave the state defenseless. Such states would, long ago, have been easy prey for their enemies. Nevertheless, these two arguments persist; the latter being a constrained-rational efficient motivator for artificially budget-constrained, Pascalian, bureaucrats. In any case, the arguments can be reckoned-with in our statistical model by: (1) letting T, the extent of the country's exchange controls be a proxy for the country's bureaucratic corruption variable; and (2) letting I, dependence of international agencies, be a proxy for the fiscal exhaustion of the country.

Although the interaction between these two commonly alleged forces might conceivably have a superadditive effect on inflation, such extreme governmental weakness would also create an exceptional degree of political instability and therefore systematically positive interactions with our war variable, W. The absence of such systematic effects in our data, as apparent in Tables 5.2-5.4, leads us to reject this conceptual possibility.

TABLE 5.2

PREDICTING INFLATION: 1989-1990

Dependent Variable is I^a

Regressor	Coefficient	T-Ratio
k	221.913	3.804
SQI	-.310	-4.361
I	-1.942	-.830
SQT	.019	3.327
T	9.277	5.324
IT	.481	11.788
SQW	177.374	8.599
W	-386.289	-6.11
TW	-10.132	-5.173
IW	4.560	2.497

R^2	.975	
Mean of Dependent Variable	107.487	

B. Estimates for Earlier Years

Going back to the preceding, more peaceful period, 1986-88 (the period following the drop in oil prices in 1986), we ran another regression of the same form. Similar results appeared, as reported in Table 5.3. IT was again the single most powerful predictor among the 9 competitors, and the R^2 was again in the .98-9 region. Finally, for the 1970s we again ran our test regression for the relatively stable, 1976-78, period. As reported in Table 5.4, similar results occurred. IT was -- for the third-straight test -- again the most powerful of the 9 competing variables!

TABLE 5.3

PREDICTING INFLATION: 1986-1988

Dependent Variable is I^a

Regressor	Coefficient	T-Ratio
k	21.548	1.789
SQI	-.174	-2.464
I	-2.686	-1.298
SQT	.005	3.427
T	-.458	-1.370
IT	.092	4.158
SQW	.115	.350
W	-7.659	-1.388
TW	.167	1.369
IW	2.169	2.847

R^2	.990
Mean of Dependent Variable	38.240

TABLE 5.4

PREDICTING INFLATION: 1976-1978

Dependent Variable is I^a

Regressor	Coefficient	T-Ratio
k	10.652	2.701
SQI	-.060	-.321
I	.140	.109
SQT	.008	11.509
T	-.425	-3.397
IT	.152	12.246
SQW	.295	.656
W	1.516	.576
TW	-.122	-2.797
IW	-.516	-1.871

R^2	.933
Mean of Dependent Variable	14.985

V. GRAPHICAL SUMMARY

There is an alternative way to illustrate the power of the theory. This is to simply plot Inflation against IT, including all IMF and GATT members who were not at war (e.g., Graph 1), comparing it to a plot (e.g., Graph 2) of Inflation against our exchange-control index, T, for non-warring non-members. The idea is to check to see if inflation is not somehow generating severe exchange controls or if there was some common causation between inflation and exchange controls. For these non-members, there was indeed no visible increase in I^a with T (see Graph 2). Graphs 3 and 4 present the same contrast for the earlier 1986-1988 period. Graphs 5 and 6 present the same, stark, contrast for the 1970s sample.

In words rather than numbers, what is going on in each pair of Graphs is quite simple. There are only a few countries with persistently stringent peacetime exchange controls. These countries are, according to our theory, trying to avoid suffering from what are for them extremely high costs of low import tariffs. Now some of these countries have no serious peacetime inflation. These are predictably the countries that are not directly dependent on that theoretically deadly combination of ideologues located at the GATT and the IMF. But if a country has persisted in maintaining stringent exchange controls and has also lived with a substantial dependency on both the GATT and the IMF, peacetime hyperinflation is -- empirically as well as theoretically -- essentially guaranteed.

VI. CONCLUSIONS

A. On Economic Ideology: A Test for Political-Economic Hubris

Very few of us are surprised when we find functional members of our broader society adopting beliefs that grossly exaggerate the relative benefits of engaging in exchange with an organization to which they belong. We should therefore not be surprised to find similar hubris in the political-economic beliefs of members of the economics profession. Consider, for example, how standard political-economic theories predict the reaction of typical, national-tariff-supporting, local governmental representatives in a national legislature to suggestions of barriers to internal, intranational, trade. Inherited political economy tells us that approximately the same political failure that explains observed barriers to international trade also predicts that the same politicians will support analogous domestic barriers to intranational trade (either for local protectionism or local revenue). But the actual politicians almost universally condemn intranational trade barriers!

We are not arguing that the reasoning of observed politicians resembles that of an enlightened economist, who understands that since the defense-externality is the same wherever in a collectively defended nation the traded property is located, the tax rate on the property should be the same regardless of where the property is located in that nation. Rather, the political sense of economic efficiency comes from historical policy experience and a political system that has evolved to entrust legislation to pragmatic Pascalian, minds. As it is in the professional self-interest of a cartel of economists to heavily discount the efficiency of the policy thought of our

GRAPH 1: INFLATION AND EXCHANGE CONTROLS: 1989-90 (IMF MEMBERSHIP)

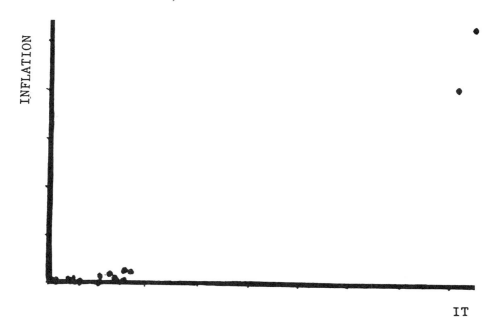

GRAPH 2: INFLATION AND EXCHANGE CONTROLS: 1989-90 (NON-IMF MEMBERSHIP)

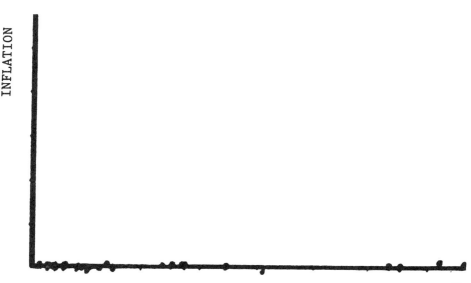

GRAPH 3: INFLATION AND EXCHANGE CONTROLS: 1986-88 (IMF
          MEMBERSHIP)

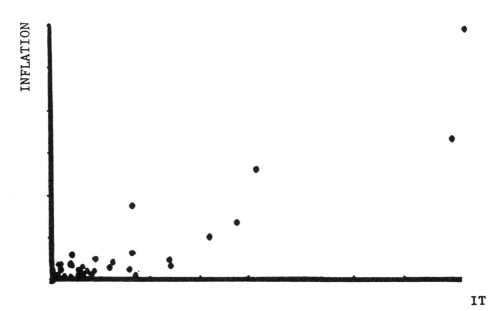

GRAPH 4: INFLATION AND EXCHANGE CONTROLS: 1986-88 (NON-IMF
          MEMBERSHIP)

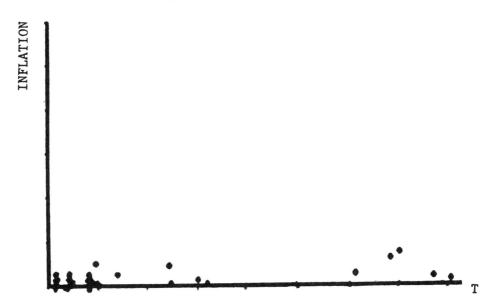

GRAPH 5: INFLATION AND EXCHANGE CONTROLS: 1976-78 (IMF MEMBERSHIP)

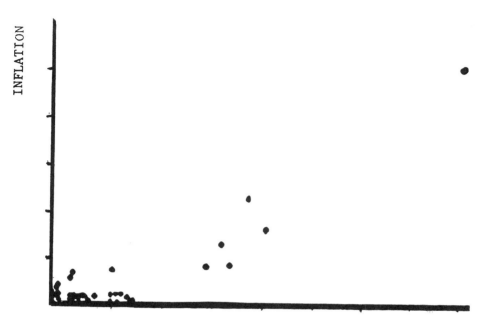

GRAPH 6: INFLATION AND EXCHANGE CONTROLS: 1976-78 (NON-IMF MEMBERSHIP)

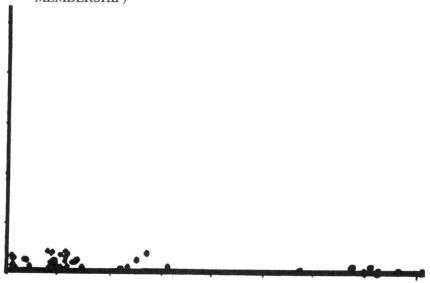

elected officials, the evolved social constraints facing professional economists similarly lead their professionally respected, themselves Pascalian, members to criticize their intellectual substitutes in the political arena.

Nevertheless, we expect that critical-minded, rationality-driven, economists would readily acknowledge the failure of the standard, highly evolved, political-economic paradigm to explain the above-noted inconsistency regarding foreign and domestic trade barriers. We correspondingly invite these special economists to compare the received ideology of international economics with the political economic theory of this chapter as alternative ways to enlighten our view of the actual world economy.

1. *Does Economic Ideology Enlighten Our View of the Past World Economy?* Consider the "Dollar Shortage" arising after WWII, wherein virtually all independent foreign nations allowed their post-war money supplies to rise in their already-booming economies to where there was dollar rationing and significant domestic exchange controls. This largely unpredicted phenomenon has never been explained to be the result of economically efficient governmental policy. Yet the great post-war expansion of the GATT, and the correspondingly widespread imposition of artificially low tariff rates, could have led to no other response from independent nations separately evolved to efficiently internalize their respective defense-externalities. Moreover, as NATO began to strengthen and the IMF's gold-exchange standard was extended to Western European nations during the late 1950s, exchange controls and the "dollar shortage" quickly dried up, but only in those regions. Again, nothing in standard economics prepares us to predict or explain the simultaneous maintenance of substantial exchange controls in the other, relatively high-defense-externality, countries.

Or recall that Germany and Japan, and subsequently the "baby tigers" of southeast Asia, being only semi-independent and unable to employ exchange controls in order to avoid the U.S.-imposed tariff reductions, had to rely on substantially undervalued currencies, and correspondingly significant subsidies to non-coveted capital imports, to reduce their consumer-goods imports toward internally-optimal levels. Again, nothing in standard economics predicts these policies or the apparent "economic miracles" that followed.

Yet these simple efficiency-explanations of widely discussed post-WWII economic mysteries are relatively innocent examples. The above three chapters have been spent in showing how economic ideology, by failing to integrate often vital defense activities and defense-externalities into its theories, has given us a series of systematically dangerous misinterpretations of economic reality and economic history.

2. *Does Economic Ideology Enlighten Our View of the Present World Economy?* The recent break-up of the Soviet Union, by dramatically reducing the external support for domestic rebel-groups in various parts of Latin America, has substantially decreased the defense-externality faced by many of these previously unstable countries. As our defense-oriented theory predicts for more than one reason, the severity of exchange controls in these countries has subsequently diminished, the frequency of Latin American hyperinflation has correspondingly fallen, and economic

growth has been impressive.

Yet almost all involved economists have cited the relative prosperity of the trade-liberalizing 1990s as convincing evidence confirming the accuracy of standard economic theory. They do this despite the theory's systematic historical failures and despite the obvious alternative theory that a fall in defense costs simultaneously decreases the efficient levels of import restrictions and increases economic prosperity.

Meanwhile, in the initially less rebel-threatened parts of Latin America, and on the other side of the globe where an emboldened China has created a new set of dependencies in southeast Asia, the strengthened IMF has been able to limit exchange controls similar to the way that the U.S. had previously limited the exchange controls of subsequently currency-undervaluing West Germany, Japan, Korea, Taiwan and Singapore. Since this earlier experience had shown that high-defense-externality countries with externally limited exchange controls rationally undervalue their currencies by artificially importing large amounts of foreign capital and creating domestic export booms, these more recent exchange-control-limitations immediately induced large temporary influxes of direct foreign investment, which fed the artificially induced savings and export booms and delayed the inevitable currency depreciations. The inevitable decline in export prices then triggered the inevitable cessation of foreign investment and real currency depreciations despite the subsequently large U.S. and IMF "bail-out" loans as part of their unrelenting pro-trade policy. In contrast to the above story, the massive contemporary literature on the subject, tied as it is to standard economic theory, offers no rational explanation for either the boom, the bust, or the trend.

3. *Does Economic Ideology Enlighten Our View of the future World Economy?* Finally, consider a world with a single, dominant empire, where there is no international competition forcing the dominant country to acknowledge the claims of the other countries. Standard international economics forecasts more of the same. However, there is little reason for a genuinely world-dominant imperial leader to tolerate exchange controls. Exchange controls and hyperinflation would be eliminated from the resulting, excessively investing and exporting, debt-dependent, third world. While it is likely that a more efficient, lump-sum colonial form of rent would soon come to replace these Cold-War-ideology-based inefficiencies, another, probably even more serious, currently emergent, distributional, problem would arise. We shall consider the problem, and a political solution to it, in the following chapter.

B. Optimal Economic Policy

In any case, the economic policies of international agencies such as the WTO (or its predecessor, the GATT) and IMF should not be predicated on economic ideology. Each country should, we have seen, be assumed to be fully capable of acting in its informed self-interest. Small-country trade barriers should be assumed to be rational and efficient as a matter of course. The WTO and other free-trade associations should be restricted to preventing various countries from exploiting their effects on prices to achieve monopoly gains from other countries.

Perhaps the easiest way to achieve these goals would be to allow international organizations to freely compete. However, in the case of a naturally monopolistic free-trade association, a suitable regulatory principle would be to disallow all-or-nothing, discriminatory price negotiation, as has been used by the GATT and WTO to bargain for much more than the simple elimination of nationally monopsonistic or monopolistic trade practices. Such efficient free-trade agreements would be largely restricted to a few large-country tariffs, a few domestic export taxes, and national grants of domestic monopolies for the purposes of foreign trade. And the IMF, in case it also turned out to be a natural monopoly, would be restricted to using non-discriminatory methods in assisting members in their attempts to finance national emergencies. Loan conditions encouraging small-country trade-liberalization, or other non-cost-justified conditions, amount to international price discrimination. They work against the justifiable role of the IMF and should be constitutionally eliminated.

STATISTICAL PROCEDURES

Explanation of Variables

The Variable E

In order to gauge the magnitude of each country's exchange control, we have developed a qualitative measure, which we call E, of the extent of each country's import licensing. Based on information reported in the International Monetary Fund's Annual Report on Exchange Arrangements and Exchange Control, we have determined the value of E according to the following formula:

E = 6   if every category of imports requires an import license and many categories of consumer good imports are prohibited.

E = 5   if every category of imports requires an import license but just a few categories of consumer good imports are prohibited.

E = 4   if every category of imports requires an import license but no category of consumer good imports is prohibited.

E = 3   if import licenses are required for a very wide range of categories of consumer goods.

E = 2   if import licenses are required for only a few categories of luxury consumer goods.

E = 1   if import licenses are required for only a few categories of consumer goods.

E = 0   if no import licenses are required whatsoever for any category of goods.

The variable MC

In order to measure the extent of instability in a particular country we have developed a qualitative "military conflict" variable, called MC, to measure it. Based on information reported in the SIPRI Yearbook we have determined the value of MC based on the following criteria:

MC = 3   if the country is presently experiencing military conflict, or the country has experienced or will experience significant military conflict within a 2-year period of the sample period.

MC = 2   if the country has experienced significant conflict during the sample period decade.

MC = 1   if the country is not a member of the defense pacts mentioned on category 0 but has experienced no significant conflict during the sample decade.

MC = 0   if the country is a member of NATO, ANZUS or SEATO and has experienced no significant conflict within the sample decade.

The variables IMF and GATT

The variables IMF and GATT are qualitative measures of a country's membership in the International Monetary Fund and the General Agreement of Trade and Tariffs respectively, according to the following rule.

IMF = 1   if, during the sample period, country is a member of the IMF and   0 otherwise.

GATT = 1   if, during the sample period, country is a member of the GATT and   0 otherwise.

The variables x, gdf, ofd, and I^a

The following three quantitative variables are based on data reported in the World· Bank's World Tables and World Debt Tables Star Retrieval System

x   measures the importance of a country's foreign trade and is measured by the log of one plus the average value of the country's exports divided by the average value of its GDP for the sample period.

def   measures the extent of the increased vulnerability of a country as reflected in the change in its government's fiscal solvency. Thus def is defined as the log of one plus the change in the government deficit over the sample period divided by GDP.

ofd   measures the extent of the dependency of the country on international agencies, and it is defined as the log of one plus the accumulated government guaranteed short term external debt plus any accumulated interest arrears at the end of the sample period.

I^a is the average inflation for the sample period.

The transformed variables I, T and W

Based on the above variables we determine the following variables as follows:

I = IMF GATT (ofd + 1) (x + 1),
T = antilog(E),
W = 2MC(def+1).

The actual data

The extensive raw data is available and will be furnished by either one of the authors on request. It is, to match our three Tables in the text above, separated into data for 1976-78, then for 1986-88, and finally for 1989-90.

CHAPTER 6

SUMMARY, POLICY IMPLICATIONS, AND A FINAL TEST

"Science: The Endless Frontier" -- Vannevar Bush, 1945

"Science: The Endless Expenditure" -- Response of Harold Smith,
Budget Director For President Harry Truman (Zachary)

I. VITAL INSTITUTIONS AND CIVILIZATIONAL UPTURNS

The vital components of an organism, whether biological or social, are unique in that each one lives or dies according as the organism lives or dies. Nature or design has presented them with an environment in which they have no strictly private opportunity cost. Narrowly rational, perfectly informed, behavior by each vital component, each member of the nonconflictual team, would then generate jointly efficient behavior (Appendix A.2). The decentralized interactions among the vital components of any organism therefore produce a relatively direct and inexpensive path to a joint optimum, one lacking the wasteful status-seeking involved in ordinary strategic interaction (Appendix B.1). Moreover -- regarding the institutional evolution of a method of selecting and suitably constraining a team of incompletely informed but objective, "Pascalian", individuals who are to make decisions about their society's vital institutions -- pragmatic imitation and a necessarily harsh level of natural selection work together to produce a rapid adjustment path.

A paradox nevertheless arises once we allow a set of initially non-existing organs to become vital as a result of the subsequent evolution of another, non-vital, organ. How could the non-vital organ ever evolve? The non-vital organ puts the entire organism at risk; its origination suddenly forces the organism's survival to be dependent upon the timely appearance of otherwise inessential, non-pre-existing, organs. The only conceivable answer is that there is (a) an essentially simultaneous, Lamarckian, evolution of the newly vital organs and (b) an extraordinary increase in the efficiency of a surviving organism containing the non-vital organ, an increase more than offsetting the sudden decrease in the robust character of the organism.[1]

---

[1] Modern game theorists will nevertheless see this as still a problem because it appears to set up a coordination game with two Nash equilibria, a so-called "stag hunt" game. Thinking of the row player as selecting a new town's political system and the column player the town's economic institutions, an early example of the resulting payoffs would be:

	Guilds	No Guilds
Early Medieval Democracy	10,10	0,0
Authoritarian Government	5,5	6,6.

The Nash Equilibria, of course, are at (6.6) and (10,10).

(continued, next page)

The non-vital social organ that we have studied is democracy. The extraordinary increase in a society's theoretically expected efficiency comes through an effective democracy's elimination of otherwise undetectable underinvestment traps (Appendix A.1). Since democracy also creates a unique need for a particular set of economically "vital" organs, a potentially fatal social burden (Appendices B.2 (Note 4) and B.3 (Section II.B)), the mere survival of democracy in the face of various changes in the nature of these vital organs provides substantial confirmation of our theory of the extraordinary efficiency of long-surviving democracies.

More specifically, an otherwise effective democracy in a world of militarily competing states will soon lose its territorial integrity and die unless it regularly overcomes a legislative time inconsistency wherein each decision in a sequence of decisions reflects a voter-willingness to trade state property for peace.   The sophisticated and flexible legislation required for this task demands an externality-sensitive and cooperative legislature, as well as a civilly reverent bureaucracy. But the same political efficiency characteristics also suffice to generate a wide variety of economically efficient civilian laws, including investor-vital laws that eliminate many of the laissez faire economy's above-mentioned underdevelopment traps.

So each long-surviving democracy has a glorious story to tell, one with a steady stream of both military and civilian highlights.   In particular, these surviving democracies are unique, both in having passed a long series of singularly difficult efficiency-tests in the area of war preparation and finance, and in having uniformly displayed a remarkable degree of economic development.

II. CIVILIZATIONAL DOWNTURNS AND HOW TO AVOID THEM

Nevertheless, a predictable end to each of these success stories has been occasioned by: (1) a loss of democratic effectiveness through civilizational dominance and a corresponding, advanced-education-produced, replacement of investor-sensitive

---

Assuming, as is implicit in the empirical argument of Chapter 3, that, in the absence of learning, both democracies with guilds and authoritarian governments without guilds survive at the same, maximal, rate despite their different payoffs, the evolutionary path converges to the popular, boundedly rational, non-socially-optimal, "risk-dominant" equilibrium introduced by Kandori, Mailath, and Rob, i.e., 5,5. Authoritarian government, for example, can be thought of as being selected because its initial expected value to the row player (i.e., 5 1/2) exceeds that of democracy (i.e., 5).

We, of course, have been defending the socially optimal, perfect-information solution, 10,10. The difference rests upon the assumption that institutional learning is, as Lamarck would have it, evolved to be conditional on other institutions. Surviving medieval democracies were thus those that had learned the conditional payoffs, i.e., that they could survive only in the presence of guilds. (This conditioning creates an asymmetric normal form game with a unique pure strategy equilibrium and hence, again applying a convergence theorem of Weibull, an asymptotic evolutionary path to the equilibrium.) Neither Nash assumptions nor bounded rationality can be defended when there is a substantial payoff to full strategic learning. Once the civilization is almost all authoritarian (the initial condition in the text), it would indeed be paradoxical if democracy survived under purely Darwinian evolution.

legislative pragmatism and civil reverence with an economic or social ideology taught by the state's ascendant intellectuals, or (2) a loss of democracy through a switch to a military technology demanding professional personnel and expensive military capital rather than widespread civilian wartime sacrifices.

By the mid-20th century, the U.S. -- like Great Britain and Austria in the mid-19th century, Provincial France in the mid-18th century, Holland in the mid-17th century, Spain in the mid-16th century, Florence-Tuscany in the mid-15th century, the French provinces again in the late 13th-century, Byzantium in the 11th and 12th centuries, and a similar string of successful investor-democracies in antiquity (Thompson, et al., Vol. II, Ch. 6) -- had become economically dominant in the same way that had the prior investor-democracies. The U.S.'s resulting role as the setter of international economic standards at the end of WWII, just as in the other cases, freed our ruling classes from the pressures of institutional emulation, generated a boom in advanced education, and soon created a kind of U.S. civilizational dominance in the West. The subsequently steady economic ideologization of our bureaucracies in the U.S. in the second half of the 20th century (which first became visible in the emergence of "legislative judges" during the 1950s) and the related economic ideologization of our legislatures (which first became visible during the anti-labor legislation of the late 1950s, and later during the "great society" legislation of the mid-1960s, the deregulation wave of the 1970s, and the 1986 tax "reform") has brought a predictable reduction in the efficiency of the U.S. democracy, although the familiar secular decline in productivity and related string of costly military defeats has fortunately been interrupted by a sharp improvement in the U.S. terms of trade that has been fundamentally the result of the decline and fall of the even more ideologized Soviet Union toward the end of the 1980s.

Moreover, the military technology has <u>also</u> been shifting. Motivated largely by our increasing technological sophistication but also by our ignominious defeat in Vietnam, there has been a rapid switch from civilian to professional armies. As in other such historical episodes, this jump in expenditures on military manpower has been rationally followed by an increasingly capital-intensive military technology, whose emergence is indicated by our high-tech operations in the Persian Gulf and Serbia.

The world's previous shift toward a highly capital intensive military technology came with of the mobile cannon during the latter half of the 15th century.[2]

---

[2]This eventually quite anti-democratic, imperializing, shift was similarly presaged by a switch to expensive professional armies, which initially concentrated in the threatened territories of various French provinces and Italian city-states early in the 14th century. What immediately followed this military professionalization in the most democratic of these late medieval states, viz., Florence, was a rapidly accumulating national debt, reflecting an unwillingness of the masses to pay for the increasingly financially expensive defense systems. Equally understandable was the decreasing fraternalism of the wealthier citizens and the subsequent, debt-induced, surrender of the popular democracy over to (1) large-scale bankers and aristocrats, who were more willing and able to finance emergencies and cannon-equipped professional armies, and (2) the existing bureaucratic elite, whose gradual ideologization led to the loss of Florentine sovereignty early in the 16th century (Chapter 3).

The inflated U.S. national debt and deflated humanism of our higher-income groups since

The following century saw a wholesale abandonment of democratic legislatures by the imperializing European governments. The military-technology cause of these ultimately anti-democratic, imperializing, movements is revealed by the simultaneous maintenance of democracy in atypically independent towns (e.g., the German "free towns" and various mountainous enclaves that were practically out of the reach of the new weapons and defended with ordinary civilians.) With the gratitude of Renaissance ruling-class elites for wartime sacrifices no longer due the immobile masses, no favors were granted. Since there was no reason for these elites to incur the costs of granting politically enforceable legal assurances to ordinary people, widespread indifference to human suffering quickly evolved (Appendix B.1).

Our post-Cold-War efforts to establish a high-tech-army-based, globalized, world economy have been essentially identical to the cannon-induced, oppression-producing, European efforts to establish centralized empires beginning in the late-15th century. Even before the end of the Cold War, since the debacle in Vietnam, we had been witnessing a professional army-based movement away from popular democracy through a steady decrease in the willingness of our higher-income groups to financially support our no-longer-militarily-sacrificing youth and a corresponding weakening of the fiscal benefits and political power of the young and the poor by way of an easy purchase of their acceptance of campaign-contribution laws favoring the wealthy. But this loss of economic and political power is only the tip of an iceberg. Soon thereafter, the post-Cold-War U.S., the world's high-tech military leader, began to develop the same sort of secure military and political dominance enjoyed by imperial Rome during the *Pax Romana* (29 BC-192 AD), the so-called *pax Americana*. By working with its European allies to subtly strip most of the world's nations of their sovereignty through the devise of making them dependent upon IMF discretion for emergency finance, the post-Cold-War U.S. has been able to demand a whole series of ideologically inspired, quite inefficient, dependent-country trade favors (Chapter 5). The resulting downward pressure on U.S. input costs has produced a corresponding boom in the value of U.S. non-human capital, which has temporarily masked the decreased efficiency of the ideologized U.S. So this is not the time to offer a plan for improving U.S. efficiency. But this is the time to offer a plan for improving world efficiency, one recognizing the severe allocational defects in our current system of international economic cooperation.

An efficient world constitution would work by assuring each nation of complete local autonomy in all local matters, including domestic fiscal policy and tariffs. Much like the German free cities, whose independence was guaranteed by the Holy

---

the Vietnam debacle are both essentially identical to the responses of early-14th to mid-15 century medieval Florence to the professionalization of its army. A similarly costly but rational surrender of the U.S.'s popular democracy over to large investors, bankers and a bureaucratic elite (like the temporary barrier to the eventual surrender of the Florentine democracy to the Medici's and the later surrender of the local French assemblies to the early Bourbon Monarchs) has, however, been delayed by the fortunate absence of an expensive military emergency and correspondingly fortunate absence of an expressed unwillingness of the masses to voluntarily pay the huge resulting war debt.

Roman Emperor throughout the imperializing period from the late 15th to the late 17th century, non-dominant states would be freed of the ideologically-inspired policy impositions of dominant states. International anti-monopoly laws, besides either breaking-up or regulating worldwide monopolies, would prevent large companies from serving as conduits for promoting dominant-country policies by limiting their political involvement beyond the protection of their local investments to a single state. International lines of credit, fixed exchange rate agreements, and free trade agreements, etc., would be permitted as part of free international contracting. However, international anti-monopoly laws would either break-up existing lending monopolies or regulate these lenders, preventing them from discriminating between borrowing countries by basing their leading rates on domestic policy variables that are not directly related to lending costs. Such an anti-imperial constitution would create an international policy environment that invited legislative pragmatism because politically independent and competing states are able to freely criticize, freely innovate, and independently evaluate the real consequences of observed policy innovations, much like existing provinces or states within observed national federations. Although wealthy, intellectually advanced, nations would still tend to be internally victimized by their intellectuals, their subsequent economic failures would not produce an entire civilizational decline. Rather, their economic rivals would simply replace them as civilizational leaders. Such is the enormous economic advantage of international political competition.[3]

Even if we disregarded the substantial economic efficiencies involved in freeing the rest of the world from the domination of the economic ideology of the hegemon, large future allocational benefits would emerge from our preliminary world constitution in that the pending international struggle for world military leadership would be substantially obviated by a timely international constitutional commitment to a political-independence-assuring world government.

The advantage of the timely adoption of such an independence-generating world constitution is even more apparent as regards the distributional benefits of the suggested constitution.

III. AVOIDING THE PENDING DISTRIBUTIONAL DISASTER

Whenever a world-dominant state emerges, that state can easily end the free competition among states for people, such as the free international competition for immigrants that has accounted for the remarkable wage-growth that began at the end of the Napoleonic wars. A world-dominant state effects this monopsonization simply by inducing all of the ostensibly competing states to impose sufficiently high tax burdens on potential laborers (e.g., through stingy welfare programs, anti-progressive income-tax rates, and large governmental expenditures on practical education and

---

[3]A complementary set of theoretically ideal institutions for a liberating world constitution is contained in a more idealistic political economic study (e.g., Thompson, et al, Vol. I) featuring an anti-cartel policy for certain intellectual pursuits. The point is to induce a break down of intellectual cartels in pursuits where they have no value-creating justification.

crime prevention).   Under such world-organization-imposed tax "reforms", the decreased attractiveness of alternatives to work and labor's loss in wealth causes worldwide labor inputs to increase so that before-tax wages fall, meaning that after-tax wages fall by more than the tax-increase.   (Externally imposed increases in a country's education and crime-prevention levels, by artificially increasing the country's effective labor supply, lower its wage level to below what the country considers to be optimal.)   The dominant-state-serving elimination of the competition of free and independent states for people, an elimination currently working through the conditions that the IMF and World Bank impose on the world's many dependent countries, thus immediately places in jeopardy the entire 15-fold expansion in real wages that has occurred since the birth of a competitive international labor market in the 1820s.   The only obvious way to prevent this pending worldwide return to subsistence wage rates and debt-peonage is to constitutionally prevent dominant states from determining the domestic economic policies of the other states.

Only under such a constitutional commitment can we maintain a free and independent international competition for people and thereby avoid the permanent mass oppression that would surely result from the emerging world empire.[4]

---

[4]Casual readers of this work -- reading this concluding chapter without having become accustomed to seeing an abstract model repeatedly explain broad historical observations that we were all taught to accept as beyond simple explanation -- will probably believe it impossible to make rational economic predictions as stark as the ones above, especially when accompanied by such a simple policy implication.

Such readers require a different kind of evidence regarding our hypothesis that the Third-World countries are generating a new force towards substantially lower real wages.

For example, the July 15, 1996 edition of the IMF Survey reports the IMF President announcing in late June a new, joint IMF-World-Bank policy of "globalization", wherein the dominant (G-7) countries are going to impose a new set of loan conditions on the world's 41 most heavily indebted poor countries.   These new conditions on loan-renewals to any one of these countries go beyond the exchange-rate conditions described in Chapter 5.   The new conditions represent a bold attempt to impose a common, wage-decreasing, tax-system on these otherwise fiscally-competing nations.   Nevertheless, the "globalization" advocate argues that the effect of the new policies on a given nation are designed to improve "the quality of its economic policies ... and hence its ability to attract investment" (p. 235).   The new policies (p.236) are concentrated in the area of "human development" (education increases and crime-rate reduction), where the term "globalization" then clearly applies because it induces the Third World countries to develop the same set of human-resource-development policies common in the more developed countries.   Later in the Survey, where the direct investor benefit of such globalization policies (viz., an expanding world supply of qualified workers and hence lower real wage rates), is reluctantly conceded (p. 238), the IMF representative placates the justifiably concerned representatives of the International Confederation of Free Trade Unions by arguing that such labor confederations have an expanded role in oppressive labor markets a role that implicitly requires more international trade-union representatives!

Still more recently -- our writing here can barely keep pace with the events -- the highly U.S.-dependent nations of southeast Asia have suddenly begun to witness the effects of the recently intensified efforts of the more developed nations to induce higher levels of industrial work-effort in this region.   The mid-1997 terms-of-trade-led collapse of real wages in southeast

As long as all potential aggressors are included in the constitutional cooperative, all of the desired freedoms -- from the external imposition of an economic ideology, from an expensive arms-race, and from radically inegalitarian world taxation -- can be maintained. The internationally destructive influence of economic ideology and the inexorably distributionally-devastating elimination of the free competition for ordinary people among independently bidding states can thus be simultaneously eliminated by returning to the original democratic ideals of Samuel Adams, Patrick Henry, Richard Henry Lee, Thomas Paine and the young Thomas Jefferson. These are the ideals of decentralized democracy, or "radical republicanism", and unfettered interregional competition that were reflected in the U.S.'s original Articles of Confederation. These constitutional ideals were found impractical at that time (just as the same ideals were found impractical in the Macedonian Empire almost 2000 years earlier) because the presence of large foreign aggressors created a need for occasionally high levels of federal taxation. But the ideals <u>are</u> appropriate to a world government run by the most powerful state, where foreign aggressors do not exist and where a primary goal of the informed initial leaders is to prevent future leaders from exploiting their awesome power over the distribution of wealth.

A constitutionally constrained world empire may, in general, have legitimate occasion, in its role as an aid in the maintenance of international order, to spend more than it has raised through initial contributions. Borrowing for such purposes may then, as in the formative years of the United States, put a debilitating strain on the world government because of the future rationality of debt abrogation. The only solution is to have the dominant country bear the costs of the emergency expenditure as a matter of constitutional obligation. The dominant country must then be compensated and continuously motivated. The now-familiar way to achieve this is through a constitutional grant of emergency control, and corresponding restriction of the top executive positions, of the world government to politically approved representatives of the dominant states. The constitutional prohibition of world taxation would prevent the executives from unilaterally asserting imperial taxation powers. While it is unlikely that the existing world government, the United Nations, would support such a reform of their existing constitution, the inclusion of the earlier-described regulation of international monopolies, and thus the inclusion of a world-regulatory discipline over large international agencies (e.g., the IMF, WTO and World Bank) and politically active multinational corporations in order to prevent implicit forms of international taxation and transfers, would probably suffice to induce the members of the United Nations to welcome such a proposal.

Finally, while our purpose remains one of advising currently humanistic world

---

Asia, as in similarly dependent Mexico in 1995, has generated massive U.S. and IMF loans to these areas rather than industrial liquidation and natural output reductions. (The difference between the pre-1990s IMF-style foreign-exchange loans discussed in Chapter 5 and these relatively new, longer-term international loans to high-work-ethic countries is that the former were there to support the country's movement toward free trade while the new-style loans are there to support massive increases in industrial production.) The emerging result, of course, imposes a kind of debt-peonage on the future taxpayers in these third-world countries.

leaders, we should contrast our plea for prompt constitutional reform to the advice of a broadly rational strategy that would alternatively be given to more distant future political leaders. It is pleasant to imagine these distant future leaders as possessing their current degrees of humanism. But theory and history do not support such a fantasy. First of all, the ongoing monopsonization of the world's labor force that is withering its middle class would, before long, make a modern-day humanist appear, as did Thomas More or Erasmus in High-Renaissance Europe, to be a hopeless romantic or a dangerous liberal. Secondly, absent the guarantees of a prior world constitution, the likely prospect of several strong nations competing for the enviable position of world hegemon implies, we have seen, that the alternative world leaders would rationally compete by developing and displaying their capacities for human brutality! Recall the dehumanization trends among the rivals for leadership in the early Roman Empire, the competitively re-imperializing 9th and early 10th century heirs of Charlemagne, the many competing confederations of 15th century Italian cities, and the would-be sultans of the Ottoman Empire. We should all want to avoid this pending distributional disaster.

IV. DOES ECONOMICS HAVE ANOTHER LESSON FOR BIOLOGY?

Returning to the biology discussion in Section I.A.10 of Chapter 2, one might well insist that an acid test of the power of any new view of economics is whether it can also help create a new view of biology. Performing such a test also helps lay bare the essentials of our evolutionary argument.[5] Of course, any such test requires some knowledge of the existing view of biology and therefore is not advised to readers who do not at least share our rudimentary knowledge of the subject.

Consider relatively high-surplus, territorial, animals. Like survivable democratic states, we high-surplus animals have long been successful in that our various generations have typically lived our lives at far-above-subsistence levels. Mobile microbiological predators have been continually attracted by our steadily high total biological surpluses and, because they have not been visible to our evolved species, it has been vital that we be hard-wired to defend ourselves against such attacks.

Moreover, since the detrimental microbes have, throughout the evolution of territorial organisms, steadily expanded their cumulative abilities to live off of territorial bodies, our associated immune systems must have been able to keep pace by continually evolving new sorts of immune responses, all the while saving many of the old immune responses to stave-off the increasingly versatile parasitic attacks. To achieve this: (1) the various warriors of our evolved immune systems (like the various warriors of an evolved of mercenary army) are starved to near-extinction and replaced by fresh recruits unless they consume the resources of their defeated

---

[5]By some standards, we already passed this test in Chapter 2 by providing an explanation of the explosive evolution of sophisticated and cost-reducing internal organs prior to the emergence of territorial organisms. The current test is a policy-oriented extension of the associated biological analysis to territorial, Ricardian-rent-receiving, organisms. So the theory in the current test is analogous to our theory of the social evolution of states.

enemies, in which case they multiply and find a much larger presence in the immune army, and, to complement this "simple" immune system, this autonomous, within-organism, harshly Darwinian, form of natural selection, (2) the DNA of previously successful warriors has found ways of traveling from the hostess-mother into her offspring's inherited immune system, thereby creating a strictly Lamarckian inheritance of the previously acquired immunity. In this way, the evolution of the immune systems of territorial organisms have, of necessity, become "adaptive".

Few immunologists would deny that the vital character of the autonomously evolving adaptive immune system is what lies behind both the harshly Darwinian evolution of existing immune cells and the singular Lamarckian process involved in the immunal inheritance systems of territorial animals. The remarkably coordinated, ordinarily quite reliable, interaction that exists among the several different kinds of immune cells is similarly easy to understand as the natural consequence of the vital character of the system.

Besides its unique evolutionary speed and corresponding ability to emulate human societies by continually exploiting both harshly Darwinian and Lamarckian forces, the adaptive immune system is special because of its evolutionary history. Other vital biological organs, including simple immune systems, were all evolved in the Malthusian world that preceded the emergence of territoriality. The constant pressure of living near subsistence, and the correspondingly persistent likelihood of a premature demise, led to the formation of enumerable experimental organisms, the more obvious successes being initially Lamarckian partnerships wherein merging partners were able to cooperatively specialize in their respective comparative advantages for the new, more versatile, organism. But adaptive immune systems were not present in these early, subsistence-living organisms. Adaptive immune systems emerged only about 475 million years ago, just slightly after the emergence of vertebrates and related territorial animals (e.g., Beck and Habicht, G. Litman). This is an elementary implication of our theory. Since an expanding variety of undefended parasitic attacks on a territorial organism was no less deadly than that of the attackers featured in our social theory, it was vital that the early territorial organisms analogously rapidly supply a continuously Lamarckian defense system.[6] In particular, the adaptive immune system can be viewed as originating in a primordial competition between different parasites in which some of the survivors were phagocytes that multiplied by specializing in both the Darwinian consumption of other parasites and a regularly Lamarckian transfer into their host's offspring, thereby kicking-off the necessarily rapid, Lamarck-Darwin, process and creating an

---

[6]The first specific organism in which an adaptive immune system has been found is the long-extinct placoderm (G. Lipman, ibid.), whose evolution into a shark reveals that its initially acquired armor had been made superfluous by its innovative development of a toothy jaw some 480 million years ago. Placoderms were perhaps the first group to totally dominate their environment. This is important because such domination implies a unique potential for territoriality in our sense (viz., "nesting territoriality" (Brown) in that all the totally dominant organism need do to be fully territorial is evolve offspring that, like shark offspring, remain close to their parents.

adaptive immune system.[7]   Without some such evolutionary pattern, territorial animals would never have survived, just as our high-potential-surplus democracies would never have survived, without the timely co-evolution of institutions such as guilds, the gold standard, and certain forms of modern international cooperation.

Our theory also tells us that long-term survival of significant numbers of an organism requires the organism to have evolved a way to receive positive net benefits from their common mobile parasites (e.g., their primordial immune cells) so as to more than offset the costs of harboring such parasites (the benefit being the consumption of more dangerous parasites). Without such a mutualistic relationship, the host organism will evolve to eliminate its non-beneficial common parasites, which invites retaliation by the parasites until one of the two generalized organisms wins the war. Even if the host wins, a new kind of mobile parasite will soon evolve to feed off the organism, etc. Thus, if the primordial host fails to respond to common mobile parasites by re-evolving in order to benefit from the parasites, thereby converting the parasites into welcomed and joint-survival-motivated partners, the continual sequence of wars means that gambler's ruin will sooner or later virtually destroy the organism. Plants, although evolving various chemical defenses against the spread of parasites (Mieras and Leach), have never evolved an immune system. This is true in spite of their approximately 400 million years of territorial existence, which began when plants started spreading large horizontal leaf systems (e.g., Vermeij, p. 19) to claim the underlying turf from other plants. The reason is that, plants, unlike animals, learned very early on to directly consume the by-product of their common parasites. They had little reason, therefore, to import an immune system to consume the more dangerous parasites. Even viruses are generally beneficial to plants in that a territorial plant can secrete toxins to isolate the infected area, drop it off, and directly consume the by-product of the bacteria that feed off of the remains. Animals are more mobile and therefore more attractive to deadly parasites, whose survival requires a convenient mode of transportation. Large-scale animal populations therefore had to co-evolve immune systems.

They have even had to re-evolve these ancient immune systems to account for more advanced levels of warfare. We have, for example, just seen how territorial organisms, whose above-subsistence living attracts an ever-expanding variety of parasites, have had to co-evolve more versatile, regularly Lamarckian as well as Darwinian, "adaptive", immune systems. More recently, surviving species have successfully re-evolved in ways enabling them to: (1) convert their specialized mobile parasites into microbial allies in germ warfare against competing omnivoirs (Ryan, Ch. 16); and (2) convert their common disease germs into allies in fights

---

[7]This Lamarckian effect was no great feat when we discussed the merger of two prokaryotes. However, for the eukaryotic hosts under discussion, it generally requires the transposition of phagocyte DNA into the nuclei of the hosts' germ cells, the penetration of the so-called "Weismann barrier" described in the text below. The recently discovered abundance of the enzyme normally required for this intercellular transposition ("reverse transcriptase") in both Drosophila and virtually all vertebrate genomes is evidence for the early evolutionary significance of such transpositions (e.g., Alberts, et al., pp. 606-09).

against less common, but more deadly, mobile parasites.

This happy story of the rapid evolution of vital defense organs would continue, just as the happy story of our most recent long-term civilizational advance would continue, were it not for the 20th century maturation of advanced professional education, advanced Enlightenment thought. We have already seen how the teacher-serving, and subsequent ruling-class, exaggerations of the value of certain <u>social</u> sciences has systematically disserved the broader society. Shouldn't we expect something similar from the <u>physical</u> sciences?

First, returning to our evolving adaptive immune system, we have seen how surviving territorial animal hosts have been able to keep pace with the rapidly evolving parasites (mainly viruses and bacteria) by combining Lamarckian with Darwinian evolutionary effects. The Lamarckian part of the process includes having the germ-cell chromosomes of the host's semi-autonomous immune system penetrated by experience-evolved DNA. But if a virus could come to imitate the experience-evolved DNA, it, too, could easily enter the host's germ-cell chromosomes. It could thereafter safely remain to employ the machinery of the host cells to send out more and more copies and near-copies of itself to <u>both</u> hosts and their offspring. Such "retroviruses" (so named because of their ability to reverse the usual Weismann process, chromosomal DNA --> RNA --> RNA + protein) eventually disarm the immune system and cause malignant tumors or AIDS, which is currently spreading in pandemic proportions because of the relatively long period during which the virus spreads throughout the blood stream before the adaptive immune system is noticeably incapacitated. Once this viral innovation mutates to where it spreads through the air like the common cold, very few of us will survive (e.g., Ryan, Ch. 19).

Where did these remarkable new imitator-viruses come from? Recent studies uniformly conclude that they came about through the radical increase in the rate of inter-species transfers of infectious organisms introduced by 20th Century immunologists (see, e.g. Myers, et al., and Morse). Thus, regarding the more advanced levels of immunological warfare noted above, professional immunology appears to have initiated, through its perennial abuse of "preventative medicine", a fatal process when it began exposing humans to the deadly viral allies of competing omnivoirs such as monkeys and rodents. In the same demand-creating fashion, modern microbiologists and anti-biotic-prescribing physicians have been ridding us of common germs that, because of their long-term co-existence with us, had presumably been co-evolved with our immune systems to provide us with more than fully offsetting immunological benefits against more deadly actual and potential microbiological aggressors, (e.g., Van Vlem, et al., and Gonzales, et al.)

It took many thousands of years for our species to re-evolve to where we could survive the microbiological attacks of competing species and where we could immunologically benefit from our common microbial parasites. We clearly have insufficient time to naturally evolve new defense systems. So we have been thrust into the middle of an escalating war between our society's increasingly valuable biologists and a whole slew of suddenly dangerous mobile parasites.

More generally, then, perhaps physical scientists can learn from our various studies that evolved defense systems are highly vulnerable to the profession-serving experiments of intellectual leaders. Time and again, dominant states have quickly collapsed from such experiments, from the self-serving and short-sighted failures of educated elites to appreciate the nature of the defense problem and their corresponding failures to appreciate the sophistication and vitalness of their inherited, practically evolved, defense systems. Experience, then, should teach responsible biologists as well as economists that this is not the time for business-as-usual.

V. LIFE IN THE FAST LANE

We should not forget, in the same vein, the bomb-producing physicists and nuclear scientists of the 1930s and early 1940s, who could probably have agreed among themselves to an international cessation of such research in the interest of world safety, but instead wound-up convincing their governmental backers (and somehow themselves) of the controllability of nuclear technology. Or, if that was infeasible, they could have agreed in the late 1940s that only <u>one</u>, constitutionally constrained, country was to have the technology instead of actively <u>encouraging</u> the spread of the technology to the other countries (Albright and Kunstel; Chapman), which set-up a radically science-serving arms race.

Nor is the problem restricted to the subconsciously demand-creating activities of trusted, heavily governmentally supported, scientists. There has also been, through the governmental encouragement of private invention and a worldwide spread of industrial technology, a corresponding acceleration in global warming and worldwide pollution problems. An objective, science-neutral, dominant state would have used its power over taxes, the international patent system, and external loan subsidies to ward off these problems before they became pending technological disasters.

The modern victory of Hellenism over state religion has been wonderfully conducive to efficient large-scale organizations of many varieties. However, as in the ancient world, it has also resulted in exaggerations of the value of professionally produced knowledge in the civilizationally dominant states of the past two and a half centuries. These exaggerations, of course, include the value of the science that is taught to future ruling classes by professional scientists or their students. The predictable dangers of this Enlightenment-style ruling-class overvaluation are now visible at every turn, but especially in the looming disasters, whether biological, nuclear, atmospheric, or economic.[8] Indeed, every one of these broad areas of rapid expansion of post-WWII governmental research support have witnessed a predictably even-more-rapid expansion in the future dangers to our civilization.

This long-term education problem, wherein educated legislators are induced to overvalue the productivity of their society's professional scientists, can be solved, at

---

[8]The Enlightenment, like the analogous mid-17th century spread of laissez faire thought in dominant Holland and the anti-guild-elitism of late 15th century Florence, and late 12th century Byzantium, can thus be thought of as natural children of the Renaissance, which irresistibly tempted its policy-professionals to over-assert their proficiencies to their Hellenistically educated ruling classes. The ease with which the Ancient Roman Empire was able to conquer these once-effective democracies during the late-Hellenistic era (Toynbee, 1959) apparently left no lasting impression on subsequent educators.

some cost, by simply eliminating the non-professional (i.e., undergraduate) teaching role of the scientists, leaving the activity of non-professional instruction to separately and independently trained teaching professionals. But this is a solution that would benefit only <u>future</u> generations of social decisionmakers.

As for the present, we are living life in a fast lane that has been continually growing faster. We cannot simply slow down. There are serious intellectual problems to be solved in all of the above sciences. And both theory and history tell us that we will crash, and fairly soon, if intellectuals do not quickly switch to a much less ideological approach to their problems, an approach induced by a research environment that is rid of its currently severe, worldwide, demand-creating, feature.

VI. AN INTELLECTUAL EFFECT OF THE PROPOSED POLICY

In other words, to survive, we must finally heed the methodological advice of Francis Bacon and J.S. Mill by creating an environment of true intellectual competition, where it is profitable to criticize as demand-creating the exaggerations of one's own colleagues. A timely breaking down of the subtle intellectual hierarchies that have dominated our world's scientific fields since the Enlightenment, an elimination of the gentlemen's agreements that have long preserved the confusion and glorified the nonsense that exists in all of these fields, is not an easy task. Although a theoretically ideal solution, an optimal intellectual anti-monopoly policy, does exist (Thompson, et al., Vol. I, Chs. 1 and 2), its development here would take us far beyond the scope of the current study. However, in solving the problem, we can recommend a significant first step.

A states-rights-type of world constitution, one administered by a world-dominant nation, would not only prevent the unfortunate economic ideology of a currently dominant country from being imposed upon other countries, substantially reduce the profit to global military confrontation, and save the world from an otherwise inexorably distributional trend toward the elimination of its middle classes; it would also substantially reduce the material rewards that now flow from following the intellectual positions of scientific leaders of dominant countries. Under such a constitution, national policymakers would likely guard their intellectual independence with the same healthy jealousies that we currently observe among the states or provinces of a given nation.

While various intranational scientific hierarchies would surely remain profitable, a genuine intellectual competition between national associations would produce a much more logically and factually disciplined, a more open and less ideologically presumptive, debate. International conferences and international policy agreements would continue to be a frequent occurrence. But the participants from the constitutionally independent, non-dominant, separate-policy-forming, nations would face much less of a loss in wealth or status by challenging the logic or facts of the participants from the dominant countries.

Thus, the anti-monopolistic, states-rights-type, dominant-country-administered, decentralized world constitution that we are proposing, while not by itself sufficient to induce an ideal world, would create a more objective intellectual climate as well as eliminate the inevitability of an allocational and distributional disaster.

APPENDIX B.1

SOCIAL INTERACTION UNDER TRULY PERFECT INFORMATION

Earl A. Thompson
University of California, Los Angeles
and
Roger L. Faith
Virginia Polytechnic Institute and State University

1. INTRODUCTION

Classical sociologists have long been distinguished from political philosophers, economists, and other social thinkers by their insistence that orderly social interactions require certain individuals to be governed by "moral principles" or "social values" guiding their responses to others and thereby enforcing the norms of the group. While most social thinkers, including most modern exchange theorists, regard moral principles as merely an incidental part of social reality, the authors of the various classics in sociology -- especially Durkheim (1957), Weber (1978) and Parsons (1937) -- required moral principles to be somehow necessary to the existence of social norms and the creation of order in a Hobbesian jungle. While their views emerged largely out of critical examinations of empirical phenomena, modern interaction theory provides theoretical support for their observation. The consideration leading to this theoretical support is simple: while rewards or punishments are generally necessary to induce certain individuals to behave in the social interest, providing these rewards or punishments -- i.e., "enforcing the social contract" -- requires responses that are ultimately irrational and therefore forthcoming only when some higher moral principle governs the response.[1]

---

[1]The game-theoretic foundations of such arguments have become increasingly clear in recent years (see, e.g., Rapoport and Chammah, 1965; McFarland, 1971; Selten, 1974). Consider a world containing a known future date beyond which social interaction will not occur. Devoting resources to meting out rewards or punishments on this last possible date cannot be narrowly rational because there would be no future behavior to influence and the past behavior, having already occurred, is water over the dam. It would be a waste of time and trouble to reward or punish anyone. Therefore, on the next-to-last conceivable date at which socially relevant actions are chosen, behavior is undisciplined and thoroughly noncooperative. But then it doesn't pay to devote resources to punishing or rewarding behavior in the second-to-last period either because behavior in subsequent dates will be noncooperative anyway. The argument thus proceeds backward in time to the present so that it never pays to cooperate when individuals are rational in the above, narrow sense.

Journal of Mathematical Sociology, 1980, Vol. 7, pp. 181-197
60022-250X/80/0702-0181$06.50/0, Reprint.
© 1980 Gordon and Breach, Science Publishers, Inc.

While a moral principle or ethical code allows an individual to carry out behavior that, at the time of its occurrence, is irrational, there is a prior calculation determining the choice of a particular ethical code. At this level, the choice is not simply a choice among various possible actions. It is a choice among various possible principled reactions to the actions of others, each reaction valued in large part for its effect on the subsequently chosen actions of others. Yet we can find no precise statement of this optimality problem in the literature. Sociologists have apparently not developed their theories of moral principles sufficient to endogenously derive moral principles and the corresponding role sets and norms from a theory of individually rational choice. As a result, they have not provided us with a theory from which we can derive the nature of social institutions and social behavior from basic technological data.

This paper provides a first step in closing this gap in the literature by constructing a "pure" theory of social institutions, a theory stripped of all informational imperfections in order to expose certain underlying tendencies characterizing such systems. The theoretical tendencies we shall derive are very similar to those found in the relatively empirical writings of Weber and, more recently, of numerous sociologists and game theorists. In particular, we find that, under perfect information regarding the reaction functions of others: (1) there is a hierarchy of decisionmakers(Section 2); (2) if everyone has strict preferences over the entire set of social alternatives, the decision hierarchy -- once formed -- will produce economically efficient roles, norms and social actions (Section 3); but (3) substantial resource losses occur in the stratification process (Section 4).

These primary efficiency results suggest that a leader, once established, will attempt to impose systems that reduce the economic wastes due to further stratification without sacrificing the efficiency of the institutions evolved by the lower members of the strata. Along these lines, we shall find that a private property system has this characteristic. That is, a private property system reduces the resource wastes involved in middle-level stratification while still allowing for the creation of efficient, middle-level roles and norms (Section 5). Private property institutions are thus seen to represent systems that reduce the amounts of resources devoted to stratification without sacrificing the natural ability of a "free", or unregulated, social system to develop efficient social institutions.

While private property systems do not deter the achievement of efficient roles and norms by subgroups in the system, when norm selectors are indifferent between more than one solution norm, a special problem arises that requires higher-level intervention in order to assure efficiency. After showing this, we apply the result to an actual historical institution -- slavery -- in order to test some of the detailed workings of the general model (Section 6).

Our secondary efficiency results help explain the survival of hierarchial organizations within private property systems despite their extra stratification costs -- and despite the perennial attacks on their efficiency -- while our primary efficiency results will be seen to offer an explanation for the survival of hierarchial social systems in nature at large (Section 7).

In terms of game theory, our general approach is unusual in that it explicitly models strategic communication. Standard noncooperative game theory does not permit such communication; it allows only the communication of simple actions, leaving the communication of principled reaction functions, i.e., strategies, to be handled by something called "cooperative game theory". Unfortunately, however, cooperative game theory has never developed an explicit communication structure and consequently has not provided us with a consistent theory of how individuals cooperate.

Our particular model of strategic communication is developed for the special case of an unrestricted communication of (and hence, perfect information regarding) the strategies of others. As conventional "perfect information" games have each player perfectly communicating only his actions while our game has perfect communication of both actions and strategies, we label our assumption, for lack of a better term, "truly perfect information". A basic feature distinguishing our game under truly perfect information from cooperative games and "supergames", both of which are designed to allow sufficient communication to prevent Pareto non-optimal solutions, is that we do not assume Pareto optimality to be a characteristic of solutions or of points on rational reaction functions. We even find an exception (the case containing non-strict preferences discussed in Section 6) in which Pareto non-optima may result no matter how perfect the information structure. Also, our solution set, being based on an explicit model of communication of strategies, does not have the problem, chronic in cooperative game theory, of being either empty or too large to be of much practical interest.

Conventional game theory's treatment of the communication of strategies has also been noted and criticized, albeit indirectly, by Schelling (1960) and Howard (1971). Our contributions relative to Schelling's seminal work on 2-person bargaining are: (1) To derive Schelling's game from a prior specification on the information structure; (2) To generalize it to n-players and (3) most important, to characterize the resulting general solutions as to their Pareto optimality and, correspondingly, to apply the model of Pareto optimality to observed social institutions. The fact that these extensions of Prof. Schelling's work on communicated strategies have not been heretofore developed is perhaps because Schelling did not property contrast his implied model with more conventional games. In particular, he failed to note that he was merely applying the standard, von Neumann-Morgenstern, perfect information solution concept to strategies rather than actions (or "plays of a game"). While von Neumann and Morgenstern (1944, Sec. 11.3) explicitly recognized that games could be constructed in which strategies are communicated in the same way as the actions in their perfect information games, they saw nothing novel about such games. For such games posed no new problem in the development of solution concepts or the existence of solutions. We conjecture that had they been more interested in evaluating the Pareto optimality of solution actions, or in formally capturing the microsociology of social institutions, they would have devoted more intellectual resources to games with perfect information concerning strategies as well as actions. But von Neumann and Morgenstern also expressed rather serious doubts about having players rely on the rationality of others, a reliance required by their perfect information solution concept. Their argument supporting these doubts is that it may pay a player to deviate from "rational" responses if he knows that another player's strategy depends on his responses.[2] But it is precisely these deviations which are at the heart of any theory of perfect strategy communication. For example, in Schelling's two-person bargaining problem, the first strategy selector is that player who can first prevent himself from following his narrowly rational responses to the actions of the player and communicate the fact to the other player. Von Neumann and Morgenstern did not see that their justifiable skepticism with respect to their perfect information game leads toward the development of games with truly perfect information rather than toward the imperfect information games which they so elegantly explored.

Prof. Howard's work, developed as a generalization of von Neumann-Morgenstern's majorant-minorant game, has strategies contingent on strategies, thus apparently implying perfect information of strategies. But Howard employs a conventional, Nash-type (Nash, 1951), solution set, where a prior strategy selector takes as given the strategies of subsequent strategy selectors. This is not generally consistent with the model we are presenting, one in which rational prior strategy selectors can communicate their strategies to subsequent strategy selectors. The result is a solution set which lacks the powerful optimality and distributional characteristics of the solution set of a game with truly perfect information (Section 2).[3]

2. THE BASIC MODEL AND ITS SOLUTIONS

2.1 The Physical Environment

An individual is denoted i, $i = 1,...,n$. An action of individual i is denoted x_i, where $x_i \in X_1$, a finite set of feasible actions of individual i. A possible social action is defined by an n-dimensional set of individual actions, and is denoted $x = \{x_1,x_2,...,x_n\}$, so that $x \in \prod_{i=1}^{n} X_i$. To describe individual preferences, each individual, i, is given a complete, transitive, irreflexive, anti-symmetric, binary relation, $\succ_i$, defined over $\prod_{i=1}^{n} X_i$. This description, in effect, assumes away indifference between any pair among the finite set of possible social actions. The motivation for this assumption and the effects of indifference on our central results will be discussed later. A Pareto optimum is a social action, x', $x' \in \prod_{i=1}^{n} X_i$, for

---

[2]von Neumann and Morgenstern (1944, Sec. 4.1.2).

[3]The following two sections follow the first two sections of Thompson and Faith (1980).

which there is no alterative, social action x'', $x'' \in \prod_{i=1}^{n} X_i$, such that $x'' \succ_i x'$ for all i. Several Pareto optima may exist.

2.2 <u>Institutional Possibilities Under Truly Perfect Information</u>

The institutions facing an individual can be completely described by the reactions of other individuals to his own actions. But institutions, or reactions, are not taken here as given; they are derived. This is done by allowing each individual to select, among all feasible reaction functions, a function which is maximal with respect to his preference relation. But we want individuals to <u>know</u> the institutions and thus the reaction functions of others. And for this to generally hold, the functions must be communication in sequence. Thus, for the individuals to know the institutions, i.e., for truly perfect information, the first communicator, say individual 1, presents the reaction function,

$$x_1 = f_1\{x_2,...,x_n\}, \tag{1}$$

to the other individuals; the second communicator, say individual 2, then presents

$$x_2 = f_2\{x_3,...,x_n\} \tag{2}$$

to individuals 3 through n; the third communicator then presents

$$x_3 = f_3\{x_4,...,x_n\} \tag{3}$$

to individuals 4 through n, and so on up to the n-1st communicator, who presents

$$x_{n-1} = f_{n-1}(x_n) \tag{4}$$

to the nth individual, who has no need to communicate. Once the action of the nth individual is taken, the action of the n-1st individual is determined. Once this pair of actions is taken, the action of individual n-3 is determined, and so on up until a social action is determined as a chain reaction from the nth individual's action. The set $(f_1,f_2,...,f_{n-1})$ is thus a complete institutional description. The feasible choice set, or strategy set, of individual 1 is the set of <u>all</u> functions from $\prod_{i=2}^{n} X_i$ to X_1.

This can be represented by the functional variable, F_1. Similarly, $F_2,...,F_{n-1}$ can be used to represent the respective strategy sets of individuals 2 to n-1. The product space, $\prod_{i=1}^{n} F_i$, thus represent the world's institutional possibilities. The strategy set of individual n is X_n.

A question may arise as to why some individuals do not present reactions functions to other individuals who are higher up in the communication hierarchy. Consider individual n. Facing the prior strategies of the other n-1 individuals, he sees that the eventual social action must be consistent with the chosen reaction functions of each of the n-1 prior selectors. Hence, if individual n responds to the prior selectors with a simple action, he will have a free choice over all social actions consistent with the prior reaction functions. But if n responds with a function of prior actions, thus giving further choices to the prior strategy selectors, he can only reduce his original choice out of the same set of possible social actions. He cannot expand the set of possible outcomes because any eventual outcome must be consistent with the given $n-1$ reaction functions. Similarly, if the $n-1^{st}$ strategy selector presents a reaction function rather than an action to his prior strategy selectors for a given action of individual n, he is giving them the choice of actions consistent with the set of reaction functions he faces and thus can be no better off. This also applies, in like fashion, to individuals $n-2$ to 2, so that it is in no individual's interest to present a reaction function to a prior strategy selector.

The above world, which can now be viewed as a "game," differs from the standard, von Neumann-Morgenstern, "perfect information" game in that some individuals are allowed to communicate their strategies to others before the latter select their own strategies. Thus, in the von Neumann-Morgenstern world, a player will not adopt a special strategy in order to influence the subsequent strategies (and actions) of others simply because he cannot communicate it and therefore cannot use it to influence the subsequently chosen strategies. In contrast, in the above world, each of the first $n-1$ players communicates his strategy to all subsequent, strategy selectors. And response strategies of the subsequent selectors are known a priori by the prior strategy selector because they are the rational responses to the given strategy of the prior selector.

While Howard has produced a general class of games (called "jk-metagmes") containing strategies contingent on the strategies of other strategy selectors, he does not assume truly perfect information. Correspondingly, he does not adopt a perfect information solution concept. Rather, he adopts, without substantive justification, the von Neumann-Morgenstern-Nash "no-regret" solution concept in which each strategy selector accepts as given the strategies of all other strategy selectors. This amounts, as Howard recognizes, to assuming uniformly zero information regarding the strategies of others at the time of strategy selection. For if the choice of strategy selector were perceived by subsequent strategy selectors, it would, in general, influence the latter's selections. Such games, besides being theoretically unsatisfying in that they typically generate a multiplicity of solution points, some of which are optimal and other non-optimal (Howard, p. 58), are empirically unsatisfying in that observed commitments are, as pointed out in the Introduction, typically communicated to others in order to influence their strategy selections.

It may be convenient to think of this problem as one in classical sociology: The individuals are pre-stratified according to their "power", or ability to influence others. The individuals above the lowest stratum can "punish" certain "deviant" behavior of others, thereby serving as members of "reference groups" who induce others to conform to certain "norms", i.e., to adopt particular actions. The middle-status individuals are in turn punished by higher-ups in ways that induce them to adopt certain "roles", i.e., to select certain reaction functions. After defining solution norms and roles, we shall look for certain properties of these solutions. Due largely to our previous work in economics, we look for economic efficiency, or Pareto optimality, properties. After that we inquire into the process of stratification and the efficiency problems that arise therefrom. The last few sections of the paper deal with the efficiency properties of various extensions of the basic model. Because we wish to avoid terminological squabbles, and also because we are hoping for an audience beyond sociology, we shall maintain our rather neutral terminology instead of adopting that of classical sociology.

2.3 Equilibrium Institutions, or "Solutions", Under Truly Perfect Information

A solution, $(f_1^*,...,f_{n-1}^*,x_n^*)$, is a set in which the ith variable is maximal with respect to $\succ_i$ for given values of $f_1,...,f_{i-1}$. A solution can be constructed as follows: first we find, for individual n, x_n^*, the point in X_n such that, for all $x_n \neq x_n^*$,

$$(f_1(f_2,...,f_{n-1},x_n^*), f_2(f_3,...,f_{n-1},x_n^*),...,x_n^*) \succ_n$$

$$(f_1(f_2,...,f_{n-1},x_n), f_2(f_3,...,f_{n-1},x_n),...,x_n).$$

This solution determines a dependency of x_n^* on $f_1,f_2,...,f_{n-1}$, which we write $x^*[f_1,...,f_{n-1}]$. Then, for individual n-1, we find a reaction function, f_{n-1}^*, such that for all $f_{n-1} \in F_{n-1}$, $f_{n-1} \neq f_{n-1}^*$,

$$(f_1\{f_2,...,f_{n-2},f_{n-1}^*,x_n^*[f_1,...,f_{n-2},f_{n-1}^*]\}, ...,$$

$$f_{n-2},f_{n-1}^*,x_n^*[f_1,...,f_{n-2},f_{n-1}^*]) \succ_{n-1}$$

$$(f_1\{f_2,...,f_{n-2},f_{n-1},x_n^*[f_1,...,f_{n-2},f_{n-1}]\}, ...,$$

$$f_{n-2},f_{n-1},x_n^*[f_1,...,f_{n-2},f_{n-1}])$$

This solution determines the dependency of f_{n-1}^* on $f_1,f_2,...$ and f_{n-2}, which we describe as $f_{n-1}^*[f_1,...,f_{n-2}]$. Then for individual n-2, we find a reaction function, f_{n-2}^*, such that, for all $f_{n-2} \in F_{n-2}$, $f_{n-2} \neq f_{n-2}^*$,

$$(f_1\{f_2,...,f_{n-2}^*,f_{n-1}^*[f_2,...,f_{n-2}^*].x_n^*[f_1,...,f_{n-2}^*,f_{n-1}^*[f_1,...,f_{n-2}^*])\}$$

$$...,f_{n-2}^*,f_{n-1}^*[f_1,...,f_{n-2}^*],x_n^*[f_1,...,f_{n-2}^*,f_{n-1}^*[f_1,...,f_{n-2}^*]]) \succ_{n-2}$$

$$(f_1\{f_2,...,f_{n-2},f_{n-1}^*[f_1,...,f_{n-2}],x_n^*[f_1,...,f_{n-2},f_{n-1}^*]f_1,...,f_{n-2}])\},$$

$$...,f_{n-2},f_{n-1}^*[f_1,...,f_{n-2}],x_n^*[f_1,...,f_{n-2},f_{n-1}^*[f_1,...,f_{n-2}]]).$$

This solution thus determines the dependency of f_{n-2}^* on $f_1,f_2,...$, and f_{n-3}, which we write as $f_{n-2}^*[f_1,...,f_{n-3}]$. The process continues until we have determined f_1^*. Since f_1^* does not depend on any prior functions, we can use it to determine the succeeding reaction functions by successively substituting starred values into $f_2^*[f_1]$, $f_3^*[f_1,f_2]$, and $f_{n-1}^*[f_1,f_2,...,f_{n-2}]$.

In this way, a solution, $(f_1^*,f_2^*,...,x_n^*)$, which implies a social choice, $(x_1^*,x_2^*,...,x_n^*)$, is determined.

The finite structure of the successive maximization problems, along with the completeness and transitivity of $\succ_i$, assures us that a solution <u>always</u> exists.

3. PARETO OPTIMALITY

Besides unqualified existence, the solution has the important property of Pareto optimality. That is, institutions formed under truly perfect information always imply Pareto optimal allocations.

To prove this, suppose the solution allocation, $(x_1^*,...,x_{n-1}^*,x_n^*) = x^*$, is not Pareto optimal. Then there is a point, $x^o = \{x_1^o,...,x_n^o\} \in \prod\limits_{i=1}^{n} X_i$ such that $x^o \succ_i x^*$ for all i. A set of reaction functions generating x^o as a social action is given by $(f_1^o,...,f_{n-1}^o)$. Of course, $(f_1^*,...,f_{n-1}^*,x_n^o) \neq \{f_1^o,...,f_{n-1}^o,x_n^o)$, otherwise x^o would be the solution. Now let individual 1 consider:

(A) $f_1\{f_2,...,f_{n-1},x_n\} = \left\{ \begin{array}{l} f_1^o \ \text{if} \ (f_2,...,f_{n-1},x_n) = (f_2^o,...,f_{n-1}^o,x_n^o) \\[2mm] f_1^* \ \text{otherwise.} \end{array} \right.$

This may induce each subsequent strategy selector to reorder his strategy in $f_2,...,$ f_{n-1}^o,x_n^o relative to $f_2^*,...,f_{n-1}^*,x_n^*$. However, as it does not alter the social actions resulting from non-solution strategies <u>other than</u> $f_2^o,...,f_{n-1}^o,x_n^o$, it does not alter anyone's ordering of these other strategies relative to $f_2^*,...,f_{n-1}^*,x_n^*$. Therefore, because $x^o \succeq x^*$, individual 1 is no worse off under (A) than under his original strategy.

We next let individual 2 consider, in view of (A),

(B) $f_2\{f_3,...,f_{n-1},x_n\} = \left\{ \begin{array}{l} f_2^o \ \text{if} \ (f_3,...,x_n) = (f_3^o,...,x_n^o) \\[2mm] f_2^* \ \text{otherwise.} \end{array} \right.$

This similarly cannot hurt individual 2. We continue on to individual n, who now faces (A),(B),.... Thus, $(f_1^o,...,f_{n-1}^o,x_n^o) = x^o$ will result if he picks $x_n = x_n^o$; and $(f_1^*,...,f_{n-1}^*,x_n^*)$ if he picks his solution action. Since $x^o \succ_n x^*$, he picks the former. The supposition that there is a Pareto non-optimal solution is thus immediately contradicted: For the supposition implies that the players individually prefer a non-solution set of strategies $(f_1^o,...,f_{n-1}^o,x_n^o)$ to the solution set, $(f_1^*,...,f_{n-1}^*,x_n^*)$.

4. STRATIFICATION

There is, in general, a significant advantage to being the first to establish a reaction function. If, for example, any individual can adopt actions that punish any single other individual sufficiently that the other individual would be better-off serving as a slave than suffering the punishment, then the equilibrium social action is that most desired by the first strategy selector (Thompson & Faith, 1980, Pt. IV). Correspondingly, there is a game, preceding our own, representing a competition to be the first strategy selector. This higher-order game is a generally inefficient, war-like, Nash-VNM noncooperative affair because strategic communication is -- by definition -- not yet established. The obvious qualities conducive to winning this game are the abilities to: (a) inflict physical punishment on potential competitors while withstanding their attacks, (b) adopt flexibly moral principles assuring broadly rational (but narrowly irrational) responses and (c) act benevolent toward potential competitors under normal conditions in order to reduce their net profit from challenging the leader. The resource wastes involved in this competition, while of some descriptive-historical significance (Section 7), are socially unavoidable and of no direct relevance to social policy. Regarding the potential resource wastes involved in acquiring subsequent hierarchial positions, several theoretical reasons exist to believe that these possible resource wastes are insignificant. For one, the first strategy selector, aware of the possibility of such waste, may use his prior commitment ability to assign the remaining hierarchial positions, punishing individuals who attempt to deviate from their assigned status. For another, since the return to hierarchial positions below the first is plausibly insignificant in our world (Thompson & Faith, Pt. IV), significant resources would not be devoted to acquire such positions.

However, the analysis, to apply beyond family and small village societies, must admit the possibility that several individuals have substantial informational advantage over the first strategy selector. Once this is admitted, certain, systematic changes appear in the subsequently chosen reaction functions. In particular, the subsequent strategy selectors, being sometimes able to escape the discipline of a reaction by prior selectors and also being generally less wealthy and therefore less generous toward the lower strata than the prior selectors, will adopt reaction functions generating solution norms that are systematically less beneficial to the lower strata (and, of course, more beneficial to themselves) than the reaction functions under truly perfect information. In other words, the members in the middle of the decision hierarchy will tend to "exploit their power positions" over the lower members. This not only produces solutions that differ from our own, optimal solution, it gives these decisionmakers an incentive to devote resources to hiding their true reaction functions from higher authorities in an attempt to gain personal redistributions from those lower in the social hierarchy. This latter effect generates pure economic waste. Similarly, efficient middle-level decisionmakers would tend to be competed out of their position by less efficient decisionmakers who are, nonetheless, relatively talented at deception.

The first strategy selector, understanding this problem, should then look for special institutions or reaction functions in order to reduce these economically wasteful, and, to him, distributively undesirable tendencies. If, for example, he imposes a common-law private-property system, a system with tort and contract law provisions serving to compensate those whose centrally determined "endowments" are somehow reduced by the actions of others, he can limit the ability of middle-level members of the hierarchy to punish lower level members in order to obtain redistribution benefits from them and, at the same time, assure certain minimum benefit levels for the lower strata of the social decision hierarchy. While institutions other than common-law private-property -- e.g., central direction of final consumption activities or enforced egalitarianism -- could also achieve these goals, private property systems free the central authority from the job of figuring out the various preferences of the others while allowing more informed individuals to cooperate in a less centralized fashion. The key question that arises, however, is: Does a private property constraint distort reaction functions in the ways that induce inefficient allocative solutions? The following section shows that the answer is negative -- that perfect cooperation achieves a Pareto optimum despite a common-law private property constraint. In economics, this theorem, although heretofore more of a conjecture than a theorem, is called the "Coase Theorem".

When communication between various, higher-level decisionmakers is costly, serious inefficiency problems arise that are alleviated -- both theoretically and empirically -- by other institutional selections of the first strategy selector (Thompson & Faith, Pt. IV). A discussion of this would take us into the history of social organization and thus be beyond the scope of this paper.

5. THE PARETO OPTIMALITY OF INTRAGROUP INTERACTION UNDER PRIVATE PROPERTY AND TRULY PERFECT INFORMATION

We now let n be a subset of a larger group that has imposed a private property constraint on the interactions between the n individuals. The constraint has the

effect of limiting the set of feasible social actions to $\prod_{i=1}^{n} \bar{x}$, the subset of $\prod_{i-1}^{n} x$

such that no one can be made worse off than he would be under a certain, "endowed"

set of benchmark actions, x^B, $x^B \in \prod_{i=1}^{n} X_1$. That is, private property restricts social

actions to the set,

$$\prod_{i=1}^{n} \bar{X}_i = \{x \in \prod_{i=1}^{n} X_i: \text{ either } x = x_B \text{ or } x \succ_i x^B \text{ for all } i\}.$$

While this constraint may dramatically alter the solution social choice, the alteration being obtained by replacing the original X-constraint with an $\bar{X}$-constraint, the altered solution is still Pareto optimal.

Our proof of this is a simple variant of the above proof for the unconstrained case: Suppose the new solution $\bar{x}^*$ is not Pareto optimal. Then there is an x^0

$\in \prod_{i=1}^{n} X_i$ such that $x^o \succ_i \bar{x}^*$ for all i. Individual 1 could, as in the Section 3 proof, be no worse off with an altered reaction function that delivered x_1^o if everyone else chose his part of x^o and $\hat{f}_1^*$ otherwise. Since $x^o \succ_i \bar{x}^*$ for all i and $\succ_i$ is transitive, $x^o \succ_i x^B$ for all i so the private property constraint cannot be violated by 1's altered reaction function. This is the key. Individual 2 similarly has a feasible reaction function that he could be no worse-off choosing in which he selects x_2^o if the subsequent strategy selectors choose their parts of x^o but $\hat{f}_2^*$ otherwise. This continues on to individual n, who would rationally pick x^o instead of $\bar{x}^*$, thereby contradicting the supposition that $\bar{x}^*$ is a Pareto non-optimal solution.

The most immediate application of this secondary optimality result is apparently to hierarchial organizations such as are found in firms and small societies within a private property system. The results suggest that, except for deadweight resource costs in the process of establishing hierarchial position, such organizations produce Pareto optimal decisions. This, perhaps, explains the persistent survival of bureaucratic, hierarchial forms of organization despite the perennial intellectual attacks on their efficiency.

Since, however, strategic communication costs are obviously not trivial, we should consider an alternative form of organization suggested by the use of the polar alternative, game-theoretic assumption of zero information with respect to the strategies of others. Here, a Nash solution is appropriate. The incentive system inducing actions that are Pareto optimal from the standpoint of the firm under this assumption is equivalent to one which pays each decisionmaker in the firm the entire total profits of the firm and has these decisionmakers pay lump sums for the right to join the firm. [This is related to the incentive system of Groves (1973). It has the important advantage of solving the "shirking" problem emphasized by Alchian-Demsetz (1972).] But we do not observe these "optimal" incentive systems! The reason is presumably that the Nash assumptions which underlie their "optimality" are completely untenable. That is, under such incentive systems, there would be an irresistible incentive to members of the organization to communicate strategies and thus cooperate so as to induce substantial overworking by the group. The fact that these "optimal" incentive systems have been rejected in favor of hierarchial systems in real world organization therefore provides strong empirical evidence for the applicability of our strategic communication assumptions relative to Nash assumptions to analyze behavior within organizations.

When communication between subgroups is sufficiently costly and hence rare, these groups, empirically speaking, become labelled separate "organizations", and, at the same time, Nash assumptions become appropriate in describing certain interactions between these organizations. Correspondingly, the first strategy selector may find different kinds of institutions desirable in responding to inter-organizational interactions. An analysis of such institutions is beyond the scope of this paper (see Thompson & Faith, Pt. IV, for such an analysis).

6. THE DIFFICULTIES PRESENTED BY INDIFFERENCE

If someone other than the first strategy selector were indifferent between two or more possible solution strategies, a prior selector, who would otherwise have no way of knowing what the indifferent one would do, would -- assuming that he could perform a reaction that would leave this later selector uniformly worse off than in a solution -- simply adjust his reactions to all but one of the later-selected strategies so as to make these strategies suboptimal for the later selector. The resulting solution in this case is also Pareto optimal, as can be seen by noting that our above optimality proof also applies here as long as the Pareto dominating strategy used in the proof is still feasible, which is the case because no prior strategy selector, in inducing a specific choice of a later selector between strategies about which the later selector would otherwise be indifferent, would eliminate a Pareto superior strategy choice.

However, when the <u>first</u> strategy selector is indifferent, Pareto non-optima may easily arise. Consider the "slave master's insensitivity" payoff matrix illustrated in Figure 1. The standard, VNM-Nash, no-regret solution has the slave resting while the master insults the slave; this is both non-optimal <u>and</u> empirically unrealistic: The solution set under perfect strategic communication, with the master as the first strategy selector, contains the Pareto optimum (10,0) where the master will beat the slave if he rests and leave him alone if he works. But the set also contains (10,-4), as the master may also insult the slave, lowering the slave's benefit to -4 without altering either the master's payoff or the slave's optimal decision. (The point, (10,-4), is obviously Pareto inferior to (10,0).) To see this, set up the majorant of the payoff matrix (Figure 2), which defines, in the master's column, the F_1 functional. A standard, VNM, perfect information solution -- which has the player with the expanded strategy set waiting for the other play to move first -- has the slave choosing between his two actions on the basis of what the master's best response would be. This would obviously lead to the (1,0) solution where the slave doesn't work and the master insults the slave, a quite unsatisfactory solution. Our game -- which differs in that the player with the expanded strategy set is the first to move -- has the master picking f_1^*, that f such that the slave's best response yields the maximum payoff to the master. It is easy to see using Figure 2, that only f^{VI} and f^{IX} will assure the master of his maximal payoff, 10. Since the master is indifferent between these two strategies, he may pick either. Since the slave is clearly worse off at f_1^{VI}, where he gets -4, then he is at f_1^{IX}, where he gets 0, the solution set obviously contains a Pareto nonoptimal as well as a Pareto optimal point.

The exercise of Section 3 can be repeated for a weak preference relation to show that if x^*, a Pareto nonoptimum, is a solution, so is x°. Hence, although the solution set with weak preference relations may sometimes contain a Pareto nonoptimal point, it must always also contain a Pareto optimum.

Because all standard <u>competitive</u> equilibria are Pareto optimal, economists have grown accustomed to the thought that individual indifference between various possible equilibria is unimportant. But, as individual indifference between the possible equilibria of a master-slave relationship can induce Pareto nonoptima, we should guard against the habit of ignoring solution indifference when examining decentralized slave economies. Apparently, the real world has not ignored the

FIGURE 1: The Slave Master's Insensitivity -- Actions and Payoffs

		WORK x_2'	REST x_2''
BEAT THE SLAVE	x_1'	5,-10	0,-6
INSULT THE SLAVE	x_1''	10,-4	1,0
LEAVE THE SLAVE ALONE	x_1'''	10,0	0,4

(Master/Slave)

problem. As our model would predict, observed decentralized slavery systems have arisen only through the capture of social "outsiders" toward which initial benevolence could hardly have been widespread among insiders (Finlay, 1972) and have dissolved not by slave uprisings or voluntary manumissions but, at least in modern times, by the intervention of politically powerful humanitarians armed with a "moral argument" (*ibid.*) based on examples in which slaves were torn from their families, worked to death, tortured, or broken of spirit for the minor conveniences of their only mildly benevolent, and therefore effectively indifferent, masters. Thus, as predicted by the model, solution indifference created inefficiencies only when the leaders were also indifferent; when the leaders lost their indifference, the institution permitting the inefficiencies was dissolved. While abolition has sometimes also served to redistribute away from the masters, as it did in the American South, albeit gradually, in view of the slow pace of Southern Reconstruction, in most cases freed slaves have become serfs or debt-peons who provide about the same benefit as do slaves to the capitalist class (*ibid.*). The social advantage of serfdom and debt-peonage is that they prevent local slave master's insensitivity problems, the former having central authorities rigidly controlling the taxation of the immobile serfs and the latter, by granting a choice of creditor-employers to the peon, inducing the prospective employers to compete away payment systems which harm the worker without benefiting the employer.

7. BIOLOGICAL APPLICATION

The optimality results also have some descriptive, biological relevance to the entire population. To illustrate this, we add the following biological assumptions: (1) each player's payoff is an increasing function of only the survival probabilities of himself and, perhaps, some others in his n-player group; (2) the "action", x, which determines survival probabilities, include the physical characteristics of the

FIGURE 2: Normal Form of the Slave Master's Insensitivity

f_1	MASTER \ SLAVE		
f_1^i	x_1'	5,-10	0,-6
f_1^{II}	x_1''	10,-4	1,0
f_1^{III}	x_1'''	10,0	0,4
f_1^{IV}	$x_1' \mid x_2', x_2'' \mid x_2''$	5,-10	1,0
f_1^{V}	$x_1' \mid x_2', x_1''' \mid x_2''$	5,-10	0,4
f_1^{VI}	$x_1''' \mid x_2', x_1' \mid x_2''$	10,-4	0,-6
f_1^{VII}	$x_1'' \mid x_2', x_1''' \mid x_2''$	10,-4	0,4
f_1^{VIII}	$x_1''' \mid x_2', x_2'' \mid x_2''$	10,0	1,0
f_1^{IX}	$x_1''' \mid x_2', x_1' \mid x_2''$	10,0	0,-6

NOTE: "$x_1^\phi \mid x_2^\psi$" means "player 1 chooses x_1^ϕ if player 2 chooses x_2^ψ.

players (i.e., their size, shape, mobility, etc.) In other words, each player is considered an abstract, amorphous unit that selects strategies defined over physical characteristics and behavior patterns so as to maximize its survival probability.

If preferences (i.e., survival probabilities) over x were identical for all players, there would be no conflict as all players would share the same set of optimal actions, x*. Each player, i, would rationally select x_i^*, and there would be no need for reaction functions (i.e., social institutions). Indeed, the "players" representing the vital parts of living creatures have such preferences. The heart and lungs of a given person share a common survival probability so that their abstract representations need no reaction function to achieve a joint optimum. To avoid these situations, we combine such "players" into units, thereby shortening our list of relevant players to include only those with unique preferences over x.

Applying our central optimality theorem, with exogenously fixed hierarchial positions, the social equilibrium has the property that there is no alternative set of physical characteristics or behavior patterns such that the survival probability is greater for at least one player and no lower for the others. This helps explain the marked tendency toward group efficiency and apparent self-sacrifice in nature (e.g., Wynne-Edwards, 1963) without resorting to implausible group-selection arguments. [See Ghiselin, 1974, for a critical evaluation of such arguments.]

As indicated above in Section 4, the mere existence of our process induces a higher-order competition for hierarchial position favoring those with characteristics of battle superiority, benevolence, and abilities to carry out reactions despite their narrow irrationality. Hence, the general theory also helps explain the socially inefficient, competitive evolution of size, speed and cunning observed by Darwin and others, the concomitant survival of extra-familial benevolence among possible leaders (e.g., Lorenz, 1964), and the survival of socially instinctive behavior towards carrying out one's promise, such as emotion-induced, punitive reactions (e.g., Dawkins, 1976).

An example indicating how joint efficiency tends to emerge once hierarchial positions are fixed may be helpful. Many modern biologists (especially Maynard Smith, 1971, and Dawkins) consider the phenomenon of sex (or meiosis) somewhat of a paradox in the absence of group selection because, put in our own, crude terms, the abstract player-female appears to have a much higher chance of survival if all, rather than half, of the offspring which she nurtures have her own, female, characteristics. While the greater biological flexibility of the offspring in the world with sex produces a somewhat higher survival probability for each of the offspring (e.g., Ghiselin), there are many examples in nature in which sexual and asexual units live stable existences with almost indistinguishable physical characteristics other than their differing reproductive apparatus (Dawkins, Ghiselin). Why wouldn't the asexual organisms in these circumstances compete out the sexual organisms, the female has only insignificant use for the male. But what makes the survival and predominance of sexual reproduction a paradox is a Nash assumption. Once we allow males to commit themselves to physically punish shirking or asexual females (in patriarchal societies) or (in matriarchies) allow females to commit themselves to punish males who do not participate in child rearing (or otherwise compensate the females), then it is easy to see that jointly efficient, sexual individuals will not be driven out by the self-interested calculation of those who specialize in child-rearing.

Similar arguments apply to explain the supposedly paradoxical existence of "warning coloration" and other such self-sacrificial characteristics (Wynne-Edwards), characteristics that cannot be easily explained with conventional Nash assumptions.

ACKNOWLEDGEMENTS

The authors benefitted substantially from discussion with Armen Alchian, Ron Batchelder, Phil Bonacich, Jack Hirshleifer, David McFarland, Louis Makowski, Joe Ostroy, and Lloyd Shapley.

REFERENCES

Alchian, Armen A., and Harold M. Demsetz, "Production, Information Costs, and Economic Organization," American Economic Review, 62, 1972.

Dawkins, R., The Selfish Gene, NY: Oxford University Press, 1976.

Durkheim, Emile, Professional Ethics and Civic Morals, London: Routledge, 1957.

Finlay, M.I., "The Origins of Slavery", in A.W. Winks (ed.), Slavery: A Comparative Perspective, NY: New York University Press, 1972.

Ghiselin, M.T., The Economy of Nature and the Evolution of Sex, Berkeley, CA: University of California Press, 1974.

Groves, Theodore, "Incentives in Teams," Econometrica, 41, 1973.

Howard, Nigel, Paradoxes of Rationality, Cambridge: MIT Press, 1971.

Lorenz, V.Z., "Ritualized Fighting," in J.D. Carthy and F.J. Ebling (eds.) The Natural History of Aggression, NY: Academic Press, 1964.

Maynard Smith, J., "What Use is Sex?" Journal of Theoretical Biology, 30, 1971.

McFarland, David D., "Notes on the Hobbesian Problem of Order: Individual Rationality, Collective Rationality, and Social Control in Prisoner's Dilemma Type Situations," unpublished ms., 1971.

Nash, John, "Noncooperative Games," Annals of Mathematics, 54, 1951.

Parsons, Talcott, The Structure of Social Action, NY: The Free Press, 1937.

Rapoport, A., and A.M. Chammah, Prisoner's Dilemma, Anne Arbor, MI: University of Michigan Press, 1965.

Schelling, Thomas C., The Strategy of Conflict, Cambridge, MA: Harvard University Press, 1963.

Selten, Reinhart, "The Chain-Store Paradox," WP #18, Institute of Mathematical Economics, University of Bielefeld, 1974.

Thompson, E.A., and R.L. Faith, "A Pure Theory of Strategic Behavior and Social Institutions," American Economic Review, in press, 1980.

von Neumann, J., and O. Morgenstern, Theory of Games and Economic Behavior, 3rd ed., NY: John Wiley, 1944.

Weber, Max, Economy and Society, Berkeley, CA: University of California Press, 1978.

Wynne-Edwards, V.C., Animal Dispersion in Relation to Social Behavior, NY: Hofner, 1963.

Taxation and National Defense

Earl A. Thompson

UCLA

Contrary to traditional models of national expenditures and taxation, national defense is not a consumer or a producer good. Rather it is a good produced to protect the ownership of other goods from foreign takeover. Using a model of international distributional equilibrium containing national defense and aggression decisions, a Pareto-optimal national tax structure is derived. The entire U.S. tax structure is then shown to be roughly equivalent to the optimal structure. This empirical result indicates that the U.S. political system has somehow been able to create a roughly efficient tax structure in spite of the systematic misguidance of economists.

In the traditional theory of national taxation, the government provides only collective consumer or producer goods. Because governmental provision of such goods does not alter any of the familiar necessary conditions for the efficient utilization of the resources remaining for private use, efficient taxation when the private-goods sector is perfectly competitive is achievable only with lump-sum taxes (such as head taxes, land taxes, or equal, ad valorem taxes on all consumer benefits). Any tax other than a lump-sum tax yields violations of the familiar necessary conditions for achieving Pareto optimality given the resources remaining for private use.

In the real world, lump-sum taxes have been consistently rejected despite the *obiter dictum* of the traditional theory of taxation.

This paper begins with a development of a theory of efficient national taxation in a world in which each government provides collective defense of the property of its citizens. While the traditional model is frequently

This research was supported by a Lilly Foundation grant for the study of property rights at UCLA. The author benefited from comments on previous drafts made by Armen Alchian, Arnold Harberger, Louis Makowski, Bob Rooney, and a referee of this *Journal*.

alleged to apply to collective defense, it is an error to describe collective defense as a collective consumer or producer good. A tank is neither a consumer nor a producer good. In the descriptively more accurate model of collective defense developed in Section I below, the private accumulation of certain kinds of capital creates an extra defense burden for the country protecting that capital. Efficient taxes are then not lump sum taxes; efficient taxes discriminate against the accumulation of capital that is coveted by potential foreign aggressors.

Section II shows that the optimal capital tax is achieved by the use of a simple income tax complemented by: (1) realistic depreciation allowances, (2) tax write-offs for charity and abnormal, noncosmetic, medical expenses, and (3) a theoretically specified, positive: (a) percentage depletion allowance to natural resource owners, (b) degree of progression in the income tax rates, (c) minimum income exemption for each individual and his dependents on his income tax, (d) corporate-profits tax, (e) excise tax on each consumer durable, and (f) tax break on capital gains.

In contrast, in the traditional economic theories of government expenditures and taxation all of these special features of the income tax—and the income tax itself—are inconsistent with a Pareto optimum.[1]

Section II also presents rough-and-ready quantitative estimates of the six optimal rates in consideration 3 above. The results are compared with actual U.S. rates and indicate a striking degree of overall efficiency of the U.S. tax structure. Our recommendations for policy changes have relatively minor effects on economic incentives.

The results raise the question of what in the U.S. political system has permitted the evolution of such an efficient tax structure in spite of the fact that the only existing tax theories deprecate every major feature of the structure.

I. The Basic Model

The Environment

We shall employ a capital model with discrete time, an infinite horizon, no joint production, and perfect knowledge about the environment.[2]

---

[1] Samuelson (1964) has attempted to provide some kind of rationalization of realistic depreciation allowances in an apparently traditional environment, but we shall find a simple economic error in his exercise. Also, some authors have assumed that an income tax does not generate a "double taxation of savings" and an inefficiently discriminating tax on future (relative to present) consumption in the traditional model. Since the double tax is only on the interest from savings in the traditional model and there may be a zero interest rate, these authors can be defended, but only in a special case.

[2] The central results in this paper have also been established for a mathematically less familiar model containing continuous-time and Marshallian joint production, although dropping this assumption requires a substitute assumption, as noted at the

corresponding to original creation for a natural resource. Because tax collectors cannot be assumed to know the value of the natural resource at any given date in the past, they cannot be assumed to know the change in its value over time. However, once a natural resource is utilized by converting it into some other good by an act of withdrawal from nature, there is, we assume, always a sale of the withdrawn resource. Hence, the obvious method of achieving the effects of a tax on the accumulation of natural resources is to apply taxes at withdrawal in a way which subsidizes early withdrawal. The ordinary income tax does not do what it may appear to—tax early withdrawal—because the profit from withdrawal increases with the rate of interest so that delaying withdrawal merely increases future taxes by the rate of interest and has no tax-saving or tax-increasing effect in a world with a constant income tax rate. Obversely, a subsidy to net withdrawal income would not encourage early withdrawal. We can specify a tax or subsidy on transactions which will encourage early withdrawal only after specifying some special, technological features of the natural resource industry.

In particular, (a) in producing a natural resource for next year, the only input one uses is the same resource in the current year, and (b) the amount of the natural resource produced is identical to the amount of the resource devoted to its production. That is,

$$K_{nt+1}^i \equiv I^{nti} \equiv K_{nnt}^{ii}, \tag{39}$$

where n is the natural resource. From this and (18), in an optimum,

$$P_{nt}(1 + a_{nt}) = P_{nt+1} = P_t C_n^t. \tag{40}$$

Similarly, the same physical units of natural resources become consumable once they are withdrawn so that, letting Q_t^i be i's withdrawal of natural resources in time t, $P_{Qt} K_{nQt}^i$ represents the consumption value of the withdrawn resource. It follows that

$$P_{Qt} - P_{nt}(1 + a_{nt}) = P_{Qt} - P_{nt+1}$$

is the direct withdrawal cost per unit of the resource assuming linear homogeneous withdrawal functions.[11] Thus,

$$P_t C_n^t = \frac{P_{Qt} \, \partial K_{nQt}}{\partial K_{nCt}} - (P_{Qt} - P_{nt+1}) = P_{nt+1}$$

[11] Thus, an implicit production function for j, a withdrawer of natural resources, can be written:

$$Q^{tj} = \min\, [K_{nQt}^j, g^t(K_{1Qt}^j, \ldots K_{n-1Qt}^j, K_{n+1Qt}^j, \ldots K_{MQt}^j)],$$

where Q is the withdrawn resource. If we select "derivatives" of this function to be such that (6) and (7) are satisfied, as we are free to do, this specification is not inconsistent with our general model. The cost of g^t is the "withdrawal cost" described above, while

$$P_{Qt} Q^{tj} = P_{Qt} K_{nQ}^j = P_t C_t^{tj}.$$

as in (40) above. Finally, there is the observation that the spot price of withdrawn natural resources has not substantially changed over time (see Barnett and Morse 1963). Thus we can write $P_{Q_t} = P_t$ and $Q_t^i = C_t^i = K_{nQ_t}^i$ for a withdrawer of a natural resource.

With a constant spot price of the withdrawn natural resource, an obvious encouragement to natural resource exploitation (when there is a positive marginal rate of time preference) is a subsidy which is a fixed percentage of the revenue from the sales of the withdrawn natural resource. For the producer would rather have a given subsidy this year than next. Thus we set

$$X_{nt} = \lambda P_t K_{nt}^{im}. \tag{41}$$

The λ is the "percentage depletion rate."[12] Hence,

$$T_b^{ni} = \sum_t b_{nt}[P_t C_n^t(K_{nt}^i - K_{nnt}^{ii}) - \lambda P_t(K_{nt}^i - K_{nnt}^{ii})]. \tag{42}$$

Using (39) and (40),

$$T_b^{ni} = \sum_t b_{nt}(P_{nt+1} - \lambda P_t)(K_{nt}^i - K_{nt+1}^i). \tag{43}$$

Assuming $b_{nt} = b_n$ and using (40) and (19),

$$T_b^{ni} = b_n(P_{n2} - \lambda P_1)K_{nt}^{i*}$$
$$+ \sum_t b_n\left[P_{nt+1}(1 + a_{nt+1}) - \lambda P_t\left(\frac{1}{1 + \rho_t}\right)\right]K_{nt+1}^i$$
$$- \sum_t b_n(P_{nt+1} - \lambda P_t)K_{nt+1}^i, \tag{44}$$

or

$$T_b^{ni} = b_n(P_{n2} - \lambda P_1)K_{nl}^{i*} + b_n\sum_t\left(a_{nt+1}P_{nt+1} + \frac{\lambda\rho_t P_t}{1 + \rho_t}\right)K_{nt+1}^i. \tag{45}$$

Hence, for an optimal tax, letting the first lump-sum term in (45) be absorbed in T^{oi} and using (32),

$$a_{t+1}^o = b_n^o\left(a_{t+1}^o + \frac{\lambda^o\rho_t}{(1 + \rho_t)}\frac{P_t}{P_{nt+1}}\right). \tag{46}$$

[12] The traditional, Harberger (1955) analysis of such percentage depletion allowances assumes that manufacturing and oil "investments" should be taxed equally if they generate the same streams of cash income. It fails to recognize that if the oil "investment" is not undertaken, there is still an accumulation of oil reserves, which is a true social investment. Therefore, it is necessary to net the disinvestment of oil reserves out of Harberger's oil "investment" before taxes should be equated on his equal investments. The Harberger study should also be corrected for the fact that a depletion allowance is capitalized in the value of the land, thus serving to increase the costs as well as the returns to current oil "investments." Making these adjustments in Harberger's analysis and making intertemporal investment possibilities and taxes explicit leads to our own analysis.

We assume that each of the N^α individuals in country α has a utility function defined over all feasible sequences of his consumption benefits,

$$U^i(B_1^i, B_2^i, \ldots), \qquad i = 1, 2, \ldots, N^\alpha,$$

where $U^i(\cdot)$ is a monotone increasing, differentiable, strictly quasi concave function.[3] Aggregate consumption benefit over these individuals during the tth period is given by the differentiable, quasi concave production function

$$\sum_{i=1}^{N^\alpha} B_t^i = C^t(K_{1Ct}, K_{2Ct}, \ldots, K_{MCt}), \qquad t = 1, 2, \ldots, \tag{1}$$

where K_{kCt} represents capital of the kth kind ($k = 1, \ldots, M$) devoted to the production of consumption benefits at time t. Aggregate capital in country α in each future period is the result of devoting capital in the preceding period to its production or acquisition so that

$$K_{kt+1} = I^{kt}(K_{1kt}, \ldots, K_{Mkt}), \qquad t = 1, 2, \ldots, \tag{2}$$

where $I^{kt}(\cdot)$ is differentiable and quasi concave. Foreign aggression is treated as a form of investment, the capital obtained from a current act of aggression being unavailable for consumption until the following period.

National defense effort at time t is

$$D_t = G^t(K_{1Gt}, \ldots, K_{MGt}), \tag{3}$$

where $G^t(\cdot)$ is also differentiable and quasi concave. The aggregate capital stock of kind k in any period is the sum of the amounts of capital used in the above activities plus the amount taken by foreign aggressors, K_{kAt}. That is,

$$K_{kt} = K_{kCt} + \sum_{y=1}^{M} K_{kyt} + K_{kGt} + K_{kAt}. \tag{4}$$

---

end of this section of the paper. In the case of a finite horizon, several of our tax-equivalence theorems hold in only an approximate sense. The perfect-information assumption can be substantially relaxed and is made largely to simplify the discussion.

[3] The "strict quasi concavity" of a function here means that if $f(x) = f(x')$, $x \neq x'$, then

$$f[ax + (1 - a)x'] - f(x) > \delta \sup_j (x_j - x_j') f_j$$

for some $\delta > 0$ where $1 > a > 0$ and $x = x_1, x_2, \ldots$. This may also be termed "asymptotically strict quasi concavity." It assures the absence of infinite quantities in maximizing f over all x subject only to linear equalities in x with positive coefficients. This type of quasi concavity, as well as the standard quasi concavity assumptions stated below [$f(x)$ is quasi concave if $f(x) = f(x')$, $x \neq x'$ implies that $f[ax + (1 - a)x'] - f(x) \geq 0$], also are used to insure the existence of a competitive equilibrium. The differentiability assumptions in this paper, together with the absence of traditional nonnegativity assumptions, are made to facilitate the mathematical argument, since it is obvious that technical nonsubstitutabilities do not disturb the optimality of incentives in our efficient tax system.

Relations (1)–(4) insure the absence of joint production and collective goods in that they state that no particular unit of a capital good serves several functions simultaneously, such as producing consumption goods and producing itself in the following period.

Similar relations hold for each country.

We assume that the distribution of capital between countries is an equilibrium distribution, meaning that each of the countries has rationally decided (rational in the Paretian sense) which property to claim and defend in each period and that the decisions are mutually consistent given the world's aggregate stocks of capital. The equilibrium initial capital stock of country α is given by

$$K_{k1} = K_{k1}^*, \qquad k = 1, 2, \ldots, M. \tag{5}$$

We assume that each country knows the rational strategies of the others so that no actual aggression occurs in determining this equilibrium distribution of capital between countries. In equilibrium, the country possessing a unit of capital in a given period is the country that has made a prior commitment to impose on any other country attempting to acquire the capital damages which are at least as great as the value of the capital to that country.[4] Since the only way to subvert the prior commitment of another country is to take control over the entire country, all foreign aggression is all or nothing. So if the net return from aggression is ever positive, it is greatest for $K_{kAt} = K_{kt}$. Hence, we can write the profit to aggression against country α for a particular aggressor as

$$\pi_{At} = A(K_{1t}, K_{2t}, \ldots, K_{Mt}) - C(D_t), \tag{6}$$

where $A(\cdot)$ is the aggressor's evaluation function of the assets he acquires and $C(D_t)$ is his corresponding cost of the aggression, which we assume

---

[4] It may be of interest to note that such commitments are generally impossible to make in a pure democracy, as the voters can always vote against a war by voting down war appropriations. Such a government is sure to lose, bit by bit if not all at once, all of its transferable capital to a nondemocratic foreign aggressor that can make commitments to fight wars over property at war costs to both parties which are greater than the value of the property at stake. (The reason such commitments are rational is that once they are made, the democratic country rationally surrenders its capital so that fighting the war is unnecessary.) However, in a constitutional democracy, where certain government policies are not subject (except at great cost) to future voter disapproval, the constitution, by giving proper incentives to the government leaders and by allowing them to command war resources without voter approval, may effect the necessary war commitment. Constitutionally granted wartime finance policies such as the draft, debt financing and government currency creation, and price controls are thus a necessary part of our wartime financial structure. An important implication of this necessary, confiscatory, wartime financing is that there is an insufficient accumulation of war-relevant capital during peacetime. This is the economic basis of the classical "national defense argument" for peacetime subsidization of certain domestic industries (see Thompson [1968] for an elaboration and empirical application). In the formal model above, such subsidies appear as government purchases of capital used to produce national defense.

to be a monotonic increasing function. The rational foreign aggressor acquires no K_{kt} if and only if the profit to the aggression is never positive.

Equilibrium also implies that each country always retains its rationally produced capital. This is true because if a subsequent unit of capital were not successfully defended, it would have been better for the country to consume the capital which was devoted to its production. This follows from the monotonicity of utility functions and the consumability of capital expressed in relations (2)–(5). In equilibrium, then, α makes D_t just high enough in each period that for each potential aggressor, $\pi_{At} \leq 0$ for all $K_{kAt} > 0$. That is, it makes D_t just high enough that the solution value of K_{kAt} is equal to zero for all potential aggressors. From (6), this level of D_t obviously depends upon $K_{1t}, \ldots, K_{Mt}$, which determines the return to foreign aggression. Hence, we set D_t equal to $D^t(K_{1t}, \ldots, K_{Mt})$, the defense requirement of the country at time t—the level of defense required to dissuade all potential aggressors. Also, since there are no foreign aggression activities in equilibrium, the only output of the "government" is D_t. Hence, equations (3) and (4) are written:

$$D^t(K_{1t}, \ldots, K_{Mt}) = G^t(K_{1Gt}, \ldots, K_{MGt}), \qquad (3')$$

$$K_{kt} = K_{kCt} + \sum_y K_{kyt} + K_{kGt}. \qquad (4')$$

Conditions for Pareto Optimality

Maximizing $U^1(B_1^1, B_2^1, \ldots)$ subject to $U^j(B_1^j, B_2^j, \ldots) = U^{j*}$, $j \geq 2$, and equations (1), (2), (3'), (4'), and (5), we find that necessary for a Pareto optimum in our environment is that the allocation of resources (i.e., $K_{kCt}, K_{kyt}, K_{kGt}$, and B_t^i for all k, y, t, and i) satisfies, in addition to the constraint equations above, the following marginal equalities:

$$\frac{C_k^t}{C_y^t} = \frac{I_k^{zt}}{I_y^{zt}} = \frac{G_k^t}{G_y^t} \qquad \text{for all } t, k, y, \text{ and } z, \qquad (7)$$

and

$$\frac{\partial U^i/\partial B_t}{\partial U^i/\partial B_{t+1}} = \frac{C_y^{t+1} I_k^{yt}}{C_k^t}, \left(1 - \frac{D_y^{t+1}}{G_y^{t+1}}\right) \qquad \text{for all } t, k, y, \text{ and } i, \qquad (8)$$

where subscripts on function symbols indicate partial derivatives of the function with respect to capital of the type specified by the subscript.

Equation (7) states the familiar condition that in an optimum, different kinds of capital are allocated between sectors so that their relative marginal productivities are equal whatever they produce. Equation (8) states that in an optimum, the marginal rate of time preference of B_t over B_{t+1} is less than the familiar marginal rate of time productivity by a percentage equal to the increase in defense requirement caused by the capital which is produced to create the extra B_{t+1} relative to the defense productivity of this capital.

Competitive Equilibrium

We now give each individual in country α an initial endowment of capital $(K_{11}^{i*}, \ldots, K_{M1}^{i*})$ such that

$$\sum_i K_{k1}^{i*} = K_{k1}^* \qquad \text{for all } k. \tag{9}$$

We also give each of these individuals a set of quasi concave production functions for each period which read:

$$C^{ti} = C^{ti}(K_{1Ct}^i, \ldots, K_{MCt}^i) \qquad \text{and}$$
$$I^{kti} = I^{kti}(K_{1kt}^i, \ldots, K_{Mkt}^i) \qquad \text{for every } k. \tag{10}$$

The aggregate functions described in (1) and (2) must then be derived by maximizing aggregate output for given aggregates of inputs devoted to the production of the output. That is,

$$C^t(K_{1Ct}, \ldots, K_{MCt}) = \max \sum_i C^{ti}(K_{1Ct}^i, \ldots, K_{MCt}^i)$$

subject to

$$\sum_i K_{yCt}^i = K_{yCt},$$

and

$$I^{kt}(K_{1kt}, \ldots, K_{Mkt}) = \max \sum_i I^{kti}(K_{1kt}^i, \ldots, K_{Mkt}^i) \tag{11}$$

subject to

$$\sum_i K_{ykt}^i = K_{ykt}, \qquad \text{all } k, y, \text{ and } t.$$

We assume that each individual may economically participate somewhat in the production of each output (which will imply nonincreasing returns to scale in the individual functions), so that the above maximizations obviously occur when and only when

$$C_k^{ti} = C_k^{tj} \ (= C_k^t),$$
$$I_k^{yti} = I_k^{ytj} \ (= I_k^{yt}) \qquad \text{for all } k, i, j, \text{ and } t. \tag{12}$$

Hence, if the equilibrium in the economy satisfies (12), it generates the aggregate production functions in (1) and (2) given the constraints in (11).

We now introduce prices. Our prices are all initial-period, unit-of-account prices; that is, they describe the amount of wealth one must currently surrender in order to obtain delivery of a good at a specified date. To obtain such prices from prices that would rule in actual transactions in future periods, a suitable discount must be applied to the price in the future to reflect the value of early payment in the form of initial wealth. The price of capital of type k delivered in period t is written P_{kt}, and the price of consumption goods delivered in period t is written P_t. An individual is also taxed an amount whose present cost is given by T^i.

TAXATION AND DEFENSE

Each individual is assumed to choose B_t^i, K_{kCt}^i, and K_{kyt} so as to maximize $U^i(B_1^i, B_2^i, \ldots)$ subject to the production functions in (10) and his budget,

$$T^i + \sum_t P_t B_t^i = \sum_k P_{k1} K_{k1}^{i*} + \sum_t P_t C^{ti} + \sum_{ty} \sum P_{yt+1} I^{yti} \quad (13)$$
$$- \sum_{tyk} \sum \sum P_{kt}(K_{kCt}^i + K_{kyt}^i).$$

The solutions represent a competitive equilibrium when prices are set[5] so that, for all t and k,

$$\sum_i Z_t^i = \sum_i C^{ti}, \qquad \sum_i (K_{kC1}^i + \sum_y K_{ky1}^i) = K_{k1}^*,$$
and
$$\sum_i (K_{kCt+1}^i + \sum_y K_{kyt+1}^i) = \sum_i I^{kti}. \qquad (14)$$

The Case of Lump-Sum Taxation

When taxes are lump sum so that they do not vary with the individual's behavior, the individual utility-maximizing choices are seen to satisfy the following marginal equalities:

$$\frac{C_k^{ti}}{C_y^{ti}} = \frac{I_k^{zt}}{I_y^{zt}} = \frac{P_{kt}}{P_{yt}}$$
and
$$\frac{\partial U^i/\partial B_t}{\partial U^i/\partial B_{t+1}} = \frac{C_y^{t+1} I_k^{yt}}{C_k^t} = \frac{P_t}{P_{t+1}}, \qquad \text{all } k, y, z, t, \text{ and } i.$$

These conditions are inconsistent with the condition for Pareto optimality in (8) except when $D_y^{t+1} = 0$ for every y and t, which is the implausible special case in which the returns to aggression by the marginal foreign aggressors are never affected by the size of the victim's capital stock.

The Pareto Optimality of a Competitive Equilibrium with Certain Capital Taxes

We now assume that

$$T^i = \sum_{tk} \sum a_{kt} P_{kt} K_{kt}^i + T^{oi}, \qquad (15)$$

[5] We assume that
$$\liminf_{t \to \infty} \left(\sum_{ty} \sum P_{yt+1} I^{yt} - \sum_{tyk} \sum \sum P_{kt} K_{kyt} - T^i \right)$$
exists to assure finite solutions. Our prices are therefore "Malinvaud prices" (Malinvaud

where a_{kt} is a constant present tax rate on capital of type k at date t and the T^{oi} is a lump-sum tax or subsidy to the individual set so that $\sum_i T^i$ satisfies the government's budget condition,

$$\sum_i T^i = \sum_{tk} P_{kt}(1 + a_{kt})K_{kGt}. \tag{16}$$

Equation (16) reflects the fact that the capital tax is levied on sellers of capital rather than buyers and that prices are the net prices to sellers. We assume that the government minimizes costs using fixed-factor prices so that

$$\frac{P_{kt}(1 + a_{kt})}{P_{yt}(1 + a_{yt})} = \frac{G_k^t}{G_y^t}. \tag{17}$$

Maximizing $U^i(\cdot)$ subject to (10), (13), and (15) yields the following marginal conditions:

$$C_k^{ti} = P_{kt}(1 + a_{kt})/P_t \quad \text{and} \quad I_k^{yti} = P_{kt}(1 + a_{kt})/P_{yt+1}, \tag{18}$$

$$\frac{C_k^{ti}}{C_y^{ti}} = \frac{I_k^{zti}}{I_y^{zti}} = \frac{G_k^t}{G_y^t} = \frac{P_{kt}(1 + a_{kt})}{P_{yt}(1 + a_{yt})}, \tag{19}$$

and

$$\frac{\partial U^i/B_t}{\partial U^i/B_{t+1}} = \frac{C_y^{t+1} I_k^{yt}}{C_k^t} \frac{1}{1 + a_{yt+1}} = \frac{P_t}{P_{t+1}}, \quad \text{all } k, y, z, t, \text{ and } i. \tag{20}$$

Equation (17) satisfies the conditions in (12) so that (11) holds. We now need only set

$$a_{yt+1} = a_{yt+1}^o = \frac{D_y^{t+1}}{G_y^{t+1} - D_y^{t+1}} \tag{21}$$

in order for (19) and (20), together with (9), (11), (14), (3'), and (4') to represent the same equation set as (7) and (8) together with (1), (2), (3'), (4'), and (5)—in order for any competitive equilibrium with such capital taxes to be a Pareto optimum.[6]

---

[6] Since we have not precluded decreasing marginal costs of defense with respect to the protected capital, there may be several allocations satisfying (7) and (8) for given utility levels of $N^\alpha - 1$ individuals. And some of these allocations may be Pareto nonoptimal. In such cases, however, we assume that the government picks tax rates (a_{kt} and T^{oi}) which correspond to their shadow values in a global Pareto optimum. That such taxes succeed in inducing global Pareto optima despite the possible economies of scale in protecting capital is easily proved. First note that our quasi concavity, nonincreasing returns and bounded-wealth assumptions insure that all solutions to (19) and (20)—given (9), (11), (14), (3'), and (4')—are privately optimal. It follows that we need only pick the levels of a_{kt} and T^{oi} that correspond to their shadow equivalents in any specified Pareto optimum in order to have the privately selected allocations of the equilibrium coincide with the Pareto optimum. For if this were not the case, then one allocation satisfying (19) and (20)—given (9), (11), (14), (3'), and (4')—would make someone worse off than would another such allocation.

Note that no particular tax rate on capital in the initial period is implied by optimal capital taxes. This is reasonable because such capital has already been produced so that taxing it is equivalent to applying a lump-sum tax. Nevertheless, we oftentimes below apply the harmless procedure of applying the optimal tax rate on future capital to capital in the initial period. Note also that the optimal capital tax is equivalently a tax on the value of the capital output, I^{kt}.

It is easy to show, using (18), allowing the optimal capital tax rate to apply in period 1, and assuming linear homogeneity of $D^t(\cdot)$ and $G^t(\cdot)$ with respect to their respective arguments, that $T^{oi} = 0$ so that optimal capital taxes alone are just sufficient to finance government expenditures. While we do not maintain these homogeneity assumptions in the paper, the result indicates, to the extent that the homogeneities are roughly plausible, a relatively minor role for lump-sum taxation or subsidization in a world employing an optimal capital tax.

Specification of the Marginal Aggressors' Marginal Profit Functions

Since the marginal aggressors' profits are kept at zero by the potential victim's defense effort, we have, differentiating (6),

$$\frac{\partial A}{\partial K_{xt}} = A_{xt} = \frac{dC(D^t)}{dD^t} D_x^t. \tag{25}$$

Hence,

$$\frac{A_{xt}}{A_{yt}} = \frac{D_x^t}{D_y^t} \qquad \text{if } A_{yt} > 0. \tag{26}$$

We assume that for some subset of $(k) = (1, 2, \ldots, M)$, written $a(k) = (1, 2, \ldots, M_a)$, $A_{kt} > 0$. We call any kind of capital in this subset a part of the country's "coveted capital." For the rest of the capital stock, $A_{kt} = 0$.

Equations (21) and (25) tell us that if $A_{xt+1} = 0$, $a_{xt+1}^o = 0$. That is, if a particular kind of capital is not part of the country's coveted capital, the optimal tax on the capital is zero. Now we assume that for all x and y in $a(k)$,

$$\frac{A_{xt}}{A_{yt}} = \frac{P_{xt}}{P_{yt}}. \tag{27}$$

That is, the relative marginal values which foreign aggressors place on different kinds of the country's coveted capital are equal to the corresponding relative values to the defending country. There are several reasons that this is not a strictly justifiable assumption. It does, however, serve to maintain reasonable orders of magnitude. A jet plane is a lot more valuable than a light bulb, to the aggressor as well as the defender. From (26) and (27),

$$\frac{P_{xt}}{P_{yt}} = \frac{D_x^t}{D_y^t} \qquad \text{for all } x, y \in a(k). \tag{28}$$

Hence, from (28), (19), and (21), optimal capital taxes are nondiscriminatory, that is,

$$a_{xt}^o = a_{yt}^o = a_t^o \qquad \text{for all } x, y \in a(k). \tag{29}$$

Problems in Implementation

We have as yet produced no model specific enough to indicate which types of capital comprise a country's coveted capital stock. Also, since it is practically very costly to tax the value of capital in every period when there are not transactions in the capital during every period, a problem arises as to how one can create, if possible, a tax system which levies only on transactions but which is still equivalent in effects to the idealized system of optimal capital taxation described above. These problems of implementation are the subject of Section II.

A Possible Generalization

Admitting Marshallian joint production of consumption and investment goods would open up the possibility that some units of produced capital would be optimally surrendered in the future to a potential foreign aggressor. To have determinate units of such capital, we would, in effect, have to introduce different defense costs for different units of equally valuable capital, thus violating (28) and giving rise to discriminatory taxes. While these cases of "surrenderable capital" are excluded from our formal analysis below, an informal discussion is provided at the end of Section II.

II. Achieving an Optimal Capital Tax

The Transaction Structure and Income Taxes

We now allow our economy to have an explicit transaction structure—a particular set of trades between individuals which achieves the optimal competitive equilibrium described above. Suppose each producer sells his entire output, purchasing all of his inputs all over again for his production in the following period. Then there would be no difficulty in implementing the optimal capital tax. A simple income tax, a tax on all producer sales, with tax exemptions granted for sales of the outputs of noncoveted capital, would obviously be sufficient to produce an equivalent to the optimal capital tax. However, this supposition is far from realistic; in our model, producers may retain some of their capital output for their own future use. To acquire an equivalence between an income tax and the optimal capital tax then requires amendments to the simple income tax besides exemptions for sales of outputs from noncoveted capital. The income tax on the kth kind of capital of individual i is given by

$$T_b^{ki} = \sum_t b_{kt}(P_t C_k^t K_{kt}^{im} - X_{kt}^i), \tag{30}$$

where b_{kt} is the income tax rate, X_{kt}^i represents deductions from the tax base, and K_{kt}^{im} represents the capital that i uses to produce goods for the market in period t. By definition,

$$K_{kt}^i = K_{kt}^{im} + K_{kt}^{ii}, \tag{31}$$

where K_{kt}^{ii} is the capital that individual i uses to produce goods which are not sold in the market. The optimal income tax exists when, for each k and i, b_{kt} and X_{kt}^i take on values that make (30) equivalent to (15) and (21), or,

$$\sum_t b_{kt}(P_t C_k^t K_{kt}^{im} - X_{kt}^i) = \sum_t a_t^o P_{kt} K_{kt}^i + T^{oi} \qquad \text{for all } K_{kt}^i, \tag{32}$$

or

$$dT_b^{ki}/dK_{kt}^i = a_{kt}^o P_{kt}. \tag{33}$$

Solutions to (32) and (33) are written (b_{kt}^o, X_{kt}^{io}).

Note that income taxes have an independence property expressed as

$$\sum_k T_b^{ki} = T_b^i. \tag{34}$$

Noncoveted Capital

Capital may generate benefits which apply to only certain, specified individuals within a country—such capital is "people specific." One's psychic capital—for example, acquired ability to appreciate nature and various activities, stock of pleasant memories, acquired ability to entertain himself—is part of the country's people-specific capital stock. The rest of a country's "people-specific capital" is "friendship capital"—where a specified individual (e.g., a husband) can command the services (e.g., good cooking) of another (e.g., a wife) because the other either feels a sense of gratitude or indebtedness to the specified individual or has confidence that the specified individual will reciprocate in the future without an explicit agreement, the cost of which would preclude such favors from having a positive net value to the recipient. People-specific capital is of no value to individuals outside the country and is not part of a country's coveted capital stock.[7] Since the returns on people-specific capital do not generate market transactions so that $K_{kt}^{im} = 0$ for people-specific capital, an income tax operates in an optimal fashion by not taxing people-specific capital.

While returns from friendship capital frequently come in the form of a monetary payment in the cases of gift and charity income, such income is, appropriately, substantially disregarded for tax purposes in the United States.[8] However, large gifts (including inheritances) frequently only partially represent a payment for friendship services, with another part representing a payment for services that a foreign aggressor could acquire. Large gifts and inheritances should therefore be taxed to some degree, with the tax rate increasing with the size of the gift or inheritance and never exceeding the income tax rate. We do observe such taxes, although we have no way of estimating optimal rate schedules to compare to the actual schedules.

When an aggressor takes over a country, he does not benefit from human capital to the extent that such capital is necessary for the "subsistence" of the individual. An individual is below "subsistence" if he would sooner die in rebellion than pay the taxes of the successful foreign aggressor. One's subsistence is comprised of normal support for his family and any abnormal, noncosmetic, family medical expenses. Hence, one's human capital below that required for his family's subsistence is not part of his country's coveted capital stock. As a result, an optimal income tax has an exemption, X_{ht}, on incomes from human capital required for normal family subsistence of market goods and for abnormal, noncosmetic medical expenses. The observed U.S. income tax exemption of about $750 per person appears to approximate the normal subsistence level fairly well, while the observed write-off for abnormal, noncosmetic medical expenses corresponds nicely to the treatment of these expenses under an optimal income tax.

It is likely that a modern foreign aggressor would support those citizens of an acquired country who were unable to produce their own subsistence. Assuming this to be the case, any increase in the assistance requirement of

[7] It should be pointed out that our assertion that people-specific capital is noncoveted rests on an assumption that a successful foreign aggressor cannot substantially switch this kind of capital into the production of benefits which are not people specific. Thus, it is assumed that the human capital that an individual devotes to producing benefits for himself (i.e., producing "leisure") cannot be substantially converted to the production of goods for the aggressor. Our foreign aggressors therefore do not make slaves out of their victims; they merely tax them to subsistence. This implication appears to be fairly realistic. The behavioral basis of it appears to be that an individual acquires certain work-leisure habits, which cannot be substantially broken at any reasonable cost by the foreign aggressors.

[8] A gift which does not represent a payment for a particular service but a mere redistribution of wealth based upon directly interdependent utilities, while not contained in our formal model, is clearly a mere transfer and should not be taxed.

below-subsistence individuals in a defending country has the same external social product as any other decrease in the coveted capital stock of equal value. The decrease in the coveted capital stock in this case appears as an increase in expenditures on charity. Hence, a receipt of charity is not only a return on noncoveted capital; it is also a reward to individuals who produce less than their subsistence for reducing their country's stock of coveted capital. So expenditures on charity should be treated for income tax purposes as any other expenditure which reduces the capital stock of the country. In fact, charitable expenditures in the United States are treated substantially the same as business expenditures for income tax purposes.[9]

Certain consumer durables such as furniture, portraits, trophies, and certain antiques are also part of the country's noncoveted capital stock. While there are no taxes on these goods as $K_{ct}^{im} = 0$, consumer durables which are part of the coveted capital stock are discussed below.

Cash, that is, paper currency, may exist in the economy with explicit transactions as an intermediate asset which allows for the achievement of the no-transactions-cost economy described in Section I. However, with costless currency creation, a successful foreign aggressor can also costlessly create any feasible level of real cash balances by altering the rate of growth of the currency supply. Hence, the level of real cash balances used by the defending country is irrelevant to the aggressors and not part of a country's coveted capital stock.

The definitions of capital which Marshall (1925), Knight (1935), and Smith (1937) inferred from discussions of men of affairs excluded people-specific capital, subsistence-producing capital, certain personal consumer durables, and paper money. Using our theory, we can rationalize the exclusion of these forms of capital from the concept of capital used by men of affairs by arguing that these men are only discussing coveted capital because it is the only capital which should be taxed. The only remaining types of private-good capital in the Smith-Marshall-Knight taxonomies— the types comprising the capital stock as seen by men of affairs—are natural resources, produced producer durables, human capital above subsistence requirements, and the remaining consumer durables. These forms will be assumed to comprise the country's coveted capital stock, and the achievement of an optimal tax on each of these forms of capital is examined separately below.

---

[9] Note, however, that a standard-type competitive model such as that developed above applies only to cases of private-good charity—cases in which each individual enjoys *his* giving charity rather than enjoying the beneficiary's receipt of the charity (i.e., in which there are no external economies in the giving of charity) and in which an individual can costlessly avoid the knowledge of another's suffering (i.e., in which there are no external diseconomies in the creation of charity-inducing attributes). Including both of these excluded realistic cases would probably have little total effect on the tax treatment of charity because their separate effects are substantially cancelling.

Producer Durables Which Are Originally Produced for Sale

No tax on the gross income from capital which is not sold in every period is equivalent to the optimal tax. The derivative of taxes with respect to K_{kt}^i is positive in (33), and, in view of (31), is zero in (30) for fixed K_{kt}^{im} if $X_{kt}^i \equiv 0$. So, for optimal taxation, $X_{kt}^i \not\equiv 0$. To achieve the effects of an optimal capital tax, we wish to consider a tax on k's gross income reduced by an estimate of its depreciation.

Depreciation, however, is generally estimable only for a good which is originally produced for sale, meaning that whenever a good other than itself is used to produce it, it is marketed. Without loss of generality, we assume that when a producer good that is originally produced for sale (labelled e for equipment) is not used to produce current marketed output, it is used to produce only itself in the following period. That is, $K_{et}^{ii} = K_{eet}^{ii}$.

Letting X_{et} represent realistic depreciation of the original purchased capital in terms of current consumer goods, (30) becomes

$$T_b^{ei} = \sum_t b_{et}[P_t C_e^t(K_{et}^i - K_{eet}^{ii}) - P_{et+1}(K_{et}^i - I_e^{et} K_{eet}^{ii})].$$

Using (18) this becomes

$$T_b^{ei} = \sum_t b_{et}(P_t C_e^t - P_{et+1})K_{et}^i. \tag{35}$$

Hence, to obtain an optimal net income tax on e in time t, in view of (32) and (35), we need only pick a b_{et} which satisfies

$$b_{et} = \frac{a_t^o P_{et}}{P_t C_e^t - P_{et+1}}. \tag{36}$$

Using (18), this optimal income tax rate becomes

$$b_{et}^o = \frac{a_t^o}{1 + a_t^o} \cdot \frac{I_e^{et}}{I_e^{et} - 1}. \tag{37}$$

From (20) and (18) we can see that when there is a stationary solution such that $a_t^o = a_{t+1}^o$ and $C_k^t = C_k^{t+1}$,

$$b_{et}^o = \frac{a_t^o(1 + \rho_t)}{(1 + \rho_t)(1 + a_t^o) - 1}, \tag{38}$$

where $1 + \rho_t = (\partial U/\partial B_t)/(\partial U/\partial B_{t+1})$, the marginal rate of time preference.

Thus, the use of realistic, physical depreciation allowances converts the inefficient income tax into an efficient one under an appropriate income tax rate.[10]

---

[10] In the real world, depreciation allowances are typically granted on a fixed schedule for a particular kind of capital good regardless of how the good actually wears out. But, also in the real world, depreciation typically takes the form of Marshallian joint pro-

The only other existing rationalization of the realistic depreciation write-off this author has seen is by Samuelson (1964). Samuelson shows that a write-off on income taxes of all forms of interest expense will create a tax structure with no effect on prices only if the tax on income includes a write-down for realistic depreciation. However, no tax system in existence subsidizes interest expenses and taxes net receipts so as to have offsetting revenue and incentive effects. Such a system would be a lot of trouble for no purpose. The tax system Samuelson claims to represent is a United States-like system, a system containing a tax on interest income as well as a corresponding write-off of interest expenses. But in such a system there is no net tax or subsidy on borrowing or lending—nor should there be in our optimality model because borrowing represents a mere redistribution of purchasing power rather than the creation of any real asset. Samuelson erred by failing to allow the after-tax contractual rate of interest to rise to reflect the equal shifts up in the interest-demand price for loans and the interest-supply price of loans resulting, respectively, from the tax write-off of interest expenses and the tax on interest income. Once gross market rates of interest are raised to reflect the tax on interest income, the reduction of the gross market rate by applying the tax write-off on interest expenses (or income) to obtain the after-tax borrowing (or lending) rate relevant for discounting only serves to pull the discount rate back down to the original real interest rate for the original allocation of real resources. And with no reduction in the discount rate in Samuelson's model, no positive income tax rate satisfies Samuelson's price invariance condition, whether or not there are depreciation allowances.

Natural Resources

Natural resources (i.e., minerals and oil and gas) pose a different problem in the lack of transactions to correspond to each act of production. Like producer-goods which are purchased upon their original creation, natural resources are accumulated by the owner without any corresponding transaction. But unlike such producer goods, there can be no transaction

---

duction of marketed output and future capital. Under such depreciation, the optimal tax on a new investment under stationary conditions is a single tax on the present value of the capital in each future period resulting from the investment, while an income tax without a depreciation allowance is a tax only on the initial capital value. It is easy to see by an argument similar to that used above that a realistic depreciation allowance converts the income tax into a tax on the present value of the future capital values implied by an investment and thus leads to an optimal choice of investments in a world in which actual depreciation takes the form of Marshallian joint production of marketed output and future capital for the firm.

There are real-world cases of physical depreciation of producer durables which have been produced for sale in which the depreciation does not take the form of Marshallian joint production. This appears for originally produced timber, wine, and various agricultural products. Here, we observe in the United States, the variable depreciation allowances of the kind which our formal model describes; these are frequently called "cost depletion allowances."

Assuming that the income tax rate is that optimal rate applied to equip-ment, and again assuming that $a^o_{t+1} = a^o$, we find, substituting (38) into (46), that

$$\lambda^o = \frac{P_{nt+1}}{P_t} \tag{47}$$

Hence, the optimal percentage depletion allowance is the ratio of the market value of the conserved natural resource to the value of the product obtained by currently exploiting the resource.

The most reliable data on natural resources we have cover the oil industry. Here, the ratio of mineral right value to output value has been relatively constant at about 23 percent (see Rooney [1965]). This mineral right value is obtained by adding amortized oil lease payments to royal-ties. The current U.S. percentage depletion allowance is 22 percent. There is thus a close correspondence in this industry between the optimal and actual percentage depletion allowances.[13] While precise data are not available, there is also a correspondence between the low 5 percent depletion allowances given to producers of gravel, peat, pumice, shale, and stone and the obviously low value of mineral rights to these natural resources relative to the prices of the withdrawn resources to consumers. And in the extreme case in which mineral rights are essentially free—such as for soil, dirt, moss, minerals from sea water, and air—there is a zero percentage depletion allowance.

We now estimate the optimal allowance for the minerals industry in the aggregate. Note first that because of the constancy over time of the spot price of withdrawn natural resources, spot withdrawal costs must fall over time so as to make the spot price of a natural resource rise at the productive rate of interest. In particular the percentage reduction in spot withdrawal costs over time times withdrawal costs relative to the spot price of a particular natural resource at withdrawal must equal the rate of interest. Therefore, the price of a natural resource at withdrawal relative to the withdrawn resource equals the capitalized rate of cost reduction divided by one plus this capitalized rate. Since the rate of decrease of withdrawal costs in the minerals industry is about 2 percent

---

[13] Oil producers are also allowed to write off most of their capital expenses (their "intangible drilling expenses") as current expenditures rather than depreciating them over the life of the producing wells. This write-off can be justified by the "national defense" argument mentioned in fn. 4; that is, the efficient price controls that are applied during a war imply an insufficient amount of domestic capacity for wartime in the absence of special subsidies. Based upon the frequency of past wars and the extent of wartime price controls on oil, a conservative estimate of the optimal subsidy to domestic drilling is 20 percent of the peacetime price of crude oil (see Thompson [1968]). The value of the write-off of intangible drilling expenses can be estimated at around 17 percent of the normal price of crude oil (see Rooney [1965]). The extension of the formal model to admit the possibility of future, successful, defensive wars for a given country is straight-forward.

per annum (Barnett and Morse 1963), and we are using a productive interest rate of 10 percent, the price of natural resources at withdrawal relative to withdrawn resource price over all valuable minerals is estimated to be 16.67 percent. In fact, the bulk of the statutory depletion allowances fall between 14 and 22 percent (with effective rates slightly lower because of a limitation of the allowance to 50 percent of the net income of the taxpayer).

The observed spot price of natural resources relative to withdrawn resources may be constant over time despite its increase for a given natural resource because the quality of the resources exploited may decrease over time. For example, the ratio of oil royalties to the value of the withdrawn oil, a well-known empirical constant, could never have remained constant had not the more easily withdrawable oil deposits been tapped at the earlier dates.

Consumer Durables

Consumer durables, like producer durables, are sold when they are originally created but, unlike producer durables, do not create future benefits for others. There is therefore no "income" from consumer durables to tax. Hence, an excise tax on the production of consumer durables goods is in order. Using again an interest rate of 10 percent, equation (37), and an optimal income tax rate of approximately 25 percent, we have an optimal capital tax rate of 2.5 percent. Therefore, consumer goods lasting 5 years and depreciating in a sum-of-years digits fashion, should be taxed at an initial excise tax rate of

$$2.5 \text{ percent } \times \left(1 + \frac{10}{15(1.1)} + \frac{6}{15(1.1)^2} + \frac{3}{15(1.1)^3} + \frac{1}{15(1.1)^4}\right)$$

$$= 5.35 \text{ percent,}$$

and consumer goods lasting 15 years should be taxed at 10.29 percent using these assumptions. Until very recently, U.S. federal excise taxes on consumer durables ranged between 5 percent and 10 percent with the lower rates generally applying to the relatively short-lived goods.[14]

---

[14] For the various excise tax rates, see Commerce Clearing House (1957, *Federal Taxes*, Subtitle D). For relative depreciation rates, see Prentice-Hall (1971, par. 15,000). As excise tax rates have recently been volatile, there is no simple method of evaluating the post-1964 excise-tax structure. Some federal excise taxes fall substantially on producer durables, the most notable of which are "business' machines (such as typewriters and computers) and cars and trucks. The business machine case is fairly easy to understand once it is recognized that the sellers of the more expensive machines normally avoid capital taxation by renting their outputs. The less expensive machines are frequently used by consumers, so that an excise tax is in order. The same applies to cars and trucks. However, businessmen should be allowed to expense their purchases of this already-taxed equipment.

An important consumer durable that is not federally taxed in the United States is an individual's home. And apartment building depreciation write-offs are so generous that, in view of the ease of transferring these buildings, there are also no substantial federal taxes on these consumer durables. But local property taxes seem to compensate for these apparent inefficiencies as effective property tax rates typically are about 2 percent per year, which is close to the federal rate on the other durables treated above. My guess is that the cumbersome local property tax and the provision of free education to minors is somehow required by the federal government before a locality can exercise local police power or float tax-exempt bonds. In this view, the locality is merely an adjunct of the federal government. The chief reason for this suspicion is that it is not plausible that freely competing localities would offer free education to a partially mobile, heterogeneous populace or would use the property tax as a means for financing it. Yet the proper education of minors is an activity whose federal subsidization is easy to support—not as a collective good—as a good falling within our model which would be privately underproduced without governmental subsidy because the private decision makers (parents) are not entitled to the increase in future productivity which their decisions (education for their minor children) create.[15] We shall employ still another implication of the lack of appropriate parental rewards in the following section. While it is fairly obvious that the inefficient parental reward structure serves to rationalize special laws against polygamy, prostitution, divorce, child labor, the minimum wage for teenagers, and social security (which removes a parent's inefficient incentive to instill feelings of guilt in his children in order to illicit their financial support after his retirement), the traditional, inappropriate theory of public finance has buried the important effects of an inappropriate parental reward structure on the efficiency of the tax system in a sea of imagined inefficiencies.

Although local property taxes in the United States are also observed to fall on the plants of small businessmen, these capital taxes are roughly offset by the national investment credit. And while larger, corporate enterprises are normally able to bargain tax breaks out of small localities

[15] Parents may capture part of the increase in productivity that their decisions create by (inefficiently) training their children to feel sufficiently indebted to transfer some future income to their parents, but even then the parent generally has a bias toward educating the child in ways which make it relatively easy to capture returns. So privately provided education would generally surrender too much of the child's leisure to "character building," which makes the children feel indebted to the parents and would overly train the child toward occupations with relatively low nonpecuniary rewards.

However, parents who have sufficient utility for their children's utility that they give their children unconditional gifts or inheritances, will make efficient child-rearing decisions (see Ruhter [1974]). Thus, public education need not accommodate the rich, who are generally observed to make some unconditional gifts to their children.

in some form or other and therefore effectively avoid local property taxes on their plants, we will find below a substantial reason for applying the current investment credit to U.S. corporations.

Human Capital

"Human capital" as used below is coveted human capital, or "skill," that part of one's human capital stock which he uses to produce goods for the market (or to produce future skill) in value exceeding his subsistence. Newly created skills are reproduced in each future period through the worker's taking care of himself and making any necessary expenditures to retain his skill, the latter being treated as the former for tax purposes by granting it a write-off as a current expense.

Since skill carries its own maintenance out of what would otherwise not have been coveted capital, its value to the aggressor in each period is the present value of its entire future product. Thus, optimal capital taxes on i's skill amount to

$$T_a^{sio} = \sum_a a_t^o K_{st}^i \sum_{\tau = t} P_\tau C_s^\tau \frac{1}{1 + a_\tau^o}.^{16} \tag{47}$$

On the other hand, income taxes are

$$T_b^{si} = \sum_t b_{st} P_t C_s^t (K_{st}^i - K_{sst}^{ii}). \tag{48}$$

We assume a stationary optimum so that $a_\tau^o = a^o$, $C_s^\tau = C_s$, and $\rho_t = \rho$. We consider an accumulation of a durable skill from the time v onward equal to ΔK_{sv}^i, where $v > 1$.

First consider the case in which the accumulation in v is not the result of foregoing income from skill so that $\Delta K_{sst}^{ii} = 0$ for all t. Then,

$$\Delta T_a^{sio} = \frac{a^o P_{v-1} C_s \, \Delta K_{sv}^i (1 + \rho)}{(1 + a^o)\rho^2} \tag{49}$$

and

$$\Delta T_b^{si} = \frac{b_s P_{v-1} C_s \, \Delta K_{sv}^i}{\rho} \tag{50}$$

where $b_{st} = b_s$.
Hence, equating ΔT^{sid} and $\Delta T_b{}^{si}{}_3$

$$b_s^o = \frac{a^o(1 + \rho)}{(1 + a^o)\rho}. \tag{51}$$

---

[16] In a case in which produced skill is maintained out of that skill itself, eq. (47) would, of course, take the standard form of eq. (15) above. It is easy to verify that our results below also hold to a close approximation for that case. (One need only note below that in such a case $K_{sst}^{ii}(1 + \rho_t + a_t) = K_{st}^i$ for $t > v$ so that [50] and [53] are correspondingly reduced to approximately match the reduction in [49].)

Tax write-offs for expenditures on education, job search, and worker-owned equipment would substantially subvert this efficient income tax. The optimal income tax in (51) is only slightly different from the optimal income tax on purchased producer durables.

Now consider the case in which the initial accumulation of a durable skill is accomplished by foregoing income from current skill and keeping leisure time constant. Here, (49) remains the same, but

$$\Delta T_b^{si} = -b_{sv-1}P_{v-1}C_s(\Delta K_{ssv-1}^i) + \sum_{t=v} b_{st}P_tC_s \, \Delta K_{sv}^i$$

$$= -b_{sv-1}\frac{P_{v-1}C_s \, \Delta K_{sv}^i}{1 + \rho + a} + \sum_{t=v} b_{st}P_tC_s \, \Delta K_{sv}^i. \tag{52}$$

Assuming $b_{st} = b_{sv}$ for $t > v$,

$$\Delta T_b^{si} = -b_{sv-1}\frac{P_{v-1}C_s \, \Delta K_{sv}^i}{1 + \rho + a} + b_{sv}\frac{P_{v-1}C_s \, \Delta K_{sv}^i}{\rho}. \tag{53}$$

Using (49), for optimal taxation, we have,

$$\frac{a^o(1 + \rho)}{(1 + a^o)\rho} = b_{sv}^o - \frac{b_{sv-1}^o\rho}{1 + \rho + a^o}. \tag{54}$$

Equation (54) states that an optimal income tax is progressive, as the marginal tax rate applying to increases in future wages, b_{sv}^o, must exceed the average tax rate, b_{sv-1}, which one avoids by training rather than working in the $v - 1$st period. For individuals whose marginal investments in human capital appear at an average level of foregone earnings, we use (51) and set $b_{sv-1}^o = a^o(1 + p)/p(1 + a^o)$ so that (54) can be written as

$$b_{sv}^o = b_{sv-1}^o\left(1 + \frac{\rho}{1 + \rho + a}\right). \tag{55}$$

Using 10 percent time-preference rates, year investment periods, and 2.5 percent optimal capital tax rates, we can fit (55) to actual data on U.S. tax rates.[17] The result is that the actual U.S. marginal income tax rates are within one percentage point of the optimal rates for all approximately average levels of foregone annual income (those between $5,000 and $10,000).

The fit is again very close. The actual U.S. marginal income tax rates are always within 2 percentage points of these theoretically optimal rates for all reasonable levels of human capital investment (i.e., for all levels of foregone annual incomes of $25,000 or less). Equation (55) implies higher tax rates on the leisure-produced accumulation of human capital of

---

[17] Future tax rates were computed assuming the individuals will be married, while current rates, b_{v-1}, were computed assuming the investor is single (Lasser 1971).

individuals with above-average foregone earnings on their marginal investments and lower tax rates on individuals with lower than average foregone earnings. But it is not implausible that the truly optimal tax rate on leisure-produced skill rises with income rather than remaining at the constant expressed in (51) because the excess of the foregone earnings of an individual over average foregone earnings is a plausible measure of the extent of his parental overtraining to surrender leisure (as the reward structure given parents induces them to instill greater lifetime estimates of the value of work relative to leisure in their young children than they would if they could collect as much of their child's leisure benefits as they can the child's work benefits), while the deficit of an individual's foregone earnings below average foregone earnings is a plausible measure of an individual's parental undertraining concerning the value of work and investing in human capital relative to consuming leisure. So we assume, rather crudely, that the optimal tax rates on leisure-produced skill are approximated by the degree of progression implied by the successive application of (55) across all levels of income. Then, since the analysis of (49)–(54) with proportionately adjusted optimal tax rates reveals that (55) still describes the optimal taxation of skill accumulation by foregoing current income, (55) describes an optimal degree of progression over all levels of income.

The above analysis applied to accumulating durable skill so that depreciation could be ignored. This appropriately describes most education and training, as most education and training is undertaken by young people who are going to use their training for very many years. However, some training is undertaken by older people and some training of youth is for short-term or risky careers. In these cases, the above tax on human capital accumulation is too high. Some sort of subsidy for retraining or for training in occupations with short durations is called for. A depreciation allowance on human capital investments would be insufficient. For since the wage increases required to justify a short-term human capital investment are greater than those required to justify a durable investment, the progressive income tax effects a greater tax rate on short-term human capital investments than on long-term investments. We do observe a tax break for risky and short-term human capital investments in the form of an "income averaging" opportunity, but we have made no attempt to quantify the effects of this tax provision.

Producer Durables Used by the Original Producer

An original producer of producer goods may avoid the taxation of his produced capital by writing off its cost of original production as a current expense and then using it himself for future production. The difficult problem of the government is to detect these activities and to apply special taxes whenever such activities occur. We now let the progressive income tax extend over from human to nonhuman capital but also apply only half of the ordinary income tax rate to "capital gains" income, income from the sales of the outputs of producer goods that can be used by the original producers of the goods. The most wealthy individuals are thereby drawn into industries in which produced producer goods can be used by the original producer, thus driving the less wealthy out of these activities. The wealthy are induced by the tax break to identify the capital gains situations, those where they have produced their own producer goods, and the government may now treat the previous expenses of producing this capital as capital expenditures, still leaving the wealthy better off than with ordinary-income treatment of both expenditures and receipts and with a higher value on the entire enterprise than the less wealthy individuals.[18] The resulting tax on producer goods used by the original producer is therefore about half as large as the highest tax bracket, reduced by about 25 percent, when, as in the United States, the capital gains tax is collected at the time of sale rather than as the gains accrue. The highest tax bracket in the United States is currently 70 percent, which puts the effective U.S. tax rate on the income from producer goods used by the original producer at about its optimal level of 25 percent.

However, the above procedure efficiently taxes only the producers' *originally* produced capital that he uses for himself. It does not tax the internal accumulation of the successive capital outputs of the originally produced capital. We have already seen in the case of human capital that in order to tax capital accumulated by foregoing current income, some sort of progressive tax schedule is required. In the present case the relevant tax brackets are very high, so that significant progression is no longer possible. One solution to this problem, which is informationally impractical, is to tax capital gains as they accrue, at about one-third of the ordinary income tax rate. More practically, we may tax realized capital gains at tax rates which increase to the date of realization with the real rate of interest, starting from one-third of the ordinary income tax rate. However, this latter solution would remove the present discouragement to *transact* in the type of capital covered by capital gains taxation. (This discouragement is also reflected in the harsh tax treatment of capital losses and realized short-term capital gains.) A rational basis for this discouragement, although not contained in the current model, is that there is a redistributional element in most transactions involving capital gains, one in which the buyer is more optimistic than the seller regarding the future value of the goods. The tax discouragement therefore serves to

---

[18] When the government fails to treat the previous expenses of the investor as capital expenditures, an inefficient "tax haven" exists—such as has recently been the case in the United States in cattle, timber, and crop development. The U.S. government ordinarily shuts down these tax havens, although rather slowly.

save the socially wasteful transaction costs involved in these transactions. Thus, we have no practical way clearly to improve the capital taxation of the capital output of those producer goods which an individual produces for his own use.

There are numerous cases in which capital gains treatment cannot be afforded to the sale of the goods produced by capital that the producer produces for himself. These occur when there is a continual stream of marketed outputs and expenditures over time, so that it becomes difficult, if not impossible, to attribute any measure of marketed outputs to the inputs that produce them. Thus, for example, a producer's maintenance expenditures are treated not as capital costs but as current business expenses, while the returns from such expenditures are treated not as capital gains but as ordinary income when the final products are marketed. In order to avoid the application of the high progressive tax rates to the nonhuman capital of individuals with continual streams of marketed outputs and expenditures on such capital, we allow these individuals to incorporate their nonhuman capital, taking their returns from the corporation in a form in which they pay only about a 10 percent tax rate.[19] Our problem is then to specify an efficient tax on corporations in light of their ability to produce their own capital. The simplest policy is to tax the value of the company (or the value of its stock, still taxing the interest income of the creditors) at the efficient, 2–3 percent capital tax rate and drop the tax on dividends and capital gains. Such a policy would directly tax any capital in the company—regardless of how it is accumulated. The costly implementation of realistic depreciation and efficient depletion allowances would be avoided, as would the taxation of dividends, capital gains, and corporate profits. But we assume that such a policy is not available, or, if it is, that corporations remain whose stock does not trade at observed prices. The problem then is to specify an efficient corporation income tax in view of the corporation's ability to produce some of its own capital. Now purchased capital is recorded on the books of a company as an asset, but internally produced capital which the company expenses is not included on the books as an asset. However, this latter kind of capital is included in the market evaluation of the company so that the depreciated stock of externally purchased assets in a corporation relative to its total capital stock can be represented by the ratio of the company's book value to its market value. We assume this is constant within each corporation.

Letting B_{ft}/K_{ft} represent the ratio of book to market value of the assets of the firm, replacing K_{et}^i in (35) with B_{ft}^i, using (32) and (36), and

---

[19] Partial dividend exclusions and taxes on realized capital gains at about half the tax rate applicable to ordinary income seem to achieve about this effective rate for the typical investor. The number may seem a little low, but it reflects the significant advantages to delaying realized gains, and giving charity and bequests in the form of appreciated stock.

adjusting for a 10 percent effective tax on dividends and capital gains, the optimal corporation profits tax is:

$$b_f^o = \left(\frac{K_f}{B_f}\right) \frac{b_e^o}{1.10} . \tag{57}$$

The average K_f/B_f has been estimated to be 1.6.[20] Thus, given our other estimates, the average optimal tax rate on corporate income is about 37 percent. While this is somewhat lower than the statutory rate of 48 percent for a large company, the presence of the 7 percent investment tax credit in recessions has served to substantially lower the effective tax on produced producer durables. Assuming that half of the years are "recession" years, the annual investment credit $3\frac{1}{2}$ percent. And assuming that the typical age of produced producer durables is 10 years, the optimal effective excise tax (using the formula for consumer durables) on corporate purchases of producer durables is about 7 percent $\times$ 1.6. This means that the effective $3\frac{1}{2}$ percent investment credit subsidizes capital by about 30 percent of the optimal capital tax. But since the corporate profits tax rate is greater than the optimal rate by about 30 percent of the optimal rate, the combined 48 percent corporate profits tax and 7 percent investment credit in recessions effects very close to an optimal tax on producer durables in corporations.

Surrenderable Capital

Apparently, the only empirical cases in which the costs of defending certain units of capital are significantly higher than the costs of defending equally valuable coveted capital are cases in which the capital is located on foreign soil. In accord with our general results, the U.S. government neither substantially commits itself to defend such capital nor significantly taxes the income from such capital.[21] Rather, the United States sells insurance against foreign confiscation to the various companies with foreign holdings, in effect charging a price for providing only those pro-

[20] This was done by multiplying an estimate of the rate of return to book value of equity for U.S. manufacturing corporations in 1966 (Pechman 1971, p. 307) by an estimate of the price-earnings ratio for U.S. industrials for the same year (Moody's Investors' Service 1967, p. a 23). This was then adjusted to represent the ratio of the book value of companies relative to their market value by adding on the ratio of debt to net worth and dividing by one plus this ratio (Pechman 1971, p. 307).

[21] An exception applies to overseas earnings of U.S. companies when taxes paid to foreign countries are below what domestic taxes would be. The United States taxes such earnings as domestic earnings and credits the foreign taxes against the tax bill. This is a significant exception only when foreign tax rates are very low, in which case the United States is probably protecting the foreign country, so that the domestic U.S. tax rates should apply.

tection services that it would rationally supply as an insurer in order to avoid claims by the insured much as private medical insurers rationally supply proper medical care in order to avoid future insurance claims.

III. Conclusion

Our results indicate that the U.S. tax structure does not produce the deluge of malincentives and economic inefficiencies that one finds when using the traditional theory of public finance. Rather, using a more accurate theory of the nature of national defense, our tax structure produces roughly optimal incentives. Because no model such as our was available to the advisors or decision makers during the development of the U.S. tax structure, our results strongly suggest that our political system, using the self-interested calculations of its citizens, has somehow been able to systematically produce a substantially more efficient tax structure than our economists, using the traditional theory of taxation, have been able to recommend.

While incentives under the U.S. tax system appear to be remarkably efficient, we are not advocating the status quo. In particular, we have argued that the current U.S. tax system could be improved by reinstating excise taxes on those consumer durables which are not used for business purposes and replacing corporate income taxes on companies with publicly traded shares with an annual tax of about $2\frac{1}{2}$ percent on the market value of their common and preferred stock, dropping the personal income tax on dividends and capital gains on such stock.

References

Barnett, H. J., and Morse, C. *Scarcity and Growth*. Baltimore: Johns Hopkins Univ. Press, 1963.

Commerce Clearing House. *Code of Regulations*. Chicago: Commerce Clearing House, 1957.

Harberger, A. "The Taxation of Mineral Industries." *Federal Tax Policy for Growth and Stability*. Washington: Joint Econ. Committee of Congress, Government Printing Office, 1955.

Knight, F. H. "Professor Hayek and the Theory of Investment." *Econ. J.* 45 (December 1935): 77–94.

Lasser, J. K. *Your Income Tax*. New York: Simon & Schuster, 1971.

Malinvaud, E. "Capital Accumulation and Efficient Resource Allocation." *Econometrica* 21 (April 1953): 233–68.

Marshall, A. *Principles of Economics*. 8th ed. New York: Macmillan, 1925.

Moody's Investor Service. *Moody's Industrial Manual* (June 1967).

Pechman, J. *Federal Tax Policy*. Washington, D.C.: Brookings Inst., 1971.

Prentice-Hall. *Federal Taxes*. Vol. 2. Englewood Cliffs, N.J.: Prentice-Hall, 1971.

Rooney, R. F. *Taxation and Regulation of the Domestic Crude Oil Industry*. Ph. D. dissertation, Stanford University, 1965.

Ruhter, W. "Childhood, Human Capital Development, and Parental Incentives." Unpublished manuscript, UCLA, 1974.

Samuelson, P. A. "The Pure Theory of Public Expenditure." *Rev. Econ. and Statis.* 36 (November 1954): 387–89.

———. "Tax Deductibility of Economic Depreciation to Insure Invariant Valuations." *J.P.E.* 72 (December 1964): 604–6.

Smith, A. *Wealth of Nations.* Vol. 2. New York: Random House, 1937.

Thompson, E. A. "Statement." *Governmental Intervention in the Market Mechanism: The Petroleum Industry.* Hearings before the Subcommittee on Antitrust and Monopoly of the Committee on the Judiciary, May 1968.

An Economic Basis for the "National Defense Argument" for Aiding Certain Industries

Earl A. Thompson

University of California, Los Angeles

Two alternative theories, each generating a "national defense argument" for protectionism, are developed and tested. The theory surviving the tests states that wartime price controls imply an undervaluation of peacetime stocks of capital which produce the war-controlled outputs. Optimal policy responses to these undervaluations are derived. For example: Nonimported, undervalued capital goods should receive domestic subsidies; undervalued capital goods, imported in peacetime but not in wartime, should receive import protection; and undervalued capital goods which are imported in wartime should be granted cartel status. An application to the United States indicates that the theoretical optimum is approximated by observed policy.

The "national defense argument" has long been a favorite of those who support governmental aid to various domestic industries. Yet the argument traditionally has been framed as an appeal to patriotic emotions, amounting to little more than the statement that the military has an unusually high wartime demand for the products of the favored industry. As such, we can hardly accept it as a sufficient economic argument for aiding an industry. This paper is an attempt to

This paper owes much to several discussions with Bob Rooney about 10 years ago, comments by Edward Miller on a previous paper, financial assistance from the Foundation for Research in Economics and Education, and helpful comments on previous drafts of this paper from Ron Batchelder, Harold Demsetz, Jack Hirshleifer, Walter Oi, George Stigler, Cliff Stone, and referees of this *Journal*. The paper also benefited substantially from the critical and enthusiastic research assistance of Bob Williams, a UCLA graduate student.

Journal of Political Economy, 1979, vol. 87, no. 1
0022-3808/79/8701-0010@02.67, Reprint.
© 1979 by The University of Chicago.

specify an economically acceptable national defense argument and to apply the argument where it appears most appropriate.

An important result of the theoretical analysis is a specification of the efficient form of the aid. This result tells us, for example, whether the efficient aid comes in the form of an output subsidy, a particular input subsidy, or a protective tariff. Another important result is a theoretical quantification of the subsidy justified by an economically acceptable national defense argument. These two results serve to distinguish an economically acceptable national defense argument from the more vague, emotional arguments. The empirical applications in this paper will employ these results.

I. National Defense as an Economic Activity

Two possible national defense arguments will be developed. Each will be built upon an aggregative simplification of the author's previous general equilibrium model containing national defense (Thompson 1974). We shall outline this aggregative simplification before proceeding to the generalizations which permit the derivation of national defense arguments.

In this model, each "nation," or given subgroup of individuals, must defend its assets in order to own them, and each capital good is owned by some nation. In such a world, national defense is a necessary social expenditure rather than a waste of the world's resources. For any distribution of property between nations, there is a set of minimal national defense efforts required to prevent one nation from taking the property of another. When property is distributed so that rationally chosen defense efforts reach these levels, there is an equilibrium distribution of property across the various nations. We assume throughout that such an equilibrium is achieved. At time t, a particular nation in this world will have a total capital stock, K^t, part of which, K_D^t, is devoted to national defense, D^t; a second part, K_C^t, to consumption, C^t; and the third and remaining part, K_I^t, to investment, I^t, that is, to the creation of next period's capital, K^{t+1}. Thus, for the particular country, the current resource conservation equations and three production functions are, respectively:

$$K_D^t + K_C^t + K_I^t = K^t, \tag{1}$$

$$D^t(K_D^t) = D^t, \tag{2}$$

$$C^t(K_C^t) = C^t, \tag{3}$$

and

$$I^t(K_I^t) = K^{t+1}, \tag{4}$$

for $t = 1, 2, \ldots$, etc. The production functions in equations (2), (3), and (4) are assumed to be differentiable, concave, and monotonically increasing.

Since there is a distributional equilibrium, the country will undertake the defense effort required to deter all foreign aggressors. That is, D^t is set so that it is just sufficient to make nonpositive the most efficient aggressor's profit from successful aggression against the country, Π_A^t. In particular, letting $f^t(D^t)$ be the least-cost aggressor's resource cost of successful current aggression and assuming that $df^t(D^t)/dD^t > 0$, K_D^t, and thus D^t, are set for every t so that:

$$\Pi_A^t = K^t - f^t(D^t) = 0.^{[1]} \tag{5}$$

Substituting (2) into (5) produces a simple dependency of K_D^t on K_t, where $dK_D^t/dK^t > 0$ in view of the monotonic increasing nature of both $f^t(\cdot)$ and $D^t(\cdot)$. The solution value of K_D^t for a given K_t is hereafter written $\overline{K}_D^t(K^t)$.

Giving consumers in the country under consideration a differentiable, quasi-concave utility function, $U(C^1, C^2, C^3, \ldots)$, we can determine a socially optimal allocation by maximizing it subject to equations (1)–(5). Substituting (2) into (5), this yields the following marginal condition for social efficiency:

$$\frac{\partial U}{\partial C^t} \Big/ \frac{\partial U}{\partial C^{t+1}} = \left|\left(\frac{\partial C^{t+1}}{\partial K_I^{t+1}} \cdot \frac{\partial I^t}{\partial K_I^t}\right) \Big/ \frac{\partial C^t}{\partial K^t}\right| \cdot \left(1 - \frac{d\overline{K}_D^t}{dK^t}\right). \tag{6}$$

Inspection of (6) reveals the left side to be the familiar, Fisherian marginal rate of time preference, while the first term in brackets on the right side is the marginal rate of time transformation. In competitive markets, these two terms are equated by rational individuals, as the former is set equal to one plus the market's real rate of interest by utility-maximizing consumers while the latter is set equal to the same rate by profit-maximizing producers. The fact that capital which is produced for the next period generates an extra defense requirement is irrelevant to individuals in a standard competitive model because the government will bear the extra defense cost (their share of the extra cost in terms of lump-sum taxes being insignificant when the number of individuals is large). In this way an inefficiency would exist

---

[1] We are assuming here, for simplification, that the successful foreign aggressor obtains all of his victim's capital. It is clear that he cannot do this in the real world, that only a certain part of a nation's capital stock is "coveted" by foreign aggressors. While the presence of noncoveted capital, which was allowed in my 1974 paper, has no effect on the national defense arguments or applications below, we shall allow noncoveted capital to exist in testing the general empirical validity of our national defense arguments. To make the above theory consistent with this test, subtract a constant from K^t in eq. (5), where the constant represents the fixed supply of noncoveted capital in the country.

in a competitive economy with neutral, or lump-sum, taxes (such as a simple consumption tax in every period). This competitive inefficiency is easily cured through the introduction of a tax on capital in all periods, which amounts to a tax on I^t, so that the return to devoting a unit of K^t to the production of K^{t+1} is reduced by $d\overline{K}_D^t/dK^t$. That is, since a capital accumulator in a competitive private-property system in which the government provides for the collective defense of the nation's capital creates an external diseconomy in that he increases the level of defense expenditures his nation requires to protect its capital stock, a periodic, ad valorem capital tax is justified. (For a formal proof, see Thompson [1974, pt. 1]). Assuming that all capital goods are sold when they are originally created, an equivalent to such a tax is an income tax with depreciation and depletion allowances (see Thompson 1974, pt. 2).

II.   "National Defense Arguments"

Two distinct national defense arguments, that is, reasons for subsidizing certain activities based on the special nature of national defense, emerge from a two-step generalization of the above model of national defense. We shall now take the first step.

A.   *Argument Number 1: Private Capital Deters Foreign Aggressors*

The first argument is the result of an extension of the above model in which the capital used in the private sector simultaneously aids in the provision of national defense as a joint product. Thus, equation (2) becomes:

$$D^t = D^t(K_D^t, K^t), \tag{2'}$$

where the partial derivatives of (2') are always positive. This change occurs because the costs of successful foreign aggression against a nation are now affected by the resources that the nation has on hand to mobilize in order to withstand an enemy attack (see, e.g., Miller 1976).[2] Substituting (2') into (5) will again yield a simple dependency of K_D^t on K^t, a Pareto optimum described by (6), and an efficient tax formula which subtracts $d\overline{K}_D^t/dK^t$ from the return on a unit of invest-

---

[2] In a more realistic model, one complicated by heterogeneous capital goods, some kinds of capital goods cannot be economically converted to wartime use. However, such goods often serve either as substitutes for others that are economically converted to wartime use or as inputs in the production of (or trade for) some war-related goods. Hence, it is probably safe to assume, at least for expositional purposes, that the entire peacetime capital stock is useful in producing current defense services as a joint product. The empirical test below, however, will explicitly assume that some kinds of private capital do not, even indirectly, aid a country's war effort.

ment. But it no longer follows that $d\bar{K}_b^t/dK^t > 0$. That is, an increase in the nation's capital stock may now decrease its national defense requirement given (2') and (5) because an increase in the capital stock may provide a greater deterrent than an attraction to the relevant foreign aggressor. If this were the case, a subsidy to capital would be in order; that is, the first national defense argument would apply. If the opposite were the case, then the generalization of (2) to (2') would simply reduce the magnitude of the efficient capital tax, no capital subsidy would be rationalized, and the first national defense argument would not apply.

Assuming observed defense expenditures are rationally undertaken, we can test which is in fact the case by relating observed defense expenditures to the observed capital stock. If there is a positive relation, then the positive external value of private-sector capital resulting from its ability to discourage foreign aggressors would fall short of the negative value of private-sector capital resulting from its attractiveness to foreign aggressors. No net subsidy would be justified, and our first national defense argument would not apply.

Some complications do arise in applying this test to a more realistic world, one with heterogeneous capital goods. For, in the more realistic environment: (1) only part of a nation's capital stock is "coveted," that is, relevant to foreign aggressors as an asset; and (2) only part, a generally different part, of its private capital stock is a potential input into the defense effort. But we can safely exclude nonmarketable capital assets (such as memories of pleasant experiences), domestic cash balances, and most private-sector technology from both types of capital. Also, since a large subset of consumer durables is noncoveted and a large, but generally different, subset of consumer durables is not even an indirect input into the defense effort, it is perhaps best to exclude all consumer durables from the capital stocks used to test the first national defense argument. These considerations limit the test to commonly measured, industrial capital stocks plus human capital. Since data on aggregate industrial and human capital stocks are available for very few countries, while NNP data are available for most countries and allow us to approximate the relative sums of the human and nonhuman, industrial capital stocks of the various countries, we use NNP data for our test. But one important defect in such a measure is that it fails to net out the maintenance of the country's human capital. For a given NNP, the lower a nation's subsistence requirement, the greater are both the stock of capital which its enemies covet and the stock of capital which it can divert to a war. So a lower subsistence requirement, ceteris paribus, will lower the country's defense requirement if the first national defense argument is valid but raise it if it is invalid.

In view of the above, we regressed national defense expenditures, taken from a 1970 cross-section of 96 countries, on: (1) NNP, taken from data published by the Stockholm International Peace Research Institute (1974), and, to account for subsistence requirements, (2) population, obtaining data from the UN *Statistical Yearbook* (1973). The assumption here is that the subsistence requirements of our countries are proportional to their populations.

The least-squares fitted equation, where Y is income and P is population, is:

$$D = \underset{(t=43.10)}{.07Y} - \underset{(t=-2.53)}{8.49P} \quad ; R^2 = .96.$$

The addition of a constant term did not have any economically significant effect on the regression, nor did the exclusion of various groups of the poorest countries, nor did the use of a two-step weighted regression procedure (Glejser 1969) to eliminate significant heteroscedasticity in the least-squares residuals, nor did the inclusion of a variable representing an age distribution parameter.[3] The sign and significance of the coefficients are ample evidence for us to confidently reject our first national defense argument.[4]

Our estimate of per capita subsistence income based upon this estimated equation, the annual income per capita which would make defense expenditures zero, is $8.49/.07 = \$121.29$. The reasonableness of this figure is additional evidence in support of our general theory of the nature of national defense.[5]

---

[3] The coefficient of the age distribution parameter which we used, namely, the proportion of the country's population which is of fighting age (19–34 years of age), also provided an additional test of the first national defense argument. For if the deterrent effect of the availability of capital especially useful in supplying defense were dominant, then having a high proportion of fighting-age citizens would, ceteris paribus, significantly reduce a country's defense requirement. Obtaining our data from the UN *Demographic Yearbook, 1975*, we found the effect of an increase in the fraction of a country's population which is of fighting age on the country's defense expenditures to be highly insignificant ($t = -0.22$ on raw data and $t = +0.23$ for data transformed to remove the significantly heteroscedastic residuals).

[4] An objection to the above (raised by Ken Arrow and an astute referee) is that our test is inconclusive because it is based on a certainty model of protection: In a model with uncertain protection, a greater capital stock might induce a country to spend more on defense even though the increased capital stock reduced the probability of aggression against it simply because wealthier people rationally purchase more security as well as other goods. If this argument held, we would observe significantly more national security and hence a lower frequency of war in wealthier countries. We surely do not observe this. The fact that observed security does not increase with wealth despite the induced increase in defense expenditures implies that an increase in a nation's wealth, ceteris paribus, decreases its national security. This implied effect is sufficient for the optimality of a capital tax in a model with uncertain protection.

[5] As subsistence would probably be higher than this for the highly developed countries, we could improve the model by making the theoretical coefficient on population rise in a linear fashion with income per capita. This would yield the same estimation

B. National Defense Argument Number 2

1. The Basic Argument

Our second national defense argument is based on the observation that price ceilings and rationing are periodically imposed on certain products during certain recurrent "national emergencies," or "wars." A direct consequence of these controls is that the owners of the capital goods which produce such products are unable to capture the wartime social values of their capital. This in turn implies that the production of such capital goods during peacetime is undervalued by private investors. A policy which raises the peacetime value of such capital up to its social value is a peacetime subsidy to this capital. With such a subsidy, $\partial I^t/\partial K_1^t$ as perceived by peacetime producers increases because the total subsidy payment to $I^t(=K^{t+1})$ will be increased if and only if more K^{t+1} is produced while the total subsidy payment to K^t is given at time t and independent of the division of K^t between K_1^t and K_C^t. The second national defense argument thus implies that the peacetime increases in the $\partial I^t/\partial K_1^t$ terms as perceived by private producers due to the optimal subsidies just exactly match the artificial, privately perceived, increases in the $(\partial U/\partial C_t)/(\partial U/\partial C_{t+1})$ terms due to the existence of future price controls and rationing.[6]

Since there is already a tax on capital in every period when we apply the argument of Sections I and IIA, this special national defense subsidy is achievable by simply reducing the peacetime tax rate on capital which produces the goods which are undervalued during a war, assuming that the subsidy rate does not exceed the tax rate of Sections I and IIA above.

This should, perhaps, be shown more formally. First, taking C to be a type of consumer good whose price is effectively controlled during a war, and taking t to be the upcoming peacetime period and $t+1$ the subsequent wartime period, private maximization of $U(\cdot, C^1, \ldots, C^t, C^{t+1}, \ldots)$ subject to a constant wealth equal to $\ldots + P^1C^1 + \ldots + P^tC^t + (1+\alpha)P^{t+1}C^{t+1}, + \ldots$ implies:

$$\frac{\partial U}{\partial C^t} \Big/ \frac{\partial U}{\partial C^{t+1}} = P^t/P^{t+1}(1+\alpha), \tag{7}$$

where P^t is a competitively determined parameter representing the

---

form but would change the interpretation of the Y coefficient to the effect of income on defense minus the effect of per capita income on subsistence. Since the latter effect is positive, our estimated Y coefficient is a downward-biased estimate of the effect of income on defense in a nation for a given level of subsistence.

[6] When, realistically, there are heterogeneous capital goods, this exact equality implies that I^t is not economically useful in producing wartime outputs other than the price-controlled output. The optimal subsidization of undervalued capital which is not specific to the price-controlled output during wartime will be discussed in Sec. IIIA.

present price to a producer of commodity C at date t, while α, which exceeds zero, represents the present value of the ration coupon enabling the wartime consumer to buy a unit of the commodity. Since privately optimal production decisions are such that profits at time t, $P^tC^t(K_C^t) + P_K^{t+1}I^t(K_I^t) - (1 + \lambda_t)P_K^t(K_C^t + K_I^t)$, are maximized, where P_K^t is the parametric present price of capital goods in period t and λ_t is the parametric tax rate on the use of capital in time t,

$$P^t \frac{\partial C^t}{\partial K_C^t} = P_K^t(1 + \lambda_t) \tag{8}$$

and

$$P_K^{t+1} \frac{\partial I^t}{\partial K_I^t} = P_K^t(1 + \lambda_t). \tag{9}$$

Since this holds for all time periods, including $t+1$, we can divide (8) by itself in the next period to obtain:

$$P^t/P^{t+1} = \left(\frac{P_K^t/P_K^{t+1}}{\dfrac{\partial C^t}{\partial K_C^t} \Big/ \dfrac{\partial C^{t+1}}{\partial K_C^{t+1}}} \right) \left(\frac{1 + \lambda_t}{1 + \lambda_{t+1}} \right). \tag{10}$$

Using (9), this becomes:

$$P^t/P^{t+1} = \left(\frac{\partial C^{t+1}}{\partial K_C^{t+1}} \cdot \frac{\partial I^t}{\partial K_I^t} \Big/ \frac{\partial C^t}{\partial K_C^t} \right) \left(\frac{1}{1 + \lambda_{t+1}} \right). \tag{11}$$

Combining (11) with (7),

$$\frac{\partial U}{\partial C^t} \Big/ \frac{\partial U}{\partial C^{t+1}} = \left(\frac{\partial C^{t+1}}{\partial K_C^{t+1}} \cdot \frac{\partial I^t}{\partial K_I^t} \Big/ \frac{\partial C^t}{\partial K_C^t} \right) \left(\frac{1}{(1+\lambda)(1+\alpha)} \right). \tag{12}$$

Hence, using (6), for Pareto optimality, the capital tax rate, λ, must be set so that

$$(1 + \lambda) = \left(\frac{1}{1 + \alpha} \right) \left(\frac{1}{1 - d\bar{K}_b^t/dK^t} \right). \tag{13}$$

This is the desired result: The existence of wartime controls simply lowers the optimal peacetime capital tax rate on the kinds of capital that produce the war-controlled consumer goods.

Since the capital tax was achieved by taxing the return to capital via an ordinary income tax, in which original investment costs are written off in the future according to the rate of depreciation or depletion of the capital, a natural method of achieving this subsidy is to allow peacetime purchasers of such capital to expense a portion of the original capital cost in the year of the original investment. A 100 percent initial write-off would completely neutralize the capital tax, as the tax rate on the future income produced by the capital would then be completely offset by the equal subsidy rate on the capital through the 100 percent initial write-off of the investment. Similarly, allowing p percent of the initial investment to be expensed, with the rest depreciated at the rate of actual depreciation times $(1-p)$, would be equivalent to a special capital subsidy of λp percent. Observed U.S. tax policies corresponding to this theoretical policy are the immediate write-off of intangible drilling expenses granted to oil and gas drillers and the immediate write-off of certain investment expenditures given to cattle breeders. These will be discussed in greater detail in Section IIIB.

An inefficient protection policy would be a peacetime subsidy to the products which suffer wartime price controls. While this policy would encourage a redirection of investment toward the kinds of capital that produce goods which suffer wartime price controls, it would fail to encourage the reaccumulation or adoption of relatively durable forms of such capital. In terms of our notation, an output subsidy has the effect of proportionately increasing both the $\partial C^{t+1}/\partial K_C^{t+1}$ and $\partial C^t/\partial K_C^t$ terms that appear to the private producers, leaving unaffected the $\partial I^t/\partial K_C^t$ term which also goes into determining the time rate of transformation, thereby leaving the time rate of transformation at the same allocation unaffected. So final output subsidies are inefficient as they fail to remove the undervaluation of future outputs relative to present outputs.

2. Tariffs and Subsidies

We now open up the discussion to allow international trade, assuming that the country imports capital during peacetime in quantities sufficient to affect the world prices of these imports. Under this condition, of course, the classic "optimum tariff" argument applies (see, e.g., Johnson 1961). That is, in the absence of international cooperation and of tariff collection costs, it is optimal for the country to impose a tariff on its capital imports. But there is an additional advantage of a tariff when (*a*) the protected capital good is undervalued through wartime price controls and (*b*) the abnormally high international transportation costs which arise during wars preclude substantial wartime importation of the capital. By increasing the domestic price and production of capital in every period, the tariff has the effect of reducing the wartime capital shortage and therefore reducing α, the degree of wartime undervaluation of the products of the capital. In this sense, the tariff serves as a substitute for a capital subsidy. If the wartime undervaluation is sufficiently small, an optimum tariff will drop α to zero. In that case, there is no need for the extra policy machinery necessary for an efficient capital subsidy, and the tariff serves a dual role.

Of course, when the pretariff level of α is sufficiently large that α is still significantly positive once the familiar "optimal tariff" level is reached, then a domestic capital subsidy is also in order. But the tariff still has the advantage of reducing the magnitude of the optimal domestic capital subsidy and therefore of correspondingly reducing the evasion and enforcement costs of capital subsidization.

While it appears to be quite likely, from the high frequency of observed tariff agreements, that international cooperation costs are sufficiently low to preclude many tariffs which would otherwise impose the familiar monopoly welfare losses from "optimal tariffs" on the world, it is much less likely that international cooperation costs would be sufficiently low to preclude a tariff which has a social advantage through its effect on α (and therefore on domestic subsidization costs) to counteract the familiar welfare cost of monopoly.

The above tariff argument will be applied in Section III.

The case in which there are significant wartime imports of the undervalued capital or its products is discussed later in this section.

3.   Alternative Methods of Capital Subsidy

a) Subsidies to investments in skill.—Since an individual's accumulation of skill is achieved to a significant degree by the foregoing of current income, and the capital good—skilled labor—is not sold when produced, there is no taxable transaction approximating the value of the current investment when labor accumulates its skill. Investments in skill are taxed indirectly when there is a higher tax rate on future, higher skilled wages than on foregone, current wages. The observed U.S. progressive income tax accomplishes this, taxing skill accumulation approximately neutrally with other kinds of capital accumulation (Thompson 1974). One way to subsidize certain investments in human capital under the second national defense argument is to reduce the degree of progression for those occupations warranting a subsidy. We observe very little of this. However, an alternative form of investment subsidy, justifiable by the extraordinarily high marginal transaction costs of lending to the young investor in his own skills, is to directly subsidize the financial part of the human capital investment. We do, of course, observe this form of subsidy. Since the second national defense argument applies quite obviously to the accumulation of certain skills because of wartime conscription (a particularly effective form of price control), an obvious rationalization of some such investment subsidy exists. Furthermore, since the United States has been a small net importer of human capital, the above argument for some degree of human capital import protection applies. (A more detailed empirical analysis appears in Section III*E*.)

b) Investment subsidies to foreign suppliers.—A difficulty arises when the wartime price controls apply to products which are substantially imported during wartime. It is apparently impractical for a country to directly subsidize foreign capital because there is no obvious way for the subsidizing country to collect for the increase in benefits such a policy confers on numerous other foreign countries. A solution to this dilemma is for the importing countries to simply allow the foreign countries to "cartelize" their industry. This means that the exporting countries are allowed to jointly purchase a significant part of the capital output of their industry or to force prorationing on their otherwise unrestricted producers based on their respective productive capacities. In either case, the result is an increase in the price and production of foreign capital but a decrease in the normal, peacetime consumption of the products of this capital. During wartime, when the industry demand for this capital becomes infinitely elastic (in the relevant range) at the effectively controlled price (which is no lower than the peacetime price), the jointly accumulated foreign capital is no longer rationally held off the market, and wartime use of the capital jumps to an amount which exceeds that which would exist without the cartel. Viewed in this way, cartels of exporters merely act as replacements for the private speculators in inventories or excess production capacity that are discouraged by the wartime price controls. For appropriately set price parameters, the economic behavior of these cartels is identical to that which would result if there were competitive markets and no wartime systems of effective price controls. To prove this, we treat the exporting and importing countries as a single country and represent the cartel as an institution which induces its members to cut back its peacetime production of consumption goods so that equation (8) is rewritten, for peacetime, as

$$P^t \frac{\partial C^t}{\partial K_C^t} = (1 + \beta)P_K^t(1 + \lambda), \beta > 0. \tag{8'}$$

The cartel does not restrict entry so that the investment equations in (9) remain the same. Dividing (8') by (8) for $t+1$, the next wartime period, and then using (9),

$$\frac{P^t}{P^{t+1}} = \frac{P_K^t(1+\beta)}{(\partial C^t/\partial K_C^t)} \Big/ \frac{P_K^{t+1}}{(\partial C^{t+1}/\partial K_C^{t+1})}$$

$$= \left(\frac{\partial C^{t+1}}{\partial K_C^{t+1}} \cdot \frac{\partial I^t}{\partial K_I^t} \Big/ \frac{\partial C^t}{\partial K_C^t} \right) \left(\frac{1 + \beta}{1 + \lambda} \right). \tag{11'}$$

Using (7),

$$\frac{\partial U}{\partial C^t} \bigg/ \frac{\partial U}{\partial C^{t+1}} = \left(\frac{\partial C^{t+1}}{\partial K_C^{t+1}} \cdot \frac{\partial I^t}{\partial K_I^t} \bigg/ \frac{\partial C^t}{\partial K_C^t}\right)_i \left(\frac{1+\beta}{1+\lambda}\right)_i \left(\frac{1}{1+\alpha}\right). \quad (12')$$

Hence, we may set the degree of peacetime monopoly, β, equal to α, so that the cartel agreement induces a Pareto optimum with no alteration in the optimal capital tax rate given by equation (13). Alternatively, a cartel may act directly as an accumulator of inventories beyond peacetime competitive levels. In this case, the only change in the system is that equation (9) for peacetime becomes

$$(1+\beta)P_K^{t+1}\frac{\partial I^t}{\partial K_I^t} = P_K^t(1+\lambda). \quad (9')$$

Substituting (9') into (10) and using (7), we again arrive at (12').

The formal argument extends easily to the case of heterogeneous, industry-specific, capital goods in that the cartel also offsets the undervaluation of K_I relative to capital which produces consumption goods whose wartime prices are not effectively controlled. For sufficiently high cartel prices appropriately attract investment away from other industries, any possible loss in profit from the enforced peacetime production cutback being offset by the increase in profit from the sale of wartime production at higher prices.

It may be argued that the observed degree of monopoly is set at the simple profit-maximizing level for the producers and is independent of negotiations to achieve joint efficiency. But evidence to the contrary is found in the fact that the two most durable post–World War II cartels, those in tin and coffee, set quotas approved and even enforced by the consuming countries. Furthermore, the newest effective international cartel, that in crude oil, is encouraged by U.S. energy policy and apparently charges substantially less than simple monopoly prices because of political considerations.

Additional evidence that observed international cartels are not simple monopolies is that the cartel countries have not jointly imposed monopolistic export taxes, such taxes representing the optimal monopoly policy when side payments are precluded (see, e.g., Johnson 1961, chap. 2). These taxes would discourage entry and investment (changing the $[1+\beta]$ coefficient in [9'] to $1/[1+\beta]$, interpreting β now as the ordinary degree of monopoly), thereby preventing the achievement of joint optimality.

An empirical application of the second national defense argument to foreign suppliers is contained in Section IIIB.

c) *Regulated industries.*—Certain industries in the real world have their peacetime prices set by government agencies.[7] If peacetime prices of the products of these industries are set so as to induce competitive supplies and clear markets, but wartime prices are effectively controlled below their marginal social values, underinvestment will characterize the regulated industries. However, if peacetime prices are set above competitive levels, and either industry supplies are optimally prorationed among the producers to prevent excessive quality competition or capacity-specific quality competition is permitted, then an investment subsidy equivalent to that achieved in the international cartel model above will be achieved as long as investment and entry are not both artificially limited by government policy.

The view that federally regulated industries in the United States, largely the ICC-controlled transport industries, receive above-competitive prices but are induced to develop more capacity than is in the joint interest of the individual firms has become increasingly popular, and the view has received substantial theoretical and empirical support in the pathbreaking article of Stigler (1971) and more recent studies by Douglas and Miller (1974), DeVany (1975), and Moore (1975). The contribution of our theory is to point out the possible equivalence of this type of cartel to a real investment subsidy rather than a simple monopoly or inefficient quality subsidy and to suggest the possible social optimality of this type of cartel.[8] An empirical application of the second national defense argument to regulated industries appears in Section IIIC.

4. Why Argument Number 2 Is Not Necessarily a Second-Best Argument

It may appear that our national defense argument, resting as it does on the existence of special wartime controls, is a "second-best" policy

[7] This is perhaps because the underlying legal structure induces sufficient divergences from perfectly competitive supplies. For federally regulated transport industries, which will furnish our most interesting empirical applications of the second national defense argument to regulated industries, a plausible justification for some regulation is the legal imperfection that people who die do not have to compensate their friends (toward whom they are not sufficiently benevolent to unilaterally transfer lump sums). Without intervention, people would overly risk their lives. For certain goods, government-imposed safety standards suffice. For others, where government safety detection is sufficiently costly, the nominal price may be set sufficiently above the free-market price, and nonsafety dimensions of product quality may be sufficiently restricted, that safety-quality competition will induce a social optimum. The prices and supplies which we shall call competitive for such industries are those generated by the regulatory policy described above.

[8] The difference in interpretation of these institutions stems from our inclusion of the positive effects of higher-than-competitive peacetime price controls on (*a*) the conservation of capital for emergency use and (*b*) the allowed wartime price, and therefore the general profitability of investment, in the regulated industries.

in that it may appear more efficient to simply remove the wartime controls and so end the peacetime capital subsidy. This may be true. However, we shall argue in this section that under quite realistic conditions, efficient wartime policy requires a system of price controls.[9] Our argument is provided by the following elaboration of our national defense model, an elaboration ultimately admitting individually rational decisions about the level of national defense.

As above, a nation protects its capital by committing itself to devote sufficient resources to the punishment of foreign aggressors that the costs of aggression to all potential aggressors are never below the returns. Such protection generally requires that the protecting nation commit itself to lose more utility in punishing an act of foreign aggression against it than the gain in utility from having the protected capital (Kahn 1960). National defense expenditures communicate this commitment. While a certain level of defense expenditures is always necessary for a nation to display its ability to sufficiently punish a foreign aggressor, occasionally additional defense expenditures must be incurred in order that the defending nation also display its willingness to apply the requisite, narrowly irrational punishment in case of actual foreign aggression. That is, a nation's willingness is occasionally tested by its potential aggressors. These test periods are the "national emergencies," or "wars," referred to above.[10]

We now assume that decisions with respect to the magnitude of peacetime defense expenditures are made in the respective periods by the nation's citizens, say, by a majority vote. During peacetime, when there is no act of foreign aggression against the country, defense

[9] The popular argument for emergency price controls, of course, is that they represent the most practical method of preventing large redistributions toward those individuals who happen to be the owners of war-scarce inputs just prior to the news of the emergency. The main problem with this equity-efficiency trade-off explanation, besides the fact that historic price controls must be given very low marks in achieving egalitarian redistributive goals, is that relatively neutral excess-profits taxes on all industries would fill the hypothesized demand for redistribution in an administratively cheaper and much more systematic way (see Hicks, Hicks, and Rostas [1942], esp. pp. 29–35, 65–71). In fact, wartime U.S. excess-profits taxes have generated relatively insignificant revenues (see Rolph and Break [1961], pp. 26–27 and chap. 11, esp. p. 252). Furthermore, the logic of the equity-efficiency trade-off argument would dictate the extension of excess-profits taxes to peacetime, but this has not occurred. Therefore, one must doubt the overall empirical significance of the argument.

[10] Since costly aggression does not occur in a distributional equilibrium, our wars are generally between countries who are each simultaneously displaying their own defense commitments and testing the defense commitments of others. Our theoretical model can be generalized to admit costly aggression in "equilibrium" by replacing our certainty equilibrium with a more general sequence of temporary equilibria in which various nations may incorrectly estimate the costs of aggression. While the substitution of the resulting statistical equilibrium concept for our certainty equilibrium has no effect upon our theoretical results, it does have some effect on the calculations of optimal subsidy rates. Our estimates of optimal subsidy rates in Sec. III will be based on a relatively realistic statistical equilibrium concept.

expenditures are rationally chosen to be $\bar{K}'_D$. Any lower level would mean that country would surrender its capital, and a higher expenditure level would be a 100 percent deadweight loss (Buchanan and Tideman 1976). But during wartime, when there is an act of aggression against the country to test its willingness to devote sufficient resources to protect its capital, the citizenry cannot be counted on to choose the level of K'_D which would display a commitment to protection. This is because it is not in the interest of the citizenry to defend its capital against a foreign aggressor who commits himself to imposing more damage on the citizens if they do not surrender their capital than the capital is worth to them. The only way for the protecting nation to defend itself against a commitment of the latter kind is to precommit itself to fight the foreign aggressor anyway, and the citizens cannot be so committed if they are free to choose any level of K'_D during wartime. So a rational military leader retains the power to choose K'_D during a defensive war. He maintains his own share of the nation's capital if, and only if, he defends it and pays no part of the cost of the war. He is willing for his nation to lose more in defending its capital than the capital is worth because he personally does not pay the costs of war. The military leader thus will choose $\bar{K}'_D$ during a war, thereby demonstrating the nation's defense commitment. In a distributional equilibrium, these displays of willingness to fight are communicated without making the citizens actually suffer more from the wars than the nation's capital is worth to them.

While the peacetime defense expenditure level, which is efficiently determined by the rational votes of the nation's citizens, is achieved by a familiar tax-expenditure process (Buchanan 1968), the wartime defense expenditure level, which is militarily determined, is achieved by other means because the military has no direct power of taxation in a democracy. In particular, the military leaders, living within a dollar expenditure budget set by the voters, set the real defense expenditures by establishing a system of price controls, where the government forces private producers to sell to the military at government-determined prices. Without such controls, given the well-known limitations of alternatives such as money creation and debt financing, the military's confiscatory wartime powers would be generally too limited to provide the requisite level of defense.[11]

[11] Several perceptive readers of an earlier draft of this paper have pointed out that it is unnatural to constrain the military by disallowing it direct taxation power. By applying direct taxation during a war, the military could avoid the inevitable misallocation costs of wartime price controls. However, we are not forced to the conclusion that the second national defense argument is a second-best argument. We can assume, we believe realistically, that people are sufficiently better off living under the illusion that they are the employers rather than the slaves of a benevolent military (the illusory nature of this thought is shown in Thompson [1977]) that the illusion of freedom from

332 THOMPSON AND HICKSON

In summary, based on the politico-military model outlined above, it is not unreasonable to assume that price controls during a war are efficient economic policies despite the inevitable wartime misallocations generated by the controls. The model serves an additional function which is key to any empirical application of the second national defense argument. It is easy to see (from eq. [7]) that the second national defense argument is based on a definition of wartime price controls which includes any form of taxation of the wartime returns to capital beyond those levels implied by λ_1, λ_2, ... Assuming nonstrategic, Cournot-type voting, the above political model allows us to identify these additional taxes as taxes which are nondemocratically selected. We have described these nondemocratically determined taxes with the term "price controls" simply because such taxes have

military domination induced by the absence of direct military taxation is worth the misallocation costs of wartime price controls. An optimal response to this preference is a benevolent deception in which military leaders avoid the use of direct taxation even though it is a feasible policy. An implication of this assumption is that prior to the rapid development of the modern, popular governments of the past 2 centuries, when military leaders could not afford to be so charitable (Thompson 1977), there would be no deception and no special authoritarian wartime price controls. But national authoritarian price controls would be ubiquitous among developed countries in recent wars. Correspondingly, we observe (see, e.g., Nef [1968, chaps. 5, 12, 13] and Schuettinger [1976]) that while virtually all major powers involved in World Wars I and II had comprehensive, national, authoritarian wartime price controls, such controls were a rarity prior to the American and French Revolutions. The only pre-eighteenth-century cases in western civilization noted in Schuettinger's historical survey were the famous Edict of Diocletian A.D. 305 and the subsequent adoption of similar controls by Emperor Julian 60 years later. However, historical studies of this period (Gibbon 1906; Michell 1947) clearly indicate that the near bankruptcy of the Roman Empire, all practical sources of direct taxation being long exhausted, accounted for these attempts to enhance the Roman military effort by forcing down the prices which the military had to pay for their consumption goods. Thus, even these ancient wartime price controls can be rationalized by an argument in which the marginal economic return to direct taxation is below its marginal economic cost. The particular forms of direct wartime taxation and borrowing relied upon prior to the eighteenth century, and the switch to the use of price controls, rationing, and modern conscription from the eighteenth century to World War II, are described by Nef. Modern military organizations probably come closest to direct taxation through their conscription of human capital. But even here they steer clear of the surface efficiency of allowing draftees to buy their way out. Allowing such purchases would apparently overly expose the citizens to the power of the military leaders. Evidence for this is the extreme political unpopularity of the U.S.'s Civil War draft in which the draftees could buy their way out (Lindsay 1968), despite the obvious objective benefit which this draft conferred on the mass of nonwealthy voters. The hypothesis that people have a substantial demand for feeling more politically powerful than they really are suggests that people will also devote some of their own resources to enhance the feeling. Such self-deceptive investments are in fact commonly observed in voter turnouts and political contributions which are normally many multiples above the levels one would predict with objective rationality theory. A more conventional, alternative formulation of the above rationalization of the modern prohibition of direct military taxation would read: "The military cannot be trusted with such power." However, this more palatable alternative reflects a view of social organization which is inconsistent with rationality, accurate strategic communication, or realistic punishability (Thompson 1977).

largely taken this form. The nature of this form of taxation is elaborated in the application below.

III. An Empirical Application of the Second National Defense Argument

Due to the ubiquity of wartime price ceilings in modern developed countries, we can select any modern developed country which has been involved in a major war over its claimed capital for an empirical application of our second national defense argument. However, studies of the degrees of effectiveness of various wartime price controls were found only for the United States. So the United States is our only candidate for quantitative application of the second national defense argument. The last U.S. war over significant amounts of U.S.–claimed capital, World War II (1941–45), will serve as our empirical model of expected future wars over U.S.–claimed capital.

Since the prices of virtually all marketed products were formally controlled during most of World War II, it is tempting to apply the second national defense argument to all marketed capital goods. But it would be grossly naïve to accept blanket price ceilings as a generally effective policy. This is made abundantly clear in the study of U.S. white-collar crime during World War II by the sociologist Marshall Clinard (1952).[12] Nevertheless, since the social benefits of wartime price controls stem mainly from charging artificially low prices to the military, higher, above-ceiling, essentially free-market wartime prices charged to civilians through quality deterioration, tie-in sales, or other forms of hidden charges do not undermine the controls.[13] In any case, significant capital undervaluations may occur only: (1) in those industries where wartime price ceilings on civilian trades cannot be easily evaded, or (2) in the production of outputs which are sold intensively to the military at significantly subcompetitive prices. The

---

[12] This book, together with the U.S. Government Office of Price Administration's *Historical Reports on War Administration* (1943–47), is the source for most of the empirical generalizations below regarding the nature and effectiveness of wartime price controls.

[13] The effectiveness of price controls in lowering the nominal war costs faced by the military is quite apparent from numerous OPA industry studies. Aggregate statistical evidence also exists. During the precontrol years, 1940–41, the implicit price index of federal government purchases of goods and services rose about seven times faster than an implicit GNP deflator. In contrast, during the peak control period, 1942–44, the implicit price index of government purchases rose at about one-half the rate of the GNP deflator (U.S. Bureau of Census, Series F-67, 82, 87, and 101 [1959]). The low price inflation for government relative to private purchases cannot be explained by a relatively slack government demand during the peak control period. Real government purchases rose over 63 percent, while real GNP rose only 19 percent from 1942 to 1944 (U.S. Bureau of Census, Series F-87 and 101 [1959]).

following discussion uses these criteria in an attempt to identify the set of capital goods which may be significantly undervalued.

A.   *Capital Goods Which May Be Significantly Undervalued*

In industries where rational quality deterioration would create severe economic wastes due to the sheer magnitudes of the wartime short-ages, we observe the development of governmental rationing systems to complement the price ceilings or direct production controls. With a rationing system, civilian quantities demanded at the controlled price are limited by the supplies of available ration coupons so that sellers have no incentive to apply the above evasive devices. The effective demand does not justify hidden charges. Hence, for significantly rationed commodities, the real prices paid to producers by civilian as well as military customers are significantly below the corresponding real commodity values to the customers. Relatively large capital under-valuations are therefore possible when the capital produces com-modities which are significantly rationed during wartime. In World War II, significant coupon rationing programs existed for the fol-lowing commodities: gasoline, meat, shoes, dairy products, canned goods, coffee, and sugar.[14] With direct production controls, the gov-ernment directly restricts the production of certain consumer dura-bles in order to hold down the prices of the capital used to produce them. In World War II, the government restricted the production of numerous consumer durables (e.g., autos and copper and nylon products). In other exceptional industries, none of the various devices to evade price controls will work. These industries are largely the so-called regulated industries, where a government agency closely regulates transactions during peacetime and thus is prepared to sub-stantially prevent wartime quality deterioration, tie-in sales, and other hidden charges. The only such industries we could find for World War II were in the transportation and utility sectors.

Finally, among the few capital goods whose owners evade wartime price controls on civilian transactions but which warrant a significantly positive investment subsidy anyway because of the sheer magnitude of the military's underpayment, skilled human capital is by far the most important. While other, quantitatively less important undervaluations of this latter variety will be considered, most of the remainder of the paper is devoted to estimating optimal investment subsidies for each

---

[14] Other, apparently much less stringent noncoupon rationing programs existed for tires, rubber footwear, stoves, typewriters, and used cars and trucks. Here an applica-tion to a nearby government administrator demonstrating a "need" (nonspeculative value) for the commodity was required in order to have the right to purchase the good. Such discretionary rationing will be included in our analysis under the heading of direct controls.

of the cases of significant undervaluation mentioned above. But our empirical argument first requires the following pair of additional limitations on the set of capital goods to which the second national defense argument may significantly apply.

First, final goods held by consumers are precluded from substantial subsidization under the second national defense argument. For such goods normally are consumed by their holders and are therefore impervious to any kind of wartime price controls. Thus, rational consumers do not require any significant subsidy to induce them to accumulate the optimal peacetime stockpiles of consumer goods in anticipation of wartime shortages. This does not, of course, preclude the possibility that wartime price controls induce an undersupply of producer goods which create consumer goods during wartime.

Second, to limit the set of producer goods eligible for a significant subsidy under the second national defense argument, recall from Section IIB that the degree of wartime undervaluation of a capital good was equal to the degree of wartime undervaluation of its product in a world containing heterogeneous capital goods only when the undervalued capital good is specific to the production of undervalued products. When it is nonspecific, the optimal capital subsidy rate must be reduced: (a) because only a fraction of the value of all its wartime products is represented by the value of its effectively price-controlled product, and (b) because wartime reallocations of this capital to the production of goods which are effectively price controlled lower its marginal product there. Thus, due to the large total value of non-controlled, wartime products which it produces, labor used to produce effectively price-controlled wartime products would merit little peacetime subsidy if it were not for the extreme wartime undervaluation of labor's product via conscription. And normal plant and equipment which will be used in producing undervalued wartime products apparently warrants a relatively small subsidy because a given plant worked more intensively during a war (say, by use during nights and weekends), while implying a lower, future, peacetime capital stock, normally efficiently provides sufficient extra services to make its marginal social wartime product fall significantly toward peacetime levels. But large subsidies are possibly warranted for semidurable, specific capital inputs, that is, industry-specific capital inputs whose existing inventories are normally largely used up within a period of time equal to the expected duration of a war.

B.   *Application to the List of Industries Facing Wartime Coupon Rationing*

Therefore, our second national defense argument, when applied to our list of industries facing wartime coupon rationing, applies mainly to its specific raw material inputs. That is, the argument should concentrate not on gasoline stations or refineries but on crude oil inputs; it should concentrate not on slaughterhouses, dairies, and shoemaking plants but on cattle; it should concentrate not on sugar refineries but on raw sugar; not on canneries but on tin; not on coffee-roasting plants but on coffee beans.

Since the U.S. imports virtually all of its tin and coffee beans, the cartel argument applies here. Correspondingly, we observe that the only two international commodity cartels in existence throughout most of the post–World War II period were in coffee beans and tin (Kindleberger and Herrick 1977, chap. 20). And the recent development of an effective cartel of oil exporters has come pari passu with the rapid development of a U.S. dependence on foreign oil. All this seems to suggest that there has already been a significant policy response to the peacetime underinvestments which would have otherwise occurred.

Moreover, the two most substantial specific raw material inputs in the production of the domestic products on our list of war-rationed commodities, oil reserves and cattle, both receive a special subsidy in an optimal form, namely, by an immediate tax write-off on a large part of the investment expenditures which create the capital. But are the magnitudes of these subsidies optimal?

To provide more realistic estimates of these magnitudes, we now drop our extreme, simplifying assumption that the starting date of future wars is known with certainty. In its place, we assume that the current, peacetime probability that a major war will begin during a given future year is the same for all future years. While the qualitative conclusions of Section II remain unaffected by the introduction of such uncertainty, we shall rely on the simple estimation exercises below to illustrate this fact rather than explicitly reformulating the theory.

The excesses of implicit values over normal money prices of crude oil and cattle during World War II, using black-market price data found in Clinard (1952), can both be roughly estimated to be about 400 percent of the controlled prices. Hence, a current, peacetime, year-long, \$1.00 oil-drilling or cattle-raising investment, which yields four subsequent annual payments having present values of 25 cents each, would have an additional, total social value of \$4.00 if a major 4-year war started in the following year, \$3.00 if it started 2 years hence, \$2.00 if it started 3 years hence; and \$1.00 if it started 4 years hence. From the historical experience of the United States, we estimate that the current peacetime probability that a major 4-year war will start during any future year is 1/50. Hence, the expected present value of external social value from the investment is $4/50 + $3/50 + $2/50 + $1/50 = 0.20, or 1/5 of the market value of the investment.

That is, the expected loss to a peacetime investor in an oil-drilling or cattle-raising project due to the presence of emergency price controls and rationing is roughly 1/5 of the market value of the total return, or 1/5 of the cost of the project.

Are the orders of magnitude of observed U.S. subsidy rates comparable to this rough estimate of the optimal rate? First we consider an oil investment. Since about 4/5 of the capital expenditures of a typical oil-drilling firm are expensed as "dry-hole" or "intangible drilling" expenses and the value of an immediate tax write-off on an oil-drilling investment over a realistic depreciation allowance on the investment is about one-half of the marginal tax rate times the investment (Rooney 1965), the value of the immediate tax write-offs for a typical oil-drilling investment, using a marginal tax rate of 50 percent, is about $\frac{4}{5} \cdot \frac{1}{2} \cdot \frac{1}{2} = \frac{1}{5}$ of the cost of the investment. This rough estimate of the actual rate is the same as our rough estimate of the optimal subsidy rate. While the exact equality should certainly not be taken seriously, it does strongly suggest that the orders of magnitudes of optimal and actual subsidy rates to oil investments are about the same.

A breeder and raiser of cattle in the United States can write off a large portion of his investment expenditures, largely feeding and labor expenditures, as current expenses. As the magnitude of these expenses relative to total capital expenditures is similar to the magnitude of dry-hole and intangible drilling expenses relative to total capital expenditures in the oil industry, the investment subsidy resulting from this "loophole" is similar in magnitude to that for the oil industry.

Natural gas, a joint product of oil exploration, also benefits from the dry-hole and intangible drilling expense write-offs. But the product also warrants an investment subsidy because its product price has, since 1954, been effectively federally regulated at prices which do not exceed competitive levels and would likely be so regulated in a future war. And the order of magnitude of the optimal investment subsidy for gas is likely the same as that for oil because oil and gas are considered to be close substitutes in the aggregate, normally selling for around their Btu equivalency.[15]

Finally, sugar was also rationed in the United States during World War II. And, again according to examples in Clinard (1952), the

[15] The fact that the prices of domestic crude oil and natural gas are currently controlled at levels which are significantly below competitive would—if permanent—be a major error in U.S. economic policy. However, a possible, second-best economic rationale for temporary controls of this sort is that even more severe unemployment would have resulted since the value of oil and gas jumped in 1973–74 if all firms had to pay the true increase in the value of oil and gas in 1973–74 (Thompson 1978).

percentage wartime undervaluation of raw sugar was roughly the same order of magnitude as the percentage undervaluations of cattle or crude oil. Corresponding to this wartime undervaluation, the United States has had, for most of the post–World War II period, a special, indirect subsidy to U.S. investment in raw sugar production. Through various Sugar Acts, the United States paid 10–25 percent output subsidies to domestic and a few allied foreign producers of raw sugar who accepted prorationing of their outputs (see, e.g., Ballinger [1971] or Johnson [1974]). As above, the magnitude of this subsidy is in line with the optimal subsidy suggested by World War II sugar rationing.[16]

Following the optimal-tariff argument of Section IIC, moderate tariffs or import quotas, whose benefits are largely terms-of-trade advantages, are also in order for imports of crude oil, cattle, and sugar, all of which were imported to moderate degrees during most of the post–World War II period. Furthermore, to generate the smaller net capital subsidies due oil refineries, slaughterhouses and dairies, and confectionary plant and equipment, positive net, or "effective" (see, e.g., Balassa 1965), tariffs on imports of refined petroleum products; meat, leather, and dairy products; and confectionaries are also in order. In fact, significantly positive effective tariffs or import quotas on *all* of the above inputs and products have existed during much of the post–World War II period.[17]

C. Industries Facing Effective Civilian Price Controls without Rationing

As argued above, federally regulated industries, which are largely transportation industries in the United States, cannot practically employ large-scale quality-deterioration or other hidden charges during wartime to circumvent wartime price ceilings. Furthermore, World War II price ceilings were relatively unfavorable to this sector. In fact,

[16] The Sugar Acts, which were developed when Cuba (an important source of raw sugar) was a close ally of the United States, were finally repealed in 1975, after 15 years of disappointing attempts to replace Cuba in the scheme. The emerging 1977 system is following an outline suggested by our theory: First, a system of unusually high domestic raw sugar price supports through governmental purchases has just passed into law. Second, a large group in the U.S. Senate is aggressively encouraging previously monopsonized foreign sugar producers to break from the past by establishing a cartel and stepping the world price of sugar all the way up to the supported domestic U.S. level.

[17] Since crude oil import quotas were shared by the U.S. oil refineries, there was an obvious net subsidy to oil refineries. Since live cattle imports, mostly from Canada, were very small compared to meat, leather, and dairy imports, even before the relatively small 10 percent cattle tariff (U.S. Department of Agriculture 1959), the substantially higher rate of protection for these processed imports (Balassa 1965) implies substantial effective tariffs on them. References for the effective tariff on U.S. refined sugar imports are Ballinger (1971) and Johnson (1974).

the nominal BLS price index of transportation services actually fell during the widespread inflation of 1942–45. Yet very little World War II nonprice rationing of transport facilities was observed, and the relative quantity of transportation services rose dramatically during the war as transportation output grew at a rate which was several times larger than the GNP growth rate.[18] It is a problem to explain the increased supply, since there were neither a massive introduction of cost-saving innovations in consumer transportation during the period nor significantly decreasing costs for the somewhat competitive transportation sector. The peculiar supply and price pattern can, however, be explained by regarding the sector as one of our cartels, wherein the prior peacetime output prices are set above their competitive levels and peacetime industry outputs are prorationed among producers according to their respective capacities while investment is basically unrestricted.

A recent estimate of the degree of transport "overcapacity" due to transport prorationing and an estimate of the degree of net abnormal wartime demand appear to be about the same. According to Moore (1975), the "artificial" overcapacity in the domestic U.S. surface transport industry has been about 20 percent. And the magnitude of the abnormal transport demand during the peak years of World War II was only slightly in excess of 30 percent.[19] Since it is not unreasonable to assume a 10 percent expansion of transport services from any given stock, it is not unreasonable to conclude that the estimated degree of excess capacity in the U.S. transport sector does not significantly differ from the optimal degree of excess capacity.

Perhaps the most direct evidence for the existence of significant excess capacity in U.S.-regulated industries since World War II is the notorious absence of peak-load pricing in these industries.

Local public utilities, which provide water, electricity, telephone service, etc., also have their prices regulated. And World War II controls also appear to have maintained an effective ceiling on these prices at about peacetime levels. But the observed demand for utilities during World War II, in contrast to the observed demand for transportation, did not rise dramatically. And we expect, from the relative durability of the capital in the utility sector, that marginal costs would not rise as fast for public utilities as for the transportation industries.

---

[18] Taken from U.S. Bureau of Census (1959), tables E 113-39 for price data, F-29 for value-added data, and table F-87 for GNP data.

[19] By dividing the average of the real values added by transportation in the years 1941 and 1947 into the average of the real values added in the peak war years, 1943 and 1944, we obtained an estimate of abnormal wartime transportation activity of 31.3 percent (U.S. Bureau of Census, 1959, tables E 113–39 for price data and F-29 for value-added data).

As a result, a much smaller peacetime investment subsidy is apparently due the public utility sector than the transport sector based on the second national defense argument. The existence of some "overinvestment" by public utilities through their peculiar incentive structure is strongly suggested by the well-known Averch-Johnson model (Averch and Johnson 1962). However, in agreement with our view of the optimum, the estimated magnitude of such overinvestment is relatively small (Petersen 1975; Graham 1976).

D. Industries Facing Relatively Ineffective Price Controls on Civilian Transactions

As indicated above, for goods and services which are undervalued during wars only to the extent that they are sold to the military at artificially low prices, the resulting capital undervaluations can also normally be expected to be relatively small. The one obvious exception, the undervaluation of skilled human capital due to the extreme underpayment for the wartime services of such capital, is discussed in the next subsection. The largest of the other, relatively small undervaluations of this type presumably occurs for those semidurable capital inputs whose wartime products are sold intensively to the military at prices closely supervised by the price-controlling agencies. An examination of the Reports of the Office of Price Administration reveals that by far the most significant inputs of this kind were most agricultural commodities, various chemicals and nonferrous metals, iron and steel, and wool and cotton. For most agricultural commodities, extra peacetime inventories are induced in the United States through various agricultural price support programs. Moreover, "set-aside," or "land bank," programs also exist which subsidize farmers to create fresh, fertile croplands. These correspond closely to our cartel model of Section IIB3. For various chemicals and nonferrous metals such as copper, lead, and zinc, we observe the governmental accumulation of large peacetime stockpiles. This policy shortcuts the various subsidy methods we have been discussing. Iron and steel, wool and cotton are not so substantially stockpiled by the government. (Neither is aluminum, but its production was subsidized heavily during the war.) These goods are, to moderate degrees, imported during peacetime. Correspondingly, we observe significant import protection rather than domestic investment subsidies for iron and steel, wool and cotton producers. The optimality of concentrating on import protection rather than domestic subsidies for moderate imports with sufficiently small undervaluations was implied by our special optimum tariff argument of Section IIB2. Furthermore, the requisite, significantly positive, effective tariff rates which are due processors of iron and steel, wool and cotton are also observed (Balassa 1965).

Optimal import protection for national defense reasons differs from classical, monopsonistic import protection in at least two observable ways. First, inputs warranting import protection under the second national defense argument normally warrant a larger degree of protection than other imports. This follows from the argument of Section II*B* 2 and the fact that the financial gain from a given amount of protection is larger for an undervalued input because the more a country becomes dependent on imports of such an input, the more likely its optimal policy is to switch from simply enforcing a monopsonistic tariff to bearing the relatively heavy burden of an international cartel. For, as we have argued above, once sufficient import dependence is developed, it pays to allow a costly international cartel in order to induce the optimal, peacetime foreign accumulation of the input. In fact, import protection in the post–World War II United States has been heavily concentrated on the narrow group of goods we have been discussing, namely, cattle, oil, sugar, iron and steel, wool, cotton, and their products. For example, according to a survey by Bergsten (1974, p. 140), over 85 percent of the protection in the post–World War II United States has concentrated on this small group.

Second, when import protection is a simple monopsony device, then tariffs are superior to import quotas in that random fluctuations in the levels of demands or costs for a given policy cause much smaller deviations from the optimal monopsony policy with fixed tariffs than with fixed quotas (see Fishelson and Flatters 1975). But when import protection is also used to prevent dependence on wartime imports, then import quotas may well be superior to tariffs. In fact, the set of postwar imports which suffered most from our World War II price controls (crude oil, cattle, sugar, cotton, wool, iron and steel, various agricultural commodities, and products of these materials) is virtually identical to Bergsten's list of commodities which have been subject to significant U.S. import quotas!

E. Skilled Human Capital

As argued above, military conscription—part of our general system of price controls in which the government can buy at the artificially low, controlled price—was particularly injurious to skilled labor in World War II because the military's payment to a significant fraction of the U.S. supply of skilled labor was far below the marginal supply price. The second national defense argument thus provides a rationale for the significant subsidization of investments in skilled labor. Such subsidies are observed in the form of general subsidies to higher education.[20] An apparent difficulty is that these observed subsidies also apply to the development of skills in the fine arts and humanities, skills which suffer little wartime undervaluation. However, Marshall's (1962) externality argument for supporting higher education—that we subsidize everyone's education because we cannot identify future creative geniuses, most of whom cannot collect the huge benefits they provide to society—applies significantly to these latter skills but very little to ordinary, practical skills that are undervalued during a war. So Marshall's argument must be added to the second national defense argument in order to rationalize observed subsidies to higher education. Since both the second national defense argument and the Marshall argument apply to science skills, the observation of a discriminatory subsidy in favor of science education is rationalized.

In order to isolate a significant area where the national defense undervaluation is large relative to Marshall's, we considered 2-year colleges, schools which appear to be largely directed toward developing standard, low-risk technical skills. We estimated the observed rate of subsidy to investments in these skills to be about 18 percent.[21] But what is the optimal rate?

To estimate the degree of wartime undervaluations of labor via military conscription, we first estimated the percentage increase in labor's supply price to the military from the predraft (1940) level of our armed forces to the average World War II level. To do this, we divided the percentage increase in the U.S. military personnel from the 1940 level to the average 1941–45 level (U.S. Bureau of Census 1959, Series Y-763) by a typical estimate of the elasticity of supply of military manpower, 1.25 (Cooper). The result, $(8.66/.452) \div 1.25 = 1,533$ percent, is an estimate of the percentage increase in military

---

[20] A rationalization for the observed subsidization of earlier childhood education emerges quite naturally from a model admitting parental malincentives (Thompson 1974; Ruhter 1976).

[21] Total governmental noncapital expenditures per student to all 2-year colleges in the United States in fiscal 1973–74 (from U.S. National Center for Education Statistics 1976) was $950 per student. Adding 5 percent interest on the book value of the assets of public 2-year colleges (from U.S. National Center for Educational Statistics 1976) brings this total level of governmental support to $1,068 per student. Total 1973 investment cost per student—the sum of noncapital total expenditures, $1,229 (U.S. National Center for Educational Statistics 1976), 5 percent interest on the book value of all 2-year colleges, $130 (U.S. National Center for Educational Statistics 1976), and the 9-month average 1973 income of full-time workers with only a high school degree, $4,672 (U.S. Department of Commerce 1975)—is $6,031. Hence, our estimated government subsidy rate to trade education for young adults is 1,068/6,031, or 17.7 percent.

wages which would have been necessary to fight World War II on an all-volunteer basis. Since military pay relative to civilian manufacturing wages decreased from 1940 to 1941–45 by about 15 percent (U.S. Bureau of Census 1975, Series D-3, D-4, F-164, and F-167), the underpayment to the armed forces during World War II is estimated to be $1,533 \div .85 \approx 1,800$ percent. But this estimate is biased on the high side in that it fails to adjust for the patriotic shift in the supply of military labor during the war, a shift which we have been unable to objectively estimate from World War II observations. However, during the U.S. Civil War, when the Union's average armed force was only 18 percent of the 15–39-year-old male population compared to about 29 percent for World War II (U.S. Bureau of the Census 1959, Series Y-763 and A 74-78), there was only an inconsequential draft (accounting for only about 2 percent of those actually serving compared to 60 percent for World War II [U.S. Bureau of the Census 1959, Series Y715, 724]). The Civil War military wage grew at about the same rate as the average manufacturing wage during the war (Shannon 1928). If instead the relative military wage had dropped the 15 percent that it did during World War II, then using our 1.25 supply elasticity, we would have had a $.15 \times 1.25 \approx 19$ percent smaller Union army. Thus, with the World War II wage pattern, the 18 percent volunteer army would have shrunk to about 14½ percent of the eligible male population during World War II, or ½ of the actual average World War II armed force. The number of men which would have required higher wages to volunteer during World War II is thus estimated to be about ½ of the observed armed force. Hence our revised estimate of the wages necessary to induce the observed average World War II armed force is $4.33/[(.452)(1.25)(.85)] \approx 9$ times the actual wage rather than 18 times.[22] Now about ⅓ of those registered for the draft actually served during the average World War II year (U.S. Bureau of Census 1975, Series Y-904 and Y-917). So the wartime undervaluation of the product of this group drops down to about ⅓ of 800 percent.

To compute the resulting undervaluation of investments in human capital, we add the assumption that workers are equally eligible for the draft during the first 20 years of their working life and are not during the remaining 20 years of their 40-year working life. Then, using our above assumptions on war probabilities, war length, and real interest rates, the present, expected percentage undervaluation

---

[22] An independent estimate arriving at about the same figure but relying mostly on Civil War pay differentials between volunteers and draftees is available on request from the author.

of a young adult's investment in human capital which increases his
wages by $\Delta W(t)$, is:

$$\sum_{t=1}^{20} \frac{8}{3} \cdot \frac{\Delta W(t)}{(1.05)^t} \cdot \frac{4}{50} \bigg/ \sum_{t=1}^{40} \frac{\Delta W(t)}{(1.05)^t}.$$

Assuming that $\Delta W(t)$ grows with aggregate real wages at the rate of 2
percent per annum, this ratio is easily calculated to be 14 percent.[23]
While the actual rate is a little higher than this optimal rate, the
Marshall argument should count for at least a couple of percentage
points. So again, since our rough point estimates of actual and optimal
subsidy rates are in very close agreement, the evidence does not
contradict the hypothesis that the orders of magnitude of optimal and
actual subsidy rates are about the same.

The international trade results of Section IIB also apply to human
capital. Since (1) a large human capital subsidy is justified by the
second national defense argument and (2) mild peacetime imports of
human capital exist, import quotas to protect our skilled human
capital can be justified. In fact, such protection exists. Since the
United States pays domestic rather than world market prices for its
imported human capital, the conventional international trade argument for the existence of a net pecuniary gain to a small amount of
protection does not apply. Nevertheless, under fairly plausible assumptions, it can be shown that there is still a positive pecuniary
benefit to initial U.S. citizens to some degree of immigration restriction.[24]

---

[23] Statistical evidence of rising relative wages of the relatively better trained persons
(Taubman and Wales 1973; Mincer 1974) might appear to contradict this assumption.
However, this evidence can be explained by the existence of greater on-the-job training
by the relatively educated and thus does not directly bear on the validity of our
assumption regarding the effect of a single period's increase in training.

[24] This is based on manipulation of the theoretical model of Usher (1977, pp.
1003–7) under the assumption that factors are paid the domestic marginal social
products. The calculations will be sent on request. The source of the pecuniary benefit
from an immigration restriction is the fact that the country may own a significant part
of the foreign nonhuman capital stock. An immigration restriction raises the domestic
profits from such investments, while the foreign countries lose from the lower net
payments to their owned factors. This redistributional benefit must exceed the cost of
the increased wages paid to intramarginal, future immigrants in order to justify even a
small immigration restriction. The evidence is that the wave of U.S. foreign investment
in the late nineteenth and early twentieth centuries pushed the marginal returns from
an immigration restriction up to around the costs by the early 1920s. The undoubtable
net fiscal liability posed by new immigrants would then suffice to rationalize a net
benefit to immigration restrictions by the early 1920s. The sudden emergence of U.S.
immigration restrictions, coming as it did after the significant labor conscription of
World War I and a long boom in U.S. foreign investment, is quite plausibly rationalized
by our theory.

F. Industries Facing Direct Allocation Controls

As noted above, the production of several kinds of durable consumer goods was restricted by fiat through direct allocation controls during World War II. The salutary effect of these controls again was to reduce the nominal cost of certain resources so as to artificially lower the cost of the defensive war. It may appear that an additional peacetime subsidy is due semidurable producer inputs into several consumer durables industries based on our second national defense argument. However, the demand for consumer durables, taken as a group, is known to become substantially "pent up." Indeed, the post–World War II pent-up demand for consumer durables is widely considered to be the primary cause of the macroeconomic boom that followed World War II. Under such a condition, it is not likely that any significant subsidy is in order based on the second national defense argument. For with such intertemporal substitution possible, it is likely that even without controls the wartime increase in the competitive equilibrium price of new consumer durables would have reduced the rational purchases of these goods to insignificance anyway.

G. A Note on Rent Controls

A typical observation of World War II bureaucrats and contemporary economists was that while World War II price controls were largely ineffective in keeping down quality-adjusted civilian prices other than for industries facing rationing or government regulation, the ceiling on apartment rentals was a singular exception (see, e.g., Harris 1945, esp. chap. 12). However, while there was some effective rent control during the war in a few military zones, enabling the military to acquire ancillary services at artificially low costs, wartime ceilings on civilian rents were largely nonbinding given the shift of people of household-formation age into military housing. Nevertheless, the post–World War II surge in U.S. housing demand was met with a 2-year extension of World War II price controls which was somewhat effective despite the high incidence of hidden charges via tie-in furniture sales, security deposits, early rent payments, and quality deterioration (Clinard 1952). (Direct evidence for this effectiveness is the somewhat lower rate of price appreciation for apartment buildings than for owner-occupied housing in the 1945–47 period [Gage 1947].) Since the resulting capital undervaluation must be considered relatively small, only a small peacetime subsidy to nonowner-occupied real estate is justified. Since the postwar increase in housing demand was concentrated on low-income units, the effective price controls were apparently concentrated there (see Friedman and Stigler 1946). So these controls justify small subsidies to investments in low-income housing. But the argument lacks power as an explanation of the small subsidies to low-income housing observed in the United States, for (1) the observed subsidies can also be rationalized by the parental malincentive problem (Thompson 1974; Ruhter 1976) and (2) postwar rent controls lack the efficiency justification of wartime price controls and therefore cannot be comfortably expected to recur given our other results.

Real estate tax shelters cannot be justified with the second national defense argument. However, observed U.S. tax shelters for non-owner-occupied real estate can be rationalized by the fact that without such a tax shelter there would be an inefficient, double capital tax on this real estate compared to owner-occupied units, both having been taxed at approximately the normal U.S. capital tax rate through local property taxation (Thompson 1974).

H. Trends

Since the likelihood of another U.S. war of World War II variety has probably been decreasing over the past couple of decades (see, e.g., Brodie 1973), the magnitudes of the above optimal investment subsidies have probably been decreasing over time. Correspondingly, we have in recent years observed decreases in: (1) the effective write-off for intangible drilling expenses, (2) the effective write-off for cattle feeding, (3) the cartel-held inventories of tin and coffee, (4) excess capacity in the regulated industries, (5) the subsidy rate to expenditures on higher education, (6) real agricultural price supports and subsidies, and (7) import quotas. Nevertheless, the great uncertainty of the secular continuation in the trend away from warfare prevents us from confidently forecasting anything like the dramatic trend away from mercantile subsidies, protectionism, and regulation which accompanied the unprecedented century of European peace from 1814 to 1914.

I. A Perspective on the Results

The results in the empirical part of this paper complement those in the author's 1974 paper. In fact, tax shelters, where individuals are allowed to expense certain original capital investments, were one of only two elements of the explicit U.S. tax structure which could not be rationalized using the simple theory in that paper.[25] The current extension of that simple theory appears to largely explain these shelters, for the significant ones are widely recognized to exist only in cattle, oil and gas, real estate, and, to lesser extents, in certain agricultural investments. The other, implicit, capital subsidies discussed above, that is, government inventory accumulation, crop-land conservation payments, provision of higher education, cartelizing regulation, and import protection were not considered in the 1974 paper and also cannot be rationalized with the simple model there.

The capital goods which do not merit significant domestic subsidies under the second national defense argument, are, from above, consumer goods, plant and equipment, and mature human capital. Correspondingly, we do not observe large subsidies to capital goods within these categories other than those subsidies rationalized in the 1974 paper as warranted by the noncoveted nature of the capital or by a parental malincentive problem.

The two papers thus combine to strongly indicate that a more realistic model of national defense than that which is implicit in traditional economic doctrine leads to a description of a Pareto optimal overall economic fiscal policy for the United States which is surprisingly close to the actual policy.

Since no such theory of national defense was available to the government decision makers who evolved these policies, we conclude that existing political processes in the United States, rather than being dominated by broad social thinking, have simulated an allocation system guided by a compensation principle. Under such a system, the potential gainers from proposed legislation always amend the proposal if the change is perceived to raise the expected utility of any individual without reducing the expected utility of any other. For such an amendment can only increase the political support of the bill's proponents, decrease the resistance by the bill's opponents, or both. If perceptions of individual gains and losses are accurate in such a system, any allocation generated by the system must obviously be Pareto optimal. Our results thus suggest that the ability of individuals

---

[25] The other unrationalized feature of the U.S. tax structure was the alleged absence of taxation on luxury consumer durables other than residences. Since valuable art, precious metals, jewelry, and furs are fairly easily hidden from a foreign aggressor (as evinced in the German occupation of France in World War II), the list of coveted luxuries is probably fairly short. What I had in mind were yachts and expensive cars. But I was unaware of the fact that the one kind of consumer good which is taxed almost uniformly throughout the United States by local personal property taxes is the pleasure boat. And the capital tax rates appear to fall in the optimal range of 1–3 percent! I was also unaware of the fact that state auto license fees typically have an ad valorem capital-tax component which also falls within this range.

in a large political system to act under their enlightened self-interest and the resulting efficiency of the invisible hand in government have been substantially underestimated.

IV. Summary

Two independent national defense arguments have been developed. The first states that an increase in the private sector capital stock of a nation raises the costs of successful aggression against the country and thereby lowers the country's required level of national defense expenditure. Since this effect is external to the private holders of such capital, the argument implies the optimality of a capital subsidy. However, an increase in the nation's capital stock may also increase the return to successful aggression to foreign aggressors. Furthermore, this latter effect appears to exceed the former, as empirical evidence strongly indicates that an increase in a nation's measured private capital stock increases rather than decreases its national defense expenditures. This suggests the optimality of a net tax on capital. The first national defense argument does not appear to be an empirically valid justification for any form of subsidization.

The second national defense argument states that certain kinds of capital are undervalued by private investors during peacetime because the products of the capital are subject to effective wartime price controls. The capital goods which are generally most qualified for significant support are semidurable producer goods which are specific to industries suffering effective wartime price controls. But, because simple price controls are ordinarily readily avoided by quality changes and other forms of hidden charges, the argument applies significantly to only a very restricted set of industries.

For domestic industries facing significant wartime coupon rationing as well as price controls, the efficient subsidy is granted by treating a certain part of its expenditures on specific, semidurable capital as ordinary business expenses for tax purposes. The most important U.S. products affected by World War II rationing were gasoline and meat. These products were produced largely by domestic industries. Correspondingly, significant tax write-offs of specific, semidurable capital expenditures in these industries are justified. In fact, such tax breaks are given, and the magnitudes of the observed tax breaks roughly approximate the optimal rates.

For foreign industries suffering from both wartime rationing and price controls, an efficient investment subsidy is provided by allowing the foreign exporters to jointly raise the peacetime prices of their outputs by accumulating a stockpile of their outputs or by forcing prorationing according to capacity on the producers in the industry.

The foreign industries supplying the United States in World War II which suffered significantly from U.S. rationing programs were the tin and coffee industries. Correspondingly, the tin and coffee cartels have been the only significant international cartels in operation throughout most of the postwar period. And the recent development of a U.S. dependence upon foreign oil was soon followed by an oil cartel with significant price and production effects. In this view, observed international cartels are not simple monopolies which gain by restricting output and the entry of inputs into their industries; they are institutions which simulate what would be competitive behavior in the absence of wartime price controls and rationing by encouraging peacetime capital accumulation in these industries.

For federally regulated industries, procedures for effective government control of the quality of privately traded goods are relatively highly developed during peacetime so that wartime price controls are very difficult to evade. Efficient peacetime incentive systems are those which induce more capacity than the companies would freely choose given their artificially low wartime product prices. Such incentive systems appear to exist, and the estimated amount of overcapacity where estimates are available appears to be of the same order of magnitude as the optimal amount.

For industries which largely evade wartime price ceilings on sales to civilians and therefore suffer from effective wartime price ceilings only on sales to the military, a generally much lower level of support is justified. However, one exception appears in the "industry" which sells the services of human capital. The singularly low wage paid by the military for skilled labor services, together with the large magnitude of the armed forces during the last world war, indicates that a significant subsidy is due youthful producers of skilled labor inputs. A plausibly efficient form of subsidy is a direct subsidy to educational expenditures by young adults. Our rough estimate of the optimal U.S. subsidy to higher education closely approximates the observed subsidy rate.

For the other industries whose wartime products are not effectively price controlled in civilian sales but are sold in significant quantities to the military at subcompetitive prices, some, relatively small aid is due their specific, semidurable capital inputs. For the most important inputs in this category, we do observe some relatively low levels of economic aid: For easily storable, specialty chemicals and nonferrous metals, we observe special government stockpiles. And for most agricultural outputs, we observe governmental commodity price supports and cropland development subsidies. For the less easily storable commodities in this category—iron and steel, wool and cotton—we observe significant tariff or import quota systems. These restrictions on international trade are optimal to rely on when there are realistic constraints on international arguments and when the magnitudes of both the wartime import and undervaluation levels are relatively small.

Significantly undervalued inputs which are not substantially imported during wartime warrant peacetime import quotas as well as domestic subsidies under realistic constraints on international bargaining. Effective protection should also be extended to processors of these inputs. In fact, our significantly undervalued inputs which were moderately imported during most of the post–World War II period were all afforded import quotas during the period. And effective protection was also apparently extended to their processors. In fact, well over 85 percent of U.S. import protection in 1970 was concentrated on our short list of qualified commodities under the second national defense argument.

Finally, plant and equipment, consumer goods, and mature human capital warrant no significant domestic subsidies under our second national defense argument. Correspondingly, no significant domestic capital subsidies are observed within these categories other than those rationalized in a related analysis of national defense.

The gradually decreasing probability of conventional U.S. warfare during the past couple of decades implies a decreasing extent of optimal national defense aid to the various industries discussed above. Correspondingly, actual aid to these industries has been gradually decreasing.

In view of the above results, a more refined economic analysis is required if we are to derive suggestions for improvements in U.S. economic policy based on our surviving national defense argument.

References

Averch, Harvey, and Johnson, Leland L. "Behavior of the Firm under Regulatory Constraint." *A.E.R.* 52 (December 1962): 1052–69.
Balassa, Bela. "Tariff Protection in Industrial Countries: An Evaluation." *J.P.E.* 73, no. 6 (December 1965): 573–94.
Ballinger, Roy A. "A History of Sugar Marketing." Agricultural Economic Report no. 197, U.S. Dept. Agriculture, 1971.
Bergsten, Fred C. "The Cost of Import Restrictions to American Consumers." In *International Trade and Finance: Readings*, edited by Robert E. Baldwin and J. David Richardson. Boston: Little, Brown, 1974.
Brodie, Bernard. *War and Politics.* New York: Macmillan, 1973.
Buchanan, James M. *Supply and Demand of Public Goods.* Chicago: Rand McNally, 1968.
Buchanan, James M., and Tideman, Nicholas. "Thompson Taxes and Lindahl Prices." Working Paper, Virginia Polytechnic Inst., 1976.
Clinard, Marshall B. *The Black Market: A Study of White-Collar Crime.* New York: Rinehart, 1952.

Cooper, Richard V. L. "Military Manpower and the All-Voluntary Force." Rand Report R-1450, Rand Corp., Santa Monica, Calif., 1977.

DeVany, Arthur S. "Capacity Utilization under Alternative Regulatory Constraints: An Analysis of Taxi Markets." *J.P.E.* 83, no. 1 (February 1975): 83–95.

Douglas, George W., and Miller, James C., III. *Economic Regulation of Domestic Air Transport: Theory and Policy.* Washington: Brookings Inst., 1974.

Fishelson, Gideon, and Flatters, Frank. "The (Non)equivalence of Tariffs and Quotas under Uncertainty." *J. Internat. Econ.* 5 (November 1975): 385–93.

Friedman, Milton, and Stigler, George J. "Roofs or Ceilings? The Current Housing Problem." *Popular Essays on Current Problems* 1, no. 2 (September 1946): 7–22.

Gage, Daniel D. "Wartime Experiment in Federal Rent Control." *J. Land and Public Utility Econ.* 23 (February 1947): 50–59.

Gibbon, Edward. *The History of the Decline and Fall of the Roman Empire.* Vol. 4. New York: Bigelow-Brown, 1906.

Glejser, H. "A New Test of Heteroscedasticity." *J. American Statis. Assoc.* (March 1969), pp. 316–23.

Graham, David. "A Test of the Averch-Johnson Model." Ph.D. dissertation, Univ. California, Los Angeles, 1976.

Harris, Seymour E. *Price and Related Controls in the United States.* New York: McGraw-Hill, 1945.

Hicks, J. R.; Hicks, U. K.; and Rostas, L. *The Taxation of War Wealth.* 2d ed. Oxford: Clarendon, 1942.

Johnson, D. Gale. *The Sugar Problem: Large Costs and Small Benefits.* Washington: American Enterprise Inst. Public Policy Res., 1974.

Johnson, Harry G. *International Trade and Economic Growth: Studies in Pure Theory.* Cambridge, Mass.: Harvard Univ. Press, 1961.

Kahn, Herman. *On Thermonuclear War.* Princeton, N.J.: Princeton Univ. Press, 1960.

Kindleberger, Charles P., and Herrick, Bruce. *Economic Development.* 3d ed. New York: McGraw-Hill, 1977.

Klein, Burton H. *Germany's Economic Preparations for War.* Cambridge, Mass.: Harvard Univ. Press, 1959.

Lindsay, Cotton M. "Our National Tradition of Conscription: Experience with the Draft." In *Why the Draft? The Case for a Volunteer Army*, edited by James C. Miller III. Baltimore: Penguin, 1968.

Marshall, Alfred. *Principles of Economics.* 8th ed. London: Macmillan, 1962.

Michell, Humfrey. "The Edict of Diocletian: A Study of Price Fixing in the Roman Empire." *Canadian J. Econ.* 13 (February 1947): 1–12.

Miller, Edward M. "The Defense Externality." *American J. Econ. and Soc.* 35 (July 1976): 271–74.

Mincer, Jacob. *Schooling, Experience, and Earnings.* New York: Nat. Bur. Econ. Res., 1974.

Moore, Thomas G. "Deregulating Surface Transportation." In *Promoting Competition in Regulated Markets*, edited by Almarin Phillips. Washington: Brookings Inst., 1975.

Nef, John U. *War and Human Progress: An Essay on the Rise of Industrial Civilization.* New York: Russell & Russell, 1968.

Petersen, H. Craig. "An Empirical Test of Regulatory Effects." *Bell J. Econ. and Management Sci.* 6 (Spring 1975): 111–26.

Rolph, Earl R., and Break, George F. *Public Finance.* New York: Ronald, 1961.

Rooney, Robert F. "Taxation and Regulation of the Domestic Crude Oil Industry." Ph.D. dissertation, Stanford Univ., 1965.

Ruhter, Wayne E. "Human Capital Development and Parental Incentives." Ph.D. dissertation, Univ. California, Los Angeles, 1976.

Schuettinger, Robert L. "A Survey of Wage and Price Controls over Fifty Centuries." In *The Illusion of Wage and Price Control*, edited by Michael Walker. Vancouver: Fraser Inst., 1976.

Shannon, Fred A. *The Organization and Administration of the Union Army, 1861–1865.* Vol. 2. Gloucester, Mass.: Peter Smith, 1928.

Stigler, George J. "The Theory of Economic Regulation." *Bell J. Econ. and Management Sci.* 2, no. 1 (Spring 1971): 3–21.

Stockholm International Peace Research Institute. *World Armaments and Disarmament, SIPRI Yearbook.* Cambridge, Mass.: M.I.T. Press, 1974.

Taubman, Paul J., and Wales, Terence J. "Higher Education, Mental Ability and Screening." *J.P.E.* 81, no. 1 (January/February 1973): 28–55.

Thompson, Earl A. "Taxation and National Defense." *J.P.E.* 82, no. 4 (July/August 1974): 755–82.

———. "A Pure Theory of Social Organization." Working Paper, Univ. California, Los Angeles, Dept. Econ., 1977.

———. "A Reformulation of Macroeconomic Theory." Working Paper, Univ. California, Los Angeles, Dept. Econ., 1978.

United Nations. *Demographic Yearbook.* New York: United Nations, 1975.

———. *Statistical Yearbook.* New York: United Nations, 1973.

U.S. Bureau of the Census. *Historical Statistics of the United States from Colonial Times to 1957.* Washington: Dept. Commerce, 1959.

———. *Historical Statistics of the United States from Colonial Times to 1970.* Washington: Dept. Commerce, 1975.

U.S. Department of Agriculture. *Agricultural Report No. 196.* Washington: Government Printing Office, 1959.

U.S. Department of Commerce, Bureau of Census. *Current Population Reports.* Series P-60. Washington: Government Printing Office, 1975.

U.S. Government Office of Price Administration. *Historical Reports on War Administration.* Washington: Government Printing Office, 1943–47.

U.S. National Center for Educational Statistics. *Financial Statistics of Higher Education, 1972–73.* Washington: Government Printing Office, 1976.

Usher, Dan. "Public Property and the Effects of Migration upon Other Residents of the Migrants' Countries of Origin and Destination." *J.P.E.* 85, no. 5 (October 1977): 1001–20.

THE THEORY OF MONEY AND INCOME
CONSISTENT WITH ORTHODOX VALUE THEORY

Earl A. Thompson

University of California
Los Angeles

Introduction

The challenge of Metzler's classic article, "Wealth, Saving, and the Rate of Interest" [17], has gone unanswered. The literature has remained without a model which captures the full logic of the classical theory of money and income. The main purpose of this chapter is not to specify such a model; it is to derive the theory of money and income that is consistent with orthodox value theory (i.e., Ricardian and neoclassical value theory and the competitive model of Arrow and Debreu). However, quite by accident, it turns out that any such theory of money and income must have all of the essential properties asserted by classical monetary economists.

The chapter proceeds as a development of the properties of any money economy which is constrained to be consistent with orthodox value theory, a theory which has a perfectly competitive, private supply of all goods. The central theoretical results are: (1) there is a money economy that is consistent with orthodox value theory, and (2) in any such economy, which we will call a "perfectly competitive money economy," there is: (a) a classical dichotomy between the real and monetary sectors, (b) an absence of real balance effects,

Reprinted from:
TRADE, STABILITY AND MACROECONOMICS
Essays in Honor of Lloyd A. Metzler
©1974
Academic Press, Inc.

(c) an absence of effects of expected inflation on the real sector of the economy, and (d) an imperviousness of output prices and employment in a sticky-wage economy to shifts in capital productivity, thrift, liquidity preference, and the money supply of any individual.

These results are in sharp contrast to the central propositions of numerous modern monetary theorists. With respect to the first result, leading modern day authors have alleged an inconsistency between any money economy and orthodox value theory. Some of these authors (e.g., Friedman [8] and Pesek and Saving [22]) have claimed that money cannot attain a positive equilibrium value in an orthodox model in which nominal money is costless to create and competitively supplied. Since a good with a zero price cannot be used as a medium of exchange, this implies that the orthodox model cannot be extended to include money. Other authors (e.g., Marschak [15] and Radner [25]) have argued (each for a slightly different reason) that money, however supplied, would have a zero total value under the informational perfections of the standard competitive model. In working out the basic money model implied by the standard competitive model in Sections I.A and I.B, we shall see that these modern day authors have failed, each in his own way, to characterize accurately the information structure implicit in the standard competitive model. Section I.C then demonstrates the existence and Pareto optimality of an equilibrium consistent with orthodox value theory in which money emerges as an individually selected, specialized medium of exchange.

Regarding the second result, the set of properties we derive for any money economy consistent with orthodox value theory contains all of the properties that modern monetary theorists have represented as *logical* fallacies in the classical view of a money economy. Keynes in his *General Theory* [12], and all later writers of note, have considered the classical view of a money economy logically defective in that it does not allow shifts in capital productivity, thrift, and liquidity preference ever to affect prices or employment. As Metzler pointed out, Pigou [24] and others have implicitly *criticized* classical monetary theory by alleging that real cash balances have belonged in the excess demand functions for nonmonetary goods all along. Patinkin [21] has criticized classical monetary doctrine for having equilibrium relative prices between nonmonetary goods determined in the nonmoney markets and a unique level of equilibrium money prices determined in the money market. Friedman [7], Bailey [4], Marty [16], and Kessel and Alchian [11] have argued that shifts in the future money supplies, when prices are correctly anticipated and money is neutral, will generally have real effects on the economy, a fact which classical writers did not include in their theoretical discussions. Sections I.D and II.E show how each of these criticisms is inapplicable to a competitive money model and that the so-called fallacies in the classical view of a money economy are in fact necessary properties of any perfectly competitive money model.

Sections II.F and II.G specify the possible sources of involuntary unemploy-ment in a perfectly competitive money economy and note the substantial evidence for the resulting theory of economic fluctuations in pre-1934 indus-trialized economies. Previous theories, by failing to specify the basic infor-mational imperfection leading to involuntary unemployment, or by treating a Say's law economy [27] as if it were somehow immune to aggregative un-employment, have apparently failed to bring out the vulnerability of employ-ment to certain shifts in technology and tastes in a classical money economy. As a result, previous theories have misled us as to the cause of the Great Depression, misled us into searching for Keynesian or Quantity Theory-type explanations. Correspondingly, we have been led away from understanding the fundamental change in the relevant macrotheory and the fundamental improvement in potential employment stability that occurred with the de-struction of the fully convertible gold standard in 1934.

Section II.H shows the impossibility of *permanent* involuntary unemploy-ment despite the absence of Pigou effects in a perfectly competitive money economy.

I. The Theory of Money Consistent with Orthodox Value Theory

A. PROPERTIES OF ANY MONEY MODEL CONSISTENT WITH ORTHODOX VALUE THEORY

The standard competitive model (e.g., Debreu [6]) specifies equilibrium allocations of real resources for given initial allocations. But it does not specify the *process* of achieving equilibrium allocations. Money is used as an intermediate good in transactions, achieving final allocations from initial ones. Therefore, since our model is a money model, our "equilibrium" necessarily specifies more information than the "equilibrium" of a standard competitive model. In particular, our equilibrium specifies a complete set of transactions in a private property system.

Despite the fact that our money model specifies more information than is provided by a standard competitive model, consistency with the standard competitive model implies a very special kind of money economy. First, in the standard competitive model, there are no transaction costs resulting from an equilibrium set of transactions. Equilibrium transactions leading to a standard competitive equilibrium's final allocations of resources must all be costless transactions. Transaction costs are dead-weight losses—losses due to imperfect contract information that an idealized central allocator could avoid. The laissez faire implication of the orthodox model, monetary or not, would not exist if transaction costs were to appear in achieving the equilibrium's final allocations of resources. (This is elaborated by Thompson [33].)

Second, in any economy with a determinate money, there are positive total transaction costs for some *conceivable* transaction sets. For if all *conceivable* transactions sets yielding the equilibrium's final allocations were totally costless, there would be no determinate money; one good could serve as a medium of exchange as well as any other, and no good would have to serve as money, which is defined as a specialized medium of exchange. However, no costly transaction set can be an *equilibrium* transaction set; the use of a particular asset as a specialized medium of exchange must be so efficient that it drives equilibrium transaction costs down to zero if the equilibrium is to contain a standard competitive equilibrium.

It is not correct to infer, as have several modern authors, from the fact that an economy with a determinate money implies informational imperfections for *some* sets of transactions, that an economy with a determinate money implies informational imperfections for *equilibrium* sets of transactions. A widespread argument, probably best developed by Marschak [15], goes: "No rational individual would hold a positive amount of money in the absence of transaction costs, for he would always prefer to buy, hold, and later sell an interest-bearing asset rather than hold onto barren money before his next ordinary purchase." But money need not be barren; indeed we shall find that in a money model consistent with orthodox value theory, money bears as much interest as the purchased asset. This, however, raises the objection: "If money bears interest, why should anyone, in the absence of transaction costs, hold anything but arbitrary amounts of their assets in the form of money, for they should be indifferent between (a) holding onto their money and (b) buying, holding onto, and later selling a different interest-bearing asset before their next ordinary purchase?" The answer to this, as we have seen, is that while there are zero costs of the monetary transactions that characterize the equilibrium set of transactions in a money economy consistent with orthodox value theory, there are positive costs of some unchosen, or disequilibrium, transactions.[1]

In a similar slip, Radner [25] argues that since a money economy implies an advantage to transactions in the future and therefore positive transaction costs in using only current transactions (including transactions in commodity futures) to allocate future resources, a money economy implies positive transaction costs, which is inconsistent with the standard competitive model. The error here is again the tacit neglect of the case in which the reliance on trans-

---

[1] Although not yet widely recognized, it is true of *any* model of orthodox value theory, monetary or not, that there are zero transactions costs in equilibrium and positive transactions costs in some disequilibria. This is developed by Thompson [33]. Transaction costs out of equilibrium are, for example, generally necessary to prevent the breakdown of decentralization by way of the monopolization of selling activities.

actions in the future, working through money, operates to remove the contract information costs from the equilibrium set of transactions.[2]

Since any real cost of providing the specialized services of a medium of exchange would be a transaction cost, a money model consistent with orthodox value theory has a zero cost of providing the services of the medium of exchange. We shall adopt the standard convention that money is paper, rather than commodity, money. (A rationalization of this assumption appears at the end of Section C.) Zero costs of providing the service of the medium of exchange therefore implies zero costs of creating and transferring the paper money.

A third property which characterizes orthodox value theory is that all assets are created according to a rule of wealth maximization for the price-taking creators, who receive all of the returns from their creation as long as the creation and sale does not reduce the property of others. Thus money is privately rather than "governmentally" produced. We shall hereafter refer to a money economy consistent with an orthodox value theory as a "perfectly competitive money economy."

B. THE POSITIVITY OF THE PRICE OF MONEY IN A PERFECTLY COMPETITIVE MONEY ECONOMY

A recent proposition regarding the production of money under competitive conditions is the following: "Since the cost of producing money is zero, the perfectly competitive real price of money is zero." (See, for example, Friedman [8] and Pesek and Saving [22].) Since an asset with a zero price cannot be used as a medium of exchange, the proposition implies the impossibility of a perfectly competitive money economy. But the proposition implies a violation of private property because the holders of one creator's money suffer a loss in utility from the reduction in their real cash balances occasioned by the supplies of the other money creators. To avoid these violations of private property, each money creator in the competitive model must be able to freely enforce his claim to issue money with a unique physical characteristic.[3] For

---

[2] Actually, Radner does not put his argument in terms of transaction costs, but rather in terms of uncertainty with respect to future demands under given future states of nature. While this uncertainty is neither necessary nor sufficient for markets in the future (see Thompson [33]), Radner infers both. We have therefore dealt with a repaired version of Radner's argument.

[3] My colleagues Armen Alchian and Benjamin Klein have independently uncovered this characterization of competitive money production (see Klein [13]). The difference between our analyses is that their argument has been that the appearance of "competing monies" or of "brand names" alters some models, while mine is the stronger claim that the conditions of the zero-price competitive money model represent a violation of the private property condition of orthodox value theory.

example, one money creator can obtain the sole right to issue blue money; others then must issue money of a different color. This prevents competitive sellers from depreciating the real product of one another. After a certain nominal money supply is produced, a seller's permanent doubling of his own produced money stock will simply halve the price of his money in terms of all other assets. Since the money creator's product is then the real balances he creates, he finds that to induce people to hold more of his product, he must make it more attractive. This is done—when direct interest is not paid on money—by committing himself to repurchasing some of the money with commodities (or other monies) at future dates, thereby decreasing his customer's cost of holding onto his money because of its subsequent real appreciation. Zero profits to a money creator will emerge once the principal and own interest on the asset initially obtained by selling money equals his corresponding future sales in the process of retiring his initially issued money. No money creator who offers a less generous repurchase plan can receive a positive price for his money. Although the return to the money holders comes in the indirect form of price-level deflation, the money creators are, in effect, paying real interest to the holders of their money at a rate equal to the own rate of interest on the assets initially sold to the money creators.

We now remove the artificial prohibition of the direct payment of interest on money. Our general argument becomes: Since it costs nothing to produce the nominal money, a competitive producer-seller will find that in order to sell it for a positive price—which is necessary for there to be any positive quantity of the money demanded—he must pay what amounts to real interest on the asset, devising through the tie-in sale of monetary services and commodity (or other money) interest, a salable money. Money, which yields the joint benefit to the buyer of real interest and monetary services, has a price which is equated in competitive equilibrium with the cost of providing the entire money asset. This cost, in an equilibrium without transaction costs, is the cost of the real interest payments on money. Thus, an equilibrium in a perfectly competitive money economy yields an allocation at which the marginal service value of money is zero. Many recent authors (e.g., Samuelson [26], Friedman [9], and Kessel and Alchian [11]) have conjectured that an equilibrium in a money economy (implicitly one with no transaction costs in equilibrium) is Pareto optimal only when the marginal service value of money is zero. But they have failed to see that the free market production of money achieves this condition. Pesek [23], for example, claims that competition cannot possibly achieve the optimum. He argues: Since an optimum requires a zero marginal use-value of monetary services, the price of money in this optimum would have to be zero. But we have seen that this does not hold when competitive interest is paid on money.

For the remainder of this chapter, we assume that our competitive money creators, rather than committing themselves to eventually retiring their issues, compete by offering direct interest on paper money (in the form of real commodities or the monies of other money creators) equivalent to the real return on a specified real good. This implies that money is "convertible" into the specified real good (or its value equivalent) at an intertemporally fixed rate. If the good into which money is explicitly convertible generates no commodity return, but only continual relative price inflation while it is serving to back money (e.g., noncoupon debt or undeveloped land), then there are no transactions representing interest payments on money even though direct real interest accrues on money equal to the real return on the specified real good. There appears to be a reasonable similarity between our competing money creators and bankers in the gold standard era; and we shall hereafter call our money creators "bankers."

C. THE EXISTENCE AND PARETO OPTIMALITY OF AN EQUILIBRIUM IN A PERFECTLY COMPETITIVE MONEY ECONOMY

We can now prove that an equilibrium in a perfectly competitive money economy exists and is Pareto optimal. First consider final equilibrium allocations of real resources. Since the marginal service value of money is zero, money does not, in equilibrium, enter the wealth constraint, utility function, or feasible production set of any individual apart from its generating an interest return. The fact that a real interest return is the sole return provided on a nonreal asset makes the asset equivalent to a real bond in an orthodox model which contains real bonds as well as real assets. If the real bonds serving as money create individually nonoptimal intertemporal allocations, borrowing and lending through the nonmonetary bond market will reestablish the individual optima. A final equilibrium allocation of resources in such an environment, according to the well-known results of Arrow [2] and Debreu [6], exists and is Pareto optimal (assuming a finite horizon, no collective-type goods, positive wealth, continuous preference relations, nonsatiation, and closed, convex consumption and feasible production sets).

Now consider the equilibrium set of transactions.[4] We wish to show that an equilibrium set of transactions in a perfectly competitive money economy exists and achieves the final allocations of the standard competitive model. We shall do this for the following special case: We assume that there is a "natural" transaction process. In this process (a) following Ostroy [19], each individual meets separately with every other individual in sequential fashion

---

[4] The question of the existence of a competitive equilibrium set of transactions implying the existence of money is novel and our proof is rather technical. The novelty of the question perhaps indicates that most economists are willing to simply assume the existence of such an equilibrium. The reader so inclined is advised to skip the remainder of this subsection and proceed on to Section D.

during each trading period (which is of sufficiently short duration that no transaction costs arise due to delays in achieving the final commodity allocation of each period), and (b) following Starr [30], each individual transfers a good when and only when he has an excess supply of the good and his trading partner has an excess demand for the good.[5] These specifications imply, when "prices" are standard competitive equilibrium prices and there are no costs of any transaction in this "natural" exchange process, that once every individual has met with everyone else in a given period, he will have no excess demand for any commodity in that period.[6] (This is Ostroy's "Principal Proposition.")

We add to the natural transaction process that the asset which one receives in exchange for positive net commodity supplies is an IOU denominated in a specified good but payable in goods of the debtor's option at the time of repayment (where the relative values between these goods are the then-ruling relative prices). Once the period's final allocation of real resources is reached, an individual will still generally own some of these debts of others and owe some of these debts to others, although the *sum* of these positive and negative debts is zero for each individual (Starr [30, Theorem I], Ostroy [19, "Misleading Existence Theorem"]). The natural exchange process thus continues on into a second round after the final allocation of real commodities is reached, where now the bilateral exchanges are all exchanges of IOU's and each indi-

---

[5] Part (b) of the "natural" process is also a rational transaction strategy for individuals to adopt. This holds for the same reason that a bird in the hand is worth two in a bush. Given part (a) and assuming that an individual does not know his later transaction opportunities within the period, an individual is never assured of being able to reduce commodity excesses with later trading partners when he refuses the opportunity of reducing them in transactions with his current trading partner. On the other hand, as we shall note, by adopting the strategy in part (b) of the process, all excess commodity demands of all individuals at equilibrium prices will become zero. The "natural" transaction process is thus also an equilibrium process, given the assumption in part (a).

However, if other individuals do not adopt the strategy in part (b), then an individual who does adopt it will not generally be able to satisfy all of his excess commodity demands in the period. Then, if some goods are complements, an individual may be worse off by adopting the strategy in part (b). For his purchase of a left glove today is a loss if he cannot purchase a right glove tomorrow. Therefore, under such complementarities, there may be an *equilibrium* set of decentralized strategies which does not satisfy the conditions of a competitive equilibrium—it may pay to go without gloves rather than endure the risk of buying a right glove without being able to find a seller of a left one. To avoid these breakdowns in market communication, we would assume that each individual knows his future trading possibilities within the period. This assumption, which is implied by an alternative to the "natural" transaction process discussed later in this subsection, would make part (b) of the "natural transaction process" an arbitrary, but still rational, trading strategy.

[6] This result uses single-period budget constraints so that claims for delivery of assets in future periods are included as "commodities." This general definition of commodities is maintained throughout this chapter.

vidual *in turn* meets all of his creditors. The transactions in this round do not generally lengthen the previously specified trading period because such IOU's may be traded in the subsequent round of trading in commodities. A holder of a mature debt has an excess supply of the debt, and the debtor has an excess demand for the debt. For payment, creditors receive their own IOU's or the IOU's of third parties, which are acceptable because these third parties could not have already taken their turn at meeting all their creditors. No new debt is created, because each debtor owns sufficient IOU's of others. Each such trade therefore reduces the total stock of existing debts by at least the amount one party owes to the other. And since each debtor must meet all of his creditors in turn, no debts are outstanding at the end of this second round.

So our "natural" set of transactions in a world with no costs of the transactions in this set achieves competitive equilibrium allocations of resources without the appearance of any specialized medium of exchange. This is an apparently new, but rather trivial, result.

To move on to the possibility of a *competitive equilibrium* set of transactions, let us alter the hypothetical condition on transaction costs by assuming that IOU contracts of many—but not all—debtors are now costly to trade to third parties because third parties do not costlessly know the precise conditions and legal validity of these primary debt contracts or of contracts guaranteeing the default-risk status of the debtor. The *natural* transaction set now entails positive transaction costs. In the natural process, some individuals, those whose default-risk status and contractual debt obligations are now not costlessly recognizable by third parties, would have to pay a premium for some of their commodities to reflect the future costs to their commodity suppliers of verifying their default-risk status and contractual obligations to others. Such individuals will, before trading in commodities, *separately*, *rationally* trade debts with individuals whose default-risk status and contractual debt obligations are known by everyone. This begins a rational revision of the natural exchange process. In what was the first round and is now the second, individuals pay to their net suppliers of commodities debt obligations of the individuals whose default-risk status and contractual obligations are understood by everyone. The commodity suppliers in turn have no trouble purchasing goods with the costlessly recognizable debt. This debt is thus chosen as the common medium of exchange, so we may call it money and its creators, bankers. Our model is thus unique in that not only may it be efficient for a group of individuals to use a common medium of exchange, but the use of that medium of exchange results from the decentralized, rational decisions of the individuals in the model. On the third round of transactions, where debts are the only assets traded, first the nonbankers meet their creditor-bankers to pay off all of their bank debts. (This is possible because the value of each individual's accumulated intraperiod debt liabilities still equals the value of his accumulated intraperiod debt assets.) After that, the bankers meet one another for debt collection according to the natural process. The monies of third parties are accepted to clear debts between bankers, and the total debt of each banker to the others equals his total money holdings. Therefore, as above, once each of these debtors has met all of his creditors in turn, there is no longer any debt (money) outstanding. The rationally revised natural exchange process thus produces an equilibrium set of transactions which has zero transaction costs and achieves a standard competitive equilibrium.

In the above exchange process, money is serving only as a medium of exchange; it is not held for durations sufficient for time productivity or time preference to exist within holding periods. Consider, however, the possibility of borrowers' supplying longer-term debts to bankers. To guarantee that competitive bankers will make some such loans and still retain the zero-transaction-cost feature of the standard competitive model, assume that the demand for these longer-term loans exceeds the amount which nonbankers can supply at zero transaction costs, while bankers can always supply such loans at no transaction costs. The assumption is, in a sense, plausible because bankers, in contrast to nonbankers, make these loans by simply extending the maturities on existing loans. Since bankers now make loans maturing beyond the end of a trading period, they cannot pay off their current obligations with the repayments of their debtors. However, because profits to banking are zero in equilibrium, bankers must offer the interest they earn on their loans to the holders of their money; and an individual who, under zero lending costs, made loans now being made by bankers is now best off by accepting interest-bearing money in light of his preference for the future return and his positive costs of such lending. (An individual in the world without direct lending costs, who did not lend at maturities exceeding the end of the trading period, is faced with the same opportunities and will therefore still not hold any debt past the end of the trading period.) Consequently, we can specify a new competitive equilibrium set of money–commodity transactions, in a world in which there are positive lending costs to some individuals, but zero costs to others. It is the same equilibrium set of transactions as in the previous case, only with bankers now providing the loans which are now costly for some nonbankers to negotiate and providing these same individuals with a money which they will hold in place of their original loans because it bears the same interest as did those loans. Specifically, the transaction process proceeds as follows: First, bankers exchange their monies for personal debts maturing within the period. Second, all individuals meet one another sequentially to clear excess demands for all commodities (including bonds). Third, nonbankers other than those who wish loan extensions pay off their bank debts, leaving an outstanding aggregate money supply held by nonbankers at the end of the period equal to the aggregate monetary value of these loan extensions. Finally, each banker in turn meets all of the other bankers to exchange monies, paying his debts with his own interest-bearing money whenever he, because of his loan extensions, has insufficient receipts to cover current obligations, and the others, because their money is being held by nonbankers (i.e., the excreditors of the bank-debtors), have insufficient interest-bearing debt to meet their future obligations as bankers.

In this way a competitive equilibrium set of transactions with money is achieved out of a natural set of transactions by introducing certain transaction costs. While the particular description of the equilibrium set of transactions is dependent upon our description of a natural transaction process, none of our results will depend on the particular set of transactions representing the equilibrium set. It is only necessary that there exists a competitive equilibrium set of transactions in which money is employed to reach the real allocations described by a standard competitive equilibrium. We have shown that there is a model of the transaction process yielding such a solution set of transactions.

The model is based, however, on the thoroughly unrealistic assumption that each individual naturally meets separately with every other during each period. An alternative model, which does not contain this assumption, is provided by assuming, realistically, that whenever there is a change in the individuals who receive the benefits from real commodities, a technical transformation, including an act of transportation, is required. Then, since an individual cannot be in two places at the same time, deliveries from one individual to the others must be sequential. Since each delivery at a given time goes to a unique location, each delivery represents a different market. The transaction process in real commodities is then given by the optimal delivery pattern of real commodities determined in a standard competitive equilibrium.[7] Personal debts are, once again, used to match commodity deliveries. In some cases these debts may be repaid without a sale of the debts to third parties. But in an unrestricted technology, there are always cases in which these debts must be sold to third parties in order for the creditor to receive his efficient commodity return. Allowing, once again, the transaction costs of such sales to be positive for the debts of some individuals and zero for the debts of others, the latter debts are individually, rationally purchased with the former debts. The resulting monetary theory is not different than that developed above with respect to any of the properties of economies treated in this chapter.

---

[7] The problem with such a formulation is that the requirement of overhead transportation costs implies nonconvexities in production or preference sets and thus nonconvex demand or supply correspondences for some price vectors. Such nonconvexities may easily present situations in which no parametric prices can exist which equate quantities demanded and supplied.

We now proceed by deriving properties of a perfectly competitive money economy that distinguish it from the money economy described by modern monetary theorists.[8]

D. The Validity of the "Invalid" Classical Dichotomy

Classical and neoclassical monetary theorists, as Patinkin [20] has stressed, assumed that equilibrium relative prices between real assets (including rights to future assets, or "bonds") were determined solely in the real asset markets. This, Patinkin claims to have shown, is consistent with a general equilibrium only if there is an "indeterminate" level of money prices regardless of the money supply. The now familiar argument can be paraphrased to read: "If equilibrium relative prices between real assets are determined in the markets for real assets (i.e., determined with Casselian demand and supply functions for real assets only), then, by Walras' law, the money market must be in equilibrium for such relative prices regardless of the level of money prices and the money supply. Thus the money price level under a classical dichotomy may be anything; it is arbitrary even for a fixed money supply."

But Patinkin's analysis implicitly requires all nonmonetary assets to generate real services (which include contractually specified future services). And this requirement is inconsistent with a money economy consistent with orthodox value theory because in such an economy some asset must yield current money-backing services, and these are obviously not part of the productive or consumptive services appearing in orthodox value theory.

Suppose, following Patinkin's standard example, we start out in an equilibrium in an economy admitting a classical dichotomy and then experimentally increase all money prices in the same proportion, keeping the money supply constant. In the absence of money illusion and distribution effects, the demand for nominal money increases. Patinkin claims that the resulting excess demand for money implies an inconsistency because an excess supply of real assets would then have to arise to satisfy Walras' law, but cannot because we have not altered relative prices. But an equivalent excess supply of *nonreal, nonmonetary* assets only need arise given that relative prices between nonmonetary assets have not changed. In fact, this is exactly what happens in a perfectly competitive money economy. The individuals who want more money necessarily plan to offer correspondingly more real goods to the money creators for money-backing purposes; and this *in itself* creates an excess supply of nonmonetary assets *equivalent* to the excess demand for money. And since the individuals will receive a return on their extra money equivalent to that which they received when they owned the real goods being sold to obtain the

---

[8] A mathematical development of the remainder of Section I is available (Thompson [34]). A mathematical development of Section II.A–E is also available (Thompson [35]).

money, the demand and supply relations for nonmonetary assets relevant for determining relative prices do not change. The point is that the real goods brought to the money creators now perform the *added* function of backing the medium of exchange. Before the excess demand for money appeared, these goods had only the potential of generating an asset that yielded money-backing services. The excess demand for money creates a nonmonetary asset. Thus, an equivalent excess supply of a nonmonetary asset, one providing backing services for a medium of exchange, is induced by the excess demand for money; the zero excess demand for those assets which appeared in the original equilibrium will remain. The market for money (and thus for money-backing services) can then be used to determine an equilibrium price level for a given money supply or, more descriptive of classical monetary analysis, an equilibrium money supply for a given price level.

Since the money-backing *services* of a good are provided free of cost, we might alternatively place a zero-price weight on the positive excess supply of the assets representing streams of money-backing services. But then, evaluating each asset at the price of its corresponding *service stream* and *not* at the price of the *good* generating the asset and its service stream, the original increase in demand for money would be a positive excess demand for a freely supplied service. So the excess demand for money services would also be of zero value. Either way, no positive excess supply of commodities would be implied by the excess demand for money in being consistent with Walras' law. Assuming that the increase in the price level represented an increase in the conversion rate of money into commodities, the excesses are cleared once the excess demand for monetary services induces the nominal money supply to increase to meet the higher demand. So, once again, we have a classical dichotomy and a determinate supply of real cash balances.

The classical dichotomy is easy to construct for a perfectly competitive money economy. Let the relative prices between real assets, and equilibrium in the real asset markets, be determined by the conventional method of orthodox value theory—without reference to money or any decentralized exchange process (e.g., Debreu [6]). Then impose transaction possibilities on the economy such that transaction costs are zero in achieving final, competitive allocations if and only if money is used in certain exchanges. At a given level of money prices, this implies that each individual has at least a certain nominal cash balance at each point in the transaction process. The balances comprise the money demands in the economy. Under perfectly competitive money supply conditions (described previously), these demands will be filled at no real cost. In this way, equilibrium money supplies, and thus real balances, are determined, but only after relative prices between nonmonetary assets have been determined in the real markets.

This construction implies the validity, in a perfectly competitive money economy, of Say's law [27], viz., that the aggregate value of the excess demands for all real goods is identically zero. Say's law is supposed by modern analysts to imply (1) an identically zero excess demand for money, (2) an indeterminate price level, and (3) the impossibility of recessionary forces in some industries without expansionary forces in others. We have seen that the first two supposed implications are false. The third supposed implication—which was also apparently held by classical writers—will be shown to be false in Section II.G.

E. The Real Balance Effect

As noted in the Introduction, classical monetary theory has been implicitly criticized for failing to include the "real balance effect," i.e., an increase in aggregate wealth implied by a small drop in all commodity prices and a constant nominal money supply. There is no such effect in a perfectly competitive money economy with a money market initially in equilibrium, so that the classical theorists cannot be logically criticized for omitting it. This result is not entirely new; it is implied by Patinkin's claim that there is never any real balance effect in a model with only "inside," or privately produced, money [20]. While the argument of Patinkin has been shown to be incorrect by Pesek and Saving [22], we shall now see that there is a case in which the conclusion (but not the argument) holds, the case of a perfectly competitive money economy.

An overall price level reduction, i.e., a proportional reduction in all prices, for a given rate of conversion of money into a real asset, will create an arbitrage profit to the purchase of goods which back money, followed by their sale to the bankers at the conversion dates. The price level must return to its original level in order to restore equilibrium in the capital markets. But even if the real money supply were slightly increased, say by increasing the nominal money supply beyond its equilibrium level, there would be no increase in aggregate real wealth. This is simply because the increase in the real value of the monetary holdings of any individual is exactly matched by the increase in the real value of the debts that the bankers owe the individual as long as the competitive money market was initially in equilibrium.[9]

This result may be used to rationalize the absence of real balance effects in classical monetary discussions.

---

[9] In Section II.H we consider the closely related question of the presence of "Pigou effects," the effects on excess demands of changes in the general price level. Pigou effects follow almost immediately from real balance effects in a modern money economy, but in the perfectly competitive money economy the flexible money supply makes the two effects different in nature. Nevertheless, the magnitude of the Pigou effect in a perfectly competitive money economy will be seen to be the same as that of the real balance effect—zero.

F. Effects of Anticipated Inflation

It has become standard, through the papers of Friedman [7], Bailey [4], Marty [16], and Kessel and Alchian [11], to argue that even if money is neutral, increases in *future* money supplies, for a given current money supply, do not merely increase *future* money prices in the same proportion when the future price increases are fully anticipated (and the demand for money is influenced by the cost of holding money). The reason is that the inflation will depreciate the real value of one's cash, thereby increasing the cost of holding cash relative to other assets in the current period. Switching into nonmonetary assets bids up the *current* price level and thereby lowers the current real cash balances in the system. The same effect is present in succeeding periods if the inflation is then expected to continue. The analysis makes the effects of inflation equivalent to the effects of a tax on money balances.

But, once again, the argument requires that competitive interest not be paid on money. When perfectly competitive interest is paid to the holders of money, bankers must pay interest on money equal in money value to the sum of the current rental and the expected price appreciation on the assets they obtain for their money. This sum would change with a change in expected future money supplies and proportionate change in future prices by an amount equal to the change in the expected inflation if no real effects were induced by the change in expected future prices and money supplies. But since the change in inflation would then not alter the return to holding *any* asset—including money —relative to any other asset, the hypothesized original allocation of real resources is an equilibrium allocation. So no real effects are induced by a change in expected inflation. A proportional increase in expected future prices and money supplies has no effect on the current price level. The returns and costs of holding money must change by the same amount when competitive interest is paid on money.

This result rationalizes the absence of distinctions between real and money interest rates and the absence of a monetary theory of interest in classical monetary theory, absences which are traditional bases for criticizing classical monetary theory.[10]

---

[10] While our results so far have displayed, and will continue to display, a detailed correspondence between the properties of a perfectly competitive money economy and the properties which most classical economists explicitly or implicitly believed to hold for a "laissez faire" money economy (see Schumpeter [28, pp. 729–731]), it is not clear that classical economists were considering a perfectly competitive money economy. However, these economists did uniformly assume fixed convertibility of bank notes into nonmonetary assets in their laissez faire systems. Under perfect competition, such assets would have to generate their valuable returns solely in terms of expected real price appreciation and not in terms of current services. This does correspond somewhat to the classical support of gold

II. The Theory of Income Determination Consistent with Orthodox Value Theory

A. The Problem

We now proceed to examine the short-period effects of various exogenous shifts on "involuntary unemployment" in a perfectly competitive money model. These effects are compared with the effects that emerge in a modern money model. We shall use the same theory of "temporary equilibrium" for both economies. (See Hicks [10] or Arrow and Hahn [3]). A temporary equilibrium is an equilibrium over an interval of time sufficiently small that expectations of all prices within the period are correct, while expectations of prices in trades in future periods are, in general, incorrect. All the properties of a perfectly competitive money economy which were developed previously (except for Pareto optimality) obviously hold for temporary as well as full equilibria. A temporary equilibrium containing "involuntary unemployment" is said to exist when the current-period supply curves of labor are based on incorrect perceptions of future wage offers or output prices and, as a result, laborers waste their current-period labor services on bargaining, searching, so adopting nonmarket vocations. We assume that a permanent reduction in the values of the marginal products of labor at the preshift, full-equilibrium quantities of labor will create involuntary unemployment. This amounts to assuming "sticky money wages."

Rudiments of a theory rationalizing this assumption are found in the book by Alchian and Allen [1]. We rationalize sticky money wages here with the hypothesis that some workers mistakenly regard reductions in their current wage offers as a result of their lower value productivities at those jobs *relative to* alternative jobs or the result of an attempt at tougher wage-bargaining by their employers. An economy which experiences no changes in technology or tastes and whose prices are not substantially bargained—i.e., the traditional

---

(which, during the classical era (ca. 1775–1850), significantly appreciated in real terms (see Viner [37].)) as backing for all note issues.

Furthermore, there is abundant evidence of the assumption by leading classical monetary economists of the applicability of much of modern monetary analysis in the presence of an inconvertible, government-supplied, paper money. One example is Thornton's famous analysis [36] of employment dynamics under inconvertible paper money. Another is Say's recognition of the fact that anticipated inflation with inconvertible paper money leads to increases in the transactions velocity of money (see Schumpeter [28, p. 710n]). Another prominent example is the analysis of Mill [18], which has deceived several modern authors not aware of the theoretical importance of convertibility into believing that Mill, and ergo the classical economists, were essentially modern monetary theorists (e.g., Becker and Baumol [5], Samuelson [26]).

underdeveloped economy—will experience no involuntary unemployment because workers there know from experience that lower money wage offers by their current employers are common to all employers. Involuntary unemployment can arise only in countries which have sufficient shifts in technology, tastes, or bargaining from one firm to another to lead some workers to confuse a shift down in the full equilibrium wage level with a shift in technology, etc., which is particular to only certain employers. The empirical presumption that business cycles containing substantial inefficient unemployment are a disease only of modern industrial societies is rather strong evidence in favor of the hypothesis we are using to rationalize sticky wages.

We shall first examine the effects on involuntary unemployment in a perfectly competitive money economy of those exogenous shifts which have long served to distinguish modern unemployment theory: shifts in the demand for money, the supply of money, the marginal efficiency of capital, and the propensity to consume. These effects are contrasted with those that arise in a modern, Keynes–Patinkin monetary environment. We then examine the effects of shifts in the marginal product of labor and input supplies. Finally, we complete a taxonomy of shifts by considering shifts which alter the relative prices between different outputs.

B. Shifts in the Demand for Money

Suppose that transaction costs become positive in present exchanges of real assets occurring in an original equilibrium and that the extended use of money would obviate these costs. (For example, suppose the original equilibrium included present trades in which each of two capital owners accepted output futures from one of two producers, and now these trades become costly because each of the capital owners now plans to consume the future output of the producer who does not use his capital. And these producers and capital owners can, if they are given the extra money, costlessly adjust to the change by switching to present trades of capital for money and future trades of money for output.) This shift increases the demand for money at original equilibrium prices. Since bankers can supply the money at no real cost, we immediately arrive at a new equilibrium with no change in prices or the allocation of scarce resources. More money is demanded, more is supplied, and no utility or price is altered. (Completing the above example, in a perfectly competitive money economy the capital owners avoid transaction costs by first selling capital to a producer for a money on which he is paid the real return on the capital and then purchasing the output of the other producer at the end of the period; and each of the producers borrows the money from a banker to pay for their capital input, paying real interest on their loan, and finally repaying the principal at the end of the period with the proceeds from the sale of their capital outputs.)

This argument for the dynamical efficiency of an elastic free-market money supply was seen and emphasized by most classical writers, including Adam Smith and J. B. Say. But the argument has gradually fallen into ill-repute as it has come to be interpreted to mean that a money supply that does not bear *competitive interest* should expand (and contract) as aggregate money income expands (and contracts).[11]

In contrast to the perfectly competitive money model, the modern Keynes–Patinkin–Friedman money model has upward shifts in the demand for money (or increases in " liquidity preference ") recessionary in that the resulting excess demand for money can be cleared only through reductions in output prices and thus value marginal products and employment rather than through market-induced increases in the supply of money.

C. Shifts in the Supply of Money

If there is an increase in the supply of money (without a corresponding change in the conversion price) in the original equilibrium of a perfectly competitive money model, it would represent an overissue and holders would, rather than trade it to nonbankers, hold it as a real asset or return such money to its creators. This effect was popularly emphasized by classical monetary writers, especially leaders of the " Banking School," such as Tooke and Fullarton, who had the support of the greater part of the scientific community, including Mill in the 1840's. (See Schumpeter [28].) Thus there is obviously no effect of changes in the supply of money on prices or employment in a perfectly competitive money economy as long as the conversion price of money is retained.

In a modern money model, money does not bear competitive interest, so an increase in supply is not held as if it were a real asset, and money cannot be simply returned to an issuer because of the finite elasticity of the money-supply function. Hence the money is spent and prices are bid up. The analysis is similar for reductions in the money supply.

D. Shifts in the Marginal Efficiency of Capital

Suppose now that the perceived future productivity of currently produced assets shifts down. In a modern money economy, this shift results in a decrease in the return to capital and bonds relative to money and thus induces an excess

---

[11] The standard critique of the dynamics under the classical policy of a flexible private money supply has consequently been that under such a policy an increase (decrease) in the nominal prices of real assets generates an increase (decrease) in the nominal money supply, thus creating the possibility of procyclical variations in the money supply. The critique is obviously based on a failure to retain convertibility at a fixed rate as part of the set of all classical monetary institutions.

demand for money. The corresponding excess supply of nonmonetary goods implies a recession in the current period. But, in a perfectly competitive money economy, where perfectly competitive interest is paid on money, the decrease in the marginal efficiency of capital creates an equal decrease in yield to the competitive bankers, who therefore must react by lowering the yield they pay on money by an equal amount. This produces a situation in which money is no more attractive than before the shift. The drop in the marginal efficiency of capital therefore simply reduces the temporary equilibrium market rate of interest by the same amount, current investment remaining at its original level. (This ignores interest-induced shifts in consumption; we shall see later that no employment effects result from shifts in the propensity to consume in a perfectly competitive money economy.)

A lower real interest on money as well as other assets does not itself induce any involuntary unemployment, even though it lowers a worker's effective real wage. The reason for this is that the lower interest payment on money, unlike a lower nominal wage offer, is known by each money holder to apply to all money holders. The lower interest payment on money cannot be regarded by a rational worker as a reason for making the changes in search, nonmarket vocation, or bargaining that he would make (and regret) in the case of a small drop in nominal wages. That is, the decreased interest on his money wage cannot be rationally regarded by a worker as the result of his lower value productivity in his current job relative to alternative, future jobs or the result of an attempt at tougher labor bargaining by his employer. (This form of argument first appears in the book by Leijonhufvud [14].) The same argument applies to changes in a conversion price of money into capital, so that shifts in such a conversion price (such as those implied in Sections I.D–I.F) in a perfectly competitive money model also have no real effects.

Thus, the most distinguishing recessionary shift of the Keynesian model is ineffective in a classical economy because a decline in the marginal efficiency of capital implies an equal induced decline in the market rate of interest on money, so that no change in the relative cost of holding money occurs.

E. Shifts in the Propensity to Consume

Suppose now there is a shift in plans so that current consumption decreases and planned future consumption increases. First assume it is a nonmonetary shift so that there is an equal increase in demand for investment goods in the form of bonds or real capital. Since there are as yet no alterations in the relative prices between consumption and capital goods, an assumption that serves to keep us in the environment of the standard income-expenditures model, the only possible effects of the shift on the aggregate demand for labor are through changes in bond prices. If bond prices are to remain the same, the increase in demand for bonds must be met by suppliers of bonds, who must *pari passu* demand real capital. Under a constant cost of financial intermediation, this will occur and no recession will result. But if there is an increasing cost of such intermediation, a lower yield on bonds to consumers and a higher borrowing cost to producers results. This induces an increase in the demand for money and an equal reduction in factor demand by the producers, so a recession results. In an economy consistent with orthodox value theory, there are no lending costs and thus no increasing spread between borrowing and lending rates and no recession. The suppliers of bonds to the consumers obtain their interest by lending to the producers at no transaction costs; hence again there is no recession.[12]

Suppose now that the reduction in consumption represents a shift into money. In a perfectly competitive money model the bankers, who must pay real interest on the extra money that they supply, must *pari passu* provide the intermediate demand for holding investment goods or bonds that the money holders have now failed to provide. So there is no induced reduction in demand for real assets. In contrast, the bankers in the modern money model do not have the flexibility to expand their money supplies and real asset demands. So a reduction in output prices and thus a recession obviously results from the shift from consumption into money.

As a check of these results that the characteristic recession-creators in modern monetary theory have no recessionary impact in a perfectly competitive money economy, we can reproduce them graphically or mathematically. We can use a simple macromodel to describe the comparative static effects of the above shifts, since they do not alter relative output prices. In particular, we may use a model with only four markets: capital goods, money, and capital and labor services for the upcoming period. (Bonds are perfect substitutes for capital goods in a standard Keynesian environment, so it is redundant to include them in a separate market with a separate price.) Removing the market for capital goods with Walras' law, we can determine the temporary equilibrium—the current price level, wage rate, and interest rate—in the money and the two factor markets. This equilibrium can be constructed graphically in price-interest rate space as follows: First find, for each price level, the value of the marginal product of the fully employed capital that results from the employment that equilibrates the competitive labor market at that price level. Since the interest rate is the value of the marginal product

---

[12] However, even in an economy with positive costs of lending, if there is a competitive supply of money and a positive, competitive interest rate paid on money, no recession results from such a shift. (See Thompson [32].) The basic reason is that a reduction in the interest paid on money equal to the higher marginal lending costs will simultaneously leave the supply price of loans from the bank unaffected and leave the supply price of loans and capital from the consumers unaffected by preventing the consumers from attempting to substitute money for nonmonetary assets.

of capital plus the given, expected rate of price inflation divided by the price level, we have thereby determined, for each price level, the interest rate implied by equilibrium in the factor markets. Then find the interest rates that equate the demand and supply of money at each different price level. An intersection of these price-interest rate pairs determines a temporary equilibrium.[13] The difference between the two economies discussed in this chapter is that a perfectly competitive money model has its money supplies infinitely elastic at the price level established by convertibility, while a modern money model has a constant money supply (or a money supply function) and has a demand function for money in which the interest rate appears as the cost of holding money. Graphically, the curve showing equilibrium in the factor markets is the same in the two economies, but in the perfectly competitive money model the money-market-equilibrium curve is a straight line parallel to the interest rate axis at the fixed conversion price, while in a modern money economy the money equilibrium curve has a positive slope, as does the curve showing equilibrium in the factor markets. The manipulation of these models to obtain the preceding results is straightforward.[14]

We now examine the effects of the remaining possible shifts.

F. Shifts in the Marginal Product and Supply of Labor

A shift in production functions generating a lower marginal physical product of labor or a shift out in the supply-of-labor curve in a modern money model will, of course, increase the temporary equilibrium rate of involuntary unemployment. The qualitative effects of these shifts are the same with classical, as with modern monetary institutions. Indeed, even the most classical of writers (i.e., Say [27, pp. 194–196]) admitted that unemployment resulted from such shifts.

In fact, still barring changes in relative output prices, it is only shifts in the marginal product or supply of labor that can alter the level of unemployment in a perfectly competitive money economy. This is easy to see: Unemployment in any temporary equilibrium can be altered only by altering the value of the marginal product curve or the money wage supply curve of labor. But since the money price of output is fixed by convertibility in a perfectly competitive money model, the only way to alter the temporary equilibrium unemployment rate is to shift the marginal physical product or real supply curve of labor.

---

[13] The above is the only atemporal model consistent with a Keynes–Patinkin environment. The standard Keynes–Patinkin model is internally inconsistent. For a verification of these propositions, and for an intertemporal model, see Thompson [34].

[14] One must note, however, that the only equilibria which count, i.e., which are stable, in a modern money model are those for which the interest rate that equilibrates the money market is more sensitive to a small change in price level than is the interest rate that equilibrates the factor markets.

With fully employed nonlabor inputs, we may conclude that the only way to change the rate of involuntary unemployment is to change input supplies or the rate of labor-favoring technical change. In fact, historical evidence (1860–1940) strongly suggests that the long (20-year) building business cycle—the largest and most widespread business cycle in modern history—has been due to a dynamic interaction between a kind of labor-favoring technical change and induced alterations in the supplies of certain inputs. (See Thompson [31].)

G. Shifts Altering Relative Prices between Real Outputs

The preceding analysis in this section has treated all outputs as if they were physically homogeneous, so that relative output prices could not vary. As a consequence, the analysis could proceed in the same technological environment as the standard, income-expenditure model. Shifts in the demand for and supply of money, in real output, in the productivity of capital, and in the productivity and supply of labor exhaust the exogenous shifts possible in such a world.

Now we consider shifts in excess demands between the various real outputs and allow these shifts to alter relative output prices. We find—at long last—a shift for which the perfectly competitive money economy is clearly inferior to the modern money economy with respect to the magnitude of the induced alterations in involuntary unemployment. An example will suffice to show this. Suppose that an initial equilibrium in an economy with two real outputs is disturbed by a shift in demand between the outputs. The shift is toward the consumption good, which is produced only by capital, and away from the capital good, which is produced only by labor and under diminishing returns. First, consider the shift under perfectly competitive monetary institutions. Suppose that money is convertible into the consumption good.[15] Since the shift cannot raise the money price of the consumption good, there must be a fall in the money price of the capital good and a corresponding drop in employment. This drop in employment may easily be more severe than the corresponding drop in a modern money model. To see this, consider the same price and thus employment change in the latter model. The lower price of one output and the constant price of the other (together with the higher interest rate implied by the constant rental on capital and the lower capital price) implies a lower demand for money than before the shift (together with a higher demand for capital as a store of value than in the perfectly competitive money

---

[15] If money were convertible into capital in such a world, no shift in output demands could create any involuntary unemployment, because no shift could alter the price of capital and therefore employment. For the shift specified above, the price of consumption goods and rental on capital would simply climb sufficiently high that a new general equilibrium would be established.

economy.) Since the money supply in a modern money model does not fall with money demand, there is an excess supply of money (together with an excess demand for the capital output) in the modern money economy at the postshift, temporary equilibrium prices of the perfectly competitive money economy. Assuming that an increase in the consumption-good price does not reduce the demand for capital output,[16] clearing these excesses requires a higher price of capital and thus a lower rate of unemployment than in the perfectly competitive money economy.

More generally, any shift in demands that increases the relative price of the asset backing money relative to other, labor-using, outputs will obviously create involuntary unemployment starting from a full equilibrium in a perfectly competitive money economy.

There can be little doubt that classical monetary analysts, who were also inveterate policy advisors, put little or no weight on the recessionary significance of a rise in the relative demand for the asset backing money, i.e., gold.[17] The policy neglect of these shifts permitted a series of sharp recessions caused by sudden increases in the demand for gold throughout the history of Europe and the United States. This is abundantly clear from the statistical work of Warren and Pearson [38]. The last such recession was the Great Depression, which saw a five-year increase in the real price of gold (1929–1934) whose magnitude was unprecedented in recorded history [38], an increase resulting from the return to the gold standard from 1924 to 1928.[18] The free convertibility of money into gold was halted from 1931 to 1934 and replaced by what has become a system of government fiat money, a system represented in the modern money model.

---

[16] Alternatively, assume that consumers all have the same, constant marginal rate of substitution between consumption and investment goods after the shift has occurred. Then the price ratio between consumption and investment goods, as determined by this rate, is the same after the shift in both of the economies under discussion. Consequently, the excess supply of money in a modern money model at the temporary equilibrium prices of the perfectly competitive model implies proportionately higher prices of all outputs in achieving a temporary equilibrium in the modern money model.

[17] Even the leading employment pessimists of the classical era—the "general glut" theorists such as Malthus and Sismondi—had their recessions due only to shifts in the supply of labor. (See Sowell [29].)

[18] The move back to the gold standard and consequent increase in the real price of gold would probably not have created a depression if the countries had made a common decision to return to the gold standard at the same time. In such a case, the countries would probably have recognized the substantial effect that the return to the gold standard would have on the real value of gold and therefore would have returned at a much higher conversion rate of money into gold, a rate which would have reflected the substantial world inflation (33% in United States wholesale prices) that had occurred since the collapse of the international gold standard in 1914. In such a case, the increase in the real value of gold would have been immediate and would not have altered money wage or price levels.

The traditional disavowal by "respectable" economic theorists of the aggregative recessionary impact of an unexpected increase in the demand for the asset which backs money has been the argument that a rise in the demand for gold will simply expand output and employment in the gold industry, so that no aggregate recession results from the shift.[19] Such an argument is based on the absence of any formal theory of employment under a gold standard and a misunderstanding of the nature of the informational imperfection leading to involuntary unemployment. Formally, a pegged money price of gold and the fact that workers' temporary equilibrium supply curves are defined in terms of money wages prevent any expansion in the gold industry despite the fact that the real price of gold has risen. One economic rationale for the higher supply price of labor in terms of nongold commodities is that some workers simply do not know that the nongold price level has dropped and so require the same wages in terms of gold for the same employment. Another economic rationale is that other workers, who know the extent of the fall in the prices of nongold commodities, expect higher real wages in nongold commodities in the post-shift economy because they believe that the lower nongold prices are due to a higher-than-normal rate of technical progress in the nongold industries, when in fact there has been a shift in demand toward gold or a lower-than-normal rate of technical progress in the gold industry.[20]

H. WAGE FLEXIBILITY AND THE POSSIBILITY OF PERMANENT INVOLUNTARY UNEMPLOYMENT

We have said nothing of the events that occur after market-learning by the unemployed lowers the future temporary equilibrium supply curves of labor. While we again cannot derive any general superiority of one of our monetary

[19] But perhaps the main reason for the academic neglect of employment fluctuations based on changes in the real value of gold was the development of central banking during the nineteenth and early twentieth centuries and the consequent development of numerous business cycle "models" in which central banking played a key role. While a central bank has no effect in a perfectly competitive money model, it has some effect in a competitive banking model with a positive transaction cost of bank lending; viz., the policies of the central bank affect the transaction cost of private lending at a given volume of total loans and hence affect the spread between borrowers' and lenders' rates of interest. While the fluctuation in central bank rates and bond purchases no doubt had some influence on the price of nongold durables and thus employment, the dominance of these fluctuations in pre-Keynesian business cycle theories obscured the causes of the larger economic fluctuations in economic history and has left us a legacy of "practical" men of affairs who believe that central banks affect our economies only through affecting the real cost of lending.

[20] A perfectly competitive money model relying solely on the latter type of rationale has some peculiar properties. First, it has the same temporary equilibria regardless of which good is used to back money. Second, all shifts which lead to contraction in some industries without expansion in others are shifts in demands or abnormal reductions in the rate of technical progress. Hence, under the latter rationale, money could indeed be called a "veil."

systems over the other, we can answer a related question. Namely, is permanent involuntary unemployment possible in our alternative monetary systems?

The answer to this question for the modern money model, as developed by Pigou [24], is well known: Permanent involuntary unemployment is impossible because the supply of real cash balances and therefore consumption demand would rise to infinity if wage reductions were to continually pull down output prices sufficiently to prevent the achievement of full employment. The argument, of course, employs a real balance effect. In a perfectly competitive money economy the supply of money changes with prices so as to retain equilibrium in the money market. Hence, even if price reductions for given money supplies generated real wealth increases in a perfectly competitive money economy (which they do not, as indicated in Section I.E), the induced reductions in the money supply would prevent real cash balances from rising during a deflation. The Pigou effect is absent in a perfectly competitive money economy.

However, while a perfectly competitive money economy lacks the anchor of a fixed money supply and real balance effect, it does have an anchor of its own—convertibility. Under convertibility at a fixed rate, when wages fall, it is impossible for all prices to fall in the same proportion. At least one price does not fall at all. In the simple case of a single output, into which money is convertible, a fall in wages produces a proportional fall in real wages because there is no change in the output price. In the general case, if we allow wage expectations and thus wages to fall continuously, adopting the macroeconomic convention that the disequilibrium is based upon incorrect wage expectations, we must, sooner or later, arrive at an equilibrium as long as one exists.

The preceding results lend rationale to the position of the classical economists that involuntary unemployment is only temporary and serve to rationalize the neglect by classical economists of Pigou and real balance effects.

III. Conclusion

A money economy consistent with an orthodox value theory in which money is competitively supplied exists, and any such economy has just about all of the properties that modern monetary theorists claim to have proved to be classical fallacies. In particular: (1) Any perfectly competitive money economy has a classical dichotomy between the real and monetary sectors and yet a determinate equilibrium quantity of real cash balances. (2) Any perfectly competitive money economy has no real balance or Pigou effects but still has an impossibility of permanent, aggregate unemployment. (3) In any perfectly competitive money economy, equilibrium allocations of resources are never affected by anticipated inflation. (4) In any perfectly competitive money economy, aggregate output is never disturbed by Keynesian or Quantity Theory shifts—that is, by shifts in liquidity preference, the marginal efficiency of capital, the propensity to consume, or the money supply.

Despite the fact that Say's law holds for any money economy consistent with orthodox value theory, the level of aggregative involuntary unemployment in a temporary equilibrium of such an economy varies substantially with certain shifts which alter relative output prices, as well as with shifts in the marginal product and supply of labor. Indeed, such unemployment in a perfectly competitive money economy is *more* susceptible to some recessionary shifts—those which decrease the demand for money—than it is in a modern money economy. The historical accuracy of a perfectly competitive money model in explaining major business fluctuations prior to 1934 appears to be remarkable, and the model highlights the danger of returning to a fully convertible gold standard.

ACKNOWLEDGMENTS

The author benefited from discussions with his colleagues, Armen Alchian, Benjamin Klein, Axel Leijonhufvud, and Joseph Ostroy. Helpful comments on an earlier draft were provided by Dan Benjamin and Robert Clower. Research support was provided by the Lilly Foundation Grant for the Study of Property Rights at UCLA. An earlier draft of this chapter, entitled "In Defense of the Classical Theory of Money and Income," was presented at the December 1969 meetings of the Econometric Society.

REFERENCES

1. Alchian, A. A., and Allen, W. R., *University Economics*, 2nd ed., Chapter 25. Belmont, California: Wadsworth, 1967.
2. Arrow, K. J., "An Extension of the Basic Theorem of Classical Welfare Economics," *Proceedings of the Second Berkeley Symposium on Mathematical Statistics and Probability* (J. Neyman, ed.). Berkeley: Univ. of California Press, 1951.
3. Arrow, K. J., and Hahn, F., *General Competitive Analysis*, Chapter 11. San Francisco: Holden-Day, 1971.
4. Bailey, M. J., "The Welfare Cost of Inflationary Finance," *Journal of Political Economy* **64** (April 1956), 93–110.
5. Becker, G. S., and Baumol, W. J., "The Classical Monetary Theory: The Outcome of the Discussion," in *Essays in Economic Thought* (J. Spengler and W. R. Allen, eds.), pp. 753–771. Chicago: Rand-McNally, 1960.
6. Debreu, G., *Theory of Value*. New York: Wiley, 1959.
7. Friedman, M., "Discussion of the Inflationary Gap," in *Essays in Positive Economics*, pp. 253–257. Chicago: Univ. of Chicago Press, 1953.
8. Friedman, M., *A Program for Monetary Stability*, p. 7. New York: Fordham Univ. Press, 1960.
9. Friedman, M., *The Optimum Quantity of Money and Other Essays*. Chicago: Aldine, 1969.
10. Hicks, J. R., *Capital and Growth*, Chapter VI. London and New York: Oxford Univ. Press, 1965.

11. Kessel, R. A., and Alchian, A. A., "Effects of Inflation," *Journal of Political Economy* **70** (December 1962), 521–537.
12. Keynes, J. M., *The General Theory of Employment, Interest and Money.* New York: Macmillan, 1936.
13. Klein, B., "The Competitive Supply of Money," *Journal of Money, Credit, and Banking.* (to be published).
14. Leijonhufvud, A., *On Keynesian Economics and the Economics of Keynes*, Chapter 2. London and New York: Oxford Univ. Press, 1968.
15. Marschak, J., "Rationale of the Demand for Money and of Money Illusion," *Metroeconomica* **2** (August 1950), 71–100.
16. Marty, A. L., "Gurley and Shaw on Money in a Theory of Finance," *Journal of Political Economy* **69** (February 1961), 57–58.
17. Metzler, L. A., "Wealth, Saving, and the Rate of Interest," *Journal of Political Economy* **59** (April 1951), 93–116.
18. Mill, J. S., *Principles of Political Economy* (W. J. Ashley, ed.), Book III. London: Longmans, Green, 1909.
19. Ostroy, J., "The Informational Efficiency of Monetary Exchange," *American Economic Review* (to be published).
20. Patinkin, D., *Money, Interest, and Prices*, 2nd ed. New York: Harper, 1965.
21. Patinkin, D., "The Indeterminacy of Absolute Prices in Classical Economic Theory," *Econometrica* **17** (January 1949), 1–27.
22. Pesek, B., and Saving, T., *Money, Wealth, and Economic Theory*, Part II. New York: Macmillan, 1967.
23. Pesek, B., "Comment," *Journal of Political Economy* **77**, Supplement (August 1969), 889.
24. Pigou, A. C., "The Classical Stationary State," *Economic Journal* **53** (December 1943), 342–351.
25. Radner, R., "Competitive Equilibrium under Uncertainty," *Econometrica* **36** (January 1968), 31–58.
26. Samuelson, P. A., "What Classical and Neoclassical Monetary Theory Really Was," *Canadian Journal of Economics* **1** (February 1968), 1–15.
27. Say, J. B., *Taite d'economie politique*, 5th ed., Vol. 1. Paris: Chez Rapilly, 1826.
28. Schumpeter, J. A., *The History of Economic Analysis*, Chapter 7. London and New York: Oxford Univ. Press, 1954.
29. Sowell, T., *Say's Law*, Chapters I–IV. Princeton, New Jersey: Princeton Univ. Press, to be published.
30. Starr, R., "The Structure of Exchange in Barter and Monetary Economies," *Quarterly Journal of Economics* **86** (May 1972), 290–302.
31. Thompson, E., "Technical Change, Its Measurement and Introduction into the Theory of the Firm with Special Application to the Explanation of the Building Cycle," Ph.D. Thesis, Harvard Univ. (1962).
32. Thompson, E., "An Optimal System of Property Rights for a General Money Economy," unpublished manuscript (1968).
33. Thompson, E., "A Reformulation of Orthodox Value Theory," manuscript (1971).
34. Thompson, E., "A Generalization of the Cassel–Patinkin Money Model," manuscript (1973).
35. Thompson, E., "A Reformulation of Macroeconomic Theory," manuscript (1973).
36. Thornton, H., *An Enquiry into the Nature and Effects of the Paper Credit of Great Britain*, reprint. London: 1939. Library of Economics.
37. Viner, J., *Studies in the Theory of International Trade*, Chapters IV and V. London: Allen and Unwin, 1955.
38. Warren, G. F., and Pearson, F. A., *Prices*, Chapter V. New York: Wiley, 1933.

REFERENCES FOR THE TEXT AND A-APPENDICES

Acres, W.M., The Bank of England From Within, Vol. I London: Oxford University Press, 1931, Ch. 12.

Adams. F.K., The Export-Import Bank and American Foreign Diplomacy, University of Missouri Press, 1976, Ch. 7.

Adams, Pythian, The Desolation of a City, Cambridge University Press, 1979.

Ady, C.M., The History of Milan Under the Sforza, London: Metheun & Co., 1907.

Alberts, B., D. Bray, J. Lewis, M. Roff, K. Roberts and J. Watson, The Molecular Biology of the Cell, 2nd ed., NY: Garland, 1989.

Albright, J., and M. Kunstel, Bombshell: The Secret Story of America's Unknown Atomic Spy Conspiracy, NY: Times Books/Random House, 1997.

Alchian, A.A., "Uncertainty, Evolution, and Economic Theory," Journal of Political Economy 58, 1950: 211-21.

Alchian, A.A., and W.R. Allen, University Economics, 3rd ed., Belmont, CA: Wadsworth Publishing Co., 1972: 70-71.

Alexander, R.D., "The Evolution of Social Behavior," Annual Review of Ecology and Systematics, 5, 1974: 325-83.

Allen, G.C., "Guilds, Japanese," Encyclopedia of the Social Sciences, 1929: 221-22.

Altamira, Rafael, "Spain, 1412-1516," The Cambridge Medieval History, Vol. VIII, Cambridge University Press, 1936, Ch. 15.

Anstey, Vera, "Guilds, Indian," Encyclopedia of the Social Sciences, 1929: 216-19.

Apostol, T.M., Mathematical Analysis, Reading MA: Addison Wesley, 1957.

Arrow, K.J., Social Choice and Individual Values, 2nd ed., NY: Wiley, 1963.

Ashley W.J., "An Introduction to English Economic History and Theory," Putnam's Sons, 1906.

Atiyah, P.S., "Liability for Railway Nuisance in the English Common Law: A Historical Footnote," Journal of Law and Economics, April 1980: 191-96.

Aumann, R., and L. Shapley, "Long-Term Competition -- A Game Theoretic Analysis," unpublished manuscript, 1976.

Bacon, Francis, The New Organon and Related Writings, 1620; reprinted in Indianapolis: Bobbs-Merrill, 1960.

Banfield, E.L., The Moral Basis of a Backward Society, NY: Free Press, 1958.

Barton, H.A., "Scandinavia in the Revolutionary Era, 1760-1815," Minnesota 1986.

Barzel, Yoram, "The Optimal Timing of Innovation," Review of Economics and Statistics, Aug. 1968: 348-55.

Bastable, C.F., The Commerce of Nations, Methuen, 1927.

Batchelder, R.W., "Optimal Compensation Under Government Imposed Rearrangement of Ownership," UCLA Ph.D. dissertation, 1975.

_____, and N. Sanchez, "The Encomiendia and the Optimizing Imperialist," UCLA Working Paper, 1988.

Baumol, W.J., "On Taxation and the Control of Externalities," American Economic Review, 62, June 1972: 307-22.

Bayley, C.C., War and Society in Renaissance Florence, Toronto: University of Toronto Press, 1961.

Beck, Gregory, and G.S. Habicht, "Immunity and the Invertebrates," Scientific American, Nov. 1996.

Becker, G.S., "Crime and Punishment: An Economic Approach," Journal of Political Economy, 76, Mar./Apr. 1968: 169-217.

Becker, M.B., Florence in Transition, Vols. 1 and 2, Baltimore, MD: Johns Hopkins Press, 1969.

Bellman, Richard, Dynamic Programming, NJ: Princeton University Press, 1957, esp. p.83.

Bengston, Hermann, History of Greece, Ottawa, Canada: University of Ottawa Press, 1988, ch. 13, esp. p. 275.

Bentham, Jeremy, Theory of Legislation, NY: Harcourt Brace, 1931.

Berge, Claude, Topological Spaces, Including a Treatment of Multi-valued Functions, Vector Spaces and Convexity, Edinburgh: Oliver and Boyd, 1963.

Bergstrom, T.C., "On the Evolution of Altruistic Ethical Rules for Siblings," American Economic Review, 85, Mar. 1995: 58-82.

Berman, H.J., Law and Revolution, Cambridge, MA: Harvard University Press, 1983: pp. 1-254.

Berner, Stanley, "Italy: Commentary in Failed Transitions to Modern Industrial Society: Renaissance Italy and Seventeenth Century Holland, Interuniversity Center for European Studies, 1974.

Bhagwati, Jagdish, The Anatomy and Consequences of Exchange Control Regimes, NY: Ballinger, 1978.

Bickerdike, C.F., "The Theory of Incipient Taxes," Economic Journal, Dec. 1906.

Biddle, Martin, Winchester in the Early Middle Ages, Winchester Studies Series, Oxford and Clarendon Press, 1976.

Black, Anthony, Guilds and Civil Society in European Political Though From the Twelfth Century to the Present, Methuen, 1984.

Blackorby, C., D. Nissen, D. Primont, and R.R. Russell, "Consistent Intertemporal Decision Making," Review of Economic Studies, Apr. 1972: 239-48.

Blok, P.J., History of the People of the Netherlands, vol. 4, NY: Putnam & Sons, 1907.

Bloomfield, A.J., Monetary Policy Under the International Gold Standard, NY: Federal Reserve Bank, 1959.

Blume, L. and D. Easley, "Evolution and Market Behavior," Journal of Economic Theory, 58, 1992: 9-40.

Bolino, A.C., The Development of the American Economy, 2nd ed., Columbus: Merrill, 1966.

Bordo, M., and F. Kydland, "The Gold Standard as a Rule," Explorations in Economic History, Oct. 1995.

Bosher, J.F., The Single Duty Project, London: University of London, Athlone Press, 1974, Ch. 3, esp. p. 74.

Botsford, G.W., Hellenistic History; revised and rewritten by Charles A. Robinson, Macmillan, 1939: 318-25.

Bowden, W., M. Karpovich, and A. Usher, An Economic History of Europe Since 1750, American Book Co., 1937.

Bowman, Linda, "Russia's First Income Taxes: The Effects of Modernized Taxes on Commerce and Industry, 1885-1914," Slavic Review, 52 #2, Summer 1993: 256-82.

Brinton, Crane, The Anatomy of a Revolution, revised ed., NY: Vintage, 1965.

Broad, C.D., Five Types of Ethical Theory, Paterson, NJ: Littlefield, Adams & Co., 1959.

Brown, J.L., The Evolution of Behavior, NY: Norton, 1975.

Buchanan, J.M., Freedom in Constitutional Contract, London & College Station, TX: Texas A&M University Press, 1977.

_____ and G. Tullock, "Polluter's Profits and Political Response: Direct Controls Versus Taxes," American Economic Review, Mar. 1975: 139-48.

_____ and _____, Calculus of Consent, University of Michigan Press, 1962.

Burckhardt, Jacob, The Civilization of the Renaissance in Italy, Oxford: Phaedon Press, 1945.

Burford, A., Craftsmen in Greek and Roman Society, London 1972.

Burgess, J.S., The Guilds of Peking, NY: Columbia University Press, 1928.

Burke, Edmund, Reflections on the Revolution in France, 1790; reprinted in Buffalo, NY: Prometheus Books, 1987.

Burt, A.L., The Evolution of the British Empire and Commonwealth from the American Revolution, Boston: Heath, 1956.

Bury, J.B., "The Ottoman Conquest," The Cambridge Modern History, Vol. I, Cambridge University Press, 1931, Ch. III.

Cagan, Phillip, "The Monetary Dynamics of Inflation," in M. Friedman (ed.), Studies in the Quantity Theory of Money, Chicago: University of Chicago Press, 1996.

Calmette, Joseph, "The Reign of Charles VII and the End of the Hundred Year's War," The Cambridge Medieval History, Cambridge University Press, 1936, Ch. VII.

Cameron, Alan, Circus Factions, Oxford: Clarendon Press, 1976.

Cameron, R.E., France and the Economic Development of Europe, 1800-1914, Princeton, NJ: Princeton University Press, 1961: 46-54.

Canovai, Tito, The Banks of Issue in Italy, Washington: U.S. G.P.O., 1911.

Carpanetto, D. and G. Ricuperati, Italy in the Age of Reason 1685-1789, London: Longman, 1987.

Cavallo, D., and J. Cottani, "Argentina," in D. Papageorgiou, et al. (eds.) Liberalizing Foreign Trade vol. 2, Cambridge: Blackwell, 1991.

Caves, R.E., J.A. Frankel, and R.W. Jones, World Trade and Payments, 7th d., Harper Collins, 1996, pp. 322-28.

Chapman, Michael, "KGB Museum Hails Oppenheimer as a Cold War Hero," Human Events, June 27, 1997: p. 6.

Clapham, John, The Bank of England, Vol. I, London: Cambridge University Press, 1945, Ch. 1.

Clarkson, J.D., A History of Russia, Random House, 1961.

Coase, Ronald, "The Problem of Social Cost," Journal of Law and Economics, 1960: 29-35.

Cobban, Alfred, A History of France, London: Penguin Books, 1961: 33-34.

Cochrane, Eric, Florence in the Forgotten Years, 1527-1800, Chicago, 1973.

Cole, C.W., French Mercantile Doctrines Before Colbert, NY: Richard E. Smith, 1931.

Collingridge, D. and C. Reeve. Science Speaks to Power: The Role of Experts in Policy Making, NY: St. Martins Press, 1986.

Commons, J.R., History of Labor in the United States, NY: McMillan, 1918.

Conant, C.A., A History of Modern Banks of Issue, G.P. Putnam's Sons, 1896.

Condorcet, Jean-Antoine-Nicolas de Caritat, Marquis de, in I. McLean and F. Hewitt (eds.), Condorcet: Foundations of Social Choice and Political Theory, Brookfield, VT: E. Elgar, 1994; originally in French, 1785-1795.

Coornaert, Emile, "Les Corporations en France Avant 1789," Les Editions Ouvrieres, 1968.

Cresswell, B.F., History of the Weavers and Fullers of Exeter, Pollard, 1930.

Cumings, Bruce, Korea's Place in the Sun, A Modern History, NY: Norton, 1997: 308-18.

Cunningham, William, Politics and Economics, London, 1885.

Darwin, Charles, On the Origin of Species, Introduction by Enst Moyr, 1960; Cambridge: Harvard University Press, originally 1859.

Davies, J.C., When Men Revolt and Why: A Reader in Political Violence and Revolution, NY: The Free Press, 1971, p. 4.

Dawkins, Richard, The Extended Phenotype, Oxford: Oxford University Press, 1982.

Dell, S., "On Being Grandmotherly: The Evolution of IMF Conditionality," Essays in International Finance, 144, Oct. 1981: 1-35.

del Mar, A., History of Monetary Systems, Kerr & Co., 1895.

_____, Money and Civilization, Franklin 1969.

Demsetz, Harold, "Toward a Theory of Property Rights," American Economic Review, May 1967: 347-59.

de Roover, R., "The Organization of Trade," in Cambridge Economic History, Vol. III, Cambridge 1963.

_____, "The Concept of a Just Price," Journal of Economic History, Dec. 1958: 428-34.

de Rosa, L., "Property Rights, Institutional Change and Economic Growth in Southern Italy in the XVIIIth and XIXth Centuries," Journal of European Economic History, Winter 1979.

de Vries, Jan, "Holland, A Commentary," in Failed Transitions to Modern Industrial Society, InterUniversity Centre for European Studies, 1974.

de Vries, Kelly, Medieval Military Technology, Orchard Park, NY: Broadview Press, 1992.

de Vries, M.G., Balance of Payments Adjustment, 1945-1986, Washington, DC: International Monetary Fund, 1987.

Diamond, Jared, Guns, Germs, and Steel, NY: Norton, 1997.

Diamond, P., and E. Maskin, "An Equilibrium Analysis of Search and Breach of Contract," Bell Journal of Economics, 1979: 282-316.

Dickson, P.G., The Financing Revolution in England, A Study in the Development of Public Credit, 1688-1756, London: Macmillan, 1967.

Dowell, Stephen, History of Taxation and Taxes in England, Vol. III, 2nd ed., London: Longmans, 1880.

Dumezel, G., "*La Tripartition Indo-Europeenne*," Psyche, 2, 1947: 1348-56.

DuPlessis, R.S., and M.C. Howell, "Reconsidering the Modern Urban Economy: The Cases of Leiden and Lille," Past and Present, 94, 1982: 49-84.

Dyer, B. and R. Obar, Tracing the History of Eukaryotic Cells New York: Columbia University Press, 1994.

Eberhard, Wolfram, A History of China, London: Routledge, 1950.

Edkins, Joseph, Chinese Currency, Shanghai: Kelly and Walsh, 1901.

Edwards, Sebastian, Real Exchange Rate Devaluation and Adjustment: Exchange Rate Policy in Developing Countries, Cambridge, MA: MIT Press, 1991.

Eichengreen, Barry (ed.), The Gold Standard in History and Theory, NY, 1985.

Eisenstadt, S.N., "Cultural Orientations, Institutional Entrepreneurs, and Social Change: Comparative Analysis of Traditional Civilizations," American Journal of Sociology, 85, Jan. 1980: 940-69.

Ellis, H.S., Exchange Controls in Eastern Europe, Cambridge: Harvard University Press, 1941.

Eshel, I., "On the Changing Concept of Population Stability as a Reflection of Changing Problematics in the Quantitative Theory of Evolution," Journal of Mathematical Biology 34, 1995: 488-510.

Evans, Paul, "Do Large Deficits Produce High Interest Rates?" American Economic Review, March, 1985.

Faith, R.L., and E.A. Thompson, "A Paradox in the Theory of Second Best," Economic Inquiry, April 1981: 235-44.

Finlay, George, History of the Byzantine and Greek Empires, Vol. 2, Blackwell and Sons, London, 1854.

Finley, M.I., The Ancient Economy, Berkeley, CA: University of California Press, 1973.

Fisher, R.A., The Genetical Theory of Natural Selection, Oxford: Clarendon Press, 1930; or 2nd ed., NY: Dover Publications, 1958.

Flick, A.C., The Decline of the Medieval Church, 2 vols., NY: Knopf, 1930.

Flink, Salomon, German Reichbank and Economic Germany, Columbia University, 1931.

Floor, W.M., "The Guilds of Iran - An Overview From the Earliest Beginnings Until 1972," Zeitschift der Deutchen Morgenlundischen Gesellshaft, 125, 1975: 99-116.

Foster, D. and P. Young, "Stochastic Evolutionary Game Dynamics," Theoretical Population Biology, 38, 1990: 219-32.

Frank, Tenney, An Economic Survey of Ancient Rome, vol. 5, Baltimore: Johns Hopkins Press, 1940.

Friedman, J.W., Oligopoly and the Theory of Games, Amsterdam/NY: North Holland, 1977.

Friedman, L.M., A History of American Law, New York: Simon and Schuster, 1973.

Friedman, Milton, The Optimum Quantity of Money and Other Essays, Chicago, IL: Aldine, 1969.

————, Essays in Positive Economics, Chicago: University of Chicago Press, 1953.

Fudenberg, D. and E. Maskin, "The Folk Theorem in Repeated Play With Discounting or Incomplete Information," Econometrica, 54, 1986: 533-54.

_____, and D. Levine, The Theory of Learning in Games, MA: MIT Press, 1997.

Garnett, Richard, "Rome and Its Temporal Power," Cambridge Modern History, Vol. I, Cambridge University Press, 1931, Ch. VII.

Ghiselin, Michael, The Economy of Nature and the Evolution of Sex, Berkeley, CA: University of California Press, 1974.

Gibbon, Edward, The History of the Decline and Fall of the Roman Empire, Philadelphia, PA: Claxton, Remsen and Haffelfinger, 1883; esp. Vol. III, pp. 633-43.

Gilbert, M., "The Gold-Dollar System: Conditions of Equilibrium and the Price of Gold," Essays in International Finance, 70, 1968: 1-49.

Gilmore, G., and C.L. Black, The Law of Admiralty, 2nd ed., 1975.

Gimbutas, Marija, "Proto-Indo-European Culture: The Kurgan Culture During the Fifth, Fourth, and Third Mellennia, BC," in G. Cardona et al. (eds.) Indo-European and Indo-Europeans, Philadelphia, PA: University of Pennsylvania Press, 1970.

Girton, L. and D. Roper, "J. Laurence Laughlin and the Quantity Theory of Money," Journal of Political Economy, Aug. 1978: 599-626.

Glasner, David, Free Banking and Monetary Reform, Cambridge, 1989.

Godeschot, J., B.F. Hyslop, D.L. Dowd, The Napoleonic Era in Europe, Holt, Rinehart & Winston, 1971.

Goldberg, V.P., "Regulation and Administered Contracts," Bell Journal of Economics and Management Science, 7, Autumn 1976: 439-41.

Goldman, S.M., "Consistent Plans," Review of Economic Studies, 148, Apr. 1980: 533-39.

Goldstone, J.A., "Revolutions and Superpowers," in J.R. Adelman (ed.) Revolutions and Superpowers, NY: Praeger, 1986: 38-48.

Gonzales, R., J.F. Steiner, and M.A. Sande, "Antibiotic Prescribing for Adults With Colds, Upper Respiratory Tract Infections, and Bronchitis by Ambulatory Care Physicians," Journal of the American Medical Association, 278 #11, Sept. 17, 1997: 901-05.

Gould, S.J., and N. Eldredge, "Punctuated Equilibria: The Tempo and Mode of Evolution Reconsidered," Paleobiology, 3, 1977: 115-51.

Gray, A., The Development of Economic Doctrine, Longmans, Green, 1956.

Greif, A., P. Milgrom, and B. Weingast, "Coordination, Commitment, and Enforcement: The Case of the Merchant Guild," Journal of Political Economy, 102, #4, 1994: 745-76.

Gross, Charles, The Guild Merchant, Oxford: Clarendon Press, 1890.

Guerdan, René, Byzantium, Its Triumph and Tragedy, trans. by D.B.L. Harley, NY: Putnam and Sons, 1957.

Gurr, T.R. and J.A. Goldstone, "Comparison and Policy Implications," in J.A. Goldstone, T.R. Gurr, and F. Moshiri (eds.), Revolutions of the Late Twentieth Century, Boulder: Westview Press, 1991: 324-41.

Haggard, S. and C.K. Pang, "The Transition of Export-Led Growth in Taiwan," in J.D. Auerbach, D. Dollar, and K.L. Sokoloff (eds.), The Role of the State in Taiwan's Development, NY: M.E. Sharpe, 1994: 74-83.

Haight, F.A., A History of French Commercial Policies, NY: Macmillan, 1941.

Halliday, Fred, Cold War, Third World, Aukland, New Zealand: Century Hutchinson, 1989.

Hamilton, W.H., "The Ancient Maxim of Caveat Emptor," Yale Law Review, XL, #8, June 1930.

Hamilton, W.D., "The Genetical Evolution of Social Behavior," Pts. I and II, Journal of Theoretical Biology, 7, 1964: 1-32.

Hammerstein, Peter, "Darwinian Adaptation, Population Genetics, and the Streetcar Theory of Evolution," Journal of Math. Biology, 34, 1996: 511-32.

Hammond, P.J., "Changing Tastes and Coherent Dynamic Choice," Review of Economic Studies, 133, Feb. 1976: 159-73.

Hansen, J.A., "Opening the Capital Account: Costs, Benefits, and Sequencing," in S. Edwards (ed.) Capital Controls, Exchange Rates, and Monetary Policy in the World Economy, Cambridge University Press, 1995: 402.

Harcave, Sidney, Russia, A History, NY: Lippincott, 1964.

Harder, F.L., Efficient Government Institutions for Water Quality Control, University Press of America, 1980.

Harris, M.D., Story of Coventry, Dent, 1911.

Harrod, Roy, The Life of John Maynard Keynes, NY: Norton, 1961.

Hart, O.D., "Perfect Competition and Optimal Product Differentiation," Journal of Economic Theory, April 1980: 279-312.

Headlam, Clinton, Medieval Towns, London: J.M. Dent & Sons, 1927.

Heckscher, E.F., An Economic History of Sweden, Harvard Press, 1954.

_____, Mercantilism, Vols. 1 and 2, 2nd ed., London: Allen and Unwin, 1955.

Hegel, G.W.F., Lectures on the Philosophy of History, London: trans. J. Sibree, 1861 (originally in German, 1825-26).

Heyman, D., and A. Leijonhufvud, High Inflation, Oxford: Clarendon, 1995.

Hibbert, A.B., "The Economic Policies of Towns," in Vol. 5, Cambridge Economic History of Europe, Cambridge, 1963.

Hicks, J.R., "Mr. Keynes and the Classics: A Suggested Interpretation," Econometrica, V, 1937: 137-49.

Hickson, C.R., and E.A. Thompson, "A New Theory of Guilds and European Economic Development," Explorations in Economic History, 28, 1991: 127-68.

Hirshleifer, Jack, Economic Behavior in Adversity, Brighton: Wheatsheaf, 1987.

_____, Price Theory and Applications, NJ: Prentice Hall, 1984, p. 8.

Hobesbawn, E.F., Primitive Rebels: Studies in Archaic Forms of Social Movement in the Nineteenth and Twentieth Centuries, 3rd ed., London, 1971.

Hodgson, N.G.S., The Venture of Islam, Vol. II, Chicago: University of Chicago Press, 1974.

Holborn, Hajo, A History of Modern Germany, Vols. 2 and 3, Knopf, 1969.

Holt, R., "The Early History of Birmingham - 1166-1600," in Dugdale Society Occasional Papers, Oxford 1985.

Houseman, W., "Excise Anatomised: The Political Economy of Walpole's 1733 Tax Scheme," Journal of European Economic History, Spring 1981.

Huang, Ray, "Fiscal Administration During the Ming Dynasty," Charles O. Hucker (ed.) in Chinese Government in Ming Times, NY: Columbia University Press, 1969: esp. 112-28.

Hume, David, Political Discourses, London, 1752.

Hyde, J.K., Societies & Politics in Medieval Italy, Macmillan 1973.

International Monetary Fund, Annual Report on Exchange Rates Arrangements and Exchange Restrictions, Washington, DC: IMF Publications Services, 1976-1994.

Irsigler, Franz, "Industrial Production, International Trade and Public Finances in Cologne (XVIth. and XVth Centuries)," Journal of European Economic History, Fall 1977.

Janssen, Johannes, A History of the German People at the Close of the Middle Ages, London; K. Paul; Trench, Triibner, and Co., 1909.

Johnson, A.H., The History of the Worshipful Company of London, vol. 1, Oxford, 1914.

Jones, Phillip, The Poulters of London, Oxford Press, 1965.

Kandori, M., G. Mailath and R. Rob, "Learning, Mutation, and Long-Run Equilibria in Games," Econometrica 61, 1993: 29-56.

Kant, Immanuel, Perpetual Peace and Other Essays on Politics, History, and Morals; trans. by Ted Humphry, Indianapolis, IN: Hackett, 1983 (originally in German, 1780s).

Karlin, Samuel, "General Two-Locus Selection Models: Some Objective Results and Interpretations," Theor. Pop. Biology, 7, 1975: 364-98.

Keen, M.H., England in the Later Middle Ages, London: Routledge, 1988, Ch. 9.

Kellenbenz, Herman, "The Organization of Industrial Production," in Cambridge Economic History, Vol. 5, Cambridge 1963.

Kelley, J. and Klein, H.S., Revolution and the Rebirth of Inequality, Berkeley, CA: University of California Press, 1981.

Kemp, M., and M. Ohyama, "On the Sharing of Trade Gains by Resource Rich and Resource Poor Countries," Journal of International Economics, 8(1), Feb. 1978: 93-115.

Keynes, J.M., A General Theory of Employment, Interest, and Money, London: Macmillan, 1936.

King, M.A., and Don Fullerton, The Taxation of Income From Capital, Chicago, IL: University of Chicago Press, 1984, Ch. 5.

Klein, B. and K. Leffler, "The Role of Market Forces in Assuring Contractual Performance," Journal of Political Economy 89, 1981: 615-44.

Klein, B., R.G. Crawford and A.A. Alchian, "Vertical Integration, Appropriable Rents, and the Competitive Contracting Process," Journal of Law and Economics, 21, Oct. 1978: 279-326.

Koht, Halfdan, "The Scandinavian Kingdoms During the 14th and 15th Centuries," The Camridge Medieval History, Vol. VIII, Cambridge University Press, 1936, Ch. 17.

Korelin, A.P., "The Social Problem in Russia, 1906-1914," in Taranovski (ed.), Reform in Modern Russian History, Cambridge University Press, 1995: 139-62.

Kramer, Stella, The English Craft Guilds, Studies In Their Progress and Decline, Columbia University Press, 1927.

Kreps, D., P. Milgrom, J. Roberts, and R. Wilson, "Rational Cooperation in the Finitely Repeated Prisoner's Dilemma," Journal of Economic Theory, 27, 1982: 245-52.

Krueger, A.O., "The Political Economy of the Rent-Seeking Society," American Economic Review, June 1974: 291-303.

Krueger, A.O., Liberalization Attempts and Consequences, NY: Ballinger, 1978.

Kuznelsova, N.A., "Guild Organization, Early Nineteenth Century," in C. Issawa (ed.), The Economic History of the Middle East, 1800-1914, Chicago: University of Chicago Press, 1966.

Lack, David, Ecological Adaptations for Breeding in Birds, London: Methuen, 1968.

Laffan, R.G.D., "The Empire in the Fifteenth Century," in The Camridge Medieval History, Vol VIII, Cambridge University Press, 1936.

Lamarck, J.B., *Philosophie Zoologique*, Paris: Dentu, 1809; reprinted, 1984; translated H. Elliot, Chicago: University of Chicago Press.

League of Nations, Report by the Economic Committee of the League of Nations, Geneva, 1936: 5-25.

Lederer, William, The Ugly American, NY: Norton, 1959.

Leijonhufvud, Axel, "In Celebration of Armen Alchian's 80th Birthday: Living and Breathing Economics," Economic Inquiry. July 1996: 418-20.

Lenin, V.I., "Selections From *Imperialism, the Highest Stage of Capitalism*," originally a 1916 pamphlet, International Publishers Inc., 1939.

Lincoln, B., Myth, Cosmos, and Society: Indo-European Themes on Creation and Destruction Cambridge: Harvard University Press, 1986, 278 pages.

Lindsay, Jack, Byzantium Into Europe, London: Clowes & Sons, 1952.

Litman, G.W., "Sharks and the Origins of Vertebrate Immunity," Scientific American, Nov. 1996: 67-71.

Litman, Simon, Essentials of International Trade, Wiley & Sons, 1973.

Lohani, P., and E.A. Thompson, "The Optimal Rate of Secular Inflation," Journal of Political Economy, Sept.-Nov., 1971: 962-82.

Luzzatto, Gino, "Per un Programma di Lavoro," Rivista di Storio Economica, 1936.

Lyashchenko, P.I., History of the National Economy of Russia to the 1917 Revolution, MacMillan, 1949.

Macaulay, S., "Noncontractual Relations in Business: A Preliminary Study," American Sociological Review, 28, 1968: 55-69.

Macdonnell, A.A., Lectures On Comparative Religion, Delhi: Bharatiya Publishing House, 1907.

MacKay, Angus, Spain in the Middle Ages, NY: St. Martins Press, 1977, Chs. 5-8..

Makowski, Louis, "Perfect Competition and Profit Criterion, and the Organization of Economic Activity," Journal of Economic Theory, Apr. 1980: 222-42.

Malthus, Thomas, First Essay on Population; reprints of Economic Classics, New York: Augustus Kelly, 1965; originally 1798.

Margulis, Lynn, The Origin of Eukaryotic Cells, Yale University Press, 1970.

Marschak, Jacob, and Radner, Roy, Economic Theory of Teams, New Haven, Yale University Press, 1972.

Marshall, Alfred, Principles of Economics, 8th ed., London: Macmillan, 1925.

Martin, T.R., Sovereignty and Coinage in Classical Greece, Princeton, NJ: Princeton University Press, 1985.

Martines, Lauro, Power and Imagination: City States in Renaissance Italy, London 1980.

Marx, Karl, Capital, v. 3, Moscow: Progress Publishers, 1977.

Massignon, L., "Guilds, Islamic," Encyclopedia of the Social Sciences, 1929.

Matsuyama, K., "Perfect Equilibrium in a Trade Liberalization Game," American Economic Review, 80(3), June 1990: 480-92.

May, A.J., The Hapsburg Monarchy, 1867-1914, Cambridge, MA: Harvard University Press, 1951.

Mayer, Herbert, German Recovery and the Marshall Plan, 1948-1952, Bonn, Germany, 1963: 54.

Maynard-Smith, John, The Theory of Evolution, Canto Edition, Cambridge: Cambridge University Press, 1993.

_____ and G. Price, "The Logic of Animal Conflict," Nature, 246, 1973: 15-18.

McCracken, W.D., The Rise of the Swiss Republic, Boston: Arena Publishing, 1892, esp. pp. 193-218.

Meier, G.J., Leading Issues in Economic Development, 5th ed., Oxford University Press, 1989.

Merino, J., "The Public Sector and Economic Growth in Eighteenth Century Spain," Journal of European Economic History, Winter 1979.

Mickwitz, G., "Die Cartellfunktionen der Zunfte," in Commentationes Humanarum Litterarum, Tomus VIII, No. 2-4, Societus Scientiarum Fennica, Helsingfors, 1936.

Mieras, van Dam, and C.K. Leach,, Defense Mechanisms, Butterworth-Heinemann, 1993, esp. Ch. 1.

Mill, J.S. [and Harriet], On Liberty, London: Parter & Sons, 1859, esp. Ch. II.

Miller, Edward, "Government Economic Policies and Public Finance, 1100-1500," The Fontana Economic History of Europe, the Middle Ages, vol. I, London: Collins, 1970.

Miller, R.L., Heritage of Fear: Illusion and Reality in the Cold War, NY: Walker & Co., 1988.

Minami, Ryoshin, The Economic Development of Japan, London: Macmillan, 1986: 203-17.

Moore, F.G., Roman World, Columbia University Press 1936.

Morse, H.B., The Guilds of China, 2nd ed., Shanghai: Kelly and Walsh, 1932.

Mundy, J.H., and P. Riesenberg, Medieval Town, Princeton: Van Nostrand, 1958.

Murdoch, James, A History of Japan, 1542-1868, Vol. I, London, 1937.

Myers, Gerald and Simon Wian-Hobson,, Viral Regulatory Structures, Santa Fe Institute, 1997.

Nash, John, "Noncooperative Games," Annals of Mathematics, 54, 1951: 286-95.

Neal, Lawrence, "A Tale of Two Revolutions, International Capital Flows, 1789-1819," unpublished manuscript, Univ. of Illinois, 1989.

Nef, John, Industry and Government in England and France, 1540-1640, The American Philosophical Society, 1940.

Nikaido, H., Convex Structure and Economic Theory, New York: Academic Press, 1968.

North, D., and R.P. Thomas, The Rise of the Western World: A New Economic History, Cambridge, UK, 1973.

Nozick, Robert, Anarchy, States and Utopia, NY: Basic Books, 1974.

Nutter, G.W., "Measuring Production in the USSR," AEA Papers and Proceedings, May, 1958: 406.

Oechsli, Wilhelm, History of Switzerland, 1499-1914, Cambridge, 1922.

O'Kane, R.H.T., Terror, Force, and States: The Path From Modernity, Brookfield, USA: Edward Elgar, 1996, Ch. 1.

Olivara, A.R., Politics, Economics and Men of Modern Spain, London: Victor Gallancz Ltd., 1946.

Olson, Mancur, The Rise and Decline of Nations: Economic Growth, Stagflation, and Social Rigidities, New Haven CT: Yale University Press, 1982.

Olson, W.K., The Litigation Explosion, Plume, 1991.

Oman, Charles, The History of the Art of War in the Middle Ages, Vol. II, London: Greenhill, 1924.

Osborne, T.R., A Grande École for the Grandes Corps: The Recruitment and Training of the French Administrative Elite in the Nineteenth Century, NY: Columbia University Press, 1983: 59.

Palliser, David, "Trade Guilds of Tudor York," in Clark and Slack (eds.), Crisis and Order in English Towns, Routledge 1972.

Papanek, G.F., "Economic Development Theory: The Search for a Mirage," in Nash (ed.), Essays on Economic Development and Cultural Change in Honor of Bert Hoselitz, Chicago: University of Chicago Press, 1977.

Patinkin, Don, Money, Interest, and Prices, 2nd ed., NY: Harper and Row, 1965, Ch. VIII.

Peleg, B., and M.E. Yaari, "On the Existence of a Consistent Course of Action When Tastes are Changing," Review of Economic Studies, July 1973: 391-402.

Pirenne, Henry, Economic and Social History of Medieval Europe, Harcourt Brace, 1933.

Pollak, R.A., "Consistent Planning," Review of Economic Studies, 102, Apr. 1968: 202-08.

Pollock, F., and F.W. Maitland, The History of English Law, 2nd ed.; reissued Cambridge: Cambridge University Press, 1968.

Polybius, History, Ch. 1, Bk. IV.

Poole, R.W., Cutting Back City Hall, New York: Universe, 1980.

Posner, R.A., Economic Analysis of the Law, 2nd ed., Boston: Little, Brown, 1977.

Postan, M.M., The Medieval Economy and Society, Berkeley, CA: University of California Press, 1972.

Prebisch, P., The Economic Development of Latin America and Its Principle Problems, NY: United Nations, 1950.

Price, Richard, Masters, Unions and Men, Cambridge University Press, 1980.

Rawls, John, A Theory of Justice, Cambridge, MA: Harvard University Press, 1971.

Renard, Georges, Guilds in the Middle Ages, London, 1919.

Reuss, Frederick, Fiscal Policy for Growth Without Inflation, Baltimore, MD: Gouches College, 1963.

Reynolds, Susan, Fiefs and Vassals, Oxford: Clarendon Press, 1994, p. 317.

Riasanovsky, Nicholas, A History of Russia, 2nd ed., Oxford University Press, 1969.

Ricardo, David, Principles of Political Economy and Taxation, London: Dent and Sons, 1965 (originally 1817).

Rice, T.J., Everyday Life in Byzantium, London: B.T. Botsford, 1967.

Robbins, Lionel, An Essay on the Nature and Significance of the Economic Science, 2nd ed., London: Macmillan, 1935.

Roemer, H.R., "The Safavid Period," The Cambridge History of Iran, Vol. 6, Cambridge: Cambridge University Press, 1986.

Rogers, J.E. Thorold, Six Centuries of Work and Wages, London: W.S. Sonnenschein, 1884.

Root, H.L., The Fountain of Privilege, Berkeley, CA: University of California Press, 1994, Ch. 6.

Rosener, Werner, Peasants in the Middle Ages, translated by Alexander Stutzer, Urbana: University of Illinois Press, 1992.

Rosenthall, Robert, "A Sequential of Games With Varying Opponents," Econometrica, 47, 1979: 1353-66.

Rostow, W.W., "The Take-Off-Into Self Sustained Growth," Economic Journal, 66, Mar. 1966: 25-48.

Rothenberg, Jerome, An Economic Evolution of Urban Renewal, Brookings, 1967.

Rowen, H.H., John de Witt, Princeton, NJ: Princeton University Press, 1978.

Rubinstein, Ariel, "Perfect Equilibrium in Bargaining Models," Econometrica, 50, 1982: 97-109.

Russell, J.C., "Population in Europe, 500-1500," in C.M. Cipolla (ed.), The Fontana Economic History of Europe, Vol. 1, London: Collins, 1972.

Ryan, Frank, Virus X, Boston: Little Brown, 1997.

Salop, S.C., "Zero Output Equilibrium," Georgetown University Working Paper, 1982.

Samuelson, P.A., "The Non-Optimality of Money Holding Under Laissez Faire," Canadian Journal of Economics, 2(2), 1967: 303-08.

_____, "Evaluation of Real National Income," Oxford Economic Papers, US 2, 1950: 1-29.

Saunders, K.S., The Ideals of East and West, NY: Macmillan, 1934.

Schmidt, Folke, The Law of Labor Relations in Sweden, Harvard University Press, 1962.

Scholz, B.W., Carolingian Chronicles: Royal Frankish Annals, University of Michigan, 1970.

Schumpeter, J.A., A History of Economic Analysis, NY: Oxford University Press, 1954, esp. p. 889.

Scitovsky, Tibor, "Two Concepts of External Economies," Journal of Political Economy, 78, May/June 1970: 526-37.

Scott, J.P., Animal Behavior, University of Chicago Press, 1958.

Sedgwick, D.H., A Short History of Italy, 476-1900, Boston: Houghton-Mifflin, 1905.

Seligman, E.R.A., Essays in Taxation, 10th ed., NY: McMillan, 1925.

Selten, Reinhard, "The Chain Store Paradox," Theory and Decision, 9, 1975: 127-59.

Sheiber, H.V., H.G. Votter, and H.O. Falbner, American Economic History, 9th ed., NY: Harper and Row, 1976.

Sherwood, Sidney, The History and Theory of Money, Lippincott, 1893.

Shyrock, J.K., The Origin and Development of the State Cult of Confucius, New York, 1932.

Sibley, Mulford, Revolution and Violence, Peace News Reprint, London: Housmans, April 1967.

Simpson, G.G., The Major Features of Evolution, NY: Columbia University Press, 1953.

Singer, H.W., "The Distribution of Gains Between Borrowing and Investing Countries," American Economic Association Proceedings, 40, May 1950: 473-85.

SIPRI Yearbook, 1970-1993, Stockholm Institute for Peace Research Institute, Oxford University Press, 1970-1993.

Sjoberg, Gideon, The Preindustrial City, Bubbs and Merrill, Free Press of Glencoe, IL, 1960.

Skocpol, Theda, States and Social Revolutions: A Comparative Historical Analysis of France, Russia, and China, Cambridge: Cambridge University Press, 1979.

Smit, J.W., "Holland, A Commentary," in Failed Transitions to Modern Industrial Society, InterUniversity Centre for European Studies, 1974.

Smith, Adam, An Inquiry Into the Nature and Causes of the Wealth of Nations, 1776; NY: Random House's Modern Library, 1937.

Smith, M.S., Tariff Reformation in France - 1860-1900, Ithaca and London 1980.

Smith, R.S., The Spanish Guild Merchant, Durham, NC: Duke University Press, 1940.

Smith, Toulmin, "English Guilds," in Brentano (ed.), Early English Text Society, 1870.

Sowell, Thomas, Classical Economics Reconsidered, Princeton University Press, 1974.

Spencer, Herbert, Progress: Its Law and Cause ..., NY: Fitzgerald, 1881.

Spengler, Oswald, The Decline of the West, NY: Knopf, 1939 (originally in German, 1923-26).

Staley, Edgcumbe, The Guilds of Florence, 2nd ed., London: Methuen, 1906.

Strayer, J.R., and H.W. Gatzke, The Mainstream of Civilization, Orlando: Harcourt Brace, 1984.

Strotz, R.H., "Myopia and Inconsistency Under Dynamic Utility Maximization," Review of Economic Studies, 23, 1956: 165-80.

Symonds, J.A., The Renaissance in Italy, vol. I, NY: Schreiber, 1935.

Takekoshi, Yosaburo, The Economic Aspects of the History of the Civilization of Japan, Vol. 3, London: George Allen & Unwin, 1930.

Taussig, F.W., The Tariff History of the U.S., Putnam, 1892.

Tawney, R.H., Religion and the Rise of Capitalism, NY: Harcourt, 1926.

Templeman, Geoffrey, "The Sheriffs of Warickshire in the Thirteenth Century," Dugdale Society Papers, Oxford, 1948.

Thaler, R.H., and H.M. Shefron, "An Economic Theory of Self Control," Journal of Political Economy, 89, Apr. 1981: 392-406.

Thomas, A.H., Calendar of Plea and Memoranda Rolls of the City of London, 1364-1381, Cambridge University Press, 1929.

Thompson, E.A., "Technical Change, Its Measurement and Integration Into the Theory of the Firm, With Special Application to the Explanation of the Building Cycle," Ph.D. dissertation, Harvard University, 1961.

_____, "Debt Instruments in Both Macroeconomic Theory and Capital Theory," American Economic Review, 57, Dec. 1967: 1196-210.

_____, "The Perfectly Competitive Production of Collective Goods," Review of Economics and Statistics, XLX, Feb. 1968: 1-12.

_____, "The Perfectly Competitive Production of Collective Goods, Reply," Review of Economics and Statistics, Nov. 1969:479-82.

_____, "Review of Arrow and Kurz's Public Investment, The Rate of Return, and Optimal Fiscal Policy," Econometrica, Nov. 1972, esp. p. 1176.

_____, "Optimal Role of Government in Competitive Equilibrium with Transaction Costs," in Auster, R. (ed.), American Re-evolution, University of Arizona 1977.

_____, "On Labor's Rights to Strike," Economic Inquiry, XVIII, October 1980, pp. 640-41.

_____, "Who Should Control the Money Supply?", American Economic Review, May 1981: 356-61.

_____, "Rationalizing Observed Health and Safety Legislation: A Pascalian Approach," American Economic Review, May 1995.

_____, "Welfare Across Generations," Contemporary Economic Policy, XIV, Jan. 1996: 10-13.

Thompson, E.A., and R.W. Batchelder, "On Taxation and the Control of Externalities: Comment," American Economic Review, 64, June 1974: 467-71.

_____ and R.L. Faith, "A Pure Theory of Strategic Behavior and Social Institutions," American Economic Review, 71, June 1981: 366-81.

Thompson, E.A., et al., viz., R.W. Batchelder, Michael Canes, Larry Ensminger, R.L. Faith, Lorraine Glover, C.R. Hickson, Wayne Ruhter, and V.M. Thompson, A Reconstruction of Economics, 3 vols., forthcoming, 2001-2003.

Thompson, E.P., The Making of the English Working Class, New York: Vintage Books, 1966.

Thompson, V.M., "Inefficient Labor Market Discrimination Under Competitive Conditions," Ph.D. dissertation, UCLA, 1977.

Thornton, Henry, An Inquiry Into the Nature and Effects of Paper Credit in Great Britain, F.A. Hayek (ed.), New York: August M. Kelly, 1965.

Thrupp, Sylvia, The Merchant Class of Medieval London, University of Chicago Press, 1948.

_____, "The Guilds," Cambridge Economic History, Vol. III, Cambridge 1963.

_____, "Medieval Industry, 1000-1500," in C.A. Cipolla (ed.), Fontana Economic History of Europe, The Middle Ages, London: Collins, 1971.

Thucydides, A History of the Peloponnesian War, trans. in 2 vols. by Wm. Smith, London: John Watts, 1757 (originally in Greek, 403 BC).

Tout, T.F., "Germany and the Empire," Cambridge Modern History, Vol. I., Cambridge University Press, 1931, Ch. IX.

Towle, L.W., International Trade and Commercial Policy, Harper, 1947.

Toynbee, Arnold, Hellenism, Oxford University Press, 1959, Chs. 11-13.

_____, A Study of History, London: Thames and Hudson, 1988.

Tracy, J.A., A Financial Revolution in the Habsburg Netherlands, Berkeley, CA: University of California Press, 1985.

Trevelyan, J.P., A Short History of the Italian People, London: Putnam, 1920.

Tullock, Gordon, "The Welfare Costs of Tariffs, Monopoly, and Theft," Western Economic Journal, 1967: 224-32.

Tuma, Elias, European Economic History, Pacific, 1979.

Turgeon, Lynn, Bastard Keynesianism, Westport, CT: Praeger, 1996.

Turgot, A., "In Praise of Gournay," in P.D. Groenewegen (ed), The Economics of A.R.G. Turgot, The Hague: Martinus Nijhoff, 1977.

Tutino, John, From Insurrection to Revolution in Mexico, Princeton, NJ: Princeton University Press, 1986.

Unger, Richard, Dutch Shipbuilding Before 1800, van Gorcum, Assen 1978.

United Nations, World Economics and Social Survey, 1998: 140-43.

U.S. Tariff Commission, The Foreign Trade of Latin America, Report #42, 2nd Series, Washington, DC, 1942.

Unwin, George, The Guilds and Companies of London, Cass and Co., 1963.

van der Wee, Herman, "Money, Credit, and Banking Systems," Cambridge Economic History, V, 1977.

van Dillen, J.G., Van Rijkdom en Regenten, Handbook tot de Economische an Sociale Geschiedenis van Nederlands Tijdensole Republiek, Martinus Nyhoff, 1970.

van Valen, Leigh, "A Theory of Origination and Extinction," Evolutionary Theory, 7, 1985: 133-42.

van Vlem, B., R. Vanholder, P. de Paepe, D. Vogelaers, S. Ringoir, "Immunomodulating Effects of Antibiotics: Literature Review," Infection, 24(4), July-Aug. 1996.

van Werveke, H., "The Rise of the Towns," in Cambridge Economic History, Vol. 3, Cambridge, 1963.

Vasiliev, A.A., History of the Byzantine Empire, Madison, WI: University of Wisconsin Press, 1952.

Vermeij, G., Evolution and Escalation: An Ecological History of Life, Princeton NJ: Princeton University Press, 1987.

Vilar, Pierre, The History of Gold and Money, 1450-1920, Atlantic-Highlands Humanities Press, 1969.

Viner, Jacob, in Jacque Melitz and Donald Winch (eds.), Religious Thought and Economic Society, Durham, NC: Duke University Press, 1978

von Grunebaum, G., "Parallelism, Convergence, and Influence in the Relations of Arab and Byzantine Philosophy, Literature, and Piety," Dumbarton Oaks Papers, 18, 1964: 89-111.

von Laue, Sergi, Witte and the Industrialization of Russia, Columbia University Press, 1963.

von Neumann, J., and O. Morgenstern, Theory of Games and Economic Behavior, 3rd ed., Princeton: Princeton University Press, 1953.

von Stromer, W., "Commercial Policy and Economic Conjecture in Nuremberg at the Close of the Middle Ages, a Model of Economic Policy," Journal of European History, Spring 1981.

Vryonis, S., "Byzantine Δημοκρατία and the Guilds of the 11th Century," Dumbarton Oaks Papers, 1963: 229-31.

Waddington, C.H., The Strategy of Genes, London: Allen and Unwin, 1957.

Wagel, S.R., Chinese Currency and Banking, Shanghai, 1915: 62-75.

Wakeman, F.J., The Fall of Imperial China, NY: The Free Press, 1975, Chs. 4-11.

Walbank, F.W., "Trade and Industry Under the Later Roman Empire in the West," in M.M. Postan and E. Miller (eds), The Cambridge Economic History of Europe, Vol. II, Cambridge: Cambridge University Press, 1987.

Waldman, Michael, "Systematic Errors and the Theory of Natural Selection," American Economic Review, 84, June 1994: 482-98.

Walker, Mark, German Home Towns, Ithaca, NY: Cornell University Press, 1971.

Wallace-Hadill, J.M., The Barbarian West, 400-1000, Blackwell, 1996.

Waugh, W.T., "The Councils of Constance and Basel," in The Cambridge Medieval History, Vol. VIII, Cambridge University Press, 1936.

Webb, Sidney, and Beatrice, English Local Government, vol. 4, London: Longmans, 1922.

Weber, Max, The Theory of Social and Economic Organization T. Parson (ed.), NY: The Free Press, 1964.

Weibull, Jorgan, Evolutionary Game Theory, Cambridge, MA: MIT Press, 1995.

Weismann, August, Das Kleimplosma: ein theorie der Vererbung, Jena: Gustav Fischer, 1892.

White, Lynn, "The Expansion of Technology 500-1500," Fontana Economic History, Fontana, 1977.

White, Morton, What is and What Ought to Be: An Essay on Ethics and Epistemology, Oxford: Oxford University Press, 1981.

Williams, G., Adaptation and Natural Selection: A Critique of Some Current Evolutionary Thought, Princeton, NJ: Princeton University Press, 1966.

Williamson, J.A., A Short History of British Expansion, London: Macmillan, 1953.

Williamson, O.E., Markets and Hierarchies -- Analysis and Antitrust Implications, NY: The Free Press, 1975.

Wilson, C.H., Anglo-Dutch Commerce and Finance in the 18th Century, NY: Arno Press, 1977.

Winter, Sidney, "Economic Natural Selection and the Theory of the Firm," Yale Economic Essays, 4, 1964: 225-72.

Wise, Terence, Medieval Warfare, NY: Hastings House, 1976.

Wittgenstein, Ludwig, Tractatics Logico-Philosophicus, London, 1922.

Woolf, Stuart, A History of Italy, 1700-1860, London: Methuen, 1979.

World Bank, The World Tables, World Bank Star Retrieval System, Washington, DC, 1993.

World Bank, World Debt Tables, World Bank Star Retrieval System, Washington, DC, 1993.

World Tax Series, Taxation in France, Commerce, 1966.

_____, Taxation in Germany, Commerce, 1966.

_____, Taxation in Sweden, Little, 1959.

_____, Taxation in the United Kingdom, Little, 1947.

Yeates, A.J., "Effective Tariff Protection in the United States, the European Economic Community, and Japan," Quarterly Review of Economic and Business, Summer 1974: 41-50.

Young, H.P., "The Evolution of Conventions," Econometrica, 61, 1993: 57-84.2

Zachary, G.P., The Endless Frontier: Vannevar Bush, Engineer of the American Century, NY: Free Press, 1997, p. 260.

INDEX

_____, et al., 2, et seq.
Thompson, E.A., and R.W.
    Batchelder, 21, 23, 28
_____ and R.L. Faith, 11, 12, 52
Thompson, V.M., 25
Thornton, H., 196
Thrasymachus, 8
Thrupp, S., 98, 99, 100, 130, 133,
    138-40, 161
Thucydides, 6, 73
Tocqueville, 5, 11, 71
Tooke, T., 195
Toulouse, 125
Tout, T.F., 147
Towle, L., 108, 179
towns (medieval) and their
    policies, 5, 84, 98-101,
    106-8, 110, 124, 149, 156,
    161, 169-78
Toynbee, Arnold, 5, 270
Tracy, J.A., 104, 158
Trevelyan, J.P., 156
Tullock, G., 43, 66, 97, 187
Tuma, E., 176
Turgeon, Lynn, 230
Turgot, A., 7, 97
Tutino, John, 220
underinvestment (underdevelopment)
    traps, 12, 20-27, 30, 33, 35, 38,
    40-45, 49, 61, 71, 73, 74, 77n,
    80, 85n, 106, 110, 114, 123,
    124, 208, 260
ungrateful future decisionmakers, 90,
    94
Unger, R., 103, 150, 158, 160
United Nations, 217, 218
United States (U.S.), 24, 42-46, 80-
    83, 86, 87, 105, 108, 109, 127,
    128, 133, 167-69, 177, 181,
    183-85, 193-98, 208-17, 225,
    227, 230, 231, 236, 238, 254,
    261-65
Unwin, G., 98, 99, 101, 130, 132,
    133, 151, 164, 165
Urukagina, 86
U.S. Tariff Commission, 209, 225

van der Wee, H., 103
van Dillen, J.G., 103
van Valen, L., 18, 66
van Vlem, B., R, Vanholder, P. de
    Paepe, D. Vogelaers, S. Ringoir,
    269
van Werveke, H., 100, 137, 138
Vasiliev, A.A., 169, 170
Venice, 125, 146, 148, 156, 189
Vermeij, G., 18, 268
Vietnam, 86, 132, 199, 224, 245,
    261, 262
Vilar, P., 163
Viner, 45
von Grunebaum, G., 170
von Laue, S., 165
von Neumann, J., and O.
    Morgenstern, 23, 52, 89, 91
von Stackelberg, 23, 89, 91
von Stromer, W., 142
Vryonis, S., 170
Waddington, 54
Wagel, S.R., 189
Wakeman, F.J., 78
Walbank, F.W., 110
Waldman, M., 67
Walker, M., 133, 147, 166
Wallace-Hadill, J.M., 59
Walras, 182
war (warfare), 17, 41, 42, 59, 71, 73,
    74, 79-84, 87, 96, 99n-104, 111,
    127, 129-37, 144-48, 157, 160-
    68, 174, 180-84, 189-97, 213,
    215, 217, 218n, 221, 222, 228,
    232, 245-47, 250, 254, 260, 262,
    268, 269
    rational warfare, 146, 181, 187
    socially costly warfare, 144
Washington, George, 44, 86
Waugh, W.T., 146
Webb, Sidney, and Beatrice, 100
Weber, Max, 6, 45, 77
Weibull, J., 14, 17, 52, 53, 56, 122,
    123, 235
Weismann, 54
West (Western Civilization), 5, 8, 54,